George Thayer has succeeded in presenting a broad and detailed picture of politics beyond the American consensus, and of the phenomena of extremism itself, its roots, the role it plays today in our society. He takes us, in fascinating—and quite often funny—detail, through the ranks of the Tax Cut Party, the Poor Man's Party, the Theocratic Party (anxious to modernize its name, and bravely fighting off take-over attempts from the extreme Left and Right), the Vegetarian Party, the Guam nationalists, the American Indian nationalists (led by a retired Brigadier General—a non-Indian), the Yockey Movement, British Israelism, the bizarre National Renaissance Party (marching proudly to the right of Rockwell), the Black Muslims, the Odinist Religion and Nordic Faith Movement ("... Odin Speed to Valhalla!"), and others too numerous to mention, from the semiparanoid to the respectable apparatus of the Left and Right.

About the Author

GEORGE THAYER was born in 1933 in Philadelphia, Pa., and educated at St. Paul's School, the University of Pennsylvania and the London School of Economics.

Since 1963 he has devoted himself to writing and political research. He worked for a year as a research assistant to Randolph Churchill on the biography of Sir Winston Churchill, and his first book, *The British Political Fringe,* was published in England in 1965.

Mr. Thayer now lives in New York City.

Also by George Thayer

THE BRITISH POLITICAL FRINGE

The Farther Shores of Politics

THE AMERICAN POLITICAL FRINGE TODAY

by George Thayer

SIMON AND SCHUSTER · NEW YORK

First printing

Library of Congress Catalog Card Number: 67–16728
Designed by Betty Crumley
Manufactured in the United States of America
by American Book–Stratford Press, Inc.

The author and the publisher are grateful for permission to quote from: *America at the Polls: The Vote for President 1920–1964* by Richard M. Scammon, University of Pittsburgh Press; *Black Nationalism* by E. U. Essien-Udom, by permission of the University of Chicago Press; *Facts About the President* by Joseph Nathan Kane, H. W. Wilson Co., *Presidential Ballots, 1836–1892* by W. Dean Burnham, Johns Hopkins Press; *Rumbles Right and Left* by William F. Buckley, Jr., Putnam's & Coward-McCann, Copyright © 1963 by William F. Buckley, Jr.; *A Statistical History of the American Presidential Elections* by Svend Petersen, Frederick Ungar Publishing Company.

To
M. S. N.

Contents

Part Six : The Independents

Part Seven : The Farther Shores of Politics

Appendices

Foreword

In writing this book, I have been concerned with examining the minor political groups in America as they exist today—those relatively small political parties and pressure groups outside the two-party system whose primary objective is to alter all or part of the existing political institutions and attitudes in America. I am not concerned here with the many groups whose fundamental interests lie outside this objective.

I have approached the subject in a spirit of neutrality and pure inquiry. As far as possible, I have tried to ignore my own political views, which fall entirely within the mainstream of American political thought. When quoting from the literature of these groups, I have conformed to the original spelling and punctuation except where it has been obvious to me that there has been a typographical error.

This book would have been impossible to prepare without the generous assistance of many people, but I would emphasize that the responsibility for the accuracy and interpretation of all facts is entirely my own. I am indebted to the more than four hundred individuals belonging to the organizations on which I have written who, with courtesy and in a spirit of cooperation, gave up their time to explain their history, activities, attitudes and objectives. I am also indebted to those in the House of Representatives, the Senate, the New York Public Library, the Free Library of Philadelphia, the Non-Sectarian Anti-Nazi League and those many other organizations and individuals who wish to remain anonymous, who so generously assisted me in my research. I am particularly indebted to Mrs. William E. Almy, Mr. J. Hampton Barnes, Dr. Arturo Morales Carrion, Mrs. Alexander F. Chisholm, Mr. Rowland Evans, Jr., Miss Kay Halle, Mr. H. S. Nugent Head, the Reverend Casey Holmes, Mr. and Mrs. Robert Hood, Mr. Robert C. Hynson, Mr. Jack Langguth, Mr. Tom Lewis, Sr. Juan Luis Marques, Mr. Harold H. Martin, Mr. Fergus Reid III, Mr. and Mrs. Charles P. Slichter, Miss Charlene Slivnick, Miss Audrey Stevenson, Mr. Charles W. Thayer, Mr. and Mrs. Landon Thomas, Mr. Landon Thomas, Jr., Mr. and Mrs. Henry Toombs, Mr. Charles L. Weltner, Mr. James A. Wheeler and Mrs. Frank Wisner for the information and help they gave me.

G.T.

Berwyn, Pa.
May 1967

PART ONE

THE
RACISTS

1

The Nazis

At once I had the answer! By being an OPEN, ARROGANT, ALL-OUT NAZI, not a sneaky Nazi—but a Nazi—with the swastika, storm troops, and open declarations of our intentions to gas the Jew-traitors (after investigations, trials, and convictions) —I would . . . make an end of the filthy "silent treatment," for they could never "ignore" NAZIS with swastika armbands and talk of gas chambers. . . .[1]

These are the words of Commander George Lincoln Rockwell, leader of the American Nazi Party—one of the smallest but most flamboyant political groups on the American scene today.

Rockwell believes in the use of shock tactics to gain attention for his views. In this respect he has few peers. Since he founded the American Nazi Party in 1958 he has added considerable lore to the American body politic.

The first act of the Party was to picket the White House with signs that read "SAVE IKE FROM THE KIKES!" and "THE ONLY COMMUNIST PARTY IN THE MIDDLE EAST IS IN ISRAEL!" Subsequent picketing has featured such signs as "GAS RED JEW SPYS!" "FIGHT RACE-MIXING" "COMMUNISM IS JEWISH!" and "FRY SOBELL TOO!" In fact, picketing the White House has become a tradition with the Party. On occasion, Rockwell has dressed several of his men in monkey outfits, particularly during counterdemonstrations against Negro picket lines. "He used to own two of them," said an ex-member, referring to the costumes, "but they kept getting ripped." Sometimes his men wear false rubber hook noses and glasses and carry such signs as "I'M FOR

KENNEDY." Usually his men appear in public in the ANP uniform: army surplus khakis, Sam Browne belt, swastika armband and paratrooper boots. As they parade to the picketing site, the American and Nazi flags are carried side by side.

In 1961 Rockwell and his men drove a "Hate Bus" through the South. The sides of the vehicle were festooned with a number of provocative slogans: "WE DO HATE RACE-MIXING," said one. "WE HATE JEW-COMMUNISM," said another. The Nazis got as far as New Orleans before being stopped, jailed and fined (the charges of "disturbing the peace and unreasonably alarming the public," however, were later reversed by a high court).

Since the "Hate Bus" days, Rockwell has continued this form of political advertisement. His men used to drive a bus around the Washington, D.C., area with the slogan: "ROCKWELL IS RIGHT! WHO NEEDS NIGGERS?" taped to the sides.

During the 1963 "March on Washington," Rockwell devised a most unusual form of protest against the Negro demonstration. He sent one of his men out with a bushel basket and told him to fill it with spiders. He then planned to climb to the top of the Lincoln Memorial and dump the contents of the basket on the massed demonstrators below. The scheme fell through only because a search for sufficient quantities of the arachnids proved fruitless.

In 1963 a number of his men went to Wisconsin and held a Nazi memorial service on Hitler's birthday over the late Senator Joseph McCarthy's grave.

Rockwell had a live advertisement at the Virginia State Fair when he ran for governor of that state in 1965.* In one cage was a cat labeled "Democrat"; in the cage next to it was a mouse labeled "Conservative"; and in the third cage was a monkey labeled "Republican."

The same year one of his followers became so upset at the possibility of home rule for the District of Columbia that he shouted, "Sieg Heil!" from the spectators' gallery of the House of Representatives. For some unexplained reason, this act took place during a debate on a bill to provide money for more research into heart disease, cancer and strokes. Earlier, another member of the

---

* Rockwell received over 6,300 votes, or 1.2 percent of the total cast.

Party—protesting the Mississippi Freedom Democratic Party's request for accreditation—painted himself in blackface and ran through the cloakrooms shouting *"Ah's yo' man! Ah's yo man! . . ."* Commenting upon his follower's action, Rockwell wrote: *". . . he successfully smashed the nigger attempt to unseat the legitimate Mississippi delegation and replace it with a gang of pro-Red coons."*[2]

The Party spent parts of 1962 and 1963 picketing the movie *Exodus.* To gain publicity, Rockwell would announce in advance that his men planned to picket the theatre at a certain time. This he knew would ensure a large crowd, made up primarily of angry Jews. The Nazis would infiltrate the crowd, their uniforms and placards covered by raincoats. At the appropriate moment, the demonstrators would shed their outer coats and wave their placards and begin chanting anti-Jewish slogans. Scuffles, some quite violent, usually ensued with the Nazi demonstrators invariably ending up in the police station charged with disturbing the peace. These demonstrations took place in many of the larger cities in America: New York, Los Angeles, Boston, Baltimore, etc. The most unfriendly city of all was Philadelphia, "the enemy capital."

"They've practically got Jewish flags flying from the flagpoles," says Rockwell.[3]

The Commander has directed many of his recent protests toward harassing peace marchers. Once, dressed as a beatnik, he grabbed a Vietcong flag and tore it up. He was punched by the pro-Red flag carrier in return. "I'm guilty as hell," Rockwell told the magistrate, "but I'd do it again." Rockwell's long-term solution for pacifists is to "Strap parachutes on [approximately 1,000 of] them and load them aboard Flying Boxcars; fly them over North Vietnam and then push the creeps out! !"

His men have on occasion mocked those pacifists who immolated themselves in protest over the Vietnam War. For instance, in early February 1965, a civil rights demonstration was being held on the steps of the Los Angeles City Hall protesting the jailing of Dr. Martin Luther King, Jr., in Selma, Alabama. The proceedings were interrupted briefly when a uniformed Nazi stepped forward and poured water from a gasoline can all over himself and then declared he was going to burn himself up in protest against "race mixing." The police led him away, but not before a television reporter had offered him a match.

Sometime in the future Rockwell plans to rent a plane and skywrite a huge swastika over New York City. The best time of year to do it, he believes, is on Hitler's birthday (April 20). He is also planning on another occasion to have one plane skywrite a Star of David over New York City, then have another plane come along and squirt brown smoke at it. He would like to do this on Ben Gurion's birthday (sometime in October).

In September 1962 Rockwell awarded one of his "Captains," Roy James, with a medal for "gallant action" in Birmingham. James had punched the Reverend Martin Luther King, Jr., in the face "for calling that nigger Jew Sammy Davis Jr. 'an example of the finest type of American.' "[4]

The previous month, one Nazi chained himself to the gate of the British Embassy in protest over something or other. Earlier two others were convicted of disorderly conduct for trampling on a Soviet flag. Over the course of the year, ANPers found themselves answering the following charges: fighting, loitering, vagrancy, assault, desertion, criminal defamation and unlawful possession of a gun. It was a typical year.

It is rare when a member of the ANP is not in jail over the course of a year. Rockwell told me that anyone in his Party who had not been in jail during the previous twelve months was considered a "virgin." "This is a rough game," Rockwell told me. "I'd like to be a nice guy, but I can't."

In the summer of 1960, Rockwell and ten of his men held a rally on the Mall of the nation's capital. There were several hundred angry spectators milling about, and they soon turned the rally into a riot. The speaker's stand was overturned; Rockwell was punched and kicked; one of his storm troopers was seized with fright and ran away; and the Party's secretary, "Lieutenant" Warner, according to Rockwell, "had his ear almost bitten off by a Jew."

Three days afterward, Rockwell went to court to face charges of disorderly conduct. To his surprise, the prosecutor recommended that he be committed to the District Hospital for thirty days of psychiatric observation to determine whether or not he was insane.

"The murmur of joy from the hoard of Jews and the ADL [Anti-Defamation League], who had filled up the Court Room, was audible," wrote Rockwell.[5] At the end of a month's study, however, Rockwell was found to be sane.

George Lincoln Rockwell was born in 1918, the eldest son of George Lovejoy "Doc" Rockwell, an old-time vaudevillian of some renown. He spent much of his early youth shuttling between his divorced parents' homes: his mother's in rural Illinois and his father's on the coast of Maine; the houseguests at the latter often included Fred Allen, Walter Winchell, Benny Goodman and Groucho Marx.*

After high school, where he was only a fair student, George Lincoln Rockwell went to Hebron Academy for a year. In 1938, he entered Brown University where he majored in philosophy and drew cartoons for the college humor magazine.

War soon interrupted his studies. He enlisted in the Navy and quickly won his wings. He spent most of the war flying anti-submarine missions in the South Atlantic and South Pacific. His only brush with disaster came when an admiral admonished him privately for failing to take precautions in storing some inflammable 35 mm film, which had caught fire and burned the top floor off a building.

After the war, Rockwell decided that he wanted to be a commercial artist. He started out as a sign painter and photographer, then enrolled at Pratt Institute in New York City. In 1948 he won a $1,000 prize in a nationwide art contest sponsored by the National Society of Illustrators. In 1950, he was recalled to active duty and was assigned to Iceland as an F8F Bearcat pilot.

It was before he left for Iceland, however, that he got his first taste of anti-Jewish literature. His first brush with a Jew—at least, Rockwell says, when he first remembered a man specifically as a Jew—was during World War II when a "300-pound, yellow-skinned, fat Hebrew," as he called him, denied him his upper berth during a train trip. But it was a little old lady whose name Rockwell forgets who first introduced him to Joseph McCarthy's

* This branch of the Rockwell family is no relation to Norman Rockwell, Rockwell Kent, or the Rockwell-Standard Company family.

speeches, Conde McGinley's newspaper, *Common Sense* and Gerald L. K. Smith's speeches. This was sometime around 1949 or 1950, at the beginning of the McCarthy period.

Rockwell read the *Protocols of the Learned Elders of Zion** and came to the conclusion that although the book itself might have been a forgery, it was still written "by a genius who knew exactly what the Jews of the world would do for sixty years, with not partial, but PERFECT accuracy."[6] He then read Hitler's *Mein Kampf* and that, according to Rockwell, "was the end of one Lincoln Rockwell, the 'nice guy'—the dumb 'Goy'—and the beginning of an entirely different person."[7]

Rockwell's political career dates from his discharge from active duty in 1954. He started a magazine called *U.S. Lady*, which he sold after what he claims was a "Red plot" to buy out the magazine. He became friends with John Kasper (who was to lead the anti-integration riots in Clinton, Tennessee, in 1956) who then ran a bookstore in the Georgetown section of Washington, D.C. Together, these two, along with several others, went on occasion to St. Elizabeth's Hospital to listen to the wisdom of Ezra Pound. They sat at the feet of the controversial poet, as Rockwell describes it, in a ward "full of raving madmen."[8]

A series of briefly held jobs plagued Rockwell for the next three years and threatened his financial stability. He worked for the

---

* This book is a bible among racists. It has an obscure history. Anti-Semites claim that it contains instructions to the Jewish people from their "Elders" on the conquest of the world. The "Elders" are supposed to be the spiritual descendants of King Solomon, the man who allegedly devised the original "protocol." Anti-Semites claim that the book recommends the use of all known forms of subversion to undermine Christianity and Western civilization: the perversion of justice through the use of perjury; the denigration of the clergy; the debasement of currency through economic and political manipulation; the weakening of morals through the sale of pornography; the masquerading of Jews as Gentiles; the "promotion of false theories"; and the physical destruction of Gentile cities.

Jews themselves claim the book to be a forgery drawn up by Czarist police at the end of the nineteenth century during one of their many pogroms. A Swiss court upheld this decision in 1935.

Others claim it was originally a political diatribe by Maurice Joly, a Frenchman, entitled *Dialogues in Hell between Machiavelli and Montesquieu,* first published in 1864, and that an obscure Russian lawyer and anti-Semite, Sergius Nilus, rewrote it (adding the word "Jew" where appropriate) and published it in 1905, claiming he had "discovered" it.

conservative-oriented Campaign for the 48 States, then for Russell Maguire's *American Mercury* magazine, then for an advertising firm in Georgia, and finally for William Stephenson's racist magazine, *The Virginian.* It was here that Rockwell once more began to draw cartoons. They were part of a series called "Odd Birds." One such "bird" was the "Red-Tinged Blackbird . . . a native of Africa . . . a rather interesting bit of wild life that tends to eat its brothers and sisters and otherwise behaves rudely"; its characteristic call is "EEEEEE-quali-TEEEEEE."

By this time Rockwell had decided that the only viable way to be a Nazi was to become an open one. He had lost patience with the right wing and the secret Nazis.

> I learned by bitter experience that the human material of the right wing consists 90 percent of cowards, dopes, nuts, one-track minds, blabbermouths, boobs, incurable tight-wads and—worst of all—hobbyists: people who have come to enjoy a perverted, masochistic pleasure in telling each other forever how we are all being raped by the "shhh—you-know-who," but, who, under no conditions would think of risking their two cars, landscaped homes or juicy jobs to DO something about it.[9]

To establish himself as an "OPEN, ARROGANT, ALL-OUT NAZI," Rockwell felt he had to form a political party; and to do this he needed a financial benefactor. He found one in Harold Arrowsmith, Jr., a wealthy Baltimorean. Arrowsmith, Rockwell notes, "never worked a day in his life, and likes this arrangement."[10]

Arrowsmith assembled some printing equipment across the river from the capital in Arlington, put Rockwell in charge, and called his new venture the "National Committee to Free America from Jewish Domination." This partnership soon splintered when things began to get rough. The bombing of an Atlanta synagogue in October 1958 was associated in the public's mind with Rockwell and his recent anti-Jewish activities. The full force of the law and public opinion descended upon the organization. The police and FBI raided his premises, anonymous telephone threats were made, homemade bombs were thrown at the house, shots were fired, fights were started, curses were exchanged. Even though Rockwell was cleared of any complicity in the bombing, the notoriety was too much for Arrowsmith; he took back his presses and fled.

The strain was also too much for Rockwell's second wife,* who returned to her family with her children. It was at this time that he changed the name of his organization to American Nazi Party. Since then, Rockwell has been carrying on his fight without a family.

Because of his notoriety, the Navy Department came under pressure to throw him out of the Reserves. Rockwell, however, convinced his superiors that he had done no wrong; he was eventually given an Honorable Discharge with the permanent rank of Commander. He felt nevertheless that his civil liberties had been abused, so he went to the American Civil Liberties Union for help. Ordinarily, Rockwell would attack such an organization as Jewish-controlled. But putting it on the spot in this manner amused him.

The ACLU did not handle the Navy case, but it later took up legal cudgels on his behalf on two other charges. Free of charge, Rockwell was assigned an ACLU lawyer named Shapiro. In his book, *This Time the World,* Rockwell describes the scene:

> The hanging jaws of the other Jews as we marched into the crowded prosecutor's offices that morning with Shapiro leading the way for his Nazi clients were worth the whole fight—just to see. And old Shapiro went to bat for us with a will and typical Jewish cleverness. He succeeded in having the charges . . . dropped. Meanwhile, out in the corridor, I was explaining to the newspapers that it might be necessary later to gas Shapiro too, as he was suspiciously active with the Communists.[11]

Until recently the American Nazi Party maintained two buildings in Arlington, one a headquarters, the other a barracks. The former was closed down in late 1965 and the contents subsequently sold to satisfy a delinquent tax bill due the Internal Revenue Service.

The headquarters building, still in operation when I visited it, was an old wood frame structure badly in need of paint. All the

---

* Rockwell has been married twice and has seven children, three by his first wife and four by his second.

windows were protected by wire mesh. A large sign on the porch roof read: "WHITE MAN . . . FIGHT! *Smash the Black Revolution!*"

I was met at the door by a young uniformed storm trooper with a loaded .38 pistol at his side. The doormat was a Jewish altar cloth. Directly in front of the door was a large sign—apparently used when demonstrating—that showed a caricature of a Negro with unusually large lips. The caption read: "MARTIN LUTHER COON, TRAITOR!"

To the left of the vestibule was a dimly lit room—part office, part shrine. The young storm trooper demanded some identification and entered my name in the log. A two-foot billy lay at one end of the desk. On one wall was a huge Nazi flag—red banner, white disk and black swastika rampant. In the center of the swastika was a blue dot. The storm trooper explained that this was symbolic of the United Nations. "Notice," he said, "how it is being consumed by the swastika."

To one side was an altar with a bust of Adolf Hitler in the center. Lighted candles were set off at the ends of the table. A picture of George Washington and a self-portrait of Rockwell hung on another wall. Behind a door, across the room, printing presses could be heard churning out propaganda. The storm trooper said that at the moment further editions of the Commander's book, *This Time the World,* were being printed and bound by members of the Party.

I was told that I had to be searched before I could see the Commander. The two storm troopers were not very proficient at their task, for they neglected two potential weapons caches. While they inspected my heels and fountain pen, they overlooked the small of my back and the pockets of my raincoat.

I was then driven to the barracks in a rather battered "staff car" by two other storm troopers. Both men were in civilian clothes, but one was armed. The storm trooper beside the driver turned to me en route and said: "You sure do learn a lot about life by being a member of the American Nazi Party."

The barracks is a sixteen-room frame farmhouse, emblazoned with swastikas, set off in the woods a few miles or so from the headquarters. A "No Trespassing" sign stamped with a skull and crossbones and a leashed Doberman watchdog warn the public away.

The building itself looked run down; plumbing and lighting fixtures obviously needed repair. The dormitory rooms, each containing two or three beds, were unkempt. The dining room, large enough to seat perhaps twenty people, was also used as a meeting room; a fancy electrified Nazi emblem hung over the fireplace. In a number of easily reached places throughout the house were wooden racks filled with eighteen-inch pieces of iron pipe.

Rockwell operates out of a bedroom-office on the second floor. When I entered, there were shouts of "Sieg Heil," a stiffening of arms and a clicking of heels by the storm troopers who preceded me.

Rockwell is a large man with a commanding presence. He was dressed in work trousers, a blue shirt, red suspenders, and wore bedroom slippers. He is not one for small talk or pleasantries, and with no word he motioned me peremptorily to a chair in the corner.

A picture of Adolf Hitler hung on one wall; a tape recorder was set up to take down our conversation; a uniformed storm trooper stood with folded arms between Rockwell and myself during the entire interview. Rockwell himself sat in a chair at the other end of the room, a loaded pistol within easy reach on the end of the bed.

There are few subjects on which Rockwell does not have an opinion. He has a gift for the pungent and shocking phrase that is noticeable in his literature as well as his speech.

For instance, he does not believe that whites should mix with "cannibals, niggers, and monkeys." In fact, he would like to see all races physically separated. "Chimpanzees do not run with baboons," he said; "they run with chimpanzees. This is the natural order of people too."[12]

He wrote the following article on Negroes in a 1965 *Rockwell Report,* an ANP publication:

MORE PROOF OF NIGGER INFERIORITY

Every time I get thrown in jail, I am forced to envy the niggers one of their abilities.

Niggers can sit staring at nothing for hours and hours and hours and hours and hours.

An intelligent being, forced to sit alone in an empty cell with no reading material, no window, no sounds, and nobody to talk to soon grows miserable just from the ache of endless, empty thinking.

Not so with the jigs. I have seen them sit for hours on end, their only movement an occasional blink, for all the world like a snake sunning himself on a rock. There are advantages to being a close relative of bugs and snakes and vegetables.[13]

The Negro's inferiority, according to Rockwell, also extends to his sexual prowess. He believes that the average white is "just as tough and ballsy as any nigger." But, he added, "I am forced to admit that a healthy nigger garbage man is certainly superior physically and sexually to a pasty-faced skinny white peace creep."

The Commander sells a "Boat Ticket to Africa" on the "Coonard Lines," which serves "bananas and choice cuts of missionary." On the back of the ticket is an advertisement for "Instant Nigger," especially for "liberal, white 'peace creeps,' race-mixers and nigger lovers."

Rockwell also issued a 45-rpm phonograph record in 1964. It is called a "Hatenanny Record" and features Odis Cochran and his guitar "plus the musical prejudice of the 3 BIGOTS!" One song is called "Ship Those Niggers Back," and the other one "We Is Nonviolent Niggers." Some of the lyrics to the latter are as follows:

> Ah's dat Sammy Davis Cat, Ah's a coon Aristocrat!
> Ah ain't no common jigaboo, Ah's a kosher, nigger Jew!

(Chorus)
> We're nonviolent niggers, peace-loving brothers
> De White folks better LOVE us, or we're gonna KILL
> them rotten mothers!

"Niggers," he told me during the interview, "have produced nothing. This has been historically true in the U.S. They have produced chaos and misery and no one will admit it. Niggers are like a disease, and to cure the disease, phony doctors keep prescribing larger doses of niggers." When he comes to power, which Rockwell predicts will be no later than 1972, he will ship all Negroes back to Africa at government expense. As for the present, "Any coon that wants to go back to Africa, I'd carry him piggy-back."

On the subject of Jews, Rockwell turns almost apoplectic. Wherever he looks he sees Jews pulling the strings, controlling the lives of Gentiles, enriching themselves from the sweat off a "white man's" brow. Jews, he believes, control the government; they control the country's finances (in fact he believes that they have a monopoly over all international finances); Jews control the arts, the press, the civil rights movement (this variety of Jew is described by Rockwell as a "nigger Jew"); they were responsible for Watts and the Harlem riots; he is convinced that most American Communists are Jews and that the Bolshevik revolution was carried out mostly by New York Jews. Every facet of American life he sees as polluted by Jews.

He believes, for instance, that Jews promote integration because it is the only way they can gain control over the more "inventive" white man. Since Negroes, in Rockwell's view, are only capable of imitating the white man's inventions, any miscegenation would produce a lower order of being easily controllable by the Jews. The sole purpose of Jews, says Rockwell, is to gain control of the world; that is why they are pro-United Nations, pro-Communist, anti-MacArthur and anti-McCarthy.

The ANP sells stickers of an anti-Jewish flavor. One says "Liberate Jewish-occupied New York"; another says "Hitler was Right!" The latter is available in six different languages. Rockwell also published a pamphlet called the "Diary of Anne Fink" which consists of photographs of Jews in concentration camps. Each picture has a caption under it. For instance, one picture shows an emaciated inmate half-lying on a barbed wire fence out of sheer physical weakness. The caption reads: "Man-o-manoshewitz, what a wine!" Another picture shows a living skeleton of a man being fed into a gas oven on a pallet. The caption reads: "I asked for a cheap pad . . . But this is ridiculous."

His literature abounds with critical references to the Jews. One cartoon shows an army bazooka team in action, the caption

reading, "Don't shoot 'til you see the hooks of their noses!!"[14]
Headlines in *The Rockwell Report* dwell constantly on the subject: "So the Jews Ain't a Race?" "How the Jews Love Christians,"
"Arrogant Jews" and "New Jew Danger" are but a few of the
titles.[15]

There is no question in Rockwell's mind that Jews should be
gassed. He is quick to say that only the traitorous ones should be
gassed, but then, he adds, "about 90 percent of all Jews are
traitors." The first thing he would do upon becoming President
would be to "set J. Edgar Hoover loose" to round up all the Jews.
"J. Edgar Hoover," says Rockwell, "is our kind of people. He
talks like a pink but when he acts, he acts like a white man!" He
would also have the Director of the FBI round up all the homo-
sexuals. He hates them almost as much as he hates Communists,
Jews and Negroes. He believes all four are often the same.[16]

As for immigrants, black or white, Rockwell would prefer they
not come to America because he believes they are "scum." I asked
him about the new immigration law and he exclaimed: "I'm
surprised you'd ask a question like that; I'd gas 'em as they came
down the gangplank!"

Rockwell sees himself as President by 1972 because by that
time, he reasons, most white Gentile Americans will be fed up with
the conniving of the Jews and the demands of the Negroes. As
President, he claims he would not set up a dictatorship; rather his
goal is to preserve the American Constitution—"the best form of
government ever." He sees his main job as achieving white hegemony throughout the world. The white, brown, yellow, and black
races would all be segregated from one another in different parts of
the world.

"We are racial counter-revolutionaries," he says, "not extremists in the ordinary sense of the word. We whites must stick
together!"

To achieve this worldwide segregation, Rockwell has in the past
flirted with the Black Muslims, advocates of an all-black nation.
On the surface, the aims of this Negro force seem to dovetail with
his own, and for a brief spell the two organizations were in
communication with each other.

In February 1962, Rockwell spoke to an audience of five

thousand at the Muslim convention in Chicago. "I am proud to stand here before black men," he cried. "I believe Elijah Muhammad is the Adolf Hitler of the black man!" Mr. Muhammad, supreme ruler of the Nation of Islam, as the Black Muslims prefer to be called, was seen to applaud this statement, as did his most talented minister, Malcolm X. Rockwell drew a warm response whenever he denounced the Jews; anti-Semitism, although not so explicitly expressed, is nevertheless a motivating force among Muslims (See chapter 11).

Eventually, however, it was clear that no working arrangement was possible between the Nazis and the Muslims. The Muslims, it seems, wanted to set up a black nation inside the United States, and this of course was anathema to the Commander of the ANP.

In the same year an attempt was made to go international. To the embarrassment of British authorities, Rockwell was smuggled into Great Britain to attend a Nazi summer camp held at Dead-and-Bury Hollow near Temple Guiting, Gloucestershire, about 130 miles west of London. There the Nazis drew up the "Cotswold Agreement," whereby all the world's National Socialist parties agreed to bind themselves together into a "World Union of National Socialists." Rockwell became World Leader, and Colin Jordan, leader of the National Socialist Movement in Britain, became Deputy Leader. (Jordan, an ex-schoolteacher, ex-soap salesman and ex-convict is married to Françoise Dior, a lifelong fascist and a niece of the late fashion designer Christian Dior.)

The day after the election, a London tabloid newspaper, *The People,* came out with a large headline which read: "THE NEW 'WORLD FUEHRER'—ELECTED BY 27 IDIOTS!"

The agreement aimed to "form a monolithic, combat-efficient, international political apparatus to combat and utterly destroy the international Jewish-Communist and Zionist apparatus of treason and subversion." No organization or individual who did not acknowledge the spiritual leadership of Adolf Hitler would be admitted to membership.[17]

Rockwell makes loyal references to some of the world's other Nazis, particularly these who have joined WUNS. Outside this sphere he has nice things to say about George Wallace, the late Senator McCarthy, Senator Harry F. Byrd, Malcolm X and the writings of Schopenhauer. He hates Robert Welch and the Birch Society; the former he calls "Rabbit" and the latter he calls "Bloomer Girl Nazis." And he has scorn for Klan leaders: first because they do not follow Rockwell's leadership, second because they are anti-Catholic, and third because they use tactics of partial terror (as opposed to *total* terror, which Rockwell would sanction under certain conditions), thus creating needless martyrs for the opposition. Above anyone else, though, he loves Adolf Hitler; in fact, he worships him. His book, *This Time the World,* is dedicated to the Fuehrer, over half the pictures in the book are of Hitler and Nazi Germany. "He produced the thoughts which propel me," Rockwell said. "Future generations will look upon Adolf Hitler," he wrote, "as the White Saviour of the twentieth century, and the Fuehrerbunker in Berlin as the Alamo of the White Race."[18]

Of the men who surround him, Rockwell had this to say: "My guys are law-abiding, decent people who I am proud to be associated with. We have no drunks, half-wits, bullies, irresponsible people, cowards, or undisciplined people like many other right wing groups."

Not everyone agrees with this assessment. Many of those who pass through the Party have had some record of criminal activity and mental disorder in the past. Rockwell claims to make a conscious effort to fend off the chronic criminal and the homosexual, but those who gravitate to the ANP generally have family problems, a history of petty juvenile delinquency, social problems —most of which stem from mental imbalance.

One man who was close to Rockwell is Karl R. Allen, an athletic ex-army lieutenant and a graduate of Florida State University. His ANP biography reads as follows:

. . . Joined August 1961. Veteran of 6 missions. Lone White Man to publicly give speech against nigger march in D.C. August 28 [1963] against police ban [for which he was jailed]; led bloody Philadelphia IV [picket-riot at ADL offices]; recently jumped on stage in Danville, Va., and told off Martin Luther King before packed hall of coons; is largely credited with getting party on organized, business-like basis internally; is holder of Party Prison Medal and Medal of Merit. . . .[19]

Allen broke with the ANP in late 1963 over what both he and Rockwell claim to be the other's personality. He took many of the ANP members with him. (Since ANP membership in Arlington rarely rises above twenty-five, a loss of ten or so men can be devastating.)

Allen's main concern is to be more "politically realistic." His new organization, called the White Party, he claims is more nationalistic, less international. He believes that the "Jewish Question" will be solved through geographic isolation rather than through extermination. He hopes to become more active against the "blockbusters," the real estate operators who want to integrate neighborhoods. He worked for George Wallace in the 1964 primaries, and hopes to be able to run his own candidates soon.

Allen calls his party a "racial political party" and claims two-hundred members—an exceedingly high estimate—in the Baltimore-Washington area alone. He is proud to be known as a white supremacist and wants all American Negroes to be "repatriated." Spengler's *Decline of the West,* Francis Parker Yockey's *Imperium* and T. Lothrop Stoddard's *The Revolt Against Civilization* are the books that have influenced him most.

Also close to Rockwell is John Patler, editor of *The Stormtrooper.* He is perhaps the best cartoonist in the ANP, better than Rockwell himself. Patler's specialty seems to be caricatures of Jews and Negroes.

Patler has been a member of a number of other racist organizations. He was associated for a while with James Madole's National Renaissance Party and briefly with Rockwell's ANP before he left to start his own organization, the American National Party.

The American National Party lasted less than two years, from 1962 through early 1963. It published a magazine called *Kill,* which carried a number of articles on world affairs. For instance, the September 1962 issue had this comment to make:

TO [sic] BAD THEY MISSED!

. . . Kwame Nkrumah, Communist boss of Ghana, was nearly killed by a bomb thrown at his car. . . . Unfortunately, the bomb didn't kill the black pig. If it had, the world would have been rid of one of the worst black swine alive. We hope the assassins keep trying.

The American National Party spent most of its time attacking Rockwell. Yet in 1963, Patler suddenly dissolved his party and rejoined the American Nazi Party. He claims this change of heart came about during a fifty-four-day prison sentence. "I did something I had not done in 2 years . . . THINK!" he wrote.[20]

Patler's sudden switch left his few followers high and dry. Most of them refused to join up with Rockwell; instead, they joined the Nationalist Party (sometimes known as the U.S. Nationalist Party), another tiny New York-based racist group which published a magazine called *The Nationalist*. This organization is not very active today, if indeed it is still alive at all. It was decidedly anti-Rockwell ("Who needs Nutzis?" read one poster), anti-Communist ("Hang Sobel"), pro-McCarthy ("America's Greatest Patriot"), anti-Young Americans for Freedom ("Goldwater's Junior League") and anti-liberal, -conservative and -Jew.

Perhaps the best known of Rockwell's associates was Daniel Burros. Burros was New York-born and -raised and had an IQ of 154. His entire life was a chronicle of personal instability. He had an undistinguished scholastic record; he received a "General Discharge under Honorable Conditions" (which is less than a straight Honorable Discharge) from the military; he could not hold a job any length of time; and he had been up before the law a number of times for fighting, using profane language and daubing swastikas on buildings. On one occasion, Burros was convicted with James Madole, of the National Renaissance Party, and several others of rioting, conspiring to circulate inflammatory literature and criminal possession of firearms and a switchblade knife. Both Madole and Burros received two-year jail terms.[21] Madole's conviction was appealed and, at the time of this writing, is still pending.

Known as "Dan the Fink" by his peers, Burros had a reputation as a "floater," one who drifted from group to group. At one time or another he had been a member of the National Renaissance Party, the American Nazi Party, the British National Party, the Odinist Religion, the Ku Klux Klan, the American Racial Fascist

Party and the Blue Shirt Legion. The last two were figments of his own imagination.

He published a magazine in 1965 called *The Free American,* subtitled "The Battle Organ of Racial Fascism." The May 1965 issue was dated "YF 76," meaning "Year of the Fuehrer," counting from the birth of Hitler.

One of Burros' old associates in the American Nazi Party claims that Burros was not insane but that he merely had an insane streak in him. For instance, he liked to torture dogs (his own dog at that time—a mongrel known as "Gas Chambers"—was not, however, subjected to this type of treatment). While he was a member of the 101st Airborne ("Screaming Eagle") Division, he is supposed to have crept out of his barracks one dark night and choked the division mascot, a bald eagle, to death in its pen.

When he was on the staff of Rockwell's magazine, *The Stormtrooper,* he often cut out pictures of spiders, swastikas, skulls, eagles and similar items from various magazines and pasted them at random on a sheet of paper which he would then photograph. With a metal plate made from the negative, he would run off hundreds of copies of his creation on the Party's press. This stack of paper he would take back to his room; once there, he would proceed to cut out all the pictures again.

Physically, Burros was a short, pudgy and sallow-faced man with thick-lensed glasses that made his eyes look larger than they were. When he sat he often put his knees up under his chin, hooked his heels on the edge of the chair, cocked his head to one side and giggled like a teen-ager. When nervous or excited he giggled uncontrollably. He walked at an oblique angle, never straight ahead, so that he was constantly wearing out the sides of his boot heels. One member recalls that he was the one who was always asking Rockwell for money for new heels.

Although blond and blue-eyed, Burros was no Nordic prototype. It was revealed in *The New York Times* in late October 1965 that Burros was in fact a Jew of Russian extraction. He had even been Bar Mitzvahed (confirmed).

This revelation proved embarrassing to Burros not only because of his long association with anti-Jewish causes, but because, at the time the story broke, he was the Grand Dragon of the United

Klans of America, Knights of the Ku Klux Klan for the State of New York. Burros had endeavored to hide his background from his associates, and for the most part, he had succeeded. Only through the persistent research of *Times* reporter John McCandlish Phillips were the facts brought to light.

Phillips related in *Times Talk*, the newspaper's house magazine, how Burros, confronted with this information, had threatened his life if the truth were ever revealed. Once Burros realized that the story could not be suppressed, he told Phillips that he would "go out in a blaze of glory." The *Times* management thought that he might try to storm the news building and shoot it up. They were also concerned for the life of Phillips himself. Security around the *Times* building was tightened, a personal set of bodyguards was assigned to the enterprising reporter, and on the day the story broke, Phillips himself was sent out of town.[22]

But Burros had other ideas. On the day the story was printed, October 31, 1965, he was in Reading, Pennsylvania, visiting Roy E. Frankhouser, Jr., the United Klans of America's Grand Dragon for the Keystone State. Furious over the publication of the story, according to Frankhouser, Burros "came raving up the stairs like a madman," demolished a bed with vicious karate kicks, found a pistol and shot himself to death.

The question that one hears most often asked about Rockwell is why does he act as he does? One reason advanced by a number of people who know him is that he is a glutton for publicity and a thwarted vaudevillian, so egotistical that he is willing to appear as a comic-opera Hitler in order to see his name in print. (Rockwell believes that the press has clamped a blackout on his activities. "I could run across the White House lawn naked," he said, "and they wouldn't report it.")

A more practical explanation is to be found in Rockwell's four-phase program for coming to power. The first phase involves making his name known to the public at any cost and by any means. He picked the swastika and his shock tactics to achieve this. The second phase is to acquaint people with his program; the third is to organize his followers into a political machine; and the fourth is to run for office and put his program into effect. Rockwell claims from time to time that he is in phase two, or three, or four, depending on the situation, the news value, his audience, and so on. But in truth, he has *never* permanently moved out of phase one, primarily because it seems to fit his personality best.

Another reason that he acts as he does lies in his genuine belief that only shock tactics will shake white Gentile Americans out of their "stupor." He believes that by openly brandishing the swastika he can so anger the Jews that they will be goaded into making rash and imprudent moves.

His controversial views and his ability to attract headlines make him much in demand as a speaker on campuses around the country. He takes advantage of his notoriety: these speechmaking tours probably now account for the major source of Party income. Rockwell seems to believe that his views are getting across to the students, although most reports are to the contrary. He tends to underestimate the intelligence of his audiences; he is apt to confuse mere courtesy for active acceptance of his views.

The effects of almost a decade in the political wilderness are plainly visible. He is extremely nervous and believes that a number of people are bent on killing him. He wears wraparound sunglasses for fear of having acid thrown in his eyes; scars from past beatings streak his face. During the 1965 governor's race in Virginia, he was seldom out of reach of a loaded pistol. He does not trust anyone. During our interview, for instance, we could not effect a simple trade of books without signed promises of delivery.

This mistrust has eroded the theoretically once-stiff entrance requirements of the American Nazi Party. Members are now taken in because they are pro-Rockwell. That is why Daniel Burros could be a member of the ANP even when there is some indication that several other members knew he was Jewish. Burros was pro-Rockwell; therefore few questions were asked.

The Commander commented during our interview that when it came to deciding just who got in and who was excluded, it devolved on him to pass judgment, regardless of the rules. American Indians have joined, he said, but "Sammy Davis, Jr., wouldn't make it."

The ANP is a minor irritant in the American body politic and is likely to stay that way in the days to come. The number of

Americans who are attracted to an active life of Naziism—even in the event of an economic decline—is limited. The Party's unpopular objectives are another antidote to success. Americans have a history of massacring Indians; they have none of gassing Jews. Thus Rockwell's message generally falls on hostile ears.

Yet Rockwell himself remains the biggest stumbling block to success. When the ANP is short of men, when finances are low, when things are going badly, then Rockwell is easy to get along with; but when the membership grows, when money begins to flow in and when his name is making the front pages of the newspapers, he turns arrogant, insufferable, boorish and uncooperative, with the result that members leave, finances fall off and publicity dries up. Thus he guarantees that his Party stays small and impotent.

Many observers have concluded that Rockwell prefers it that way, free from the problems of growth, free from rivals, free to do what he likes best: make headlines.

2

The National
States Rights Party

A much larger and far more active racist group is the National
States Rights Party.* It claims chapters in thirty-six cities, from
Massachusetts to California. The NSRP boasts that it is the third
largest political party in the United States, a statement challenged
by many other groups. Its leaders refuse to say how many members there are in the Party, although an estimate of six hundred
activists, with perhaps an additional eight thousand activist sympathizers, would be generous.

The Party was formed in 1958 by Dr. Edward R. Fields, a
young chiropractor, and Jesse B. Stoner, a Georgia attorney with
a varied political career. The NSRP's genesis, however, can be
traced back to 1946. At that time there existed an organization in
Atlanta called the Columbians, a paramilitary combat group that
actively plotted the take-over of the state of Georgia. It was
founded just after World War II by Emory Burke, a long-time
fascist. Its symbol was a lightning bolt similar to the one used by
the *Hitler Jungend,* the Nazi youth movement.

Following a series of disturbances, Burke and a number of
others were seized, along with a considerable amount of arms,
ammunition and explosives. Also confiscated was a list of citizens
who were to be exterminated once the Columbians came to
power.[1] Burke was sentenced to three years in prison.

One of the members of the Columbians was Edward Fields,
only fourteen years old at the time. He and others formed a "Free
Emory Burke Committee," which proved unsuccessful.

* No relation to the States Rights Democratic Party ("Dixiecrats") that
flourished during the 1948 election.

In 1952, Fields formed the Christian Anti-Jewish Party with fellow law student Jesse Stoner. Stoner went on to be admitted to the Georgia bar, but Fields dropped out of law school in 1953 to attend the Palmer School of Chiropractic in Davenport, Iowa. While there, he sponsored an "Anti-Jew Week" (February 21–28) and was investigated by the local police when it was reported he was putting stickers on storefronts reading: "This place owned by Jews." By 1956 he had graduated, and once more he plunged into active politics, first as an organizer for the Citizens' Councils, later as a founder of an anti-Semitic, anti-Negro organization called the United White Party.* The UWP soon merged with a segregationist group called the States Rights Party, and shortly thereafter the Party's name was changed to the present one.

Since 1958, the NSRP has absorbed the National White American Party, John Kasper's Seaboard Citizens' Council, James Bagwell's South Carolina Klan, the U.S. Klans of Florida, Dewey Taft's Conservative Party in Tampa, and a number of other small splinter groups. It is currently associated with the "Northern European Ring," an international fascist association, and with the British National Party, a strikingly similar group led by John Bean, an ex-associate of Colin Jordan's.[2]

Jesse Stoner originally came from Chattanooga, Tennessee, where his family used to own Rock City, a well-known tourist attraction on top of Lookout Mountain, south of the city. In his youth, Stoner suffered an attack of polio which has left one leg shorter than the other.

He began his political career in 1942 at the age of eighteen when he became a Kleagle (an organizer) for the Knights of the Ku Klux Klan in Chattanooga. He later became a member of the Columbians. In 1946 he founded the Stoner Anti-Jewish Party, which proposed to make Judaism a legal offense punishable by death. This party, he felt, would out-Hitler Hitler, whom he believed to be a moderate. Stoner ran for Congress in 1948 under this label and received over 500 votes out of some 30,000 cast.

---

* One of the UWP's founders was Matt Koehl, a former leader of the "SE Guard" of the National Renaissance Party, later a "Security Officer" for the NSRP and, from 1962 onward, a member of Rockwell's American Nazi Party.

With Edward Fields, Stoner changed the name of the party to the Christian Anti-Jewish Party. Stoner became the NSRP's General Counsel when his party merged with it. In 1959, he became the Imperial Wizard of the Christian Knights of the Ku Klux Klan, which operated out of Louisville, Kentucky. This Klan does not appear to be active at the moment.

Originally located in the home of a member in Jeffersonville, Indiana, NSRP headquarters was soon moved to Birmingham, Alabama. In the summer of 1965, it was moved again to Augusta, Georgia, where it remains today, in the downtown section, within sight of the tall Confederate monument.

The final move was for two reasons: first, Jesse Stoner is eventually to become the Chairman, replacing Ned Dupes, a retired salesman formerly associated with John Kasper's Seaboard Citizens' Council, and it was felt that the Party should be located in the state of its Chairman. The second reason for the move—and perhaps the chief one—stems from a split that took place within the Party in 1964, the only one it has experienced so far. Apparently three members, led by James R. McDaniels, had a disagreement over policy with Fields, Dupes and Stoner. Part of the dispute concerned the wearing of uniforms, a practice the Party had adopted on its founding. Fields' faction had come to believe that uniforms were hurting the Party and had decided in favor of wearing only an armband and a silver lightning-flash lapel pin (Stoner has a diamond one). The three dissidents wanted to keep the Sam Browne belt, white shirt, black tie and military cap of old.

Fields also claims that McDaniels wanted to be the sole leader, a common enough affliction among minority groups. What angered the young chiropractor the most, however, was the loss of their mailing list—the life and blood of any propagandist—to the dissidents.

In any event, McDaniels' group, now calling itself the American States Rights Party,* remained in Birmingham, and Fields, Dupes, Stoner and company moved to Augusta.

---

* Philosophically, the ASRP varies little from the NSRP. It publishes a newspaper called *The White American,* subtitled: "Being a politician is a sorry profession—Being a statesman is a noble one." Articles concentrate on

Membership in the National States Rights Party is limited to White Christian Americans. "Any person of Asiatic, African or Jewish blood or ancestry," states the constitution, "can never be a member of this Party and the same prohibition applies to every White person who is married to such a person."

"If a man claims he's white," Fields told me, "we take his word for it; but if a man comes in and looks like a nigger, we'd probably start asking some questions." As for Jews, Fields claims he can spot them either by their looks or by their name. Members must renounce their allegiance to other political groups, particularly Rockwell's Nazi Party, the Klan and the John Birch Society.

The Party's eschatology includes a certain amount of mysticism reminiscent of the German-American Bund of the 1930s. For instance, the NSRP constitution explains the thunderbolt as:

> . . . an ancient symbol of the White race. It is the thunder from the heavens which first awed our forefathers as they looked into the storm clouds and listened to the thunderous roar. The White race has always used different forms of the flash of light to symbolize strength and power. The Thunderbolt has always been a warning to the Whiteman's enemies. The flash was a rune in the first alphabet of our White folk. . . .

The passage goes on to describe the flag—of Confederate design with a white disk and red flash in the center:

> The red stands for the pure red [an earlier version had "Nordic" in place of the word "red"] blood of our White people which we seek to preserve. . . . The blue represents the vast

---

attacking Jews, Negroes and Protestants ("Katzenbach is a Communist JEW!"), similar to the NSRP newspaper, *The Thunderbolt.* One item, for instance, pictures Uncle Sam in his famous "America Wants You!" pose, with the following doggerel below:

> On any issue before you choose
> Check the influence of the Jews.

The symbol of the Party is a *double* lightning flash, reminiscent of the Nazi *Schutzstaffl* (SS) markings.

Physically the Party differs with the NSRP on two counts. It continues to wear uniforms and it has fewer members, perhaps twenty-five.

future of our White people stretching into time and eternity: as long as God's blue sky is above us, the great White race shall live. The cross in the background . . . is the Cross of St. Andrew which was part of the battle flag of the Confederacy. It represents the persecutions of our forefathers. . . . The white circle stands for the purity of our White womanhood and our beloved little White children who are the basic reason for our united stand; we struggle for them. We are ordained by God to save the White race so that civilization will exist as long as the world stands. . . .

The objectives of the National States Rights Party revolve around the well-being of "Whiteman." The Preamble to the constitution and bylaws puts it this way:

We of the National States Rights Party believe in our Lord Jesus Christ and the Christian heritage of our people. We believe in the great White race and the necessity for the preservation of our race and the Nation which the Whiteman created out of the wilderness of this continent. . . . We believe in preserving the Race of our forefathers which built civilizations out of jungles and which gave art, culture, inventions, freedom and justice to the entire world. We will not allow the blood of our people to be polluted with that of black, yellow, jewish or mongrel peoples. . . . All that is patriotic, good clean and decent springs forth from the foundations of our White folk. These high standards of living do not, and cannot, exist in the non-White backward areas of the world, except where the Whiteman maintains a foothold of control. . . .

We dedicate ourselves to the task of saving America and the White race and the preservation of the pure blood of our forefathers. . . .

One of the ways in which the NSRP proposes to save America for Whiteman is to rid the country of "aliens." Exactly what constitutes an "alien" is unclear, but Negroes ("Blackman"), Orientals and Jews would head the list. Fields, for one, does not believe in gassing Jews as does Rockwell; he would rather deport them to distant lands; Negroes he would ship to Liberia and Orientals to Hawaii. Although Fields originally considered Palestine unsuitable for Jewish settlement because it falls within the Christian-Arab sphere of influence,[3] he now seems to take the view that Israel is indeed the best place for them. At one time he favored Madagascar.

And what if these Americans did not want to make such a move? Well, said Fields, "later on, the country would have to be purified."[4]

> Jew-devils have no place in a White Christian nation. When our Party is elected . . . the Government will expel the Jews and confiscate their ill-gotten wealth for the benefit of the American people. When the Jews are gone, we Americans will own rich America.[5]

The fifth anniversary issue of *The Thunderbolt,* the Party's newspaper, dated April 1963, added: "We want our money back. The Jews have our money and we want it back. When we get it back, we will enjoy a genuine and lasting prosperity, with plenty for all. . . ."

The NSRP view that Communists and Jews are virtually one and the same differs little from the attitudes of other racist groups. The Party feels so strongly on the issue, in fact, that it wrote the following into its constitution:

> Communism is Jewish! Communism is one of the Jew plans, along with the United Nations organization and other world government schemes, to destroy us and conquer the world. Revolutions, no-win wars, internationalism, economic chaos, inflations, starvations, unemployment and depressions are deliberately designed by the Jews to promote their communistic plans. In every communist country, the Jews are the ruling race. Almost all communist spies are Jews. Our Party proposes for the Government to expel all communists from this Nation. Without the Jews, there would be NO communism![6]

The Party attacks the Negro on what it believes to be a scientific basis. One article, often seen in NSRP literature, entitled "Negro Skull & Brain Still in Ape Stage," attempts to show that the angle between jaw, mouth and forehead is indicative of intelligence.

Whiteman has a 70° angle, Caveman 50°, Negro 60°, and Gorilla 40°. The article goes on to say:

THE NEGRO ACTUALLY IS A HIGHER FORM OF GORILLA. GOD DID NOT WISH FOR THE WHITE RACE TO MIX WITH THESE ANIMALS. TELL YOUR FRIENDS AND CHILDREN THESE SCIENTIFIC TRUTHS SO THAT COMMUNIST TEACHERS AND PREACHERS WILL NOT BE ABLE TO BRAIN WASH THEM WITH "THE BIG LIE" THAT ALL MEN ARE EQUAL.[7]

Fields told me, with a certain amount of heat in his voice, "We not only feel the Negro is a primitive race, we have proved it in our literature. On their own they are not capable of maintaining a civilized society."

If Negroes remain on American soil, "even with segregation, it is inevitable that mongrelization of the races will take place. A mongrel, high-yellow race!"

The Thunderbolt, an eight- to twelve-page monthly, is the Party's major source of literature that "proves" Fields' and other members' points. Many of the articles are reprints from other newspapers; there is a section on NSRP activities around the country; the back page advertises, among other things, anti-Jewish literature (*Jewish Ritual Murder,* by Arnold Leese, *The Protocols of the Learned Elders of Zion,* and *The International Jew,* by Henry Ford, etc.), Thunderbolt armbands ("reduced to only $1.00 each"), and mail-order "High-powered military rifles, priced from $7.50 to $87.50."

One section is devoted to "Jews in the News." Typical headlines are: "LBJ Appoints Another Jew to U.N.," "Communism is Still Jewish" and "Jew Shoots Rabbi." Anti-Negro headlines also appear: "Negroes on Rampage, RAPE-RAPE-RAPE," "Full Blacks Most Inferior," "God Bless Ian Smith, Patriot & Hero" and "Thaddeus Stevens Whiteman's Worst Enemy, Until Katzenbach." *The Thunderbolt* exhorts its readers to "Pass [the newspaper] on to your doctor," "Pass on to a student" and "Pass on to your lawyer."

When it is not attacking Negroes and Jews, the newspaper concentrates its fire on a number of other subjects. On antiwar demonstrations, an article entitled "We Favor Burning of Beatniks" had this to say:

> On November 1st [1965] a screw-ball left winger [referring to Norman R. Morrison] burned himself alive in front of the Pentagon in protest against the war in Vietnam. He was a member of a group of degenerate beatnik Quakers who would have America surrender to Communism rather than fight. When the news reached NSRP Headquarters, we all shouted "Hooray." . . .[8]

Only six months after President Kennedy had taken office, the Party was calling for his impeachment.[9] Unlike others who would like to see Chief Justice Earl Warren impeached, the NSRP believes that all nine members of the Court should be put to death.[10] Adolf Eichmann's trial, NSRP members believe, was a "GIANT PROPAGANDA HOAX"; and they are also convinced that the death of six million Jews in World War II "has been disproved by many authorities."[11] Most right-wing groups defend the Federal Bureau of Investigation as the last bastion of "Americanism," but not the NSRP. They attack it as part of the "Communist-Jewish Conspiracy." "At one time," said Fields, "it was a good organization. But under Kennedy and Johnson it has been turned into a political police." He added, "Every member who makes a name for himself, they [the FBI] offer money to turn pimp. They even offered me $50,000 cold cash to testify against Mr. Stoner. They said: 'We're sure we can come up with some information [against him].' Every one of our leaders has been approached." The FBI, he argued, "definitely want to suppress the racist right wing in America. As soon as we find a man who is disrupting our work, we immediately suspect he is a paid pimp."

The Party claims to be different from the ordinary conservative groups throughout the country. To be sure, its members are anti-New Deal and resistant to change. Ned Dupes, for instance, distrusted President Franklin D. Roosevelt because he "had eyes close together like a rat's."[12] Fields would never vote for Goldwater because he is of Jewish descent. "That's reason enough not to vote for him," he said.

"We differ from conservatives," he added, "in that we do not oppose TVA, Social Security and Medicare. We call ourselves the 'Farmers' and Workers' Party.' We have a Social Security program that is much more generous than the present program. We would give everyone the same amount—$250.00 minimum per month— at the age of 62; and it would come out of the 'General Tax Fund.' "

Furthermore, Fields states that his Party is in favor of REA where private industry cannot step in "because the people must have electricity"; he favors free birth control devices to backward countries; and he wants low interest rates all around. He opposes: "U.N. control of the U.S. Government"; foreign aid, except surplus military weapons for allies; the Federal Reserve System because "the U.S. Government should print its own money";* and he does not sympathize with the Black Muslims because they want to set up an all-black state here in America, rather than in Africa.

The NSRP first made headlines at the time of the Atlanta synagogue dynamiting in October 1958. Five men arrested as suspects in the case were identified as members of the Party. Charges were eventually dropped after the trial of one member, George Michael Bright, ended in an acquittal. One of the witnesses who appeared in Bright's behalf was late Eldon Edwards, formerly a paint sprayer at GM's Fisher Body plant in Atlanta, and at that moment Imperial Wizard of the U.S. Klans, Knights of the Ku Klux Klan.

Perhaps the major reason why the NSRP hates the FBI today is that the key witness for the prosecution turned out to be an undercover agent from the Bureau.

The arrest of the five NSRP members helped create a rash of ad hoc committees. One of them was called the National Committee to Secure Justice for the Atlanta Five and was headed by William Stephenson, editor of the now-defunct *Virginian*. George Lincoln Rockwell, one of Stephenson's old protégés, was also active with an ad hoc committee of his own.

* See Chapter 18 on the Greenback Party.

In 1960, the NSRP fielded Presidential and Vice-Presidential candidates. For President it nominated Governor Orville Faubus of Arkansas and for Vice-President, Admiral John G. Crommelin, USN (ret.). Faubus was a most reluctant candidate and declined to run. His name was removed from the Florida ballot, but remained on the Alabama, Arkansas, Delaware and Tennessee ballots. The Party polled 7 percent of the vote in Arkansas, slightly more than 1 percent in Tennessee and much less in Alabama and Delaware.

Crommelin, the Vice-Presidential candidate, is one of the NSRP's most fervent supporters. Since his forced retirement from active duty in 1950, he has been a perennial candidate for national office. He ran for the Senate in 1950, 1954, 1956, 1960 and 1962, receiving over 112,000 votes against Lister Hill in the 1956 contest and over 51,000 against John Sparkman four years later. He ran for governor of Alabama in 1958 and for mayor of Montgomery the following year, in which he received 10 percent of the vote. With the exception of the 1960 Vice-Presidential bid, he has run as a Democrat.

Crommelin comes from a distinguished family of military men. One ancestor fought in the Revolutionary War; both his grand-fathers fought for the Confederacy. He is the eldest of five brothers, all of whom distinguished themselves in World War II. Crommelin Field, at Atlantic City's Naval Air Station, was named for two of his brothers who died in battle.

The Admiral himself was an outstanding naval aviator. He once was the leader of the famed stunt-flying squadron, "The Blue Angels." Early in the war he served aboard the carrier *Enterprise,* later as Chief of Staff aboard the carrier *Liscomb Bay.* This latter ship was sunk by enemy torpedoes; Crommelin was forced to swim from it in the nude because he was taking a shower when the ship was hit.

In 1950, Crommelin, then a Captain, became embroiled in the celebrated "War of the Admirals," a controversy centering around the unification of the services and including disputes over the relative merits of super carriers and long-range bombers. He alleged that the B-36 program was full of scandal and that the Navy was being "nibbled to death." He passed on to the press some confidential material in support of his views. This led to his being reprimanded and reassigned. In spite of this, he kept up his attacks in defiance of direct orders. His superiors then furloughed him on half pay, and soon thereafter he was retired with the rank of Rear Admiral.

Until 1956, Crommelin merely campaigned on an anti-Communist and segregationist platform. Then his anti-Semitism began to show. Addressing the North Alabama Citizens' Council, he declared that the integration efforts were being led by "Felix Frankfurter, a Jew [and] Senator Herbert Lehman, a Marxist Jew." He then went on to ask, "Don't you know it's their kind of people who are behind this whole mess? . . . We've got to keep this last frontier of the real Anglo-Saxon race. . . . And if I am wrong, my name is Finkelstein."[13]

He has since spoken in Los Angeles and Dallas under the auspices of Gerald L. K. Smith and at a number of Citizens' Council meetings. The topic of his speech is usually "The Hidden Force," his explanation of a giant "Jewish-Communist-Integration Conspiracy." Many racist publications are his loyal boosters: Conde McGinley's *Common Sense,* Smith's *The Cross and the Flag,* Stephenson's *The Virginian* and, until 1960, Frank Britton's *The American Nationalist.*

In the 1962 senatorial race (his third against Lister Hill), his campaign manager was the Reverend Oren F. Potito of St. Petersburg, Florida. Potito, a director of the racist Church of Jesus Christ-Christian, is affiliated with the Anglo-Saxon Federation of America and the "U.S. Rangers," a paramilitary organization in California. He later became an organizer for the NSRP. Also involved in Crommelin's campaign were the Reverend Gordon Winrod, then the National Chaplain of the NSRP, and son of the late Gerald Winrod (the alleged seditionist in World War II and editor of *Defender* magazine); the Reverend Wesley A. Swift, the founder of the Church of Jesus Christ-Christian and a leader of the U.S. Rangers; and James K. Warner, at various times associated with Rockwell, the NSRP and the Odinist Religion.

In 1962, the National States Rights Party sent seven of its members to Oxford, Mississippi, to protest against the enrollment of James Meredith, a Negro, in the University. Potito, one of the seven, was detained and some firearms were confiscated from his car. Later in the year, the NSRP picketed Dr. Martin Luther King in Montgomery and Arthur Dean at the University of Alabama. James Warner was convicted of trespassing in the latter instance and was sentenced to six months in jail and fined $100.

In 1963, the Party organized a "Fire Your Nigger" campaign with the hope of forcing more Negroes to leave the South. It distributed literature in Birmingham blaming the Jews for the demonstrations there. It started a riot in the same town with Negro civil rights workers which resulted in a broken hand for Warner. It sponsored a boycott of integrated stores in Birmingham by waving Confederate flags and carrying placards reading "This store serves Negroes."

Earlier in the year, several uniformed members of the NSRP became involved in a quarrel with some high school students in San Bernardino, California. In the ensuing altercation, one of the students was wounded by a shot fired from a pellet gun allegedly in the hands of one of the NSRP men. Two men were found guilty of battery and disturbing the peace. Another, "Connie" Lynch, a firebrand orator who regularly sports a Confederate vest during public appearances, and an associate of Wesley Swift's, was also found guilty of disturbing the peace.

On 15 September 1963, the 16th Street Baptist Church of Birmingham was dynamited and four children were killed. Fields denied any complicity in the act, claiming it "had disrupted everything for us." Threats of retaliation ran so strongly against him that he felt it prudent to change his address. Among the suspects arrested in connection with the bombing was an NSRP member. He and the others were charged with illegal possession of dynamite, fined and sentenced to six months in jail.

Later, Fields, Stoner and Warner and a number of others were indicted on three counts for conspiring to interfere with the Federal Court's desegregation order. The Party hired Matt H. Murphy, Jr., subsequently the defense attorney in the 1965 Liuzzo murder mistrial, and shortly thereafter killed in an automobile accident, as its lawyer. In early 1964, he succeeded in having the charges dropped.

The NSRP was also in the thick of the race riots in St. Augustine during the summer of 1963. Connie Lynch, a self-ordained Fundamentalist-type preacher, led the assault. He teamed with Stoner to tour northern Florida to revitalize the Klan in the area. Lynch at various times has been an organizer for the NSRP, a Klansman, a member of the U.S. Rangers and the Christian Defense League. He has an impressive talent for turning audiences into howling, frenzied, blood-seeking mobs such as the one in St. Augustine. A news reporter caught this statement on his tape recorder from Lynch:

> I spoke to the white people, the white people rallied behind it and we kicked the livin' hell out of the niggers—sent the out-of-town niggers to the hospitals and out of state to their own home town where they oughta been. And the niggers of St. Augustine got quiet and went back home to nigger-town where they belong. . . .

Lynch, a short, stocky, dough-faced man with curly hair, speaks with a staccato rapidity, his voice rising several octaves with excitement and rage. Alluding to what would happen if a white man seduced a Negro woman, he exclaimed:

> Those people would *kill* if you put a woman among the white-faced husbands; they'd *shoot you!* But they tell me I don't even have a right to *fight* to protect the white race! Let these black bucks come in. . . . They said it was gonna be settled in the bedrooms; well, I've got some news for them!

In late 1965, the NSRP held a rally in Anniston, Alabama, at which they advocated removing "the nigger out of the white man's streets." One member of the audience, Hubert Damon Strange, a young gas station attendant with a dreary record of assault and weapons offenses, became so fired up that he drove off with two friends and shot down a young Negro in another car who, ironically, belonged to no civil rights group, walked no picket line, was hard-working and was not even considered "uppity." Strange, defended by Jesse Stoner, was convicted of second-degree murder by an all-white Southern jury and was sentenced to ten years in prison. The case rested on the testimony of a small-time hoodlum who admitted he had turned in his friends to collect the $21,000 reward money. On the actual shooting, the turncoat had this to say: "I asked Damon [Strange] how many Negroes did he get . . . and he said 'I got one I'm pretty sure because the car was swerving off the road. I had to lean out the window to get him.' "[14]

Over the last few years, the NSRP has experienced some success in combating "blockbusting" tactics. There are two stratagems to blockbusting, the first of which is straightforward. A Negro group such as the National Association for the Advancement of Colored People or the Congress of Racial Equality will buy a house in an all-white area and move a Negro family in with the hopes of eventually integrating the entire neighborhood. In opposing this, the NSRP will often outbid the Negro group, or it will agitate against the sale of the house to a Negro (for instance, signs that read: "Zoned—a *White* community") or, as a last resort, it will turn to intimidation.

The other stratagem is for an unscrupulous real estate dealer to buy a house in an all-white neighborhood—for an exceedingly high price if need be—and move a Negro family in. He will then terrify the other homeowners with tales of Negro excesses until they sell out at bargain prices. The original Negro family is then evicted, and all the houses are resold to other whites for huge profits to the dealer.

In one of those ironies that seem to abound in a situation such as this, the Negro agencies and the NSRP are temporarily allied against the real estate dealer: the Negro groups because the dealer is not really carrying out a block-busting operation; and the NSRP because it is opposed to any Negroes moving into a white neighborhood.

In 1964 the NSRP again put forward a Presidential slate: John Kasper for President and Jesse B. Stoner for Vice-President. Their names appeared on the voting lists of three states: Arkansas, Tennessee and Montana. In all, they received slightly more than 6,000 votes, an 86 percent drop from their 1960 showing.

Since their electoral efforts have borne little fruit, the Party members have decided that future campaigns will be conducted on the local levels only. They plan to adopt the slogan that the Alabama Democrats dropped in a move to modernize their image:

"White Supremacy—for the Right." This, they believe, will win them many votes.

"We do not plan to run anyone above city council, state legislature and perhaps U.S. Congress," Fields told me. "We feel we can use the money more effectively." Also, he concluded, referring to past battles lost, "contributors balk at giving to so hopeless an effort."

3

"... Odin Speed to Valhalla"

1

There are a number of other groups and individuals on the American political scene whose outlook is predominantly racist in character. Perhaps the best-known racist in America today is the Reverend Gerald Lyman Kenneth Smith, now in his late sixties, the handsome, intelligent, spellbinding, rabble-rousing leader of the Christian Nationalist Party.

Smith's political career dates from 1933 when he joined William Dudley Pelley's Silver Shirts.* He soon moved on to serve Huey Long as an organizer of his campaign for the Presidency. When the Kingfish was cut down by assassins in 1935, it was Gerald Smith who delivered the funeral oration. He then cast his lot with the

---

* Pelley, a New Englander of "uncontaminated English Stock," founded the Silver Shirts—sometimes known as the Christian American Patriots—in Asheville, North Carolina, in 1933, the day after Hitler came to power. His followers dressed themselves in silver shirts, blue corduroy knickers and gold stockings. In its heyday, the organization claimed two million adherents. In 1936 he established the Christian Party and ran for President under the slogan "For Christ and the Constitution." His platform read in part: "I propose to defranchise the Jew by Constitutional Amendment, to make it impossible for a Jew to own property in the United States excepting under the same licensing system successfully employed against Occidentals in Japan, and to limit Jews in the professions, trades and sciences by license according to their quotas of representation in the population."

By 1939 Pelley was a Nazi sympathizer, and by 1942 he was in jail for sedition. The Silver Shirt organization collapsed with his jailing. After the war he spent his time bombarding his faithful with a curious religio-spiritual message that defied comprehension as time went on. He died in 1965.

Townsendites until he had a quarrel with Dr. Francis E. Townsend, founder of the pension-promoting scheme, and quit. Smith then teamed up with Father Charles E. Coughlin, the anti-Semitic radio priest from Royal Oak, Michigan.* By 1937, Smith had formed a group called the Committee of One Million, ostensibly organized to oppose "insidious and subversive influences that are now undermining the sanctity of our churches, the integrity of our schools, the authority of our government, and the sacredness of our family institutions." In effect, he sought to stampede the middle and lower income groups to the right as Hitler had done in Germany. He preached the general evils of democracy, advocated isolationism, and predicted a Bolshevik take-over of the U.S. unless the public woke up and followed his advice.[1]

In 1944, Smith ran for President on the American First Party ticket, an organization of his own creation. Publicly, he supported America's war effort, but his Party's platform advocated virtually none of the long-range postwar goals that the Allies were seeking, such as world peace and the end of racial and religious intolerance. He received only 1,780 votes.

After the war, Smith turned his fire upon the United Nations, the Negroes and the Jews, particularly the Jews. He claimed, for instance, that Nazi Germany was not responsible for the war. It was, he said, promoted by "power-mad internationalists operating under the direction of international Jewry."[2]

In 1946, he formed the Christian Nationalist Crusade by uniting

---

* Father Coughlin began his career in the early 1930s as a monetary reformer. He came to national attention with his attacks on the American financial community which he believed created the depression. He formed the Union Party in 1936 and ran a William Lemke for President against FDR, a person he initially admired but upon whom he soon soured. The Party ran third, receiving almost 900,000 votes.

By 1937 he was a famous radio priest, attacking the financial community with abandon, particularly the Jewish sections of it. As time went on he became more anti-Semitic; he had turned pro-Nazi by the outset of war. A group of Jewish agencies showed how one speech of his was taken almost verbatim from one of Goebbels'. By the end of the war his Roman Catholic superiors had effectively silenced him.

Today his Christian Front and National Union for Social Justice have been dead a full generation. Father Coughlin lives quietly in Royal Oak, still priest of the garish church-in-the-round, the famous Shrine of the Little Flower.

a number of right-wing groups and individuals under his leadership. Some of these included Kenneth Goff, then of Christian Youth for America, an ex-Communist, now a director of Soldiers of the Cross; the Reverend Arthur W. Terminiello from Alabama, sometimes known as "the Father Coughlin of the South"; Frederick Kister, of the Christian Veterans of America; Larry Asman, of the Christian Veterans Intelligence Service; and Jeremiah Stokes, of the Salt Lake City Pro-American Vigilantes, and also husband of the late alleged seditionist Elizabeth Dilling. Although the major leaders have since gone their own ways, the Crusade and the Christian Nationalist Party, formed in 1947, are still Smith's main political vehicles.

Smith ran for President again in 1948. His Christian Nationalist Party platform advocated deporting Jews, the shipping of Negroes to Africa, the suppression of all "Jewish Gestapo Organizations," and the closing down of the U.N. He spent some of his time attacking General Eisenhower—who was being wooed by the Democrats at that time—as a Jew. He based his contention on an apparently jocular statement in the 1915 West Point yearbook that referred to the future President as "Señor Dwight David Eisenhower, gentleman, the terrible Swedish-Jew, as big as life and twice as natural."[3]

The election year of 1952 was perhaps Smith's most active political period. He set up headquarters close to both the Republican and Democratic Conventions and began to attack his opponents with old-fashioned abandon: Eisenhower's promotion as a Presidential candidate was a hoax conjured up by "the same cheap Jew publicity machine that makes a star out of a Hollywood whore, or a hero out of a marijuana smoker"; Thomas E. Dewey should go "crawl under a log"; Averell Harriman was "an ingratiating bootlicker, a vassal of Herbert Lehman." Of the late Senator Kefauver, then a Presidential possibility, he wrote:

We have no genealogical report that would indicate that there was any Jewish blood in Kefauver, but he has the Jewish mouth, the Jewish nose and the Jewish profile. He obeys Jews, he runs with Jews, he collaborates with Jews, he allows Jews to form his strategy planning, and he performs like a Broadway actor under direction of a Jewish nightclub operator. Who wants a man in the White House that looks like this? God save us from this.[4]

Smith backed General Douglas MacArthur for President that year as did most of the racists, or "nationalists" as they preferred to be called at that time.* However, they were split among themselves and refused to unite under one banner to promote their common candidate.

One faction, the largest, was organized by Mrs. Lyrl Van Hyning, long-time leader of We the Mothers Mobilize for America. She was able to draw such people as Kenneth Goff, Conde McGinley and the late Eugene N. Sanctuary, an ex-Klansman and accused seditionist, into her sphere of influence. Another group revolved around Joseph Beauharnais, then the leader of the White Circle League and currently associated with the National States Rights Party. He and his faction were more anti-Negro than Mrs. Van Hyning's group, which was primarily anti-Semitic. Beauharnais set about establishing an organization called the National Association for the Advancement of White People.†

A third faction was the newly born Constitution Party, set up by a group of dissident Republicans who were displeased with Eisenhower's nomination. Co-Chairmen were Percy L. Greaves, an economic consultant to Howard Kershner's Christian Freedom Foundation, and Mrs. Suzanne Silvercruys Stevenson, the leader of the superpatriotic Minute Women of the U.S.A. The Party, however, was soon raided by a group of anti-Semites led by Upton Close, the ex-radio announcer and friend of Gerald Winrod's (Gorden Winrod's father), and W. Henry MacFarland, Jr., organizer of the American Flag Committee and the Nationalist Action

---

* The only prominent individual in this group who failed to endorse MacArthur was Elizabeth Dilling. She claimed she found a touch of Judaism in the distinguished General's background. She also claimed that FDR and Winston Churchill had Jewish ancestors and, furthermore, that they both were related to MacArthur.

† This group should not be confused with a later NAAWP, founded by a William Miller in Cincinnati in 1963. Although Beauharnais' group is no longer active, both organizations have taken a similarly strong anti-Negro position. Miller, who claims chapters in five states and 2,500 subscribers to his newspaper, *The American People,* is no relation to the 1964 Republican Vice-Presidential candidate of the same name.

League, the last of which was listed as "fascist" by the Attorney General.

These developments shattered the racists into many factions. All of them supported MacArthur (who, incidentally, refused to support his supporters), but none of them were able to agree on a common Vice-Presidential candidate. As a result, MacArthur's name appeared on a number of state ballots with different Vice-Presidential running mates. Jack B. Tenney, of California's "Tenney Committee," was the running mate on the Christian Nationalist Party ticket; Vivien Kellems, also candidate for Senator from Connecticut, was his running mate on the Constitution Party ticket; Senator Harry F. Byrd, against his wishes, was put in the second spot of the grab-bag America First Party. In addition, there were others who sought the Vice-Presidential nod; indeed, it was so confusing at times that C. Leon de Aryan, editor of *The Broom,* a racist, spiritualist and health-fad newspaper, suggested that all "nationalists" write in a vote for Jesus Christ.

In any event, MacArthur's combined vote was slightly more than 17,000, one quarter the Prohibitionist vote.

The 1952 election marks the end of Smith's active Presidential aspirations. He did run for President in 1956, but he lost rather badly: he received only eight votes, not quite a record low.

It also marks the end of any effort to unify the racist-"nationalist" groups in postwar America. From time to time there is talk of unification—from Rockwell, Smith, Fields, Klan leaders and others, and on occasion there is an amalgamation or two. But there has never been a regrouping, not even a united front.

Gerald L. K. Smith has a well-deserved reputation as a spellbinding speaker of the old school, one who understands what an audience wants to hear and one who knows how to exploit it. George Lincoln Rockwell, in a rare tribute to anyone outside of his own organization, wrote:

> He whispers, he sighs, he wheezes, he coos—then he BLASTS with the power of a locomotive roaring through a tunnel. He laughs, he cries, he howls, he cajoles, he mimics, he screams, he begs, he goes back to whispering, sneers, leers, yells, bursts into

hysterical laughter—then whimpers some heart-rending bit which leaves you limp.

Perhaps unconsciously, Rockwell acknowledged the full power of the man: "I sat in the balcony. . . . If Smith had said suddenly, 'JUMP!'—I think I would have done it."[5]

Smith's "whispering, sneers, leers, yells" lap over into his magazine, *The Cross and the Flag,* now in its third decade of publication. He has a name for virtually everything he dislikes. His barbs run from the acid to the near vulgar. Thomas Dewey he has described as an "impudent little villain" and as the "little man on the wedding cake"; Eleanor Roosevelt he has called "the world's most evil influence, the old hatchet gal, the villainess of American history"; Lady Bird Johnson, he tells his readers, has "a sharp Semitic profile"; Linus Pauling he dismisses as "Moscow's helper"; Rabbi Stephen Wise he considers "America's number one Jew"; Eisenhower he called "a phony who can fool only the stupid"; and Drew Pearson he criticizes as "a low-grade, highly paid renegade, hypocrite, liar, blackmailer, character assassin, working for the Jewish Anti-Defamation League."

New York he refers to as "Jew York," the United Nations as the "Jew-N"; the ADL he considers "the OGPU of Jewry"; television industry executives he calls "Jew-controlled mind-washers"; both Communism and Zionism are "the twins of the Anti-Christ."

Jesus Christ, he tells his readers, was the world's greatest anti-Semite; at the drop of a contribution to the Crusade he is willing to send you "documentary proof" of FDR's Jewish ancestry; Negroes he believes are a "child race" unworthy of equality; miscegenation, he adds, would result in white skin giving way to "a sort of Miami tan."

Smith's following is difficult to pin down, but one indication of its size can be determined by the circulation of his magazine, *The Cross and the Flag.* It reaches approximately thirty thousand people, although Smith claims a higher number.

He retains this following in large part by the use of scare tactics. His primary appeal, for instance, and one he pushes time and time again, is as a martyr for truth. He tells his reader that he is the only purveyor of truth in the United States. Because his enemies cannot stand the truth, so his reasoning goes, he is first on the "Hidden Hand's" list for assassination. "KILL HIM! KILL HIM! KILL HIM!" was written across the top of one letter he sent to his subscribers, meaning—so the reader learned later—that "Christ-hating mobsters" were trying to do Smith in for daring to tell the truth. Another one read: *"My life is on the line! Written in blood, sweat and tears! This is the Deadly Moment! Every citizen must stand up and be counted as a patriot, a coward, or a fool!"**

Most of the headlines are a precursor of a plea for money ("Fill out the enclosed coupon and insert with it the largest gift of money possible and rush it to the nearest post office.") Throughout his writings there is the vague threat of catastrophe, sinister plots, mysterious death and imminent bloodshed, all of which prod his alarmed subscribers to reach for their checkbooks.

Through it all, however, Gerald L. K. Smith plunges on, por-traying himself as the fearless, dedicated, uncompromising warrior who *alone,* among 196 million other Americans, dares speak the truth. Confident of the support he will receive to carry on the fight—having already shaken his subscribers out of their stupor—he closes his appeal on his knees: "I cannot imagine myself quitting any more than I can imagine you quitting me . . .," he wrote. "I plead with you, do not ignore this letter." It is a Smith speech set to words.

Approximately 80 percent of all the articles in *The Cross and the Flag* are concerned with the Jews or their euphemistic substi-tutes: the "internationalists," the "World Power" or the "Hidden Hand," etc. There is, however, a body of opinion that questions whether Smith is *actually* an anti-Semite. Surprisingly enough, some of this doubt comes from Jewish circles.

As an example, one person, whose job it is to keep an eye on people such as Smith, noted that Smith is an inveterate antique

---

* Smith also has a more immediate vision of his own mortality. Recently he erected a 67-foot high snow-white statue of Jesus Christ atop 1,500-foot Magnetic Mountain near Eureka Springs, Arkansas. The "Christ of the Ozarks," as it is known, reminiscent of Rio de Janeiro's statue of Christ on Corcovado Mountain, is visible ten miles away and is illuminated at night by blue, violet and purple spotlights. Smith plans to use the statue as a grave marker for himself and his wife.

collector and that virtually all the antique auctions in the Los Angeles area (Smith's main base of operations) are dominated by Jews. This man, who also collects antiques, claims that he has seen Smith at nearly every auction he has attended, sitting quietly, talking in a friendly fashion with the people around him, both Jews and Gentiles alike. "Nobody," he said, "would put himself in the position he does of associating with Jews week after week if he *really* hated them."

A number of other people, particularly news reporters who have followed Smith's career for many years, concur in this view. They believe that he is too urbane and too intelligent to believe what he preaches. They generally feel that Smith is more interested in the power he has over people's minds and that he is fascinated by the techniques of crowd psychology. Smith, one reporter said, knows how to spike a speech with just enough racism to shock the audience; he knows how to impress the naïve; he revels in his power to turn off and on a wide range of emotion in his audience —"he wheezes, he coos . . . He laughs, he cries, he howls, he cajoles, he mimics, he screams, he begs," all too good effect. The essential difference between, say, the members of the National States Rights Party and Gerald L. K. Smith is that those in the NSRP *believe* what they are saying while there is some doubt about Smith's sincerity and objectives.

For all that, Smith is still America's leading demagogue.

2

The National Renaissance Party is a small racist group in New York City. According to its founder, it was formed in 1949 with the merger of three organizations that had been or were to be declared "fascist" by the Attorney General: W. Henry MacFarland, Jr.'s Nationalist Action League, Kurt Mertig's Citizens Protective League, and the German-American Republican League.

The leader of the Party since its inception has been James Harting Madole, a balding, myopic, hawk-nosed forty-year-old bachelor who lives with his mother in a walk-up apartment on the upper West Side near Central Park.

Madole dresses conservatively but his suits are worn; when I spoke with him, his eyes never once attempted to meet my gaze; and his handshake is limp and unenthusiastic. His mother, white-haired, stern-faced, with a mole on her lip, questioned me suspiciously about my motives in interviewing her son before I had even taken off my overcoat. By the time I was seated she was in the middle of a discourse on the Jews. "When I go into restaurants after Jews," she said, "it looks like pigs ate there."

By this time, her son had entered the room and had settled himself in a chair. He began a long discourse on the Party and its objectives. It was the day before the Burros story broke in the press, so he was quite edgy. Often when he spoke he seemed to be talking to some other audience, at some other time, as if in a trance. But he speaks articulately, glibly and very quickly, one thought piled on top of another.

Marxists, he began, look at history from an economic point of view; "We in the National Renaissance Party, on the other hand, take a racial and cultural viewpoint." Race mixing, including both integration and miscegenation, cannot be achieved, he said, without creating clashes: "It would be like mixing lions and tigers together." The Toltecs, Mayans and Aztecs were "pure races," with "pure blood," who created high civilizations; when their blood was mixed with other races, he declared, their civilizations were destroyed. "The mixing of whites with Negroes will bring the U.S. down to the level of South and Central Americans and Caribbean peoples," he said with a desultory wave of his hand. He added that he was in favor of "repatriating" American Negroes to the newly independent nations in Africa.

The Jews he would like to deprive of their American citizenship because, as the NRP program puts it, they are "an alien virus in our national blood stream and as such . . . must be purged from our cultural, economic and political life." Thereafter, he proposes, only Caucasians—Nordics, Latins, Slavs, Anglo-Saxons and Celts —would be allowed to benefit from American society, as long as they are "mentally and genetically sound."

Having created this "Racial Nationalist State," he would then carry out the following program: He would abolish Congress and replace it with a strong, centralized elite of leaders; that section of the communications media that was hostile to racial theories would be suppressed; the Federal Reserve would be nationalized; the gold standard would be replaced by a "goods standard"; labor "tribunals" would settle industrial disputes; the state would own 50 percent of all industries; strong protective tariffs would be set up; income taxes would be abolished (government income would be replaced by "gross dividends accrued from the monopolistic combines in which it [the state] controls 50 percent of the stock"); the national debt would be abolished; a thirty-hour week would be instituted; and, perhaps most important of all, a white hegemony would be created among the Western nations of the world "to act as a mighty bulwark against the colored hordes of Asia."

This program is more fascist in viewpoint than Nazi,* although the question of race is given more emphasis than it was in Mussolini's Fascist state. Madole is an acknowledged admirer and supporter of Sir Oswald Mosley's, the prewar leader of the British Union of Fascists, himself an admirer of Mussolini, and currently the advocate of a "United Europe," by which he means worldwide apartheid. Madole maintains close contact with Mosley's organization, the Union Movement, as well as with several Continental fascist groups and publications.

The NRP seldom can call on more than twenty-five to thirty activists at any one given time. It may have as many as four hundred members throughout the nation. Madole claims a circulation of two thousand for his *National Reniassance Bulletin,* which is probably not too wide of the mark, although it is doubtful that this is a paid circulation.

Of the two dozen activists, perhaps half belong to the "Security Echelon Guard," otherwise known as the SE Guard. Madole dresses these men in surplus army fatigue caps, black ties, khaki shirts with collar tab insignia ("Assault Leader," "Captain," "Major," etc.), lightning-flash armbands similar to those of the NSRP, and Sam Browne belts. Madole himself wears no uniform

---

* I make the distinction that all Nazis are fascists, but that not all fascists are Nazis. Nazis are those people who subscribe to the doctrines of Hitler in particular, while fascists are those who believe in the general fascist philosophy of, for instance, the corporate state, the leadership principle, and authoritarianism, irrespective of how much these ideas might overlap with Nazi doctrines.

and has no rank—he is merely referred to by his men as "the Leader." The Guard has its own magazines: one is called *SE Guard,* which "Major" Daniel Burros once edited, and the other is *SE Man,* which apparently serves as a recruiting brochure.

One article in a 1963 issue of *SE Guard* extols the virtues expected to be found in potential candidates for this paramilitary unit. It concerns one Ed Cassidy, a chinless, sunken-cheeked youth whose only expression seems to be that of a man who has just bitten into a lemon. The article reads in part:

HERO OF THE WHITE RACE
ED CASSIDY

. . . Let us examine his record in the last half year. Firstly, he received three months imprisonment for writing anti-Jewish slogans on walls. (This was an act of personal zeal not authorized or sanctioned by the Party.)

Next he was involved in the fist-fighting on May 25th [1963], when our rally was attacked by the JWV [Jewish War Veterans]. One day later he was attacked from behind by YAF [Young Americans for Freedom] Jews. He was so badly beaten he nearly lost an eye.

Next he was attacked by a band of Negroes during a literature distribution opposing CORE. His right arm was completely covered with cuts from broken glass. After being attacked *he* was arrested by police. . . .

This is a sample of the sacrifices the young SE Men make for YOU! Stand behind your front line troops! Give us the financial help so that the sacrifices of Cassidy and the other SE Men are not in vain!!!

The motto of the National Renaissance Party is "One Race, One Nation, One Leader." The Party takes its name from Hitler's "Last Political Testament" written just before he committed suicide in his Berlin bunker. Said Hitler: "I die with a happy heart aware [that there] will spring up . . . the seed of a radiant renaissance of the National Socialist movement."

These SE Men—and the allusion to generative fluids is deliberate—are the NRP's shock troops. Wherever there is trouble, they are there. By 1954, five years after the Party was founded, there had been so many fistfights, brawls and breaches of the peace, and so much anti-Semitic and fascist literature circulated throughout the New York City area, that the House Committee on Un-American Activities spent part of the year investigating the Party. The NRP was denounced in a staff study as an "avowed neofascist organization," and a request was made to the Department of Justice to ascertain "whether prosecution of its leaders under the provisions of the Smith Act was possible." Nothing came of the request.

New York City in 1959 and 1960 experienced a wave of swastika daubings on synagogues and other Jewish buildings. Over eighty daubings were reported between the end of December 1959 and February 1960, many of them creations of SE Men. Madole believes there were others behind the acts:

> . . . the current wave of swastika paintings, like the synagogue bombings of yesteryear, were manufactured by Jewish fund-raising organizations to achieve their purposes of terrifying gullible Jews into greater financial sacrifice, to stimulate mass migration of Jews from Central Europe to Israel, to exert pressure on world public opinion aimed at keeping Germany divided, and to institute new school curricula for the German youth which will thoroughly brainwash the future generation and create a guilt complex among young Germans thus facilitating the continuation of endless German reparations to the State of Israel.[6]

In July 1963, SE Men distributed inflammatory literature to civil rights workers picketing a White Castle diner in the Bronx. Before too many minutes had elapsed, a riot was under way: fistfights, kneeings, bitings, thrown bottles, cuts, blood, screams, yells, curses . . .

Eight members of the NRP were convicted on thirty-two counts, including charges of riot, conspiracy, unlawful assembly and Sullivan Law violations, the latter because a search of the NRP truck at the scene revealed a cache of weapons, among them a pistol and crossbow. Madole and Daniel Burros were, as noted, two of those convicted. Madole, for one, is very proud of his Party's action at the White Castle diner, for he showed me, during the interview, a blue "campaign" ribbon that he had issued to all the SE Men who had taken part.

Earlier in the year, the NRP held a "Mass Open-Air Rally to kick Pro-Red and Race-Mixers out of Yorkville," as its flyers proclaimed. Four thousand spectators turned up at 86th Street and First Avenue to watch the action. Before long there was a melee of SE Men and anti-fascists struggling over an NRP flag and staff. A riot broke out. In the issue of *SE Guard* that followed this incident, a considerable amount of space was devoted to the riot. One story was written in the manner a historian might use to describe a military battle:

> When the JWV [Jewish War Veterans] attacked Mr. Madole, the SE threw itself into the fray. A short but terrible battle ensued. All the SE behaved splendidly, and covered the SE with glory.
>
> At one point 1,000 Jews broke down the center barricades and penetrated the foot police lines. It looked like certain annihilation for the small SE detachment. The mounted police then charged. The Jews broke into screams. "The Cossacks! The Cossacks are coming!" they cried. The Jew line fell back before the horse onslaught.[7]

Once again the racial nationalist SE Men were rescued from the brink by capitalist police.

The same year, the National Renaissance Party allied itself briefly with the African Universal Church and Commercial League Corporation, a small black nationalist group headed by a certain Archbishop C. C. Addison, the origin of whose ecclesiastical title is unclear. Addison has been a staunch foe of integration for years. He has promoted a "back-to-Africa" movement as well as the establishment of an independent Negro society in America. At a "Mass Rally to Support Racial Segregation and Black Nationalism," in December 1963, Madole claimed he was ready to treat the black segregationists as equals. He then began a long attack on the Jews, a particularly sensitive subject with the nationalists. His speeches were returned in kind by Addison, who also attacked the NAACP as "an association for the advancement of colored people and Gentiles in the interests of organized world Jewry." This friendship broke up, however, for the sole reason that neither group could stand being near the other.

At present, the NRP is in a quiescent stage, first, because Madole has been chastened somewhat by his legal troubles and, second, because the Party has never really recovered from the Burros affair. In fact, two weeks after Daniel Burros shot himself, another Jew was found in the Party, a Robert J. Burros, the Party's National Secretary, a dapper, articulate, near-handsome ex-shipping clerk who was no relation to Daniel. Robert Burros had stepped into the editorship of *The Free American,* Daniel's paper, and had redesigned it as a Ku Klux Klan organ, emblazoned with a cross rather than a swastika.

Madole, however, was losing considerable face among his fascist peers, so he reluctantly stripped Robert Burros of his job as National Secretary, but kept him on as an organizer in Newburgh, New York. Burros insisted he would not commit suicide, adding: "I will always be loyal to Mr. Madole as the most brilliant leader of the American Far Right—as the general and true leader of the Fascist forces of this country."[8]

Today, Madole concentrates his efforts on the written word, firing broadsides at a number of targets, particularly the "moderate" right-winger—that is, anyone to the left of his views:

> They [William Buckley, Robert Welch, Billy James Hargis] are like doctors who seek to prescribe a cure for a desperately ill American public but FAIL TO DISCOVER AND ISOLATE THE JEWISH BACILLUS WHICH IS THE SOURCE OF THE PLAGUE OF DESTRUCTIVE NIHILISM BESETTING OUR BODY POLITIC.[9]

Israel is another of Madole's preoccupations. One NRP leaflet states: "Jews like [Emmanuel] Celler and the Zionist organizations which dominate American Political circles would gladly use American soldiers as cannon-fodder to assure Israel's survival and ultimate expansion in the Middle East."

Jews in Russia, he said during our interview, "were persecuted not because of race but because Russia wants the Jews there to be Russians first and Jews second, if at all. But the Jewish hierarchy wouldn't allow it."

He went on to say that he believed that the Jews took over the United States in 1913. He listed four reasons why he believes this: first, because the Federal Reserve Act "took the power of coining money out of the hands of the government and put it into the hands of Jewish bankers"; second, the graduated income tax was passed "to finance the bankers"; third, the Anti-Defamation League was established; and fourth, the NAACP had been established a few years previously. The formation of the last two organizations, said Madole, was intended to stifle all criticism.

"No minority group can claim it is simon pure any more than a majority group can," he argued. Ignoring the fact that neither the ADL nor the NAACP have ever made such a claim, he added, by way of an example: "The Mafia," he said, "is made up mostly of Italians and Sicilians; but there is no league to stop people talking about Italian gangsters."

Madole insists that he will eventually come to power and when he does it will be by ballots, not by bullets. In the meantime one of his objectives is to infiltrate his men into other right-wing organizations in order to take them over. So far he has had no success.

"The Birch Society also uses these methods," he said, "but the Birchers want anarchy—the elimination of the state from industry. Now, with the NRP," he added, rising from his chair indicating the interview was over, "we would participate in industry and take 50 percent of the GNP to run the state." This would mean the establishment of a one-party state at first.

"But," he said, as I was putting on my coat, "think of what you would get for it!"

3

The racists have their intellectuals. One of their major groupings is a loose-knit association of individuals who are known informally as "the Yockey Movement." Its strength is found on the East and West Coasts and in Florida; Yockey Clubs, promoting intellectualized racist theories, exist in these areas.

The intellectual fount of the movement was until recently *Western Destiny,* an expensive and well-laid-out monthly magazine that was published in Los Angeles by the Noontide Press. Its

editor was Roger Pearson, an ex-tea planter from Calcutta and a
founder of the Northern League for Northern European Friendship and Cooperation. The objectives of the Northern League are
to protect, foster and bind together the true Nordic Aryan people
and their heritages. The League's badge of identification is "a
Fylfot (or tryfoss), a three-armed sun-symbol older than the
swastike or sun-wheel." Its publication, *Northern World,* which
dwelt on subjects that tended to extol all things Nordic, and its
successor, *Folk,* were replaced by *Western Destiny* in 1964.

Western Destiny was also the lineal descendant of Liberty and
Property, an organization that published a monthly newsletter
called *Right,* now out of print; back copies, however, can be
purchased from the Noontide Press. The founder of Liberty and
Property was Willis A. Carto, now the treasurer of Liberty Lobby
and the man behind the scenes at *Western Destiny.* One of the
guiding spirits of *Right,* Dr. E. L. Anderson, was until recently an
associate editor of *Western Destiny.* Noontide Press, to complete
this rather complicated picture, is also associated with Alert
Americans Association, which puts out the *First National Directory of "Rightist" Groups, Publications and Some Individuals in
the United States (and Some Foreign Countries),* published at
intervals under Carto's direction. The *Directory* lists over three
thousand right-wing groups in the country.

The Yockey Movement takes its name from Francis Parker
Yockey, a man of considerable mystery. He was graduated cum
laude from Notre Dame and spent a short time in the Army during
World War II before he was discharged for medical reasons,
"dementia praecox, paranoid type" according to his discharge
papers. He served for a while as an assistant prosecuting attorney
for Wayne County (Detroit). He then served on the War Crimes
Tribunal in Nuremberg from 1946 to 1948. Apparently he became
converted to the German criminals' point of view, believing that
the tribunal was entirely the work of Jews. For some reason still
not clear today, the U.S. government refused to renew his passport. He fled to Ireland and lived in hiding there while he wrote a
long book called *Imperium,* now the handbook of most all American racists.

In 1960 Yockey was apprehended in Oakland, California. His

suitcase had been lost at the Fort Worth airport, and airlines officials, opening it to identify it, found three passports bearing different names but the same picture. Yockey was arrested in the home of a Jewish school administrator, a survivor of Auschwitz. An unusually high bail of $50,000 was set. No one has ever explained why government officials were so pleased to have caught him.

Yockey attempted suicide twice, and tried to break out of jail once. Eleven days after his arrest he died; the general verdict was that he poisoned himself, although his admirers—particularly Carto, who was one of the last visitors he had—say he was murdered. One way or the other, an air of mystery still surrounds his death.

Imperium was first published privately in London in 1948 under Yockey's pen name, Ulick Varange. Only two hundred sets of the two-volume work were printed. Since then, Noontide Press has published a one-volume edition that has given the book a wider circulation. Willis Carto wrote an introduction to this edition. Yockey dedicated the book to "the Hero of the Second World War"—presumably Adolf Hitler.

The message the book imparts appears to be a compendium of ideas gathered from Oswald Spengler's *Decline of the West*, Nietzsche's *Thus Spake Zarathustra*, Alfred Rosenberg's *The Myth of the Twentieth Century* and Hitler's *Mein Kampf*.

Yockey sees all cultures as stratified: at the upper end are "Culture Bearers" and at the lower end are the "Culture Distorters." According to Richard Kelly Hoskins, writing in *Western Destiny*, Culture Bearers are a small group of people, an elite, from which future leaders are recruited. This group assumes responsibility, according to Hoskins, for "collecting, preserving, and passing to future generations our Civilization's soul."[10]

Yockey himself provides a definition of Culture Distortion: *"Culture-distortion is the condition in which outer life-forms are warping the Culture from its true life-path."*[11] The Distorters, those who create the Distortion, are sometimes otherwise referred to as "The Sub-Europeans, the Retarders, the Michel element, the money-worshippers, the lazy and the stupid." The biggest Distorter of all is the Jew, according to the author: "One group, however, has brought about a major Culture distortion throughout the entire Western Civilization and its colonies on every continent, and that is the rear-guard in the West of the fulfilled Arabian Culture, the Church-State-Nation-People-Race of the Jew."[12]

The author then claims that "the total alien-ness of the Jew made him *politically invisible* to the West."

Yockey can seldom break away from his culture fixation. He speaks of high cultures, low cultures, culture feelings, culture disease, culture retardation, cultural vitalism. On occasion, he will lapse into the inscrutable—for instance, in a chapter entitled "The Law of Constancy of Intra-Organismic Power."

Yockey has little to say that is complimentary about the United States. "America," he writes, "with its total lack of spiritual resistance, springing from the inherent *soul-weakness* of a Colony, became the host to other large Culturally-parasitic groups." The author believed that Slavs, Levantines and Japanese are typical parasitic groups.

The difference between the "ideal Culture" and what exists today is best reflected in Yockey's chapter "The Abyss":

> The sacred soil of our Culture is [now] occupied by armies of Barbarians and distorters of our Cultural instincts and heritage. Once Rolo, William of Normandy, the Hohenstaufen, Coeur de Lion, de Bouillon, the Teutonic Knights, Rainald van Dassel, Gustav Adolf, Wallenstein, Alba, Cromwell, Richelieu, Turenne, de Saxe, Frederick the Great, Pitt, Napoleon, Bismarck, trod this soil. Today, as I write, it is occupied by Kirghizians, Mongolians, Armenians, Turkestani, Sengalese, Negroes, Americans, Jews. These Culturally alien armies rule through traitor governments, whose members have sprung up from between the cracks in the pavement, and who deal in hatred of the Spirit of the Age."[13]

Imperium has come to be regarded by many racists as the postwar *Mein Kampf* and is almost more popular than *The Protocols of the Learned Elders of Zion*. It is required reading for neophyte racists with intellectual pretensions. It is a dull, pompous, wordy book, perhaps only slightly less unreadable than *Mein Kampf*.

Willis Carto's introduction to the Noontide Press edition makes
better reading. He claims that "the only real crime of Francis
Parker Yockey was to write a book, and for this he had to die."
Carto also has a gift for the provocative statement, such as, "It
should be remembered that the individual enjoyed far more liberty
in Europe under the Monarchs than in America today."[14] On the
Peace Corps, he has this to say: "The ultimate expression of this
militant water-pistol imperialism is the hilarious yet deeply symbolic 'Peace Corpse,' the true expression of the *zeitgeist*. Created
out of the typically American combination of abysmal do-good
stupidity and inability to gauge the feelings of others, and enlight-
ened greed, this is the perfect symbol for today."[15]

Western Destiny was the one magazine that consistently pushed
Yockey's ideas. Yockey was not, however, the only source of
inspiration: the works of Ezra Pound, Heinrich von Treitschke,
Gustave Le Bon, Richard Wagner, Thomas Carlyle and Oswald
Spengler were also promoted. Yet nearly every issue of *Western
Destiny* carried an article or two on either Yockey, *Imperium*,
Culture Bearers, or Culture Distorters.

Often Yockey's ideas are reflected in the writings of people
outside the active racist world. Taylor Caldwell and Professor
Revilo P. Oliver, both of whom write for the Birch Society, are
vocal admirers of Spengler, from whom Yockey drew much of his
material.

Western Destiny carried a long list of contributing editors which
some people consider to be the *Burke's Peerage* of Western racists.
Although the list changed from time to time, it included: William
Stephenson, former editor of *The Virginian;* Ned Touchstone, of
The Councillor; Dewey Taft, formerly with the National States
Rights Party; C. M. Goethe, the honorary President of the Ameri-
can Coalition of Patriotic Societies; and Jack Tenney, the 1952
Vice-Presidential candidate on Gerald L. K. Smith's Christian
Nationalist Party ticket.

Foreigners include John Bean and Andrew Fountaine, of the
British National Party; A. K. Chesterton, a nephew of the writer
G. K. Chesterton, and leader of the League of Empire Loyalists;
Arthur Ehrhardt, of *National Europa;* F. A. France, of *The North-
lander;* Fabrice La Roche, a European fascist much admired by

Madole; and Admiral Sir Barry Domvile, KCB, CB, CMG, a founder of the prewar pro-Nazi "Link" in Britain.

Ex-editor Pearson is now the moving force behind a new quarterly called *The New Patriot*. It is intended to be a high-quality, professionally produced, "prestige" magazine, the purpose of which is to conduct "a responsible but penetrating inquiry into every aspect of the Jewish Question." The editorial advisory board consists of Admirals Crommelin and Domvile; Edward Fields of the NSRP; Brigadier General William L. ("Jerry") Lee, listed in 1962 as a member of the Board of Advisors of Billy James Hargis' Christian Crusade, and as an Endorser and Field Coordinator for the John Birch Society; and retired Marine Lieutenant General Pedro A. del Valle, who runs the Defenders of the American Constitution.

Recently, the torch of Yockeyism has passed to *American Mercury,* a magazine with a varied history. In the 1920s, *Mercury* was made famous under the iconoclastic editorship of H. L. Mencken. In the early 1950s, however, it was purchased by wealthy Russell Maguire, who turned it into a racist publication. Maguire sold out in 1960, and three years later ownership passed to a Texas organization called the Legion for Survival of Freedom. At this stage, *Mercury* had been changed from a monthly to a quarterly; its racist point of view, however, had not changed.

In 1966 *Mercury* underwent a major reorganization. The chairman of the board is now Bruce Holman, formerly with Liberty and Property. The new organization announced that it was taking over subscriptions to *Western Destiny.* Many of *Western Destiny*'s contributing editors have accepted the same post with *American Mercury.*

4

In addition to intellectuals, the racists have their own religion. It is called the Odinist Religion and Nordic Faith Movement and is run from Los Angeles by James K. Warner. (It was Warner who sent George Lincoln Rockwell an eighteen-foot-long Nazi flag in 1958 to honor the birth of the American Nazi Party.) Not all racists are Odinists, but no one except Aryans is eligible to join.

Odinists have no church, just a symbol (the sun-wheel) and a magazine (*Viking Age*). The sun-wheel, a circle encompassing a Greek cross, is "the signal expressing the divine will of GOD, to combat the Evil, wheresoever it approaches," according to Odinist literature. *Viking Age* is a mimeographed periodical of varying lengths edited by Warner.

Warner entitles himself at various times "Rev.," "OP" and "Hofgodi," all references to his current ecclesiastical station. Warner did receive a Doctor of Divinity degree in 1961 from the Church of God, but he renounced it to devote his time to Odinism.

Historians are an integral part of this religion. They are known as "Skalds." The most famous Odinist Skald was Daniel Burros. He was welcomed into the fold with the following article in *Viking Age:*

NEW SKALDS

. . . We wish to welcome DAN BURROS . . . to our ranks. Dan Burros is one of the most able historians of our time, concerning our race and its accomplishments. Skald Burros, is also editor of the well written historical newspaper *The Free American.* One just has to meet Skald Burros, and he is immediately impressed with the great mass of knowledge he can call to mind at a moment's notice.[16]

The Odinist Religion was founded either in 1925 or 1933— Warner is not sure which. In any event, in 1933, "after almost a thousand years of the dark ages (Christianity)," the Odinist Church was reorganized by an Australian racist, A. Rud Mills. It was closely tied to Alfred Rosenberg's Nordic Faith Movement.* A. Rud Mills wrote a number of books on Nordic religions; he also wrote articles for *Right* during its five-year life. In 1964, Mills died. He was held in such high esteem by Odinists that he was given the posthumous title of "Archbishop." A memorial article to him in *Viking Age* said: "All true White men wish him Odin speed to Valhalla."

Apparently the roots of Odinism can be traced back over eighty

---

* Alfred Rosenberg was Hitler's ideologue and a master Jew-baiter, whose belief in Nordic mysticism was so strong as to seem ridiculous even to his colleagues. He was hanged as a war criminal in 1946.

centuries: Warner dates *Viking Age* not only as "Calendar Year 1967" but also "Odinist Year 8180."

Warner wrote a pamphlet called "The Law of Odin" in which he outlined the roots and purposes of his religion. If I understand him correctly, the earth's moon is the fourth to be caught in the gravitational pull of the earth. The first three moons were drawn into the earth's orbit many millions of years ago, causing all sorts of life to grow on earth: enormous vegetation, dinosaurs, giant human beings. Out of the last-mentioned [who have since perished] and sometime during the "third moon," evolved the white race— "the almost perfect creation of the SUPREME BEING OF THE UNIVERSE."

Unfortunately for Warner and fellow Odinists, other species survived, "not men but resembling men in some close features."

After the third Moon fell the inferior species of animal life were confined to the parts of the Earth which were almost unlivable swamps, and along with the hideous crawling creatures these freak mutations of nature somehow managed to survive.[17]

"While other species degenerate," Warner writes, "the White race is working towards perfection." This evolutionary process, he adds, is based on eugenics.*

The highest goal of the White race is to use genetics to breed itself into a higher and purer race thus in the end becoming one with God. When the SUPREME BEING gave us Creative Intelli-

* In order to initiate "the correct eugenic outlook into politics," the American Eugenics Party was founded in 1964. Samuel Andrisani, a Los Angeles bachelor, is the Party's leader and possibly its sole member. In 1965, he ran for the Los Angeles Board of Education. He campaigned on a platform of "hereditary inequality." Schools, he believes, should make no effort to concentrate on bettering defective students, since he considers it impossible. He received over 15,000 votes and plans to run for the State Assembly in the future.

The AEP also believes in "offspring control," to limit inferior people from having children. Those who qualify as inferior include those with hereditary health defects, ugly appearance, negative achievements, and deficient ana-tomical structures. He would sterilize criminals who have gross mental deficiencies. As for Negroes, Andrisani would send them to Africa through the good offices of Alberta Spain's Peace Movement of Ethiopia, a Negro nationalist group, with whom Andrisani works closely.

gence he placed this part of HIMSELF within us, putting the spirit of God within our bodies, minds, and souls. The body then is the TEMPLE OF THE LIVING GOD, and is a sacred thing not to be defiled by foreign substance or impurities.

The greatest objective and duty of the White race is proper breeding to produce a perfect race. With the coming of "modern" thought and inventions, the White man has all but forgotten his TRUE MISSION in life.[18]

Warner then says that "GOODNESS (GOD-NESS) is striving through Eugenics to be closer to God." It follows, therefore, that those who break this "natural law of God," by mixing with other races, are sinners. Sinners, he writes, are doomed to "freakedness which causes their off-spring to be sickly and mal-formed."

At one point in time, writes Warner, the white race—the "original race"—split into many factions, most of which traveled about the earth mating indiscriminately with "other species of life": "negroes," "yellow asiatics" and the like. The group that went to Europe remained fairly pure, genetically speaking, although a few impure genes were detected from time to time. Eventually, some "Wise Men" decided to halt what amounted to the genetic backsliding of these people. They isolated the community and banished all outsiders.

This was done and the White man's "CREATIVE GENES" were saved. An aberration, however, sprang up in the form of a group with "shrewd SELF-INSTINCT ABILITY" that compensated for its lack of "CREATIVE ABILITY." This group, according to Warner, became so inbred that another genetic type was created, otherwise known as "JEWS."

Once they began to mingle outside [their own] area they found that their self-instinct ability had a repellent effect upon pure Whites who still had their full CREATIVE INTELLIGENCE. This in turn created hatred which led to physical clashes between the groups. . . .

Jewish leaders KNEW that they could only gain victory over the CREATORS by lowering the CREATOR's genetic balance below their own, thus putting them on top. To do this they would have to get the SONS OF GOD to inter-breed with the Asiatics and Negroes until they reached the point of no return.[19]

Warner goes on to give some indication of what he believes must be done in order that the white race remain pure:

> . . . in accord with GOD's NATURAL LAW either isolate the hybrids and inferior species or ensure that the hybrids and inferior species are no longer able to spawn inferior offspring. THIS IS GOD'S LAW.

Whether Warner seeks forced sterilization, mandatory birth control devices, or legal extermination of the "inferior species" is unclear. He is confident, however, that whatever the means, he has God's blessings. And in the closing pages of his work he reminds his reader, in case of doubt, that "this book was compiled in the spirit of LOVE."

5

Racists are generally inveterate newspaper readers, always scanning such organs of the enemy as *The New York Times,* Washington *Post,* Los Angeles *Times, Wall Street Journal,* Chicago *Tribune,* Baltimore *Sun* or St. Louis *Post-Dispatch,* the leading Jewish and Negro newspapers and many of the "liberal," "internationalist" and "race-mixing" magazines such as *Life, Harper's, Saturday Evening Post, Newsweek,* and *The Reporter.*

These publications are gleaned for every scrap of information that may help the cause—rapes, riots, mixed marriages, Jews appointed to positions of importance, fluoridation of the water supply, international cooperation, and other subjects close to their hearts. To a racist, these are the publications that "maintain a conspiracy of silence over racist views and activities"; these are the ones that are owned by Jews—no question about it in racist eyes—and these are the ones that have brainwashed the American public so that it can no longer see the racist "realities" of the world.

On the other hand, there exist a number of newspapers that present their readers with the racist point of view. The one with the largest circulation is *Common Sense,* a four-page semi-monthly published in Union, New Jersey, and devoted almost entirely to attacks against Jews. It was founded in 1947 by Conde McGinley, Sr., and was published by him until his death in 1963. It still carries on but circulation has declined: at its peak in 1962 there were 90,000 subscribers, today there are only 52,000-odd readers.

McGinley had considerable influence on the careers of a number of racists: it was his newspaper that propelled George Lincoln Rockwell into his anti-Jewish crusade; Mrs. Ann Bishop, recently the Vice-Chairman of the National States Rights Party, claims that it was *Common Sense* that "educated [her] on the Jews"; Admiral Crommelin was so impressed by McGinley's message that he invested in the Christian Education Association, the legal owner and publisher of the newspaper.*

Contributors to the newspaper have included Upton Close, Merwin K. Hart, Dan Smoot, Pedro del Valle, Kenneth Goff, and Robert Williams, editor of the anti-Semitic *Williams Intelligence Summary* from Santa Ana, California.

McGinley's influence stemmed from his adept advocacy of the "worldwide conspiracy" theme, a cornerstone of racist thought. According to racists, in league with each other to take over the world are Communists, Jews, Wall Street bankers, Negroes, Protestant clergy, and sections of the Eastern "Establishment." How this actually works is not very clear, but the syllogism usually runs like this: the Money Powers in the West are predominantly Jewish; the U.S. is actually run by a "secret government" in New York; Jews financed the Russian Revolution; therefore the Western Money Powers are sympathetic to communism and are in secret alliance with the Reds to destroy Western civilization.

There are variations to the conspiracy theory that will be examined later in the book, particularly the theory that minimizes the activities of Jews but plays up those of the "internal communist threat" and other enemies.

Common Sense favors the conspiracy theory (racist version) for all it is worth. In one recent issue a picture of Anastas Mikoyan, U Thant, Ralph Bunche and Adlai Stevenson carried the caption: "Internationalists seal world slavery plot with treason handshake." The newspaper claimed that Sidney Weinberg, senior

---

* I have seen the newspaper on the desks of many people who would ordinarily be considered outside the sphere of racist activities.

partner in the investment banking house of Goldman, Sachs, & Co., "took the place of Bernard Baruch, head of the Zionist Invisible Government, and advisor to seven presidents." Douglas Dillon, the former Secretary of the Treasury, according to *Common Sense*, "is determined to strengthen the international monetary system in order to bankrupt America and further sink us into World Government under Zionist rule." A 1953 headline read: "THE COMING RED DICTATORSHIP. ASIATIC MARXIST JEWS CONTROL ENTIRE WORLD AS LAST WORLD WAR COMMENCES. THOUSANDS OF PLOTTERS PLACED IN KEY POSITIONS BY INVISIBLE GOVERNMENT. FEW WERE EVER ELECTED."

McGinley's newspaper was investigated in 1954 by the House Committee on Un-American Activities. The Committee's report stated that, while *"Common Sense* represents itself as 'the Nation's anti-Communist paper,' . . . such patriotic claims provide poor disguise . . . for some of the most vitriolic hate propaganda ever to come to the attention of the Committee."

Other literature, if one is a conscientious racist, must include Gerald L. K. Smith's *The Cross and the Flag,* the circulation of which is on the rise. The middle-aged or elderly racist might peruse back issues of William Dudley Pelley's *Valor* magazine (published by "Soulcraft Fellowship, Inc."), Frank Britton's three-color newspaper, *The American Nationalist,* or Gerald Winrod's *Defender* magazine, all three long-time racist publications, the first two of which have been discontinued.* Perhaps, out of loyalty, one might take out a subscription to *The Winrod Letter.* It is published by the Reverend Gordon Winrod, Gerald's son, once the National Chaplain of the National States Rights Party, who resigned to start "The Winrod Hour," a weekly radio broadcast from station XEG, Monterrey, Mexico.

The White Sentinel is a monthly published in St. Louis by John W. Hamilton, a former lieutenant of Gerald L. K. Smith. Hamilton runs the National Citizens Protective Association, Inc., a Negrophobic, anti-Jewish organization that has been involved in many

---

* Pelley's publication passed into history with his death. Britton's newspaper folded in 1960 when he was convicted of attempted bribery of a public official and given a one-year-to-life sentence.

segregation-integration conflicts. His *White Sentinel* appeals mainly to Southern racists.

Another magazine, *The Truthseeker,* based in San Diego, attacked both Presidential candidates during the 1964 election. Senator Goldwater, it complained, had made no provisions to thwart "the eventual take-over [of the U.S.] by more fertile Blacks." As for LBJ's Democrats, "more Jewized and therefore more dedicated to Negro-breeding policies," they would probably win; and as long as the voters, "drunk on Jew talk," continued to ignore the race problem, "the decline of the White race would continue."

The dedicated racist will read at least one foreign magazine with similar views. A. K. Chesterton's *Candour* from London, *Jeune-Europe* from Brussels, *Europa Korrespondenz,* from Vienna, *National Europa* from Paris and *Canadian Intelligence Service* from Flesherton, Ontario, are only a few of those available.

Of particular interest are those magazines that promote a strange mixture of theories: racism, British-Israelism, vegetarianism and spiritualism.

The oldest is *Destiny,* the journal of the New England-based Anglo-Saxon Federation of America, which preaches the British-Israelite creed—also known as the Anglo-Israelite creed, Celto-Saxon, Destiny of America, Pyramidology, and Kingdom Message.

British-Israelites are not confined to the political world but are often found in the religious field. Sometimes they belong to both. Some of the better-known British-Israelites are Gerald L. K. Smith, Wesley Swift, Kenneth Goff (all of whom are Protestant ministers), William Kullgren, and a clutch of Fundamentalist preachers located mostly in the South. One of the more unusual expressions of this cult is found in the "White House Crusade and Church of Jesus Christ of Israel," whose leader calls himself "Jasper VII." Jasper VII, based in Los Angeles, urges his followers to "denounce the creed of Judaism openly," keep Jews out of public office and "throw out of this land that beast of international Babylon, the United Nations."

The British-Israelite creed can be traced back to the late eighteenth century and the bizarre theories of a religious fanatic called Richard Brothers, who preferred to be known as "the Prince of Hebrews." He believed that he was a direct descendant of King David and, as such, was the rightful heir to the British throne. The creed actually blossomed into a movement in the late 1920s under Howard B. Rand when he began publishing *Destiny*.

From Brothers' crude beginnings, British-Israelites today believe that Anglo-Saxons are God's Chosen People. By selective reading from the Bible, they maintain that Anglo-Saxons were originally the ten "lost" tribes of Israel. By further selective reading, the Jews are considered "remnants of Judah," a nation separate from Israel, and are, therefore, "a curse, a hiss, and a reproach."[20]

These cultists go to great pains to prove that they, and not the Jews, are God's Chosen People. The word British, they will tell you, originally was *berith-ish, berith* being Hebrew for covenant and *ish* meaning man, in other words, "men of the covenant." Saxon, they will say, stems from Saac's sons, or Isaac's sons, thus fulfilling God's promise in Genesis 21:12: "In Isaac shall thy seed be called." The most tortured logic concerns the etymology of the word England. It is not, they will assert, a corruption of the Old English *Engla-Land,* meaning land of the Angles (as opposed to that of the Saxons); rather it comes from the Hebrew *engle* meaning bullock because, they say, Isaac's sons killed bulls there. They are reinforced in their logic by the name for the symbolic Englishman: John Bull.

These theories are not held in high regard by most scholars.

Nevertheless, the British-Israelite creed has an estimated two million followers throughout the world, mostly in England and Canada. Not all of the followers are outright anti-Semites; they range in degree from the mildest, who harbor perhaps a slight hostility toward Jews, to the most fervent activists, who openly boast of anti-Semitism.

In the South there are two major British-Israelite publications. One is called *National Forecast Magazine* ("Current Events in the Light of Bible Prophecy"), whose editor is Charles O. Benham from Topton, North Carolina. The other publication is *Kingdom Digest,* edited by John A. Lovell of Fort Worth, Texas.

On the West Coast there are four British-Israelite newspapers. One emanates from Portland, Oregon, and is called *The Reminder of Our National Heritage and Responsibilities;* the second is the *Prophetic Herald,* of the Bethel Temple in Spokane, Washington, whose pastor, Alexander Schiffner, once assigned all the world's ills to a "Fabian, Rhodes Scholar, Zionist, Pinko, Communist, New Deal, Fair Deal, Socialistic-minded gang";[21] a third is William Kullgren's *Beacon Light Herald.*

Kullgren, like Gerald L. K. Smith, is a link with the past. He has been operating on the political fringes ever since 1933 when he was a Silver Shirt. He was indicted for sedition during World War II, but the charge was dropped when the judge died. Since then he has limited his activities to publishing the *Beacon Light Herald* from his home in Atascadero, California. When I went to visit him he was in hospital recuperating from a heart attack. His wife, who was minding the editorial chores in their home on the edge of town, loaded me down with back issues of the magazine, culled at random from an office that looked as if it had not been neatened or dusted in a generation.

The *Beacon Light Herald,* according to Kullgren, is a magazine "devoted to the problems of humanity," some of which he lists: "astrology, prophecy, education, philosophy, social problems, public ownership, health and healing, institutions, poultry raising, fruit culture, recreation, economics, and California's Mission trails."

In 1941 he wrote: "Mr. Hitler is going to go places, in spite of Mr. Roosevelt and the rest of his kikes . . . he is the divine instrument to break the hidden control of international Jewry." Two years earlier, in another issue of the *Beacon Light Herald* (then the *Beacon Light*), he wrote that Anglo-Saxons "must regain the liberty they once enjoyed under the laws of Israel." To achieve this, the entire New Deal, its leaders and its program, "the whole damnable Talmudic, Babylonian system," had to be swept away.

> What are we waiting for? The firing squad to clean us up? If we allow the New Deal program to be completed, and it is now 95 percent complete, all who believe in Christian ethics will be exterminated, whether you are leaders or not. . . .
> What are we waiting for? Again I say,
> IMPEACH ROOSEVELT, AND REPEAL THE TALMUD INSPIRED NEW DEAL LAWS.[22]

Through a process known as "non-astronomical transformation," most of Kullgren's enemies were supposed to have been turned into Jews, among them FDR, Churchill, Truman and Eisenhower.

Kullgren laces his magazine with astrological predictions of doom, disaster and death. One of his favorite targets in this field was, again, the late wartime President:

> The Lunation is exactly in opposition to Mr. Roosevelt's Uranus in the 12th, and sextile to Jupiter; and as Uranus is in the 12th of his chart, he is going to make some sudden, secret move, of an expansive nature, in connection with the army and the navy; but you will not learn the details of same except partially; it looks like a move to aid some foreign army and navy, for his Jupiter is on the cusp of the 9th; so I am convinced that he is going to secretly violate the Johnson Act.
>
> This Mars is right over Roosevelt's Neptune and square to his Sun posted in the 8th house, another indication of secret financial manipulation; but he is going to lose a powerful supporter by death. To sum it up, the chart of the United States and Roosevelt's chart have plenty of dynamite packed into them.[23]

Often he predicted worse catastrophes: fire, famine, epidemics, pestilences, atomic war and, periodically, the end of the world. To protect oneself against these hazards, he promoted health foods which, coincidentally, he sold: nostrums, lotions, powders, concentrates, oils, syrups, herbs. Most of all, he sold medical theories. "The science of raw juice therapy is sweeping the country like a prairie fire," he once wrote. "Raw carrot juice will positively cure cancer," he wrote on another occasion. He sold a number of books that reflected his medical theories: *True Chromotherapy, Astro-Diagnosis, Craniopathy, The Grape Cure, Intestinal Gardening, Health and the Sun Signs,* and *Cocoanuts and Constipation* were just a few of the titles available to interested followers.

Kullgren also claimed he maintained a clairaudient relationship with a number of people out of the past. Information of a vital nature from them would be imparted to the public through Kullgren. His most frequent messages came from Jesus Christ.

The fourth newspaper mixing its anti-Semitism with other

matters is C. Leon "Kosti" de Aryan's* *The Broom,* or more accurately, *Sun-Work-Shop and the Broom,* until recently published monthly from San Diego. De Aryan, born Constantine Lagenopol in Roumania, is eighty years old and combines vegetarianism and his own brand of Zoroastrianism with his British-Israelism and anti-Semitism. He also opposes Negroes, Catholics, vaccinations, the American Medical Association, the Federal Reserve, fluoridation, and a number of other standard racist targets.

Like Kullgren, De Aryan was indicted twice for sedition during World War II. The indictments, however, did not actually get to trial.

The newspaper's masthead carries Zoroastrian phrases: "Hu-Hata" (Good Word), "Hu-Mata" (Good Thought), "Hu-Var-ashta" (Good Deed), for instance. Occasionally there will be an inscrutable article on his version of Zoroastrianism; sometimes he mixes these beliefs with vegetarianism. For instance, one article reads in its entirety: "The unfailing KARMA protected Jesus. There was no decaying animal matter in his body. There was no killer's Karma in the vegetarian body."

A fairly regular column carried in his four-page newspaper is one called "Seasonable Hints" and is written by a Dr. O. Z. Ha'nish, or Hanish, or Otoman Z. A. Ha'nish, depending on which issue you read. It contains hints to vegetarians for the month.

> *TO OXYGENATE the system* so as to chemicalize the nerve-ganglia get perfume laden air and eat aromatic foods.

> *Dried olives and celery* will be found an excellent kidney regulator—use moderately.

> *The Stomach* desires particular attention this month and prefers a mild, hot tea rather than a cold drink.

The circulation of the *Sun-Work-Shop and the Broom* is small and is becoming smaller with time. Much of the space is given to obituaries of friends and subscribers. Those that are left are the hard-core individuals who have stuck by De Aryan for many years. It seems that no one under sixty-five reads the paper and that no

* Shortly before publication I learned that De Aryan had died.

one under seventy writes letters to it. One man claimed that, after years of physical suffering and big medical bills, he turned to fruit, vegetables and nuts and now, at eighty-eight, feels better than he has in years. Another writes in saying that the cure for crippling strokes is wheatgrass. Still another, sensing that death is nearby, waxes poetic: "I must go down this last street with an irrepressible sigh, where the weather-beaten houses sleep and calmly wait to die. . . ."

And there is a letter from Lyrl Van Hyning, of We the Mothers Mobilize for America, thanking De Aryan for remembering her seventy-third birthday and complimenting him on his article, "Jesus Christ was not a Jew." She is most grateful, she continues, for their conversation on vegetarianism, for it has helped her breathing. She ends her letter with a blessing. She gives her home address, but when it comes to adding her zip code number, all she writes is "NO!"

4

The Ku Klux Klan

Of all the racist groups in America, the only major home-grown one has been the Ku Klux Klan. For over one hundred years on and off it has been active on the political scene and is further distinguished by a consistent history of terror and violence.

There have actually been three Klans during the last century, all springing from the same roots, yet each different from the other. The first Klan lasted only twelve years—from 1865 to 1877. It was started in Pulaski, Tennessee, as a lark by a few Confederate soldiers just out of uniform. From all indications it was innocent in its intent, nothing more serious than a social secret society of war comrades. These men took their organization's name from the Greek word *kyklos,* meaning circle; they added some mumbo jumbo to their rituals, much like any other fraternal order, and they wore hoods and robes.

Within weeks it had turned racist. Coming into existence at the time of Reconstruction, the occupation of the South by Union troops, the carpetbagger, the scalawag and the Negro legislators, the Klan was an instant success with the disillusioned and embittered white Southerner. It had three aims which remain virtually unchanged today: intimidation of the Negro (then in power) into submission, the destruction of all Negro political power, and the purging of carpetbaggers from the South.

The masks and robes worn by the Klansmen, it was discovered, frightened the superstition-prone Negroes. A hooded member of the Klan, for instance, once rapped on the door of a poor Negro's shack and demanded a bucket of water. When it was produced, he pretended to drink the entire contents, pouring the water into a sack inside his robe. He then patted his stomach and said to the frightened Negro: "That's the first drink I've had since I was killed at Shiloh!"

But not all terrorist activities were as innocent. Within four years of its founding, a congressional investigating committee uncovered thousands of cases of hangings, shootings, torturings, whippings and mutilations. Most of the victims were Negroes, carpetbaggers, scalawags and whites arbitrarily deemed immoral, unfaithful or impecunious. In Louisiana 2,000 people were murdered or wounded in the few weeks preceding the 1868 Presidential elections. There were 75 murders in Georgia and 109 in Alabama during the same period. The commanding general of Federal troops in Texas complained of so many murders taking place that it was impossible to keep track of them.

The forms of punishment were both unique and brutal. A man might be whipped with rawhide until his bones were exposed; others might be quartered; still others were hung from a tree until they were strangled to death. On one occasion a suspected Negro murderer was himself murdered. His body was then boiled in a sugar boiler to remove the flesh, and his skeleton, wired together by an ex-Confederate surgeon, was then hung from a tall pine tree "as a warning of the fate of other evildoers."[1]

Things became so bad that General Nathan Bedford Forrest, Confederate hero and the Klan's Grand Wizard, ordered the Klan disbanded in 1869. It was not until 1871, however, that the country first learned of the true nature of the organization. Klan membership, 500,000 at its peak, began to melt away following the congressional investigation of that year. The Klan itself eventually died out when Reconstruction ended in 1877.

A highly romantic legend sprang up around this early Klan. It was pictured as an Invisible Empire of Galahads who were trying to save all that was good with the South. The legend was fed by Thomas Dixon, Jr.'s novel, *The Clansman* (1905), and later by D. W. Griffith's 1915 motion picture, *The Birth of a Nation*.

In the same year that Griffith's masterpiece was being shown in Atlanta, the Klan itself was revived by a lanky Alabama Methodist minister named William Joseph Simmons. Simmons was reportedly an ex-garter salesman, a "colonel" of the Woodsmen of the World, and an inveterate joiner of fraternal orders. He had been denied a pulpit in 1912 by his church's elders for "inefficiency and moral impairment."

He started his Klan by burning a huge cross on top of Stone Mountain, Georgia. For five years his Invisible Empire of the Knights of the Ku Klux Klan drifted along with some two thousand members. The organization was billed as "a classy order of the highest class." Then in 1920 Simmons hired two publicity agents, Edward Clark Young and wealthy widow Elizabeth Tyler. Through the work of these two, the Klan grew rapidly. By 1925 there were some five million Klansmen in America. Unlike the first Klan, this one was nationwide in scope and middle-class in temperament.

Its power was such that it controlled the legislatures or statehouses, or both, in Colorado, Texas, Oklahoma, Louisiana, Maine and Kansas. In New Jersey there was a Klan organization in every county; in Ohio, twelve mayors were Klansmen and countless sheriffs, schoolboard members and city councilmen were as well; in Indiana, Grand Dragon D. C. Stephenson held virtual control over the politics in the state; and in Oregon the Klan was so powerful that it elected Klansmen as President of the State Senate and Speaker of the House. Many politicians joined simply to survive. One of the better-known ones to have signed up is Supreme Court Justice Hugo Black. (He quit in 1925 before he ran for senator from Alabama.) At the 1924 National Democratic Convention an estimated 350 delegates were Klansmen and were the ones primarily responsible for the defeat of Al Smith (as they were to be again in 1928). In August 1925, forty thousand robed Klansmen marched down Pennsylvania Avenue in Washington; one group carried a huge American flag to catch money thrown by spectators.

Simmons added many frills to his Klan. Along with Young and Tyler, he pushed a more Fundamentalist line which included—besides the original Klan's hatred of Negroes and carpetbaggers—hatred of Catholics, Jews, "the international conspiracy," loose women, liquor and all foreigners not of Anglo-Saxon stock. Simmons revived such spicy tales as the nuns who supposedly carried around little gingham bags, with drawstrings, which were used to transport the fruits of priestly lust to the furnaces;[2] or the tale that the "dago" Pope was planning to take over the U.S. and had arms cached in Catholic churches for that purpose. He also added considerably to Klan regalia and terminology. Robes were made of satin and had peaked hoods and fancy embroidery. Such terms as Kleagle, Klabee, Kladd and Kludd entered the American lexicon for the first time; so did fanciful names for months, weeks and days.*

These five million Klansmen contributed to the organization's coffers some $75 million per year. Such fortune marked another aspect of this Klan: it was (and, indeed, the third Klan today still is) a haven for the fast-buck merchant, the shoddy financial manipulator and the slippery opportunist. While the first Klan was poor, decentralized and fairly honest in its intent, the new Klan was a huge promotional project run for the benefit of its leaders and at the expense of the rank and file.

Violence was still common. One newspaper found that from October 1920 to October 1921 there had been 4 killings by the Klan, 1 mutilation, 1 branding with acid, 5 kidnappings, 42 floggings, 27 tar and feather parties, 43 persons warned to leave town, 14 communities threatened and 16 masked parades of intimidation.

But by 1924 the heady days of this Klan were over. Many states had passed antimasking laws, corruption among the leaders weakened the organization's solidarity, an investigation in 1921 revealed more sordid details and, in 1926, Indiana's posturing Grand Dragon, D. C. Stephenson, was convicted of murder after a lower-berth Pullman-car rape of a young girl. By 1927 membership had fallen to some 350,000. The second Klan did not die, however, until World War II when the Internal Revenue Service hit the organization for $685,000 in back taxes. James Colescott, then Imperial Wizard, closed up shop rather than pay them.

It should be noted that in its decline, from 1926 to 1944, the Klan turned more vicious and brutal, perhaps a portent of things to come with the present third Klan. In 1935, Florida Klansmen

* See Appendix II for a complete list.

flogged and castrated one Joseph Shoemaker, a white man and a founder of an independent political organization called the Modern Democrats. Shoemaker was then tarred and feathered, one leg being plunged into a bucket of boiling tar. He died nine days later in agony. Eleven men, most of them Klansmen, were subsequently acquitted. Five years later, near Atlanta, one Ike Gaston was beaten to death with bullwhips. His only crime was being the town drunk. At the same time the Klan was courting the pro-Nazi German-American Bund. They held a joint rally in New Jersey's "Camp Nordlund." A forty-foot-high cross was burned and everyone sang German marching songs. Several years later, Klansmen carved a large "KKK" with a penknife on the chest and stomach of a Houston Negro. They then hung him by his knees from an oak tree and flogged him with a chain.

The third Klan was revived after the war by Dr. Samuel Green, an Atlanta dentist. It grew appreciably after the school desegregation decision by the Supreme Court in 1954, and expanded rapidly in 1961 when an ex-rubber worker, Robert M. Shelton, Jr., brought together many of the bickering and ineffectual Klans.

This Klan again differs in many significant ways from the previous two. It inherits, to be sure, the goal of white Anglo-Saxon Protestant supremacy, the subjugation of the Negro as a second-class citizen, the xenophobia toward outsiders and the hatred of Jews, Catholics and Eastern liberals. It is also nationwide in scope, although its strength is centered in the South. But this Klan is not middle-class; it is lower-class. Nor is this Klan a single unit. Today there are some fifteen Klans and perhaps a dozen more that have not yet surfaced. Each one guards its individuality most jealously, refusing to subordinate itself to any one man's rule. The current strength of all Klans together is estimated to be from 50,000 to 100,000 with an additional one million sympathizers.

There are two major Klans, one a fiefdom, the other a loose coalition of independent Klans. The United Klans of America Knights of the Ku Klux Klan is the personal empire of Imperial Wizard Robert Shelton, a young and energetic man who has been a Klansman for a decade. Headquarters are in Tuscaloosa, Alabama, and the 35,000 or so members are scattered throughout at least eighteen states.

Shelton's Georgia "realm" is headed by Grand Dragon Calvin Craig of Atlanta. He controls some 49 Klaverns (local Klan units) with some 9,000 members. "I can take five men in a city of 25,000 and that is just like having an army," said Craig. "That five men can almost control the political atmosphere of that city." In many parts of the South it has happened.

Shelton's Mississippi realm of some 27 Klaverns is controlled by Grand Dragon E. L. McDaniel, a Natchez truck driver and teamster. The Alabama realm is run by Grand Dragon Robert Creel of Bessemer; he controls some 12,000 members in over 70 Klaverns. The South Carolina realm, run by Grand Dragon Robert Scoggin, of Spartanburg, has 2,500 supporters in 20 Klaverns. The Florida Klaverns are controlled by Don Cothran and contribute some 1,000 members. The Virginia realm is run by pistol-packing Marshall Kornegay; and the North Carolina realm, the fastest growing of all with some 113 Klaverns and perhaps 8,000 members, is controlled by Grand Dragon James Robertson Jones of Granite Quarry.

In addition to those throughout the South, United Klan realms have been established in New York (run, until his death, by Daniel Burros), Pennsylvania (Burros' one-eyed friend, Roy Frankhouser, is the Grand Dragon), New Jersey (Frank Rotella), Delaware, Ohio, Wisconsin and Indiana.

The second largest Klan is run by James K. Venable, a lawyer from Tucker, Georgia. Venable is Chairman of the National Association Knights of the Ku Klux Klan, a loose confederation of nine separate Klans. Venable is Imperial Wizard of his own National Knights of the Ku Klux Klan, which claims memberships in forty-eight states but has Klaverns in only three: Georgia, Alabama and North Carolina. There is Earl E. George's Improved Order of U.S. Klans based in Lithonia, Georgia; there is Houston P. Martin's thousand-member Original Knights of the Ku Klux Klan (now known as the Anti-Communist Christian Crusaders) in Louisiana; there is Imperial Wizard A. E. Bolen's Association of South Carolina Klans; Jason Kersey's 25-Klavern United Florida Ku Klux Klan; Grand Dragon Charles Maddox's Association of Georgia Klans from Savannah; Imperial Wizard H. J. Jones' U.S. Klan Knights of the Ku Klux Klan; William H. Morris' Federated

Knights of the Ku Klux Klan from Buchanan, Georgia; and, finally, Dixie Klans, Inc., from Chattanooga. All these Klans together may have eight thousand hard-core members, although no accurate estimate is available.

In addition there are some unaffiliated Klans. There is Sam Bowers' militant and secretive White Knights of the Ku Klux Klan, located in Mississippi, which boasts forty-three Klaverns and three thousand members (although there has been a drastic falling off of members as of late); there is the small Association of Arkansas Klans; the Militant Knights of the Ku Klux Klan, located in Florida; the Mississippi Knights of the Ku Klux Klan, run by a Walter A. Bailey; and the one-man Aryan Knights of the Ku Klux Klan run by a crippled World War I veteran named Horace Sherman Miller from Waco, Texas.

This picture is further complicated by the fact that many of these associated and independent Klans maintain relations with Shelton's United Klan. Sometimes there are membership raids between one group and another; at other times these small groups split and re-form; more often they spring into being during a racial crisis only to die a slow death long after peace has returned. The current situation is extremely fluid.

Who are these Klansmen? Unquestionably most of them come from the working classes of white society, where the technological rejects, the insecure, the unassimilated, the despairing and the frightened congregate. The average Klansman has a fifth-grade education and is usually a day laborer, a mechanic or an industrial worker who works where job security is virtually nonexistent and where competition with Negroes is immediate and real. He lives in an urban society but his heart is in the country. He sees himself as a poor white and knows that he is unwelcome in the city; but he also realizes he cannot return to the simple rural life he prefers. Often he straddles the two societies, operating a gas station, selling cars or lightning rods or quick lunches—businesses that usually congregate along the "neon strip" border between center city and the farm. His slight education does little to ease his plight, for it gives him enough knowledge to be aware of his predicament, but not enough to escape it. He is not a part of the white power structure, and in this respect his actions reflect the same frustrations as the Negro, Catholic and Jew who are also excluded, for the most part, from it. He feels trapped and sees no way out except by lashing out viciously at the Negro below him and the white power structure above him.

With a few notable exceptions, the Klan is an urban movement, not a rural one as it is often thought to be. The Klan is filled with "rednecks" and "wool hats" but mostly those who have recently moved to town. Klan strength, for instance, is found more in northern Georgia and between Atlanta and Augusta, not in the rural south; it is found in central Alabama between Birmingham and Montgomery where the industry is located, not in the northern or southern farm belts of the state; it is found to be most potent in Mississippi within an area encompassed by Jackson, McComb, Hattiesburg and Meridian, not so much in the rural Delta country where Negroes outnumber whites more than two to one; and it is found along Florida's more industrial east coast rather than along the rural west coast and panhandle. In truth, the Klan is a sociological phenomenon, a reaction to life in the South where it is changing the fastest.

Stewart Alsop believes that all Klansmen are essentially escapists. They swagger about with pistols and shotguns, confident that they are invincible, important and on the side of the good. Alsop points out that the Klan is much like a young boy's secret club— with oaths, rituals, costumes, a sense of belonging, no girls and an enemy. When Grady Mars, Grand Klaliff (vice-president) of Shelton's North Carolina realm, said, pointing to his snub-nosed .38 Smith & Wesson pistol, "Mister, with this little gun, I can drop a man at a hundred yards, every time," he obviously thought he could. (It would be an impossible feat even for an expert sharpshooter.) Mars wore silver eagles on his collar as head of the "VIP Security Guard," an organization assigned to protect Klansmen at their rallies. Apparently his dream world was shattered somewhere along the line for he shot himself to death the day after Alsop interviewed him.[3]

Judge Daniel Duke, of Atlanta, a dynamic and gregarious man, a graduate of Christ Church, Oxford, and a lifelong opponent of the Klan, believes that the Klan mind is similar to the minds of people who watch professional wrestling matches. Klansmen, he says, go to cross-burnings and cornfield harangues for the same reason that a neatly dressed bank clerk will go see exotically named wrestlers. As soon as the contestants begin to grapple, the clerk, until then the model of decorum, begins to shout *"Give it to him! Get that sonofabitch! . . . ,"* his face contorted with rage, his hat mangled in his hands. When the match is over the man regains his composure and once again can face his nagging wife and empty future. So, too, the Klansman finds his catharsis among people who damn everything that he believes keeps him from being the person he thinks he should be. "It's kind of an amateur group therapy," said Judge Duke, but, he added, "it becomes dangerous when some elements believe what their leaders say."

Part of the catharsis is readily evident in Klan ritual. Although initiation ceremonies vary from Klavern to Klavern, the following, briefly, is a typical one:

Klexter guards the "outer den"; Klarogo guards the "inner den." Inside the darkened, candle-lit meeting room are Klaliff (vice-president), Kludd (chaplain) and Exalted Cyclops (president) on his "throne." To the left is Kligrapp (secretary). In front sits Night-Hawk who is in charge of the candidates and the fiery cross. To the right is Kladd (conductor), Klokard (lecturer) and Klokann Kommittee (a three-man board of advisors or investigators). In the center is the altar.

Cyclops begins the Konklave by shouting, *"All aliens who have not attained citizenship in the Invisible Empire of the Knights of the Ku Klux Klan will retire to the outer den!"* Klexter and Klarogo take up their posts and guard the doors.

Signs and countersigns are given among Klansmen who then enter the inner den. Klexter greets the initiates with "Tsog," and the newcomers are instructed to respond "Tsog." In the inner den Klokard prepares the altar. Kludd advances with a Bible and a vessel of "dedication fluid." Both are placed on the altar, the Bible opened to the 12th Chapter of Romans.

Cyclops asks: "Faithful Klokard, why the fiery cross?"

Klokard replies: "Sir, it is the emblem of that sincere, unselfish devotedness of all Klansmen to the sacred purpose and principles we have espoused."

"My Terrors [the collective name for all Klansmen in a

Klavern] and Klansmen, what means the fiery cross?" asks Cyclops. All respond: "WE SERVE AND SACRIFICE FOR THE
RIGHT!" Then all Klansmen rise and sing stanzas from their
opening "Koke" (to the tune of "From Greenland's Icy Mountains"). Kludd then prays to God "to invoke Thy blessings upon
our Emperor, the Imperial Wizard. . . ."

Now comes the initiation of the "aliens." Klarogo first speaks
the password "allw" to Klexter, who repeats it to Night-Hawk,
who, in turn, raps on the outer door seven times. Klexter asks,
"Who dares to approach so near the entrance of this Klavern?"
Night-Hawk responds and gives the countersign. Klarogo opens
the door and Night-Hawk gives another signal: "gallws."

The aliens at the door face Cyclops. More ritual is exchanged.
Klokard examines the aliens' qualifications and eligibility (those
who are white, male, Protestant, believe in "clannishness," white
supremacy, government of U.S.A., Klan rules and have paid their
initiation dues of twenty-five dollars).

Klarogo steps aside, Kladd and the aliens cross the room. All
Klansmen rise and give "Tsog," then face the altar with the
command "Tsoc-L." Other orders are repeated, the signals "allw,"
"Tsoc-L," "Gstog" and "LLW" reverberate around the room.
Kludd addresses the aliens, followed by Cyclops, who outlines
their duties and responsibilities.

Cyclops then consecrates the aliens with the sacred fluid while
Klansmen sing a song to the tune of "Just As I Am Without One
Plea." Cyclops then greets each alien with "Tcok" and invests
them with the title of "Klansmen." The new members are then
taught the "way of the Klavern" and the "Klan Konversation."
Finally they receive "mioak," the sacred symbol of the Klan after
which Klokard reads the first lesson from the Kloran, the Klan's
bible.[4]

This is just one instance of Klan ritual. Klan signals, countersigns, grips and codes change from time to time. Sometimes there
is confusion. Donald Appell, for instance, the House Committee
on Un-American Activities' chief investigator, tells the story of
being in the South during his investigation and stopping in a small
town to ask the way to a Klan rally. He directed his question to a
local policeman who, before he answered, slipped Appell the Klan

grip, a rotary motion of the clasped hands. A variation, according to Appell, is tapping the middle finger against the other's wrist when shaking hands. There are supposed to be a number of secret signals by means of which one Klansman can tell if another one is around (such as grasping one's elbows with one's hands, which is also supposed to mean that that Klansman needs help). Imperial Wizard James Venable of the National Knights says he can tell whether a man is a Klansman just by looking at him. The Klan salute, at least in private, is a fascist-type stiff-arm effort.

The 1965 Klan hearings in Washington brought out the fact that Klansmen operate behind a number of fronts, much like the Communist Party. Most of them are known as "gun clubs" or "sportsman's clubs" and serve the dual purpose of giving a Klansman an excuse to have a gun and of giving the club an opportunity to buy ammunition cheaper through the National Rifle Association. One fully armed group is called Nacirema, Inc. (American spelled backward), whose members wear black robes. It is supposed to be one of the most violent of all Klans. Very little is known about it.

One group of Klaverns in North Carolina uses numbers to identify its members. The Rowan Sportsman's Club, for instance, a Klan front, had as its Klabee (treasurer) one Fred L. Wilson, otherwise known as "200-001." With obvious glee, the New York *Herald Tribune* reported (26 October 1965) that Wilson was a convicted numbers operator.

The hearings also disclosed that some Klans have been holding field exercises, much like the Minutemen. Two in particular, in 1961 and 1964, were cited, the trainees being taught how to handle dynamite, fuses, fire bombs and booby traps. The 1964 exercise allegedly included a course in how to take over radio stations and power plants.

(To digress briefly, the 1965 HCUA hearings were instructive in other ways. As one after another Klansman came forward to hide behind the First, Fourth, Fifth and Fourteenth Amendments, the ignorance of the men soon became apparent. With the exception of the more intelligent Klan leaders, most had trouble reading their stock response. Some never were able to master "Sir, I respectfully decline to answer the question on the grounds previously stated," but had to have it repeatedly whispered to them, phrase by phrase, by the Klan's lawyer. Dotted throughout the hearing room were perhaps twelve U.S. marshals, each one identified by a tiny colored pin stuck in the seam of his lapel. Some marshals faced the Klansmen sitting in the witnesses' section while others faced the audience. Noticing an equal number of blue-clad policemen lining the walls, I asked one marshal whether his job was to protect the audience from the Klan or the Klan from the audience. Without cracking a smile, he answered in a long Southern accent, "Bo'f . . .")

Klansmen are given lessons in the proper construction of a burning cross. There are several varieties of such crosses. One is the standard thirty- to forty-foot variety made of a pine tree trunk with a notched crosspiece nailed to it. Burlap is then wrapped tightly around the wood. Then a liberal mixture of gasoline and motor oil, at a ratio of one-half gallon of gas to five pounds of oil for every foot of cross, is applied. (Sometimes the ratio is changed, depending on the desired effect.) A hole is dug, the cross is raised with ropes and wedged in. Often when the torch is applied a cross-shaped ground fire is started where the cross lay as it was being soaked.

Another type of cross is known as the "cross of intimidation." It comes in two varieties. One is about six feet high with a pointed end that can be planted quickly on someone's lawn. The other is the same but with .32 caliber bullets wrapped in the burlap.

I once went to a cross-burning in Dagsboro, Delaware—or at least I *thought* it would be a cross-burning from what I read on the advertisements stapled to the telephone poles. It was held at night in a cornfield, and policemen were out on the main road directing traffic into the field. A naked lightbulb illuminated a wooden speaker's platform set up next to a housetrailer. The American and Confederate flags flanked the microphone. Some two hundred spectators, including the press, milled around the trailer with over forty Klansmen in their robes. There were white robes, white robes with red stripes on the arms and hems, red robes, red robes with green and white stripes, green robes, and green robes with red stripes, but no purple robes (only Shelton, the Imperial Wizard, wears purple, and he was not there).

Another hundred or so spectators sat in their cars and watched. A loudspeaker blared forth with "That Old Rugged Cross" and "Move Them Niggers North," making conversation almost impossible. Over by a stable hot dogs were being sold by a Klanswoman in a mustard-covered white robe; one fellow was doing a brisk business selling "Never" buttons and the Klan's newspaper, *The Fiery Cross,* from the trunk of his car; another robed Klansman was passing out application blanks to everyone not in uniform; a policeman was taking down license-plate numbers, including mine ("Don't give me no argument, fellah, I'm jes' doin' what I'm told. . . ."), and a light-skinned well-dressed elderly Negro watched the entire proceedings from the shadows.

A group of Klan "security officers," dressed in white helmet liners, combat boots, gray shirts and trousers, and white fourragères, and carrying ominously long flashlights, patrolled the area. One man wore captain's bars; another held a police dog on a chain.

I was told by the Kludd for Delaware, that no cross was to be burned that night because of "a local drought." There was a rumor that a cross with lightbulbs on it was to be raised, but it never materialized.

Eventually the music was turned off and, one after the other, Klan speakers mounted the platform to give their pitch. Unfortunately, my tape recorder batteries went dead so I only caught fragmentary bits of what was said. There was Layton Braun, Sr., from Baltimore, who started things off with a long extemporaneous prayer. Then came Joseph Alpert, a local Klan leader, who peered out into the night through dark glasses. He began his speech with: "Now, ladies and gentlemen, let's get down to some nigger business. . . ." This remark was greeted by vigorous clapping from the standing spectators and by a cacophony of horn-blowing from those in their cars. One reporter, a veteran of many Klan rallies, noted that this was the first drive-in one he had ever been to. Then came Charles J. Luthardt, who was then running for office in Maryland on the Fighting American Nationalist ticket. He was dressed in civilian clothes and wore a "Never" button. Before his turn to speak, he passed through the crowd handing out little slips of yellow paper. On them were stamped: "VOTE WHITE. This is your *LAST* chance. Charles J. Luthardt for Governor." The only thing I recorded him saying was: "I want people to say to me: 'We don't care if you're a thief, we don't care if you're incompetent. . . .' I want people to vote for me because I'm a white man!" As I was listening to him, a little old woman, in pink hair curlers and a gingham dress, struggling into her Klan robes, came running up to a Klansman standing behind me. Totally out of breath she gasped to him, snapping the hood over her forehead, "I thought I'd *never* make it!"

Then came Vernon J. Naimaster, Grand Titan of Maryland, who also spoke to the crowd from behind dark glasses. Eventually there came the featured speaker, Robert Scoggin, Grand Dragon of the realm of South Carolina. Scoggin, for thirteen years a Klansman and a veteran on full disability and winner of two Purple Hearts, is a master of invective. Pointing his finger to the press, he said in measured tones: "Turn on your tape-recorders, Katzenbach kids. . . ." Martin Luther King, he said, "is the only man who can black fifty miles of highway in a day" (vigorous horn-honking). The Vice-President he called "Hen House Humphrey"; the President himself he referred to either as "Lame Brain Johnson" or "Light Bulb Johnson"; and Washington, D.C., he called "Hershey city—80 percent chocolate and 20 percent nuts." The crowd lapped it up, laughing at his racial jokes and his uncomplimentary references to Negroes, Jews, Catholics and liberals.

Then came the pitch for money; Klansmen passed through the crowd with hats, shaking them ostentatiously when they came near the press. Someone else made a plea for a wheelchair for a crippled boy who was paraded by two Klansmen before the spectators.

Then with a final prayer and a plea to join, the rally broke up to enthusiastic clapping, whistling and horn-blowing. As a policeman motioned my car onto the main highway nearby, I could hear the recorded voice of "Colonel Sharecropper," strumming his electric guitar, singing over the loudspeakers: "Move them niggers North/ Move them niggers North/If they don't like our Southern ways/ Move them niggers North. . . ."

How much this kind of rally or a real cross-burning contributes to Klan violence is questionable. Undoubtedly, as Judge Duke points out, not all spectators find such activities a sufficient release for their tensions.

Most Klans, for instance, have an inner group, unknown to other Klansmen, which is composed of the most dedicated and fanatical members. They often plan and carry out the acts of violence and terrorism. Since the ordinary Klansman is not privy to their secrets, he can say with a straight face that the Klan is nonviolent. In spite of rank-and-file ignorance, these inner groups do exist and go by a variety of names. The most common are known as "wrecking crews"; sometimes they are known as the "ass-tear committee," "the enforcers," "the underground" or the "secret six." Most of the members are trained in the use of rifles, explosives and violence. Collie LeRoy Wilkins, for instance, was supposed to have been a member of a "secret six." Another one of these groups was supposed to have threatened the life of Martin Luther King in 1965 (one of the numerous threats he receives every year).

Whether these inner groups, the Klaverns as a whole, or an individual fired by a highly developed sense of outrage commits Klan violence is known only to the Klansmen themselves or the FBI, and neither group talks too much about it. In any event Klan violence is impressive by any standard. The total number of acts of violence of all types has never been counted, but between 1 January 1956 and 1 June 1963, for instance, there were 138 cases of dynamitings in the South associated with the Klan. There were 29 bombings in Birmingham alone between 1957 and 1965. Among all the rubble were Negro homes, churches and integrated schools, a YMCA in Chattanooga, an auditorium in Knoxville and synogogues in Miami, Jacksonville, Gadsden and Nashville.

Specific examples of Klan violence should be noted. In 1957, a defenseless Negro was castrated by four Klansmen who then poured turpentine on the open wound. This was part of a Klan sacrificial initiation ceremony, and the four culprits, followers of one Asa "Ace" Carter,* were sent to prison for twenty years. In April 1964, three men in black hoods abducted a millworker in

* Carter's followers eschewed moderation. They have attacked Nat "King" Cole on a Birmingham stage, they fought the admission of Autherine

Bogalusa, Louisiana, and beat him with a pistol and a whip, claiming he had failed to support his child. In June of the same year a group of armed men surrounded the Mt. Zion Methodist Church in Philadelphia, Mississippi, beat the Negroes and burned the church to the ground. Five days later, in the same town, three civil rights workers—Andrew Goodman, James Chaney and Michael Schwerner—disappeared. Their bodies were discovered six months later. Twenty-one men, many of them Klansmen, were charged with conspiring to violate the constitutional rights of the three. So far no one has been convicted of the crime. Three weeks later, Lemuel Penn, a Negro educator on his way north from military training at Fort Benning, Georgia, was shot down by a man in a passing car. Two men linked to the Klan were convicted under the Federal civil rights conspiracy statute and given ten-year jail terms. Four other men were acquitted.

Later in the year a gang of masked men kidnaped a union official in Laurel, Mississippi, and flogged him with a heavy strap, after which they poured a hot liquid into the wounds. Apparently the man was beaten because his union had approved of a federal order giving Negroes equal treatment at the local Masonite plant. The suspected floggers were all Klansmen. In December 1964, several armed men poured gasoline on a shoe shop in Ferriday, Louisiana, and set fire to it. A Negro was prevented from leaving the building and he subsequently died of burns. In February 1965, another group of armed men—this time in "bloody" Lowndes County, Alabama—disrupted a church service and warned the minister to leave town lest he disappear forever. A month later the Reverend James Reeb from Boston was clubbed to death by four men. The suspects were identified as Klansmen. Two weeks later Viola Gregg Liuzzo was shot down by a night rider on the Selma-Montgomery highway. Three men identified as Klansmen—Wil-

---

Lucy into the University of Alabama, and they helped John Kasper during the Clinton riots of 1956. Once, Carter was questioned by some of his Klansmen about their Klan's finances. Offended by such arrogance on the part of his own followers, Carter drew a revolver and blasted away, wounding two of the insurgents. Attempted murder charges were later dismissed. As of this writing Carter is a special assistant to ex-Governor Wallace of Alabama.

liam Eaton, Eugene Thomas and Collie LeRoy Wilkins—were later convicted by an all-white Southern jury of conspiring to deprive the civil rights worker of her civil rights.*

Such acts of violence are denied by Klan leaders. "We do not believe in violence," said Imperial Wizard Robert Shelton, "despite that certain individuals have committed acts of violence under cover of darkness, shielded by masks and robes resembling the official regalia of the Knights of the Ku Klux Klan. 'Ballots not Bullets' is our motto."

HCUA investigator Donald Appell disagrees. During a break in the Klan hearings he told me the following story, quite revealing of the Klan mind. Said Appell: "I asked one member of the Klan, off the record, how he kept out violent elements from his group and he said, 'Well, we don't have that problem because we're not a violent group.' Then I said, 'Well, what procedure do you use to get rid of a member if he, say, goes out and shoots a Negro?' And he answered, 'I don't care if he goes out and shoots a *hundred* niggers!' "

Appell later stressed the existence of fear among Southerners that has been spawned by such remarks and actions of the Klan. He said that this fear is real and bone-chilling and has been the secret of the Klan's past successes. "If we did anything in the hearings," he said, "we dissipated that fear."

Imperial Wizard Shelton, for one, is annoyed that all violence is blamed on his United Klans. "There is several Klans, you know," he said. "That is the trouble of throwing every nut in the same bag and saying it's all the same kind of nuts."

Indeed there is a variety of Klans. There is, for instance, the Reverend James "Catfish" Cole, whose Klan was subjected to considerable ridicule in 1958 when he held a cross-burning in Robeson County, North Carolina. Robeson County differed from other Southern areas in that it maintained a three-way segregation between whites, Negroes and a tribe of proud and prosperous

---

* In early 1966, a retired Birmingham businessman put the following classified ad in the Birmingham *News:* "NOTICE. Do you need a crowd-getter? I have a 1963 Oldsmobile two-door in which Mrs. Viola Liuzzo was killed. Bullet holes and everything still intact. $3500." Anthony Liuzzo, the widower, sought an injunction to prevent the sale of the car for what surely would have been a macabre freak show.

Indians called Lumbees, whom many believe are descendants of the lost colonies of Roanoke. In any event, at the sight of these Indians, many of whom were armed and had donned warpaint for the occasion, Cole's meeting was broken up, his Klansmen fleeing in terror. The story was carried in all news media from coast to coast, and everyone laughed except the Klan.*

Then there were the Bryant brothers, Arthur and Joseph, from North Carolina who ran their own Klan. They also had impressive criminal records ranging from larceny and bad-check passing to juvenile rape and senior solicitation for prostitution. There was plumbing contractor Bill Hendrix, who had his own Klan in Florida. He ran for governor in 1952 and received eleven thousand votes but soon thereafter was convicted of sending vulgar postcards to his political opponents.

There is Walter Bailey, of the Mississippi Knights of the Ku Klux Klan, who wrote to me: ". . . Your Senators and Congressmen nail our Caucasian hides to the barn door every chance they get and that especially applies to that infamous louse, Hugh Scott. That goon hates everybody and everything white. . . . Hate? They're the hatingest shysters in the nation along with J. Edgar Hoover, Earl Warren, Katzenbach, Lyndon Johnson and Hubert Hooligan Humphrey."

Horace Sherman Miller, a crippled war veteran from Waco, Texas, runs the Aryan Knights of the Ku Klux Klan. He puts out a mimeograph sheet called *Aryan Views—White Folk News,* which leans heavily on attacking Jews. Every once in a while his *News* carries a boxed insert reading:

> **Jew Communists**
> **say**
> **integrate**
> **rob-rape-riot-kill**

* In 1966, Grand Dragon James R. Jones of the North Carolina realm offered Klan memberships to the Lumbees, apparently on the theory that if you can't lick 'em, recruit 'em. So far there have been no takers.

He is something of an international Klansman. His literature is eagerly sought by "Klansmen" in Canada, Austria and Britain. (There is a British KKK and it is closely associated with the tiny neo-Nazi parties on the island.)

One of the most violent Klans of all is the White Knights of the Ku Klux Klan located in central Mississippi. Although he denies it, the Imperial Wizard has been identified as Samuel A. Bowers, Jr. He is a thin, blond forty-two-year-old native of Laurel who runs the Sambo Amusement Company, a vending-machine enterprise. Bowers lards his ideology with considerable historical and religious overtones and once called on his followers to prepare for a Communist invasion from the Gulf of Mexico. When I wrote to him asking for information he replied by accusing me of possibly being part of "some foul and subversive plot" worthy of the FBI's attention.

As it turned out the FBI was more interested in him. The Bureau has linked the White Knights to six civil rights murders from 1964 to 1966 alone. Recently fourteen White Knights, including Bowers, were picked up in connection with the 1966 firebomb slaying of Vernon Dahmer, a prosperous Hattiesburg Negro. When the government agents (the leader of whom was named, ironically, Robert E. Lee) raided Bowers' house, they found a large arms cache, diagrams of bombs and Hallowe'en-type masks, one of which was the likeness of President Kennedy.

Despite these other Klans, Shelton's United Klans of America, the largest, is still considered the most violent. The evidence, if not admitted by Shelton and his followers, is still substantial. All those arrested in the Lemuel Penn, James Reeb and Viola Liuzzo murders, for instance, have been identified as United Klansmen. A number of dynamitings, assaults, shootings, beatings, kidnapings, floggings and threats have also been linked to them. Governor Paul Johnson of Mississippi, by no means a liberal (yet not the black reactionary he is often made out to be), claims that this Klan indulges in violence. So do many other Southerners of less than liberal stripe. The atmosphere of violence was so pervasive during the first Liuzzo trial (in which Wilkins was acquitted of murder), for instance, that Alabama's Attorney General, Richmond Flowers, deemed it prudent to have a man stand up and face the audience every time he, Flowers, rose to conduct the prosecution.

Shelton's Klan has also been accused of being more interested in the dues-paying capacities rather than in the quality of its members. This has undoubtedly brought into the organization a number of individuals who are not particularly concerned about the finer points of the law or the more subtle nuances of social behavior. It has also provided Klan leaders with a style of life to which they were never previously accustomed. Shelton, for instance, rides around in a large black Cadillac with a two-way radio. He has built himself a nice house in the suburbs of Tuscaloosa and wears expensive, well-tailored suits that make him look like a banker. He carries an expensive briefcase and wears a large diamond ring. This is a considerable step up in the world for an ex-rubber worker. James R. Jones, the dynamic Grand Dragon, also shows the fruits of affluence. A grammar-school dropout, an ex-lightning-rod salesman, sailor and bricklayer, he, too, rides around in a large Cadillac (known as "the Dragon Wagon") and wears expensive suits. Recently he has asked his faithful to turn over their green-stamp books so that he can buy an airplane for Klan business. Jones hopes he can learn to fly before the 2,000-book (representing $240,000 worth of groceries) goal is reached.

Many ex-Klansmen say that the profit from the sale of robes, for instance, is exorbitant, often running as high as 300 percent over investment. They also complain that considerable money is raised by the Klan going into an area (such as Dagsboro), elevating the political temperature with their rallies and cross-burnings, collecting money from the agitated spectators and then disappearing until the next year, when the same process is repeated.

Robert M. Shelton, Jr., as host to many of these rallies and as a leader of particular talent, is a man of considerable interest. He rose to power in 1960–1961 at a point where Klan fortunes were fragmented and disoriented. He was able to weld a number of groups together and since has left all competitors far behind.

Shelton was born in 1929, the son of a "retired merchant" who currently works for ex-Governor Wallace. After three years in the Army, Shelton worked for the Goodrich Tire Company in Tuscaloosa but was fired because of his Klan activities. From then on

"Ku Kluxing," as he called it, became a full-time job. He is a craggy-faced man, ascetically thin, with blue eyes, a soft voice and a sad countenance. In conversation he seldom smiles and seems to want to convince the listener that his Klan is nothing more than a Protestant counterpart to the Knights of Columbus and B'nai B'rith.

Although Shelton claims that his United Klans has nothing to hide from the government, he offers very little information. At the Klan hearings, for instance, Shelton took the Fifth Amendment 73 times in 100 minutes. In all, he took the Fifth 158 times. (In the fall of 1966, he was convicted of contempt of Congress and was sentenced to one year in prison and fined $1,000.) His personal views, however, are something else. Here he is quite voluble.

"Our research and studies have found," he said, "that there is more stirring and movement of the nigra when they have a full moon. They show a higher increase in the rate of crime and sex during the full moon."[5]

Desegregation, he said, "is disrupting and breaking down all connections and communications, so people who five years ago would think nothing of throwing fifty cents or a dollar into the hat of a nigra now won't do it."

One of Shelton's Kludds, Roy Woodle—now no longer a Klansman—perhaps best reflected Klan fears of integration. Said he to a crowd: ". . . You raise hawgs and you know when them hawgs have a gang o' little pigs, she'll tries to protect 'em; you know a dawg, when they have a gang o' pups, they'll tries to protect 'em; and you tell me you got a gang o' white chill'un runnin' 'round your yard and you're gonna stand by and see 'em sold out to a bunch of niggers God help you to wake up and gotta do what God'll have you do. . . ."

Shelton is also a believer in the international conspiracy theory, or "One Worldism" as he calls it. He is convinced, for instance, that the Wall Street investment bank of Kuhn, Loeb & Company actually controls the entire world, giving orders to Washington, London, Paris, Moscow and Peking alike. These people, he says, have been responsible for all America's troubles—the depression, all the wars, the fluoridation of the water, the civil rights strife and the assassination of President Kennedy.

James R. Jones, a near-handsome man with obsidian eyes and a scar on his cheek, is even more talkative than his boss, Shelton. "I don't hate niggers or Jews or Catholics," he said. "I just love white people. Our forefathers confiscated the land from the Indians and it looks like some of them are doing their best to give it back to the niggers. I'm against that."

Jones believes that the civil rights movement is financed "from the Communist Party, from the Zionist, Christ-killin' Jews. And I say Christ-killin' Jews 'cause they have not been absolved since they crucified Christ and their relatives can be traced back to the ones that run in the streets today."

Everyone in this country, continued Jones, is organized "with the exception of the white Protestant Gentile. Your niggers have your NAACP and CORE along with your sorry white trash. You've got B'nai B'rith for your Jewish people, your Knights of Columbus which is a secret fraternal order, as they say, and nobody has ever talked about investigating that which they should. But the white Protestant Gentile, the only hope, the only salvation they have left in this United States today is the United Klans of America, Incorporated which saved the South twice, or the Klan has, and it looks like we just have to do it again."

Grand Dragon Jones has the reputation of being a superb organizer and a rough customer. I caught some hint of this latter quality when I talked with him and three other Klansmen in the Klan suite in the capital's Congressional Hotel. On the off-chance that some Klansmen were in, I went to the hotel and called them on the house phone. Surprisingly, they invited me up. In the suite were Jones, Lester V. Chalmers, the Klan's lawyer, and two other Klansmen whose names I missed. For the first forty minutes I was grilled by all four of them—who was I, what did I want, what were my beliefs ("If you ain't for us, you're agin us," said Jones).

One of the Klansmen, a well-dressed middle-aged man with unusually long and wavy hair for a Southerner, semi-humorously backed me against a wall and mockingly began to search me, saying, "Okay, Mr. FBI, where's the tape recorder. . . ." He then put his face about two inches from mine, opened his mouth wide and burst into a forced staccato laugh, all the time poking me for the alleged tape recorder. Then he put his index finger on the center of my chest, put his whole weight on it and, with his face right back up to mine, asked "I'n' it fun-nee?" The other three seemed to think so because they all laughed. They no doubt enjoyed the idea of trying to shock people.

Eventually Chalmers called the fellow off, and a bourbon and water was thrust into my hand. Jones began to talk away. He needs very little prompting for he loves to ramble on about the Klan. But just as soon as he started, Chalmers got up, raised his hand and ordered Jones to stop. He said it might jeopardize the contempt of Congress hearings that they had to attend the following day. So just as quickly as my interview had begun, it ended. I sat there for another twenty minutes exchanging idle talk as Chalmers from time to time kept re-emphasizing the importance of not talking. "I never caught a fish that didn't have his mouth open," he said.

As I rose to leave, Jones too rose and, leaning over the table between us, said to me in a Southern drawl—his eyes by now cold and disdainful: "If'n you don't write somethin' nice about us, one of these dark nights you're gonna get a knock on your door and you'll know who it is."

The long-haired Klansman, in a last effort to horrify me, put his arm on my shoulder and led me to the door, saying, "I'm going downstairs too. I'll take the elevator, you can take the shaft." He broke out into laughter and all the others joined in.

The only other Klan leader of interest is Shelton's rival, James K. Venable, the Imperial Wizard of the National Knights of the Ku Klux Klan. Venable comes from an old Georgia family that first settled in America in 1608. He says he can trace his family's history back to A.D. 806. One ancestor sat in the Virginia House of Burgesses and a great-great-uncle, also named James Venable, was Dr. Crawford W. Long's "guinea pig" during the famous doctor's pioneer work in anesthesiology. Venable's family for many years owned Stone Mountain, a Georgia landmark, an old Klan shrine and now state property.

Imperial Wizard Venable is an elderly man with a red face and a friendly and warm manner. He speaks with a soft voice in private conversation (in public appearances he can harangue) that betrays

a certain inner hopelessness and cynicism. He has been a Klansman since 1924, and some who know him (most of whom are not
Klansmen, but lawyers, judges and politicians) say he is generous,
unstable and not personally violent.

He is an enigmatic type of Klansman, not the cool, public-
relations-conscious type like Shelton. For instance, he has a large
volume of law business in Atlanta that includes many poor Negro
clients. The day I visited him his anteroom was filled with Negroes
seeking legal help. On occasion he has defended Jews, Catholics
and even Black Muslims. Venable maintains a number of Negro
families on his property in Tucker, Georgia, near Stone Mountain.
"There's a nigger on my place belongs to the NAACP," he told
me. "Hell, I don't charge him any rent."

Venable best reflects W. J. Cash's contention, in his book, *The
Mind of the South* (Random House, 1941), that the more the
South is attacked by outsiders, the more Southerners love to shock
their critics for what seems to be a perverse pleasure in proving
that the criticism is true (much like my experience with Jones and
his friends in Washington). One anti-Klan friend of Venable's
claims, for instance, that the Imperial Wizard is not really anti-
Semitic even when he gets up and says: "What I don't like about
the Jews is that they took the pork out of pork and beans."
Venable is smart enough to know that critics in the North—Jews
and Gentiles alike—rage at such a remark. Venable, of course,
wants them to rage, and revels in the fact that they react on cue.

Venable sees life as inconsistent, hypocritical, unrealistic and
fragmented. He hates the junior executive type who lives in the
white suburbs and who withdraws from the realities of life.
Venable believes he knows what is going on and is angered that he
cannot do anything about it. He has come to the conclusion that
America is living on borrowed time, and his use of shocking
statements is his way of jolting people out of their stupor.

He looks at the Klan as a fraternal order of white males rather
than as an aggressive group of night riders. "Our attitude is
interpreted as hating niggers," he said. "Well, it's just not true. I
have no damned sympathy for any man who goes out and takes
the law into his own hands whether he's a member of the Klan or
any other group." The ballot box and boycott, he said, are the

Klan tools to victory, "and the sooner they [referring to Shelton's Klan] realize it the better off they'll be."

He went on: "If this country is ever saved from communism, it will be by the little man: the carpenter, the farmer, the filling station attendant. I'd like to see a [Klan] constitutional change to bring Catholics in. They're not in because their primary allegiance is to the Pope. But I know there are very many dedicated Catholics who would make good Klansmen.

"If we Americans don't make a radical change in the next three years," he continued, "we're going into a communist world. I am just as much to blame for it . . . because few take the proper interest in electing the right people to office." The Communists, he believes, will strike America through Mexico, Cuba and Alaska. "We don't have enough manpower," he complained, "to defeat our enemies with all the traitors we have within our country."

Venable opposes the exchange of foreign students, he has advocated an underground artesian well system to give water to the population in emergencies, he believes that the only limitation on owning firearms should be on high-caliber weapons, not "domestic" ones, and he wants to see a realignment of the two major parties.

"You shouldn't have one party having all the power," he said. "It shouldn't be allowed. It's like letting one hog have all the slop. The white Protestant Gentile sits back and says, 'Hell, what does my vote count?' Well the nigger, he's out there registerin' and votin' and that's why our government's gone to hell. If we'd adopt that attitude, we'd get somewhere."

Richmond Flowers, Alabama's maverick Attorney General, holds no brief for any Klansman, Shelton or Venable alike. He believes that they are one of the major stumbling blocks to progress in the South. Flowers has pointed out, for instance, that a number of Klansmen surround ex-Governor Wallace—a situation, says Flowers, that can pollute the state's politics. Whenever he has tried to move against the Klan he has been thwarted by the ex-Governor. In fact, Wallace demanded his impeachment on the grounds that he was "collaborating with the Federal Government." Having labeled the Klan "a hooded bunch of killers and night riders and floggers that this nation and this state [Alabama] have no use for whatsoever," Flowers is naturally enough not welcome down at the Klavern. As a matter of fact, the White Knights once asked Alabama Klansmen to kill him as a fraternal favor.

Flowers believes that strong state leadership and a few stiff sentences would destroy the Klan in no time at all. But the long-range answer, he believes, is education. Otherwise the Klan mind will never be able to pull itself out of the trough that encourages a Klansman to say, for instance, as one did recently: " 'We're on the move!' That's what the niggers are hollerin'! 'We're on the move; we're on the go; we're gonna run the white people down; we're gonna kick 'em in the teeth; we're gonna take our place in society!' Well, I got news for you, nigger, *you* nigger! [laughter from the crowd] We're on the move too! [cheers] . . . I don't believe in segregation, I believe in slavery [more cheers]!"[6]

5

The Citizens' Councils

Some people call the Citizens' Councils the *White* Citizens' Councils; others call them "the white power structure." Hodding Carter calls them "the uptown Klan." But by whatever name they are known, there is no doubt that the Citizens' Councils of America are blood kin to the Ku Klux Klan. To be sure, the Councils and the Klan are not on speaking terms, but the aims are the same: the maintenance of segregation and the preservation of "the Southern way of Life." The Councils appeal to the better educated, more sophisticated Southern segregationist because their tactics are more subtle, more clever than Klan activities. There are no cross-burnings, demonstrations, or cornfield harangues to interest the uneducated, "wool hat" or "redneck" racist. If the mark of a Klansman is cracking skulls, then the mark of a member of the Citizens' Councils is twisting arms.

The Councils, as did the Klan, blossomed into full flower as a direct result of the Supreme Court's 17 May 1954 ruling on *Brown vs. the Board of Education;* the Court held that "separate but equal" school systems were outside the pale of constitutionality.

Within two months of "The Decision," as it came to be known in the South, the first Council was organized in Indianola, Mississippi. It was the first of hundreds of Citizens' Councils to spring up throughout Dixie during the next twelve months.

In November 1954, the Citizens' Council published a pamphlet in which it described its own place in the political scheme of things. Part of the five-page document declared:

The Citizens' Council is the South's answer to the mongrel-
izers. We will not be integrated! We are proud of our white blood
and our white heritage of six centuries. . . . If we are bigoted,
prejudiced, un-American etc., so were George Washington,
Thomas Jefferson, Abraham Lincoln, and other illustrious fore-
bears who believed in segregation. We choose the old paths of our
founding fathers and refuse to appease anyone, even the internationalists.

Hard-core members in a local Council varied in number from
ten or so to two dozen; nearly all of them represented the more
prosperous segments of the community: businessmen, lawyers,
planters, political officials. The structure of each Council was
uncomplicated and flexible, free of Klan jargon and fancy titles.
Usually four committees were set up, each one a reflection of
major Council concerns: an information and education committee
to educate both whites and Negroes on the advantages of segregation and the dangers of integration; a membership and finance
committee to create a well-financed white bloc vote; a legal
committee to anticipate the moves of the opposition, to carry out
countermoves and to recommend the application of "economic
pressure to troublemakers" (this reference to economic pressure
was later dropped from official CC literature); and a political
committee to discourage, among other things, Negro voting.

Council strategy sessions, often held during lunchtime at a
downtown club, were brief affairs. The members would meet,
argue, plan, agree, then disperse to meet once again briefly at some
future specified time and place. In its early days the Councils were
most elusive: there were no central offices, no signs on doors, no
calling cards, no letterheads, no literature. It was a crusade at its
most efficient stage, with a maximum of zeal and a minimum of
overhead.

By 1956, the idea of Citizens' Councils as a buffer against
federal incursions into the South had become so accepted by Dixie
segregationists that a more formal organization was established to
coordinate the activities of the many independent groups. This new
organization was called the Citizens' Councils of America and
came into being at a spring convention in New Orleans at which

delegates representing Citizens' Councils from Alabama, Arkansas, Florida, Georgia, Louisiana, Mississippi, North Carolina, South Carolina, Tennessee, Texas and Virginia were present. (The Oklahoma Councils had been unable to send a delegation but gave its proxy to the Texas group.) *

Its headquarters were first located in Greenwood, Mississippi, but later moved to the state capital, Jackson. Robert B. Patterson, the founder of the Indianola Council, was appointed executive secretary.

The purposes of the new group remained essentially unaltered from those of the many independent Citizens' Councils: it sought "the preservation of the reserved natural rights of the people of the states, including primarily the separation of the races in our schools and all institutions involving personal and social relations; and . . . the maintenance of our States' Rights to regulate public health, morals, marriage, education, peace and good order in the States, under the Constitution of the United States."[1]

Tactically, the Citizens' Councils of America sought to have all its member organizations actively encourage the whites to organize and protest and to fight to preserve the separate schools; it encouraged the local groups to intervene forcefully where necessary to guard against federal incursions into the South; and it suggested that a concerted effort be made on a national level to promote "the cause of constitutional government and freedom of personal association." One of the primary objectives of the Councils was also to provide a sharp counterattack against the NAACP.[2]

From their inception the Councils have been led or inspired by some of the South's most prominent segregationists. Taking them in the order that they appeared on the scene, the ideologue and godfather of the whole movement is a man virtually unknown outside the South. His name is Tom P. Brady, a state supreme court justice of Mississippi who lives in Brookhaven, a small,

---

* Most of these statewide Councils were the descendants of smaller states' rights groups that had sprung up immediately after The Decision. The Caucasian League (Miami), Grass Roots League (Charleston, S.C.), Knights of the White Christians (New Orleans), National Association for the Advancement of White People (Washington), Pro-Southerners (Memphis), Southern Gentlemen's Organization (Baton Rouge), White Brotherhood (Atlanta) were but a few of them.

sleepy town of eight thousand located fifty-five miles south of Jackson, the capital. Judge Brady (pronounced Braddie, as it used to be spelled) is a trim, dapper man in his early sixties with a silvery mane, a gray mustache, and courtly manners. He is a native Mississippian, a graduate of Lawrenceville School in New Jersey, Yale, and the University of Mississippi Law School.

Brady published a book a few weeks after The Decision called *Black Monday,** a hastily produced little paperback full of typographical errors. It has become the bible of the Citizens' Councils. In his book, the author claims that the Supreme Court's action was a Communist plot and that it had "arrested and retarded the economic and political, yes, the social, status of the Negro in the South for at least one hundred years." That Monday in May, he went on, "ranks in importance with July 4, 1776, the date upon which our Declaration of Independence was signed. May 17, 1954, is the date upon which the declaration of socialist doctrine was proclaimed throughout this nation. . . ."

The judge called for an all-out war against The Decision. He suggested that all nine Supreme Court Justices plus the Attorney General be elected to office instead of nominated by the President; he called for the formation of a grass-roots organization to fight the verdict; he proposed a number of legal maneuvers to circumvent desegregation; he toyed with the idea of a "third political force" in the South to do battle with the liberals in both major parties; he felt that economic pressure should be applied against those favoring integration; and he proposed that Negroes be transshipped to some distant place.

Brady rekindles all the Southern fears of Negro sexuality. "Whenever and wherever the white man has drunk the cup of black hemlock, whenever and wherever his blood has been infused with the blood of the negro, the white man, his intellect and his culture have died." Intermarriage, he believes, will create a "hybrid yellow mulatto man," an outcast and a potential Communist. Negroes, writes the judge, are little better (or little worse, it is not clear) than the chimpanzee:

* A term attributed to Mississippi Congressman John Bell Williams. Brady claims that all income he has received from the book has been turned over to the Citizens' Councils.

You can dress a chimpanzee, housebreak him, and teach him to use a knife and fork, but it will take countless generations of evolutionary development, if ever, before you can convince him that a caterpillar or a cockroach is not a delicacy. Likewise the social, political, economical, and religious preferences of the negro remain close to the caterpillar and the cockroach. This is not stated to ridicule or abuse the negro. There is nothing fundamentally wrong with the caterpillar or the cockroach. It is merely a matter of taste. A cockroach or caterpillar remains proper food for a chimpanzee.

Brady produced some startling prophecies in *Black Monday*. His most famous one, and perhaps a reason why the book has become the Councils' bible, was fulfilled barely a year after publication date. In his book, Judge Brady wrote:

The fulminate which will discharge the blast will be the young negro schoolboy, or veteran who has no conception of the difference between a mark and a fathom. The supercilious, glib young negro, who has sojourned in Chicago or New York, and who considers the councils of his elders archaic, will perform an obscene act, or make an obscene remark, or a vile overture or assault upon some white girl.

In the first week of August 1955, the battered body of Emmett Till, a Negro teen-age schoolboy from Chicago, was fished out of the Mississippi River. Till died because he allegedly "wolf whistled" or leered at a young, attractive white girl in a little town called Money (population 100), just a few miles north of Greenwood, the home of the Citizens' Councils at the time. Two defendants, one the husband of the girl, were acquitted of any complicity in the crime. The Councils denied any involvement. To this day the killing has gone unpunished.

One person who was deeply moved and inspired by Brady's book was Robert Patterson—"Tut" to his friends—a farmer from the Delta town of Itta Bena. Red-haired, blue-eyed, hard-working, in his mid-forties, Patterson was a star end and captain of the 1942 Mississippi State football team; after graduation he served as a paratroop officer, fighting with distinction in the Battle of the Bulge. Several years after the war he returned to Sunflower County

in the Delta—also the home county of Senator James Eastland—
to run a plantation.

Three years later The Decision was handed down and Patterson's life changed considerably. He and some friends had set up
the first Citizens' Councils in Indianola by the middle of July
1954. For the rest of the year Patterson stumped the state, quietly
pushing his and Brady's message, organizing branches and seeking
new members at five dollars per person. Since then his evangelistic
endeavors have expanded to encompass the entire South. Today he
is secretary of the Citizens' Councils of America, based in Jackson, and executive secretary of the Association of Citizens' Councils of Mississippi, located in Greenwood just a few miles from Itta
Bena.

One of the first things Patterson did after the May 17 decision
was to mail out a form letter to CC members enclosing a suggested
reading list. Most of the publications were anti-Negro in content,
although a few were anti-Semitic. Frank Britton's *The American
Nationalist,* Gerald L. K. Smith's *Cross and the Flag,* Conde
McGinley's *Common Sense,* and John Hamilton's *The White
Sentinel* were a few of the suggested titles.

The ADL noted in 1956 that Patterson had previously written
for a number of anti-Semitic publications, including James
Madole's *National Renaissance Bulletin.* Patterson, however, denies that he is anti-Semitic; he once told representatives of B'nai
B'rith that if their ADL branded him an anti-Semite, he would *not*
deny it. Obviously pleased at outbluffing them, he said, "That was
the last I heard from 'em."[3]

Although anti-Semitic viewpoints can be detected on the fringes
of the movement, the body of the Citizens' Councils seems free of
any distinct Jewish bias. Members are content to train their fire at
Negroes, integrationists, liberals and Communists, all of whom are
considered by Southern segregationists to be one and the same
thing.

Patterson's views vary only marginally from Brady's. He believes without question in the inherent inferiority of the Negroes;
he does not envision the day when Mississippi will be desegre-
gated; he half-jokingly accepts the Black Muslim idea that a few
states should be set aside for Negroes, suggesting with obvious

relish New York, Michigan, Illinois and California; he sees integration as Communist-inspired; the white South must unite against outside interference; whites, he adds, must vote as a bloc; and intermarriage, he avers, will destroy Western civilization.

One of the best known Southern segregationists is Roy V. Harris, the chairman of the Citizens' Councils of America. Harris is a graduate of the University of Georgia, Class of 1917, and currently is a member of the Georgia Board of Regents, the body that governs school policy in the state. For twenty-two years he was a representative in the Georgia Legislature, eight of which were served as speaker. For two years he was a state senator. Today he lives in Augusta, a senior partner in the law firm of Harris, Chance, McCracken & Harrison.

He is a short man, in his early seventies, on the rotund side, with thinning hair, rimless glasses and a cigar that seems permanently welded to the corner of his mouth. He is gregarious, confidence-inspiring and has a short, staccato laugh that is almost a giggle. Like many heavy men he is exceedingly nimble and quick on his feet; this applies to his political activities and viewpoints as well.

He said that back in 1954 he realized the South would have a year of grace before the federal government began enforcing the law. He took the opportunity to brush up on the history of Reconstruction. "It dawned on me," he said, "that it took twelve years to get the bayonets out of our backs and fifteen to twenty years to bring about harmony. I started to preach that we couldn't win this fight in under twenty years. We had to overcome this brainwashing that segregation is un-Christian.

"So we advocated resisting in every way we could, to keep it off as long as possible; and when it came to going to jail we'd do"—here he drew the words out—"just enough to keep out of jail."

He said he did not think that the South would ever convince the North on the value of segregation, but, he said, "we had to hold the line until they came around to our way of thinking. We had to wait until they got enough nigras up there—until they got a bellyful of the proposition."

Part of the problem, says Harris, is that the North thinks they are integrated when in fact they have de facto segregation. As long as they think that, said the peppery lawyer, the courts concentrate their attacks on the South.

"If the Supreme Court had held that *every* school had to mix 'em all over the country," he said, "hell, there would have been a revolution throughout the entire country and our fight would have been won."

He added with a mischievous smile, "We aren't mean enough to force it on anyone, but we thought it would help our case."

Most people, he said with an exaggerated cadence to his Southern drawl, "don't *know* the nigras; they don't *deal* with 'em. Now you get some of these lawyers who deal with 'em, *they'll* tell you about 'em."

Harris takes the common Southern stance that civil rights legislation is unconstitutional, that it is contrary to the spirit of states' rights, and that it is one more instance of fuzzy liberal thinking in Washington. "Boys . . .," he said, obviously orating to an imaginary white audience, "if you're going to be raped, make damn sure it's rape; you don't have to cooperate!"

He feels that over the years the Citizens' Councils have been a lot luckier than they originally thought they would be. "We have not been responsible for any violence," he stated, noting as well that every Citizens' Council conference charges twenty-five dollars as a registration fee to keep the "crackpots" out. "The Klan, antifluorides and anti-Jews would ruin the meeting," he said.

The size of the Citizens' Councils has always been a subject of speculation. Current estimates put the membership near the 300,000 mark, with 80,000 in Mississippi alone. Many observers dispute these figures. Harris, for one, says that Councils grow and die over a short span of time. "When Martin Luther King comes to Georgia," he said, "there are Citizens' Councils all over the place; when he's not around you can't even get a meeting." Yet, he added quickly, "there are some very small, dedicated groups such as here in Augusta." Transplanted Yankees, Harris claims, form the backbone of many a Council. "Damn," he said, "after they've been down here awhile they becomes worse'n we are."

Politicians, he continued, "are scared to hell of the nigger bloc vote; we've got to take a page from the nigger book and vote together."

Harris spearheaded the Goldwater campaign in Georgia, feeling that the ex-Senator was the first person for whom a Southerner could cast a protest vote. But, he said, "it's difficult for any hard-boiled Southerner to vote the Republican ticket; to get the movement going we had to organize 'Democrats for Goldwater.'" Harris claims credit for Mississippi going for the Republican nominee.

Harris publishes one of the more flamboyant newspapers in America, called *The Augusta Courier*. He started it in 1946 and claims a current national weekly readership of 10,000. It is delivered to his readers in an ordinary brown, grease-resistant paper bag. The headlines of the four-page paper are usually printed in flaming red and predict one catastrophe after another. "DEFEAT BY INTERNATIONAL COMMUNISM IS PREDICTED FOR THE UNITED STATES," reads one. At the bottom of the front page he asks, again in red type: "ARE YOU GOING TO SURRENDER TO THE LEFT-WINGERS?" Most of the articles are concerned with Negro "inferiority," the "impossibility" of integration and the "benefits" of segregation. Under his own byline in a column called "Strictly Personal," Harris dwells virtually on no other themes.

Occasionally he attacks his enemies, one of his favorites being Ralph McGill, the publisher of the Atlanta *Constitution*. "McGILL'S RACE MIXING PHILOSOPHY WON SWEEPING VICTORY SEPTEMBER 12," reads one red headline. McGill thought this so amusing that he had a copy of the edition framed and hung on his office wall, along with his many awards, trophies and mementos.

Harris is most anxious to spread the news of his *Courier* as widely as possible. "You have the authority," he told me, "to reproduce any part or all of them at any time you want."

With a vigorous handshake, a short cackle of a laugh, a pat on the back, and a few jocular references about how much fun it is outwitting the North, he eventually ushered me out of his office, wishing me well. Before I had left the anteroom he already had a client firmly gripped by the hand and, with his ubiquitous cigar still welded in place, was assuaging the man's legal fears.

Another cog in the Citizens' Councils wheel is William J.

Simmons, the editor of *The Citizen,* the Council's official publication.* Tall, well over six feet, he is distinguished by a Kitchener
mustache and a rather soft appearance. He is the son of a fairly
wealthy retired Jackson banker and a graduate of Mississippi
College in Clinton. During World War II he served as a civilian
with the Royal Engineers of the British Army and later briefly in
the U.S. Navy. He says that his views on race hardened while he
was in Jamaica, claiming that a caste system had sprung up there
among Negroes of various shades creating, he says, endless
problems.

The Citizen claims a circulation of 34,000, perhaps a realistic
indication of hard-core Council strength throughout the nation.
Articles in it are by a wide variety of people, such as ex-Governor
George Wallace of Alabama, General Edwin A. Walker, ex-
Governor Ross R. Barnett of Mississippi, Robert C. Ruark, James
J. Kilpatrick, editor of the *Richmond* (Virginia) *News-Leader* and
author of *The Southern Case for School Segregation,* and Medford
Evans, a contributing editor of the Birch Society's *American
Opinion.*

Simmons himself writes a number of articles and most of the
editorials. One recent issue was devoted entirely to "How to Start
a Private School," reflecting one of the Citizens' Councils' major
objectives at the moment. Virtually all the articles in *The Citizen*
are devoted to the segregation-integration controversy. The 114
pieces of Citizens' Council literature listed in the back of nearly
every issue of *The Citizen* range in outlook from a pamphlet called
"Why Segregation Is Right," by Simmons, to "Zoological Sub-

---

* *The Citizen* should not be confused with *The Councilor,* a publication
put out in Shreveport, Louisiana, by Ned Touchstone. It claims a paid
national readership of 191,000, which is optimistic. Articles in Touchstone's
paper are anti-Semitic and far more crude in their treatment of Negroes
than those in *The Citizen.* "Westbrook Pegler Will Write for *The Councilor,*" says one; "Rothschilds Fail in Court Effort to Suppress French Book,"
states another headline, referring to Roger Peyrefitte's book, *Les Juifs.* One
article, entitled "Witch-doctor Nation Seeks the Moon as Its Very Own,"
shows a Zambian "astronaut" climbing a pole. Yet another article attacks
the "new set of 'Minority' Heroes and Cowboys." Crispus Attucks, says the
article, is not a bona fide American hero; Wyatt Earp is of "Khazar
ancestry"; and Deadwood Dick, so the article concludes, was "a paleface
who didn't have a paleface."

species of Man," by Dr. E. Raymond Hall. If one were to buy one piece of all the literature listed in the back (this would include such items as a "NEVER" button and a miniature Confederate battle flag), it would cost the zealot $186.20, giving some idea of the volume of propaganda that must flow out of the Jackson headquarters.[4]

Simmons is perhaps the Councils' most indefatigable speaker and as such reflects much of the members' attitudes. He believes, for instance, that a three-pronged attack is being mounted by American "egalitarian socialists" against constitutional freedoms. It began, he said, with our attempt to reach an agreement with Soviet Russia, giving our recognition of the country and the Test Ban Treaty as two examples. He said that there is also under way an attack on business, in which a double standard is created— "one set of rules restricting and hamstringing business while another set bestowed power and unlimited monopoly upon socialist labor leaders like Walter Reuther, who is a Vice President of the NAACP." The third attack has been an attack on the white race: "Under the idealistically glowing phrases of 'brotherhood' and 'tolerance' all races were to be submerged in a sea of egalitarianism through integration. And all were to be ruled by a liberal 'Elite' in a planned society."

He claims that two slogans have been used—or, rather, "misused"—to further this three-way attack. One is *peace,* "that is, peace on terms satisfactory to the Kremlin." It has led, he said, "to such outlandish situations as the military invasion of my own home state by 30,000 troops to put one negro in Ole Miss solely because of the color of his skin while Russia built its strength in Cuba with absolute impunity, under an umbrella held by the Kennedy-Johnson Administration." The other slogan is *civil rights.* "Most people think only of race when they hear the term 'civil rights,' " he said. "Many are persuaded through some kind of blind emotional, collective guilt, which the liberals have worked very hard to establish, that whatever the negro complains he lacks is what he should have, regardless of the consequences."

This attack on segregation, he continued, stems from the current situation in which "the white liberals hold the balance of power through the leverage of the negro bloc vote." To hold this vote, says Simmons, "the liberals promise more and more special privileges for the negro in the form of 'civil rights' bills, which not only would give them social and political preference, but economic as well."

Simmons derides the Northerner as a hypocrite, pointing out that Harlem is the "largest *segregated* Negro community in the world." Despite years of "integration," propaganda, brotherhood and tolerance, "the result . . . is that a white man or woman will not—I repeat—will not live in Harlem." The composition of an average American city, Simmons stated, finds a white business core in the middle, surrounded by a ring of Negro slums, which in turn is surrounded by white suburbs. "Liberals," he said, "may invariably be found inhabiting these suburbs."[5]

There are a number of other luminaries who are associated with the Citizens' Councils of America. One is Leander Perez, Sr., the political boss of Plaquemine (pronounced Plackman) and St. Bernard parishes in Louisiana. He was one of the founders of the CC of A. Perez, known by everyone as "Judge," is a man of intimidating mien. In his seventies, with wavy gray hair offset by bushy black eyebrows, with hooded eyes that miss nothing, and rimless glasses, he is capable of volcanic wrath, scorn and anger. He is a rich and powerful man not only in his two swampy parishes south of New Orleans but in the city itself and throughout the state. He has a prosperous law practice, he is a cattleman, a leader in the establishment of private schools, an assistant district attorney (for thirty-six years he was district attorney for his two parishes but in 1960 turned the job over to a son, Leander, Jr., who promptly appointed his father his assistant), a statewide political string-puller, a wealthy oilman, a favorite hero of the NSRP, and a tireless speaker in the cause of segregation. In 1962, he was excommunicated from the Catholic Church because of his persistent attacks on Archbishop Joseph Rummel's decision to desegregate the New Orleans parochial schools.

Perez is a hard-line anti-Negro segregationist. He expresses a minimum of Southern paternalistic feelings. When he gets worked up he is likely to call Negroes "Congolese" or "burr heads." He explained to a Senate hearing in 1965 that few Negroes registered in his parishes because they were "a low type of citizen" with little interest in politics. He admitted that he did not "go out and beat the bushes for Negroes" adding that a Negro registration of 3.3 percent (96 out of 2,897 eligibles) in Plaquemine Parish was all that reasonably could be expected. He considers all civil rights activities as part of a "Black Belt Communist conspiracy" which will bring the Negro to power in the South; once in power, he said, they will declare their independence of the Union and set up their own all-black nation.[6]

Richard Morphew runs the Citizens' Councils forum, the major propaganda effort of the organization. It produces and distributes radio and TV programs to approximately 450 stations per week, which means that over 23,000 CC programs go out over the air each year.

Morphew, whose office is down the hall from Simmons', his boss, is one who would like to see the Negro returned to Africa. He objects to being labeled a racist because he thinks it is a scare word. "If you realize there are differences between the sexes," he told me, "then you are a sexist." He believes that the Mississippi Freedom Democratic Party, started by SNCC workers, "exists solely to fulfill a need of the New York papers." It operates, he concluded, "out of someone's hat."

He has a number of complaints that stem from his background and experience as a radio and TV newscaster. "Police dogs," he said, "never snarl north of the Mason-Dixon Line; and white segregationists always seem to have bad grammar but integrationists never have." He also objects to the term "White Citizens' Councils" so often used by the press. "Why not Black NAACP?" he asks.

Perhaps the one point that distinguishes the Citizens' Councils from the Klan is tactics. While the Klan depends on physical violence, the Councils call on their powers of economic, political and social pressure to keep the white community in line and the black one "where it belongs." The Councils today reject the notion that they use any pressure whatsoever in the furtherance of their aims, even though in their earliest brochures they were calling for the "application of economic pressure to troublemakers." Councilmen will argue that they seek to achieve their aims only through the written and spoken word. However, there is considerable evidence to the contrary, indicating that a formidable amount of economic pressure of a most basic sort has been applied by Councils to those individuals and groups who have strayed from the path of segregation.

There are literally hundreds of examples of coercion by the Councils. A few examples of the variety of tactics they use will suffice.

In 1955, the Councils were responsible for the closing down of twenty-year-old Providence Farm near Tchula, Mississippi. This 2,600-acre farm was a cooperative venture started by a group of idealists in the 1930s to help relocate uprooted sharecroppers. Most of the labor on the farm was performed by Negroes, who also were the primary recipients of the produce.

To the white hierarchy in the area, such activities in the land of free enterprise and white supremacy had long been suspect. After an extensive and involved campaign, the Citizens' Council succeeded in having the farm branded as a center of social integration, basing the contention on the most misleading evidence. The verdict was the kiss of death to the farm and it was eventually closed down, not so much because it lost the faith of the town fathers, but because of the boycotts, anonymous telephone threats, the cutting of telephone and electricity wires, the fear that the place would be burned down, and the lack of cooperation from the local police.

One person who had the temerity to defend the operators of the farm was the Reverend Marsh Calloway, a Presbyterian minister from nearby Durant. He was forced to resign from his pulpit only eight days after having spoken up in defense of them.

Another person who has spoken out against the Councils' activities has been Mrs. Hazel Brannon Smith, perhaps the best known of all Council targets. She owns the Durant *News,* the Lexington *Advertiser* and the *Northside* (Jackson) *Reporter,* all small but once healthy newspapers covering the local scene. Her success in the past had been due to her outspokenness on subjects other editors feared to touch. With the advent of The Decision, however, total conformity against it was demanded, a condition Mrs. Smith would not accept.

She is an admitted segregationist but she has refused to condone the activities or even the existence of the Citizens' Councils and the Mississippi State Sovereignty Commission;* she would not overlook white weaknesses, nor play up Negro ones, a favorite pastime of most segregationists; she has demanded that the law be blind to both white and black skins; and she has suggested on occasion that various sheriffs, deputies, political bosses and the like were incompetent to hold office. Such a stance led to Hazel Brannon Smith being branded a "moderate," a "liberal"—in other words someone who cannot be trusted. (A moderate, in Judge Brady's words, is someone "who is going to let a little sewage under the door.")

Shortly after the Providence Farm closure, economic presure was applied to Mrs. Smith's papers to bring them into line with Council dogma. Before long advertising dropped off to nothing, her papers shrank to four pages each, and she went considerably into debt. Her husband lost his job at the hospital because he was "too controversial"; a rival newspaper was started, edited by a man Mrs. Smith had trained. An article in *Ebony* magazine at that time did not help matters much. It pictured Hazel Smith as a lone white warrior in the cause of integration. This article was widely circulated by the Councils.

To look at her newspapers today, one wonders how she survives at all. All have virtually no advertising and a shrunken circulation. She is, in fact, supported in large measure by silent Southern moderates who sympathize with her stand but who, for various reasons, will not support her publicly.

Another target of Citizens' Council ire was and continues to be P. D. East, the young publisher of the *Petal Paper* at Petal Mississippi. East has been a persistent critic of the Councils and many of their attitudes. When economic pressure was brought to

* The State Sovereignty Commission was a creation of the Citizens' Councils and was Mississippi's official apartheid agency. Its functions were similar to the Councils' but on occasion could become more totalitarian. It had its agents tape sermons and lectures of ministers and professors who were suspected of being soft on segregation; it had a pack of informers to weed out the unfaithful in colleges and schools; it took polls on "racial attitudes" to find out who was wavering; and it has forced over thirty ministers and a number of prominent professors to leave the state since its founding.

bear upon his enterprise, he ran a large headline in his column taunting his adversaries. "GO TO HELL IN A BUCKET!" it read. His local circulation and advertising have dried up, but he has survived and fared better than Hazel Brannon Smith because he maintains a fairly sizable national circulation.

East's most famous work was a full-page ad in a 1958 edition of the *Petal Paper* in which he mockingly described the advantages of joining the Citizens' Councils. The ad pictured a braying jackass in one corner and began: "Yes, YOU too, can be *SUPERIOR*. Join The Glorious Citizens Clans . . .!" The ad went on to list various "freedoms" that would accrue to members: ". . . Freedom to yell 'Nigger' as much as you please without your conscience bothering you! Freedom to wonder who is pocketing the five dollars you pay to join! Freedom to take a profitable part in the South's fastest growing business: Bigotry! FREEDOM TO BE SUPERIOR WITHOUT BRAIN, CHARACTER, OR PRINCIPLE!" It ended with: "This Wonderful Offer Open to White Folk Only. . . . Remember: not to join means you're a nigger lover! . . ."[7]

"It appears," he wrote elsewhere, "to be something of a rat race in the South today to see which state can first attain complete and total assdom."[8] Councilmen positively *hate* P. D. East, which is the way he prefers it.

Other examples of intimidation come to mind. Citizens' Councils were responsible in large measure for the defeat of moderate Representative Brooks Hays of Arkansas in 1958, a year after the Little Rock difficulties; they were responsible for the campaign to elect independent electors in the 1960 and 1964 elections; they have been responsible for most of the obstructionist legislation passing through Southern state legislatures; they had a hand in the WBOX radio boycott in Bogalusa which eventually destroyed that enterprise; and they attempted a character assassination of a Billy Barton, once managing editor of the Ole Miss student newspaper, apparently because he had attended a sit-in demonstration in Atlanta. (The Councils were subsequently subjected to a certain amount of ridicule when it was learned that Barton *had* attended the sit-in, but as a reporter, not as a demonstrator.)

Councils have led the fight against integrationist Negroes. Threatening a man with the loss of his job, foreclosing the mortgage, demanding the withdrawal of his money from the bank, taking his name off the voters list and annoying him by acts of petty vandalism are some of the more common tactics employed. In Yazoo City a school desegregation petition was signed a year or so after The Decision by fifty-three residents of the town. The Yazoo Council ran an ad in the local paper listing the names of the petitioners and asking the readers to "look them over carefully." Within a short period of time all but a handful had publicly asked that their names be withdrawn from the petition.

The Councils' power was such that it was able to bring the Falstaff Brewing Company to its knees. A story, published in John Hamilton's *White Sentinel* in the fall of 1955, stated that the brewing company had bought a life membership in the NAACP for one of its salesmen. The article went on to suggest that those who disagreed with such activities should refrain from drinking that brand of beer. Sales must have slipped considerably in the South, for in no time at all a Falstaff vice-president was on his way to talk things over with the Council. To the immense satisfaction of Council officials, the Falstaff Brewing Company released a statement disavowing any support for the NAACP; thus the boycott, if there ever was one, was called off.

Although the Citizens' Councils of America have not been directly involved in any violence, there is no doubt that such activities as these have added measurably to the climate of bitterness and hatred in the South.

There is considerable agreement among impartial observers that the Citizens' Councils are in decline. They will be around perhaps for a generation or so, but their passing is assured. They are faced, first, with a rising Negro registration to which Southern politicians will have to cater. Second, the once solid South is fragmenting into many autonomous groups, not all of which have turned their eyes from the future. But it will be violence that will destroy the Councils. Eventually they will have to choose between respectability and violence. This is not a problem so long as the Councils are a force; but once the members feel that the reins of power are slipping from their grasp, the "uptown Klan" will be forced by temperament and circumstance to relocate itself in a less savory section of town.

PART TWO

THE
FAR
RIGHT

6

The Armed Right

1

The Minutemen organizations that dot the landscape fall into no easy classification of radical activist political groups. Essentially they are not racists, yet there are some groups that show a pronounced antipathy toward minorities; nor can they be called "respectable" conservatives, since their viewpoints are more pessimistic than those of, say, the John Birch Society, often considered to be on the very edge of acceptability; yet at times they can articulate a few reasoned thoughts. What makes Minutemen unique is the way they go about "saving" America from the clutches of her enemies.

Robert Bolivar DePugh, a forty-four-year-old businessman from Norborne, Missouri, is the leader of the most publicized and perhaps the largest Minuteman group in the country. The impetus for such an organization grew out of a duck-hunting trip in 1960 when one member of the party said jokingly, referring to the international political scene, that if worse came to worst and the Russians invaded, they—the duck hunters—could at least take to the hills and fight as a guerrilla band. DePugh and his friends took the remark seriously. In the belief that the world situation was fast disintegrating in favor of the Communists, they thought it might be a good idea if more Americans knew how to defend themselves and their communities.

The sportsmen decided to study the problem more closely. DePugh records that "it came as a shock to suddenly realize that in the seventeen previous years the Communists had succeeded in taking over seventeen sovereign nations. We were surprised also to learn that only one had been taken over by military conquest. The other sixteen were lost to communism by internal subversion or negotiations."

Eventually DePugh and the others came to the following conclusions:

1. Our diplomatic war against communism has already been lost by bunglers or traitors within our own government. . . .
2. This diplomatic war has been and continues to be lost by appointed government officials beyond the reach of public opinion.
3. We cannot win a diplomatic war against communism abroad until we first establish a genuinely pro-American government here at home.
4. A pro-American government could no longer be established by normal political means. . . .
5. The minority vote blocs, controlled labor unions and corrupt political machines so completely monopolize the American political scene that there is no chance for the average American citizen to regain control of his own destiny at the ballot box. . . .
6. . . . any further effort, time or money spent in trying to save our country by political means would be wasted. . . .
7. . . . the leaders of most other conservative organizations privately agree that it is politically impossible to elect a conservative government. . . .
8. . . . We concluded that the American people are moving inexorably toward a time of total control and frustration such as must have been felt by the people of Budapest and East Germany when they finally staged their suicidal revolts.

   Therefore, the objectives of the Minutemen are to abandon wasteful, useless efforts and begin immediately to prepare for the day when Americans will once again fight in the streets for their lives and their liberty. We feel there is overwhelming evidence to prove that this day must come.

DePugh heightens this starkly pessimistic view of the political situation by larding his rhetoric and prose with a deep strain of potential violence. The most celebrated example, and the one that brought DePugh's Minutemen to national attention, appeared in the 15 March 1963 issue of *On Target,* the group's newssheet. The story was directed to twenty U.S. congressmen who had voted against an appropriation for the House Committee on Un-American activities, and read, in part:

> . . . See the old man at the corner where you buy your papers? He may have a silencer-equipped pistol under his coat. That extra fountain pen in the pocket of the insurance salesman that calls on you might be a cyanide gas gun. What about your milkman? Arsenic works slow but sure. Your automobile mechanic may stay up nights studying booby traps.
>
> These [Minutemen] patriots are not going to let you take their freedom away from them. They have learned the silent knife, the strangler's cord, the target rifle that hits sparrows at 200 yards. Only their leaders restrain them.
>
> Traitors beware! Even now the cross-hairs are on the back of your necks.

DePugh believes that counterinsurgency troops—the Green Berets—are being trained in Vietnam to be used against Americans at some future time to protect the power of "self-seeking bureaucrats." He has speculated in the pages of *On Target* on the possibility of Russia having smuggled A-bombs into the United States (through our embassy in Mexico City) to be set off at some future date. Two of DePugh's West Coast cohorts caused a stir in 1962 by claiming that Red Chinese troops were massed on the Mexican border ready to invade the country. Said one Minuteman: "There are several hundred thousand of these crack shock troops. Of course, if they invaded they wouldn't get very far, maybe only up to Long Beach. One American is worth ten chinks."[1]

DePugh was also one of the few who had no words of sorrow for the assassination of President Kennedy. "Now that John F. Kennedy is dead," he wrote within a month after the event, "we can expect to hear millions of words about his greatness. . . . We will not be hypocrites—we will not soon forget that he ignored the best interests of his country from the day he took the oath of office to the day he died."

The Minutemen leader believes that the day has come where bacteriological warfare can be administered by an amateur. "Do you realize," DePugh said, "that I could kill everyone in the United States except myself, if I wanted to." To do this, he said, it would be merely a matter of assembling certain viruses from his own Biolab Corporation laboratories and spreading them throughout the country simply by coughing on enough outbound passengers at a large municipal airport. Of course, he added, he would have to immunize himself, but within two weeks he would be the only person alive in the nation.[2]

DePugh believes that within five years or so America will be under Communist control. "I don't think there's one chance in a thousand of us having a thermonuclear war," he said. "But all this propaganda against it and for peace is designed to do just one thing: it is designed to make the American people feel that the difference between communism and Americanism is not worth fighting a war over—that it's not worth defending.

"If the Communists can convince us of that, then they are going to win. They don't have to have a war. All they have to do is convince us that it is not worth it. We'll sit on our cans and let them take over piece by piece by piece by internal subversion, negotiation and sell-out and they won't have any need for war."

Once the Communists have taken over, he sees a long internal struggle between the left and the right. "In other words, this may be a long period of assassination and counterassassination, of terror and counterterror. In this I feel we have one big edge because we feel that our knowledge of the left wing is far greater than their knowledge of the right wing, so far as identities are concerned.

"And the thing that is really a little terrifying about it is that we could very easily be sitting on the edge of a bloodbath in this country."[3]

Perhaps what terrifies DePugh the most is the possibility that the constitutional right to bear arms might be abridged in some manner. In *On Target*, he has warned that "ALL PATRIOTIC AMERICANS WHO HAVE BEEN ACTIVE IN THE ANTI-COMMUNIST MOVEMENT ARE NOW FACING A PERIOD OF EXTREME DANGER," basing his fear on impending gun legislation. He goes on to advise his readers: "If you are EVER going to buy a gun BUY IT NOW!" Recommended selections for adult males are, .30-06 Garands, 7.62mm NATO FN's, .30-06 bolt action Springfields or .303 Lee-Enfields, and a variety of sporting rifles and shotguns; for the adult female, the Winchester model 100 in .308 caliber or .30 caliber military carbines; for older children, sporting rifles in 6mm, .243, .270, or .222 calibers; and for the young tots, semiautomatic .22 rifles. DePugh recommends also that each gun be stockpiled with three hundred or more rounds of ammunition.[4]

DePugh is a soft-spoken, neatly dressed man, beginning to suffer from middle-age spread. He was born in Independence, Missouri, the son of a local deputy sheriff. He went to the University of Missouri for a few semesters then joined the Army in early 1942 and served throughout the war as a radar technician. He sympathized with McCarthy during the Army hearings, recalling that some of the scientists he had known in the service "seemed not to hold allegiance to the same flag I did."

He went back to college, to Kansas State, to the University of Colorado and to Washburn University in Topeka but received degrees from none. While at Kansas State he formed a national organization called "The Society for the Advancement of Canine Genetics," which was affiliated with the International Genetics Society. DePugh claims that his society had a membership of two thousand, mostly dog breeders.

In 1954, he organized the Biolab Corporation in Independence. Its major product was dog food supplements. The business collapsed the following year due to "differences of opinion" among the owners. For the next four years he worked for a dog food firm. By 1959 he had reorganized Biolab, moved the company seventy miles east to Norborne, and with his brother Bill built the company into a sizable business with a wide range of veterinarian products and a net worth of approximately $350,000.

"One reason for starting the Minutemen," DePugh said, "was due to my experience in business. I was filling out so many forms I got to the point where I was saying 'When are they going to give me a few hours to run my business?'" He claims that the volume of business was reduced intentionally and did not come about as the result of his political activities. "Four years ago we had three factories and were in debt. We cut back and now we have no debt. By keeping the business small and compact we don't have to worry about persecution. They can't starve us out."

Norborne, to the irritation of the townspeople, is often described as "a dusty little farm town of 950." The citizens there are dour, hard-working and suspicious of outsiders. Very few had any comments to make on DePugh, although it was clear that they did not like the publicity he had brought them. When I asked one person where DePugh lived, she answered, "That's easy, it's the house with the lights on all night."

Biolab Corporation is located on Norborne's main street and serves, presumably, as Minutemen headquarters. The day I was there business was fairly slow. DePugh's wife was acting as secretary, and his daughter-in-law was sticking labels on jars in the back room. A farmer came in asking if Biolab sold any medicine to cure arthritis in pigs. He was turned away by Bill DePugh, the active manager, who explained that Biolab products were available only to veterinarians in wholesale lots. The entire building smells of vitamin A.

The outer office was drably furnished but had a bookshelf in one corner that held Minutemen reference books. There was *Realistic Combat Training,* by Lieutenant Colonel Robert B. Rigg; *Assault Battle Drill,* by Major General J. C. Fry; *Combat Intelligence in Modern Warfare,* by Irving Heymont; a three-volume edition of *On War* by Von Clausewitz; a handbook on the Thompson submachine gun; field manuals on pistols and revolvers; another three-volume work called *Materials Toward a History of Witchcraft,* by H. C. Lea; and a book called *The American Fluoridation Experiment.* On a table nearby were stacks of a Minutemen pamphlet called *The Use of Sodium Nitrates in Explosives.*

DePugh is reluctant to see strangers because he feels he has been mistreated by many of them in the news media. He would not even answer my letters. I was fortunate because when I arrived at Biolab Corporation and announced myself, it just happened that DePugh's assistant, Patrick "George" Peyson, was at that very moment reading *Guerrilla*—written by my uncle, Charles W.

Thayer. "Hey!" he said. "This book's our *bible!*" and dashed out of the building in search of DePugh.

The personal office of the "National Coordinator," as DePugh prefers to be known, was crammed full of paperwork and more reference books on irregular warfare. Under a table was a cardboard box with perhaps fifty clips of either .30 caliber or .30-06 caliber ammunition. An antiaircraft shell stood on the desk. On one wall was a "Let Freedom Ring" chart, listing telephone numbers in various cities where interested parties could hear "patriotic messages." On another wall was a sign that read: "God . . . Give us men!" The office had no windows.

DePugh described the structure of his organization as more like a sponge than a tiger. Break the back of a tiger, he said, and the beast cannot fight. But cut a sponge into a thousand pieces and each fragment can grow back into a new sponge. He claims that all states have Minutemen units, each broken down into "bands" which, in turn, are broken down into teams of six to eight men. "There is no chain of command above band," said DePugh; "we can have a loose structure like this just as long as the other bands believe in the same doctrines and policies." No membership list is kept, nor a central mailing list. Most members are identified by number. For instance, one Minuteman from Pennsylvania, complaining in a letter that his group was denied rifle range facilities, signed the letter simply "7005."[5] DePugh noted that there has been a considerable turnover among his followers, but he says he expects that. "It is a matter also of continuously cleansing the organization of those who want to use it for some selfish purpose."

The Minutemen are not an army, he went on, for four reasons: there are no uniforms, no chain of command, no paid personnel and no collective ownership of equipment. Each individual is asked to own a minimum of one rifle and one pistol and ample ammunition for both; beyond that, a member can purchase what he wants. DePugh, for instance, used to keep an 81mm mortar in his car.[6]

In January 1967, DePugh, Peyson and Troy Houghton, the Minutemen's West Coast coordinator, were sentenced to four, two and three years in jail respectively for violating the Federal Firearms Act. All three have appealed their convictions. DePugh has also resigned as the Minutemen's leader because he believes that for the long-term good of the organization the leadership should be anonymous, with power vested in an "executive committee." Whether this has in fact happened is not clear; not enough time has elapsed since his resignation in 1967 for any trend to appear.

Total membership DePugh puts above 25,000, of which he says, for security reasons, he knows less than 10 percent. Other sources put the membership figure as low as 200; perhaps a realistic figure would fall between 5,000 and 6,000.

"Our people are part-time people," said DePugh. "This is partly to conserve money but also because it gives a different solidarity to the organization. Birch Society Coordinators get $12,500 salary; he may be working for the money or through dedication, you never know which. With us we don't pay anyone so when things get tough our organization is still intact."

DePugh puts a high premium on intelligence and security. "The answer to the problem of defending ourselves against dictatorship is to identify the enemy specifically: name, address and phone number. We try to find out who these people are, what their connections are, their weak points and their strong points."* In one pamphlet, DePugh explained the virtues of intelligence and illustrated his point as follows:

> Suppose you pick up a telephone book, opened it to any page at random, closed your eyes and put your finger on one name. Now suppose you read that name for the first time and said to yourself, "Sometime in the next 30 days, I'm going to kill this man."
>
> Consider the situation—one man, picked at random, is marked for death. He might be the most powerful, the wealthiest, the most influential man in that city, but none of these things would help him in the least. He would be defenseless. Why?

---

* Much of their research shows up in *On Target*. Their information seems to be gleaned primarily from literature supplied to them by the organizations they are analyzing and gives little indication of any independent research on their part. An analysis of the ADA, for instance, gave short sketches of the major individuals concerned, a brief outline of its policies; and then came to the conclusion that the organization is "very red indeed."

Because you would have one thing that he did not have—intelligence. You would know his identity and he would not know yours. So long as that condition continued, there would be no possible way in which he could arrange an adequate defense against you.

Exactly the same situation exists between ourselves and our Communist-Socialist enemies. Our success will be directly proportionate to our knowledge of them and inversely proportionate to their knowledge of us. . . .

As for security, DePugh has many suggestions. "Use deceptive measures," he advises: Subscribe to left-wing periodicals to keep an eye on the opposition (this, adds DePugh, "will keep the postal inspector guessing as to which side you are really on"); use two envelopes in sending mail, never put a return address on the outside one, send the letter indirectly, preferably through a friend; place opaque material such as tin foil inside the envelope to keep the letter "from being read by infra-red cameras"; prepare telephone codes in advance; make sure a prospective recruit is not an infiltrator before identifying yourself as a member; undercover Minutemen should not fraternize with known Minutemen; do not write patriotic letters to newspapers; classify all correspondence "top secret," "secret" or "restricted"; prepare secret rendezvous points and mail drops and change them frequently; contribute money to Minutemen with cash (checks can be traced); observe the "need to know" rule; keep records in code; avoid being followed, take evasive action if necessary; and so on.

Tactically, DePugh sees his Minutemen as an underground force rather than a guerrilla organization. He wants his men to blend into the human landscape because he feels they can be more effective in population centers. (He also admitted that most Minutemen have jobs to hold down and that it would be impractical to have a guerrilla band roaming around the hills living off the land with nobody to fight.) He boasts of having penetrated a number of left-wing groups, but he would not elaborate on the point. "You understand," he said, patting the air in my direction, "I won't prove it to you." He did admit that a few Minutemen had joined the Communist Party, but added that he did not trust them very much.

He offered to have his men infiltrate the campaign staff of President Johnson during the 1964 contest. He planned to have his men sabotage the Democratic Party's efforts by being rude to important contributors, by leaking information to the Republican Party and by confusing the speaking engagement schedule. Senator Goldwater did not accept his offer of assistance.*

DePugh has lately turned his gaze upon the rash of left-wing demonstrations throughout the country. He feels he can neutralize the leaders by infiltrating the crowds. On how he would specifically neutralize the leaders, he would only say "maybe with drugs."

Although intelligence and security matters take first consideration, guerrilla warfare tactics are also emphasized. DePugh stresses knowledge in "sabotage, espionage, subversion, infiltration, escape and evasion, clandestine fabrication of supplies, counterfeiting enemy documents, recruiting, training, communications and propaganda." He sometimes offers advice, such as how explosives can be fashioned from a pool cue ball or a deck of ordinary playing cards. He suggests the reading of judo and karate booklets which show how a man may be killed silently and with one blow. He claims he is planning to mass produce for his followers an inexpensive "Minute mask"—a plastic hood of his own design with chemically filled breathing tubes—against the day Russia starts a nerve gas war.[7]

DePugh's assistant, Patrick Peyson, added that the Minutemen seek recruits with a wide variety of talents. Most members, he said, had experience as pilots, demolition experts, radio operators, parachutists—"enough for a couple of companies"—electronic surveillance or judo instructors. "We are always looking for men with technical skills," he continued, "because the fight in this country as opposed to, say, Vietnam will be a much more sophisticated fight."

When it comes to guerrilla exercises in the woods, DePugh turns silent. His reticence is due to a combination of factors: he no

* In July 1966, DePugh started his own party called the Patriotic Party. His platform calls for "severely limited government and a maximum of individual freedom" and the abolition of the personal income tax. The success of the Party, said DePugh to the four hundred enthusiasts attending the founding convention, depends on the "explosive enthusiasm" of its members.

doubt revels in the mystery which he can draw around his organization; he quite justifiably fears legal reprisals; and finally, and perhaps most important of all, he fears ridicule that would destroy his group for good.

The quality of training on these "field exercises," judging from what few reports there are, indicate that much is left to be desired. In 1961, thirteen Minutemen (one a woman, another a teen-age boy) met together early one morning on an isolated ridge in southern Illinois, east of St. Louis, and partook of some varied irregular warfare tactics. DePugh and his assistant, Rich Lauchli, instructed them in the use of terrain for concealment, the proper method of destroying a hilltop enemy outpost, the proper way to advance behind a smokescreen, and the formation of a skirmish line advancing against a concealed enemy. Lauchli then gave a demonstration of rapid-fire mortar shooting using dummy rounds.[8] Similar maneuvers were reported in Texas, Nebraska, Pennsylvania, Ohio, New Jersey and Missouri.

In the early fall of 1963, a field training exercise was held near Temecula, California, on private property. A memorandum, entitled "General Notes and Hints from September Seminar 1963," listed some of the instruction material presented to the fifty-odd Minutemen in attendance. Excerpts:

> The best set-up for making "Molotov Cocktails" is as follows. Using the small disposable type beer bottles, fill with a home-made napalm mixture of ⅔ gasoline and ⅓ "Duz," fill the bottles and cap them with an inexpensive bottle-capper available at most drug stores. Tape a regular "Tampax" sanitary device to each bottle with masking tape. . . .
>
> A good cheap explosive can be made by distilling iodine, or buying iodine crystals. When kept in ammonia they are very stable but when dried out become highly explosive. . . .
>
> Methane gas (or nerve gas) is obtained when small slivers of pure teflon plastic are inserted in a cigarette. The results are always fatal, and almost immediate. The only known antidote is Atropine, which must be taken immediately.
>
> The complete formula for the manufacture of Nitroglycerine is given on Page two. Warning.....!!! NOT to be attempted by amateurs. This stuff is BAD!!!...

There is some indication that St. Louis is a major center of Minutemen activities. Two years after the above-mentioned maneuvers took place, a large cache of ammunition, canned food and survival equipment was found in a wooded area approximately thirty miles southwest of St. Louis. The cache consisted of four heavy metal drums inside of which were more than a thousand rounds of ammunition, field manuals, machetes, army fatigues, blankets, pup tents, tarpaulins, shovels, canned water and food.[9] The same year, a cache was discovered in Prince William County, Virginia, in the vicinity of the Manassas Battlefield. Thirty-six sticks of dynamite—enough to destroy a multi-story building— were found stored in jars. There were pop-up targets scattered throughout the woods as well as stationary targets, in one case an old car door, riddled with bullet holes.[10]

New York is also a center of Minutemen activity. In the fall of 1966, 19 Minutemen from the New York City area were arrested on the eve of a planned attack upon three rundown rural camps that at one time or another had been used by left-wing or pacifist groups. Police seized an awesome array of weapons from various Minutemen cells: 115 rifles, 9 machine guns, 5 mortars, 26 pistols, 50 camouflage uniforms and steel helmets, 30 walkie-talkies, 10 cans of black powder, 2 bazookas, 3 anti-tank grenade launchers, over one million rounds of ammunition and assorted brass knuckles, trench knives, machetes, crossbows (with arrows) and cleavers.

One of the men taken into custody was a milkman, whose nickname was "Nathan Hale," who stored plastic bombs in his icebox. Another man was a 40-year-old college sophomore. Still a third was an individual who spent his leisure hours firing cans of peas from a mortar at a pasture full of cows while a forward observer—his brother—called back range corrections.

What seldom makes the newspapers, however, are such items as these: often Minutemen maneuvers are little more than "shoot-'em-ups" at which tin cans, bottles, saplings and small game are targets; in many cases game is shot out of season; dynamite and ammunition, particularly in the case of the Prince William County cache, often change their chemical composition due to exposure and become highly unstable and unsafe; in a few cases, forest fires have been started from the muzzle blast of weapons; and, finally, perhaps the primary reason the caches have been discovered has been due to the debris that usually surrounds the area: unburied garbage, paper, old targets, broken branches, campfire ashes, etc. "Far from saving America," one critic said, "these people seem bent on destroying it, by burning or littering it to death."

This singular lack of military discipline is often reflected in the activities of individual Minutemen. During the rioting in Watts in 1965, a number of uniformed individuals calling themselves Minutemen were involved in a minor fracas on the edges of the strife-torn area. DePugh claims the men were kicked out of his organization because they were uniformed, because they acted as "Minutemen" and because they disobeyed orders. "Watts," said DePugh, "was provoked to draw people in to increase destruction; so we stayed out."

One of DePugh's followers from California has made almost as much of a name for himself as has his leader. His name is Troy Houghton, alias Don Alderman; he was the one who claimed Red Chinese troops were massed below the border preparing to invade the U.S. Houghton has been in police custody fifteen times in the last eleven years, mostly in burglary cases. He has been convicted on a number of charges, from auto violations (tampering with a vehicle) to indecent exposure.

In 1964, Houghton dressed himself up as an Army colonel and infiltrated the Army's mock war exercises in the Arizona-California-Nevada deserts called "Operation Desert Strike." He was not caught; in fact, he was assigned a jeep and a driver.[11]

Another California Minuteman is William N. Holstine, alias Jim Mitchell. He says he sleeps with two carbines and fifteen hundred rounds of ammunition by his bed and brags that he knows where howitzers and a complete field hospital are hidden, ready to be put to use. Still another West Coast Minuteman is William F. Colley, a free-lance photographer, who runs an organization, affiliated with DePugh's group, called The Loyal Order of Mountain Men. Colley, also party to the Chinese-massed-on-the-border scare, is, like Houghton, a sex offender. After being convicted in 1957 on three counts of sexual molestation of young children, he was put on ten years' probation provided he submit to an orchiectomy (the removal of his reproductive powers).[12]

Yet another Minuteman is Keith Dwayne Gilbert, a fugitive from justice in 1965, suspected by police of stealing fourteen hundred pounds of dynamite from a California storage magazine earlier in the year. He is known to have violent anti-Negro opinions; he stands convicted of an unprovoked assault on a Negro motorist in 1964, and he was under suspicion for a telephone threat against the life of Martin Luther King. Gilbert has been denounced by both DePugh and his Minutemen.

A small faction of Minutemen who believe DePugh to be a political moderate once conceived of a plan to plant a lethal dose of cyanide gas in the UN building's air-conditioning system. The plot progressed to the point where one man actually obtained ten gallons of potassium cyanide for $56. DePugh loyalists were outraged at this development and made plans to shoot the faction's leader in a room lined with butcher paper. To obliterate any trace of the crime, the bloody paper was to be burned, the body buried in a deep grave somewhere in Missouri, and the gun smelted down. Both the plot and counterplot fell apart when the authorities got wind of them and stepped into the picture.

A Stockton, California, gun shop owner, while perhaps not a Minuteman but one who certainly pushes the organization's literature, said: "The private citizen has an inalienable right to carry around his own machine gun, howitzer or atomic device." DePugh concurs, adding: "We're only exercising our constitutional rights of freedom to bear arms, freedom of assembly and freedom of speech."

DePugh justifies all this activity by quoting from a statement made by President Kennedy shortly after taking office:

> Today we need a nation of Minutemen—citizens who are not only prepared to take up arms but citizens who regard the preservation of freedom as a basic purpose of their daily life and who are willing consciously to work and sacrifice for their freedom.

He also refers to the 1960 Annual Report of the House Committee on Un-American Activities, in which was written:

Events of the past year have provided convincing evidence that the American people cannot rely completely on this country's armed forces to protect themselves from communist domination and slavery. This is not because our military forces lack the power or the will to defend this country, but rather because the nature of the attacks being made on the United States by its major and only significant enemy are so designed as to render conventional military forces as ineffective as possible for defense purposes.

DePugh's vision of a perfect American involves "a return to limited government." He said that government should be a service rather than a commodity and that it should be paid for—no deficit spending or large bureaucracy. He added that there is a blurring of lines between state and federal governments going on that is destroying checks and balances. "When LBJ can do things in Missouri without worrying what the Governor of Missouri thinks," said DePugh, "this is bad."

He would like to have the U.S. get out of the United Nations because "the blurring of lines would be just one step higher." America should also pull out of Vietnam because the liberation of Cuba is more important and should come first. "We are in Vietnam," he said, "to use up the limited amount of military stockpiles to weaken our potential." President Johnson, continued DePugh, "is a traitor; if he is sincere, there are other places where men, money and material could be put to better use, so he must have another motive."

In DePugh's estimation, President Johnson wants "to put this nation in a position where we have to surrender our national sovereignty to a U.N. government in order to survive."

Such a situation fully justifies the existence of his organization, says DePugh. "Obviously," he went on, "guerrilla warfare is of great interest to many people and if it is a device we can use to get people interested in the political field, then so much the better." His job as leader of the Minutemen, he explained, is to "train leaders who will defend us against this tyranny," for, as he wrote in one of his recruiting pamphlets:

When murdering communist bands come roaming through your community, they must not find a lazy, disarmed people waiting like lambs for the slaughter. They must find instead a vigorous and well-armed civilian population—able and determined to protect their families and their property.

"The only trouble is," broke in Patrick Peyson as I was about to leave, "we first have to erase the image that we are machine-gun toting fanatics who plan to storm the White House steps."

2

There are two other groups that qualify as paramilitary, both of which are described below.

It should be noted, however, that organizations with the word "Minutemen," or variations of it, in their titles are not necessarily paramilitary groups. They are mostly very conservative pressure groups, usually activist and militant. Some are letter-writing groups, others push legislation, still others back candidates; usually all pride themselves on being able to mobilize at a moment's notice when they sense a breach of our freedoms. There are various "Minute Women" groups throughout the country; there is a Minutemen for Christ group in Pasadena, and a Minutemen group in New Orleans that is nothing more than a small gun club whose president is a Southern "colonel" on Governor McKeithen's staff.

The Counter-Insurgency Council, a paramilitary group located in Collinsville, Illinois, is run by Richard "Rich" Lauchli, an ex-member of DePugh's Minutemen. Lauchli has been arrested a number of times on violations of firearm laws. He was fined $100 in 1957 for possessing firearms unlawfully transferred or made, and he was fined $500 in 1960 for stealing twenty-three bazookas. In 1964 he was indicted for trying to sell submachine guns, a flame thrower, aerial bombs, mortars, automatic pistols, rifles and considerable ammunition to supposed agents of South American revolutionaries, who turned out to be Treasury agents.

Lauchli, an ex-World War II paratrooper, claims his CIC is merely "a loosely knit homogenous alliance composed simply of individuals with a love of country and a will to do something about it." He says that his group is limited to the St. Louis area and numbers no more than thirty-six individuals.

The essential difference between Lauchli's and DePugh's groups is that the members of the CIC wear uniforms on maneuvers and DePugh's Minutemen do not.

Lauchli's ties to DePugh's group are sentimental at best. Other independently formed paramilitary groups seem far more closely associated with the Norborne-based Minutemen. Examples of the latter include the Sons of Liberty in New Jersey (whose manual on garroting and other guerrilla techniques closes with a quote from Isaiah), the Brothers of the Iron Cross in California, the Paul Revere Associated Yeomen (PRAY) in New Orleans, and Kenneth Goff's Soldiers of the Cross, based in Englewood, Colorado. One of Goff's compatriots was the Reverend Dallas Roquemore. He believed that the Russians were trying to corner the horse market in order to launch a Cossack-style attack on the west coast. Roquemore set up a Minutemen camp in California's Santa Ana range of mountains but was soon thereafter shot to death by a recruit whose alertness he was testing.

Considering their ephemeral nature, these groups may no longer have any ties with DePugh's organization.

The other paramilitary group worth noting in any detail is known either as the U.S. Rangers or the California Rangers. It is the only Minuteman-type organization that is clearly racist in character. It is tied in very closely to the Ku Klux Klan, the National States Rights Party, the Christian Defense League and the Church of Jesus Christ-Christian.

The founder of the Rangers is Colonel William P. Gale, U.S. Army (ret.), who served under General MacArthur in the Philippines organizing guerrilla forces. In 1957, Gale ran for governor of California on the Constitution Party ticket, and in 1962 he announced his candidacy for the same office on an independent platform pledged to abolish both federal and state income taxes. He is now a self-appointed pastor of a church he chooses to call "the ministry of William P. Gale."

The purpose of the Rangers is similar to, if not identical with, the objective of DePugh's Minutemen: to build a secret underground network for the conduct of guerrilla warfare activities.

From all indications the membership has always been small. Training activities run along the lines of the Norborne Minutemen, each member being required to own several weapons and quantities of ammunition.

Gale, however, injects racism into his paramilitary operations. One of the phrases he uses to describe both Negroes and Jews is, "Turn a nigger inside out and you've got a Jew." He once said of the six million Jewish dead in World War II: "I can show you top-secret documents that prove that the 6,000,000 Jews Hitler was supposed to have killed are right here in America. They're here. And if we run them out of here, they'll go down to South America somewhere and start screaming about how we burned them in gas chambers. I've got two chambers ready for them now—two ovens ready for them now."

In 1963, Gale and a cohort captured control of an American Legion Post in the Los Angeles area and turned it into a part of his Rangers operation. The power grab was exposed in the newspapers; the "Signal Hill Situation," as it came to be known, proved an embarrassment to the leaders of the American Legion and the charter of the post was revoked.

Gale is closely associated with the Christian Defense League, the founder of which is the Reverend Wesley A. Swift, of Lancaster, California, and pastor of the Church of Jesus Christ-Christian.

In 1945, Swift was identified as a Klan organizer, and was once described as "a former Ku Klux Klan rifle-team instructor." He was a legal representative of Gerald L. K. Smith's Christian Nationalist Crusade in the early 1950s and he launched a number of organizations on his own: The California League against Communism, the Anglo-Saxon Christian Congregation, and the Christian Defense League.

Swift founded the Church of Jesus Christ-Christian in 1946, and it has since grown into a string of churches stretching from southern California to the San Francisco Bay area. The church's symbol is a thunderbolt, similar to the NSRP's. The Reverend Oren Potito, associated with the NSRP, is the church's "Eastern" representative in Florida; the Reverend Charles Conley "Connie"

Lynch, perhaps the nation's most vituperative racist firebrand, is also a minister of the church.

Everything Lynch says appeals to the emotions. For instance, on the Jews: "All the non-whites, not only in America, but throughout the world, are being marshalled against the white race by these Christ-hatin' Jews and it's going to come to a bloody race war." Lynch went on to say, "I encourage every white American, if they don't have a gun, get them a gun." On Negroes, Lynch does not mince words: "White America, all over, not just the South, ought to rise up and demand that these niggers go home and stay home, or get 'em out of here and send 'em back to Africa and let their kinfolk eat 'em."

Another minister in Swift's church is Neumann Britton, a plasterer by trade. His home serves as Lynch's permanent West Coast address. Britton was reported, in 1963, to be the San Bernardino County chairman of the National States Rights Party.

The Christian Defense League is actually a militant arm of Swift's church. Ostensibly, the purpose of the CDL is to protect the Christian heritage, but in fact it is an armed group preaching racial intolerance.

Besides Swift and Colonel Gale, those most closely tied to the organization include Harold Burroughs, a veterinarian, who sometimes acts as an usher at Swift's church; Shreve "Duke" Nielson, Swift's son-in-law and bodyguard; Clinton Wheat, a member of the Ku Klux Klan who carries a .45 Colt automatic in his belt at the small of his back; James Oviatt, an elderly Los Angeles haberdasher who was one of the financial backers of the Christian Defense League; Admiral Crommelin, who is the CDL's Eastern Regional Director; several ex-Baptist ministers; and, finally, an individual who invariably wears a Boy Scout shirt and carries a .38 caliber snub-nose revolver around in a hollowed-out Bible.

One member of the CDL, William H. Garland of Cucamonga, California, maintained a considerable armory at his residence. A police raid revealed eight machine guns and one hundred rifles, shotguns and pistols. Garland's barn contained an ammunition dump for heavy-caliber rockets, bombs, highly volatile chemicals and thousands of rounds of ammunition.

Swift himself is reported to have one of the largest gun collections in California. He also maintains a rifle range on his Kern County ranch.

Most of these individuals will claim that each one of these organizations is a separate entity, unconnected with any other group. This undoubtedly is true in the sense that the nature of these groups prohibits close relations of any duration. Too many men want to be captain. Yet, a number of them, specifically the American Nazi Party, the Christian Defense League and the Church of Jesus Christ-Christian, have explored ways and means of working together. In June 1964 these groups met to discuss a merger for the purpose of exchanging information, for keeping an up-to-date roster of agents, double agents and informers, and for exchanging views on matters of interest.

Although the possibility that such negotiations would produce a unified group under one name is remote, they may very well produce a loose association of organizations, the combined noise-making capacity of which would be vastly increased and whose hard-core nucleus would revolve around a secret guerrilla force such as the Rangers.[13]

7

The Proselytizers

1

Anyone wishing to take an active part in right-wing political activities would have no trouble finding the appropriate group to join. For three dollars he can buy from the Alert Americans Association a small pamphlet called *The First National Directory of "Rightist" Groups, Publications and Some Individuals in the United States (and Some Foreign Countries)*. The fifth edition, published in 1965, lists 3,406 groups, publications and individuals, all pushing a variety of right-wing views. Omitting churches, individuals, foreign organizations and multiple listings of the Citizens' Councils (42), American Opinion Bookstores (32), "colleges requiring the loyalty oath for student loans" (16), Conservative Party (7), Constitution Party (25), Ku Klux Klan (19), Liberty Amendment Committee branch offices (69) and Young Americans for Freedom offices (12), there are 2,598 right-wing organizations remaining, not taking into consideration cross-referencing or individuals operating under a variety of names. This figure represents a threefold increase over the number of organizations listed in the 1962, or fourth, edition of the *Directory*.

No count has ever been made of the people who belong to these groups, but a conservative estimate would put the hard-core activists at 300,000 with an additional three to four million part-time to casual supporters. Although small in absolute terms (four million people are only 2 percent of the population), these figures are far larger than anything on the left.

It is beyond the scope of this work to delve into the affairs of all 2,598 right-wing groups in this country. Nevertheless, a variety of them should be mentioned—some briefly, others a little more fully and a few in considerable detail.

For a start, if a person with right-wing sympathies felt at loose ends he might join the Watch Washington Club (if he lived near Columbus, Ohio), or the Grass Rooters (in Los Angeles), the Shocking Truth Committee (Glendale, California), or Internal Intelligence (Dalton, Illinois), or the First Anti-Communist International (New York City), or Freedom's Legion U.S.A. (Denver), or the Committee to Study the Record (El Cajon, California). If he wanted more information or more verbal ammunition, he might write away to Jab A Liberal Series (Arcadia, California), Tapes for Patriots (Houston) or Fight Communism Stickers (Minneapolis). Undoubtedly he would be in contact with Suppressed Books (Shreveport, Louisiana), the Joe McCarthy Bookstore (Boston), and the Patrick Henry Book Store (Los Angeles) as well as two of the largest publishers and distributors of right-wing material in the country: Omni Publications (Hawthorne, California) and The Bookmailer (Linden, New Jersey).

If the newcomer's tastes ran to militaristic-sounding groups, he could join Fighting Homefolks of Fighting Men (Glenwood Springs, Colorado), Here We Stand, Inc. (Cincinnati), Marching Men (St. Petersburg), Marching Truth (New York City), We Fight On (Phoenix), Freedom Fighters (Ft. Worth) and World War III Victory Campaign (Houston).

If he feels that fluoridation of the water supply seems to be part of a Communist plot or otherwise a threat to the health of the nation he could subscribe to *Fluoridation Digest* and join any one of the twenty organizations listed in the *Directory* with "Fluoridation," "Pure Water" or "Clean Water" in their titles. If he has doubts about mental health he can join Mental Health Crusaders in Dallas or Arizonans for Mental Freedom in Phoenix. Were he to perceive an erosion of American values he could join fifty-five groups whose names begin with "Freedom," or he could join ten "Americanism" groups, twenty-two "Liberty" groups, fifteen "Patriotic" groups or nine "Truth" groups. If he is plagued by high taxes he might join the Committee for the Repeal of the Income

Tax in Evanston, Illinois; or if he objects to Yugoslavian pilots being trained in the United States he can join the National Indignation Convention; or if he is concerned about communism among professors at Harvard he can join Veritas run by Colonel Archibald Roosevelt. If he lives in Tennessee and his hatred of Communists has no outlet, he might join the Society to Exterminate Neo-Communist Harbingers—or STENCH, for short. If he is shocked by the number of "obscene" publications on the newsstands he can join the Citizens for Decent Literature in Cincinnati and read their publication, *The National Decency Reporter*. In the event his tastes run to the inscrutable, he might join the Understanding Group at Large (Fresno), the Foundation for Divine Meditation (Thornfield, Missouri) and subscribe to "Why Why Why" (Port Angeles, Washington).

However, for anyone wishing to move into the big-time right-wing groups, there are other organizations that warrant more attention. For a start, there is "Life Line," a series of radio programs that are broadcast daily over 387 radio stations. Life Line, which until 1957 was known as "Facts Forum," is owned by Haroldson Lafayette Hunt, reportedly America's second richest man (after J. Paul Getty).

Hunt is a self-made millionaire many times over. With a $2,000 inheritance he became a millionaire by the time he was twenty-one by speculating in cotton. He lost it all in a panic in 1921; however, he was soon back in the chips when he bought up all the oil leases he could find in the then untapped and vastly rich east Texas oilfields. Today his wealth is estimated between $700 million and $2 billion. No one knows for sure, not even Hunt himself.

Hunt lives in Dallas in a house that is a reproduction of Mount Vernon, only this one is larger—Hunt claims 10 percent, others say three or four times larger. He is something of an eccentric. He is, for instance, a food faddist. He drinks goat milk and insists that all bread he eats be baked at home with a high fluoride wheat grown only in Deaf Smith County, Texas. He carries his own lunch to the office in a plain paper bag, not because it is cheaper than a lunch at the Petroleum Club (on the top floor of the downtown Dallas building that he owns), but because it is the only way he can get the health foods he enjoys. Some bags are humorously marked

"H. L. Hunt Gourmet Lunch," and one of his four sons insists that he saves the bags. Hunt also has bragged of new culinary delights having been discovered in his own kitchen, such as prune muffins and carrot cakes.

Hunt wears store-bought suits and clip-on bow ties, drives his own car to work, lets his hair grow long and his dandruff go unchecked, and displays no ostentatious public habits at all except for his home which is his only hobby. One of his favorite pastimes is sitting around the family hearth singing old-time tunes. His favorite is "We Ain't Got a Barrel of Money." Hunt used to chain-smoke cigars but gave them up, he said, "because it was costing $300,000 of my time per year just to unwrap them."

Hunt's office is large and comfortable and is protected by a squad of secretaries. His desk is littered with products from his HLH Products Company. His favorite is an item called Gastro-Majik for upset stomachs. He is its own best salesman. Once, for instance, he contributed to a local opera company's production of "The Barber of Seville." The management was so delighted that they asked Hunt to say a few words to the audience. He devoted his entire speech to the medicinal benefits of Gastro-Majik.

Hunt is exceedingly difficult to interview. He began our conversation with: "I suppose you think I'm just some sort of screwball rich man. . . ." After every question that I asked he would say: "Now what you want me to say is . . ." My avowals of good intentions were to no avail. Each question that I asked he would answer by summoning one of his many secretaries into the room, asking her to get out such-and-such a Life Line brochure, giving it to me and then saying, "This should answer your question." Apparently there is no subject he has not at one time or another touched upon with the written word, for at the end of an hour I had sheaves of Life Line brochures and very few spontaneous comments from the man on the other side of the desk. Whenever he did venture an off-the-cuff remark, he had the habit of mumbling inaudibly into his hands then stopping and smiling.

Life Line (then Facts Forum) was set up in 1951 to organize "small discussion groups devoted to the study of the art of living, social advancement, the science of government and agriculture." Ostensibly, it was to present both sides of any controversial subject, but no matter how hard it tried to accomplish this it kept coming up conservative. The programs were so one-sided, according to the IRS, that Life Line's tax-free status as an "educational" group was revoked in 1963. This ruling is now being appealed. Earlier, Life Line lost its "religious" exemption when it was found that one of the two sponsoring churches did not exist; the other one failed to answer letters concerning its sponsorship.

Life Line claims it pays its own way but it is, in fact, underwritten by Hunt-owned companies: HLH Products, Hunt Oil Company, HLH Parade Company, etc. I have never heard anyone else's products advertised on one of its programs. Reportedly, HLH Products alone spends $100,000 per month advertising on Life Line. There are some five million daily listeners to the programs.

The IRS ruling is disputed heatedly by Life Liners because it means that contributions are no longer deductible; it also means that the organization can no longer qualify for a post office subsidy that reduces its postal bill by two thirds. Life Line does a brisk business sending out radio tapes, *Life Lines,* a four-page publication, and *Life Line Links,* a book club leaflet. Without its exemption, the squeeze is on: postal rates have tripled and contributions have fallen off.

Despite Hunt's reticence, his views and attitudes are observable through the murk. He sees himself as a "constructivist patriot," rather than as a conservative, whose sworn enemy is "the mistaken," his way of saying Communist without being sued. The last President whom Hunt approved of was Calvin Coolidge because he reduced the federal debt and did not do much else. He said in 1961 that it was just as well that the Cuban invasion failed because it was "just one Communist government trying to overthrow another." His programs reflect the belief, for instance, that foreign aid was originally the idea of Stalin; that the United States has been pouring dollars down an "economic rathole"; and that "teachers, psychologists, sociologists, psychiatrists, economists and politicians" are nothing more than "practiced braintwisters turned loose on our defenseless children."

In his "romance" novel, *Alpaca* (published by the H. L. Hunt Publishing Company, which also prints telephone books), H. L.

Hunt created a Utopian constitution in a mythical country in which a graduated system of suffrage had been set up. Those paying the highest taxes were given seven votes. Two extra votes were given to each citizen who waived his old-age pension. Everyone was given at least one vote, but a person was allowed to delegate others he thought were better qualified to cast his vote for him. Hunt insists that he did not devise this system as a possible alternative to the present one in America. Rather, he said it was created "to stimulate people in the emerging countries to adopt a constitution whereby they would try to govern themselves instead of yielding to a dictatorship." In late 1966 he made a concerted effort to sell the idea to the South Vietnamese government with no visible results.

2

Another program one might listen to for its right-wing views is the "Dan Smoot Report." It is carried on eighty-nine radio stations and fifty-two TV stations in thirty-one states. A staff of fifteen, besides producing the shows themselves, publishes an eight-page transcript of each day's program. It is known as the *Dan Smoot Report* and is sent to 28,000 paid subscribers and to an additional 1,300,000 people as a gift. Robert Welch of the Birch Society believes that Smoot's *Report* is the ideal literature to be placed in barbershops and doctors' offices.

Smoot himself is a handsome and rugged-looking individual, a graduate of Southern Methodist University. He taught English for a year at Harvard and then joined the FBI as an investigator. After nine years with the Bureau he quit in 1951 to work for Hunt's Facts Forum. Four years later he left because he did not like to present both sides of an argument. For a while he put out a sheet called *Dan Smoot Speaks,* prompting many to ask "But who wants to listen?" Eventually Smoot himself admitted that the title was "frightfully pompous" and changed it to the present one.

Smoot's programs were financed in large measure by Dallas Bedford Lewis, the late millionaire president of the Lewis (pet) Food Company. Lewis claimed once that "approximately 80 percent of everything the federal government is doing" is unconstitutional. Smoot tends to agree. Not only Earl Warren but all nine Justices, he feels, should be impeached; America, he believes, should pull out of Asia and let Chiang Kai-shek fight our wars for us. "If you want the government to provide you with clothing, housing, food, medical care, training in an occupation and security in old age," he once wrote, "get yourself a life term in prison." On the subject of fluoridation, Smoot writes: "Mental-control drugs have already been developed—drugs which pacify and make human beings tractable and amenable to discipline. When will our public officials begin to add these to our water systems?"

In the 7 June 1965 issue of his report, Smoot argues that the only "fruits of liberalism" are street crimes. The article leads the reader to believe that *all* street crimes are committed by Negroes. In 1956, Smoot became worked up over the Alaska Mental Health Bill, a plan to create community health services in what was then a territory. Smoot believed that the bill was a Communist plot to set up a concentration camp—"Siberia U.S.A." he called it—where dedicated anti-Communists would be railroaded out of the way.

Smoot's vast appeal among right-wingers stems from his past FBI training. The argument goes that anyone who had such training *must* be an expert on communism. Harry and Bonaro Overstreet, in their book *The Strange Tactics of Extremism* (a book not appreciated on the right), point out that his legalistic background does not hinder his slanting a case in such a way that a distorted picture is given (such as, for instance, his article on street crimes). The Overstreets also note that Smoot believes that it is more American to decide in advance what is to be proved and then prove it rather than letting the facts speak for themselves.[1] One way Smoot does this—and he is not alone in using this tactic—is to use the material of other right-wingers as unimpeachable sources. Thus, in the 1 June 1964 *Report* entitled "Communism in the Civil Rights Movement," he quotes material from *The National Program Letter,* the Richmond *News Leader,* Manning Johnson, Fulton Lewis, Jr., Circuit Riders, Inc., HCUA Reports and Senators Eastland and Thurmond—all right-wing sources. The few other sources he uses only highlight the conclusions his right-wing sources draw.

3

The most sophisticated of all the radio programs is the "Manion Forum." It is broadcast over some 265 radio stations and 15 TV stations in 42 states and the District of Columbia. The Forum differs from the other broadcasts on three counts: it is the most reputable one of them all, its programs are produced with considerable professional skill, and its appeal is primarily to Midwest isolationism rather than American fundamentalism (although the two overlap somewhat).

The man who runs the Forum is Clarence E. Manion, for eleven years (1941–1952) Dean of the College of Law at Notre Dame. In his early political life Manion was an up-and-coming Democrat who was regarded highly enough to be named at the age of thirty-six the keynote speaker at the 1932 Democratic State Convention in Indiana. He was touted for senator in 1938 but never received the nomination. By the time war broke out Manion was involved with the isolationist America First Committee, and two years later he was lashing out against the "super-duper planners of what they call 'the brave new world.'" In 1952 he supported Taft for the Republican nomination, but when it went to Eisenhower, with Adlai Stevenson as his opponent, he bolted the Democratic Party and organized "Democrats for Eisenhower."

The new President appointed Manion chairman of the Commission on Inter-Governmental Relations, an organization set up to study the functions of, and the conflicts between, the federal and local governments. But within a year Manion had become a political liability to the President because he, Manion, came out strongly in favor of the Bricker Amendment (a proposal to limit the President's treaty-making powers), which Eisenhower vigorously opposed.

Manion resigned and from that point on has been deeply involved in the politics of the right. He was one of the founders of For America, an organization to build grass-roots support for conservative candidates. He is a member of the National Council of the John Birch Society, an adviser to Billy James Hargis' Christian Crusade, and a legal adviser to the Citizens Foreign Aid

Committee (which opposes foreign aid). In addition, he was an adviser to the Campaign for the 48 States (later to become Americans for Constitutional Action, with which he is not associated), and he played a part in the 1956 Third Party movement that ran T. Coleman Andrews for President on the States Rights Party ticket. He has also been an adviser to the Intercollegiate Society of Individualists and a sponsor of the American Committee for Aid to Katanga Freedom Fighters.

Manion operates out of the law offices of Doran, Manion, Boyton & Kamm in the St. Joseph Bank Building in downtown South Bend, Indiana. His office is well appointed, filled with the usual memorabilia of a politician. But the bright green rug clashes rudely with the off-green cloth wallpaper. Manion himself is on the short side with a square face and has hooded eyes that nevertheless sparkle with intelligence. He has an expressive face and uses his hands when he talks, occasionally rubbing them over his balding dome when he speaks. He is urbane and articulate and talks exceedingly fast.

Manion holds no grudge against Eisenhower over the Bricker Amendment imbroglio, although he has not changed his own views on the subject. "Ike," he said, "is just like a Rotarian; you can't help liking him personally." The Dean does not agree with Robert Welch's thesis that Eisenhower was a "dedicated, conscious agent of the Communist conspiracy." Manion is an admirer of Barry Goldwater's and worked hard for his election in 1964. His loss, he said, was not the fault of the candidate but was Nixon's and can be traced back "to the midnight cabal in New York with Rockefeller" in 1960.

The Forum was started, according to Manion, by accident in 1954 after a number of friends suggested that a radio program was needed to explain to the people the facts about the Bricker Amendment. The stated purpose of the Forum today is "to provide a speaking platform for great numbers of prominent and knowledgeable people," a platform, he added, that they otherwise would not have. Manion claims that his speakers cover a wide spectrum of political opinion; but, in truth, he must mean views on the right alone, because of the 218 Forum speakers from 1955 to 1965, not one was noted for his liberal or left-wing views.

The business manager of the Manion Forum, at least up to 1964, was Leo F. Reardon. In their book *Danger On The Right* (Random House, 1964), authors Arnold Forster and Benjamin Epstein point out that Reardon's past political activities included stints as adviser to Father Charles Coughlin, fund raiser for Upton Close and broadcaster for Merwin K. Hart—three men who had at one time or another a distinct bias against Jews. Whether Forster and Epstein wished to drag the tarbrush of anti-Semitism across the Manion Forum is not clear. In any event, there is no evidence that any anti-Jewish feelings are expressed in the organization. Dean Manion's and the Forum's message is straight Midwest conservative isolationism, larded now and again with Birch-like suspicions of conspiracy.

The Forum tends to associate many of America's ills with an international devil. Therefore it is violently anti-Communist, strongly anti-British, distinctly anti-United Nations and fervently pro-Bricker Amendment. Its programs plead for a hard-line foreign policy, the end to foreign aid "giveaways," victory in Vietnam and a rolling back of the Iron and Bamboo Curtains. It calls for a smaller federal government, the end to income taxes, stronger anti-union laws, the restoration of states' rights, the return of God to the classrooms, the end of "gigantic and unnecessary" federal subsidies and an end to that "palpable fraud" Social Security.

As a Birch Society member, Manion tends to see traitors everywhere: in Washington ("addle-pated 'Liberal' Internationalists steering us down the river to 'One Worldism' and slavery"), in the Supreme Court ("the most subtle sort of subversion"), in the churches, in the civil rights movement and, indeed, in "every facet of our society." This, he says, is the alarming condition upon which the imminent destruction of America is now predicated. His many radio shows (costing an estimated $400,000 per year for air time) will help reverse the trend, he believes.

There are other right-wing radio shows one might listen to as a neophyte on the right. Howard Kershner, for instance, President of the Christian Freedom Foundation and editor of its magazine, *Christian Economics,* speaks to the nation for fifteen minutes weekly over 148 stations. His messages promote "the Christian religion and education in the field of economics." Much of this activity is underwritten by Sun Oil millionaire J. Howard Pew and his Pew Freedom Trust. In addition there is America's Future, Inc., of New Rochelle, New York, which claims its messages reach twenty million Americans over 483 stations. The principal moderator and commentator is Rudolph K. Scott.

4

Once past the small right-wing groups and the radio shows, a serious student must move on into the middle-sized right.

One such group, for instance, is the Liberty Amendment Committee with sixty-nine branch offices. Its headquarters is in Los Angeles, and it claims four thousand members. This committee wants at least three quarters of the fifty states to pass an amendment to the Constitution that would bar the government from engaging in any business, professional, commercial, financial or industrial enterprise except as specified in the Constitution. All government property that falls into the above category would have to be sold. Three years after the ratification of the amendment the federal government would be prohibited from levying taxes on personal income, estates and gifts. In other words, the Sixteenth Amendment would be repealed.

Willis Stone, the committee's chairman and a descendant of Declaration of Independence signer Thomas Stone, lamented to me that too many people believe that his committee wishes only to abolish a personal irritant (income taxes) with no thought being given to how the revenue would be replaced. Not at all, says Stone; the purpose of the committee, he explained, is to get the government out of the "more than seven hundred federal corporate activities" that it now operates. Stone claims that if the government were out of these businesses, the corporate income tax of these organizations—as privately owned corporations—would bring in more revenue than now received through personal income taxes. Thus Stone sees his Liberty Amendment Committee performing four worthwhile services: getting the government out of private enterprise; somehow turning those now money-losing fed-

eral enterprises into private money-making corporations; reducing
the overall size of the federal government and its bureaucracy; and
abolishing the personal income tax.

Some of those companies and/or activities that Stone feels the
government has no business being in include the Bureau of Indian
Affairs, the Panama Canal Company (one of the few federal
companies that does make a profit), the General Services Administration, Rural Electrification Administration, Small Business Administration, Island Trading Company of Micronesia, Alaska
Railroad, Virgin Islands Corporation (including a distillery, a
magazine and a hotel), Food for Peace, the School Lunch program,
Tennessee Valley Authority, Cuba Nickel Company, the Forestry
Service, Military Air Transport Service, the Federal Crop Insurance Corporation and map-making operations, postal savings systems, savings bond sales and fertilizer and mineral production
(including uranium, zirconium, magnesium, helium, rubber and
scrap metal). It is unclear from LAC literature how some of these
organizations would suddenly start making a profit once cast out
on their own.

To date, seven states have passed the Liberty Amendment:
Wyoming, Texas, Nevada, Louisiana, Georgia, South Carolina and
Mississippi. It was closely defeated in Colorado and Minnesota.
The amendment was first introduced in Congress by the late Ralph
Gwinn of New York; today its major sponsor is Representative
James B. Utt of California. The possibility of such a bill being
passed in the near future is felt by most observers to be remote.
Nor is it likely that thirty-eight states will pass the amendment in
order for it to pass into law.

5

The Liberty Lobby, no relation to the Liberty Amendment Committee, is another one of the middle-sized organizations worth
noting. It was first conceived in 1955 as a massive conservative
pressure group organized to counterbalance "an aggressive coalition of minority special interest pressure groups" that had "captured" Washington, D.C. It dates its beginning, however, from
1961 when it began to publish its *Liberty Letter*.

"We are an *action* group," writes Colonel Curtis B. Dall, the Lobby's chairman (and an ex-son-in-law of Franklin D. Roosevelt). "Our aim is to supply accurate and timely legislative information to thousands of Conservatives so that they will be inspired to effective action." The Lobby's executive secretary, W. B. Hicks, Jr., a Texan and formerly associated with the newspaper *Human Events,* sees the Lobby exerting pressure by taking an active part in congressional hearings and by having its followers pressure congressmen directly with letters, telegrams, phone calls and personal visits. Liberty Lobby does not try to elect individual conservative congressmen to office but attempts to move the entire country as many notches to the right as it can. In this regard it distributed over twenty million pieces of literature during the 1964 campaign.

Liberty Lobby has some 175,000 subscribers to its *Letter.* In 1963 it began publishing a "confidential Washington report" known as *Liberty Lowdown.* This goes to all financial contributors of twenty dollars or more. It also puts out *Liberty Ledger,* a biennial publication that rates senators and congressmen on the basis of their voting records.

The Lobby has bitterly fought the recent civil rights bills and the changes to the immigration qualifications. It is against federal aid to education, foreign aid, GATT, recognition of Red China, tax-supported housing and power facilities, the Genocide Treaty, the U.N., "world government" and "socialized medicine." It promotes states' rights, less farm controls, reduced federal expenditures, the McCarran-Walter Immigration Act, independence for Puerto Rico, a free gold market, repeal of the Sixteenth (income tax) Amendment and lower taxes.

It has published a number of highly critical books and pamphlets on those who oppose its views. One is called *The Ev and Charlie Show,* a thirty-one page pamphlet subtitled "How the GOP Leadership Sells Out the Party." Senator Everett Dirksen and Representative Charles Halleck are pictured as trained seals performing for President Johnson. Another publication is a twelve-page tabloid called *LBJ: A Political Biography.* Liberty Lobby claims that over ten million copies of it were distributed before the 1964 election. The author of this critical piece was W. B. Hicks, Jr., who seems to have gleaned much of his information from millionaire rancher J. Evetts Haley's book, *A Texan Looks at Lyndon*. On the back page of Hicks' publication we are told that this nation has never seen a politician like Lyndon Baines Johnson. "Only in Germany and Italy," says the author, "have there ever been personalities so well equipped to appeal to the 'gut-issues' of politics." Lest the point be lost, it continued: "Just as Hitler and Mussolini made allies of millionaires and paupers . . ."

Another booklet is *J. William Fulbright: Freedom's Judas Goat*, which claims that the Arkansas senator hates "patriots and patriotism with a passion beyond description"; that he was instrumental in the Senate's censure of McCarthy; that he was responsible for the failure at the Bay of Pigs; and that he is an archetype of the "liberal-internationalist phenomenon." "Holding the fiction of the equality of men to be the primary fact of all life," states the pamphlet, "he would drag down the superior in order to fit his ideology—so long as he, himself, remains on top."

The most notable characteristic of Liberty Lobby is its racist flavor. Its Policy Board, for instance, has listed as members the Reverend Kenneth Goff, an ex-Communist and a former associate of Gerald L. K. Smith's; Robert Kuttner and Louis Zoul, once contributing editors to *Western Destiny;* and Ned Touchstone of *The Councilor*. In addition there is Edward L. Delaney, a former broadcaster for the Nazis during the early period of World War II (he says he quit when America entered the war; later an indictment for treason was dismissed); Tyler Kent, an American who spied for Germany while an employee of the U.S. Embassy in London; W. Henry MacFarland; Judge Tom Brady, the author of *Black Monday;* and, finally, Joseph P. Kamp of the Constitutional Educational League, whose writings over the years some claim "have been marked by ill-concealed anti-Semitic innuendoes." A thinly disguised affiliate of Liberty Lobby is the National Coordinating Committee of Friends of Rhodesian Independence and is headed by Taylor Caldwell, the best-selling novelist who often writes for the John Birch Society.

The man behind Liberty Lobby, however, is Willis A. Carto, whose name does not appear on any of the organization's literature. He is understood to be the Lobby's treasurer. In the past he has been associated with *Western Destiny,* the Yockey Movement, We, The People!, the Congress of Freedom, the John Birch Society and Christian Crusade.

Carto is a secretive and elusive individual who prefers to remain in the background, pulling the strings while Dall and Hicks work the public face of the organization. On occasion, however, he surfaces, usually to be critical of one thing or another. He has, for instance, called Chief Justice Warren a "trotskyite"; he opposed Hawaiian statehood on the grounds that it would bring about "the gradual watering down of the idea of American nationality and nation-hood to a meaningless, characterless cosmopolitan univer- sality"; and he has attacked the churches because, he says, al- though they oppose the atheism of Marxism they are otherwise communistic, "with the impertinence added of their daring to invoke Divine blessing for the apostasy."

A comparison of the current Policy Board with the 1961 Board shows that in its early days Liberty Lobby was relatively free of racists. There were always a few around such as Merwin K. Hart and Verne P. Kaub (who, until his death in 1964, was slated to become the Lobby's president), but the majority were just right- wing, not racist. There was Salt Lake City's long-time Major J. Bracken Lee; Tom Anderson, a member of the Birch Society Council and Editor of *Farm and Ranch;* A. G. Heinsohn, also a member of the Birch Council and the president of Cherokee Textile Mills; and Harry T. Everingham, the asthmatic president of We, The People!, an activist group that organizes "constitution day" rallies and bombards individuals with letters through a front called The Minute Men Network.

Other indications of the Lobby's racism can be found in its literature. Another twelve-page tabloid, similar to the one on President Johnson but this time flattering, is called *Stand Up for America, The Story of George C. Wallace.* Throughout, the em- phasis is placed on racial troubles and how the ex-Governor "solved" them in his state. An *Emergency Liberty Letter,* to cite another example, once began: *"FINAL DEATH NOTICE OF OUR REPUBLIC. Civil Rights Passage Would Insure Dictator- ship."* In yet another publication, *Conservative Victory Plan,* the Lobby blamed Goldwater's 1964 loss on a poor campaign and a "defensive" strategy. The twenty-three-page memorandum then went on to advocate the exploitation of "backlash" and immigration issues, and the establishment of "parties within parties," rather than a third-party movement.

6

The Lobby's *Ledger,* an analysis of the voting records of congressmen and senators, is but one of the many studies designed to educate and influence both the general public and the lawmakers. The most influential analysis on the right is published by a relative newcomer to the scene, Americans for Constitutional Action.*

According to Charles A. McManus, ACA's executive director, the reason for the organization grew out of conservative congressmen's irritation over being given a 0 percent rating on the Americans for Democratic Action's voting index. "This," he said, "was negative; we wanted something positive."

ACA was founded in 1958 and is the direct descendant of the Campaign for the 48 States. The godfathers to ACA are retired Admiral Ben Moreell and Senator Karl Mundt. Moreell, a broad-shouldered, square-jawed ex-athlete was the commander of the famed Seabees during World War II. From 1947 to 1958 he was chairman of the board of Jones & Laughlin Steel Corporation. Today, at seventy-five, he is one of the major forces within the right wing. He is a trustee of the Foundation for Economic Education and the Intercollegiate Studies Institute, an adviser to Young Americans for Freedom, a sponsor of the 1962 Committee for Aid to Katanga Freedom Fighters and a near-perennial recipient of Freedoms Foundation awards. Moreell told a 1963 Human Events Conference that he was "fed up to here with Robin Hood government that promises to rob the rich to pay

* Other voting analyses are published by the Chamber of Commerce, the American Farm Bureau Federation, Civic Affairs Associates, Inc., Kent and Phoebe Courtney's Conservative Society of America, Dan Smoot, and the National Rural Electric Cooperative Association.

Analyses with a more liberal or neutral slant are published by Americans for Democratic Action, the National Farmer's Union, the Industrial Union Department AFL–CIO, the Committee on Political Education, the *Congressional Quarterly* and, on occasion, the *New Republic*.

the poor and, when there are not enough rich left to pay the bills, robs rich and poor alike to pay Robin Hood. . . ."

The trustees of ACA are by and large a distinguished group of conservatives. Major General Thomas A. Lane, a member of General MacArthur's wartime staff, serves as ACA's president, Brigadier General Bonner Fellers, also a member of MacArthur's wartime staff, serves as ACA's vice-chairman. Fellers, like Moreell, spreads his talents among a number of other groups: the Citizens Foreign Aid Committee, the Birch Society, Christian Crusade, ISI and YAF. Other trustees are actors Walter Brennan and John Wayne, ex-Congressman Bruce Alger and Ralph de Toledano, a writer for *National Review*.

The *ACA Index,* a selective voting record of all the lawmakers in Washington, determines to what degree an individual is an ACA "constitutional conservative." Not all bills presented in the House and Senate are included in the *Index,* only those which ACA feels are important. As each bill is voted upon, ACA chooses the side it believes to be "pro-Constitution" and "anti-Socialist." It notes its position on any bill—as, for instance, the 1965 Medicare Bill— with such remarks as: "NAY votes are: FOR Sound Money & AGAINST Inflation. FOR Private Competitive Market & AGAINST Government Interference. FOR Local Self-Government & AGAINST Central Government Intervention. FOR Individual Liberty & AGAINST Coercion." Thus, a senator or a congressman who followed the ACA line all the time would get a 100 percent rating while those who always voted against it would get a 0 percent rating.

Those who most consistently followed the ACA line in the Senate in 1964 were Tower (100 percent), Goldwater (98 percent, down from 99 percent the year before), Simpson and Mechem (97 percent). Those lowest on the *Index* were Senators Ribicoff, Inouye, Edward Kennedy, Long, and Nelson. All had 0 percent ratings.

In the House the ACA favorites were Edward J. Gurney (R., Fla.), Charlotte T. Reid (R., Ill.) and John Ashbrook (R., Ohio). All received 100 percent ratings in 1964. Conversely there were 35 Congressmen who rated 0 percent and another 88 who fell below the 10 percent mark.

To receive a 100 percent ACA rating takes some doing. It means one is bucking the majority 90 percent of the time. Votes must be registered, for instance, against cutting the cost of federal farm programs, against federal aid to depressed areas, against aid to educational TV, against a minimum wage increase and against foreign aid, slum clearance, health research and civil rights. Very few votes are cast in favor of something for the simple reason that such bills never reach the floor of the House or Senate to be voted on. Thus, for all ACA talk of positive action, its position on most questions is strictly defensive.*

In 1961 ACA began a "distinguished service award" program in which parchment testimonials are presented to those lawmakers who scored well on the *Index*. Everyone scoring over 65 percent is eligible. On occasion, the awards have been turned down because they constituted a political liability to the recipient, just as an ADA award might burden a moderate liberal.

ACA is also involved directly in election campaigns. It provides a number of services to a candidate if he asks for them (and if he, in turn, is approved by ACA). It will, for instance, provide professional campaign managers, money and literature. If the candidate wishes, ACA will give him a public endorsement; if it is felt more prudent to withhold it, then nothing is said. In 1962, ACA provided field men for eleven senatorial and 35 congressional candidates. A total of $28,000 was spent in 16 states by ACA, 2 of the 46 candidates getting direct financial aid. After the election, ACA claimed that it had "actively assisted a total of 184 candidates"—a far larger number than originally stated—and added that 74 percent of all 184 were successful. What must be noted, however, is that most of the 184 seats were "safe" to begin with. A more realistic measurement of ACA's success can be gained by considering the results of the 46 races in which it was actively involved, ostensibly with the hope of providing the extra margin needed for victory. In this case, 25 of the 46—or 54 percent—of the ACA-backed candidates won.

* The *ACA Index* received considerable publicity when General Edwin A. Walker was forced to resign from the Army in 1961. Walker had urged troops under his command in Germany to consult the *Index* before casting their military ballots.

In 1964, ACA stepped up its direct participation in elections. It spent $110,000 in that election year, spread out among 70 individuals or firms in 28 states and the District of Columbia. It also provided speeches (probably written by Frank Kluckhohn) to those ACA-assisted candidates who wanted them. Nor did ACA neglect the Presidential race itself. It published a special *Index* on President Johnson's own voting record, rating him a poor 10 percent.

While admitting with considerable understatement that the 1964 election results "did not equal those of 1960 and 1962," ACA still claimed success in 54 percent of the contests in which it was involved. How this was figured is difficult to say, because 10 of the 14 Senate candidates it backed lost; and in addition, of the 103 House incumbents rated 80 percent or better, 28 went down to defeat while only 1 of the House incumbents rated less than 10 percent was defeated.

ACA operates on a budget of nearly $200,000 per year, and all of what it spends comes in in the form of nondeductible gifts. The largest contributions in 1963–1964, for instance, were from E. Ainsworth Eyre of New York City ($11,400), an Endorser of the Birch Society and a director of W. R. Grace & Company; DeWitt Wallace of Mt. Kisco, New York ($3,500), the founder and editor of *Readers Digest;* three members of the Pew family from the Philadelphia area ($9,000 total); Mrs. Seth Milliken of New York ($2,650), an Endorser of the Birch Society and an adviser to YAF and Liberty Lobby; and Helen Clay Frick of Pittsburgh ($2,000).

Undoubtedly, ACA is here to stay as a fixture on the right, to counterbalance the pulse-taking and behind-the-scenes-string-pulling activities of Americans for Democratic Action on the left. What we will probably see in the future is ACA moving more directly into active politics. Already it has forged close ties with Young Americans for Freedom and the Free Society Association, Dennison Kitchel's organization. Given the opportunity, which means the money, it also plans to jump into the field of electronic data processing, particularly that section dealing with strategy and forecasting. The results of such research and analysis and, indeed, active participation will be enough, it feels, to give its conservative

candidates a sufficient margin to win over any left-wing candidates
who might oppose it.

7

Another group warranting some consideration is Young Americans for Freedom. YAF, as it is known, is an action group open to
all conservatives below the age of forty. It claims 25,000 members
from 1,000 campuses and high schools and in a number of communities. The Washington, D.C., head office has a paid staff of
eighteen.

YAF is an amorphous organization whose ideological position
is difficult to pin down. Members, for instance, do not fall into any
one category: there are neat ones, sloppy ones, bearded ones and
clean-shaven ones; there are Negro, Catholic, Jewish and Protestant members; many are college graduates, others are not.

Generally speaking, a line can be drawn between the libertarians
and the authoritarians in the organization. An uneasy truce is
maintained by both sides. The libertarians oppose statism—the use
of the federal government to promote improvements in living
standards, social conditions and "the general welfare." They talk
in terms of rugged individualism, *laissez-faire,* reduced federal
spending and less restrictive laws. The authoritarians, on the other
hand, emphasize the value of order, law, virtue and experience.
They are more distrustful of the American system and generally
are easier prey to a conspiracy complex. These two attitudes are
common to the entire right; they are only more pronounced here
among the more volatile young.

Both libertarians and authoritarians, however, advocate victory
in Vietnam, the retention of the student loyalty oath, continued
nuclear testing and the withdrawal of aid from Communist satellite
countries. The typical YAFer will be of above-average intelligence,
middle-class in his desires, a fervently pro-Goldwater fan (wearing
his gold "27" pin to prove it—the number referring to the 27
million voters who pulled the lever for Goldwater in 1964), pro-
fraternity (many believe there is a plot afoot to do them in) and a
fan of Noel E. Parmentel, Jr.'s and Marshall J. Dodge III's

recording called "Folk Songs for Conservatives," a spoof of all conservatives.

The conception of YAF can be traced back to 1959 when a bill was introduced into Congress seeking to repeal the loyalty oath required of students accepting federal aid under the 1958 National Defense Education Act. Two Washington, D.C.-based students, Douglas Caddy and David Franke, both of whom were members of the Intercollegiate Society of Individualists, began organizing students to oppose the bill. By January 1960 they had expanded to thirty campuses and had created such a fuss that the bill was shelved. Later on in the year this group began to call for the nomination of Goldwater for Vice-President (Nixon, it was felt, had the Presidential nomination wrapped up). This fell through, but Goldwater, in praising the young for all the work they did on his behalf, suggested that a more permanent organization be established for young conservatives.

Thus, in September 1960, over one hundred young conservatives from forty-four colleges met at William F. Buckley, Jr.'s family home in Sharon, Connecticut, to set up just such an organization. Some who helped draw up the YAF guidelines were not of the young. In particular, there was M. Stanton Evans, author of *Revolt on the Campus* (a prediction of a conservative revival) and Marvin Liebman who acts as a public-relations consultant to a wide variety of right-wing groups.

The document that emerged from the three-day session at Buckley's home has come to be known as "The Sharon Statement." This 400-word manifesto; allegedly drafted by Evans, is printed in full below because it illustrates a number of points germane to the right wing in general today. It reads as follows:

IN THIS TIME of moral and political crisis, it is the responsibility of the youth of America to affirm certain eternal truths. WE as young conservatives, believe:

That foremost among the transcendent values is the individual's use of his God-given free will, whence derives his right to be free from the restrictions of arbitrary force;

That liberty is indivisible, and that political freedom cannot long exist without economic freedom;

That the purposes of government are to protect these freedoms through the preservation of internal order, the provision of national defense, and the administration of justice;

That when government ventures beyond these rightful functions, it accumulates power which tends to diminish order and liberty;

That the Constitution of the United States is the best arrangement yet devised for empowering government to fulfill its proper role, while restraining it from the concentration and abuse of power;

That the genius of the Constitution—the division of powers—is summed up in the clause which reserves primacy to the several states, or to the people, in those spheres not specifically delegated to the Federal Government;

That the market economy, allocating resources by the free play of supply and demand, is the single economic system compatible with the requirements of personal freedom and constitutional government, and that it is at the same time the most productive supplier of human needs;

That when government interferes with the work of the market economy, it tends to reduce the moral and physical strength of the nation; that when it takes from one man to bestow on another, it diminishes the incentive of the first, the integrity of the second, and the moral autonomy of both;

That we will be free only so long as the national sovereignty of the United States is secure; that history shows periods of freedom are rare, and can exist only when free citizens concertedly defend their rights against all enemies;

That the forces of international Communism are, at present, the greatest single threat to these liberties;

That the United States should stress victory over, rather than coexistence with, this menace; and

That American foreign policy must be judged by this criterion: does it serve the just interest of the United States?

It is apparent that YAF has opted for a government of very limited powers, more limited than what the Founding Fathers conceived. According to this statement, the amount of freedom at large in the country varies inversely with the size of the government. Much like Students for a Democratic Society and other groups on the left, YAF equates smallness and powerlessness with goodness. There is no mention here of the government's right to lay and collect taxes, to provide for the general welfare, to regulate interstate commerce, to borrow, coin and regulate money, to make treaties, and so on. From this statement one gathers that the federal government's only job is to protect the country's freedoms through the preservation of internal order, the maintenance of national defense and the carrying out of justice; apparently nothing else is it allowed to do. This viewpoint is a commonly held one among right-wingers; again YAFers seem to express it more clearly than others.

The Statement also wraps itself in the Constitution and then tries to draw into the same folds the concepts of the market economy and economic freedom, a process never attempted by the Founding Fathers. It seems to be an unconscious effort on the part of YAF to weld together the propertarian-anarchic-"objectivism" concepts of Ayn Rand* with the *laissez-faire* economic theories of Ludwig Von Mises and the foreign policy ideas of Barry Goldwater.

Finally, YAF is transfixed by the Communists. Unlike the Birch Society, however, which believes that the only remaining anti-Communists in America are we and thee and we're not so sure of thee, YAF does not lay all the blame for America's failures on internal traitors or "Comsymps." Rather, it reflects the more moderate right-wing viewpoint that the Communists are deadly conspirators whose guile and cunning have duped a number of ignorant and stupid Americans into following their line. YAFers believe that *most* of America's enemies are found outside the country and that only *some* are on the inside. In spite of this moderation, however, YAF is still quick to jump to the conclusion that every shortcoming, every failure and every enemy gain is due to the work of "the Communists."

---

* A cult of worshipers has grown up around Ayn Rand, author of *The Fountainhead, Atlas Shrugged* and other novels. She takes individualism to the extreme of near anarchy. This point of view, coupled with her reverence for private property and objectivism and her hatred of collectivism, emotionalism and pragmatism, is best reflected in the words of her hero, Howard Roark, in *The Fountainhead* (Bobbs-Merrill, 1943, p. 678). Said he: "I came here to say that I do not recognize anybody's right to one minute of my life. Nor to any part of my energy. Nor to any achievement of mine. No matter who makes the claim, how large their number or how great their need. . . . I wish to come here to say that I am a man who does not exist for others."

YAF is an action group above anything else. It has, for instance, set up a Speakers Bureau much like the Birch Society's that will provide speakers for YAF gatherings. Barry Goldwater heads the list and will usually speak free of charge to any major YAF function. There is also a film library where such films as "A Generation Awakes" (featuring William Buckley and Goldwater) and "Operation Abolition" (a thirty-minute "exposé" of Communist agitation during the 1960 anti-HCUA riots in San Francisco) are sold or rented. YAF also cooperates with the Manion Forum, which distributes weekly tapes suitable for YAF-sponsored meetings.

The Young Americans also put out two major pieces of literature. One is *The New Guard,* the first issue of which (1961) boasted:

> Ten years ago this magazine would not have been possible. Twenty years ago it would not have been dreamed of. Thirty-five years ago it would not have been necessary. Today *The New Guard* is possible, it is a reality, and it is needed by the youth of America to proclaim loudly and clearly: we are sick unto death of collectivism, socialism, statism, and other utopian isms which have poisoned the minds, weakened the wills and smothered the spirits of Americans for three decades and more.

The other publication is called *Report on the Left* and confines itself exclusively to talking about the activities of young left-wingers around the nation. Bettina Aptheker is a favorite target and Martin Luther King's "record of affiliation with pro-Communist causes" is trotted out periodically.

YAF attacks the National Student Association—the closest thing students have to a U.N.—with particular bitterness and ruthlessness. It believes that the liberal views of the NSA do not reflect the views of the one million students it is supposed to represent. At the 14th Annual NSA Congress in Madison, Wisconsin, in 1961, YAF made an all-out effort to take it over. Its tactics were reminiscent of Trotskyist tactics in the 1930s. First, busloads of young right-wingers poured into Madison, in far greater numbers than would otherwise have been expected. YAF then began its take-over bid from behind a front called the Committee for a

Responsible National Students Organization. At the Congress itself, YAFers kept in close contact through short-wave radios; orders were issued from a central command post; sympathizers were strategically placed throughout the hall to give the appearance of strength; and at one point a YAFer seized the microphone to make a fiery speech—an act that would probably bring forth tears of nostalgia in an old-time Trotskyist. The YAF takeover did not succeed, even with the aid of senior YAFmen William Buckley and Fulton "Buddy" Lewis III, but the NSA was definitely shaken up and has never been the same since.

YAF has not given up. As the years have passed it has become clear that its goal is nothing short of destroying the NSA. Periodically it puts out a list of colleges that have either withdrawn from or refused to affiliate with the NSA. Sometimes YAF helps this process along. In 1962, for instance, Winfield Scott Stanley, Jr. (now the editor of the Birch Society's magazine, *American Opinion*), and Bill Cotter (who at one time had worked for the National Association of Manufacturers) went to the University of Oklahoma in order to ensure that a referendum on the question of withdrawing from the NSA was passed. The YAF troops were well organized in the area, and by the time the votes were to be cast it was evident that the NSA was to be the loser. YAF had branded it a leftist front and the tag stuck. The students voted two to one to disaffiliate.

In the 1964 elections, YAFers were the Young Turks who provided much of the groundwork that gave the Republican nomination for President to their hero. During the campaign in the fall, it was YAFers who provided the zeal in what was by then considered a near hopeless effort. Even today YAFers will say that Goldwater was defeated because of poor campaign tactics, not for his ideas. Not *all* YAFers believe this, but most do.

Two years before, YAF counterdemonstrated against a group of peace marchers in Washington. The young conservatives carried signs that read: "They're not Red, they're Yellow" and "A Test a Day Keeps the Commies Away." YAFers were also involved in the Dallas U.N. Day incident in which Ambassador Adlai Stevenson was spat upon, shoved about and struck on the head with a placard.

In the spring of 1965, YAF mounted a campaign against the Firestone Rubber Company which was planning to build a $50 million synthetic rubber factory in Roumania. Picket lines were thrown up around many Firestone tire dealers, who, in turn, put the pressure on their superiors to call off the deal, since the salesmen claimed they were losing business to the Goodyear dealers (Goodyear had previously turned down the Roumanian business as not in "the best interests of the U.S."). YAF then began handing out flyers showing Roumanian equipment being used in the war in Vietnam. Apparently Firestone decided to cancel the Roumanian business when the company's officials learned that YAF was planning to set up a "Committee of Slave Labor" in Indianapolis and advertise Firestone's plans during the 500-mile Memorial Day Race. This event is Firestone's biggest yearly advertising splash (most racing cars there use Firestone tires), and the company obviously did not want it ruined by a group of noisy youths who were questioning the company's patriotism.

Perhaps YAF's biggest moment came in 1962 when it held its "World Liberation from Communism" rally in Madison Square Garden. All 18,000 seats were filled, and another 6,000 conservatives were turned away at the door. Many of the featured speakers could not make it: Moise Tshombe, General Edwin Walker, Senator Dodd, David Lawrence, Herbert Hoover, John Wayne and Dr. Edward Teller. But it did not make any difference. Awards were handed out to many right-wing heavyweights: Roger Milliken of the Deering Milliken Company, Senator Thurmond, Ludwig Von Mises, John Wayne (*in absentia*), former Governor Charles Edison of New Jersey, John Dos Passos, Marvin Liebman and M. Stanton Evans.

Wild cheers greeted the mention of Katanga, states' rights, victory over communism and William Buckley; boos were heard at the mention of President Kennedy, the U.N., coexistence and Harvard. L. Brent Bozell, an editor of *National Review* and Buckley's brother-in-law, both bored and electrified the audience during his speech. For much of the earlier part he dwelt on the dangers of Gnosticism, a malady not fully grasped by his audience. But then he stirred the crowd to wild cheers when he called for the following new orders to be issued from Washington:

To the Joint Chiefs of Staff: Make the necessary preparations for a landing in Havana.

To our Commander in Berlin: Tear down the Wall.

To our Chief of Mission in the Congo: Change sides.

To the Chief of CIA: You are under instructions to encourage liberation movements in every nation in the world under communist domination, including the Soviet Union itself.

By the time YAF's hero mounted the rostrum to give his talk there were not too many balloons left to let free, not too many streamers left to throw. Nevertheless, they cheered lustily as Goldwater predicted the end of radical liberalism and the dawn of a new conservative renaissance. Receipts for this rally totaled $80,000, more than YAF's 1960–1961 budget. Hopes were running so high that some YAFers were talking of renting Yankee Stadium.

But it was not to be. For a number of reasons, not all of them clear, YAF has become atrophied in the past few years. Part of the reason has been due to Goldwater's defeat in 1964. Many conservative hearts were broken over the poor showing. Also, it is questionable how much farther YAF could grow on the campuses beyond the 5 to 10 percent of students who make up the conservative fringe. Although there are many more conservatives on campuses than that, the others are not interested in politics and do not want to take part. YAFers often forget that fully 70 percent of all students are apolitical. Undoubtedly, YAF has also failed to grow because students have been repelled by the ruthless, Trotskyist-like tactics it employs.

In spite of these problems, YAFers see hope for the future. They believe that YAF has proved that there is a legitimate place for the conservative viewpoint in America (which they say was not so prior to 1960). They see YAF as the instrument to keep the conservative dialogue alive and growing and as a body that continually offers new ideas for evaluation. Lastly, they view YAF as a positive benefit to the two-party system, giving hope to the conservatives within, thus keeping them from breaking away into third-party splinters out of sheer frustration.

8

Birchers and Others

1

The largest of all right-wing groups is the John Birch Society. It has been on the scene only since 1958, and for all but the first two years of its existence it has been subjected to a constant and withering barrage of criticism from all quarters. Whenever brickbats are to be thrown at the right in general—whether in a spirit of fairness or with malice aforethought—the John Birch Society invariably catches the brunt of the onslaught. It has been called an example of "warmhearted main-street vigilantism," a group that turns responsible criticism of the Communists into a dirty joke, an organization that diverts the nation into a game of Patriots and Traitors, and many things much worse.

The question naturally arises, then, why is it the subject of such abuse; why do its enemies attack it so vehemently; and why is it defended so tenaciously by its friends?

To begin to understand why this is so, it must be appreciated that a Bircher is quite different from every other individual on the right. To be sure, there are variations and degrees of "Birchers" in other organizations; a Birch Society member is just the superior example of the species.

The Society is a direct spiritual descendant of those right-fundamentalist groups—the Barn-Burners, Know-Nothings, Townsendites, America Firsters, etc.—that have always been a part of the American political scene. In this sense, the Society is not a new phenomenon, just a current one that must be understood as our predecessors tried to understand the phenomenon in their day. Like all these right-fundamentalist groups, the Birch Society stands directly between the racist and armed, or "untouchable," right and the "semirespectable" right.

There are five characteristics that distinguish Birchers from all other individuals on the right. First of all, their image of America and the world is wholly conspiratorial. They believe that they live in a world in which they are spied upon, plotted against, persecuted, betrayed and undoubtedly destined for total ruin. They assume that there are always solutions capable of producing victories, and when none are found the blame is placed on a conspiracy of evil men and their dupes. How else can it be, they ask, when America is the most powerful nation in the world? Virtually every facet of life is seen as part of this conspiracy. To give but one example from my own experience, I recall that on one visit to the Society's head office in Belmont, Massachusetts, I mentioned to a secretary as she was driving me from the office to the warehouse that the roadwork being done in front of the head office must be a bother to those inside. My remark was by way of idle conversation, but she replied without a trace of a smile on her face: "Yeah, it's all part of the conspiracy."

Second, Birchers refuse to believe in the integrity and patriotism of their fellow Americans. All institutions—the President, Congress, State Department, Supreme Court, the churches, business, the unions, civil rights groups—are attacked with extraordinary bitterness as part of the conspiracy. Through Birch eyes, these groups are seen as more a threat to America's freedom than external groups such as the Soviet Union and Red China.

Third, they reject the political system as a betrayal of truth, as a compromise of principle and as a circus to divert the people. They see the country so rotten with internal subversion that there is little hope left for its salvation.

Fourth, they reject even the most minimum programs dealing with the current social, economic and international problems. In fact, they reject virtually every program put into effect over the last thirty-five years. Yet their own *positive* program advocates nothing more than the repeal or removal of things—the end to the income tax, foreign aid, NATO, Social Security, the United Nations, and so on.

Finally, they advocate, among other things, the use of dirty tactics to change the situation, tactics that are entirely alien to the American political tradition.[1]

They differ from the racists, on the one hand, because they have no exclusive fixation about Catholics or Jews (indeed, right-fundamentalism is not the exclusive domain of Protestants but includes Catholics and Jews as well); and on the other hand, they differ from the "semirespectable" right and conservatives in that the latter accept the recent past (even though they may not like it) and acknowledge the good intentions of their political opponents and refuse to believe that all acts are part of a conspiracy. Furthermore, Birch criticism is seldom presented within the framework of rational discourse and civic responsibility. They are not interested in learning through the exchange of ideas; they insist that knowledge is a one-way street.

The Birch Society is the product of prosperity, not hard times. Its members, therefore, are not motivated by immediate needs but by a vast unease, an inner frustration that cannot be defined precisely. A member of the Society, for instance, is likely to be most sensitive to changing social mobility particularly if he believes that he himself is sliding down the social scale. He would prefer to perpetuate the distinctions of caste and class rather than take his chances in a shifting, amorphous society. In a traditionally rootless environment such as ours, he seems to be in a desperate search for secure identity. For instance, he seems tormented by the possibility that his own loyalty to the country may be questioned. Since an ancestor, or perhaps even he himself, gave up his birthright to move to America, he feels a compulsion to prove that he has cast off the shackles of the old and is a 100 percent true, loyal American. He is expressing rootlessness at its most desperate stage.

Nor is a man moving up the social and economic ladder immune to Birch Society appeals. This type of individual often tends to exaggerate the causes that made him successful, fearing that change will not only alter the conditions that allowed him to move up but that change will destroy the ladder itself, dropping him back to where he was.

In truth, then, Birchers can be anyone; they are not drawn from any one stratum of society. They can be rich on the way down, rich on the way up, poor on the way down or poor on the way up, white or Negro, Catholic, Jew or Protestant. The Society definitely is not made up solely of disgruntled WASPs, as is so commonly thought. There are an extraordinary number of Catholics (usually the more doctrinaire variety who oppose, for example, their Church's moves toward ecumenicalism), some Jews (particularly the more orthodox ones) and some Negroes (usually middle class, who see the civil rights movement as promoting individuals who might one day constitute a threat to their own jobs).

The difference between a Bircher and a Klansman is important. Outside of ideology, a Bircher can be found anywhere in the social and economic spectrum and is—or feels he is—in a state of flux. A Klansman, on the other hand, feels he is trapped between the Negro below him and the white power structure above him. I never met a really rich Klansman (although many wealthy individuals contribute to the Klan) nor one that had been successful before he joined the organization. This, of course, is not true among Birchers.

There is also the element of the provincial rebelling against the cosmopolitan in the average Bircher. Any shift away from the provincial—and few Birchers think of themselves as cosmopolitan—is resisted fiercely. The migration to the cities, the congressional and statewide reapportionment, the increasing interest by the federal government in the problems of the cities, all have tended to heighten the Bircher's sense of frustration, since he believes that all true American values are nurtured in the countryside—independence, integrity and honesty, among others. A Bircher also tends to be a Fundamentalist. He takes his Bible and the Constitution literally; he thinks, acts and dresses in an orthodox manner; he demands absolute conformity in all spheres of endeavor; and any deviation from the norm is seen not only as an illness in society but as a threat to the very meaning of his existence.

Collectively, the Birchers view the whole world around them as so horrendous that they subconsciously refuse to face it. Like the man who kicks the cat because he cannot face up to his wife, Birchers lash out at every cat in sight. Indeed, their hostility and frustration are so intense that the thought is raised that Birchers subconsciously hate the entire country. One hesitates to suggest such a possibility were it not for considerable evidence before us.

In December 1958, Robert H. W. Welch, Jr., an ex-candy manufacturer, met with eleven other men in an Indianapolis hotel. For two days he delivered a monologue on world affairs. It was taken down on tape and soon thereafter was published as the John Birch Society's *Blue Book*. It was at this time that Welch proposed the formation of the Society, to be named, he suggested, after an army captain and Baptist missionary who was killed shortly after the end of World War II by the Chinese Communists. To Welch, John Birch was the first victim of the cold war.

Communism, Welch told his audience, "is wholly a conspiracy, a gigantic conspiracy to enslave mankind; an increasingly successful conspiracy, controlled by determined, cunning, and utterly ruthless gangsters, willing to use any means to achieve its end." (Russia, he said, became our ally in World War II so that it would be in a better position to infiltrate us.) He sees the conspiracy as having been so successful that Norway, Finland, Iceland, Bolivia, Venezuela, India, Indonesia and a number of other countries outside the satellite camp are "for all practical purposes" in Communist hands. He believes that western Europe is so far down the road to collectivism that it could be taken by telephone anytime the Soviets wished. America, according to Welch, maintains "at least thirty huge communist espionage rings" that are paralyzing the people and destroying their will to resist. "The communist stranglehold on the economic life of Hawaii [then still a territory]," he said, for example, "is so great that it constitutes virtual political control as well." To grab continental America, he added, the Soviets will not need to invade; the country will soon be so softened up that the *coup de grâce* will be nothing more than a "mopping-up" operation. America, he concluded, has been supporting the international Communist conspiracy for many years and constitutes the backbone of its strength.

"You may think I am an alarmist," said Welch with considerable understatement to his listeners. "Frankly, I am."[2]

Most Birchers agree with this view; they would argue only over minor details. One member of the Society with whom I spoke expressed a similar viewpoint in light of current events. Soviet Russia, he said, pushes forward until pressure is built up, then backs off until the pressure eases. Then it advances once again. The State Department, he said, is aiding and abetting this process, first, because there are those in the department who are soft on Communists and, second, because they are afraid to act "lest Russia *do* something, like drop the bomb." He believes that, as a result, America's foreign policy is reactive rather than bold and creative.

"If we had *won* the war in Korea," he said, "by bombing China and fighting her, there would be no Vietnam now." Why not fight China, he asks? "We are scared of what she *might* do but are too scared to be bold and aggressive. So we never know what she actually *will* do. We are scared by phantoms. How do we know that China isn't a hollow shell? Are we so certain that Russia would come to her aid? Russia would probably be delighted to see China knocked into a cocked hat. In the meantime, nibble, nibble, nibble until today we have in essence a government much like Russia's—authoritarian, centralized, bureaucratic, socialistic—everything but the concentration camps."

John Rousselot, the articulate ex-congressman who now runs the Society's West Coast office, speaks of other problems. He sees the civil rights movement as being dominated by leftists and the legislation on its behalf as establishing a privileged minority. He defends Rhodesia, since in his estimation most of the remaining countries in the world are too willing to accept left-wing governments. In the United Nations, he says, the Communists exercise an inordinate amount of control over the committees. The organization, he believes, is being used by the Soviet camp to prevent any decisive actions against its aggressions.

Welch proposed to his eleven listeners in Indianapolis a number of remedies to this "alarming" state of the world. First, he proposed to establish *American Opinion* reading rooms throughout the nation (350 have been set up to date), stocked with anti-Communist literature. There would be a strict limitation on the taking out of books "so as to avoid too much loss through communist sabotage." Then he would distribute *American Opin-*

ion (formerly *One Man's Opinion*) as widely as possible. *National Review* should be in every fraternity house, the *Dan Smoot Report* should be in every physician's and dentist's office. *Human Events* in barbershops and airplane magazine racks. He would support the radio shows of Dean Manion and others, and put his weight into the political scales and harness the "letter-writing weapon" of "a million truly dedicated and controlled supporters." He would organize fronts, said Welch, "little fronts, big fronts, temporary fronts, permanent fronts, all kinds of fronts." Finally, he said, he proposed the use of dirty tactics—the innuendo, the "exposure," the "bombshell" and "shock tactics"—to jolt the American public into a state of awareness. "Join your local PTA at the beginning of the school year," he advised his followers just like any other public-spirited citizen, but then added, ". . . and go to work and take it over."

"This is no cream-puff war we are in," he told his eleven rapt listeners, "and the stakes involved are not those of a pillow fight."

Welch confuses his readers somewhat in the *Blue Book*. In the beginning of the book he says that the only enemy is "the communists and we do not intend to lose sight of the fact for a minute." Then, toward the middle, he talks of "turning our searchlight on . . . hazy characters and their even hazier activities." His own term for someone he thinks is a Communist but fears to say so lest he be hit with a libel suit is "Comsymp," now a very popular word with nearly everyone on the right. Finally, toward the end of the book, Welch writes: "The greatest enemy of man is, and always has been, government." (Welch is of the opinion, for instance, that "ambitious men with criminal tendencies naturally gravitate into government.") Thus it is clear that a Bircher has many precedents for striking out indiscriminately at everything he dislikes.

Welch believed that a "hardboiled, dictatorial and dynamic boss" had to lead the new organization. Not surprisingly, he had himself in mind. As he has set it up, his John Birch Society is a monolithic organization, semi-secret, operating under completely authoritative control at all levels, and subject to "smoothly functioning direction from the top." There is no internal democracy because, as Welch wrote: "Democracy is merely a deceptive phrase, a weapon of demagoguery and a perennial fraud." Prospective members of a chapter are *asked* to join and can be fired with absolutely no recourse or explanation. Welch has no intention of turning the Society into a collection of debating clubs. Recently the Society has been wracked with dissension. Because there is no machinery for the redress of grievances, Welch has found himself tied down with disciplinary problems which only he is authorized to resolve.

The founder and absolute boss of the John Birch Society is of particular importance because it is the stamp of his ideas and attitudes that have made the Society what it is today. Welch was born in 1899 in North Carolina and entered the University of North Carolina at the age of twelve. He then went on to Harvard Law School and the Naval Academy (where he spent only two years). For many years thereafter he was a vice-president of a candy manufacturing firm in the Boston, Massachusetts, area. In a biographical sketch written in the third person he acknowledged "one wife, two sons, a Golden Retriever dog and 14 golf clubs— none of which he understands but all of which he loves."

He left the candy company in 1956 and has had no connection with it since. By that year Welch had become sufficiently alarmed by the Communist menace that he decided that direct action was the only course remaining for Americans who cared. Previously he had sought the Republican nomination for lieutenant-governor of Massachusetts, and in 1952 he had ardently supported the candidacy of Robert A. Taft. Both his own and Taft's failures only fortified his opinion that the world was fast slipping into the collectivist morass of the Communists and "one-worlders." From 1956 to 1958 Welch studied the "conspiracy"; he came to the conclusion that the many anti-Communist groups in America were ineffective because they allowed internal differences of opinion to exist and they relied on "democratic" procedures to get things done. He concluded that only through dynamic personal leadership could the Red "tide" be rolled back. All this led up to the fateful meeting in Indianapolis in 1958.

Welch is a short, white-haired man who in private is gentle and thoughtful but in public is brusque, short-tempered and even rude.

He is nervously energetic and will often put in sixteen to twenty hours of work a day. On occasion he will work through the night, his office staff in Belmont being greeted in the morning by their bleary-eyed, stubble-chinned boss. Welch likes to foster this image as a hard worker, and in the main it is true. He is constantly on the move—flying back and forth over the country, writing, dictating, issuing orders, making speeches, planning future moves and investigating previously unexplored areas of "the conspiracy." But on at least one occasion the whistle has been blown on him. A janitor in the building, going about his nocturnal duties, reportedly once discovered the founder sound asleep on an air mattress in his office.

He is not without a sense of humor. Once while he was in India he had someone write a memo to his staff in Sanskrit. He was pleasantly surprised upon his return to find that the message had been translated and the orders carried out. His office is on the ground floor of one of the three Society buildings in Belmont. One wall is lined with an estimated two thousand books—a passion with him, especially poets—and on another wall, facing his desk, hangs a large map of the world. Behind his desk are framed pictures of his heroes: General Douglas MacArthur, Senator Joseph McCarthy and Captain John Birch.

Welch is an inveterate public speaker, but he does not appreciate an audience that coughs or makes any other noises. Sometimes when he believes that the crescendo has reached a particular peak, he will halt his speech and accuse the noisemakers of being part of a "dirty communist trick." His hatred of the press is ill-concealed. He believes that they twist his views out of shape and print only the most uncomplimentary pictures of him. Once he told some fellow-Birchers, who were surrounded by the press, to keep silent because they were "among enemy ears."

As absolute ruler of the Society who takes orders from no one—not even his twenty-five-man Council of Advisors—every view of the Society's is in reality Welch's; in his own words, "we are not going to have factions developing on the two-sides-to-every-question theme." Some of these views should be noted. In the July–August 1965 edition of *American Opinion* he had this to say:

On Selma: . . . a horde of termites from all over the country, led by half-crazed ministers and professors, swarmed over the small town of Selma, Alabama, in typical demonstration of Communist activism.

On the Supreme Court: The theory that the Warren Court is working for a domestic, as distinct from foreign, dictatorship becomes less tenable every day.

On the object of Medicare: . . . to destroy the independence and integrity of American physicians [which] will inevitably create a "pressing shortage" of physicians and nurses. Communist provinces are sure to have a surplus of medical workers they will be glad to export to the United States to relieve the "shortage."

On the Kennedy assassination: . . . the *Worker* was certainly indiscreet when it nominated Earl Warren for the cover-up job before he was appointed to head an illegal and un-Constitutional Cheka.

On deGaulle: . . . the real advancement of the plot of the Communist Conspiracy against Europe clearly comes from President deGaulle himself.

On Vietnam: No action really detrimental to the Communists is conceivable, or even *possible,* so long as Rusk, McNamara and Katzenbach remain in power. . . . The important point is that Americans can expect *only* defeat so long as they are commanded by their enemies.

In the *Blue Book,* Welch wrote: "I had rather have for America, and I am convinced America would be better off with, a government of three hundred thousand officials and agents, every single one of them a thief, than a government of three million agents with every single one of them an honest, honorable, public servant. For the first group would only steal from the American economic and political system; the second group would be bound in time to destroy it."

One issue of the Society's *Bulletin* carried the following diagram of what Welch and most other Birchers believe to be "the Liberal mind":

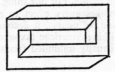

Other writers for the Birch Society follow these trains of thought. W. Cleon Skousen, for instance, an ex-FBI man and a former police chief of Salt Lake City (later fired by Mayor J. Bracken Lee), believes as does Welch that the West Coast Communist newspaper, *People's World,* is a key transmission belt in the Communist conspiracy. In other words, orders are issued from afar to *People's World,* which then, through its news stories, issues the marching orders and current Marxist line to such publications as *Time, Newsweek* and *The New York Times.*

Another writer until recently was Revilo P. Oliver (it can be spelled backwards as well), a classics professor at the University of Illinois at Urbana. In the summer of 1966 Oliver was pressured into resigning from the Society and its Council because of his anti-Semitic views. Previously Welch had described him as "an authentic genius of the first water, *and quite possibly the world's greatest living scholar."* Oliver looks and acts like a tea planter. He is a large man with a flat face, a mustache, swept-back hair and bad teeth.* His dress and manners are impeccable. Often at the sight of a female he will bow from the waist and sweep his hat past the ground. He has a deep, mellifluous voice and a way of intimidating those he deems inferior by quoting long passages in Latin. He once described himself as a "monarchist." One academic acquaintance remembers seeing him by chance at the local veterinarian's. The vet, holding out a bottle of pills, was suggesting to the distinguished classics professor that he give his dog one or two tablets in the event the animal showed any further signs of emotional disturbance.

Oliver created a considerable stir in 1964 when he wrote two long articles in successive issues of *American Opinion* called "Marxmanship in Dallas," in which he argued that President Kennedy was killed by The Conspiracy because he was falling

* Oliver is an outspoken opponent of fluoridation. He wrote in the April 1965 issue of *American Opinion:* "Categorical proof of direct damage to the human organism is hard to obtain. For one thing, the Department of Health, Education and Welfare makes every effort to prevent or suppress honest research on the subject and, of course, it accomplishes a great deal. Since the Department is now milking American taxpayers at the rate of five billion dollars per year, it has virtually unlimited funds for bribery, intimidations, and smears."

behind schedule in a Communist timetable for taking over the United States. Oliver wasted very few words of sympathy for the then recently assassinated President. Kennedy, he wrote, "procured his election by peddling boob-bait to the suckers." The late President also "in close collaboration with Khrushchev, staged the phony 'embargo' that was improvised both to befuddle the suckers on election day in 1962 and to provide for several months of cover for the steady and rapid transfer of Soviet troops and Soviet weapons to Cuba for eventual use against us." Finally, he wrote: "And if the international vermin succeed in completing their occupation of our country, Americans will remember Kennedy while they live, and will curse him as they face the firing squads or toil in a brutish degradation that leaves no hope for anything but a speedy death."[3]

The best-known Birch view of all, however, and the one that catapulted the Society into the limelight, is Welch's statement that ex-President Eisenhower is a "dedicated, conscious agent of the communist conspiracy." This statement first appeared in Welch's book *The Politician* (also known as the *Black Book* because of its cover), which is exclusively concerned with the public life of Dwight Eisenhower and how he, supposedly as Moscow's little helper, singlehandedly turned the country into a Soviet appendage. According to Welch, Eisenhower—whose motivation, he conceded, was "more ideological than opportunistic"—was a "fanatic" because his mother was a Jehovah's Witness; his brother, Milton, was actually "Dwight Eisenhower's superior and boss within the Communist Party"; Welch called John Foster Dulles "a communist agent"; Allen Dulles, as head of the CIA, he called "the most protected and untouchable supporter of communism"; and Chief Justice Warren he labeled as "an extreme left-wing socialist as well as a consummate hypocrite."

Welch believes that these views were first attacked by the West Coast Communist newspaper, *People's World,* which was followed soon thereafter by attacks from *Time* and the *Saturday Evening Post.*

The Society's founder claims that *The Politician* was originally a private letter to friends that in no way was intended to reflect the views of the entire Birch Society. But because so many people believe that Welch *is* the John Birch Society and that his private views cannot be separated from his public ones, Welch felt he had to counter the outcries over his opinion of Eisenhower by publishing the letter as a book in 1962. "Read it and judge for yourself," said the full-page ads in many of the nation's leading newspapers. An eight-dollar price tag was placed on this extraordinary document (500 pages long, 200 of which are notes).

But what Welch did not tell his readers is that the published version was not the same document as the original letter. Much of the material had been altered. For instance, the damaging phrase "dedicated, conscious agent of the communist conspiracy" appears nowhere in my edition, part of the sixth printing. I understand from those who own copies of the first five printings that theirs are similar to mine—that none of them read as the original. Other alterations are readily evident. Milton Eisenhower, we learn, is no longer "Dwight Eisenhower's superior and boss within the Communist Party," but his "superior and boss within the whole Left wing Establishment"—a considerable backing off from the original charge. Eisenhower's "fanaticism" having stemmed from his mother's religion, we find, is entirely omitted.

Perhaps the second best-known statement Welch made in his letter was: ". . . there is only one possible word to describe his [Eisenhower's] purpose and his actions. The word is treason."[4] In my version it reads: ". . . it is difficult to avoid raising the question of deliberate treason. For his known actions and apparent purposes certainly suggest the possibility of treason to the *United States,* no matter how he may rationalize it to himself as loyalty to an international dream."[5]

Welch finds himself in a bind because of his anti-Eisenhower statements. As the absolute boss and infallible anti-Communist leader he cannot admit to being wrong without losing considerable face and seriously damaging the cause. Thus his rank and file are stuck with all his pronouncements—public and private—and many do not like it. *The Politician* has been repudiated by the Birch Society Council and by nearly every Bircher that I met; yet the stigma that because this is what Welch thinks this is what *all* Birchers think cannot be erased. Birchers are in much the same position as were members of Moral Re-Armament during the late

1930s. When the founder, leader, prophet and, with his death, the saint of the movement, Frank Buchman, said in an unguarded moment "I thank heaven for a man like Hitler," his followers could not reject the statement because to do so would have destroyed the infallibility of the man and would have discredited the movement's claim of being "superior" and "close to God." Thus Birchers cannot renounce Welch because it would be a tacit admission that perhaps their mission is not divine nor guided by a man of destiny.

One of Welch's pet theories is known as the "principle of reversal," a tactic the Communists are supposed to use to good effect against the free world. Scott Stanley, the editor of *American Opinion,* described it to me as "one step backwards and two steps forward." In other words, when the Communists seem to be retreating they are actually softening up the West for a major advance. More commonly, the theory translates out as things being just the opposite from what they appear to be. Thus Eisenhower is a Communist because he appears to be so American. Welch believes, for instance, that Boris Pasternak's novel, *Dr. Zhivago,* was actually pro-Soviet and that the Russians persecuted the author intentionally in order to stir up interest in the West where it would be read. Stanley, for instance, views the Hungarian Revolution in the following manner: "Russia set up the Revolution . . . they knew it would happen. They let the Revolution take place and held off until they saw we wouldn't move. Then they crushed it. The Russians now know we won't go into other countries to save them." He told me this in the fall of 1965 at a time when the United States was in the process of substantially increasing its commitment to South Vietnam.

Carried to its logical conclusion, this principle of reversal convicts all Birchers of being Communists. More important, though, it serves as a convenient escape hatch for all acts in the world that do not fit the Birch view of things.

Welch claims to be an expert on communism who documents his material with the care of a true scholar. "I have a fairly sensitive and accurate nose in this area," he wrote in the *Blue Book.* Yet both his scholarship and knowledge are constantly under attack as shoddy and illogical. Three major examples should suffice. Welch, for instance, claims that before Lenin died in 1924 he laid down to his followers a strategy of Communist conquest. Paraphrased and summarized, Lenin is supposed to have said: "First we will take East Europe. Next, the masses of Asia. Then we will circle that last great bastion of capitalism, the United States of America. We shall not have to attack; it will fall like overripe fruit into our hands." Harry and Bonaro Overstreet, in their book *The Strange Tactics of Extremism,* point out that there is no evidence whatsoever of Lenin ever having laid down this strategy. With mild drollery, the Overstreets wrote: ". . . we leafed through Lenin's *Selected Works* to confirm our conviction that nothing of the type appeared there." They went on to say that neither those who had read Lenin's *Complete Works* in Russian nor research scholars at Stanford nor the Curator of the Slavic Room at the Library of Congress nor ex-Communist Louis F. Budenz could recall having seen it in any of Lenin's works. The Overstreets go on to suggest that perhaps Welch had not read his Lenin and that his "leading anti-Communist" scholars, upon whom Welch relies for much of his information, were not up to the mark.[6]

In October 1961 Welch charged in a speech that "about 3 percent of the Protestant clergy could now be described as Comsymps." This worked out to approximately 7,200 individuals at the time. Later he claimed that one half of 1 percent of Roman Catholic priests were Comsymps. That figured out to be 273 priests. Welch provided no names or proof.

The *Pilot,* the official newspaper of the Roman Catholic archdiocese in Boston, challenged Welch to name the priests and promised to print the names and charges. A number of Protestant groups issued a similar challenge. In a letter to Monsignor Francis J. Lally, editor of the *Pilot,* Welch admitted that the figures had been "pulled out of a hat," expressing surprise that anyone would expect him to name names.[7] Yet such backtracking has not prevented Welch from making charges anew, particularly toward the Protestant clergy who have no single body to answer for them. The 3 percent figure so handily used by Welch was first brought into play in 1953 when J. B. Matthews, a leftist turned rightist, wrote an article in *American Mercury* magazine in which he said that 3 percent, or 7,000, Protestant churchmen had served the "Kremlin conspiracy." This article created a storm of protest among church leaders and eventually led to Matthews' resignation from Senator McCarthy's Permanent Committee on Investigations. To Welch, because an "expert" such as Matthews says 3 percent, then it *is* 3 percent—in 1953 or 1961 or possibly even today. The percentage apparently never needs to be revised, perhaps because it is never proved.

Lastly, note should be taken of the Birch Society's "Scoreboard," an annual tally and analysis of all the countries in the world, showing the percentage of Communist control in each. In the July–August 1965 *American Opinion* we read that the United States was 60–80 percent Communist in that year, up from 20–40 percent in 1958 (at that rate, the country will be 100 percent Communist by 1969). Britain was also 60–80 percent Communist in 1965; Iceland, a NATO partner, was 80–100 percent; so were Kenya, Syria, Egypt, Venezuela and Bolivia.

What disturbs many who read these "Scoreboards" is, first, no experts are quoted except Revilo P. Oliver, a classics scholar, and "our correspondents on six continents." Therefore there is no way to judge the authoritativeness of the news. Nor is there any explanation of how these percentage figures were arrived at or what they mean. Scott Stanley explains that, in the case of America being 60–80 percent Communist, if the Communist Party launched an all-out effort, they could control 60–80 percent of the country. It does not mean, he said, that 60–80 percent of Americans are Communists, rather that that many would succumb to the Communists under pressure. Reed Benson, the Society's Washington, D.C., representative and the son of ex-Secretary of Agriculture Ezra Taft Benson, told me that the degree of communism in the country is decided by Welch and six or seven of his friends. Benson believes that Welch is the foremost authority on communism in the world.

Scoreboard percentages seem to be too loosely applied. The 20-point spread between 60 and 80 percent, for instance, represents nearly 40 million Americans. For one who claims to have "a fairly sensitive and accurate nose in this area," Welch has consistently refused to prove his olfactive talents to the American people.

But so much for theories, ideas and attitudes. If they do not fit together too well and there are gaps here and there, it makes no difference because what really motivates a Bircher most of all is action. ACTION.

Welch gives the orders, a steady stream of them. They are issued to the fifteen Major Coordinators, who pass them on to the sixty Coordinators, who in turn feed them to the Section Leaders, Chapter Leaders and the approximately sixty thousand members of Welch's army. The orders come thick and fast.

Set up some fronts. Any name will do: College Graduates Against Educating Traitors at Government Expense, for instance, or Committee to Warn of Arrival of Communist Slave Labor Goods on the Local Business Scene, or Support Your Local Police, or Truth About Civil Turmoil (TACT), or Committee to Impeach Earl Warren, or Committee to Investigate Communist Influence at Vassar College, or Committee Against Summit Entanglements. Put them to work educating the people. Hold a "card party": have your chapter members go into the local store selling, say, Bulgarian wicker baskets and secretly distribute cards among the shelves reading, "Buy your communist products at ——." Go out and heckle a few Comsymp speakers. Spread yourselves among the audience so that no one will realize you are working together. Ask embarrassing questions. Boo when they mention President Roosevelt, the U.N. or Medicare.

Write letters praising the radio programs of Dean Manion, Kent Courtney and Dan Smoot. Write to your congressman and ask why the Pentagon is muzzling the military; thank Senator Thurmond for his support in this campaign. Farley rated Truman among the great Presidents; write him. Write United Airlines and tell them to take the U.N. seal off their planes. Send postcards. We have some that say: "The UN—get US out!" or perhaps you would prefer one that said: "The house that Hiss built." If Ike is going to a summit conference, send him a telegram: "Dear President Eisenhower, If you go—don't come back!"

Get to work in your community and take over the running of the

library, the school board, the PTA or the Police Benevolent
Association. If you cannot control them, harass them. Try the
school board this month since attendance is low in the summer.
Boycott UNICEF cards. Get *your* church out of the National
Council of Churches. Call for the reintroduction of the Bricker
Amendment. Try common stocks or gold in Canada as a hedge
against inflation. Distribute the Warren Impeachment Packet—a
$2.45 value for only $1. Read one of our approved books. We are
pushing *The Kohler Strike* by Sylvester Petro. Make sure your
library has it.

Hire a plane and have it drag a trailer—reading "GET US
OUT"—over the crowd at, say, the Michigan–Minnesota football
game. Speaking of banners, get your school to fly one reading
"One Nation Under God." As a gimmick, hand out boxes of candy
on which are printed the local "Let Freedom Ring"* telephone
number. Tell the Purex Company what you thought of their TV
program that was sympathetic to Sacco and Vanzetti. Show
"Operation Abolition" or "Communism on the Map" to the local
schoolchildren or ask the American Opinion Speakers Bureau to
send a man down to address the Chamber of Commerce. We can
offer you Colonel Victor J. Fox, Dr. Hans Sennholz or Mrs.
Virginia Shackelford this week or Willis E. Stone next week. "Why
the Communists are Winning World War III" or "The Way Out"
might be good topics. Watch nails. They are being shipped in from
Yugoslavia. We found some in Connecticut. If you disagree with a
newspaper's point of view, threaten to boycott the advertisers,
picket the building, flood them with mail, jam the classified
telephone lines or, better yet, buy the paper out.

* "Let Freedom Ring" is the brainchild of William C. Douglass, a physician from Sarasota, Florida. It is a ninety-second "patriotic message" that can
be heard by dialing certain unlisted telephone numbers in most of the larger
cities throughout the United States. The voice is usually anonymous and the
message is changed every week. Typical of the messages is the one broadcast
in February 1964: ". . . a plan is being developed for the systematic house-
to-house search of the entire United States for arms of any kind. The search
is to be made by the U.S. Army by blocking off five states at a time,
beginning in the western part of the country. The entire civilian population
is to be disarmed by the end of 1965." This information seems to have been
taken bodily from the October 1963 issue of *On Target*. Recently the
telephone company has demanded that those who operate the local LFR
outlets identify themselves in their messages.

Show your colors.* Form a Committee for the Return of Morality to check these American history textbooks that are subversive, particularly those written by that "meritricious hack" Arnold Toynbee or that "eternal sophomore" Oliver Wendell Holmes. Then campaign for the return of the McGuffey Reader. Make sure you have your "Card-Carrying American" card in your wallet. Complain about the Panamanian flag being flown over the Canal Zone. Write to Syngman Rhee in Hawaii; it's his birthday.[8]

And so it goes, day after day, month after month.

I had the chance to meet one target of the Society's wrath. In 1964, the Xerox Corporation planned to underwrite six 90-minute TV specials at a cost of some $4 million dealing with the United Nations. The July *Bulletin* of the Birch Society stated: "Let's begin that campaign [to "get the US out of the UN and the UN out of the US"] by a veritable flood of letters to the officers and directors of the Xerox Corporation. . . ." The article went on to say that they hoped that up to a hundred thousand letters would be sent. The names and addresses of the seven officers and six directors were then listed.

The Xerox official with whom I talked—who prefers to remain anonymous—said that he received over three thousand letters. Most of them came in two waves, one after the July 1964 *Bulletin* article and the other after the February 1965 *Bulletin,* which urged on the members of the Society to new efforts. Apparently the volume of letters was disappointingly low.

Many letters to this particular official were identically mis-addressed because the *Bulletin* had listed the wrong address. Some mail contained letters to other Xerox officials by mistake; others enclosed literature from a number of other right-wing organizations. A few letter writers lambasted Xerox's TV plans but then noted at the bottom how much they liked the product. There were virtually no anonymous letters.

Xerox refused to knuckle under to the pressure and the TV programs went off as planned.

---

* This refers to wearing a red, white and blue "handkerchief" in the breast pocket. This item is actually three pieces of cloth stapled to a cardboard insert to fit the pocket. They are manufactured by a "patriotic" group in Portsmouth, Virginia.

A tabulation of all letters received on the subject—both pro and con—was undertaken by Xerox in 1965. It showed that the corporation received 45,000 negative letters from 11,000 writers and 12,000 favorable letters from as many people. So although the volume of negative letters was heavier, the ratio pro and con of actual writers showed a majority in favor.

The Birch Society is big business. Its monthly overhead in 1966 exceeded $400,000. (Birch staffers are well paid: a Major Co-ordinator, for instance, gets $12,500 a year.) The monthly print-ing bill alone comes to $125,000, and the Society spends $35,000 a year on postage. Total yearly operating expenses for 1965 were near $5 million, dwarfing all other minority groups. But this is not all gravy. In 1965, Welch admitted that he spent nearly $5 million but then confessed that receipts had added up to only $4 million. With a 20 percent deficit such as this, the Society could go broke very quickly. Realizing this, Welch began a crash campaign for additional money under the title "A Stick of Dynamite" (to blast "apathetic minds"). The goal was $3 million to be raised as soon as possible. It has not been reached as of this writing—mid 1967—but not through any lack of trying. Taking his cue from the Republican and Democratic Parties, Welch has been holding $25- and $50-a-plate testimonial dinners all over the country. He has added the twist of a "dine now, pay later" scheme whereby reluctant Birchers pleading poverty have no excuse but to attend. The recent faction fights within many chapters have not helped this effort.

Birch Society strength can be found primarily in three geo-graphical areas. There is a solid core of members in Florida centered mainly in Jacksonville, Palm Beach, Daytona, Sarasota, St. Petersburg and St. Augustine. Texas is the second pocket of strength, with several thousand members in the Houston area alone, another 1,500 in the Dallas–Ft. Worth area and a small concentration surrounding Amarillo. There are teen-age chapters in five Houston high schools. Birch strength is on the increase in the South in general, particularly in those areas where the Citizens' Councils are in decline. Throughout the Midwest there is some strength in Indiana, Ohio, Michigan and Wisconsin. Kansas, Utah,

South Dakota and Washington also have numerous Birch chapters. The worst recruiting grounds of all are the Eastern seaboard, Illinois (particularly Chicago) and most of Appalachia.

The biggest Birch center of all, southern California, deserves special attention. Although membership is secret, there are an estimated 15,000 Birchers in the southern half of the state. They are organized into 1,200 chapters and employ 16 full-time organizers. The San Marino headquarters is Welch's West Coast base and is where the Society's rising number two man, John Rousselot, guides the fortunes of the organization.

These Birchers are a force in California politics. They have infiltrated the Young Republicans, the PTA and various civic committees throughout the area. They were responsible in large part for Rockefeller's defeat in the 1964 primary. The local politicians court them for the extraordinary zeal they possess. Birchers there are dedicated enough to march 5,000 strong through the streets of Los Angeles protesting a major speech by President Kennedy. The state's Attorney General, Stanley Mosk, told of nearly 80 Birchers showing up at a meeting sponsored by some local clubs. They cheered on cue and shouted *"republic!"* whenever the speaker said "democracy." Some Birchers have been so restive at meetings that the police have been needed to restore order.[9]

Why southern California turns a person into a Bircher (or, perhaps, why a Bircher is drawn to southern California) is difficult to answer. Some of the reasons are political, some are not. People come to California at the rate of 2,000 per day every day of the year. This figure represents a 1,000 net increase over departures. Most of the newcomers are in their early thirties and they believe that by coming to California they are leaving their troubles behind. There is a sense of pioneering, the belief of an attractive life awaiting them that accompanies anyone moving into the state. But these people are often naïve and ignorant of the world; they usually are fleeing a small, dull, middle-class town where morals, religion, dress and speech are conventional. These people, therefore, are vulnerable because, in a land where they have few friends, the Birchers offer conviviality, a "clubby" atmosphere, a chance to be a member of an elite.

Since there is no obvious power structure in Los Angeles or in any part of southern California, people tend to form their own independent ones. The Birch Society offers one that promises hard work for the bored, a cause for the agitated, a superficial sense of sophistication and a militancy that breeds loyalty and tenacity. Generally speaking, the women are the workhorses in these groups; the men usually just give the money.

The Bircher in Southern California can attempt to lead what he supposes to be, in his own opinion, a complete "right-wing life." For instance, he probably will read the *National Chronicle* (formerly the *Shasta Valley Chronicle*) or the *Valley News and Greensheet* (a four-day-a-week throwaway newspaper of 150 pages or so); he might attend James W. Fifield Jr.'s First Congregational Church of Los Angeles (ironically, not too far away from left-winger Stephen Fritchman's First Unitarian Church of Los Angeles) or the First Baptist Church of Van Nuys. He would buy his food at Hughes Supermarkets, where Birch literature is available, and his gas from the Richfield Oil Company (because their slogan used to be "give me some of that all-American gas"). He would bank at Joseph Crail's Coast Federal Savings & Loan Association and send his children to either Pepperdine College or the University of Southern California's Research Institute on Communist Strategy and Propaganda, founded by oilman Henry Salvatori.

Because Patrick Frawley, a backer of right-wing causes, is associated with a number of companies, this same Bircher might persuade himself to use only Schick razors, stay in Hilton hotels and watch only Technicolor movies. But he would limit his Technicolor movies to those that starred such right-wingers as John Wayne, Walter Brennan and Rhonda Fleming. More often he would stay home and watch right-winger Raymond Burr in "Perry Mason." Every once in a while he might take the whole family out for dinner to Knott's Berry Farm and Ghost Town in Buena Park. Walter Knott, the creator of this enterprise, also runs the California Free Enterprise Association, the purpose of which is "to sell Americanism back to Americans."

This insulated right-winger would probably buy his books at the local American Opinion Bookstore and his clothes at Oviatt's. He would most likely feed his dog or cat or parakeet Dr. Ross Pet Food, a product of the late D. B. Lewis' Lewis Food Company. Finally, he would make sure he did not miss the daily episode of "Orphan Annie" drawn by Harold Gray, who has been pushing right-wing causes in his comic strip for years.

In time, a right-winger who so surrounds himself could and often does believe that those who do not follow his example are subversive or at least suspect.

A few further comments are necessary on the John Birch Society. One of the most noticeable characteristics of the Society, for instance, is its similarity to the Communist Party of the United States. Both are authoritarian; they organize fronts, set up reading rooms, advocate underhanded tactics; they have internal machinery to purge dissident members (in both cases, the decision of one man), they operate in small units with cover names (Birch Society chapters have four-letter code names), and both try to disrupt political activities from behind the scenes.

The Overstreets point out that the Birch Society unintentionally renders a sevenfold service to the Communists. It creates confusion by its loose and irresponsible use of derogatory labels; it is, as noted, a totalitarian organization; it confuses people by claiming that the Communist threat is mainly internal; it hinders many necessary efforts by labeling them Communist-inspired or Communist-controlled; it is vague about what it wants; it encourages its members to believe that they are acting like responsible citizens when in fact they are parroting the orders of one man; and, finally, whatever solutions it does propose are usually far oversimplified.[10]

Because its philosophy is not sophisticated—indeed, Welch is proud that *American Opinion*, for instance, avoids "eggheadism" —the Society repels the country's youth, because although the young may themselves lack sophistication, they respect it in others. The great bulk of Birch members are over thirty and are decent, honest and loyal Americans but nevertheless frightened and confused. One marked characteristic I encountered among them was their defensiveness. "Why don't you tell the truth about us?" they would ask. "Don't you realize how few people know that this country is a republic and not a democracy?" they would continue.

Birchers have a stock answer to criticism: "The same old smear methods employed by the liberals is used," they will say, "namely, condemn the man and what he stands for but don't dare try to refute his facts." What Birchers fail to grasp is that most Americans do not believe Welch's facts, and furthermore they do not believe it is their job to refute every charge made by the Society. Rather it is the Birchers' job to substantiate the charges to the satisfaction of their critics, which—despite Birch denials—they consistently refuse to do. Birchers still believe that an unsubstantiated charge must be proved false by the accused rather than proved true by the accuser. This attitude qualifies the Birch Society as the vanguard of the new McCarthyism.

Because of its ideas and tactics the Society finds itself totally outside the mainstream of American politics. It is certainly not conservative in the sense Everett Dirksen, Barry Goldwater or William Buckley might use the word. Nor is it in my opinion even reactionary; rather, it seems more an aberration on the political scene, a manifestation of social disquietude that periodically crops up in our history for reasons stated previously. It is so far from the mainstream, for instance, that Welch feels it necessary to tell his rank and file that they need not do anything as a Bircher that offends their conscience—a statement that would not even occur to anyone within the mainstream.

There are three factors that will play a considerable part in shaping the Society's future. One is the authoritarianism of the organization. Although Welch's absolute control may make the Society more effective and keep the Communist infiltrators at bay, it still creates a situation where Hitlerism could sprout up overnight. So far this has not happened, but it easily could, given the lack of checks and balances. Already there are signs that there is considerable internal dissatisfaction with the authoritarianism of the organization.

Second, the forces of bigotry—particularly anti-Jewish and anti-Negro sentiments—are constantly hovering around the edges of the Society (the removal of Revilo Oliver is one manifestation of this). Sometimes bigots join and cause considerable damage before they are purged. The xenophobic, elitist attitude of the members tends to make them sympathetic to racist appeals. A constant vigilance is required to police the Society's fringes. If the guard is ever lowered and the racists take over, it will spell the doom of the Society.

Finally, there is Robert Welch himself, who in many people's eyes constitutes the biggest stumbling block to growth. His unsubstantiated charges and the cavalier way he treats the reputations of other repel those who might otherwise be attracted to the cause. William Buckley put his finger on the Birch dilemma when he wrote: "How can the John Birch Society be an effective political instrument when it is led by a man whose views on current affairs are, at so many critical points, so critically different from their own, and, for that matter, so far removed from common sense?"

Barring any catastrophic change, the Society will undoubtedly be on the scene for many years to come. Two trends will help keep it here. First is the domestic racial situation which, if the past is any indication, will continue to agitate various sections of the population. Those who feel threatened by this change in the status quo will tend to gravitate toward the Society. Second, American foreign policy will undoubtedly continue to be just as frustrating as it has been in the recent past. There will be few clear-cut victories or obvious defeats, just a large gray area of half this and half that. This will continue to be a frustrating situation for many people, and those who cannot take it any longer or who feel the urge to change it will drift into the Society.

Undoubtedly the John Birch Society will profit from both trends.

2

If the Birch Society were not hostile to third-party movements, it would surely throw its support to Kent and Phoebe Courtney's New Orleans–based Conservative Society of America.

Compared to the Birch Society, the CSA is small. Its yearly budget runs to $460,000: the *Independent American,* the CSA's newspaper, published every two months and sold to a claimed 27,000 people (probably on the high side) accounts for $250,000 of the budget; the activities of the CSA itself account for $60,000; and the Associated Pelican Printing Company accounts for the remaining $150,000. The organization has twenty-two employees who, until recently when a new headquarters building was erected, used to work in three nondescript buildings a few miles from the downtown New Orleans business district. The Courtneys are planning to add a fourth operation to their organization: a mass-mailing company called Southern Automated Mailers, Inc. (Motto: "Let SAM do it.") One sidelight of the current organization is the weekly radio edition of the *Independent American* which Kent Courtney claims reaches half a million listeners.

Kent Courtney, the National Chairman of the Conservative Society of America, has been in right-wing politics since 1954. Previously he had taught economics, banking and marketing at Tulane. He served in the Navy during World War II and then worked as a pilot for Pan American World Airways. When Senator McCarthy was censured in 1954, Courtney chaired the New Orleans branch of Ten Million Americans, a movement to circulate petitions opposing the Senate's action. It was also the year Courtney began publishing *Free Men Speak,* later renamed *The Independent American.*

In 1960 Courtney ran for governor of Louisiana on the States Rights Party ticket. Democratic candidate Jimmy H. Davis received nearly 400,000 votes; Courtney received less than 13,000, but he claims he forced Davis to make more conservative promises because he, Courtney, "had all the sheriffs in north Louisiana on my side." Courtney quit the States Rights Party of Louisiana in 1961, claiming that it was a "vest pocket party . . . a caudal appendage of a Democrat by the name of Leander Perez." Since then, Courtney has been a registered Conservative.

The Conservative Society of America was formed in 1961—so legend had it, with eighteen dollars in capital—in order to promote the election of conservative congressmen to office. Indirectly, Senator Goldwater was partly responsible for this because, in the eyes of the Courtneys, his biggest weakness was insisting on calling himself a Republican and not an "Independent Conservative." As long as Goldwater supported the Republican ticket—which included the Courtneys' two arch enemies, Governor Nelson Rockefeller and Senator Javits—there seemed to be little hope for conservatism. The drive for a New Party or Conservative Party—it is called both—received fresh impetus after Goldwater's 1964 defeat. "If

Goldwater had purged the Republican Party of the Liberals,"
wrote Kent Courtney, "such as Rockefeller, Romney and Scranton,
then there would have been no need to establish a new conservative
political party."[11]

Kent Courtney is currently trying to set up independent Conservative Parties in as many states as possible. The immediate goal
is thirty states by 1968. Over half have been set up already in such
states as Florida, Georgia, Missouri, Illinois, Colorado, Washington, New Jersey, Pennsylvania and Kansas. Some of these parties
were set up independently of Courtney's efforts; others, such as the
Conservative Party of New York, will have nothing to do with
him. Nevertheless, Courtney is encouraging them all. Publicly, he
claims no interest in controlling the majority of these new organizations. "My only purpose is to get the conservative movement
going. If Buckley comes along and says 'I am the leader' and the
people follow him, God bless them." He sees his own CSA as "the
Agitprop of the conservative wing."

Physically, Kent Courtney is one of the largest men on the right.
He weighs some 230 pounds, has two chins and an outsized
waistline. Recently he told an audience of which I was a part that
he had lost 35 pounds so he could no longer claim to be "the
biggest patriot around." Courtney has reddish hair, a self-confident
air and a powerful platform delivery. One of his speaking techniques is to encourage audience participation. Whenever the name
of, say, Mrs. Roosevelt is mentioned, the audience boos, when Ike
is mentioned it hisses, and with Goldwater it applauds. Courtney
also uses the "wake-up technique" to good effect, shouting at the
top of his lungs at a key point in his speech. For instance, at a
speech he gave in 1965 to some sixty people in a Baltimore high
school auditorium, he said, his voice soft and persuasive: ". . .
Without hurting the civilians in South Viet Nam, without bombing
North Viet Nam, we could say to our 'allies' who are supplying
our enemies, [here Courtney shouted in shrill tones] *'THESE
SHIPS ARE SUPPLYING OUR ENEMIES; THIS I CALL
TREASON! . . .'*" The entire audience jumped about two inches,
a young YAF placard-carrier off to one side almost fell out
of his seat, and a Birch Society matron, arranging literature in the
lobby, came dashing around the corner to see if anything was

wrong. By this time Courtney had resumed speaking in his normal well-modulated voice.

Among men, Courtney's language often turns pungent. For instance, to me and three or four other men, he expressed his displeasure with a well-known newspaper columnist by saying, "The next time I see [him]"—here Courtney grabbed imaginary lapels and jerked a knee into the air—"I'm going to . . . kick him in the *cajones!*" He also has the gift for the colorful phrase and story, which he often uses in his speeches. The 1960 Republican Vice-Presidential candidate he refers to as "Henry Sabotage"; newspapers, he says, subject Americans to "mass Pavlovian brainwashing every day," particularly, as he told the high school auditorium audience, the Baltimore *"Fun."* His favorite story concerns the Republican elephant and the Democratic donkey, which, he tells us, were two different animals before 1952. "But then they began sleeping together and the product," he said, his arms spread in mock horror, "was wond'rous to behold: the blood line of the ass was stronger so they called it the 'Donkeyphant.' Others called it the 'Elephonkey.' You couldn't tell which end which noise was coming out from. . . ." The same audience laughed and clapped.

Kent Courtney describes his wife as "so far right that the only thing beyond is outer space." Phoebe Courtney is an ebullient, fast-talking woman with braided hair. Her language is almost as colorful as her husband's. She is supposed to order her steaks, for instance, "communist blood red."

Kent Courtney, who is proud to be known as a "professional patriot," has been stumping the country since 1965 trying to arouse interest in a third-party movement. I attended a one-day "Congress of Conservatives," held the day after his Baltimore high school auditorium speech. There were forty-eight others in attendance from Delaware, Maryland, New Jersey, Pennsylvania and New York. The purpose of the congress was to discuss the reasons for and the problems of setting up a third party.

"We're the only party who says we want freedom for America, Cuba, Tibet, etc.," he told his audience. "We want to destroy the Communists and want to live in freedom on our own terms, not on anyone else's! . . ." The American conservative, he went on, "stands today in the center of the political spectrum. To the left are the National Socialists, the Communists, New Deal, Raw Deal, Fair Deal, New Frontier and the Great Society. To the right is anarchy. We conservatives want the minimum amount of laws."

In a one-party state, he said, "there is no two-party press, there is no criticism of goon-ism, there is no criticism of give-aways, there is no criticism of crime, of Democrats and Republicans, of leftists or the press."

Much of the blame for this Courtney puts at the feet of conservatives. "We've been active eating lunches, vigilant in keeping our money in our pockets and brave in retreating from the Communists," he scolded. But, he added, that does not mean conservatives cannot be successful. "Let us examine the statement 'New parties are never successful.' Well, Norman Thomas' Socialist Party was most successful; it never got one electoral vote but it captured both the Democratic and Republican parties with its philosophy."

There are four burning issues, Courtney went on, which the Conservative Party must solve. First, he said, "every American is a slave one day in five because he pays 20 percent in income taxes"; second, he said, there is "treason in high places" that must be rooted out; third, America is financing her enemies, which must cease; and fourth, the "Communist-dominated U.N." must be opposed. "If we don't win," Courtney told his audience, "we're going to be the best educated anti-Communists inside a concentration camp you ever saw."

To educate his conservative legions, Courtney publishes a wide variety of literature. As a third-party advocate, his best-known piece is a sixty-four-page booklet giving many useful tips on how to set up a new political party. Backing it up are slim pamphlets called *Tax-Fax*—the highest number in my possession being No. 67—which give the CSA view of things. For instance, No. 5, entitled "Nixon in '68?" is, according to the subtitle, "An Exposé of the Leftwing Record of Richard Nixon, Possible Presidential Candidate of the Liberal-Controlled Republican Party." Quoting from the *Dan Smoot Report, US News & World Report* and Ralph de Toledano, Courtney pictures the ex-Vice-President as a phony anti-Communist, a civil rights hypocrite and one who would "take a gamble" with America's national security in order to coexist peacefully with the "aggression-crazed" Soviet Union.

"The Income Tax *Can* Be Repealed!" reads *Tax-Fax* No. 15, giving a boost for the Liberty Amendment. "Communist Infiltration in Religion" is the title of *Tax-Fax* No. 31, subtitled "Does the National Council of Churches Speak for You?" Courtney's source material is drawn entirely from right-wing sources such as Myers Lowman's Circuit Riders, Inc., books and articles by Billy James Hargis, Edgar C. Bundy, Fulton Lewis, Jr., and HCUA. *Tax-Fax* No. 65 is called "Treason on the Campus" and asks "will the communists 'infect' your son or daughter?" Courtney's answer is a very firm "yes" in view of the fact that such groups as the DuBois Clubs, Progressive Labor Party and Berkeley student "rioters" are tolerated. What the dedicated anti-Communist can do, suggests Courtney, is to purchase extra copies of *Tax-Fax* ($75 will get you 1,000) and send them to your congressman, senators, your children and relatives in college, professors, regents and members of the local board of education and youth groups.

Both Courtneys are fervent members of the John Birch Society. In fact, Kent Courtney is a chapter leader in New Orleans. On occasion he feels that Robert Welch is too mild. For instance, when I asked him how he felt about the founder's well-known remarks on Eisenhower, he said, "Hell, I pick up where Welch leaves off."

Part of the trouble, says Courtney, "is that people don't believe us when we say that there is a conspiracy. . . . Buckley, for instance, says that the communists are not domestically dangerous, rather the mistakes come from misguided liberals. Well, anyone who knows how to read the reports of the House Un-American Activities Committee [HCUA] and the Senate Internal Security Subcommittee can only come to the conclusion—'Yes, Mr. Buckley, there is a conspiracy.' " He sees a link-up between the civil rights activists and domestic Marxists. "Yes, I do believe you can tell a man by his associates," he told the Baltimore congress. "Blackbirds fly together and redbirds fly together; but recently both the redbirds and the blackbirds have been flying together."

He is particularly annoyed at the FCC's "Fairness Doctrine," which he thinks is not at all fair to him. Painstakingly, he said, "I outline the pro-communism of, say, Dr. Martin Luther King. Immediately the NAACP and other Federally-financed [*sic*] agencies demand equal time at government expense. They call us smearers, liars and fanatics."

Courtney has turned his ire on other targets. "Secretary of Defense McNamara," he told the congress, "will go down in history as 'Secretary of No Defense'!" This remark was greeted by clapping and shouts of "Right!" from the audience. " 'We're no longer losing,' says McNamara. What an inspiring piece of information *that* is!" he added, the audience breaking out into laughter. "De Gaulle," he said, "is a phony Communist and [François] Mitterand is a real Communist!" Later on, when I interviewed Courtney in his old New Orleans office (on one wall hung a portrait of General Robert E. Lee and on his desk were two phones, one of which he referred to as "the hot line"), he said, "There is nothing worse than a man such as Otto Passman who makes fine conservative speeches but then votes for foreign aid. I much prefer a man such as Hale Boggs who says he's a liberal. At least he's not a hypocrite."

Courtney still seems confused over how he should treat Barry Goldwater. Courtney was friendly in 1960, but from 1961 to 1963 there was a coolness. Then he backed the Senator in 1964, although he had his doubts, yet not before he, Courtney, had "nominated" Robert Welch for the Presidency on a third-party ticket. Yet, all in all, Courtney felt that Goldwater did as well as he could in 1964. "The twenty-seven million votes," he said, "is the maximum number of votes you could get for a philosophy. They [the voters] had to fight their way through a fall-out of torn Social Security cards to vote!" But, in retrospect, Courtney is not so sure Goldwater was the best man. Governor Wallace, he told his audience, "was ready to run in thirty-six states if Goldwater had not been nominated." Looking back, he added, "I wish Goldwater had not been nominated."

The man Courtney's Conservative Parties nominate for President in 1968 will tell much of where his parties are headed in the future.

The Congress of Conservatives that I attended brought to light many of the problems this third-party group faces. Besides the usual problems of qualifying for the ballot, building an organization and raising money, there are the hostility from the press, the skepticism of the voter and the "you can'ts" from the pessimists. Robert Schlachter, who ran as a Conservative for governor of New Jersey in 1965, stood up and told the audience that a Conservative Party campaign might be called a "Robinson Crusoe campaign— you think you're all alone on the beach; then you see a footprint. Well, that's us!" Schlachter, for one, has little regard for William Buckley's candidacy for mayor of New York. Buckley, he said, "is the clown of conservatism, the Judas goat. If you are serious, get in there and fight; if you want to play marbles, get out!"

These conservatives are convinced that there is no hope for the Republican Party. "They say the Republican Party is up!" said Schlachter. "But how far more up can you go from the balcony? You must be on the playing field!" Another participant in the Congress was Harold P. Poeschel who runs the New Jersey Conservative Party. He attacked the Republican Party as a "legal ghost" that is "controlled by the internationalists." Poeschel, an insurance agent, ran for governor of New Jersey in the 1965 primary as an "Unreconstructed Republican." He believes that the "international bankers seek to control the world," along with the Council on Foreign Relations. He also believes that the U.S. Army is being trained in counterinsurgency to put down a revolt in America.

In an effort to shake loose Republicans from their party he asked those assembled at the congress: "Which is more important to you, loyalty to your country or loyalty to your party?" When you build in a city, he continued, "you need a wrecking crew as well as a builder." It is high time, he said, for a new party to be built. He then strode to the front of the room and held aloft a few copies of a paperback book, saying that it should be read by all those who are tired of the present two-party alignment. The title of the book was *It is HIGH TIME, the Case for a New Party,* by Harold P. Poeschel.

Courtney has had his problems with anti-Semites. He is smart enough to know that his conservative movement would be dead if they ever came into control. Several years ago he personally wrote to twenty-five people well known for their prejudice toward Jews,

Negroes and other minorities, and told them they were not welcome at an organizational meeting he was planning to hold in
Chicago. Nevertheless, two female anti-Semites showed up and
caused such a scene at the door that Courtney had them thrown
out. On another occasion, a former member of the CSA, W. Henry
MacFarland, Jr., former head of the Nationalist Action League,
became temporary chairman of the Conservative Party in Pennsylvania. When objections were raised because of his biased views,
Courtney tried to get him to back down, which he refused to do.
All ties were broken after two weeks of argument. "MacFarland is
no longer a member of the CSA," said Courtney, "because I
returned his money."

The growth of the Conservative Party movement will depend on
two factors, neither of which will Courtney or his followers have
any control over. The first hinges on the fortunes of the Republican Party. If it collapses in the near future (which it shows no sign
of doing), Courtney may benefit. The second factor hinges on
the John Birch Society, which, in essence, is doing exactly what
Courtney's CSA and Conservative Party movement are doing
except running men for office. As long as the Birch Society stays
away from the hustings, Courtney's organization will fill a need
among right-wingers. If the two become competitors, however, there
seems to be every indication that those who favor this type of
activist-political organization would gravitate to the John Birch
Society because it is larger, richer and better known than Courtney's group. Courtney does not believe the Birch Society will join
the third-party camp. His survival is based on the belief that
more publicity can be garnered quicker and cheaper in an election
than from the corporate promotional efforts of an organization
such as the John Birch Society. This may bring many new recruits
into these Conservative Parties. Courtney, for one, is convinced it
will.

3

The Conservative Party of New York deserves special attention
because it is one of the few conservative groups that is a political

reality. It was founded in 1962 for three major reasons. The first was to move the whole spectrum of New York politics to the right. "We Conservatives quit trying in 1962 to influence the Republican Party from within," said Kieran O'Doherty, one of the Party's founders. "We just couldn't do it." An independent, strong Conservative Party, he said, was the answer. The second reason, hinged to the first, was to eliminate the Liberal Party's leverage by corralling the conservative vote, previously lost or at least dissipated by default. Thirdly, the formation of the Party reflected a reaction to "interest-group politics"—the playing off of one group against another, long a staple of New York and American politics.

The state chairman is J. Daniel Mahoney, a New York City attorney. His associates include David H. Jaquith, the President of the Syracuse Board of Education and an unsuccessful candidate for governor on the Party's ticket in 1962; Suzanne LaFollette, a journalist and the niece of the late Senator Robert LaFollette; Professor Henry Paolucci of Iona College, who ran unsuccessfully against Robert Kennedy and Kenneth Keating for senator in 1964; two writers for *National Review,* Frank S. Meyer and William F. Rickenbacker; and Kieran O'Doherty, an attorney who looks like actor George C. Scott. O'Doherty, who ran unsuccessfully for senator in 1962, was William Buckley's campaign manager during the 1965 mayoralty race.

The Party claims a working strength of 31,000 registered voters, split evenly between New York City and upstate. It claims another 15,000 who work for the Party but have not changed their old registration. Martin Burgess, Jr., the Party's executive director, said that no survey has ever been made of the type of people who join, but in his estimation the average Conservative is a middle-class homeowner, a policeman, a veteran, a Catholic in the city, a Protestant upstate. Conservatives in New York City are not, as many believe, exclusively the WASPs of Manhattan.

For example, in the 1965 mayoralty race, candidate Buckley received 120,549 votes in Queens (or 17.2 percent of those cast in that county), 20,427 votes in Richmond (25.1 percent), 62,988 in The Bronx (13.8 percent), 97,115 in Brooklyn (12.5 percent) and 38,048 in Manhattan (only 7.3 percent, well below the 13 percent overall vote he received).

In the 1966 governor's race, the Conservative Party outpolled the Liberal Party by 2,789 votes. Dr. Paul L. Adams, the Conservative candidate for governor and the dean of Roberts Wesleyan College near Rochester, edged out Franklin D. Roosevelt, Jr., his Liberal opponent. Since the election of governor alone determines the order of precedence on the ballot in New York State, the Conservatives will be placed at least for the next four years on Line C and the Liberals will be dropped to Line D. To hold Line C on the ballot is considered to be of the utmost importance to both minor parties, since they are convinced that such a position affords them the opportunity to exercise a balance of power in the state.

How permanent is the Conservatives' hold on Line C is difficult to say at the moment. Many of the 510,000 votes for Dr. Adams undoubtedly came from that section of the electorate which strongly opposed a referendum seeking to create a permanent Police Review Board in New York City. The Party's militant stand against the Board was consistently pushed throughout the campaign, almost to the exclusion of other issues. One result was that the Conservatives outpolled the Liberals in their own stronghold of New York City (since the Review Board issue was essentially a local one) and lost to the Liberals upstate, a Conservative stronghold. Without such an issue to galvanize them, it remains to be seen whether the Conservative Party can consolidate its position on Line C four years hence and beyond.

"The Liberal Party power," said Burgess, "is totally unjustified when you consider how few races hinged on Liberal support— Lindsay yes, but others no!" An analysis of the citywide results of the 1965 state assembly elections shows that, out of 76 districts in the New York City area, 56 were contested by Liberals and Conservatives. In only 46 percent, or 26 of the 56 districts, Conservatives outpolled the Liberals, but the total Conservative vote in these districts was slightly more than the total Liberal vote. Liberals held the balance of power in two districts, but it was not exercised. The Conservatives held the balance of power in five districts, and in one case these votes were crucial in electing a man to office. The results of the 1966 Congressional and local elections were similar, with particular improvements recorded in Queens and Richmond.

The views of the Conservative Party of New York differ considerably from those of Kent Courtney and his group. The New York Conservatives seek a balanced state budget, no increase in taxes, a revision of unemployment insurance laws, the enactment of right-to-work laws, the repeal of any legislation that encourages featherbedding, no busing of schoolchildren, a return to the local school concept, the end to state financial support of rent control, the requirement of one year's residence to qualify for welfare, stronger laws and punishment for crimes of violence, and an end to public housing.

There is virtually no evidence of a conspiracy complex within the Party, even though a number of Birchers are known to belong to it. The Party's view towards small-l liberals is that they are stumbling, bumbling, naïve and fatuous individuals whose loyalty and good intentions are seldom questioned but whose mental probity and philosophical scope leave much to be desired.

One persistent criticism of the Party is that its appeal is to racists, particularly the anti-Negro vote. Undoubtedly some of this criticism is justified, but in many cases it is overstated. Most of the criticism revolves around the Party's opposition to the busing of schoolchildren. "We object to busing 'other' students into 'worse' schools," said Burgess; "we do not object to Negroes being bused to 'better' schools." Another Conservative put it this way: "The whole question is a Liberal *canard* to pin the racist tag on us. It is questionable who is more race conscious, those who advocate busing or those who oppose it. For the Liberals to call us racists is absurd."

4

There is another conservative political group on the current scene. It is called the Constitution Party. It was founded in 1952 by a group of "nationalists" who objected to the nomination and eventual election of Dwight Eisenhower to the Presidency. Before long the Party was raided by a group of anti-Semites who were to dominate the Party until around 1960 when the more blatant ones were kicked out. The Party still has a racist flavor today but it is muted; most members tend to be more circumspect in their criticism.

In 1952 the Constitution Party ran General MacArthur for President in Texas and he received 3,089 votes; in 1956 it backed ex-IRS Commissioner T. Coleman Andrews, who was also running on the States Rights Party ticket. In 1960 the Party was on the ballot in Texas and Washington. In Texas it ran Charles L. Sullivan for President and the late General Merritt B. Curtis for Vice-President. In Washington, General Curtis was the Presidential candidate, thus running for both offices simultaneously.* Over 18,000 Texans voted for Sullivan, but Curtis could win no more than 1,401 votes in Washington.

In 1964 the Party was only on the ballot in Texas. It ran Joseph B. Lightburn for President and Ted Billings for Vice-President. Lightburn is the grandson of Civil War General Joseph Lightburn and is currently a shopkeeper from Jane Lew, West Virginia. Lightburn, who is proud of the fact that his initials are the exact opposite of the current President's, campaigned under the slogan "Let a Lightburn in the White House." His running mate, Ted Billings, was born in Whitehouse, Ohio, and currently owns a health food store, Lifeguard Foods, in Denver. Together Lightburn and Billings polled 5,060 votes.

The Party's platform at first glance seems little different from that of any other extremely conservative group. Every issue of the Party's monthly *Newsletter,* an eight-page pamphlet, usually carries a full page on the Party's planks entitled "★★★★ Here It Is—The World's Greatest Platform!★★★★" The Party advocates the repeal of many things: federal aid to education, the Civil Rights Act, the Mental Health Bill, the Sixteenth Amendment, the United Nations Treaty Act, the Disarmament Act, reciprocal trade agreements and GATT. It calls for the outlawing of the Council on Foreign Relations, breaking off diplomatic relations

* Oddly enough, he has not been the only one to do so. Senator William E. Jenner was a candidate in 1956 for both President and Vice-President— in Texas for the Constitution Party, and in Kentucky for the States Rights Party respectively.

with Communist countries, the suspension of "immigration beyond the quotas of the McCarran-Walter Act and [the deportation of] the millions of illegal entrants already in the United States"; it calls for an annually balanced budget and the retirement of the U.S. debt. In a positive vein, the Party calls for the teaching of the free enterprise economic system in the schools, Bible reading in schools, the expansion of the states' rights concept and the withdrawal of government participation in business.

But what makes the Party different from all the others is the emphasis it puts on two questions. Plank 1 reads: "THIS IS A CHRISTIAN NATION . . . nothing in the Constitution shall be construed so as to interfere with the free exercise of religion." Exactly what the Party means by this is not clear, because the usual complaint over the abolition of prayers in public schools is, if anything, downgraded by the members. Party spokesmen constantly stress the point that "this is a *Christian* nation, . . . this is a *Christian* nation, . . ." but seldom offer to explain why they choose to emphasize the point at all.

Some observers believe that the constant use of these words reflects either extremely narrow religious fundamentalism or thinly veiled racism. For instance, Bert Ellis, the Party's chairman and a fire-extinguisher distributor by trade, wrote the following in a letter to Kent Courtney, his political opponent, in the fall of 1965:

> . . . I can appreciate your mention of your pledge to love of God. But you need to be stronger in that regard. You need to use the words "Jesus Christ" or "Christian" to really let people know where you stand. As you probably know, Jesus Christ is the offense to the unbeliever. It is He who turns away the agnostic. Unitarians, the Theosophists, Moslems, Jews, Jehovah Witnesses, and many other religious sects believe in God, but do not acknowledge Jesus Christ as man's personal savior. The original colonies in America were set up to edify the Lord Jesus Christ. . . .[12]

Richard K. Troxell, the state chairman of the Constitution Party in Texas, believes that all past American laws have been Christian in character but that recently, he says, they have not been. "The government is no longer servant but master," he said. "This is an Eastern philosophy and we are diametrically opposed to it." One possible explanation for the emphasis on "Christian" is that Troxell and Ellis and their followers refer to this "Eastern philosophy" as the philosophy of the Anti-Christ. Thus, all who deny *Christ* (not necessarily God), deny America.

The second question that distinguishes this Party from others is its emphasis on "the money question," which is usually expressed in the slogan "Buy Back the Federal Reserve." To Ellis, this is one of the two most important issues of the times.

This is a hoary argument that is similar in many ways to the current Greenback Party view. Essentially, Constitution Party members argue that the Federal Reserve System is a private corporation that is run for the sole benefit of "international financiers," whom they name as "the Rockefellers, Rothschilds, Kuhn, Loeb & Company, etc." "Warburg," said Troxell, not making it clear to whom or what he was referring, "is number one among them."

The sole purpose of these international financiers, so Party members believe, is to control "the world's monies." The struggle to gain control of them is viewed as having been a long and bitter one dating from the days of the Babylonian goldsmiths. Napoleon, members believe, was lured by the financiers to take over the world. He did not succeed. The American Civil War, they add, was started by international financiers to destroy this country and to gain control of its money. This, too, was unsuccessful. But the international financiers, they assert, finally did succeed in taking over the world in December 1913 when the Federal Reserve Act was passed. From then on the financiers have had things pretty much their own way, say the Constitutionalists: they control the United States because it is "in debt to the Federal Reserve"; "they coin their own money" and have taken it "out of the hands of the people"; they have created wars, depressions and revolutions to solidify their control over the monies of the world. One Party member recently told an audience that these financiers are encouraging the United Nations to step in and "regulate the peace" in America. The plan, he said, calls for "Red Chinese [troops] to 'police' the South."

The Party's leading guru on the subject is a Houston insurance executive named Wickliffe B. Vennard, Sr. He wrote a book called *The Federal Reserve Hoax* in which he laid most of the country's ills at the feet of "the International Zionists who steered our ships of state from Wall Street by means of money control." Besides the international financiers and Zionists, Vennard believes that the "Illuminati," Bilderberger conferences, Bandung conferences, the "Hidden Government," the Council on Foreign Relations, communism and the Atlantic Union are also enemies of the United States.

Vennard even thinks that anti-communism is a bankers' racket:

> Hundreds of speakers are tirading from coast to coast denouncing Russia, communism, Socialism, United Nations, etc. They are aiding and abetting the International Bankers who constitute our Public Enemy No. 1. . . . Their plan now is to sap the energies of Americans in an all-out hate campaign against Russia and vice-versa. Any person who points his finger at Russia and Communists and says he knows what he is talking about is doing this country a great dis-service. To kill the octopus, we must aim at the heart. Nothing is accomplished by aiming at the tentacles. If all would concentrate upon the Repeal or Repurchase of the Federal Reserve System, when accomplished, all the other un-American activities would wither like leaves on a vine.

Part of the reason the Constitution Party is considered racist is that two of its most enthusiastic boosters are well known in racist circles. One is Richard Cotten, a radio propagandist, an ex-Bircher, an ex-member of Liberty Lobby and formerly a teacher at one of Billy James Hargis' "Anti-Communist Youth Universities." Cotten broadcasts his right-wing views—similar to Constitution Party views—over three Mexican and nineteen American radio stations at an estimated cost of $150,000 per year. Cotten was thrown out of the John Birch Society because of his allegiance to one Kilsoo Haan, a Korean prophet that Welch believed to be pro-Red, and because of what the ADL calls Cotten's "fondness" for armed anti-Communist groups. The other booster is Ned Touch-stone, the editor of *The Councilor,* mentioned previously.

One issue of the Party's *Newsletter* featured a double-page spread advertising a "GIANT RALLY" in Austin, Texas. The two noted speakers were to be Cotten and Touchstone. "Let's give them a BIG Texas welcome!" said the ad.

Troxell, one of the spokesmen for the Party, is a young, handsome Texan who runs his own advertising–public relations firm located in Houston. He is a graduate of Southern Methodist University who, by 1960, "had gotten fed up with the Republican Party." He joined the Constitution Party and has never regretted it. "I got fed up with people who compromise on everything," he said. "I believe it is time to make a stand on what you believe like our forefathers did at the Alamo." Although Troxell does not see the Constitution Party winning in 1968, he does see the Party being on the ballot of all fifty states. At this writing he claims that twenty-eight states have Party organizations and are working to put candidates on the ballots. He believes, he told me, that the Party will be successful in his lifetime.

According to Party literature, success will be achieved in the following manner: In the 1964 election, six people out of ten voted for President Johnson. In the future (the literature optimistically says 1968, but not even Troxell believes that), the Party sees the "socialist" Republicans and Democrats each getting three of the six votes for Johnson while the Constitution Party will get the remaining four. Although this would be a minority victory the Constitution Party is not disturbed because there would be no runoff.

Each of the Party's state organizations is near anarchic in character. Little allegiance is paid to the main office in Houston; each Party draws up its own platform; and none need adopt the official Constitution Party candidate if it does not want to. Until September 1965 the Maryland organization was run by retired Marine Lieutenant General Pedro A. del Valle, now the president of the Defenders of the American Constitution, located in Florida.* (Until his death in 1966, DAC's secretary was ex-

* The DAC publishes *Task Force,* which periodically puts out "alerts." In one alert, Del Valle wrote that the State Department is consciously surrendering U.S. sovereignty to the U.N. This means, he said, "we may ultimately expect that savage Congolese, Ghanians, Ethiopians and Ghurkas will 'maintain law and order' in the United States, in the same manner as in Christian Katanga, by fire, murder and rapine."

Constitution Party candidate General Merritt B. Curtis.) Del Valle was formerly vice-president of Merwin K. Hart's National Economic Council and is a good friend of Robert Williams, publisher of the racist *Know Your Enemy*.

The Iowa party is run by looseleaf book manufacturer Robert D. Dilley, who was originally set up in politics through the help of Kent Courtney. Dilley has since switched his allegiance to the Texas group. This party may now be using the Constitution Party title, but Dilley sent me literature with the American Independence Party label on it. The situation is very fluid in Iowa.

The South Dakota party is run by a bearded doctor named Clarence S. Martin. His organization is known as the Christian Constitutional Party, and it stresses the Christian aspect of the platform. Martin offers fourteen slogans for his followers—for instance, "God gave us two ears and one mouth, we should listen to God twice as much as speak to Him"—as well as a "Creed," a "Credo" and a "Call to Action."

The Pennsylvania organization is called the Constitutional Party and is run by an energetic and articulate individual named Edward S. Swartz. Swartz is the owner of Indian Echo Caverns, a tourist attraction twelve miles from Harrisburg. He campaigned for governor in 1966 under the slogan "Put a Cave Man in the Capitol."

The Florida affiliate, run by one Stanley Pospisil of Miami, is called—just to confuse things—the Conservative Party, because Kent Courtney's man in Florida, Dr. William Douglass of "Let Freedom Ring," registered the name "Constitution" before the Texas group could get around to it.

This last action reflects the nature of the relations existing between Ellis' and Courtney's organizations. They have been feuding for years, each trying to outdo the other in order to become the undisputed leader of a third-party movement. "What is it, Mr. Courtney, that offends you about the Constitution Party?" Ellis asked in an open letter. "Is it because you don't run it?" When I mentioned the feud to Courtney he said that the only differences were over policies, particularly Ellis' position on the Federal Reserve. But it was obvious to me that there is more to it than that.

Ellis also takes Courtney to task for supporting Goldwater—the "false messiah"—in 1964. He also disagrees with Courtney over the latter's belief that each state party should have only "temporary" chairmen so that when better-known leadership is found it can step in and run it. "We are not organizing this great and glorious party," Ellis retorted, "so that it can be turned over to any false messiahs or stooges controlled by the International Bankers." And as a last stab at his foe, he wrote: "I . . . will pray for your salvation and God's forgiveness of your sin of supporting the Anti-Christ."

The battle still rages.

9

The Christian Right

1

The first reaction one encounters when examining the activities of the four major Christian right groups—Billy James Hargis' Christian Crusade, Carl McIntire's 20th Century Reformation Hour, Fred Schwarz's Christian Anti-Communism Crusade, and Major Edgar C. Bundy's Church League of America—is that none of its leaders believe it fair to include their organizations in a political study. Each will say, in effect, "We are a Christian organization fighting the Anti-Christ; therefore it is dishonest of you to call us political." If communism were viewed by them exclusively as a religion then their point would be valid. Most Christian right literature, however, is frankly political in content. In fact, as time has passed, the transparency of the religious-only claim has become all too apparent, and the cries of innocence sullied have become correspondingly less convincing. For better or for worse these groups and the others mentioned briefly below shall be considered to have a distinct political bias.

The largest of these groups is Billy James Hargis' Christian Crusade. Its gross receipts in 1964 were over $834,000 (up 1440 percent from 1956); current operating costs run to $100,000 per month; its news magazine, *Christian Crusade,* circulates among some 110,000 readers; over one million pieces of literature are mailed out each month (the yearly postal bill exceeds $75,000); Crusade speakers stump the country holding "Anti-Communist

Leadership Schools" and "Anti-Communist Youth Universities"; squads of advance men, front men and follow-up men fan out around the Crusade evangelists to ensure the maximum benefit from their appearances. Hargis himself usually spends twenty days a month speaking to various right-wing groups around the country; his voice is heard on 270 radio stations per week; the Crusade produces a seemingly endless array of motion pictures, television shows, books, tape recordings, tracts, pamphlets and record albums; and the Crusade operates, among other things a hotel, a thirty-five-foot executive motor coach and a $1 million "cathedral."

Billy James Hargis, the man leading this crusade, has been a minister in the Christian Church (Church of Christ) since he was eighteen years old. He was born in Texarkana, Texas, in 1925 and after his graduation from high school attended Ozark Bible College at Bentonville, Arkansas. Although he spent but one and a half years there he was nevertheless ordained a minister in his church. He then held successive pastorates in Granby, Missouri, Sallisaw, Oklahoma, and Sapulpa, the latter a suburb of Tulsa.

Throughout these years he became more and more alarmed over what he considered to be an indifferent attitude of the Protestant clergy toward communism. He was further disturbed by their apparent apostasy. In 1950, he resigned his post and within a year had founded the Christian Echoes Ministry, Inc.—later the Christian Echoes National Ministry—a "religious, non-profit-making body" whose purpose it was to awaken America to the threat of communism. The name Christian Crusade was to evolve later when it became apparent that the name Christian Echoes National Ministry had no appeal to those people Hargis wanted to reach.

Two years after he founded the Crusade, in 1953, Hargis received his first nationwide publicity when he launched his "Bible Balloon Project." During the five years that this operation was supported by the Crusade, over one million portions of the Bible, translated into seven languages, were launched via balloon into Iron Curtain countries.

In 1955, he preached a sermon on Easter Sunday before the Tomb of Christ in Jerusalem and was asked to return and repeat his efforts on another occasion, which he did. In 1957, he took a trip around the world, during which he met Syngman Rhee (a "brilliant world leader") and Madame Chiang ("the most powerful single Christian force in today's world").

In February 1960, Hargis' name was again on the front pages of the newspapers. This time it was over what has come to be called "the Air Force manual affair." This incident came to a head the previous month when the Air Force issued a manual for the training of noncommissioned officers in the Air Force Reserve. Part of the text read as follows: "Communist fellow travellers and sympathizers have successfully infiltrated our churches. . . . There appears to be overwhelming evidence of communist anti-religious activity in the United States through the infiltration of fellow travellers into churches and educational institutions." The document then went on to say: "The National Council of Churches of Christ in the United States of America officially sponsored the Revised Standard Version of the Bible. Of the 95 persons who served in this project, 30 have been affiliated with pro-communist fronts, projects and publications."[1]

The man who wrote this section of the manual was one Homer T. Hyde, a Baptist and a civilian whose knowledge of communism among the Protestant clergy was limited to asking his own minister what he knew on the subject. The minister suggested contacting Hargis, which Hyde then did. Hargis sent Hyde two small pamphlets he had written—"Apostate Clergymen Battle for God-Hating Communist China" and "The National Council of Churches Indicts Itself on 50 Counts of Treason"—plus one pamphlet from Myers Lowman's Circuit Riders, Inc., entitled "30 of the 95 Men Who Gave Us the Revised Standard Version of the Bible." These three pieces of literature provided the documentation for Hyde's critical remarks.

The NCC complained of the attack in a letter to Thomas S. Gates, the Secretary of Defense. Gates was embarrassed by this development and withdrew the document from circulation. *The New York Times* was to remark that "something is wrong in our defense organization when this kind of venomous nonsense can be put out at Government expense."

The uproar caused considerable publicity to fall the way of Billy James Hargis. Ever since that day his organization has grown to the point where it is now the largest one on the Christian right.

In 1954, Hargis received an honorary Doctor of Divinity degree from the Defender Seminary in Puerto Rico. This organization was founded by the late Reverend Gerald B. Winrod, a Wichita-based propagandist who published *The Defender,* a magazine that flourished in the 1930s and 1940s and which was openly hostile to Jews. Winrod was so pro-German during the late 1930s that he became known as "the Jayhawk Nazi." He subsequently was indicted for sedition three times, but the charges were dropped after the presiding judge died during the trial.

Hargis received his BA two years later from Burton College and Seminary in Manitou Springs, Colorado, and in 1958 he was to be given a Bachelor of Theology degree from the same institution. In 1957, Belin Memorial University, then located in Chillicothe, Missouri, and now in Manassas, Virginia, awarded Hargis an honorary Doctor of Laws degree. According to the Department of Health, Education and Welfare, both Burton and Belin Colleges are "degree mills," organizations that award degrees without requiring students to meet the standards necessary to win a degree at an accredited institution. In 1959, Dr. Clyde Belin, the head of the latter college, was sentenced to a one-year term in federal prison on six counts of using the mails to defraud.

The Crusade family is large and diversified. One of Hargis' associate evangelists is the Reverend David A. Noebel, a thirty-one-year-old native of Wisconsin who once ran for Congress in a primary election against Democrat Robert Kastenmeier of the 2nd District. Noebel joined Christian Crusade in 1964 and is considered to be the back-up man for Hargis. Recently Noebel wrote a pamphlet called *Communism, Hypnotism and the Beatles,* in which he argued that the Communists have a master music plan for American youth designed to make them mentally ill and emotionally unstable. This master music plan involves rhythmic, beat and folk music.

The Reverend Charles V. Secrest is another associate evangelist and is Hargis' brother-in-law. Dr. Fernando Penabaz, Hargis' biographer (*Crusading Preacher from the West*) and a Cuban refugee, serves as the Director of International Affairs for the

Crusade. J. E. Hargis, Billy James' father, is a trustee of the organization. The Crusade's advisers include two members of the Birch Council: Tom Anderson and F. Gano Chance, the latter of the A. B. Chance Company. Four other well-known advisers are Robert D. Dilley of Des Moines; Dr. Bob Jones, Jr., the president of Bob Jones University in Greenville, South Carolina; Brigadier General Richard B. Moran from Kerrville, Texas; and General Charles A. Willoughby, one of the most ardent of all supporters. General Willoughby was Chief of Intelligence for General Douglas MacArthur during World War II and the Korean War. He writes a column called "Foreign Intelligence Digest" for *Christian Crusade* magazine. Willoughby thinks so much of Hargis that he gave him an elaborately engraved five-foot sword from the Crusades that had been presented to Willoughby by General Franco of Spain.

One of the most important men in the Crusade is L. E. "Pete" White, a Tulsa advertising man who had previously been employed by Oral Roberts, the "faith healer" of TV fame. White claims that he built Roberts up from twenty-five dollars into a multimillion-dollar enterprise but then fell out over money. Shortly thereafter White was approached by Hargis, then at his Sapulpa pastorate. White took on the job of promoting Hargis and has been largely responsible for the growth of the Crusade that followed. White's name only appears as editor of *Christian Crusade;* he is not a trustee nor an official adviser but is nevertheless very close to Hargis' ear.

Hargis has no single large contributor to the Crusade. However, one individual, the late W. L. Foster, a Tulsan who made millions in oil leases, lent Hargis as much as $500,000 at no interest to get started. Foster also was a contributor to such groups as Liberty Lobby, We The People! (of which Hargis was the president for two years), the United States Day Committee and Gerald L. K. Smith's operations. Most money, however, comes pouring in as the result of the multitudinous appeals that flow out of the Crusade's Tulsa headquarters.

The activities of the Crusade are indeed prodigious. For fifteen minutes every day of the week Hargis broadcasts his "anti-Communist message" over 270 radio stations. His Sunday broadcast, he said, is "spiritually oriented." On occasion he will hold radio marathons, eight-hour shows exclusively concerned with the "Communist problem." They are usually beamed to the public over two powerful Mexican radio stations, XEG in Monterrey and XERB in San Diego. No one seems to know how many people hear Hargis' messages, but all agree that the audience is huge. In 1964, 10.5 percent of Crusade income came in through radio appeals.

The Crusade has produced 26 fifteen-minute color films suitable for both TV and theatres. Subjects discussed include the Supreme Court, churches of America, foreign aid, state sovereignty and Communist subversion in the U.N. They feature such stars as Captain Eddie Rickenbacker, John Rousselot, Barbara Hartle and Benjamin Gitlow, the latter two ex-Communists.

Tape recordings of Hargis' speeches are offered to the public at five dollars per tape. Hargis also sells 33-rpm phonograph records. The four best known are "Communist America—Must it Be?," "The United Nations Hoax," "Jesus Christ—The Hope of the World" and "Songs and Sayings of Billy James Hargis."

Book publishing is also big business with the Crusade. The books are cheap paperbacks most of which have no index or source notes. In 1962, Hargis published *The Facts About Communism and Our Churches* and *Communism, The Total Lie,* which he claims together sold more than 48,000 copies in two years. *The Real Extremists—the Far Left* was published in 1964 and, according to Hargis, sold 35,000 copies in the first four months after publication.

Letter writing is a major means by which the Crusade raises money. Hargis believes in the long, folksy letter that is full of inside information on the Crusade. When it comes to emotions, few plugs are left unpulled. A July 1962 letter on blue stationery in the handwriting of Betty Jane Hargis, Billy James' wife, told of the pressure on the Hargis children caused by criticism of their father by the press. "Won't each of you help to relieve some of this pressure by your contributions?" She promised to send each contributor "a snapshot of Billy and the children" if they wanted one. On another occasion, the *Weekly Crusader* announced bluntly in bold red ink: "THIS PUBLICATION WILL BE DISCONTIN-UED AS OF OCTOBER 1, [1962] UNLESS . . ."

Hargis' letters are personal and emotional. *"I am indignant, angry, aroused!"* began one. "Deep inside me I am seething with resentment over the lack of support for our boys in South Vietnam. Perhaps you can sense the white heat of emotion in my words. *Oh, the shame of it!"* The letter went on to say that Hargis was planning "to saturate the nation with an eye-catching bumper strip" reading "We Back Our Boys in Vietnam" (with the Crusade name and address printed below). Along with a plea to buy a minimum of twenty-five bumper stickers (at $6.25), Hargis added another plea for further general contributions. Part of this money, he explained, would go to "Project Clean Slate," an effort to pay off radio stations which have been carrying Hargis' debts indefinitely. The FCC, said Hargis, was trying to prove that these stations were biased in favor of him, which he thought would put the station licenses in jeopardy.

Hargis also raises money by a technique that some call a "prayer auction." The first recorded auction took place in August 1961 at a time when the Mutual Broadcasting Company offered the Crusade a six-month special low rate "for only $38,870." At the 3rd Annual Crusade Convention that year in Tulsa, Hargis stood up before the seven hundred people in the audience and cried: "I pray to God for one man to sponsor this program for six months. I know that man exists in the audience. Will he stand up?" No one stood up so Hargis continued: "Alright then, we will divide this burden. I need four men who will accept God's challenge and give $10,000 each to sponsor this program." This met with more success as two men stood up. Hargis continued: "Give us four, oh, God, who will give $5,000 each. Quickly. $2,000?" One man stood up. ". . . One thousand dollars?" Three men stood up. In the end, after calling for contributions of $500 through $100, Hargis found that seventy-nine men had pledged the exact amount needed.[2]

Hargis uses other money-raising techniques. He sells 100 back copies of *Christian Crusade* for $3 and $20-chairs for $100 as a memorial in his new "cathedral."

Two of the smallest money-raising operations, but nevertheless two that receive the most publicity, are his Christian Crusade Anti-Communist Youth University and his Anti-Communist Leadership

Schools. The Youth University is located in Manitou Springs, Colorado, in the Crusade-owned Summit Hotel and offers six two-week seminars for students over fourteen years old. According to one issue of *Christian Crusade,* "These seminars are designed to give a well-rounded education to students in the areas of Christianity, communism, socialism (communism's Marxist twin), economics. We cover specifics like the National Council of Churches, the Marxist United Nations, disarmament, etc." The article goes on to say that "we are able to judge and weigh the burning issues through the spectrum of truth—the Bible." Besides Hargis, Penabez and Noebel, the 1966 faculty included Frank L. Kluck-hohn, a former *New York Times* reporter and author of such books as *America: Listen!* and *Lyndon's Legacy;* Dr. Grace Levinson, head of the Voice Department at Bob Jones University; and General Edwin A. Walker, who is described as "the un-muzzled Army officer."

The Anti-Communist Leadership Schools, however, are better known and better attended. Limited to some 150 "constitutional conservatives," the school lasts five days and costs $125 per person, not including literature bought. The most famous of the schools was held in Tulsa in 1962. At the opening session Hargis warned that no intemperate statements from the floor or platform would be tolerated. This warning, however, did not prevent one member of the faculty, Dr. Revilo Oliver, from calling liberal intellectuals "witch doctors and fakers with a sanctified itch to save the world" who, in addition, are taxing America to death for the benefit of every "mangy cannibal in Africa." He went on to describe Drew Pearson as "one of the biggest, slimiest rats in the sewers of American journalism." (Pearson is particularly hated by Crusaders because he once accused Hargis of peddling vitamin pills, which the evangelist denied. However, *Christian Crusade* at one time did carry ads for a food supplement called Nutri-Bio, which was seized in 1961 by the U.S. Food and Drug Administration as being "of no value in the treatment or prevention of any of the diseases which commonly occur in this country.") Oliver also lashed out at Arthur Schlesinger, Jr., calling him a "mountebank and shyster," and at Secretary of Defense Robert McNamara, whom he termed a "former socialist professor."

Another speaker at the school was R. Carter Pittman, a lawyer from Dalton, Georgia, who is active in the Citizens' Councils. He caused a considerable fuss when he attacked the Negro race as being biologically and intellectually inferior to the Caucasian. He added that the major difference between American Negroes and Negroes in the Congo was that "in the Congo they eat more people than they do in the United States." Even Hargis winced at this remark.

The 1966 Anti-Communist Leadership School which I attended for three days was clearly not as provocative as the 1962 school, but nevertheless it presented a good cross-section of the Crusade, its followers and its ideas.

Hargis, of course, is the star attraction. Physically, at six feet and an estimated 270 pounds, he is one of the larger leaders on the right. His girth is enormous, but he is surprisingly light on his feet. He also looks much younger than news media photographs make him appear. He lives in a $45,000 "parsonage" and has a 700-acre ranch outside of Tulsa. Like the President of the United States, Hargis is transfixed by his own initials, BJH. His wife's name is Betty Jane and his four children are named Bonnie Jane, Billy James, Becky Jean and Brenda Jo.

Hargis calls everyone by his first name and collectively "Brother." He sprinkles his language with colloquialisms, familiarities and Biblical quotes. "You folks go over and fellowship in the dining room after the meeting . . .," he told a group of Crusaders during the school. "Honey," "dear hearts" and "y'all" are other favorite forms of address. "Praise God," "Thank the good Lord Jesus" and "God of our Fathers" are typical of his religious expressions. His favorite quotation is from Ephesians 6:12: "For we wrestle not against flesh and blood, but against principalities, against powers, against the rulers of the darkness of this world, against spiritual wickedness in high places."

Hargis can keep an audience amused with a seemingly endless collection of jokes and stories. He flatters his followers with compliments, he is something of a ham actor, he has a jolly laugh, and he is a powerful platform speaker who can make a two-hour speech seem like a twenty-minute sermon. His style is informal and can vary from spontaneous bursts of humor to foot-stomping,

table-pounding shouts of anger. He objects to being tagged as a
"bawl and jump" evangelist.

He has developed a taste for travel, particularly to Europe and
the Holy Land. Few years have passed since the founding of the
Crusade that he has not gone to Europe or Jerusalem. Hargis also
has a taste for fine clothes. The day I interviewed him he was
wearing a tan smoking jacket with a velvet collar.

There is no doubt that his followers adore him. I have seen
elderly female crusaders break into helpless giggles of pleasure
when Hargis flatters or teases them. He is a back-patter and a hand-
squeezer. Such is his spell over some individuals that they seem
eager to carry their checkbooks around at port arms.

Entire families follow the Hargis line. One family from the
Texas Panhandle said that they had been to almost every Anti-
Communist Leadership School Hargis has ever held. Their children had attended the Youth University, and they work hard for
the Crusade in their hometown. Their attractive daughter confided
in me that her entire family were being persecuted by their hometown neighbors because of their views and associations.

One elderly woman said to me, not making it clear to whom she
was referring: "I'm glad my captain never lost a battle!" Others
listen to his speeches with rapt attention, muttering, "That's right!"
or "A-men!" or "Hear, hear!" at whatever pleases them. One
white-haired woman at the school fell into a trance during Hargis'
speech and expressed her agreement with his views with arm
motions similar to those of an orchestra conductor.

Hargis' views differ only slightly from those of other groups on
the right. He favors reduced taxes, a greatly reduced bureaucracy,
a sound dollar, the elimination of foreign aid, the withdrawal of
government from business, a return to states' rights, no dilution of
America's sovereignty, the severance of diplomatic relations with
Communist countries, the fostering of patriotism, sound economics
and "time-honored virtues." He opposes inflation, "legislation by
the Judiciary," socialism and federal involvement in schooling,
housing and voting. He also believes that segregation was ordained
by God.

A common theme running through all his political positions is "we have been betrayed." The biggest traitors he believes to be "liberals, welfare staters, do-gooders and one-worlders." The Communists have infiltrated, he claims, the churches, Congress, the Pentagon, the newspapers, TV, magazines, foundations, the Supreme Court and labor unions. As Hargis sees it, their job is to smear patriots such as himself. Things are so bad, the betrayal has been so complete, believes Hargis, that the Communists will take over the country by 1974.

The 1966 Anti-Communist Leadership School was held in Tulsa at the Western Village Motel near the edge of town. Hargis' Crusade had leased the Village with an option to buy, in the hopes of turning it into a retirement home for elderly Crusaders. It soon became apparent, however, that the project would never pay for itself, and both the option to buy and the lease were eventually dropped. Nevertheless, the Crusade was running the motel at the time the Leadership School was being held, and it packed the rooms with sixty to eighty guests, many of whom had traveled from far afield to attend the sessions. Attendance, said Ruby White (the wife of Pete White), had been cut because of the bad winter weather. For the most part, all the guests were individuals well past their forties. Only a few young people were present.

The most noticeable aspect of the school was the amount of literature for sale. No matter where one went there was a rack of literature with an individual standing nearby to collect money. In the motel lobby there was a rack of slim pamphlets for which the Crusade is famous. Some of the titles are *The Strange Death of Povl Bang-Jensen, Should We Surrender to Castro or SMASH Him?, The Ugly Truth About Drew Pearson* and *Why I Left the Armed Forces,* by Major General Edwin Walker, who refers to himself as "USA (resigned)."

Over in the dining room there was another rack, this one slightly larger, carrying vast quantities of Crusade and Birch Society literature as well as general right-wing favorites such as John Stormer's *None Dare Call It Treason* and Phyllis Schlafly's and Admiral Chester Ward's *Strike From Space.* But it was at the entrance to the meeting hall where the racks and the tables were the biggest. Besides the Crusade and Birch Society material there were such items as Bibles (some of which had brightly colored plastic covers), Christian Crusade bookends, plastic trash containers—with the Crusade stamp—for the automobile, and a number of framed photographs of Billy James Hargis. One picture showed him posed before a painting of Christ, with a parchment copy of the Constitution in his hands, an American flag to one side, and a Crusader in armor to the other. This item was selling for $6.50. Another picture featured Hargis on a horse.

Also for sale was literature from Myers Lowman's Circuit Riders, Inc., and the House Committee on Un-American Activities. A "General Walker Package" sold for one dollar, but was sealed so that there was no way of knowing what was inside. Subsequent inspection revealed that the packet contained eight single-sheet flyers (two of which were identical) and eight small pamphlets, six of which were under eight pages.

A full range of records were also available. Some of them were selling quite briskly. The couple who stayed next to me at the motel, for instance, played "The Songs and Sayings of Billy James Hargis" over and over again far into the night. Tape recordings of the speeches delivered at the 1966 School could be ordered immediately following the talk itself. Any combination of fifteen speeches could be had for fifty dollars.

The first speaker I heard at the 1966 school was Dr. W. O. H. Garman, the minister of the Callendar (Presbyterian) Memorial Church of Wilkinsburg, Pennsylvania. Garman is a former public relations man and a past president of Carl McIntire's American Council of Christian Churches, an anti-NCC group. Garman's topic at the school was "The Folly of Disarmament." He said that he himself on occasion carries a gun and that he had taught two of his three children to shoot by the age of two. At six years, he claimed, his son could shoot a .45 "very well." His talk continued on this line for some time then dwelt on "fuzzy thinkers and traitors" who put Castro in power in Cuba ". . . and the Reds in power in the Dominican Republic." The Bible, he said, "is not with these fuzzy men" ("A-men," said Hargis from the back of the room). Winding up his speech on the subject of civil rights riots, he told the audience that if any Negro "tried to molest my wife or children, my gun's coming out smoking!" As for the Negro rioters in Philadelphia in 1965, Garman felt that "they should have been gunned down!"

Immediately following Garman came David Noebel, who spoke on "The Foreign Policy of the National Council of Churches." Noebel is a powerful speaker, building each point to a crescendo and then stopping suddenly to let the words sink in. The NCC, he said, was composed of "wolves in sheep's clothing" who have been calling for the collectivization of America since 1912. But the roots, he said, go deeper than that. "Bolshevism and Fabianism emanate from Marx and they came together in the NCC." Much of the radicalism in the churches, he added, came out of the—and here the slip was intentional—"Union Theological Cemetery." Because he believes that all Russian Orthodox priests are KGB spies, he asked: "Do you remember the time the Orthodox priest's beard fell off in Jerusalem?" The audience nodded knowingly. He then suggested a campaign to give peaceniks gasoline and matches.

Noebel ended his speech by asking questions to the audience. "Does the National Council of Churches speak for you," he asked, "when it advocates the recognition of Red China?" There were murmurs of "No!" from the audience. "Does the National Council of Churches speak for you," he continued, "when its leadership endorses the abolition of the House Committee on Un-American Activities?" Again there were fervent murmurs of "No!" from the audience. ". . . When it supports the law-violating 'Freedom Riders' in the South? . . . when its leadership requests clemency for convicted communist spies? . . . when it helps sponsor and train agitators for the invasion of one of our sovereign states? . . . when it endorses the unionization of farmers? . . . when it accepts a cash gift of $200,000 from the CIO? . . . when it supports the extension of the Reciprocal Trade Act?" Each time the cries of "No!" became louder and more pronounced. The NCC, concluded Noebel, "speaks for the forces of apostasy. . . . It is the single greatest fifth column force within the borders of the United States!"

The next morning Fernando Penabaz spoke on "The Case of Rhodesia." (The applause following his introduction was countered by a "Booo!" from Hargis, who had just walked into the room at that moment. The audience and Penabaz broke out into laughter.) Penabaz began his speech by giving the details of an elaborate conspiracy in which Fidel Castro was supposed to have sent an agent to Zanzibar to take over the country so that the Cubans could get their hands on the American missile-tracking station there. According to Penabaz, the station was dismantled and is now in Cuba.

Moving on to other subjects he said: "And just what is this thing called World Opinion? Most people in the world have no opinion at all!" Eventually he came around to the subject of Rhodesia, whose policies of segregation and exclusion he endorsed. The attack against Rhodesia, he said, financed by the "filthy, dirty, low-down British pound," was being spearheaded by the leaders of Ghana, Algeria, Egypt and Ethiopia. "Rhodesia is not the main target, as you know, . . ." he said; the real one is South Africa. On the subject of apartheid, he said: "Kennedy will tell us not to be segregated; but just try to climb over the ten-foot-high wall of their mansion in Palm Beach and see what happens to you . . . and you don't have to be black to have this happen to you!" We live, he sighed, "in the silliest era man has ever lived in."

That evening Dr. Charles Poling and General Richard B. Moran spoke to the school. Poling comes from a famous ecclesiastical family. His brother Daniel is editor of *Christian Herald;* another brother is pastor of the First Presbyterian Church in Salem, Oregon; a third brother was one of four chaplains who gave their lives in World War II when the U.S.S. *Dorchester* was torpedoed; his father was a minister and college president; and his mother was soloist for Dwight Moody. The topic of Charles Poling's speech was "Tears Become Us Now." Our country, he said, "is in trouble, real trouble. We are closer to losing our freedom than we realize. We have been squandering our days crying 'It can't happen here!' " Like most right-wingers, Poling resents being called "sick," "extremist," "mentally unbalanced" or "politically unreal." He, for one, makes fun of the charges leveled at him. For instance, he would sometimes preface his remarks with "Since the NCC has just declared me 'senile' and 'sick' . . ." On one occasion he said: "I'm not a lunatic but I'm an extremist because I'm extremely right!"

There has been, he continued, "a move to impeach Earl Warren. I think that's silly. I think we should impeach the whole bunch in Washington." The primary purpose of his work, he concluded, was "to stir up America to get us back on the path of Pilgrim character."

General Moran, the chairman of the Crusade's advisory board, spoke next on the United Nations. He traced the history of the "one world idea" back to the eighteenth century and the Rothschild family. Their purpose, he said, was to control the world, and they were to do this by being trained from childhood to attach themselves to rulers as advisers. This, he added, "has been true since 1773 right up to today and Walt Rostow." The Rothschilds, he explained, needed an organization through which they could control the world. They tried the League of Nations, but the Senate would not buy it. "However," he said, "after World War II, they succeeded in the United Nations. . . ."

Moran had other doubts about the U.N. Its charter, he said, is "anti-God"; it is trying to create a "Universal Brown Man—the man with no race, the neuter man . . ."; and, he concluded, there is no reference to the rights of private property in the charter.

The major speaker at this Leadership School was General Walker. Because of other commitments I was unable to hear him, but I did meet him briefly. He has become the number one folk hero of right-wingers—not only because of his enforced retirement from the Army in 1961 but also because of the treatment he received at the hands of the federal authorities during the University of Mississippi riots in 1962. Most right-wingers believe Walker was railroaded into a mental institute to be brainwashed because he was a threat to the "pro-Red status quo."

Walker himself has the reputation as the right's worst public speaker, often becoming incoherent when he mounts the podium. But in private this is not so; he is fairly articulate and not given to the monosyllabic anti-Communist clichés he sometimes uses in public. The two topics on which he spoke to the school were entitled "Moscow vs. Tulsa" and "The Great Am-Cong Society."

Billy James Hargis' speech the next day was one of three he gave that week. All three speeches were related. This topic was entitled *"Political* Planning for Victory over Communism." The previous one and the final one, neither of which I heard, were entitled *"Spiritual* Planning for Victory . . ."* and *"Educational* Planning . . ."* The following excerpts are from the second speech:

"I am a Christian conservative today," he began, "because only conservatism in the United States espouses the philosophy of Christ. . . . The liberal churches today preach a social gospel. This is misnamed; it's really a socialist gospel. Or, in the common vernacular, they preach the gospel according to Martin Luther King instead of the gospel according to Matthew, Mark, Luke and John. . . .

"I believe the Bible is inspired, I believe it's God's word, I believe in heaven and hell, I believe in God and Satan, I believe in right and wrong, I believe that God *gave* us America, I believe America was God's greatest nation under the living Sun and the ideal of governments, and I believe the only hope to maintain freedom is this orthodox Christian traditionalist viewpoint. . . .

"Then you have the anti-communists who say 'I would rather be dead than Red' and I'm one of those that say that. I would rather see my children . . . I would rather make the choice . . . and I wouldn't hesitate to make the choice: I would rather see my children destroyed and *my* life destroyed, my wife's life destroyed in a nuclear bombing than the thought of them having to live under a communist slave state. This wouldn't be living, this would be hell on earth and death would be merciful! [shouts of *"Right!"* from the audience] . . .

"Now my friends, if you don't think that . . . world government is the goal then you had better become convinced on that *one* point or you will not be an effective conservative because it all hinges on that. This is their goal: world government, as fantastic as it sounds. . . .

"I have lived through liberalism since the days of Franklin Delano Roosevelt and I have seen my country go bankrupt economically; and I've seen our churches become apostate; and I've seen our schools emphasize internationalism instead of nationalism and even turn against the faith of our fathers. I've seen this country in the name of progress become a bankrupt—morally and economically—republic and it's not even a republic any longer. I'm afraid that we have the seeds of a dictatorship in Washington, D.C., today ["A-men," "Hear, hear!"] and I'm concerned and I have a *right* to be concerned and as long as I live I will *express* that concern. . . .

"As I have already told you in Ezekiel and Revelations both, the Anti-Christ builds a world government and a world church. It's built on compromise and appeasement; it's built on surrender of convictions, not on orthodoxy, not on principles. . . . You don't achieve ecumenical unity without compromise and compromise is evil! ["A-men! A-men!"] . . . Internationalism, liberalism, welfare statism, Marxism, fascism, communism, Nazism is nothing but an attack upon a man's correct relationship with God. It is concealed atheism. . . ."

Hargis can use humor to good effect. For instance, he said this about his critics who attacked his own opposition to the "God is dead" school: "It's not hate to declare war on God," he began, "it's only hatred when you declare war on those who declare war on God. . . . In other words, my friends, we've got to learn who to hate and who to love. Now you can hate certain people and it's love. But you can love certain people and it's hate. I am therefore in favor of our getting a petition up—many of you have signed the 'Impeach Earl Warren' and all these petitions—I think we need a new petition. And I think that we need to petition the liberals of both political parties to give us a new dictonary that tells us who to hate and who to love because we want to be in step. I want to know who to hate because apparently I'm hating some of the wrong people [laughter]. And if you hate the right person it's love, don't you see? [more laughter] . . ."

Later on, Hargis turned serious again. With considerable emotion in his voice, he said: *"Don't talk to me of liberalism! It is a double-standard, Satanic hypocrisy!"* [Cries of *"A-men!"* followed by loud clapping.] Hargis continued: "The only people that I ever met in my life that I think are worth knowing are these little ol' Bible-believing Christian people who love the Lord and who love America and they're willing even in their feeble way to the best of their ability to give their lives in the defense of both ["A-*men!*"]. They're the only people I want to know, and they're the ones I want to hold my hand as I walk through the Valley of the Shadow of Death."

Hargis spent over half his speech talking about problems that face his Crusade. He believes that the federal government is out to squelch any criticism of the consensus. General Walker, J. Edgar Hoover, Barry Goldwater, Robert Welch, Fred Schwarz, Carl McIntire, George Benson and himself, in his own estimation, are the prime targets to be destroyed. Walter Reuther, says Hargis, is behind the assault because he is "perhaps the most powerful man in the United States." He controls, adds Hargis, "the largest bloc vote in the United States and now indirectly controls the second largest bloc vote—the Negro vote. . . ."

Hargis is also a big critic of the press. He is particularly nettled by what he considers to be lack of objectivity. Quoting from a newsclipping,[3] he said to the audience at the school: " 'The issue developed after Tulsan Billy James Hargis' Christian Crusade program in November 1964 attacked Fred J. Cook of Interlaken, New York [New Jersey], a free-lance writer.' Now you want to hear objectivity in news reporting?" Hargis asked. "Listen to the coming line: 'Cook had criticized . . .'—now notice, Fred Cook had *criticized.*' Isn't that sweet? It's gentle, American, Christian, humane. '. . . Cook had *criticized* the conservative Hargis operation.' Now notice, Hargis had *'attacked'* Fred J. Cook, but Cook had *'criticized'* Hargis' operation in a magazine article called 'Radio Right: Hate Clubs of the Air.' Now that's criticism. To refer to me as operating a 'Hate Club,' that's criticism; but when I expose Fred Cook, that's an *attack.* You see, dear friends, you don't know who to hate."

Hargis went on to tell of his financial troubles in 1961. Contributions, he said, fell off drastically after a few unfriendly pieces on him appeared in the national press. He told how he went into debt to his numerous radio stations to the tune of $300,000 and how some of his fair-weather friends kept writing him, saying, "You fool, this is where you went wrong . . ." He explained the "hell on earth" he went through in 1962 to drag the Crusade out of the red—how he turned to General Walker in desperation and how they both together stumped the country in a money-raising speaking tour called "Operation Midnight Ride." The debt today, he said, was down to $100,000 and was to be paid off as soon as possible. "I shall never forget," he said, "what Ted Walker did for me."

In private, Hargis is little different from his public image: folksy, energetic and pungent. He said that "the press's habit of using the guilt-by-association technique galls me to the core." He showed me a clipping of an article that begins by talking about the Klan and ends up mentioning Hargis. He is particularly irritated by the portrait painted of him by the authors of *Danger on the Right,* a book sponsored by the Anti-Defamation League. "I can't respond to it for fear of being labelled anti-Semitic. So it's a form of dictatorship," he said.

The Internal Revenue Service, after investigating the Crusade's tax-free status for several years, revoked the privilege in 1966. The IRS charged that part of Hargis' operations were "directed at the accomplishment of political objectives including efforts to influence political action by the public and government and only remotely, if at all, accomplish any educational, religious or charitable objective." It also charged that the Crusade's activities had in effect given direct or indirect support to candidates. Hargis denies all this. He believes that the IRS—and the FCC—are being used to coerce him off the air and out of business. He believes that within three years he will no longer have any freedom of speech.

Hargis told me before the IRS had revoked his organization's tax-free status, that if his tax-free status were not upheld, he planned to file six "People's Suits" against the NCC, *Christian Century* magazine, *Motive* (a Methodist magazine), the *United Church Herald* (of the United Churches of Christ), the Fellowship of Reconciliation and the NAACP (only one section of which has a tax-deductible status). They will, says Hargis, be charged with trying to influence legislation and, except for the FOR, with supporting LBJ in 1964. In any event, he says he will ask his supporters to continue to send their contributions to his Christian Crusade Church, another deductible organization of his.

Perhaps what bothers Hargis the most is that his new tax status may balloon his postal bill, now approximately 7.5 percent of his costs, into one third of his total costs. This would inhibit him considerably.

During the five-day Leadership School, Hargis gave all the guests a tour of his plant (the bus used for transportation from building to building had been purchased by Crusaders with Green Stamps). The publication and mailing facilities are perhaps the most extensive on the right—except for the John Birch Society. The Crusade owns a $35,000 mailing machine, $27,000 worth of tape-duplicating equipment, a number of letter-writing machines, a signature-signing machine, extensive printing equipment, a 20,000-book library (part of which was purchased from Allen Zoll, the former leader of American Patriots, Inc.—a "fascist" group, according to the Attorney General's list of subversive organizations), and there are rows upon rows of name index plates ready to be fed into the addressing machine. In addition there are files on Communists, "NCC pinks" and fellow travelers. There is $35,000 worth of stock in readiness at any one time—books, pamphlets, Bibles, and tape recordings of some five hundred anti-Communist speakers. Over seventy individuals handle the work, and the frantic atmosphere reminded me of the mailroom at Sears, Roebuck around Christmas time.

In another part of Tulsa is the Christian Crusade Cathedral, a concrete block-and-stucco building that cost one million dollars to construct. It has no front or back, Hargis said, nor will it have any choir. Hargis would rather hire two professional gospel singers because if he did not like them he could fire them. This way, he noted, reflecting on the experience he had in his previous pastorates, he would not be stuck with hometown *prima donnas.* The "Garden of Gethsemane," he added, off to one side of the Cathedral, will have organ music piped to it, and the water fountain there will be so rigged electronically that it will react to the tone and volume of the music inside. The cathedral itself will be non-denominational, but the baptistery, noted Hargis, will be a waterfall.

One Crusader, listening to Hargis' description of the building, suggested jokingly that the cathedral have an execution chamber—

"in case we lose the fight." All the other Crusaders present nodded in agreement.

2

Hargis is an upstart on the scene compared to Dr. Carl McIntire, who has been a member of the Christian right since 1936. McIntire is pastor of the Bible Presbyterian Church in Collingswood, New Jersey. He is editor-in-chief of the weekly *Christian Beacon* and the commentator on the 20th Century Reformation Hour radio broadcasts. He is also the founder of the American Council of Christian Churches, the president of the International Council of Christian Churches, president of Shelton College in Cape May, New Jersey, president of Faith Theological Seminary outside Philadelphia, and a director of Highland College in Pasadena, California.

McIntire was born in 1906 and was graduated from Park College in Parkville, Missouri, in 1927. He then entered Princeton Theological Seminary in preparation for the Presbyterian ministry. While there, he became an ardent admirer of Dr. J. Gresham Machen's, a well-known Fundamentalist scholar. When Machen broke with the seminary in 1929 to set up his own more conservatively oriented Westminster Seminary in Chestnut Hill, Pennsylvania, McIntire followed and secured his degree from the new institution two years later.

McIntire then began to work in opposition to the more liberal forces in his church. He and Machen set up an Independent Board of Presbyterian Foreign Missions that soon became so disruptive that the General Assembly of the Church voted to abolish it. This action, however, failed to cool McIntire's ardor, and in 1936 he was dismissed from the ministry of the United Presbyterian Church. The synod found him guilty on three charges: disapproval, defiance and acts in contravention of his church's government and discipline; lack of zealousness and faith in maintaining the peace of the church; and violation of his ordination vows.

McIntire and Machen went on to found another church, but the two men eventually split. McIntire then founded on his own the Bible Presbyterian Church in Collingswood. A few years later, in

1941, he formed the ACCC to compete with the National Council of Churches (then called the Federal Council of Churches), which McIntire has always believed to be the fount of Protestant apostasy. In 1948 he set up the ICCC to compete with the World Council of Churches, then in the process of being organized in Amsterdam.

The membership of the American Council of Christian Churches has always been a matter of speculation. Neither McIntire nor the Council publishes a figure, one of the few groups listed in the *Year Book of American Churches* (an NCC publication) that refuses to do so. Since the NCC, the major body speaking for American Protestantism, lists forty-one million members in its thirty-one constituent denominations (in 1965), a number of interested observers have sought in vain to compare this figure with McIntire's in order to assess relative strengths. The ACCC once stated that its membership was 1.25 million; the National Association of Evangelicals, an independent group with 10 million members, offered to send $1,000 to any charity if McIntire could prove to independent auditors that the figure was even 20 percent correct. The challenge was not accepted. From all available sources, there are fifteen member churches under McIntire's wing with a maximum total membership of 200,000.

The objectives of all McIntire's groups are to return to what they believe to be fundamental Christian beliefs and to purge Protestantism of all its "sinister" influences. These influences are many: at the top of the list are Communists, socialists, liberals and "one-worlders," followed closely by the NCC, the NAE, Catholics, the Gideons, the RSV Bible (McIntire applauded its burning in a North Carolina church), the U.N., Billy Graham ("a compromiser"), the International Court of Justice, ecumenicalism and "the social gospel."

McIntire, as the undisputed leader of these 200,000 churchgoers, is the ACCC's spokesman, and more often than not personally launches the attacks upon its enemies. He charges, for instance, that the U.N. is bankrupt morally and physically; but regardless, he stresses that a "one-world church" is just around the corner. He opposes the U.S.'s "give-away" policies, disarmament, consumers' cooperatives ("little outposts of Soviet Russia"), the United Protestant appeal, "One Hour of Sharing" (its purpose, said McIntire, was to raise money for "Socialist propaganda"), and the conservatively oriented National Association of Evangelicals.

The phrase "common man," he explained, "is an innocent-sounding term, but it is filled with all the tyranny of State control." The word "brotherhood" is likewise to be distrusted, particularly "racial brotherhood," because its emphasis "produces the class and racial strife in which the Communists delight." His view of nuclear war is provocative: "For us to have the Atomic bombs," he said, "and, in the name of a false morality born of a perverted sense of self-respect and pacifist propaganda, to await the hour when Russia has her bombs to precipitate an Atomic war, is the height of insanity. . . ."

In the 1960 Presidential elections the Democratic Party listed McIntire as one of five "major anti-Catholic extremists operating in the current political campaign." His antipathy toward Catholics is nothing new. In 1945, he called the church "the Harlot Church and the Bride of the Anti-Christ." It is, he added, the "greatest enemy of freedom and liberty that the world has had to face today. . . . One would be much better off in a communistic society than in a Roman Catholic Fascist set-up."[4] He has also described the Catholic Church as "a false religion which enslaves human souls in darkness and superstition," which will "sell her secret confessional system for political world power." All priests, he adds, whether they be in America or behind the Iron Curtain, are spies for the Pope.

McIntire does not believe that he is anti-Catholic, but he does take great pride in his belief that it was he who kept President Truman from sending an ambassador to the Vatican. As for President Kennedy, his office, wrote McIntire, "was used to advance the Roman Catholic Church in the United States as it has never been advanced in all the years of its existence." McIntire went on to say that "Americans respect the religion of others about them, but the manner in which the Roman Catholic Church exploited the President and the way in which the President was constantly assisting their interests and their cause, produced a deep resentment in the hearts of millions of Americans. It is still there today." But undoubtedly the galling factor to McIntire was that, after Kennedy was elected, "the President treated the American

Council of Christian Churches with the utmost disdain" by not treating it as an equal to the NCC (which is over two hundred times larger than McIntire's group).[5]

McIntire's primary target is the National Council of Churches. Of all the groups he hates, he hates the NCC the most. To him, the Council is "apostate, Communist and modernist." When the NCC replied that there had never been a Communist or a sympathizer among its officers, executives and staff, McIntire retorted that such a statement was "self-serving" and "preposterous." The NCC asked that its detractors offer proof of the charges. Here McIntire backed off, saying, "It is puerile, naïve, downright ignorant for the National Council of Churches to say that among all its numerous departments and literally thousands of clergymen there is no one with 'communist leanings.' " McIntire sheds very little light on who exactly are the clerical Communists because, at the moment of truth, he refuses to name names. He retreats to the position that any association with a "communist front" warrants the man being a suspected Red.

"How many communist fronts is it necessary for a man to be connected with," he asks, "before someone can say that he gave aid and comfort to the communists and their cause?" McIntire will call the NCC "communist," but with individuals he beats around the bush, lest he be sued for libel or slander. He gives no indication that he believes it is his job to prove the charges.

The examination of the "pro-Communist records" of two favorite McIntire targets—Bishop Eugene Carson Blake and Bishop G. Bromley Oxnam—should be sufficient to illustrate McIntire's method of attack. McIntire's source material usually comes from Myers Lowman's Circuit Riders, Inc. Presbyterian Blake, for many years president of the NCC and now general secretary of the World Council of Churches, is condemned by Lowman because he signed a petition in 1959 to eliminate the HCUA. In the same vein, McIntire condemns Blake because three years previously he had shepherded Metropolitan Nicolai, "the KGB agent," around the country under the auspices of the NCC. The mere fact that the two men would even talk to each other, in McIntire's eyes, implies that they agree with each other, both spiritually and politically, that Blake was in cahoots with the visitor. By this reasoning, Eisenhower is a Communist for inviting Khrushchev to the United States.

Bishop Oxnam, a leading Methodist who has served the NCC for many years, is also a suspect because he has forty-one "citations" after his name in one of Lowman's catalogues on the "public records" of Protestant Clergymen.[6] A close inspection of these citations shows that most of them date from 1940–1946, years when the Soviet Union was our ally. Seven of the organizations listed have made the Attorney General's list as subversive groups; but from my information, none of them were so listed when Oxnam was associated with them. Nor is there any indication that at least one of them—the National Council of American-Soviet Friendship (today listed as subversive)—was, during the war, endorsed by such luminaries as Cordell Hull, Leverett Saltonstall and General Eisenhower. Oxnam is further suspect, it appears, because he joined committees to abolish such Americana as the poll tax, lynching, HCUA and the H-bomb.

McIntire minces no words when it comes to what he thinks of Bishop Oxnam. Wrote McIntire: "Oxnam represents the popular, radical, pro-communistic element in religious circles in America. . . . In the name of Christ, Oxnam has championed the socialist principles of Karl Marx and become, I believe, the leading 'religious disciple' of Marx in the free world."[7]

But such men as Bishops Blake and Oxnam are not the real target. The NCC is the target, and yet, only insofar as it represents everything that McIntire and his ACCC oppose. If you question the Virgin Birth or the bodily resurrection of Christ, or are a believer in Darwin's thories, or promote the brotherhood of man, or suggest that "God is dead," or encourage ecumenicalism, or read the RSV Bible, or do and think any number of other "modernist" things, then according to McIntire, you are to be opposed and eventually destroyed by the forces of righteousness.

The Supreme Court's decision to ban prayer from the schools is particularly disliked by McIntire. "We are to be a Godless nation," he said, "for anything which partakes of God, appeals to God, is 'religious' and in violation of the First Amendment." He predicts the day when Bibles will be banned from court and envisions future coins with the motto "In Pluralism We Trust."

McIntire is another one of those on the right who views democracy, capitalism and Christianity as indivisible from one another. For instance, he wrote:

> God is the Author of Liberty and the church of Jesus Christ does have a responsibility to defend freedom, to state the moral foundations for a free society. This involves a Philosophy, a doctrine.
>
> The trouble with the National Council of Churches is that their philosophy is socialistic, basically materialistic. The church should not remain silent and have nothing to say. It should be the great champion of freedom and the exponent of the revealed will of God. . . . and the second table of the Decalogue is exceedingly social in its demands and concepts of man and his relationship one to another.
>
> The churches should speak against communism, socialism and alien ideologues which deny freedom. Freedom is indivisible and its greatest champion in all areas should be blessed disciples of the Lord Jesus Christ.[8]

Edward Cain, in his book *They'd Rather be Right* (Macmillan, 1963), points out that somehow theological argument over the primacy of faith is lost in an argument over economics. The law of supply and demand, he adds, suddenly becomes one of God's laws. Not only does freedom demand capitalism, according to McIntire, but so does Christianity; in fact, to his way of thinking, Christianity *depends* on capitalism. Edward Cain gingerly notes that this point of view raises the question of idolatry—a far greater sin than apostasy and a heresy that does not seem to bother McIntire.[9]

McIntire's views are spread among the public through a number of channels. He reaches the minds of the young clerics through his Faith Theological Seminary; he reaches the young college student through Shelton College (which is having problems with its accreditation) and Highland College; and he reaches selected minds through conferences held at the 333-room oceanside Christian Admiral Hotel in Cape May, New Jersey. This hotel was bought by one of McIntire's organizations for $300,000 and refurbished with another $250,000. Many of the rooms have been redecorated with special contributions and have been given such names as the Patrick Henry Room, the General MacArthur Room and the John Birch Room.

But these activities are really sidelights to his main propaganda guns: letter writing and his 20th Century Reformation Hour radio shows.

McIntire's letters, called "radio letters," follow much the same pattern as Hargis'. They come thick and fast, one every few weeks or so, each one with a return envelope enclosed for donations. Folksiness is combined with the hard sell. The letters often have such words as "Urgent" written at the top, and the faithful are addressed as "My dear Christian friend" or "Beloved." Unlike Hargis, who is often content to ask for the $5 and $10 contributions, McIntire aims high. Apparently there is no limit to the possibilities. On one occasion he appealed for one individual to give $10 million for Shelton College; on another occasion he ended his letter with: "I pray that this letter will bring the greatest single response that we have ever had from our radio audience. We need it today. Remember your will, the $1,000 gifts, too. We love God! . . ." This same letter began as follows: "Hate! Hate!! Hate!!!—we have uncovered the hate. It has been fully exposed to public view. You will be amazed when I tell you the story." McIntire went on to explain how station WXUR (owned by Faith Theological Seminary) in Media, Pennsylvania, had been subjected to a boycott and general harassment by its detractors and how he had overcome both.

The 20th Century Reformation Hour was started in 1960 and has grown from a few stations to some six hundred outlets today all over the country. It costs an estimated $1.2 million per year for air time (and another $500,000 to keep the rest of his operations afloat). McIntire keeps a large pin-studded map on the wall of his office in Collingswood, New Jersey, indicating where he has radio outlets. States with the most pins are Florida, Mississippi, North Carolina, Oklahoma, Pennsylvania, Texas, Virginia and Washington. There are very few pins along the upper Eastern seaboard and none in any of the major cities in the country. His audience is a rural and suburban one and is estimated at 20 million listeners.

His programs run to a pattern. He opens with a folksy greeting that is offset by strains of some patriotic music such as "The Battle Hymn of the Republic." His assistant, the Reverend Charles E. Richter—known as "Amen Charlie"—is also on the show; his only job is to say "Amen," "Yes," "No" or other words at the appropriate moment during McIntire's talk. Approximately one third of the program is religious in content, the message being tied in some way to the political two thirds. There is usually a long, extemporaneous prayer in the Fundamentalist tradition; then perhaps a hymn followed by a short talk on some passage from the Bible; and then a call for contributions for Korean orphans or Indian famine relief.

Then comes the political pitch. The 8 December 1965 program, one of the few that I recorded, is typical. McIntire attacks the NCC for issuing a statement on its views on Vietnam. The NCC, notes McIntire, sees no victory possible and asks that there be no escalation and that there be a move by both sides for peace. The following extract reveals McIntire's views:

. . . If we weren't in there [Vietnam] right now, resisting the communists, they would already have all of South Vietnam and they'd be well on their way to taking over Southeast Asia. As much as we hate war, as much as we want to keep away from it if we possibly can, when the aggressors come and they move in as the communists are moving, then we must stand up by the help of Almighty God and *resist* it and that's exactly what we're doing at the present time ["Amen!"] and so far as war settling anything I'd like to say to everybody everywhere it is the atomic arsenal and the military might of the United States which is keeping the peace of the world right now ["Right!"] and that's what's doing it ["A-men!"].

And furthermore let's go a little further. The National Council says that war in the Atomic Age may destroy everything. Well this is one good evidence that the National Council leaders don't believe the Bible in these matters. My Bible teaches very plainly that this old world isn't going to be destroyed until after Jesus Christ comes and then it's gonna be destroyed by fire in judgement by Almighty God. . . . And I don't believe for *one moment* that we're gonna see the atomic blast destroy this world while you and I are here. It's just not going to happen. But these communists and these liberals are using the fear of the bomb to frighten us so we won't stand up for our principles of morality and we will retreat from freedom . . . and our political leaders —some of them—are being intimidated by this type of propaganda. . . .

We don't want the peace of communism; we don't want the peace of slavery; we don't want the peace of tyranny. *We want the peace of freedom!* ["A-men!"]

The program ends with a plea for more contributions. Then the station announcer notes that Dr. McIntire can be heard twice a day six times a week over this station and that all the programs are sponsored by McIntire's newspaper, *The Christian Beacon.*

Recently, McIntire's radio programs have come under fire for presenting a distorted picture of the world. The "home" station of WXUR, for instance, has been accused of "blatant anti-Semitism" by the ADL. Other complaints have been lodged by the Catholic Interracial Council of New York, the American Baptist Convention, the United Church of Christ, the AFL-CIO, the National Urban League and the NAACP. The issue came to a head when WXUR applied to the FCC to have its license reissued when Faith Theological Seminary took over the operation of the station. To the annoyance of McIntire's critics the license was granted.

Soon afterward, the Pennsylvania State House of Representatives in the 1965 session passed Resolution 160 calling into question the fairness of the radio presentations and asking that the FCC initiate an investigation. This infuriated McIntire and he began a series of "Cow Pasture Rallies" in 1966 to rally support to his side and to rescind the resolution.

I went to one of these rallies and it was much like his radio shows, but this time curiously with more of a religious slant. It was held on a farm in rural Pennsylvania, and some three hundred people turned up carrying their own aluminum-and-plastic folding chairs. They were middle-class Americans, neatly dressed and serious; many carried Bibles. A buckboard stage had been set up, and some gospel singers entertained the crowd before the speeches. A few songs were sung, a long prayer was offered, there were a few short talks, and then eventually everyone settled back to hear the featured speaker, Carl McIntire.

He is a large man with a firm handshake who leans protectively over a person when in conversation. His speaking voice is strong; it echoed up and down the valley. His style of speaking is emotional: he waves his arms, his voice quavers, then whispers, then rises to a crescendo only to drop off into a soft purr. He calls the crowd "beloved": "Oh, beloved," he said, "my Bible says . . . that you can't serve Baal and serve God at the same time. . . . You can't talk about freedom without attacking communism and you can't talk about following God without attacking believing in a socialist state. . . ." The crowd nodded its approval. McIntire went on to discuss the injustice of Resolution 160 and asked everyone there to support him in his fight.

As the hours passed and the sun began to disappear over the horizon, McIntire turned the rally into a revival. How this was to help in his fight against Resolution 160 is unclear; it may have been the mood of the moment. With heads bowed, the audience was asked to make a decision for Christ. McIntire alternatively scolded, cajoled, pleaded, teased and begged the group, asking for those who felt they had God in their hearts to stand up. The crowd was silent. Again McIntire begged and pleaded, he offered prayers; his voice rose in anger at his enemies, softened at the mention of God and the Scriptures. First one person stood up; McIntire cried for joy. Then two more stood up, then another and another, until by the end of the evening the exhausted but happy crowd had seen six people stand up for Jesus. It was, in McIntire's words, "a very successful rally."

3

Dr. Frederick Charles Schwarz of the Christian Anti-Communism Crusade claims that it is dishonest to include him and his organization in any political study. In the main, there is considerable justification for such a point of view because his Crusade does differ markedly from all other groups. He will say that he is neither right-wing, nor conservative, nor a Fundamentalist. The only two adjectives he will acknowledge are "Christian" and "anti-Communist."

Any cursory examination of the organization will show the

following differences: he has no regular radio show; he has not built any monuments to himself such as cathedrals or seminaries; his letters to his estimated 50,000 supporters contain no drumbeat pleas for money; his speeches and writings display a modicum of good sense and intelligence; he is the most open about his finances (usually producing the latest balance sheet the instant the subject is mentioned); and his activities for the most part are limited to discussing communism and the enemies of Christianity and freedom. In spite of this, however, there is a thread of politics running through his organization and his activities; it cannot be avoided.

Schwarz's detractors are many and vocal. He has been called a "patriot for profit"; the " 'Enry 'Iggins of the Right"; a namedropper who never smiles, who is rude, "wary" and "dumpy," and who rages at his staff in a shrill, Cockney-flavored voice. All this is unfair and detracts from understanding the man and his Crusade.

Schwarz was born in Brisbane, Queensland, Australia, in 1913, the son of a well-to-do Viennese Jew who had embraced Christianity. He won degrees in science, art and medicine at the University of Queensland and for a number of years thereafter was a general practitioner and psychiatrist in the suburbs of Sydney. He was also a lay preacher in the local Baptist church.

Schwarz first became interested in the anti-Communist cause in 1940 when he took on a well-known Australian Communist in debate and was soundly trounced. His pride was hurt by his own lack of knowledge, so he began to read all the books he could find on communism—those of Marx, Engels, Lenin and Stalin for a start. In time his knowledge was such that he was asked by many groups to lecture on the subject. He eventually took his revenge on the Communists when, one day, he found himself speaking in the Sydney Domain, the Australian version of Speakers' Corner. A Communist fired a question at him: "What is dialectical materialism?" he asked. Schwarz shot back: "Dialectical materialism is the philosophy of Karl Marx that is formulated by taking the dialectic of Hegel, marrying it to the materialism of Feuerbach, abstracting from it the concept of progress in terms of the conflict of contradictory, interacting forces called the Thesis and the Antithesis culminating at a critical nodal point where one overthrows the other, giving rise to the Synthesis, applying it to the history of social development, and deriving therefrom an essentially revolutionary concept of social change."

The questioner's jaw dropped, and he looked at Schwarz with wide-open eyes. "Don't blame me," said Schwarz. "It is your philosophy, not mine. You are the one who believes it."[10]

By 1950 Schwarz was well known in Australian anti-Communist circles. He came to the attention of Dr. Carl McIntire and Dr. T. T. Shields, the latter a Baptist minister from Toronto, both of whom were visiting Australia that year. They persuaded Schwarz to make a two-month tour of the United States, which he subsequently did. In 1953 Schwarz returned to America and set up the tax-free Christian Anti-Communism Crusade in Waterloo, Iowa, in partnership with W. E. Pietsch, a local radio evangelist. The purpose of the organization was "to combat communism by means of lectures in schools, colleges, civic clubs, servicemen's organizations and other similar organizations and through radio and television broadcasts and by providing courses for missionaries and others to be used in Bible schools and seminaries and the holding of religious and evangelistic services in churches, and through the publication of books, pamphlets and literature. . . ."

In 1956, the Crusade moved to San Pedro, California, and two years later five miles away to Long Beach where it is situated today. It maintains regional offices in Waterloo, Houston, Seattle, San Francisco, Indianapolis and Sydney, Australia.

Schwarz received two assists that helped to make his name known nationally. Billy Graham arranged a meeting with congressmen whom Schwarz addressed in Washington. Shortly thereafter, in 1957, Schwarz was asked to testify before the HCUA. His topic was "International Communism (the Communist Mind)."

It was this testimony before the HCUA that perhaps catapulted Schwarz into the role as an "expert" on communism, a reputation he still enjoys today. It also best reflects his views on communism. He sees the Communists as having grown from a handful of men half a century ago to a vast and powerful dictatorship controlling nearly one third of the world. Christianity, he has said, after two thousand years can do no better. In his view, Communists are incredibly intelligent, capable, resourceful, clever, well-organized, sinister and quite mad. He believes, for instance, that they have been successful in the past because of the belief in and the application of three "scientific laws." The first is, he says, " 'There is no God.' They are proudly, unashamedly atheistic in theory and practice. When they deny God, they simultaneously deny every virtue and every value that originates with God. They deny moral law. They deny absolute standards of truth and righteousness. An entire civilized code of moral and ethical values is destroyed so that they are free to erect in their place new moral and ethical standards as the occasion demands."

The second "scientific law," according to Schwarz, "is that man is a material machine. He is matter in motion and nothing more. Man is a body, and he is completely describable in terms of the laws of chemistry and physics. Man has no soul, no spirit, no significant individual value, no continuity of life. He is entirely an evolutionary product, the species *Homo sapiens,* and subject to modification, adaptation and transformation by the applied, established laws of animal husbandry."

The final "law" is economic determinism. "It states," Schwarz told the Committee, "that the qualities of human intelligence, personality, emotional and religious life merely reflect the economic environment; that in the last analysis what we think, what we feel, what we believe, whom we love, and whom we worship is simply an expression of the environment in which we are raised, and since that environment is primarily concerned with economic forces, in the final analysis, man is a determined economic being."

Schwarz went on to tell the HCUA hearing that communism rests on a class concept, that its followers believe that capitalism creates a degenerate environment, that they believe in the universality of class war and that the ends justify the means.[11]

Brooks R. Walker, the author of *The Christian Fright Peddlers* (a book, incidentally, that Schwarz believes treated him fairly), criticizes Schwarz's view of communism. He writes that Schwarz reduces communist philosophy to the point where it appears absurd. He adds that Schwarz overplays the Communist's commitment to scientific empiricism. Walker then notes that he equates atheism with the repudiation of ethics and morality, which, if true, would impugn the name of many moral and ethical atheists.

Schwarz does these atheists a further dishonor by linking all atheism with communism.

Walker does say, however, that Schwarz *has* grasped the essence of one communist appeal: the program to change human nature. Schwarz described the ideal communist environment: "There will be no need for a police force; there will be nothing for police to do. There will be no need for an income-tax department because everyone working, according to his natural impulses, gives of his best for the general well-being, and out of the abundance thus created retains only his own personal needs. Farewell anger, lust and greed, envy, malice and strife, pestilence and war; enter golden, compassionable, cooperative brotherhood; mankind will live together in the glorious day of communism that has dawned on earth."

Behind all this, notes Walker, "is the certain knowledge that one man must be sacrificed, and he is the most important of all—the individual. Human nature has been redefined by someone, some group, other than the only person who has a right to say what human nature should be—the individual. The nature of man has been placed in the keeping of an elite, now called the Presidium, which is entrusted with deciding what is best for man."[12]

One reason I put Schwarz among the Christian right groups is that he, too, equates freedom, capitalism, free enterprise and Christianity as indivisible. None, in his mind, can exist without the other. American freedom, he writes, rests on an economic base. Walker points out that Schwarz falls into the same trap Marx did: he has reduced the complexities of history to a single-cause theory of economics. Schwarz's viewpoint, furthermore, tends to polarize the world into two camps, good and evil. There are no gray areas, just black and white, take your choice. This is a common view among all minor political groups.

Schwarz is also criticized for putting too much emphasis on the vulnerability of the student to communist ideas. He talks of the "student intellectual who is susceptible to the appeals of communism by reason of his educational conditioning" who "sees the opportunity to mold men and create history." To many people, this is a fatuous argument.

The greatest criticism, however, is directed toward Schwarz's

constant use of scare phrases. He once said to an audience—
perhaps his best-known remark: "Christians! To arms! The enemy
is at the gate! Buckle on the armor of the Christian and go forth to
the battle! When they come for you, as they have for many others,
and on a dark night, in a dank cellar, they take a wide-bore
revolver with a soft-nose bullet, and they place it at the nape of
your neck. . . ."[13] On another occasion he told an audience that
Khrushchev himself had "chosen San Francisco as headquarters of
the world communist dictatorship—the Mark Hopkins Hotel will
make splendid offices for him." Again he has said: "If you own
shares of common stock, it means you! Now, fifteen million
Americans own common stock! If the Reds win, it means the
gallows!" Another of his famous scare phrases was the remark he
made to the HCUA where he said that the Communists had
tentatively set the deadline for the conquest of America at 1973.
Critics point out that if this were indeed true, this is no time to sit
around and talk about it as Schwarz is doing; it is time to man the
barricades.

"I asked to be judged," he told me, "not on whether I frighten
people but on whether I give a true picture of the nature of
communism, the magnitude of the communist danger and the
consequences of communist conquest." He added: "I think fear is
a stimulus; it makes the adrenalin flow." In reply to those critics
who say he paralyzes people with his phraseology, he said emphatically: "I think they're wrong!"

But Schwarz does not eschew emotionalism. "Yes, my logic
makes others emotional," he said, "but *I'm* not emotional. Emotion is part of humanity. If someone tells you a member of your
family has been hurt and you don't get emotional, you're either in
a state of shock—which is protective—or abnormal. Now I can
tell about that person being hurt in a calm, quiet voice . . . ," he
said.

Schwarz is criticized also because he comes up with no solutions. But the evangelist doctor does not see it that way. His job,
he explained, is to educate, not to provide the answers. "In
medical terms," he said, "I am a pathologist. He is the one who
analyzes, describes and researches the disease. He never cured
anyone in his life; he simply provides the physician with informa-

tion." Yet, in a sense, Schwarz believes that by analyzing communism and by explaining it to the public, he is, in effect, partially providing the cure, because he is convinced that an informed public is the best defense against communism.

He is particularly irritated by many of his critics. He calls them totalitarian in nature because they apparently believe that the ordinary people are not fit to hear the truth except from some approved elite. This, he says, is ridiculous. "You can learn more in a half hour in a library," he told me, "than you can from years of reading newspapers."

The 1962 TV documentary called "Thunder on the Right," produced by CBS, particularly rankles him. He considers it the "most effective 'forgery by film' I have ever seen." Nowhere, he wrote to the producer, "was there any intelligent presentation of the message which consumes the great majority of the time at the [anti-communism] schools. This I consider basic dishonesty." Schwarz wrote to the president of CBS asking if his Crusade could buy a 16 mm film presentation of the film. "I would like to use it," he wrote, "at our anti-communism schools to illustrate great technical proficiency in the service of dishonesty." Schwarz received no reply.

Personally, Schwarz is a pleasant and informal middle-aged man. He wears short-sleeved shirts around the office and will put his feet on his desk when in conversation. He is equally as informal with his staff, his favorite phrase being "Righto!" His Australian twang seems at first to be nearer a Down East accent. He is, however, high-strung and full of nervous energy. Whenever he senses that an unpleasant question is about to be asked he will break in and say, "Just a minute . . . just a minute . . . just a minute . . ." in an attempt to have it rephrased.

His Crusade's headquarters are located in downtown Long Beach in what was at one time a bank building. Empty tellers' cages stand to the left as one enters. Along one wall to the rear of the building were 50,000 copies of Schwarz's book, *You Can Trust the Communists* (*to be Communists*) which were destined, so Schwarz said, for Louisiana schools. The book's title had been changed to *Communism—the Deceitful Tyranny,* lest the young minds misinterpret the original title. Schwarz claimed that over one million copies of the book had been sold since it was first published in 1960.

Schwarz spreads his message to the American people through "Schools of Anti-Communism," a week-long series of lectures that run from nine in the morning until nine-thirty at night. It costs ten dollars to attend all sessions, plus an additional sum for the banquet at the end. Featured speakers over the years have included ex-Communist Helen Birnie; F. Gano Chance; Major General William F. Dean; Senator Thomas J. Dodd; E. Merrill Root, the author of *Brain-Washing in the High Schools* and *Collectivism on the Campus;* J. Fred Schlafly, Jr., president of Defenders of American Liberty (a sort of right-wing ACLU); W. Cleon Skousen; and Commander Paul Terry, director of education for the Copley Press newspaper chain.

A typical school was the Greater Chicago School of Anti-Communism, held in late May 1965. Schwarz spoke eight times, on such subjects as "Communist Philosophy," "Communist Fronts" and "How to Debate Communists and Fellow Travellers." Charles Fox, editor of the California-based muckraking magazine, *Tocsin,* spoke on "Communism on the Campus." Herbert A. Philbrick spoke on "I Led Three Lives" (also the name of his book) and the "Assassination of President Kennedy." M. Stanton Evans spoke on "The Investigating Committees," and Dr. Joost Sluis, a surgeon who also runs the Crusade's Northern California branch, spoke on "British Guiana: A Case History." There were also numerous films: "Nightmare in Red," "Communist Weapon of Allure," "Schwarz-[Harry] Bridges Debate" and the old favorite, "Operation Abolition," were but a few shown to the audience. And there was Janet Greene, the Crusade's director of music, whose guitar-playing was supposed to "demonstrate the value of folk-singing in exposing the doctrine and practices of communism." Some of the songs she sings are entitled: "Termites and Comrade's Lament," "Inch by Inch," "Fascist Threats," and "Commie Lies." Schwarz confessed to me that he wrote the words to some of the songs.

The most famous of all the schools held by Schwarz and his Crusade was actually not a school at all but a rally held in October 1961, in the Hollywood Bowl before 15,000 cheering Crusaders.

On the stage were such luminaries as George Murphy, John Wayne, Ronald Reagan, Pat O'Brien, Lloyd Nolan, Robert Stack, Roy Rogers, Edgar Bergen, Andy Devine, Walter Brennan, Cesar Romero, Tex Ritter, Ozzie and Harriet Nelson, Jack L. Warner and William Lundigan. But the star of the show was C. D. Jackson, *Life* magazine's publisher. Previously, *Life* had called the Crusade "a new kind of 'revival meeting,' serving non-religious ends. . . ." Schwarz preaches, the article went on, "doomsday by communism in 1973 unless every American starts distrusting his neighbor as a possible Communist or 'Comsymp.' " The editors of *Life* apparently reconsidered their position, and as a result Jackson journeyed West to make amends. He apologized—and ended by aligning *Life* with Schwarz in the fight against communism. Two weeks later, *Life,* in an editorial, reaffirmed its hostility to the radical right but reserved more praise for Schwarz as "well informed," adding, even if the Crusade did attract those people who were "too superheated to teach or learn anything."

Life's reference to "superheated" people points up one of Schwarz's problems: the quality and stability of his followers. In many cases these people belong to the more volatile right-wing groups, those organizations sometimes known as "meet and scream" groups, who are ready to condemn, attack, harass or intimidate at the first slip of a liberal phrase. Schwarz admits he is embarrassed by them at times but says that it is the price one pays for educating a far larger group. In one instance, Schwarz parodied the more extreme individuals by saying that they were the type who referred to the Kennedy Administration as "that nest of traitors up there in Washington who are selling us down the river." To his discomfort, the audience broke out into vigorous applause, not at the parody but at the remark. "You know," he said, "they *actually* misunderstood what I was saying; they thought I meant it."[14]

Schwarz is open to considerable criticism because all follow-up work after an Anti-Communism School session is left in the hands of the local individuals who feel so inclined. Schwarz maintains no machinery to ensure that what he has taught to a certain group is being spread throughout the area after he has left. In many cases the void is filled by members of the John Birch Society who are zealous organizers and are quick to grab anyone who has become agitated by Schwarz's remarks.

The Crusade is a half-a-million-dollar operation. The bulk of its income comes from membership dues, private contributions, special meetings and schools. Half of its expenses go to advertising its meetings and administrative expenses. Other major outlays include salaries and "foreign missionary" work. Schwarz is paid $5,000 per year and his wife draws another $5,400.

The Crusade's 1965 foreign investment included gifts to various enterprises in South America (over $25,000), Japan ($7,000), and for "television programs"—exactly where is not stated ($30,000). Past investments, in this case in 1962, include financing a printing press in Kerala, India; the purchasing of a property for orphan boys in Secunderabad; the initiation of an Anti-Communism School in Japan; the publication in Spanish of *You Can Trust the Communists* for distribution in Mexico; and various other smaller programs in South Africa, British Guiana and Jamaica.

Schwarz received considerable publicity in 1963 when some of his zealous followers began distributing a twelve-page comic book below the border entitled *If Communism Comes to Mexico*. This booklet shows Communists standing over laborers with whips, other peasants languishing in prison, and a priest being driven through the streets at the point of a bayonet. The booklet concludes that, if the Communists take over, most Mexicans will lose their lives. There follow some Bible verses and a plea to all patriots to defend their homeland.

Schwarz's backers are a wealthy lot. Patrick Frawley has long been a generous donor. His Technicolor, Inc., and Schick Safety Razor Company sponsored the Hollywood Bowl rally in 1961. Frawley is quoted as saying: "Dr. Schwarz will not lack for money while I'm around." Another big contributor is the Richfield Oil Company, also a sponsor of the 1961 rally. Allen-Bradley is a big contributor; so is the Lilly Endowment and the Glenmede Trust of Philadelphia, Pennsylvania.

One of the questions that Schwarz has to parry time and time again is: "Why is it necessary for an Australian to come to

America to tell us how we can be saved from communism?" Schwarz answers by saying: "How *dare* Sister Kenny come to the United States to try and stop children from having poliomyelitis!" He went on to say that "if there were eight Soviet subs off Australian cities, there is nothing the Australian Prime Minister could do except scream to the United States and plead for help. If it doesn't come, you're sunk." Freedom, he said, "will live or die on what the United States does, so that is why I am here. Americans have always welcomed ideas from other people. They have been wonderfully generous to me."

4

A word should be said on another Christian right group. Its name is the Church League of America, sometimes known as the National Layman's Council. It was founded in 1937 by three prominent Chicago businessmen who were decidedly anti-New Deal. Roosevelt's "court-packing" is cited by the League as the reason for the original organizational meeting. Once established, the League campaigned against a third term for FDR in 1940 and against federal aid to education.

According to its literature, the purpose of the League is to "rekindle the spirit of valiant Christian Americanism." It complains that "Marxian Socialism is a growing force in this nation" and that this "organized Radicalism must be met intelligently and courageously." The American form of government, it notes, "is distinctly a limited government deriving its powers from the governed and it must always remain so. . . . An *all powerful government tends to become arrogant,* imperious, extravagant and Fascistic. . . . Those who are affiliated with the Church League of America in action or in sympathy recognize that intellectual and spiritual freedom are inseparable from the freedom to accumulate and own and that free enterprise is the only foundation upon which free institutions (churches, colleges, etc.) can satisfactorily survive. . . ."

The activities of the League fall into three categories: "research," publishing, and local activities such as lectures and seminars. The League claims to have "over five tons" of "countersubversive" files with one million three-by-five cross-reference index cards, all of which is supposed to have been accumulated since the turn of the century. These files contain information on "Communists and fellow-travelers," many of whom are supposed to be members of the clergy. The League is also supposed to have a complete library on leftist literature from the *Worker* to *New Masses* to *People's World.* There are also files on the ACLU and the ADA and a section set off by itself on John Dewey. Very few outsiders have seen these files.

For anyone contributing ten dollars or more per year to the League, "documental information" from the research section may be secured. Unlimited information is not available for the ten-dollar contributor but is calculated on a pro-rata basis—roughly one name for every additional five-dollar contribution—after the initial information on four people is obtained.

The League also publishes "special detailed documented reports on organizations, individuals, publications and movements" which are free to the ten-dollar contributor. In addition, the League publishes a monthly newssheet "of current subversive activity" called *News and Views* which goes to all those contributing five dollars or more.

These files are housed in a contemporary colonial, $225,000 building in Wheaton, Illinois, a Chicago suburb. No outsider is allowed to inspect the files, nor is one even allowed to see the area in which they are housed. When I stopped by the office, I was politely rebuffed in my attempts to see them by Mrs. Edgar C. Bundy, the wife of the executive director (who was away on business at the time). She most willingly sold me some of the League's literature but would not let me stray past the lobby. As I was leaving, she called after me cheerfully: "Now you write something nice about us or we'll hate you."

A considerable amount of literature is available for anyone who wishes to buy it. Books include *Certain Activities and Affiliations of 181 Lutheran Clergymen,* by J. B. Matthews; *Collectivism in the Churches,* by Major Edgar C. Bundy; and *I Was an NKVD Agent,* by Anatole Granovski. The League's latest catalogue (1966) lists fifty-six "valuable tape recordings for anti-Communist study groups or public meetings," two of which are seminars featuring collections of six and fifteen tapes respectively. A one-hour tape rents for four dollars and sells for eight dollars. Some of the titles on the tapes are: "Communist Penetration of Religious Groups" (one hour), "Enter the Anti-Christ" (one hour), "Will the Communists Capture the U.S.?" (two hours) and "Porno-graphic Literature in the Churches and Recommended by the National Council of Churches" (one hour and a half). Most of the tapes are narrated by Major Bundy.

Films are also for rent or sale. Twenty-one are listed in their catalogue. "By Their Fruits Ye Shall Know Them" is a favorite and is described as "a hard-hitting documentary exposing all of the Communist Party and front organization publications and their vicious attacks on Barry Goldwater, calling for his defeat and the election of Lyndon Johnson; and a host of official publications of liberal church groups which are doing the same thing in the same language. . . ." (The title of this film is also the unofficial motto of the Church League; its members will say, for instance, that the files are *not* used for name-calling purposes but simply speak for themselves.)

Other films available are the sixty-minute "Katanga" ("See the stark tragedy of how the so-called 'peaceful' United Nations . . . savagely attacked the only anti-Communist province of the Congo. . . ."), the twenty-minute "It's a Grand Old Flag," the thirty-minute "Ronald Reagan on the Welfare State" and the old standby, the thirty-minute "Operation Abolition."

One of the major activities of the League is its "Counter Subversive Seminars" sponsored by local groups throughout the country which must produce a minimum attendance of fifty indi-viduals. The "tuition" is ten dollars and is tax-deductible and includes a year's subscription to *News and Views*. The seminars last from two to four days and feature lectures by Major Bundy and others who are described as "the highest qualified men in the nation." Each seminar is built around *A Manual for Survival*, a textbook compiled by the Church League. This book begins by outlining the dangers of communism, then it discusses communist techniques, such as infiltration and subversion, and concludes with a chapter on what the individual can do about it.

On the Supreme Court the book said: "June 17, 1957, has

come to be known as Red Monday by both lawyers and anti-Communists. . . . On that day Chief Justice Warren and Justices Frankfurter, Douglas, Black, Harlan, and Brennan handed down four decisions which in effect told the Communists 'Go ahead, boys, you have nothing to worry about.' "

On American education it said: "There are about 1,391,000 teachers of all classes from kindergarten to graduate level in the United States. Of this number, roughly 300,000 are college, university or seminary teachers, professors or administrators. Dr. J. B. Matthews, a recognized authority in this field, has compiled the front records of some 6,000 educators, practically all of them at college or university level. Of this number probably not over 2,000 could be said to have long, consistent, and significant communist front affiliations. Yet to paraphrase a famous observation of Winston Churchill, never have so few served to bring so much disgrace and suspicion on so many otherwise honorable and patriotic people."

To combat these tendencies, the book recommends that the patriot undertake certain activities. First: read the *Christian Beacon, Dan Smoot Report, Human Events, National Review* or *News and Views*. Then, "do not try to fight alone. Join and actively support reputable organizations which convince you that they are doing a good job in combatting subversion." After that, mail out "countersubversive materials" or write letters to editors exposing the "leftist" letters. If no local group is available to join, then "locate a few experts with former FBI, Army, Navy or other intelligence experience and form a small study and action group"; get anti-Communists to speak at the local clubs and luncheons; and never allow anyone in your hearing "to slur the FBI, the House Committee on Un-American Activities, the Senate Internal Security Subcommittee, the Church League of America, the American Council of Christian Churches or any other organization which you know to be fighting subversion."

The man behind all this activity is Major Edgar C. Bundy, a graduate of Oglethorpe University in Atlanta and Wheaton College in Wheaton, Illinois. Bundy served in the Air Force from 1941 to 1948, which included an assignment as an intelligence officer on

General Claire Chennault's 14th Air Force staff in China. During his service, Bundy was ordained a Baptist minister in the Southern Baptist Convention but has never held a pastorate. After he left the Air Force he continued to serve in the reserves and otherwise earned his living as city editor of the Wheaton *Daily Journal.*

Bundy first came to national attention in 1950. The previous year he had testified before the Senate Appropriations Committee in opposition to the foreign aid bill. He advised that funds for Europe and NATO be diverted to the Pacific, specifically to China, because, he said, if China fell, then Japan, the Philippines, India, Burma, the Malay States and the Dutch East Indies would all fall to the Communists. And South Korea, he added, would be invaded by North Korea. When China did fall and South Korea was invaded, Bundy's stock shot up significantly. He was hailed as a political clairvoyant. His correct predictions at that time are used today to strengthen the predictions he makes for tomorrow.

Bundy was also active in the American Legion. In 1954, he sponsored the Legion's condemnation of the Girl Scout Handbook as "un-American." The next year he led the Legion forces that secured the adoption of resolutions condemning UNESCO; this group also called for an investigation of the ACLU and various foundations. Bundy's resolution asking the Legion to recommend America's withdrawal from the U.N., however, was defeated. Again, in 1961, Bundy led the Legion attack on the Foreign Policy Association. The previous year he had jumped with both feet into the Air Force Manual Affair by vigorously defending the inclusion of the material that had originated in the literature of Billy James Hargis.

This was also the year that Bundy visited General Walker in Germany. Walker had included Bundy's book, *Collectivism in the Churches,* on his recommended reading list for the "Ladies Study Groups," made up of 24th Infantry Division wives. This was a part of Walker's "Pro-Blue" program that was to bring him under such fire and eventual retirement.

Bundy took over the reins of the Church League in 1956 and since that year has built the organization up to where it now is considered the largest right-wing "research" (in this sense, of people and organizations, not of ideas) group of its kind, with a staff of twenty-three and receipts (in 1964) of $208,000. The latter figure represents nearly a tenfold increase since Bundy took charge. To be sure, many other organizations have similar files, but nobody has "over five tons" of them. Myers Lowman's Circuit Riders, Inc., maintains extensive files on church laymen; so does Lloyd Wright's American Security Council; George Washington Robnett's (one of the original founders of the Church League) Institute for Special Research is also said to have extensive files on Communists; so does Myron C. Fagan's Cinema Educational Guild, which concentrates on Reds in the movie industry; the Cardinal Mindzenty Foundation keeps files on "slanted" or "anti-anti-Communist textbooks"; Hargis' Christian Crusade, mentioned previously, has extensive files; and so does the Americanism Educational League from Los Angeles and the International Services of Information, Inc., from Baltimore.

Bundy's public utterances are little different from those of Carl McIntire, who is a friend of his. He has characterized disarmament as a "dangerous delusion"; the late Edward R. Murrow as "a smear artist against anti-Communist forces"; Harry Overstreet as a "minor rank philosophy professor"; and academic freedom as "the ultimate of insanity."

". . . The fact was and is that COMMUNISM and THEO-LOGICAL MODERNISM are as one!" he wrote in *News and Views*. "Communism and Modernism," he continued, "walk hand in hand. They are bedfellows. They complement one another. They come to each other's rescue when they get in trouble. They have a mutual defense. They maintain a mutual offense against their common enemy—Bible-believing Christians who want no part of their false doctrines."

Church Leaguers, along with the followers of Hargis, McIntire and Schwarz, would add a hearty "A-men!" to that.

10

The Educators

1

The final category of right-wing groups is the educational-intellectual one, those groups who promote new ideas, remake old ones and reflect the views that are current on the right. There are seven organizations that deserve some comment. Two are educational institutions: Freedom School and Rampart College, and Harding College and the National Education Program. Three are "idea" organizations: the Foundation for Economic Education, the American Economic Foundation, and the Intercollegiate Studies Institute. And two are publications: *Human Events* and *National Review*.

Freedom School and Rampart College are two small, private, unaccredited institutions located on the same campus—a 526-acre area outside the town of Larkspur, Colorado, a few miles north of Colorado Springs. The rustic-looking campus sits in a lovely valley of fir trees along the Rampart Range of the Rocky Mountains.

The Freedom School was founded in 1956 "to conduct a school for students sixteen years old and over to teach primarily the libertarian philosophy of individualism." The courses run for a two-week period and cost from $60 ("workshops for advanced students") to $350 (for a course in "Explorations in Human Actions," limited to executives). Faculty members are drawn from other organizations and institutions. They include Frank Chodorov, a former editor of *The Freeman* and a founder of the Intercollegiate Society of Individualists; Rose Wilder Lane, a benefactress of the school (one of the buildings is named for her) and a former editor of Merwin K. Hart's National Economic Council Review of Books; Leonard Read, president and founder of the Foundation for Economic Education; newspaper owner R. C. Hoiles; and a clutch of economists from such institutions as the University of Wisconsin, Ohio Northern, Queens College (Flushing, New York), University of Michigan and Utah State Agricultural College.

In 1963, "The Phrontistery" (Greek for "a place for thinking") was added to the school's facilities, complete with dean and visiting lecturers. Two of the better known of the latter in the past have been Milton Friedman, Professor of Economics at the University of Chicago, and Ludwig Von Mises, a visiting Professor of Economics at New York University and a consultant to FEE. The Phrontistery runs for only six months during the winter and is described as "an intensive workshop."

According to its literature, Freedom School's courses "seek to find the truth of man's nature which can enhance man's well-being." The two weeks of instruction are broken down into six sections of study: "The Nature of Man," "Acting Man," "The Nature of the Market," "The Human Record," "The Nature of Government" and "The Nature of a Free Man." The approach to these subjects will be discussed later in the chapter.

The other institution, Rampart College, was founded in 1963 and is a four-year unaccredited school specializing "on the findings already available . . . through [the] Freedom School operation." At the moment, Freedom School facilities are being used until the construction of the college's graduate school is completed. When finished, the Rampart College complex, overlapping somewhat with the Freedom School plant, will have cost some five million dollars to build and endow. The purpose of the college is to educate students "in the art of thinking, rather than memorizing. Their conclusions will be reached through logical reasoning and not through the parroting of opinions expressed by others."

Although unaccredited, courses at Rampart—primarily history, business administration, economics and "praxeology" (the study of human actions)—can lead to the awarding of a degree. Exactly what kind is not specified but college officials talk in terms of "master's degrees" and "PhD's."

Together, Freedom School and Rampart College house a library of 11,000 books which they hope to enlarge to 100,000 when the Rampart expansion is completed. The current cornerstone of the library is the works of Mill, Locke and Spencer, and the complete works of the Foundation for Economic Education.

Both schools generate a number of publications. One is called the *Newsletter* and is used to stimulate and maintain interest in the school among alumni, friends and contributors. Rampart has its own *Journal* ("of individualist thought"), a well-bound quarterly featuring articles by such writers, past and present, as Lysander Spooner, Albert Szent-Gyorgyi and Herbert Spencer. The Pine Tree Press is the name under which the two schools publish or distribute a number of works. There is *Anarchy* and *This Bread Is Mine,* both by the schools' dean, Robert LeFevre; there is *The Anti-Capitalist Mentality,* by Ludwig Von Mises; *Economics in One Lesson,* by Henry Hazlitt; and *What Has Government Done to Our Money?* by Murray N. Rothbard. The Press has its own tabloid called *Pine Tree,* which is "for the politically disenchanted." It cost ten dollars for a year's subscription, and one of its "regular columnists" is George Boardman from Chloride, Arizona, who is also associated with Kent Courtney's Conservative Society of America.

In 1962 Freedom School—then still the major operation—reported a total income of $187,000. The bulk of this money comes from private contributors. The largest in that year was the Deering Milliken Foundation, which gave $100,000. In fact, one of the biggest boosters of the school is Roger Milliken, the anti-union textile mill owner from Spartanburg, South Carolina. He serves as a trustee to both of these institutions. Other large contributors in the past have been the Donner Foundation (now called the Independence Foundation), the Winchester Foundation (supported by Pierre F. Goodrich), and the Ingersoll, Grede, Chance and Barber-Colman Foundations.

Many of the students, particularly those taking the executive-centered "Explorations in Human Action" course, come from the industrial companies that provide the funds for the above foundations. Thus Ingersoll Milling Machine, the Barber-Colman Company, Grede Foundries and the A. B. Chance Company all send their favored employees there. Deering Milliken, however, is the most enthusiastic company. In 1965, for instance, it sent a total of 167 employees to the Freedom School. This represented 58 percent of all the students that attended the school's courses that year.

The man behind all this activity is Robert LeFevre (he pronounces it "Luh Fave"), the founder and dean of both institutions. His background includes stints as radio disc jockey, sound effects engineer (one Minneapolis news story in 1935 described him as an "expert" who "made one noise or another 91 times during a 15-minute program"), real estate broker, army captain and newspaperman. He was also something of a cultist in his youth (although his own biography does not reflect it), having been an ardent follower of "Daddy" and "Mama" Ballard, leaders of the Great I AM Movement.

A slight digression is necessary here to explain this cult. The Great I AM Movement was founded in the early 1930s by Guy Ballard, an amateur theosophist, and his wife, Edna, an occultist and harpist. Their movement enjoyed some vogue between 1934 and 1940 and claimed several million followers (a doubtful estimate) at its peak. The movement took its name from Exodus 3:13–14 where Moses, in conversation with the voice out of the burning bush, asked: "Who shall I say sent me?" The answer was: "I am that I am."

If I understand it correctly, the basis for I AM, as it is known for short, stemmed from a vision Guy Ballard had on Mt. Shasta. There, he met "St. Germain," who gave Ballard a cup full of liquid from the "Universal Supply—Omnipotent Life itself." This liquid enabled Ballard's spirit to withdraw from his physical body. Then St. Germain took Ballard in his new state, wrapped in a sheet of flame, and traveled around the world, in one instance to visit Ballard's past incarnations—as a great musician in southern France and as an ancient Egyptian priest. The most important trip, however, was to Royal Teton Mountain where St. Germain kept the records of the entire world. A stone was touched, the rocks parted, huge bronze doors swung open and there, inside, were large rooms filled with gold and silver. In one room was a large golden disc with seven points to it, through which poured "the

Great Cosmic Beings," powerful currents of force received only by either the "Great Illumined" or the "Ascended Masters of Light." In another room were the records of the world written on gold sheets.

The "Mighty I AM presence" was the Ballards' way of saying God but was never clearly expressed   as such. "Ascendant Masters" were humans who, by their own effort, generated within themselves enough power and love to break away from human limitations. There were many such Masters: St. Germain, Jesus, God of the Swiss Alps, Angel Deva of the Jade Temple, Ray-O-Light, Cassiopeia, Quan Yin and, after his death in 1939, Guy Ballard himself.

The sect condemned xylophones, accordions, cymbals, banjoes and saxophones as carrying "certain destructive vibratory action." It also condemned bowling, fashion shows, going bare-legged (except in a tennis game), shirt-tails hanging out and anklets for girls under fifteen. It praised the harp, skating and swimming (except going in and out of the water, because the temperature change would "open the door to sex"). Politically, the movement was extremely conservative. Many I AM adherents were also members of William Dudley Pelley's Silver Shirts.

A certain number of I AM members were known as the "one hundred percenters." They swore to follow no other teachings and to abstain from all meat, onions, garlic, tobacco, liquor, narcotics, card playing and sexual intercourse.

Human life is maintained, they believed, as long as the "Silver Cord of Liquid White Light" is anchored in the heart. This Light comes from the Mighty I AM presence and enters through the top of an individual's head. The sect also believed in reincarnation. Guy Ballard believed he was the reincarnation of George Washington. His other reincarnations, he said, went back 70,000 years. His wife, Edna, was convinced she was the reincarnation of Joan of Arc and their only son, Donald, the reincarnation of the Marquis de Lafayette.

Part of the sect's ritual included "decrees" or "calls" whereby the power of the Mighty I AM presence was invoked to destroy the cult's enemies. One decree, directed at President Franklin D. Roosevelt and his wife, went: "Blast, blast, blast their carcasses from the face of the earth forever!" A more general one went as follows: "Send Legions of Thy Angel Devas of the Blue Lightning of Divine Love to seize, bind and remove from within and around me and my world all entities . . . forever! If they be of human creation, annihilate them! . . ." Ballard claims to have destroyed 400,000 such individuals in Philadelphia, 332,000 in New York City and one million in the rest of the United States within a single 23-hour period by just such invocations.[1]

I AM cultists also believed that whenever someone was reincarnated he always came back as someone worse than the previous person he was. Thus they thought that they were doing their enemies a favor by calling for their damnation before they got any worse.

In any event, LeFevre was a follower of the Ballards from 1936 to 1940 or so. He and one Pearl Diehl wrote a 199-page book in 1940 of their experiences in the cult called *"I AM"—America's Destiny* (Twin City House, St. Paul, Minnesota). LeFevre related how one day, when he was filing records in a radio studio, he was struck by the Great I AM presence, who spoke to him personally. LeFevre also relates a number of supernatural experiences: driving a car while asleep for over twenty miles without an accident (this was accomplished with the help of his "Higher Mental Body"), leaving his physical body for a trip through the air to Mt. Shasta, and seeing Jesus.

In 1940, Edna Ballard and her son Donald were indicted by a grand jury in Los Angeles for using the mails to defraud. Twenty-four other I AM leaders were also named in the first indictment; a supplemental indictment named LeFevre and Diehl as additional defendants. But charges against these two and a dozen others were soon dismissed at the request of the government.

The legal battles of the two Ballards is a long and complicated story involving a trial, a dismissal, a retrial, a conviction and a Supreme Court reversal. Edna Ballard, through all this, maintained the leadership of the cult, although membership had fallen off drastically. Later she was to publish a newssheet called *I AM Ascended Masters Youth in Action,* published by "Miracles, Inc." of Denver.

During World War II LeFevre served in the Army and was

honorably discharged in 1945 as a captain. Soon thereafter, he went with his wife on a cross-country lecture tour "in a pilgrimage for world peace." Their tour was financed by the Falcon Lair Foundation, a nonprofit group interested in religion, philosophy and government whose headquarters were "Falcon Lair," Beverly Hills, California, formerly the home of screen idol Rudolph Valentino. (One of the buildings at the Freedom School is named Falcon Lair.)

In 1950 LeFevre ran unsuccessfully for Congress in a Republican primary and then went to work for an anti-union organization called the Wage Earners Committee. A year or so later the committee was sued by two movie producers, Stanley Kramer and Dore Schary, for picketing and allegedly libeling their films as being pro-Communist. LeFevre and Ruth Dazey (now the editor of *Rampart Journal*) were among the defendants, but the case died out as the Wage Earners Committee disintegrated.

A few years later LeFevre went to work for the right wing in a big way. He became a vice-president of Merwin K. Hart's National Economic Council, a director of the Congress of Freedom, a director of the U.S. (sometimes United States) Day Committee—whose purpose it was to diminish in importance the observation of October 23 as United Nations Day—and an adviser to Harry Everingham's We, The People! The U.S. Day Committee made headlines in 1954, at the same time as Edgar Bundy, when LeFevre led an attack on the Girl Scout Handbook as having too many references to the U.N. The Scouts retreated, reporting that more than forty changes had been made—about half of which were due to LeFevre's criticism.

That same year LeFevre moved to Colorado Springs and began to write editorials for R. C. Hoiles' *Gazette-Telegraph*. He still writes for the newspaper today, claiming that his total output so far has been three thousand articles "all [written] in a patriotic, libertarian vein." Two years later he founded the Freedom School, where he has been ever since.

What drives LeFevre personally and the Freedom School ideologically—indeed, forms the bedrock upon which all courses are based—is a complicated philosophy that, in essence, rejects all government today as a barbaric tool of coercion. Government, although it may have had its uses at some point in the past, is seen as an anachronism in today's complicated world. LeFevre claims in his book, *The Nature of Man And His Government* (Caxton Printers, Caldwell, Idaho, 1963), that government is just another tool of man's devising, no better nor worse than the men who created it, and is calculated to make men stronger and better able to protect themselves. Strength, he writes, is found in compulsive unity. Therefore, "government, inherently, places individualism at a low point on any scale of values. Individuals are the enemy of government. Government is inescapably concerned with unity. Individuals are the necessary victims."

To maintain this unity, he writes, governments are required to use force; thus individuals, he reasons, are again the losers. When conformity is at a premium, then individuality goes for a discount. He describes it as follows:

> A peaceful and law-abiding citizen, for example, may have perfectly sound and moral reasons why he does not wish to share his money with the government or the politicians of Yugoslavia. His conviction can be logically derived, morally certain and sincerely maintained. In holding to his conviction, the individual is harming no one. His belief is not inimical to the welfare of other people. Actions which might spring from his belief are not aggressive. In other words, physically, mentally and morally, such a citizen can be above reproach.
>
> Yet, when the government adopts a policy which prescribes the sharing of his earnings with a foreign government, the man who objects to this can be treated in precisely the same manner as a bank robber could be treated and for the same reason. The government cannot brook a deviationist.[2]

Every citizen therefore, somehow, somewhere, is the victim of the aggressive tactics of government. "There is almost no activity in which human beings engage," he writes, "which is free of legality. Think what you will, do what you will, there is a law somewhere which either compels, limits or prohibits. . . . Thus the average person today, buttressed in by the government, surrounded and overshadowed by government, finds himself a lawbreaker several times during an average day."

But this, maintains LeFevre, is entirely in keeping with the function of government. Its job is to *pass* laws, not repeal them. He views government as a body selling compulsion that the people *must* buy in advance but who are never in a position to refuse to buy. Unlike the free marketplace, he adds, where man can enter or avoid depending on his own inclination, man has no choice but to join into an involuntary association with government.

Government's classic job, he continues, is to make war on government's enemies, whether it be the individual, the clan, the tribe, the community, the society or the foreign body. With the exception of the last-mentioned, each of these smaller entities can rob, pillage, riot and destroy but, he says, only government can conduct a war. The only *true* function of government, he adds, is to protect the peaceful from the belligerent; unfortunately, he says, the rules are extended and expanded to such extremes that the state itself soon becomes man's mortal foe.

Unlike other tools that man devises, government is not controllable by its creators. It becomes, he says, "a ravening monster" that knows no restraint. Therefore, the problem is, first, how do you control the tool you devised? Second, since the essence of any progress is the refining and improvement of the tools used, how can government be changed to be brought up to date?

Here LeFevre falters, for he has no answers. "We are trying to explore areas in which the nonpolitical structure can be used," he told me. He claims he is not recommending the abandonment of government for those who want it. But he does feel that not everyone should have to submit to it or receive its benefits. "Just imagine a situation," he said, "where there was no government. Just think how human relationships would change if everyone had to solve their own problems without relying on an instrument of coercion." He claims his ultimate goal is to see returned to man the qualities of character and responsibility and the recognition that he supports himself—qualities taken away, he says, by government.

LeFevre, who is a large, gregarious and pleasant man with white curly hair, denied to me that his ideas amounted to anarchy, as so many of his critics have suggested. "First of all," he said, "we [at the school] are a-political. We are Stoics and prefer the word 'autarchy,' " which he explained meant self-rule or self-sufficiency.

LeFevre's argument is based on the thesis that man is absolutely dependent on property. "This is not only true of humans," he said, "but of all animals as well." He pointed out that lion trainers, for instance, have sensed this for years; they realize that there is a certain point past which they cannot cross or the lion will attack. "Our ability to survive," continued LeFevre, "is predicated on our ability to dominate a portion of our environment. What does *me* good is the food *I* eat, not what *you* eat. Whatever the government takes that is rightfully mine, then it is a criminal." All morality, he went on, is predicated on private property: five of the Ten Commandments tell you, he notes, not to take another's property. The Latin word *proper,* he said, implies moral and proprietary conduct; in other words, proper conduct is conduct decided by the owner. The characteristics of property are that it has a value, a boundary and is subject to the control of the owner. "Every immoral act in the world," he said, "is a trespass of a property boundary. Property has no rights, but all human rights are rights to property."

LeFevre is a persuasive speaker. He fortifies his position by saying that his views are not airtight but need to be worked on by everyone. He only asks that his students snap out of the intellectual slough in which they have been living and begin to rethink things out for themselves.

His arguments are so cogently put that, at the end of a two-week session at the Freedom School, the students come reeling out of the classrooms, their self-confidence shaken and their previous notions thrown into a state of confusion. Robert Welch, for one, is furious at what LeFevre is doing because, he says, it is neutralizing many people who might otherwise be good fighters in the anti-Communist cause. Welch maintains that the students of LeFevre's philosophy come away believing that the whole system is so corrupt that there is no point in, for instance, voting (something, incidentally, that LeFevre proudly claims he does not do) or fighting Communists, since in their own minds the whole order must be overturned.[3]

LeFevre dismisses this criticism with a smile and a wave of the hand. He believes that his views are nearly to the point of becoming a vogue—soon to sweep the academic and political worlds like a prairie fire.

2

Harding College is a coeducational four-year school on a forty-acre campus in Searcy, Arkansas, a town of 7,500 situated in farm country fifty miles northeast of Little Rock. Since its early beginnings in 1910, the purpose of the college has been to provide sound education with a strong emphasis on religion and Christian morals. The curriculum is limited to liberal arts courses, and the school's Christian emphasis is restricted to the Fundamentalist dogma of the Church of Christ. Today there are 1,200 students, an endowment of over $13 million and a 96-man faculty with full scholastic accreditation.

But it is not really Harding that interests us here. It is the National Education Program, located on the Harding campus, and for all intents and purposes so intertwined with the college that the differences become meaningless. The NEP is also sometimes known as The American Heritage Center, and the whole operation is usually referred to collectively as "Harding," "the NEP" or "the Searcy complex."

Of particular interest is the man behind the entire operation: Dr. George Stuart Benson. Benson, himself a graduate of Harding, class of 1925, spent eleven years as a missionary and teacher in South China. He was a professor of English at Sun Yat Sen University in Canton for one year and then the president for six years of the Canton Bible School, which he founded. In 1936 he returned to the United States and took over the reins of his alma mater, which at that time could boast of only two buildings, 200 students, no accreditation and a $75,000 debt.

The same year he started the National Education Program. Its purpose, Benson wrote me, was and is "to emphasize the importance of Constitutional Government and private ownership of property and of faith in God as revealed in the Bible through the Old and the New Testaments. . . . We are strong for the personal freedom that we consider to be a God-given heritage to man and we have great faith in the private enterprise economy which developed into the most efficient and fruitful economy that man has ever known under our personal freedoms as guaranteed by our Constitution.

"Therefore, we look upon the three great supporting pillars of our American way of life as: Faith in God, Constitutional Government and Private Ownership of Property."

Recalling his feelings back in 1936, Benson said in a 1961 interview: "I was shocked and saddened at the lack of understanding and appreciation which most Americans seemed to have of their country and their heritage. They seemed beaten by adversity, disillusioned with democracy, ready to give up a free-enterprise system, which, even in the depths of the depression, gave them a standard of living far beyond anything else in the world. They had lost their Christian convictions and their sense of moral purpose and were listening to all manner of false prophets.

"Having seen despotism and totalitarianism at first hand in the Orient, I knew where this would lead, and I began talking about it to everyone who would listen."

Thus the NEP was founded to reverse this trend; and in the interval, it has grown into perhaps the largest right-wing propaganda source. No group distributes more literature or offers so much equipment, props and aids extolling the free enterprise system as the Searcy complex (except perhaps the John Birch Society, but, then, much of its literature and equipment comes from the NEP).

It runs on a remarkably small budget of $250,000, although much of the overhead is undoubtedly absorbed by Harding. Approximately 45 percent of contributions come in the form of grants, the rest from sale and rental of materials. Large donations in the past have come from the Sloan Foundation, whose gift of $300,000 in 1949 first put the NEP into the big leagues. This foundation also gave $597,870 to finance a series of "American Adventure" film cartoons. The Alcoa Foundation gave $1,246,168 in 1962. Other large gifts have come from the Chrysler Corporation, the Volker Fund, Independence Foundation, Armco Foundation and the Reader's Digest Foundation. The largest gift of all came from a private individual, the late Harry R. Kendall, an Evanston, Illinois, insurance executive. He gave $2.5 million in the mid-1950s. The NEP also made some money by buying radio station WHBQ in Memphis in 1946 for $300,000 and leasing it out for a fifteen-year period in 1954 for nearly $3 million.

The quantitative output of the NEP is indeed prodigious. "If you are going to move Washington to do the things it ought to do," said Benson, "you have got to move public opinion. My aim is to move public opinion at the grass roots in the direction of godliness and patriotism."[4]

The following are some of the major items that the NEP sends out among the public:

Benson writes a weekly column called "Looking Ahead" that is mailed to 3,000 newspapers and journals; it concentrates on emphasizing the advantages of the American private enterprise system. Another weekly column, called "Listen Americans," is written expressly for industrial employee publications and is published in over 900 house organs. The combined audience of these two columns together is estimated at 20 million weekly.

The National Program Letter is the NEP's main propaganda piece. It is a four-page newssheet of opinion that sells for $1 for a year's subscription. It has a circulation near 30,000. The purpose of the *Letter* is to influence the nation's "thought leaders." Approximately 35 percent are mailed out under industrial sponsorship, the remainder on individual request.

The NEP also produces films. Currently it is offering thirty-four 16 mm films—many of them in color—to anyone wishing to pay the rent on them. Some have been distributed through theatres owned by Metro-Goldwyn-Mayer; others have gone to schools, civic groups, clubs, churches and industries. The most famous of the NEP movies is "Communism on the Map," which an estimated 15 million Americans have seen. This 45-minute Technicolor production, done with professional skill, shows America lying helpless before the brutal and beguiling Communist conspiracy. It shows General George C. Marshall's efforts in the Far East as being responsible for the communization of China; it claims that Czechoslovakia succumbed because it had allowed a coalition government to be established; and it shows the 1960 student riots in San Francisco as being manipulated by members of the Communist conspiracy. At the fadeout, the entire world is either Pink or Red save for Switzerland, Spain and the United States, and upon them a question mark has been placed.

Norman Thomas, for one, is highly critical of the film because, he says, the theme is misleading; Communists and Socialists are pictured as one and the same, which, he points out, is far from the truth.

It is also apparent that much of the material for the film was taken verbatim from the Birch Society's *Blue Book* and the yearly "Scoreboard," which allegedly shows how Red is the world.

Another popular film is "Adventures in Economics," a cartoon series of ten films. The work is of high professional quality and was produced by John Sutherland, a former Disney executive. The stories promote the free enterprise system in a semi-humorous way. The major character is "Dr. Utopia," who has an ism for all ills. One film of this series, called "Fresh Laid Plans," depicts an owl as an expert on how to solve the economic problems in "Eggville"; eventually the owl's suggestions destroy the economy of the egg producers. This film has been considered by some viewers as a satire on the Brannan Plan, but it is denied by Dr Benson. Some 35 million people have seen this series.

Other films produced by the NEP are "American Adventure," another series of ten films which show how American capitalism developed; "The Republic of Apathy," a half-hour satire showing what can happen if a person does not vote (among other things: the creation of a welfare state which eventually embraces communism); "The Two Berlins," a short documentary comparing life on both sides of the wall; and "Communism in Action," a two-part film showing how communism grows and what life is like behind the Iron Curtain.

In addition, the NEP puts out a number of 35 mm filmstrips, again dealing with communism and the American citizen's responsibilities. An estimated 50 million people have seen these series.

The cartoon motion pictures, "Adventures in Economics" and "American Adventure" are also offered to television stations. More than 130 commercial and educational stations, with a weekly audience of 30 million, have used this material.

Some of the other items offered by the NEP are flannelboard presentations (one is entitled "The Power of Your Vote"; another is "Communism's Invisible Weapon"); prepared speeches; and high-school course outlines which include suggested books to read. The NEP also holds "Freedom Forums," which are one-day affairs aimed at leaders in industry, education, the press and labor unions. Summer Seminars of five days duration are held at various colleges, the purpose of which is to "inspire and challenge . . . students to become more actively interested in their American heritage." Tapes and speech reprints of these meetings are widely distributed. For instance, over 500,000 copies of a speech on brainwashing by Major William E. Meyer have been mailed out.

The Searcy complex also sells a speech called "The Structure of the American Way of Life." For twenty-five dollars, a forty-inch-high "structure" of styrofoam can be used to illustrate the speech itself. This structure shows a base labeled "Fundamental belief in God," a pedestal labeled "The United States Constitution designed to serve the people," two columns listing the "Political and Economic rights protected by our laws" (the "Right to worship," the "Right to make a profit," etc.) and, at the top, a block reading "The American way of life, our freedom," which in turn is surmounted by an American flag. This structure is very similar to the one sold by Freedoms Foundation at Valley Forge.*

* The relationship between the NEP and Freedoms Foundation has been a close one. Benson and his colleagues have won a number of Freedoms Foundations awards. Benson himself has won nine over the years, including the "George Washington Medal," the most coveted by right-wing groups and one which Benson unabashedly calls "the Nation's highest honor."

The Foundation itself was founded in 1949 by Don Belding of Foote, Cone & Belding, Edward F. Hutton of E. F. Hutton & Company, and Kenneth D. Wells, a former businessman who now serves as the Foundation's executive vice-president and director. The primary function of the Foundation is to give awards (some eight hundred a year) to those who excel in selling the American way of life. Its new colonial-style offices near Valley Forge Park feature a "briefing room," a "Congressional Medal of Honor Grove," a court commemorating the original thirteen states (around each state's flagpole are stones taken from the dwellings of the original signers of the Declaration of Independence), a "Patriots' Wall," an "American Rifleman Gate," a "Credo monument" and a "Heroic statue of George Washington at prayer." Some of these items are still in the planning stage. Despite the fact that many prominent Americans are associated with the Foundation, including President Eisenhower, it is often accused of promoting shallow jingoism and "instant tradition."

The Harding-NEP philosophy is little different from that of, say, Billy James Hargis (who, incidentally, feels very close to Benson and his views). The danger from outside the country, Benson believes, is minimal compared to America's internal fifth column. He is convinced that the day the Communists actually take over the United States is closer than most people believe. The take-over itself will be peaceful, he says, because the will to resist will be destroyed unless Americans wake up and do something about it as he is doing.

One other aspect of the NEP should be noted. It maintains "outposts" at three other colleges: Oklahoma Christian College in Oklahoma City, King's College in Briarcliff Manor, New York, and Pepperdine College in Los Angeles.

The closest relationship is maintained with Oklahoma Christian College, where Benson has served as chancellor since 1956 (he commutes back and forth in his private plane). In 1958, the college (then called Central Christian College) held its first Freedom Forum and a year later established the American Citizenship Training Center modelled after the NEP. These Freedom Forums are sometimes called Citizenship Seminars and are now yearly affairs on the campus in Oklahoma City. Past speakers have included W. Cleon Skousen; John Noble, for nine years a Soviet prisoner, who lectures on his experiences; Charles Shuman, the president of the American Farm Bureau Federation; ex-Congressman Walter Judd and Benson himself.

King's College channels its Americanism courses through a division of the institution called the National Freedom Education Center. Its executive director is Carleton Campbell, a medical doctor who was so impressed by the NEP activities that he decided to bring the same message east. Although there are many similarities between Benson's and Campbell's programs, there is no direct affiliation. The NFEC also holds forums, mostly in "enemy territory"—New York City—and features such speakers as Dr. Howard Kershner of the Christian Freedom Foundation, Clarence Manion, Herbert Philbrick and Major General Charles A. Willoughby. The Center has also produced a filmstrip, "Challenge to

Citizenship," which both the Center and the NEP offer for rental or sale.

Pepperdine College, like King's College, is not directly tied to Benson's NEP, although Benson does take credit for setting up what is vaguely called Pepperdine's "citizenship program." Its director is William C. Teague, who was formerly at Harding College; Pepperdine's director of business relations was also associated with the Searcy complex for many years. Pepperdine holds Freedom Forums featuring such speakers as Dr. Frederick Von Hayek, a well-known conservative economist who is accorded almost as much reverence by intellectuals on the right as Ludwig Von Mises, Milton Friedman and the late Wilhelm Ropke; Stefan Possony, director of international studies at Stanford University's Hoover Institute on War, Revolution and Peace, and a member of Barry Goldwater's "brain trust"; Lemuel Boulware, a former General Electric vice-president; and Richard Arens, former staff director of the HCUA.

According to a 1962 brochure, Pepperdine also produces a weekly radio broadcast on the Mutual network "presenting the message of American free enterprise," with singer Pat Boone as narrator.

One of Pepperdine's most ambitious projects is a thirteen-film series on the theme of "Crisis for Americans." The films are being produced in Hollywood and are narrated by radio personality Harry Von Zell. By 1964, three films had been completed, one on coexistence, another one on Communist imperialism and a third on the Communist accent on youth. The latter features Colonel William Mayer and Dr. Robert Strausz-Hupé, the latter a director of the Foreign Policy Research Institute at the University of Pennsylvania.

3

The three "idea" groups—Foundation for Economic Education, the American Economic Foundation and the Intercollegiate Studies Institute—vary only subtly in their own views on what the economic and political life in America ought to be, but each organization varies considerably in temper and direction.

They differ from the NEP in that they are seeking to reach the thought leaders in America—perhaps 50,000 people from students to union leaders—not the average man in the street. They differ as well from LeFevre's operations in that they do not question the need for government, only its size and true function. Because these three are interested primarily in ideas and avoid any hint of activism, they seldom make the headlines and, consequently, are virtually unknown to the public at large.

The Mecca of right-wing intellectualism is Irvington-on-Hudson, New York, where the Foundation for Economic Education is located. It was founded in 1946 by Leonard Read, now its president and formerly a U.S. Chamber of Commerce official. All the well-known conservative thinkers write for FEE's magazine, The *Freeman,* or if they do not write for it, they are honored by it. There is Hans Sennholz, an ex-Luftwaffe pilot and head of the Department of Economics at Grove City College (an institution largely financed by the Pew family) in western Pennsylvania; R. C. Hoiles; Henry Hazlitt, the *Newsweek* columnist and economist; Benjamin A. Rogge, professor of political economy at Wabash College; Milton Friedman; F. A. Hayek and Ludwig Von Mises. From times past there is Adam Smith, Herbert Spencer, John Stuart Mill, Wilhelm Ropke, John Hamilton, John Jay and James Madison.

The problem as FEE sees it, according to its literature, is as follows: "State interventionism—popularly called socialism, communism, Fabianism, Nazism, the welfare state, the planned economy or whatever—grows rapidly here in the U.S.A. and elsewhere not because this 'progressive' ideology lacks opponents but because there are so few who adequately understand and can competently and attractively explain interventionism's opposite: the free market, private property, limited government philosophy and its moral and spiritual antecedents." Leonard Read sees FEE's job, therefore, as specializing "in better understanding this philosophy ourselves while exploring ways of explaining it with ever-improving clarity. . . . In short, we specialize in aiding those who would become more skilled and eloquent explainers of the private enterprise or freedom philosophy."

The ideal American government in FEE's view is one that

applies only enough power and coercion to prevent illiberal persons from trespassing on the liberty of others. FEE men do not believe that governmental controls are a cure for every social ill. Individual liberty, they say, is being replaced by a concept that represses the actions of others by substituting the plans of rulers. Government, they believe, should get out of private enterprise— and this includes TVA and the Post Office; it should not be a regulatory agent; it should not be involved in welfare, education or any other function that historically has been reserved to the states or private individuals. Such a state of affairs—were the government out of the activities—would provide the maximum of liberty for the individual and would herald the dawn of an age where the spiritual and physical growth of America and her citizens would surpass anything anyone dreamed could take place.

FEE believes itself to be unique in that it is calling for self-improvement as distinguished from attempts to call for the reform of others. The latter, it claims, is the primary impetus which drives the current "statist" leaders in America.

According to Dr. W. M. Curtiss, FEE's executive secretary, FEE is not an action group; nor does it intend to present both sides of an argument. Curtiss believes that there are too many "liberal" points of view being promoted. The term "liberal," he adds, is a misnomer; in the classical sense of the term, those who believe in libertarian conservatism are the true liberals. Today's "liberals," he argues, are actually radicals and totalitarians who have no faith in the abilities of the ordinary citizen. The current crop of leaders, he maintains, have contempt for the citizen who wishes to take care of himself.

"The main difficulty today," he said, referring to FEE, "is that many people say our ideas are too ethereal. Well, we believe that there are things that are right and wrong. We try to find out what is right and hold it up as a light for others to follow." Curtiss reflects the general conservative's repugnance against what is believed to be the current vogue of splitting all questions down the middle— unlimited pragmatism, as some call it—where *all* questions are solved by compromise and where principles often go by the board. As one person put it to me: "There is no such thing as being half pregnant; you either are or you aren't."

This endless compromising is seen by Leonard Read as an often undetectable erosion that only becomes visible when most of the freedom has been lost. He writes:

> While most of our lost freedom is in the form of a gradual and indefinable erosion, there are instances where the loss is already completed and, thus, can be specifically named. These instances, however, are not at all impressive or persuasive except to the few individuals to whom a specific instance applies. Suppose, for example, one were to reply, "I have lost the freedom to plant all the tobacco I please on my own land." Who cares, except that infinitesimal part of the population who might want to grow tobacco? Or, "I have lost the freedom to work for anyone at less than $1.25 per hour." Again, who cares, except those unfortunate individuals whose services aren't worth this much? Or, "I have lost the freedom to pick up a passenger at the Greater Cincinnati Airport in my own taxicab." Who cares, except Cincinnati taxicab operators? Or, "I have lost the freedom to competitively price services rendered by my own railroad." Who cares, except the few owners of railroads? Or, "I have lost the freedom to raise whatever grain I please to feed my own chickens." Most voters don't raise chickens and, thus, have little concern for the plight of those few.[5]

It is the thought leaders of the nation that must be reached, FEE believes, if the trend toward "oppressive" government control is to be reversed. One thought leader of particular interest is the educator. "We need to reach the people who write textbooks," says Curtiss; "we'll never change [Paul] Samuelson; he's made up his mind. We're trying to reach those uncommitted in their economic philosophy who *will* be the thought leaders."

In this regard, FEE holds seminars through the year—some sixteen in 1965, for instance—where current and potential leaders are brought together for intensive discussions. As many as sixty individuals might attend a seminar, although the mean average is closer to thirty-five.

FEE also tries to reach the potential leaders through its monthly journal, *The Freeman,* which is mailed to over sixty thousand individuals and institutions. All the articles are scholastic in their approach to problems; never do the authors discuss day-to-day issues. "We try to provide the seedstock material for others to use," said Curtiss. Articles range in content from Herbert Spencer's "The New Liberalism" to Henry Hazlitt's "Back to Gold?"

Another weapon in FEE's arsenal is a looseleaf pamphlet called "Clichés of Socialism," a series of refutations of some of the more common clichés. My edition lists seventy-three rebuttals, some of the titles (read: clichés) of which are: "Why, you'd take us back to the horse and buggy," "I'm a middle-of-the-roader," "Federal aid is all right if it doesn't bring federal control," "Socialism is the wave of the future" and "I'm for free enterprise—BUT!"

Leonard Read has written most of the replies to these clichés, followed by Sennholz, Rogge, Hazlitt and Paul Poirot, *The Freeman's* managing editor.

FEE is supported entirely by contributions from some twelve thousand individuals. A few large corporations contribute, among them General Motors, Dupont, Chrysler, Gulf Oil, Montgomery Ward, U.S. Steel, Armour and B. F. Goodrich. The budget runs to half a million dollars a year and, in keeping with its philosophy, FEE refuses to apply for a tax-free status. FEE believes that it must sink or swim on its own merits. *"FEE receives precisely what it deserves,"* reads one pamphlet.

The Foundation believes that the educational process will be a long one. "We look at this problem as a real long-term deal," said Curtiss. "We won't return to freedom in your lifetime, certainly not in the way we would like to see it. . . . The only way we can measure success today is with individuals. I think there are more people today who understand the importance of freedom, even though the country is more socialistic today than it ever was." Curtiss pondered this thought for a moment and then said: "One of our problems is that people get discouraged. You have to develop a sense of humor in order to live with the situation." What the right wing needs, he concluded, is a Mencken.

4

A soulmate of FEE is the American Economic Foundation, located in mid-Manhattan. It was founded in 1939 "to help bring about a better understanding of American business so that friction among economic groups may be reduced and the benefits of American capitalism may become more apparent to everybody." The founder and the current chairman is Fred G. Clark, an insurance and oil executive. His assistant is Richard S. Rimanoczy, a former advertising executive. The AEF operates on a budget of $600,000 per year, much of the money being supplied by the same corporations that finance FEE.

The American Economic Foundation differs from FEE in that it concentrates on educating high school students. The more complex theories emanating from FEE are often distilled into simple terms so that the relatively unsophisticated minds of the young can better understand them. This organization also differs from FEE in that it sometimes enters the current political scene to comment on events or individuals with which it takes exception.

The AEF carries out a number of educational programs, the most recent example receiving wide notice being "The Hall of Free Enterprise" at the 1964–1965 New York World's Fair. On a more long-term basis, the Foundation provides kits, films, wall charts, pamphlets and books to high schools. Some of this material has been characterized as a "hard sell" for the American competitive system. The AEF's best-known book is *How We Live* by both Clark and Rimanoczy. It claims to present "the basic blueprint of man's economic life." Over three million copies of this book have reportedly been sold. Some of the better-known pamphlets include "Not by Bread Alone," "Let's Face the Facts of Inflation" and an "Economic Fallacy" series subtitled "The Things We 'Know' that Are Not So." The Foundation also runs "Teachers Institutes," seminars designed to stress the need for economic education. They are held in over a hundred colleges in thirty-five states and the District of Columbia. Materials supplied by the AEF at these Institutes have been placed in educational systems embracing more than seven thousand high schools.

The philosophy guiding the AEF is summed up in its "Ten Pillars of Economic Wisdom" and expanded upon in *How We Live*. The Pillars are conservative in character and read, for instance, "Government is never a source of goods," "Nothing in our material world can come from nowhere and go nowhere, nor can it be free . . . ," and "Wages are the principle cost of everything."

Clark believes that the income tax is "a law that is so bad, so poorly conceived, so inefficient, so unfair, so complex, and so debilitating, indeed so cancerous, that it must be removed from the economic body of our nation. . . ." On labor unions he has written: "Incidentally, can you name one single labor leader since Samuel Gompers who ever defended management's right to a fair profit?" Those who have worked in the New Deal, New Frontier and ADA he has called "witch doctors," and Walter Reuther he has called "a pious champion of reckless spending."

In the main, however, the AEF stays clear of personalities and day-to-day developments to dispense its economic ideas to the future leaders of this country.

5

The last "idea" group is the Intercollegiate Studies Institute (formerly the Intercollegiate Society of Individualists), located off Independence Square in Philadelphia. It was founded in 1953 and grew out of a 1950 article in *Human Events* by the late Frank Chodorov in which he said: "If Socialism has come to America because it was implanted in the minds of past generations, there is no reason for assuming that the contrary idea cannot be taught to a new generation." A businessman read these words and sent Chodorov a check for $1,000, suggesting that he start something along these lines. In its first year ISI operated as a mailing-list organization out of the *Human Events* office. Then it moved to FEE's offices in Irvington-on-Hudson, where it remained until 1958, after which it moved to its present location. The first president of ISI was William F. Buckley, Jr.—a "figurehead," as he recalls—who was soon replaced by Chodorov, the founder. The man who actually runs the Institute today is E. Victor Milione, the executive vice-president. Milione previously was associated with an organization called Americans for the Competitive Enterprise System, which organized industrial tours for high school students.

According to Milione, ISI is a nonprofit educational organization with a budget of $250,000, all of which is raised through contributions. There are no members of the Institute and no dues, but there is a 25,000-name mailing list from which contributions are solicited.

Similar to FEE and AEF, the Institute makes no effort to deal with current political issues; its approach is also academic. Most observers, including critics, acknowledge that the treatment of issues is generally of a very high caliber. ISI does differ, however, in who it wishes to influence. While FEE dispenses ideas to all those uncommitted who might be thought leaders, and while AEF concentrates on high school students, ISI is solely concerned with influencing college students and young professors.

The crux of ISI's philosophy, according to Milione, is that there is a conflict between seeking the truth at a college and the preaching of an ideology and that this conflict, whether left or right, is often weighed too much in favor of the ideology. "The seeking of truths is the most important aspect of education," he said; "the real goal is to provide a man with the ability to make his own decisions." Attendant to this view is the belief that educational institutions are caught in a dilemma trying to satisfy three needs at one time: the individual's need in terms of his own uniqueness, community needs and specialist needs. Milione believes that too much emphasis is being placed on the latter two.

"ISI objects to anyone—Schlesinger or Welch—getting up and saying 'This is the truth' and not educating the student to the point where he can make his own valid judgments," said Milione. "Harvard and Yale have tremendous prestige," he went on, "and the implication is that they *know* what is right, not only in specific disciplines but in the relationships of one to the other." He said that there is no university in the United States—particularly the large, well-known "liberal" ones—nor any body of knowledge that promotes "wholeness," that is to say, the fully educated individual. "Instead of broadening the student's knowledge," Milione added, "the universities are actually encouraging his provincialism by providing for only certain aspects of his needs." ISI hopes to fill that void.

This attitude toward education translates out as a conservative philosophy because it reflects the belief that were the scales to tip in favor of "truth" (as opposed to "ideology"), the majority if not all the students would reject the socialist, collectivist and totalitarian indoctrination that they apparently are receiving today.

In their hearts, and from a longe-range point of view, ISIers are wedded to seeking the truth—and it is certainly reflected in their intellectual efforts; but on a day-to-day basis, they seem to be saying: "If ideology must be preached, let there be more of the conservative variety."

On a more general level, ISI has no one strong philosophical thread. Some of the writers to its magazine, *The Intercollegiate Review,* are followers of Ayn Rand, others are disciples of Ludwig Von Mises, and yet others are a kind of intellectual YAFer. But all those who associate themselves with ISI stand opposed to the trends of the past thirty-five years. They oppose "relativism," Keynesianism, statism, liberalism and anything to the left of these isms. ISIers talk in terms of freedom, *laissez faire,* private property, minimum government, and other conservative thoughts much like someone from FEE, AEF and YAF.

ISI seeks to put across its point of view in five ways: publications, a club program, summer schools, lectures and a fellowship program.

The Intercollegiate Review is one of the better produced intellectual journals on the collegiate scene, showing professionalism in its layout and a very high quality in its subject matter. One issue may carry articles such as "Moral Presuppositions of the Free Enterprise Economy," by Karl Brandt, and "The Dilemmas of Disarmament," by Stefan T. Possony. Another might carry such articles as "The Relation Between Power and Values in the Nuclear Age," by William R. Kintner, "National Self-Defense and Political Existence," by Gerhart Niemeyer, and "Imperialism: The Threat to Existence," by Leo Paul de Alvarez.

Two other publications are *ISI Campus Report,* a roundup of ISI club activities, lectures and notices of new books and articles; and *Under 30,* a semi-annual digest of the best articles from many conservative campus magazines.

The club program has experienced considerable success since it was initiated back in the early days of the organization. Today there are some one hundred clubs on as many campuses with a total membership of twenty-eight thousand. The only requirement demanded of a club is that it—for a switch—*not* be closely associated with ISI headquarters in Philadelphia. Milione believes that each club should be independent, capable of standing on its own feet and only drawing material and assistance from ISI as it is needed. This enforced separation also allows ISI to disassociate itself from any group which decides to go off on its own tack, a problem aggravated by the high turnover (completely every four years or so) in all the clubs. Furthermore, every club is expected to be solely an educational group and not a political activist one.

These clubs go by a variety of names, the most common being The Conservative Club. The University of Chicago Conservatives publish the *New Individualist Review,* perhaps the best known of all these journals; the club at Harvard is called the Charles River Literary Society and publishes a glossy quarterly called *The Harvard Conservative;* The University Society of Individualists at Berkeley publishes *Man and State;* the University of Pennsylvania has its Eleutherian Society and a publication called *Analysis;* and Cornell's Conservative Club puts out a journal called *The Gentlemen of the Right.*

ISI holds numerous summer schools, a program that was initiated in 1960. Again, these meetings feature as speakers some of the most respected names among conservatives: Gerhart Niemeyer, Frank S. Meyer, Russell Kirk, Robert Strausz-Hupé and Senator John Tower. Approximately three schools are held each year, one in the East, another in the Midwest and a third on the West Coast.

Lectures and seminars are also held throughout the scholastic year at all of the clubs. The same caliber of men teaching at the summer schools is available for these sessions. A high standard of scholarship is maintained. Topics such as "The Revolt of the Sophists," "The Behavioral Approach and the Nothing-But Fallacy" and "Behavioralism and Economics" are typical of those presented.

Under ISI's fellowship program, ten fellowships per year are awarded to graduate students in economics and political science. They are each worth $1,500 plus tuition, and the money comes from private foundations. The recipient, in order to qualify, must state his intention of teaching upon completion of his studies. This is ISI's way of trying to change the educational system at its heart.

To many conservatives active on the political scene, the true value of ISI is that it is training the leaders for tomorrow's battles. Some of those exposed to the ISI view go off into the fringes, but many others do not. Most eventually gravitate into the Republican and Democratic Parties where their conservative views are beginning to act as a counterforce to the young left-wingers. The number of Young Turks active on the political scene who cut their teeth in ISI is impressive. There is William Buckley, M. Stanton Evans, William H. Regnery, John G. Pew, Jr., of the Sun Oil family, James Kilpatrick, the editor of the *Richmond News Leader,* Garry Wills, assistant professor of classics at Johns Hopkins, Richard Whalen of the *Wall Street Journal,* Edwin McDowell of the *Arizona Republic* and the author of *Barry Goldwater: Portrait of an Arizonan* and, finally, a number of energetic youths who are active in Young Americans for Freedom and *Human Events.*

Milione is confident that sometime in the foreseeable future the opinions and views of these Young Turks he has promoted will not only be listened to but be dominant in the land.

6

The two most influential publications on the Right and the two that give their heart and soul to the cause are *Human Events* and *National Review.*

Human Events is a sixteen-page weekly tabloid-type newspaper with a circulation exceeding 100,000. It is one of the few newspapers with an aggressively right-wing point of view that is available at newsstands, particularly on the East Coast.

It was started in 1944 by the late Frank C. Hanighen, a writer, editor and author of muckraking books (for instance, he was co-author of *The Merchants of Death,* an exposé of the munitions industry). At a luncheon held in Chicago early that year, Hanighen convinced General Robert E. Wood, then Chairman of Sears, Roebuck, Sterling Morton of the salt company, Colonel Charles Lindbergh, Colonel Robert McCormick, W. H. Regnery, Sr., and two others that the conservatives needed a newsletter from

Washington, D.C., that would keep the forces on the right apprised of events and developments there. Hanighen persuaded his listeners that his idea was a good one, and with $500, some advance subscriptions and their encouragement, the newssheet was started. It took its name from the first line of the Declaration of Independence and was printed in such a way at first that each sheet was a separate item capable of being distributed in part yet at the same time appearing to be a complete unit. Thus Hanighen hoped that the original subscribers would pass on the four or five sheets to as many friends.

The early days of *Human Events* were rugged. Circulation for a number of years hovered around the money-losing 10,000 mark. Schemes were devised to increase circulation (5,000 copies were offered for $25, for instance); a plan was once devised to sell *Human Events* and *American Opinion* as a package deal, but the scheme fell through because it lost money. But then, in 1961, the publication's circulation and sales figures began to climb steeply. From 10,000 in 1954, circulation passed 85,000 in 1963 and 100,000 in 1965. Its gross sales of other literature passed the $1 million mark in 1962.

In 1964 Hanighen died and his place was taken by James L. Wick, his associate of many years. Wick had previously worked for FEE as general manager of *The Freeman* and as a staffer on the 1940 Willkie campaign and the 1944 Dewey campaign. Wick has since died and his place has been taken by his son, Milton.

The newspaper sees itself, if you will, as both objective and biased. "In reporting the news," stated one flyer, *"Human Events is* OBJECTIVE; it aims for accurate presentation of the facts. But it *is not* IMPARTIAL. It looks at events through eyes that *are* BIASED—in favor of limited constitutional government, states rights, private enterprise and individual freedom."

There is no doubt that *Human Events* epitomizes those organizations on the right that "view with alarm" the recent trends and developments in the United States. "We will never have efficiency in the service of delivering mail," read a 1960 article, "until the Post Office is turned over to private enterprise." It views with alarm Walter Reuther, who, in another 1960 article, was described as "a ruthless labor dictator and one of the most mischievous

Socialist leaders in the country." Civil rights is also suspect; began a 1961 article: "Throughout the ugly activity of the bus-riding integrationist agitators who have been touring the South to cause trouble, and who have been illegally accommodated by some extremists . . ." The international conspiracy is cause for alarm; said a 1962 article: ". . . the Administration has deliberately blocked production of advanced aircraft in order to kill off the manned-bomber program . . . ," and then went on to ask: "What other weapons are we not producing because the Russians suggested it?"

The New Frontier was also cause for fear. President Kennedy, said one article, actually headed a "Fabian Socialist Administration." Another article suggested that Kennedy himself was a "High Class Beatnik." Nor is President Johnson free from criticism. One 1963 headline read: "President Johnson: Blessed Are the Poor; they'll elect me." James Kilpatrick wrote an article in *Human Events* in which he called the President a "counterfeit Confederate." Even democracy comes under fire; it was once described as "counting all the heads empty or not."

Human Events views with alarm the appointment of British poet Stephen Spender as Poetry Consultant to the Library of Congress. It views with alarm the new silverless coins, calling them "government slugs." And it views with considerable alarm CORE, Dr. Spock ("Peacenik Pediatrician"), station KTBC in Austin, Texas, the New Left and peace marchers ("People Laughed at Hitler's Marchers," read one headline), Adam Clayton Powell, the War on Poverty, "modern Republicanism," and all those congressmen who voted for foreign aid, federal aid to education, civil rights, Medicare or the repeal of section 14(b) of the Taft-Hartley Law.

Those who do the viewing with alarm represent a cross section of writers on the right. There is Morrie Ryskind, formerly of the Los Angeles *Times;* Ralph de Toledano; Walter Trohan, the Washington bureau chief of the Chicago *Tribune;* Alice Widener, the publisher of *USA* magazine; Westbrook Pegler; Senator Thomas Dodd; Ronald Reagan; labor columnist Victor Riesel; and Congressmen H. R. Gross (R., Iowa), Albert Watson (R., S.C.), Edward Derwinski (R., Ill.) and John Dowdy (D., Tex.). One of the reasons *Human Events* maintains such a large circulation is that it presents the news in such a manner that it appeals to a wide spectrum of right-wingers. The Bircher may think it too mild and the casual conservative may think it too racy, but both will read it because it presents the news in a lively way.

The result is ideological confusion. No one is sure where *Human Events* stands on the right, and it seems to be a deliberate policy. It does not, for instance, call for the impeachment of Chief Justice Warren, but it does call for Constitutional amendments that, if passed into law, would drastically change the balance-of-power concept. It does not have a conspiracy complex, but some of its writers do. Nor is it bigoted or totally reactionary, yet it features a few columnists who are. It claims it has no time for third-party politics, but it supported Buckley in the 1965 mayoralty race in New York. At times it is an ardent admirer of Barry Goldwater; on other occasions it is one of his biggest critics.

And so it goes. As long as a person has any identifiable conservative attitudes there is something in the pages of *Human Events* for him.

The newspaper has other interests besides reporting the news. Because it believes that the regular press is biased in favor of "liberals," it runs a "School of Journalism" in cooperation with ISI. Scholarships are awarded to young conservatives who wish to become reporters.

Human Events is also one of the right's major pamphleteers. The following are samples of its material: "Senator Kennedy's 'Right to Loaf' Bill," by Frank Chodorov; "Corruption Unlimited: Urban Renewal," by James Wick; "Public Enemy Number One—Taxes," by radio commentator Paul Harvey; "The Web of Warren," by Frank Hanighen; and "Communism: A False Religion," by J. Edgar Hoover.

In retrospect, it is quite clear that *Human Events* has been one of the major beneficiaries of the resurgence among conservative groups since 1960. It has prospered from the formula of embracing as many conservative views as it can consistent with its policy of presenting the right-wing side of the news. This has paid off in terms of both circulation and profitability, and there is no indication that this policy will be changed.

7

National Review, published every other week, is acknowledged to be the best-written and most articulate of all the publications on the right. It was started in 1955 and has built itself up where today it can boast an impressive circulation near the 100,000 mark. Although the magazine does not influence the power wielders in Washington, it nevertheless can shake right-wing mountains. Most of this is due to the style, intelligence and personality of its editor, William Frank Buckley, Jr.

Buckley is the son of one of America's wealthiest men. At his death, Buckley, Sr., had amassed a fortune estimated at over $100 million. The family's privately held Catawba Corporation (now run by William's brother, John) controls oil development concessions on some 60 million acres of land, equivalent to the land mass of England, Scotland, Wales and Northern Ireland. William, Sr., was the son of a second-generation Scot-Irish immigrant who had made a small fortune in merchandising and sheep-raising in Duval County, Texas. Although his father was a Protestant, William, Sr., was raised in the Roman Catholic religion of his mother.

William, Jr., inherited his father's views on individualism, free enterprise and the survival of the fittest. From the beginning he was a precocious and opinionated individual. In 1931, when he was six years old, he wrote to King George V of England and told him to pay back his country's war debt. Two days after his arrival at an English school, he confronted the headmaster with a list of things he did not like about the institution. Within forty-eight hours of his arrival at an army base, he fired off a letter to the commanding officer deploring wasteful practices and the poor quality of the staff. (The letter was intercepted before it reached the commanding officer's desk.)

Buckley graduated from the Millbrook School in upstate New York in 1943. He then studied at the University of Mexico for a year and soon thereafter joined the Army. He began as a private and was discharged in 1946 as a second lieutenant. He then entered Yale and studied history, political science and economics.

He served as the chairman of the *Yale Daily News,* got himself elected to Fence Club and Skull and Bones, and built himself a reputation as a first-class debater.

The year after his graduation in 1950, his book *God and Man at Yale* was published (by W. H. Regnery & Company). In it, Buckley argued that his alma mater was full of anti-religious and anti-capitalist attitudes. This point of view was considered quite controversial at that time, and Buckley was soon labeled as the *enfant terrible* of the renascent right.

For the next four years Buckley held three jobs, one as a "regular panelist" for H. L. Hunt's Facts Forum, another briefly as ISI's president, and a third as an associate editor of *American Mercury.* He broke with *Mercury*'s owner-editor, Russell Maguire, when anti-Semitism began to creep into the pages of the magazine. In 1954, Buckley co-authored with his brother-in-law, Brent Bozell, *McCarthy and His Enemies,* a defense of the late Wisconsin senator. The two authors argued that, although charges were sometimes hurled about with considerable abandon, McCarthy nevertheless had rendered the nation a singular service by demanding that people be concerned with their own country's internal security, particularly within the State Department.

National Review was started in 1955 with the financial help of 120 investors. By way of introducing it to the public, Buckley wrote that the magazine planned to stand "athwart history, yelling 'Stop' at a time when no one is inclined to do so, or to have much patience with those who urge it."

His magazine is of the old school of journalism, that which reflected the opinions of one man much in the tradition of, say, Colonel Robert McCormick of the Chicago *Tribune* or, today, of William Loeb of the *Manchester* (N.H.) *Union Leader*—outspoken, opinionated and right-wing.

On its fifth birthday, *National Review* could boast a circulation of 31,913 and debts totaling $860,000. Its circulation today has tripled, but the finances have improved little. Periodically, the editor has to plead for extra help from his readers, and usually he gets it. Of course, Buckley could personally make up the deficit each year from his own resources, probably without even a skipped heartbeat from his personal financial advisers, but it is apparent that he wants to make the publication pay for itself.

One reason *National Review* is constantly in difficult financial straits is it has not yet broken the advertising barrier. That is to say, most of its ads come from companies whose owners or managers are right-wing in their views. Milliken, Schick, Kennametal and Allen-Bradley are names most seen on the advertising pages. The non-ideological advertisers have, on the whole, avoided the magazine. One wonders why, when its readers comprise the bulk of conservative thought leaders in the country.

The names on the masthead are an impressive group of right-wing scribes: James Burnham (an ex-Trotskyist), Frank S. Meyer, M. Stanton Evans, Will Herberg, James J. Kilpatrick, Ralph de Toledano, Garry Wills, Brent Bozell, Frank Chodorov, Suzanne LaFollette, Gerhart Niemeyer, Morrie Ryskind, Anthony Lejeune and Elspeth Huxley. Guest writers range from Carol Bauman, the wife of a YAF activist, to Sir Shane Leslie, a relation of Sir Winston Churchill.

As if one Buckley were not enough on the staff, one sister is managing editor, another is a columnist, yet another handles the correspondence and Brent Bozell, a brother-in-law, is on the editorial board.

William Buckley differs from all other critics on the right in that he uses a rapier instead of a sledgehammer. One never gets the impression that Buckley ever loses his temper. Rather, his pen is dipped in nitric acid; he has the gift of the scintillating phrase that can be driven home with what seems to be bored understatement; he can deliver a verbal knife thrust with a toothy smile; his Henry James-like rhetoric—some sentences containing half a dozen thoughts linked together by an equal number of subordinate clauses, "howevers," "but-on-the-other-hands" and "as-I-am-sure-you-are-awares"—can destroy the most cogent arguments by the sheer weight of words. His prowess with words is such that one sometimes gets the impression that he is more concerned with the way he is saying it than what he is saying. Nevertheless, his withering ridicule, his style of delivery and his flashing wit are perhaps the most feared weapons in the possession of the right. He can, for instance, reduce such advocates of liberalism as Norman

Mailer and James Baldwin—both articulate when not under stress —to the point where they become incoherent.

Buckley's verbal manner, recently bolstered by a TV show of his own called "Firing Line," now includes visual weapons. Before a cruncher is about to be delivered, he will lick the corner of his mouth, raise his eyes to heaven as if his opponent's argument were straining his credulity, and then, voice husky and soft, deliver some devastating rejoinder such as: "I wish you wouldn't sound so fatigued when confronted by historical fact."

Some of Buckley's rapier-like thrusts should be noted. President Johnson he has called "Uncle Cornpone"; Pope John XXIII's encyclical *Mater et Magister* he believes is "a venture in triviality"; the 1963 March on Washington he described as "mob deployment"; Harry Golden he has called "the high priest of left-wing yahooism"; novelist Gore Vidal, "a philosophical degenerate"; and Vincent Sheean "the king of gemutlichkeit." He chided Norman Mailer for his "subpoena envy" when he, Mailer, was not called to testify before a congressional committee investigating the sponsorship of the Fair Play for Cuba Committee.

Buckley believes that Jean-Paul Sartre, Simone de Beauvoir, Truman Capote, James Baldwin and Mailer—"that kind of thing" —are products of what he calls "the fever swamps of the literary left." Arthur Schlesinger he has dismissed with: "No one believes anything he says anyway." John Lindsay he is convinced is "an embarrassment to the two-party system." Eisenhower, wrote Buckley, "when he was not the laughing stock of the troublemakers, was the explicit object of their contempt." On the New Frontier he said: ". . . there aren't enough psychiatrists in the world to cure this crazy administration." David Susskind he labeled "a staunch liberal" and went on to say that "if there were a contest for the title 'Mr. Eleanor Roosevelt,' he would unquestionably win it." When introducing Norman Thomas on his show, Buckley said: "If I were asked what has been his speciality in the course of a long career, I guess I would say 'being wrong.' "

Not everyone appreciates what Buckley or his magazine says about them. An editorial in *National Review*, for instance, accused Linus Pauling of "acting as a megaphone for Soviet policy" and giving "aid and comfort to the enemies of this country." Pauling sued for $1 million but lost the case because the court ruled that the distinguished chemist was a "public figure" open to the same comment that applies to public officials.

Buckley's political views fall somewhere to the left of the Birch Society's views. He accepts the standard conservative position that opposes the power of unions, the trend toward state-run welfare, featherbedding and government power. "I will not cede more power to the state," he wrote. "I will not willingly cede more power to anyone, not to the state, not to General Motors, not to the CIO. I will hoard my power like a miser, resisting every effort to drain it away from me. I will then use *my* power as *I* see fit. . . ."

The advent of the Birch Society has forced Buckley to take a stand pro or con the controversial organization. In the 13 February 1962 issue of *National Review*, an editorial, presumably written by Buckley, said: "Mr. Welch, for all his good intentions, threatens to divert militant conservative action to irrelevance and ineffectuality. There are, as we say, great things that need doing . . . John Birch chapters can do much to forward these aims, but only as they dissipate the fog of confusion that issues from Mr. Welch's smoking typewriter. Mr. Welch has revived in many men the spirit of patriotism, and that same spirit calls now for rejecting, out of a love of truth and country, his false councils." Buckley, like Goldwater, was quick to add that he had considerable admiration for individual Birchers and that he felt it was unreasonable and undiscriminating to condemn all members of the Society out of hand.

Public opinion, says Buckley, is a "paper tiger" that inhibits the United States' role as a world power. "In one week we landed Marines in Santo Domingo and bombed North Vietnam," he noted, "and everyone expected a lot of shouting and not very much really happened." American cities, particularly New York City, he believes have become hotbeds of crime, owing in part to what he calls the liberals' "anything goes" attitude. "You can't walk from one end of New York to another without standing a good chance of losing your wallet, your maidenhead, or your life," he wrote.

Nor does Buckley have much confidence in intellectuals who have the ear of politicians in power. "I would rather be governed," he said, "by the first two thousand people in the telephone directory than by the Harvard University faculty." But this does not mean that Buckley is an egalitarian. He has said that he would much rather "pothole" the road to the voting booth than broaden it. Occasionally Buckley is ambivalent in his attitude toward "statism." He favors the statism of congressional investigations and the statism of right-to-work laws, for instance, but he is against the statism of civil rights laws and aid to public schools.

Buckley is best when he is explaining what the American right stands for and what it does not stand for. In his book, *Rumbles Right and Left,* he explains it to Norman Mailer:

> The true meaning of the right wing, Mr. Mailer, is commitment, a commitment on the basis of which it becomes possible to take measurements. This is true whether in respect of domestic policy or foreign policy. For those on the radical Left with Norman Mailer, and for so many Americans on the moderate Left, the true meaning of our time is the loss of an operative set of values—what one might call an expertise in living. For then, there is no ground wire, and without a ground the voltage fluctuates wildly, wantonly, chasing after the immediate line of least resistance—which, in Cuba, is *Do Nothing.* For those, like Norman Mailer, who have cut themselves off from the Great Tradition, one observes that it is not truly important that a Laos has been dismembered, or that a great wall has gone up through Berlin, or that a Cuba has been Communized: Mailer's world is already convulsed, at a much higher level, and he has no ear for such trivia as these. For he views the world as groaning under the weight of unmanageable paradoxes, so that Euclidean formulations, Christian imperatives, Mosaic homilies become, all of them, simply irrelevant; worse, when taken seriously, these are the things that get in the way of his own absorption with himself, in the way of that apocalyptical orgasm which he sees as the end objective of individual experience.
>
> How strange it is that all the Establishment's scholars, all the Establishment's men, have not in the last half dozen years written half dozen paragraphs that truly probe the true meaning of the American right wing. They settle instead for frenzied, paranoid denunciations. Indeed the Left has discovered that the threat is really internal. There is no enormity too grotesque, or too

humorless, to win their wide-eyed faith. I have seen some of them listen respectfully to the thesis that people in America belong to the right wing out of resentment over their failure to get their sons into Groton. . . .[6]

Along with all other conservatives, Buckley took umbrage at President Eisenhower when he invited Premier Khrushchev to the United States in 1959. The following passage illustrates how a conservative such as Buckley views the matter:

Last year [1959] Mayor Wagner ostentatiously announced his refusal to greet Ibn Saud—on the ground that Ibn Saud discriminates against the Jews in Saudi Arabia, and no man who discriminates against Jews in Saudi Arabia is by God going to be handled courteously by Bob Wagner, Mayor of New York. Now, as everyone knows, Nikita Khrushchev not only discriminates against Jews, he kills them. On the other hand, he does much the same thing to Catholics and Protestants. Could *that* be why Mr. Wagner consented to honor Khrushchev? Khrushchev murders people without regard to race, color or creed—that is, on straight FEPC lines; and therefore, whatever he is guilty of, he is not guilty of discrimination, and so he is entitled to Robert Wagner's hospitality. Is that the shape of the new rationality?[7]

Buckley sees himself as occupying the dead center of the conservative movement, trying to pull the Birchers away from the more intemperate ideas of Robert Welch and, at the same time, giving hope to the fainthearted conservatives to his left. Even though his views are not airtight, he nevertheless can hold this position with some feeling of security because he is one of the few on the right who skillfully treads the narrow line between advocacy and acceptability. Buckley's views are not so far beyond the pale that reasonable people dismiss him as unrealistic; many believe that there are enough seeds of truth in what he is saying that he deserves their attention. On the other hand, he has not slipped sufficiently toward the centers of power where people regard him as one of the Establishment's more vocal household pets.

However, Buckley did put this position in jeopardy in 1965 when he ran for mayor of New York City. He made it clear that he was not too serious about it (on being asked what he would do if he won, he said, "I'd demand a recount.") and that his objective was a negative one—to defeat the more liberal John Lindsay. Barry Goldwater, who knows what it is like to lose big, called Buckley a "political kamikaze" and a "wrong-way Corrigan." Somehow Buckley's reputation survived his defeat, and he still maintains the position he seeks to hold: the most authentic and most respected voice of conservatism in America today.

A number of people have noted that there are many similarities between William Buckley and the late President Kennedy. Buckley is immensely wealthy, a Catholic, witty, articulate, athletic, from a large family and with considerable charisma and charm. But there the similarities end. Both have viewed the political world from different points in the spectrum. The Associated Press once felt that the similarities were sufficient to be worthy of comment. Said a 1961 release: "Should President Kennedy and William F. Buckley, Jr., chance to pass each other on a crowded street they would probably bless themselves and murmur: 'There but for the Grace of God go I.' "[8]

THE
NATIONALISTS

11

The Black Nationalists

1

Some several trillion years ago an unknown black scientist blew up the Moon because the people who lived on it—"original man"—refused to speak the same language. From the debris was created the earth, some 36,000 miles out of orbit. What was left of the Moon capsized and everyone fell off and died; water and life, however, were retained on the earthly fragment.

The first and only inhabitants of the earth at that time were black people, members of the Tribe of Shabazz. They lived in South Asia and built a city called Mecca.

Caucasians were the product of a 600-year experiment conducted by a genius of the Black Nation called Yakub. He discovered, roughly 6,000 years ago, that black people could be progressively bleached through "mutation," thus he produced the brown, yellow, red and white races. In the process of developing the white race, Yakub bred all the goodness, strength and ability—inherent in the Black Nation, the "original people"—from it. He had, in fact, created the first real "colored" man (that is, the extreme deviant from the black norm) who, because he was weak and generally inferior all around, was branded a "devil."

Yakub, a born troublemaker with a big head, had previously been thrown out of the Black Nation with 59,999 other dissatisfied individuals. To get revenge on Allah, Yakub had created his "devil race." Yet, there was a grand design to all this. God (or Allah), it seems, chose to allow these "devils" to rule for 6,000 years to test the mettle of the Black Nation and the capacity for justice of the white race. The whites have failed in their task of providing justice to the blacks, so their time is up. In fact, their time was up in 1914; all whites are now living in a period of grace. It is only a matter of time before the Black Nation once again asserts its authority.

Part of God's divine plan for his people called for a 400-year stint as slaves in North America, which was up in 1955.

On the day of judgment there will be a holocaust. First will come a "spiritual sounding of the trumpet"—a siren in an airplane—which will broadcast the beginning of the end. All people will have eight to ten days to decide whether or not they want to leave this "earthly hell." Come the judgment itself, a "dreadful" wheel-like airplane, one-half mile by one-half mile in size and armed with bombs, poison gas and fire, will destroy all human life (American whites first, European whites a little later) except 144,000 "so-called Negroes." These chosen few will be the vanguard in a "New World" in which peace and happiness will reign supreme.

God is black; his religion is Islam; and his bible is the Holy Quran. He teaches that the Nation of Islam or Lost-Found Nation (which is only one part of the black-brown-yellow-red Black Nation) is God's "chosen"; that his chosen are Asiatics (not Negro) who created great civilizations while the whites were still "crawling on their hands and knees like beasts of the forest and living on raw meat"; that there is no life after death; that Heaven and Hell are just two conditions of life; and that Caucasians are "wicked, evil, blue-eyed, pale-faced devils" who shall receive their punishment on the judgment day.[1]

In order to understand the Black Muslims, as they are more commonly known, it is necessary to grasp the content of the eschatology above.

> [It] shows the black nationalists' desire to free themselves
> from the exploited image of blackness and hence from the deep
> feeling of self-rejection, cultural alienation, and social estrange-
> ment which pervade and corrupt the personalities of the Negro

masses. It expresses the nationalist's need to attach himself in a positive way to something worthy and esteemed, some center of power, some tradition and, generally, some "central idea" capable of endowing his life with meaning and purpose. It offers hope in a future, one in which blackness will no longer be despised.[2]

Black nationalism addresses itself to a number of anxieties within the American Negro community. Chief among them are the Negroes' concern for their identity as a people, which is threatened by integration and assimilation. It reasserts the Negro male's superiority, particularly as head of the household. As a release for all anxieties, it identifies the cause of them as something concrete and visible ("blue-eyed, pale-skinned devils"), not as a set of vague, seemingly insurmountable pressures. Most important of all, black nationalism seeks an end to the dilemma that finds Negroes freed from bondage for over one hundred years yet still not accepted into the mainstream of American society.

Black nationalism is not a new phenomenon in America. Its roots predate the Civil War and can be traced right up to the present through such organizations and individuals as the American Colonization Society, Booker T. Washington, W. E. B. Du-Bois, Marcus Garvey and his Universal Negro Improvement Association,* and Noble Drew Ali, the "prophet" of the Moorish-American Science Temples.

Prior to the twentieth century the movements were essentially Negro nationalist in character, concerned with the problems of American Negroes only. Since 1900, black nationalism has come

---

* Marcus Garvey, the "Black Moses," was a Jamaican who sought to unite all Negroes of the world and establish a country of their own in Africa. He believed that Negroes had to be united by a common consciousness of race and nationality in order to become a great and powerful people. To this end, he set up a variety of corporations—the Negro Political Union, the Negro Factory Corporation, the Black Star Steamship Company, were but a few of them—in an effort to increase Negro self-sufficiency and in the belief that such enterprises would help pay for the eventual "repatriation" of American Negroes to Africa. He set up a provisional government, paid himself a large retainer, called himself "His Highness, the Potentate," and conferred knighthoods and peerages upon his faithful. In 1925, Garvey was convicted of using the mails to defraud. He spent two years in jail and was then deported. His UNIA collapsed around him, and he died unheralded in London in 1940 at the age of fifty-three.

to the fore, preoccupied with the problems of all nonwhite peoples of the world.

The black nationalist's God, although black in spirit, came to America in the form of a light-skinned Negro of oriental mien called W. D. Fard, also known as Walli Farrad, Professor Ford, F. Mohammed Ali, Farrad Mohammed, and Allah (God). Little is known of his background. His mother was a bleached-blonde "devil" of uncertain trade known as "Baby Gee." His father was known only as Alphonso, sometimes described as "a Jet Black Man of the Tribe of Shabazz." Fard had previous arrests on charges of narcotics, bootlegging and assault with a deadly weapon; he served three years in San Quentin Prison. Fard appeared in Detroit in 1930 as a peddler of silks in "Paradise Valley," the local Negro slum. Before long he was the leader of a small cult of "Moors" with headquarters in a Temple of Islam. By 1933 he was reputed to have eight thousand followers. Some of his faithful believed he was "the Mahdi's prophet," others the reincarnation of Noble Drew Ali himself, still others God.

Fard disappeared in the summer of 1933 or 1934, depending on what source you believe. A faction of Fard's empire, those who considered Fard to be God, broke away from the Detroit Temple and set up shop in Chicago, where it has flourished ever since. The leader of this faction was and continues to be Elijah Muhammad, born Elijah Poole in Sandersville, Georgia, in 1897. He has also been known at various times as Elijah Karriem, Gulam Bogans, Muhammad Rassouli, Elijah Muck Muhd, and Robert Poole. Elijah Muhammad, who claims to be infallible, believes that Fard, said to have been born in 1877, will live until he is 444 years old and that he—Fard, or Allah—now resides in Mecca.

The history of the Nation of Islam during the 1930s, 1940s and 1950s is distinguished by a number of characteristics. The highlight of the 1930s was its propensity for human sacrifices. One intrepid Muslim was reported to have erected an altar in his Detroit home in 1932 and convinced a boarder that he should present himself for human sacrifice so as to become "the Savior of the World." At the appointed hour, and with great ceremony, the man plunged a knife into the volunteer's heart. On another occasion, this same Muslim confessed to police that he had planned to sacrifice two women welfare workers, if only he could have found out where they lived.[3] Sacrifices were still being performed as late as 1937. One Muslim was arrested early that year as he prepared the ceremonial slaying of his wife and daughter. He was also making plans to cook and eat them.

The 1930s also witnessed the fragmentation of the nationalist movement. There was the Peace Movement of Ethiopia, still in existence, that urges Negroes to return to Africa. There was the Iron Defense League (a uniformed group of black fascists), the Pacific Movement of the Western World, an organization called "The Development of Our Own," all of which sympathized with the Japanese during World War II. There was then the short-lived National Movement for the Establishment of the 49th State and later such sects as the Joint Council of Reparation (a back-to-Africa group that was at one time willing to work with Rockwell's American Nazi Party), the Garvey Clubs, the United African Nationalist Movement, the Jamaican-based Ras Tafarians (a small, marijuana-smoking cult whose members have murdered at least six persons; this group takes its name and derives its inspiration from Emperor Haile Selassie, who was born Ras Tafari Makonnen), the Royal Ethiopian Jews, the Washington Park Forum, the American Economic League and a number of others.*

The 1940s was the time when most Black Muslims were in jail for, among other things, refusing to register for the draft, sedition and conspiracy. Elijah Muhammad himself was arrested in 1942 and sent to jail until 1946. The Nation of Islam leader and many of his followers sympathized with the Japanese during the war, claiming close kinship to the non-white Orientals. "Great Japanese victories leave few victims for us," Muhammad was quoted as saying at the time. Apparently imprisonment of its leader did not destroy the Nation; in fact, it continued to grow, most recruits coming from federal prisons.

In the 1950s, the movement began to expand rapidly, primarily

* The Nation of Islam has been the object of a number of take-over bids. In 1932, the Communist Party made a bid; later one was made by a group of Japanese who wanted the Muslims to swear allegiance to the Mikado; and still later a bid was made by an Ethiopian group led by one Wyxzewixard S. J. Challaoueliziczese. More recently, another group of Communists and a Trotskyist sect have made bids. None of them have been successful.

because of the messianic qualities of Muhammad's second-in-command, Minister Malcolm X. Its growth was helped by the concurrent migration of Negroes from the countryside into the cities. Virtually all Nation of Islam Temples are located in cities where there is a sizable Negro population. Today it has been estimated that members exceed 100,000 in number. That, as one observer put it, is more people than Billy Graham has converted.

Elijah Muhammad, like Fard, is a light-skinned Negro with an Oriental profile. He is of small stature, rather fragile-looking and suffers from high blood pressure, bronchitis and asthma. The seventh of twelve children, he worked at a variety of menial jobs before coming to Detroit in 1929, where he was subsequently converted to Islam by Fard. He admits to having no formal education and no working knowledge of Arabic. He works hard, however, has a retiring manner (except when he speaks of whites), wears an embroidered fez, conservatively cuts suits, and a white shirt usually with a white bow tie. He has six sons, two daughters and over two dozen grandchildren, all of whom, until recently, were in the movement.

Elijah is revered by his followers as the Messenger of Allah, as the Prophet, as the Divine Leader, the Savior Allah, and Our Deliverer. Every Muslim, with gushing praise, attributes all his own words, actions and thoughts to "the Honorable Prophet, Elijah Muhammad." Elijah himself seems a little embarrassed by the praise.

If W. D. Fard is the Nation of Islam's Jesus Christ, then Elijah Muhammad would be its St. Paul. He has the unsettling habit of saying, during one of his rare public appearances, in response to a reporter's query: ". . . And how do I know that? . . . Because Allah told me." He never raises his voice, never seems unsure of himself. On occasion he will vary the format with: "Ah, but you see . . . I didn't say that. Allah said that."

Muhammad's hatred of whites seems to have no limits. "The white man is more vicious," he said, "than the dogs he sets upon us. He is never satisfied with a black man no matter what his position. You can lie down and let your back be his doormat, but soon he'll get tired of that and start kicking you. 'Turn over, nigger! You're layin' on the same side too long,' he'll say." On another occasion he wrote:

> The slave-masters' every cry is to beat—beat—kill—kill—the so-called Negroes. Maybe the day has arrived that Allah will return to the devils . . . that which they have been so anxious to pour on the poor innocent so-called Negroes. Allah will give you your own blood to drink like water and your arms and allies will not help you against him. . . .
>
> America is now under Divine Plagues. One will come after the other until she is destroyed. Allah has said it.

The reference to plagues is a favorite topic of Muhammad's. Every natural or man-made disaster is played up in his newspaper as the beginning of the end: sandstorms, floods, hurricanes, airplane crashes, shipping disasters. The winter of 1966 was held to be an augury of things to come.

Of all devils, the Jews are the object of the most concerted criticism by Muslims. In fact, most poor Negroes feel a deep hostility toward Jews because, as so often is the case, Jews own many of the stores in Negro areas. They are therefore the most "visible" of whites. This is particularly true in Harlem and Watts. It was no coincidence that the Negro rioters in both areas turned their wrath on the Jewish stores first. Harlem's term for all Jews, "Goldberg," is only slightly less derogatory in meaning than "Whitey," "The Man" and "Mr. Charlie." Blazing anti-Semitism will often be the motivating force behind a person joining the Nation of Islam.

Elijah Muhammad seldom castigates the Jews directly, but his late second-in-command, Malcolm X, often was more candid and undoubtedly reflected the feelings of many other Muslims. The latter said in an interview in *Playboy* magazine:

> Make a true observation about the Jews, and if it doesn't pat him on the back, then he uses his grip on the mass media to label you an anti-Semite. . . . The Jew is always anxious to *advise* the black man. . . . But the Jew that's advising the Negro joins the NAACP, CORE, the Urban League and others. With money

donations the Jew gains control, then he sends the black man doing all this wading-in, boring-in, even burying-in—everything but buying-in. . . . No, when there's something worth owning, the Jews got it. . . .

Whatever Elijah Muhammad chooses to castigate—the Negro middle class, the civil rights movement, or all whites everywhere—his faithful lap it up with a seemingly insatiable appetite. Malcolm X writes in his *Autobiography* of Muhammad giving a speech:

". . . And, *still,* this Christian American white man has not got it in him to find the human decency, and enough sense of *justice,* to recognize us, and accept us, the black people who have done so much for him, as fellow human beings!"

"YAH, Man!" . . . "*Um-huh!*" "*Teach,* Messenger!" . . . "*Yah!*" . . . "*Tell 'em!*" . . . "*You right!*" . . . "Take your *time* up there, little Messenger!" . . . "Oh, *yes!*"

The goals of Muhammad's Nation are not clear; in fact, they seem intentionally vague. But if they are not baldly stated, they are at least implied, and no Muslim is under any illusions about them. First, Muslims seek a worldwide hegemony of black peoples; and all non-whites are considered black. They realize that only through strength will they be heeded. White fear of black unity, they add, is the reason why Muslims are persecuted.

Muslims also seek racial and economic separation. In his book, *Message to the Blackman in America,* Muhammad writes:

We must stop relying upon the white man to care for us. We must become an independent people. So-called Negroes should:

1. Separate yourselves from the "slave-master."
2. Pool your resources, education and qualifications for independence.
3. Stop forcing yourselves into places where you are not wanted.
4. Make your own neighborhood a decent place to live.
5. Rid yourselves of the lust of wine and drink and learn to love self and your kind before loving others.
6. Unite to create a future for yourself.
7. Build your own homes, schools, hospitals and factories.

8. Do not seek to mix your blood through racial integration.
9. Stop buying expensive cars, fine clothes and shoes before being able to live in a fine home.
10. Spend your money among yourselves.
11. Build an economic system among yourselves.
12. Protect your women.[4]

The Nation also seeks land, and this one demand qualifies it as a political group. Where precisely this land is, no one within the movement has ever stated. The chances that any specific site will ever be named are remote. There is some speculation that Muhammad would prefer some land in the Southwest (this may be due to his living in Phoenix, Arizona, most of the year because of his asthma); others seem to think he is considering some foreign land. Malcolm X, in 1960, before he broke with Muhammad, suggested that American Negroes be subsidized by the federal government for their "300 years without a pay day":

> The United States can subsidize Israel to start a state—Israel hasn't fought for this country. The United States can subsidize India and Latin America—and *they* tell Americans to "go home!" We even subsidize Poland and Yugoslavia *and those are communist countries!*
> Why can't the Black Man in America have a piece of land with technical help and money to get his own nation established? What's so fantastic about that? We fought, died and helped to build this country, and since we can't be citizens here, then help us to build a nation of our own. We don't have to go to Africa. We can do it right here.[5]

He was once specific enough to say that he thought "nine or ten states would be enough" but he would expand the point no further.

There are others who believe that Muhammad expects to acquire his land only on the day of judgment. At that time the prevailing order of things will be reversed, and if any whites are still alive they will be shipped back to Europe so that the Black Nation can rule America in peace.

Muhammad can profit handsomely from the fact that his organization is considered primarily a religion. Without fear of being accused of sedition, he can talk about "the judgment day," the "Battle of Armageddon," holocausts, trials by fire, the devils, believers, unbelievers, the "battle in the sky," and so forth, because they are religious terms.

Muhammad runs an exceedingly tight ship. He is absolute boss, there are no elections, he makes all the important appointments, his word is law. He demands absolute obedience from his followers; any infraction is severely dealt with.

A Muslim must not drink, smoke, swear, lie, steal, gossip or gamble. He must not commit adultery, nor socialize with Christians, nor fornicate, nor conk his hair, nor use skin bleachers, nor show disrespect to his ministers, nor carry any weapon. He must maintain a high standard of personal hygiene; he must dress conservatively, keep his home tidy, pray five times a day facing Mecca and eat only one daily meal. He must not vote in elections nor otherwise take part in public life. He must not salute the American flag nor may he join the military. Otherwise he should obey all laws. If he has a job outside the Mosque, he should do a fair day's work for his pay.

The Muslim's surname is replaced by an X to free him from his Christian "slave name." Eventually, if he is a good Muslim, he is given his "original" name—Ali, Karriem, Shabazz, Muhammad, and Sharrieff are the most common—which Elijah is supposed to learn directly from Allah. "Why should we Africans carry our slavemasters' names?" asked Malcolm X once. "Did you ever see a European white man calling himself Kasavubu?"

Food a Muslim does not eat includes black-eyed peas, collard greens, pinto beans, cornbread, rabbit, possum, squirrel, coon, carp, catfish and sucker fish. The one absolutely taboo food is pork, which Muhammad claims has 999 specific germs and is actually one-third rat, one-third cat and one-third dog. A Muslim can be suspended indefinitely from the Nation if caught eating it.

Muhammad keeps his followers very busy within the fold; in fact, he insists that all Muslims spend a maximum amount of time at the Temple. This helps to build up loyalty and cut down on old habits. Each member is supposed to contribute a certain percentage of his income to the organization, which sometimes runs as high as 33 percent, with special lump-sum assessments for occasions such as Savior's Day (February 26). If a Muslim is not out hawking his quota of the sect's newspaper, *Muhammad Speaks* (circulation approximately 200,000), he may be out "fishing" in the ghetto for new members. Or he may be collecting green stamps for a new school bus, or he may be attending classes at the University of Islam (most of which are accredited), or he may be helping in the office with correspondence, inserting yellow sheets of paper into each envelope "to keep the letter from being read by infra-red cameras," or advising correspondents not to put a return address on their envelopes.

The chances are good, however, that he will spend considerable time working in one of the Muslim enterprises, all run on a hardnosed capitalist basis. In Chicago, for instance, the Muslims own a barbershop, a gas station, two clothing stores, a restaurant (where the food is described as "Soo Deelicious"), a realty company, a radio and TV repair shop, a dry cleaning business and some apartment buildings. They own a 140-acre farm in Michigan. There is also an eighteen-room mansion and a fleet of expensive cars which must be kept in top condition in order to maintain Elijah Muhammad in the manner to which he has become accustomed.

If you are a female Muslim, the chances are you spend your time in the Muslim Girls' Training and General Civilization Class, which is a leadership group dedicated to teaching the female converts their proper role in life. All MGTGCCs wear a white nunlike habit and shun all beauty aids—lipstick, rouge, nail polish, etc.

If you are a physically large male and show unusual zeal and dedication to the Nation of Islam, you may be chosen to join the Fruit of Islam, a tough, fanatical, secret elite that comprises the inner core of the movement. Fruits of Islam are supposed to be the exemplars of the Black Nation, maintaining a standard of Muslim excellence that all followers would gladly emulate. They are both admired and feared by the rank-and-file Muslims. Fruit, so the analogy goes, is the final product of any tree; yet, fruit provides

the seed for the next tree. The FOI see themselves as the fruit
of the old tree (slavery) and the seed to the next (the Black
Nation).

The Supreme Captain of the FOI is Raymond Sharrieff, Elijah's
son-in-law and perhaps the second or third most powerful man in
the movement. He is a stocky man, always neatly dressed, with a
baleful glare who, like most other Muslims, does not talk to
whites.

New FOIs, once chosen, are given rigorous training. This
includes judo, military drill, the use of knives, blackjacks and
small arms. They are also taught such techniques as how to
incapacitate a police horse and how to kill a police dog (grab its
leash and whirl the animal around your head until it strangles).
Every FOI takes a special, secret oath.

Apparently the FOI keep small arsenals, pending the battle of
Armageddon, but the caches are not supposed to be as big as they
were in the 1930s. No FOI arms himself in public. In any event,
there is no need to be armed because, as one observer put it, the
FOI are trained to do without arms what a cook can do with
potatoes—mash, slice and fry.

The major functions of the FOI are security and discipline.
Whenever a rule is broken, the accused goes before the FOI for
judgment. Whatever decision is handed down—fine, suspension,
beating, expulsion—is final; there is no appeal. What happens
when an FOI steps out of line is less clear, although there are some
indications that the ultimate penalty is death.

FOIs are purportedly prepared to lay down their lives under a
number of circumstances, three of them being: an assault on a
black woman, an invasion of the Temple, and an attack on the
Prophet himself. Everyone is searched by FOI before entering the
Temple, members and guests alike. Un-Muslim items such as
tobacco, dope, razors and miscellaneous hardware are confiscated
until the person leaves.

The Fruit of Islam also provides Elijah Muhammad and his
ministers with a corps of bodyguards. Muhammad's personal set of
janissaries is a phalanx of the most intimidating-looking FOI
imaginable—rugged six-footers all with stony expressions. Whenever Muhammad makes one of his rare public appearances he is

escorted into the room by perhaps thirty of his FOI. He is not even visible; his guards bunch around him like artichoke leaves. When this moving mass of Muslims reaches the appointed spot, the phalanx parts and out pops Elijah Muhammad, blinking like an owl in the sun.

The bulk of Muslim recruits are drawn from what A. Philip Randolph calls those "lowest down on the totempole." They are the ones who have been hurt the worst by whites, both mentally and physically; they are the ones who feel most alienated from society. They are the ones who are uprooted from their past— usually Southern rural—and the ones who have lost contact with their church. When a Muslim goes "fishing" for recruits, he goes to the center of the ghetto, where the pimps, winos, hustlers, addicts, criminals and bums congregate.

One of the most famous of Muslim recruits was Malcolm X, the man who built the Nation of Islam into what it is today.

Malcolm was born Malcolm Little in Omaha, Nebraska, in 1925. When he was four years old, the Black Legion, a local Klan-like group, burned his parents' house down because his father was "uppity." Before he was seven years old his father was run over by a streetcar. When he was fourteen he moved from Michigan to Boston to live with his sister, Ella Mae Collins. From a self-confessed "hick," Malcolm soon turned "cool" and "hip," a "stud" and a "cat" with a zoot suit, knob-toed, orange-colored "kick-up" shoes and conked hair.*

Known as "Detroit Red" by his friends (and later as "the Harlem Asp"), he was successively a shoeshine boy, a Lindy-hopper, and a sandwich vendor on the *Yankee Clipper* running between Boston and New York. Within a year of his moving to Boston he settled in Harlem, where he was a waiter in Small's

* To conk hair, according to Malcolm, thin slice a potato into a Mason jar, pour in half a can of lye; add two eggs and stir rapidly with a wooden spoon. This "jelly-like, starchy-looking glop," as Malcolm called it, is then spread all over your scalp. Apparently this mixture burns; but the longer the pain can be endured the longer the hair will remain straight. Relief is achieved by washing the solution off with water. In his *Autobiography*, Malcolm complained that he conked his hair once in the men's room on a train, but when he went to wash off the scorching "congolene," as it is also called, he found that the pipes were frozen. He wrote: "I had to stick my head into the stool and flush and flush to rinse out the stuff."

Paradise, a hustler, a pimp, a dope addict, a gambler, a numbers pusher and a thief.

When the draft board summoned him in 1943, Malcolm broke out his wildest zoot suit, put on orange knob-toed shoes, worked up his hair into a "frizzled conk" and went, as he writes, "skipping and tipping" into the recruiting center saying he wanted to be a general. "Daddy-o," he told the psychiatrist, ". . . I want to get sent down South. Organize them nigger soldiers, you dig? Steal us some guns, and kill up crackers!" A 4-F card was sent to him in the mail.[6]

In 1946 Malcolm was sentenced to ten years in prison for armed robbery. He was not yet twenty-one years old. He spent his prison days educating himself. He read most of the books in the prison library, including the dictionary—which he read from cover to cover—to improve his vocabulary. Somewhere along the line, Malcolm got religion, specifically the Muslim religion. He first heard of it through a brother who visited him in prison, but no doubt he picked up the details from other prisoners. In his *Autobiography,* the transformation from a sharp street hustler to a Muslim mumbling "All Praise be to Allah" seems a bit unreal, particularly his adoration for Elijah Muhammad, whom he had not then yet met. But there is no question that Malcolm was a sincere convert. What it was that sparked the change—besides, of course, the usual Muslim hatred of "Whitey," "Mr. Charlie," "the blue-eyed devils"—will never be known.

In 1952 Malcolm was released from prison and for the next twelve years helped expand the Nation of Islam into the organization it is today. He rose to the number two position, the heir apparent; in fact, he became so well known he almost overshadowed Elijah Muhammad. Some say that membership in the Nation grew from 400 in 1952 to over 80,000 in 1963.

Malcolm X was one of the most dynamic and vitriolic of all Negro speakers. He had a very small personal following, but he was widely admired as one who would stand up to "Whitey" and "tell it as it is." He was one of the few Harlemites who could draw a crowd in the rain. He once declared, "We need a Mau Mau to win freedom and equality in the United States! . . ." (Taking its cue from this remark, a small group of Nationalists organized the Harlem Mau Mau Society soon after Malcolm's death. The group is distinguished by its small size, its hard hats with "Mau Mau" painted on the shell, and its members' propensity for carrying bayonets in public.) On another occasion Malcolm shouted at some whites: *"Your little babies will get polio!"* American Negroes, he wrote, "are like a black tick riding on the udder of a white cow." On the subject of black men desiring white women, he wrote, ". . . Like a Black Brother recently observed to me, 'Look, you ever smell one of them *wet?'* " As to whether the Muslims' impetus is hate, Malcolm was quite blunt:

> For the white man to ask the black man if he hates him is just like the rapist asking the raped, or the wolf asking the *sheep,* "Do you hate me?" The white man is in no moral *position* to accuse anyone else of hate!
>
> Why, when all of my ancestors are snake-bitten, and I'm snake-bitten, and I warn my children to avoid snakes, what does that *snake* sound like accusing *me* of hate-teaching.[7]

In 1962, a plane full of whites from Atlanta, Georgia, crashed on takeoff from Paris, killing 121 people; Malcolm had this to say about it:

> I would like to announce a very beautiful thing that has just happened. I got a wire from God today. He really answered our prayers over in France. He dropped an airplane out of the sky with over 120 white people on it because the Muslims believe in an eye for an eye and a tooth for a tooth. We will continue to pray and we hope that every day another plane falls out of the sky.

A year later, commenting on the Birmingham riots, he said: "I'd say this: if anyone sets a dog on a black man, the black man should kill that dog—whether he is a four-legged dog or a two-legged dog!"

It was Malcolm's propensity for strong words that triggered his break with Elijah Muhammad in early 1964. Speaking of President Kennedy's assassination, Malcolm cried: "Being an old farm boy myself, chickens coming home to roost never did make me sad;

they've always made me glad." Because of the public outcry that followed this remark, Muhammad took the opportunity to suspend his most able minister.

But his remarks were not the real reason. Malcolm was becoming a threat to the leadership of Muhammad, and this was intolerable. It was a case of a powerful evangelist versus an aging passive leader. Malcolm demonstrated his power to the world one day when he waved a mob of Harlem Muslims away with a flick of the wrist, prompting one man to say, "No man should have that much power."

In addition, Malcolm, for all his hard-nosed anti-white talk, was actually moving toward a position of accommodation, wherein he believed whites and blacks could live together in peace. He had reached this conclusion later in 1964 during a pilgrimage to Mecca where he saw peoples of all colors working together. He was beginning to beam his appeal to the nationalistic instincts in all Negroes, not limiting it to Muslims.

He still believed that American Negroes had to battle for what they wanted—in other words, Malcolm was prepared to use economic and political force as opposed to nonviolent techniques —and he announced he was prepared to lead that fight. His new stance found him being courted by a number of militant organizations: CORE, SNCC and the Socialist Workers Party being three of the most ardent.

His was also—so he claimed—being stalked by FOI gunmen. Muhammad apparently realized that Malcolm, if he were successful in his interracial approach, would undercut the entire Nation of Islam position of separation and noncooperation.

In February 1965, three gunmen shot Malcolm full of holes as he was beginning a speech in a Harlem ballroom. Over forty thousand people attended his funeral. Within days he had been deified as a savior of the Negro people. Even today young Negroes still wear Malcolm memorial buttons ("Our Black Shining Prince —Freedom By Any Means Necessary") and the black fur astrakhan hats he favored.

Despite the conviction of the three assailants, no one on the fringe can agree on a common culprit. In charges reminiscent of President Kennedy's assassination, some say Malcolm was murdered by Communists; Conrad Lynn, a lawyer who describes himself as a "Black Marxist nationalist," thinks some "police finks" were put up to it; even James Farmer, a friend of Malcolm's and considered an astute observer of the political scene, was heard to mention something about "Red Chinese."

2

Because my skin was the wrong shade, no Muslim would talk with me officially. I pestered them so much in Chicago that when I ordered a book from them, they sent it—with the spine neatly split in two. On another occasion I had a chance to talk briefly with a young Muslim in a restaurant, which was a mistake. He went into a hysterical monologue full of Muslim clichés about whites. Eventually the owner asked us to leave, saying that we were hurting business. On yet another occasion, around Christmas, I saw a neatly dressed Muslim deep in "enemy territory," Rockefeller Center. He was selling *Muhammad Speaks,* taking advantage of people's seasonal generosity. As I approached to buy a copy I could hear him calling softly to the passers-by: "Help the Negroes . . . help the Negroes. . . ."

Nor did I have a chance to meet Malcolm X, because he was dead before I began this study. But I did go to a meeting of Malcolm's breakaway group, the Organization of Afro-American Unity, now run by his sister, Ella Mae Collins.

The meeting was held in the Hotel Theresa, 125th Street and Seventh Avenue, the heart of Harlem. (One corner of this intersection is now known as "Malcolm X Square.") It was a warm, sunny Sunday afternoon in the late fall. The street-corner speakers were out in full force. Diagonally across the street from the hotel a crowd had gathered in front of Dr. Louis Michaux' House of Good Sense and Home of Proper Propaganda bookstore to hear a goateed individual on a stepladder talk about the advantages of going back to Africa. Speakers were talking to knots of people up and down both main streets. Some of the shouting could be heard half a block away. The sidewalks were full of strollers, church-goers, hustlers, children.

It is difficult for any white to understand the loneliness, the sense of not belonging, that must saturate the consciousness of many Negroes whenever they venture out into the white world. I got a taste of what it must be like that Sunday afternoon when I stepped out of a taxicab to find that I was the only white person in view.

The OAAU was meeting in a small upstairs room of the hotel. I was invited as the guest of Conrad Lynn's, one of the speakers, so the OAAU guards let me in. A strapping Malcolmite searched me at the door in a very professional manner: nothing was left to chance, everything was examined with care. I was perspiring profusely by the time he finished. The room was packed with about seventy people, all fairly well dressed, a few children here and there. I took a seat in the back. Guards, showing no emotion, lined the walls with their arms folded, feet apart. A large picture of Malcolm X hung on the wall behind the speaker's table. A loudspeaker was blaring forth with recordings of Malcolm speaking: ". . . blue eyes, pale skin, blond hair . . . *same* man . . . *same* enemy . . ."

The crowd of black nationalists in the room were beginning to work themselves up. "That's *right!*" "Tell it as it *is*, brother Malcolm!" The main speakers were not even in the room yet.

"Bloodshed . . .," continued Malcolm, "all revolutions involve bloodshed. . . ."

"RIGHT!"

"Yeah, yeah!"

"The white man sent you to Asia, Korea and Europe to *bleed* for the white man," shouted Malcolm. "If violence is wrong in America, then it is wrong abroad. . . ."

"Uh-huh!"

"Oh *yes!*"

"Tha's *RIGHT!*"

A man in a black astrakhan hat and a brown, pink and white robe paraded in front of the speaker's table with a wooden baton. The meeting finally came to order; Malcolm's voice was reluctantly turned off.

Throughout all the speechmaking there was considerable commotion and movement in the room, a constant hum of voices, an occasional shout of approval, sporadic handclapping and foot stamping; from time to time the crowd would leap to its feet and cheer. On two instances, where particularly harsh anti-white statements were made, part of the crowd turned around and looked at me, one of only two whites in the room. (I never saw the other one.)

My notes are fragmentary.

Clifton de Berry, a Mississippi-born albino, and at that time the Socialist Workers Party candidate for mayor of New York City, was the first speaker.

"If you're a black man, you've got problems," said de Berry. "Black, brown and yellow people are turning their backs on this type of government here. . . . Revolution means taking power; to do this we must develop revolutionaries—legal, terrorist, guerrilla warfare. . . . I believe it's about time revolutionaries stop allowing responsible Negro leaders teaching something *only they* believe in! . . . We must expose the Uncle Toms. . . . Watts was the first blow for the black revolution! Everyone should be proud of it . . . [cheers]! This is how you will get respect. . . . *Meet power with power* [more cheers]!"

William Epton was next to speak. He was a candidate for state senator on the Progressive Labor Party ticket and was soon to be convicted of rioting in connection with the 1964 Harlem riots and given a one-to-two-year sentence in prison.

"We are talking about overthrowing the most powerful nation in the world . . . ," he cried. "To overthrow this government, we must talk about the entire country from the East to Watts, from Canada to Texas [stamping of feet]. We must bring in the suppressed whites, the black bourgeoisie who are progressive. . . . We need a revolution because Negroes will not be free until the United States government is overthrown! ["That's *right!*"] *We are the fifth column of this country! . . .* We must cripple him wherever possible. . . . We must turn America inward with our revolution so as to free other countries for their revolutions. . . . We must be prepared to say 'I'd rather die on this street than live another day under these conditions!' "

Conrad Lynn spoke next and tried to calm down the oratory.

The audience was impatient. An African student spoke on pan-Africanism; the audience became restless. A Malcolmite rose to his feet and shouted: *"Long live the spirit of Malcolm X* [cheers]!" *"Long live the Oh-Ay-Ay-Yew* [more cheers]!" *"Long live the Black Revolution* [prolonged cheers and foot stamping]!"

"To get ready for the revolution, you must *think* like a revolutionary." Said Mrs. Collins, her red and blue sash trembling with rage, "Don't just let there be talk! Let us have unity! Let us prepare! . . .

"Blacks *work* for you-know-who, pay *taxes* for you-know-who and *die* for you-know-who! Do you know what it's like," she asked, "to be black in the belly of a whale?"

Pointing her finger at the audience, she thundered: "We have too much irresponsibilities, too many conked hair curly-haired people *talking* about a revolution! *Stop standing around on the corner swapping wit! Go in search of wisdom!* If we can get ten percent of the thirty-five [sic] million blacks in the United States, we can have a revolution! . . .

"Let us not say that the next generation of black man walking up and down the road will be begging the white man for freedom! . . . If a white man tries to molest you, *declare war on* him! You don't need a gun. That's *his* weapon, *he* needs it! . . . ['Git 'em, git 'em, git 'em! . . . ,' chanted one man.]"

A member of the Deacons for Defense spoke briefly appealing for money to buy weapons. "We're planning to buy five hundred carbines and they cost eighty dollars a piece . . . Deacons use only the best weapons! ['Get whitey, boy! . . .'] Who's gonna start the contributions? . . . ['Yeah, yeah! Yessir, yessir!']"

A long question-and-answer period followed, broken by more commotion, the hum of voices, clapping and cheering. One man got up and asked rhetorically: "Why is it that *we* don't own all the illegitimate business in Harlem; why does whitey own it?" Another person stood up and asked, "Why is it that up here in Harlem we pay first-class prices for second-class meat while down on Park Avenue they pay second-class prices for first-class meat?" Before any of the speakers could answer, a little old lady in a flowered hat leaped to her feet and, waving a finger in the air, shouted with total rage in her voice, *" 'Cause we is niggers!"*

With anything more than a cursory glance, certain trends are apparent among America's Muslims. There is no doubt that Muhammad's way of life has restored the self-respect of some Negroes; they have been weaned away from a personal corruption by Muslim demands that they "wake up, brush up and clean up." But this has not turned Muslims into paragons of virtue. In fact, the Nation of Islam has been accused on two counts of backsliding.

The first concerns Elijah Muhammad, who has been accused by some of his former followers of improprieties in his personal life. Malcolm X believed that Muhammad was not living up to the rigid standards of behavior that Muhammad himself demanded of his rank and file. This was one of the reasons that sparked Malcolm's break with the Nation in 1964.

If such activities were ever to create any disillusionment among the faithful, it may turn the Fruit of Islam into more of a Gestapo than it already is, terrifying the rank and file sufficiently to keep them in line, shaking them down if necessary. The possibility that the FOI might eventually develop into a black Mafia or Murder Incorporated is not too remote.

The second count concerns the Muslims' public activities. One of their major propaganda points is that they are law-abiding individuals. Unfortunately for their public relations department, too many crimes of violence have been committed by Muslims to sustain the claim. Muslims have been involved in most of the prison riots over the last twenty years; they were active in the race riots of 1964 and 1965; they have been involved in a number of robberies—one, a 1965 bank holdup in Newark, New Jersey, saw the mayor of the town personally pursue the Muslim bandits through the streets. Assassination attempts against other enemies were quite common before the successful one against Malcolm.

From all appearances the Muslims are shrinking in size. They grew phenomenally in the early 1960s from the publicity they received, but from all reports they have been unable to hold the new recruits. One of their star converts has been Muhammad Ali, in real life Cassius Clay. He, perhaps more than anyone else, has drawn new recruits to the organization. When his original financial backers (all of whom were white) from Louisville, Kentucky,

bowed out of the picture in 1966, Clay staffed his boxing corporation, Main Bout, Inc., with Muslims. They seem to be firmly in
control.

3

A number of other black nationalist impulses should be noted.

One was the Black Liberation Front, composed of three Americans and one Canadian girl who hatched a plan to blow up the
Statue of Liberty, the Washington Monument and the Liberty Bell
as a protest against the treatment of Negroes in America. Early in
1965, Robert Collier, a library clerk and founder of the Front,
went to Canada and arranged with Michelle Duclos, a member of
the *Rassemblement pour l'Independance Nationale,* to transport
thirty sticks of dynamite to The Bronx. This was done without
incident. But, as the result of information supplied by an undercover agent, the quartet was arrested. Police said that the dynamite
was so unstable that it was a wonder the stationwagon and driver
were not blown up on the trip down from Canada. Collier and his
two co-conspirators—Walter Bowe, a trumpet player in a combo
called "The Angry Black Men," and Khaleel Sultarn Sayyed, an
Arab-Negro, were sent to prison for ten years. Duclos was banished from America forever.

Another impulse is LeRoi Jones, the angry, bearded playwright-
author. Like many black nationalists, Jones married a white woman.
"Guerrilla warfare is inevitable in the North and the South,"
he has said. "Every black is a potential revolutionist . . . you
can't use nuclear weapons against us when we kill a few cops . . .
there is no way of saving America."[8] Jones was the founder of
the Black Arts Repertory Theatre in west Harlem that put on
"dramas of anti-white frustration and revenge." In late 1965 the
theatre received a grant of $40,000 from HARYOU-ACT, a
federal poverty agency. Said Jones: "I don't see anything wrong
with hating white people." Nor did he see anything wrong with
accepting a government grant to preach it. In March 1966, the
police discovered an arsenal in the theatre building; the rifles,
pistols, crossbows, bombs, meathooks, knives and hashish pipes

belonged to an unnamed extremist Negro nationalist secret society.

Jones is criticized because all he does is preach a "hate whitey" sermon, offering nothing better. He seems content just to have whites hate him until he establishes a name for himself, at which point he might come forward with a few original ideas.

Another black nationalist impulse is the Deacons for Defense and Justice. It was started in the spring of 1965 in Jonesboro, Louisiana, by a group of church deacons. Its membership is secret, but it claims to have fifty chapters throughout the nation, many of which are in the North. The Deacons' leader is Charles Sims, a Negro from Bogalusa, Louisiana, with a surly and suspicious disposition.

The Deacons are an armed self-defense group that was formed to counter Klan violence. Sims stresses that the Deacons' weapons would be used only in defense. "They [the whites] bring the fight to us," he said. "We guard white and black civil rights workers from white terrorists' bullets and churches from bombs."

Robert Hicks, Sims' aide, said that he does not ever envision the Deacons becoming an offensive group such as the Klan. "It is not in keeping with the law," he said. He added that the Deacons are a shell organization in quiet times; but when defense of the Negro community is necessary, a chain telephone alarm system and runner system can mobilize Negroes with weapons in a matter of minutes. "The threat of counterviolence keeps down Klan violence," Hicks said. "Our secrecy," he continued, "puts an edge of doubt on who is and who isn't a Deacon, which counters Klan secrecy."

In February 1965 Hicks was threatened by the white community in Bogalusa because he had white civil rights workers staying in his house. The police ordered the workers out. Hicks refused to comply, and the police retorted that his house would probably not be standing in the morning. The Deacons were mobilized; a confrontation took place between armed Negroes and a white mob which threatened to erupt into violence. Eventually the whites backed down.

When I interviewed Hicks at his home, he looked at me incredulously and said: "Man, a year ago if you had driven into the Negro community in broad daylight as you just did, we would have had to escort you out of town." As it was, Bogalusa was quiet and there were no incidents during my visit. The racially troubled town has seen less Klan violence of late, attesting to the strength of the Deacons.

There is also a group called "The Five-Percenters," an outgrowth of another anti-white group called the "Blood Brothers." Five-Percenters are mostly teen-age hoodlums and neophyte Muslims who have taken their name from a conviction that 85 percent of all Negroes are cattle, 10 percent are being used, leaving 5 percent self-chosen saviors who will lead the Negroes out of "bondage." The Five-Percenters were led in 1965 by ex-Muslim Clarence "Puddin' " Smith, who calls himself "Allah" and whom his followers believe to be God. Members of the group, among other things, have been ejected from a courtroom for shouting nationalist slogans, have assaulted a police officer who tried to stop them from molesting a Negro girl, and have threatened schoolteachers with such statements as "You blue-eyed white devil! You'll burn!"

Yet another group is James Lawson's United African Nationalist Movement, a tiny group of back-to-Africa street-corner speakers. He advocates that whites sell out their businesses in Negro areas; if that is not possible, then the stores should be expropriated. "If we are unable to bring about an orderly transfer of business from whites to Negroes in Harlem," he thundered, then "it will be done one way or the other." He does not rule out violence.

A more significant factor on the nationalist scene is Daniel Watts, the editor-in-chief of *Liberator* magazine. Before turning active nationalist, Watts was a rising young architect who helped design the arched arrival building at Kennedy International Airport.

Watts concentrates his magazine's fire on the liberal integrationist. "We're tired of white chauvinism," he told me. "We're tired of Bayard Rustin being imposed upon us as our spokesman." As an afterthought he asked, "Who ever voted for Bayard Rustin?" (When I told this to Rustin, he cocked his head, thought a moment and said, "Well now, who ever voted for Dan Watts?")

Liberator, says Watts, is "trying to *change* things. We are calling for the end of the castration of the black man and allow him to assert his manhood."

He went on, "We will no longer sit back and listen to this shit about integration." It has, he avers, destroyed Afro-American cooking and the Afro-American identity; it has diverted the energies of blacks and confused middle-class whites; worst of all, he said, "it has turned the focus away from jobs to some moral crap."

He adds, "It suits the white liberals to hang us up on the moral bag."

What Watts is seeking is a Negro struggle led by Negroes, not liberal whites, not do-good whites and especially not Jews, whom he attacks with considerable abandon in the pages of his magazine. "The long hot summer," he said, "will see more violence against Jewish shopkeepers. I think it should be done." The underlying complaint against the Jews, he said, was his opposition to whites in the civil rights movement. "Any cursory look at it," he explained, "shows that Jews are the dominant whites there." Every other ethnic group has its own power base, he said, then asked: "Why do these white liberals have a compulsion to love blacks when they can't get along among themselves?"

His slogan seems to be "We Can Carry Our Own Burden, Thank You!" which implies that the Negro community be Negro-owned and -operated, from small stores and banks to factories. Watts summed up his point of view logically with: "We live in a power-oriented world; those who sit at the conference table have power; therefore we must have power!"

Perhaps the most significant forces on the black nationalist front today are the Alabama "Black Panther" Party and the Mississippi Freedom Democratic Party. Both are creations of the most militant of the civil rights groups, the Student Nonviolent Coordinating Committee, or "Snick" as it is pronounced from its initials.

SNCC is a newcomer on the civil rights scene, having been founded in 1960. It is a product of the sit-ins of that year, and its growth has been due to a resurgence of interest in New Left and iconoclastic ideas. It is a tough, abrasive and self-assuredly revolutionary group, continuously at odds with all the other civil rights groups.

Its members—mostly Negroes, but some whites—are the shock troops of the civil rights movement. They come from a wide variety of backgrounds—universities, businesses, the clergy, the arts—but hold certain things in common. For instance, most of the two hundred SNCC organizers are young, under thirty. All are in revolt against American society, particularly against segregation and the existing leadership both in and out of the civil rights movement, from President Johnson to Martin Luther King. They have never been committed to a doctrine of nonviolence (even though it appears in their title), yet at the same time they do not advocate violence. (Both are considered possible tactics to be used at the appropriate moment.) They talk in terms of direct action—boycotts, sit-ins, demonstrations, registration drives, education—which has resulted in their having acquired a certain expertise in Southern penal institutions. They place great emphasis on "living free" or, as they are more likely to say, "digging freedom," which is a personal matter with them, defying any categorization.

They have a distinct distrust of anything organizational: SNCC, for instance, is one of the few groups where titles are vague and ephemeral, where economic dogma is even more obscure and where institutional literature is virtually nonexistent. They positively despise the thought of a leadership cult; anyone in power any length of time is suspect. (One of its leaders, Robert Moses, received so much national publicity that he felt obliged to change his surname to Parris—his middle name—and drop temporarily out of sight.) In this sense, there is a streak of anarchism running through the organization not unlike that found in the Wobblies of old—undisciplined, exuberant, arrogant and self-righteous all at the same time.

There is a *mystique* of "total commitment" that demands of SNCC workers the rejection of the society in which they live. They spurn all compromise, conciliation and gestures as hypocritical. They revel in their role as outsiders, much as Red China does, confident in the knowledge that their leverage to change society is potentially far greater than working within the system.

SNCC's battleground is in the rural South, among those people and in that part of America which tourists seldom see: the shanty towns, the disenfranchised Negro sharecropper, the poor, the bypassed, the disinherited. "Our job," says John Lewis, until recently SNCC's chairman, "is to organize the unorganized into a vital force for radical, social, economical and political change. Our job is to create what I like to call pockets of power and influence, where the people can say, 'This is what I want and need.' "[9] To this end SNCC workers dress poor, talk poor and act poor in order to find out and implement what is wanted and needed.

The forms these efforts take are varied: independent unions, cooperatives, "Freedom Schools." One of the most publicized to date has been the establishment of independent all-black political parties. The two best known are deep inside Dixie, in Alabama and Mississippi.

The Mississippi Freedom Democratic Party was established in the spring of 1964 and grew out of the Council of Federated Organizations (COFO), now defunct. The year before, in a COFO-sponsored mock election, Negro candidates polled over 80,000 votes; in a 1964 mock congressional election, over 60,000 votes were cast, certainly formidable totals for a new and radical political party in one state. This turnout of Negroes—previously considered to be uninterested in politics—was one of the primary reasons why the MFDP was founded. The individuals behind the elections and the formation of the new Party—Robert Parris Moses, Aaron Henry, Lawrence Guyot, Fannie Lou Hamer, and others—still play a dominant role in the organization.

The Lowndes County Freedom Organization, otherwise known as the "Black Panther" Party (the name derives from the Party's symbol which appears on the ballot), is of later origin and was the by-product of a concerted registration drive in the county under the direction of SNCC organizer Stokely Carmichael.

What both parties seek to achieve are grass roots organizations among Negroes that, with political solidarity at the polls, will force the white community to pay attention to their needs. The two organizations are concentrating their efforts on getting people elected to local offices, the offices that most affect their everyday life: sheriff, tax assessor, tax collector, circuit solicitor and school board member. To do this they have begun an all-out drive to register Negroes. How successful they have been is difficult to say, for to register a person is not the same as getting him to vote, since in many districts a Negro still puts his life on the line—at a minimum his economic life—if he is seen at the polls.

However, some trends are noticeable. In the 1966 primaries, for instance, the increased Negro registration did encourage a number of white moderates to seek office, it muted overt racism, and it actually won the nomination for local office for a few Negroes. One thing that it proved is that the Negro will not necessarily vote an anti-white ticket as long as moderate whites run as candidates.

During the summer of 1964 the MFDP sent a delegation to the Democratic Convention in Atlantic City. It demanded full accreditation, to replace the all-white Mississippi delegation. To avoid an embarrassing scene, President Johnson offered two seats to the MFDP as delegates-at-large, with a further proviso that all the insurgents sign a loyalty oath to the Democratic Party. This was rejected by the Freedom Democratic Party as an insult and as tokenism. Early in 1965 it sent another delegation to the capital demanding that the elected Mississippi congressmen be replaced. The MFDP was turned away unsatisfied.

The relations between SNCC and the NAACP have always been near the breaking point. In one instance, Roy Wilkins, the executive secretary of the NAACP, during a speech he was giving in Jackson, Mississippi, was rushed by a group of SNCC militants who wanted to challenge him to debate. The mob's leader was stopped short by an NAACP official who was sporting a pistol. Wilkins left the hall to the cries of "Uncle Tom!" and assorted other catcalls.

By 1966 a mutual disenchantment had sprung up between SNCC and those groups less militant, such as the NAACP and the Democratic Party. In fact it has taken on the appearance of total alienation. In the spring of 1966, SNCC replaced its chairman, John Lewis, and its executive secretary, James Foreman, with militant nationalists Stokely Carmichael and Ruby Smith Robinson. This move heralds a new tack by SNCC, a move out of the mainstream of civil rights. It reflects a rejection of any cooperation with whites.

The cry "black power!" is the term used to unite the organization. It is a much abused term, often frightening moderate whites who think it means an armed uprising in the streets, far worse than what happened at Watts. According to Carmichael, the term simply means a very militant union of Negro economic and political power, controlled by Negroes alone. What Daniel Watts is preaching and what Malcolm X was preaching just before he was killed vary only in nuance with this view.

The new leaders see the major parties as corrupt, racist and "hopelessly middle-class." They want to destroy the Democratic Party and replace it with a party that does not "exploit" poor people. In their eyes, only an all-Negro party can accomplish this.

Carmichael, a handsome, Trinidad-born Howard graduate, plans to exclude all whites from his organization in the future. "We will not fire any of our white organizers," he said, "but if they want to organize, they can organize white people. Negroes will organize Negroes." He plans to boycott all White House conferences on civil rights, and he does not envision ever cooperating with other civil rights groups if they have whites in them. The new chairman was the one who called for all Negroes to vote as a bloc in the 1966 primaries. However, the new voters showed considerable sophistication by choosing good candidates over ones judged solely on the basis of their skin coloration.

A member of Martin Luther King's Southern Christian Leadership Conference raised the point that an all-Negro party is a kind of reverse racism, to which Carmichael replied: "To ask Negroes to get in the Democratic Party is like asking Jews to join the Nazi Party."[10]

Negroes should not imitate white politics, he continued, "because white politics are corrupt. . . . Negroes have to view themselves as colonies, and right now is the time for them to quit being white men's colonies and become independent." Apparently Carmichael hopes that the next time he confronts the Democratic Party he will have the necessary political power to get what he wants—and with no white strings attached.

But SNCC has a number of factors working against it. The possibility of a third-party movement achieving success is remote, because as long as it is exclusively Negro it solidifies the whites against it. Furthermore, the Southern Negro has shown no great willingness to vote himself out of the civil rights movement. Finally, as the Negro on the bottom of the ladder gains power and betters his economic position, there is every likelihood that whatever militancy he has now will soon evaporate.

Perhaps the most feared of all the black nationalist groups is RAM—the Revolutionary Action Movement, which is sometimes referred to as the Revolutionary *Armed* Movement. It was started in 1964 and today has approximately a thousand members, all Negroes, mostly concentrated in America's largest cities. Until recently it published a rabidly nationalist magazine called *Black America*. RAM is thought to have large caches of weapons and ammunition to be used on the day that a revolution breaks out. Its members reportedly hold training sessions where close-order drill, the manual of arms (with broomsticks) and the manufacture of Molotov cocktails are taught.

No one knows for sure who the RAM stalwarts are. Undoubtedly they overlap considerably with the Five-Percenters, Malcolm X's group and some of the more violent Marxist groups. Their devotion to secrecy is so fanatical that often one member of RAM does not know many other members. An article in a 1966 issue of *Life* produced this exchange between an interviewer and an anonymous member of RAM:

> Q. How would you tell if a man you don't know is an extremist?
> A. Well, if I was sitting in a really good espionage movie, like—oh—"The Train" or "The Spy Who Came in from the Cold," and the guy sitting next to me was black and he was taking notes, I'd figure he's probably a brother.

RAM's spiritual godfather is Robert Franklin Williams, a bearded, soft-spoken ex-Marine who once belonged to a white Unitarian church and headed the NAACP chapter in Monroe,

North Carolina. In late summer 1957, Monroe Negroes, firing from sandbagged gun emplacements, routed an armed Klan caravan seeking to invade the town's Negro section. Four years later, Williams fled from the United States, one step ahead of the FBI, who sought to detain him for jumping a kidnaping indictment. Williams received asylum in Cuba and set himself up as the "premier of the African-American government-in-exile." He began broadcasting over "Radio Free Dixie" from Havana, suggesting that Negroes in the South take up armed resistance against the local whites.

Williams publishes a small pamphlet called *The Crusader,* which comes into the United States either by direct mail to subscribers or by being smuggled in over the Canadian border. The following passage illustrates the tone of Williams' articles in the pamphlet and comes from the June 1964 issue. Speaking of urban guerrilla warfare, he wrote:

> The weapons of defense employed by Afro-American freedom fighters must consist of a poor man's arsenal. Gasoline fire bombs, lye or acid bombs . . . can be used extensively. During the night hours such weapons, thrown from rooftops, will make the streets impossible for racist cops to patrol . . . gas tanks on public vehicles can be choked up with sand . . . long nails driven through boards, and tacks with large heads are effective to slow the movement of traffic on congested roads at night.
>
> Derailing trains causes panic. Explosive booby traps on police telephone boxes can be employed. High-powered sniper rifles are readily available. Armor-piercing bullets will penetrate oil-storage tanks from a distance. . . . Flame-throwers can be manufactured at home. . . .

The article concludes: "America is a house on fire. FREEDOM NOW, or let it burn, let it burn!"[11]

12

Separatism, Large and Small

1

The island of Puerto Rico, associated in one form or another with the United States since 1898, harbors considerable nationalist sentiment. This sentiment has not been relegated, as it has in other instances, to some political limbo; rather, it reflects the points of views of a significant segment of individuals within the political mainstream of Puerto Rico. In truth, very few Puerto Ricans would deny being one kind of nationalist or another.

Throughout its history Puerto Rico has been driven by three desires, yearnings that have often conflicted with one another. Because it is a small island, its people have feared isolation, which has often been expressed in terms of a desire for close association with a larger political entity. Also, coupled with an historical threat of starvation, its people have always had a desire for physical well-being, regardless of other considerations. And finally, they have always sought to establish an identity of their own, which is reflected in sentiment for independence. These desires can be found today in the three major political streams on the island: the Commonwealth adherents, the statehooders and the *independentistas*.[1]

The Commonwealth sentiment is reflected in the Popular Democratic Party, since 1940 the ruling party on the island. The PDP was founded in 1938 by Luis Muñoz Marin, Puerto Rico's governor from 1952 to 1964.

Muñoz's party has always been divided into three factions. The center and largest faction—now run by the current governor, Robert Sanchez Vilella—contains the Commonwealth supporters. The pro-statehood wing is called the Popular Statehood Movement; its backers are less for statehood than they are a reaction against Muñoz's strong hold over the Party. The third faction, that one seeking independence, is known as the Vanguardia, a four-year-old movement claiming three thousand followers within the PDP. One of its members, also a leader of an inner group called "The Twenty-Two," is Muñoz's daughter, Vivian Muñoz Mendoza.

Although there is some real statehood sentiment in the PDP, the largest statehood force in Puerto Rico today is the Republican Statehood Party—the Partido Estadista Republicano. Even though it received 34 percent of the votes for governor in 1964, it considers itself a minor party.*

One of the most eloquent spokesmen for the Party is José C. Barbosa-Muñiz, a grandson of the Party's founder. He is a professor at the University of Puerto Rico at Humacao, an intense man in his mid-thirties, urbane and articulate. He does not believe, for instance, that the general world trend toward the establishment of independent states makes the statehood position reactionary or anachronistic. On the contrary, he says, "there is a difference between nationalities and body politics. A nation is not necessarily a politically organized group. It is an emotional thing that makes people feel they belong.

"So I am a nationalist—a Puerto Rican all the way; but I also belong to a body politic that is a national organization of people and it is what bestows upon me my citizenship; and as a citizen I have rights and I have duties, and the full meaning of these rights and duties can only be achieved by Puerto Rico becoming a state of the Union.

* This belief stems, ironically, from the Puerto Rican government's support of both major and minor parties (each is given $75,000 per year and $150,000 in election years) and the guaranteeing of an opposition in the island's House and Senate. As one statehooder told me, "Because we are guaranteed so many seats, we do not *have* to work together. We remain fragmented and helpless and thus, permanently, a minority."

"For all the thirty-six years of my life," he said, "I have been an American citizen." But, he asked, referring to the fact that he cannot vote in American elections, "why do I only have equality when I am in the United States and not in Puerto Rico?" The idea, he went on, that statehooders do not want to be Puerto Ricans is not true. "We want to be Puerto Ricans just like Texans want to be Texans—but more," he said.

The third major force on the island is the *independentistas*. They are fragmented over tactics. Some, such as the Vivian Muñoz Mendoza faction, advocate working within the existing system. The others advocate either violence or noncooperation. Those groups advocating the latter two tactics are closest to being outside the political mainstream in Puerto Rico.

Three groups advocate violence. One is the Movimiento Armado Puertorriqueño Autonomia, or Armed Movement for Puerto Rican Home Rule, known by all simply as MAPA. It is composed of a few individuals who were caught stockpiling arms in anticipation of an uprising. Its leaders were arrested in 1965. Ostensibly the organization has collapsed, although very little authoritative information is available to substantiate this.

Another tiny group advocating violence is the Movimiento Libertador de Puerto Rico, a New York-based group run by one Pelegrin Garcia. It attacks the other pro-independence groups because they do not call for "an arms struggle." Garcia's group is distinctly Marxist in flavor, reflecting the intransigent views of— and indeed being very closely tied to—both the Progressive Labor Party and the Puerto Rican Socialist League. The latter is run by an old-time Marxist named Juan Antonio Corretjer.

The largest group advocating violence is the Nationalist Party, which dates from the early 1920s. It was founded by Pedro Albizu Campos, who in life was the leader, the inspiration and the prophet of the island's nationalists and who in death has become their saint.

Pedro Albizu Campos was the illegitimate son of a wealthy Spaniard and a Basque-Indian-Negro mother. He was educated at Harvard, and shortly after graduation, as World War I had just broken out, he registered for the American draft. Because he had inherited his mother's coloring he was posted to a Negro regiment. Later he was to say that this show of intolerance had sparked his hatred of the United States and had quickened his entrance into nationalist politics.

Called "Don Pedro" by everyone, Albizu Campos was a revolutionary from a nineteenth-century mold. He was a very dignified, cordial man of medium stature with fiery eyes, an ample mustache, sideburns and bushy hair. He was always neatly dressed, sometimes sporting a cane, a cape and a Homburg; seldom if ever was he seen in public without a coat and tie on, even in the middle of the summer while making a speech.

He believed in freedom but had no understanding of the techniques for achieving it. He was always ready to serve but would not go to the people for support; they would have to come to him, he believed, which they never did.

His view of Puerto Rico's status stemmed from his contention that the island's sovereignty dated from the Treaty of Sagasta, signed by Muñoz Rivera, Luis' father, in 1897 and predating the Treaty of Paris which ended the Spanish-American War. All subsequent acts by the United States, he added, are therefore null and void, indeed illegal; the "foreigners" should therefore pull out of their "colony" and leave the people to their own devices. This view is held in common by all the *independentista* groups today.

By 1930 Albizu Campos was in complete control of the Nationalist Party, formed eight years previously. In 1932 he ran for senator-at-large and received 11,882 votes, only 2.6 percent of the total cast, giving some indication of his strength. Three years later, as the result of a riot at the University of Puerto Rico at Rio Piedras in which four of his men were killed, Albizu declared that his party would no longer support "colonial elections."

In 1936, Albizu was convicted of conspiring to overthrow the government after two of his men had murdered the police chief, Colonel E. Francis Riggs, as he was leaving church. Albizu was sentenced to ten years in the Atlanta penitentiary. His followers were infuriated by the loss of their leader and planned a series of demonstrations on Palm Sunday, 1937. The governor, General Blanton Winship, ordered the parades and meetings cancelled, fearing more violence. In Ponce, however, communications between the nationalists and the authorities broke down, resulting in the death of nineteen people and the wounding of over a hundred. This incident has gone down in history as "the Ponce massacre."

Albizu returned to Puerto Rico in 1947. Within three years, he and his Party were back on the front pages of the newspapers. In early November 1950, on the eve of the plebiscite which subsequently paved the way for the granting of a constitution for Puerto Rico, two nationalist gunmen charged Blair House in an attempt to assassinate President Truman. Before the dust had settled, one nationalist was dead, a bullet through his ears, the other was wounded, his heels beating a rapid tattoo on the pavement. One Presidential guard was killed and two more wounded. In the pocket of the dead man was a letter in Spanish from Albizu Campos giving the gunman the authority to carry out the assassination attempt.

Several days previously, a disjointed rebellion broke out on the island in which thirty-one Puerto Ricans died. A carload of nationalists stormed the Fortaleza, San Juan's 300-year-old governor's residence, in an attempt to assassinate Muñoz Marin. Four of the six attackers died on the spot. Elsewhere, nationalists attacked some nine provincial police stations with small arms and Molotov cocktails; and a company of nationalists seized the town of Jayuya, killing four policemen and burning down the post office, police station, Selective Service headquarters and twenty homes.

After a two-day siege, Albizu was flushed from his home in San Juan. In three separate trials he was convicted of attempted murder, illegal use of arms and subversion; he was given a sentence in prison of from thirty to eighty years.

In 1953 Muñoz pardoned Albizu when doctors declared him paranoid: the aging revolutionary took to wrapping his legs in wet towels believing that the U.S. was bombarding them with death rays.

Within a year of his release his nationalists were back on the rampage, this time in the Capitol building. Three nationalists entered the Visitors' Gallery of the U.S. House of Representatives and began shooting wildly at the legislators below, one of the gunmen shouting: "Puerto Rico is not free!" Five congressmen were wounded. Albizu, in San Juan, praised the three nationalists for their "sublime heroism."

After yet another gun battle, Albizu was brought back into custody along with forty-two other nationalists and ten Communists. He was sent to prison along with the terrorists.

In 1956, Albizu Campos suffered a stroke; he was unable to walk or talk. He had filariasis which made his flesh swell. He continued to claim that he was being killed by atomic rays. Those who knew him said he was not mad but cynical, feigning eccentricity to attract attention.

When Albizu died in 1965, he had only a handful of hard-core followers (mostly, ironically, in New York and Chicago); yet over fifty thousand people turned out for his funeral. He spent more time in jail than perhaps any other contemporary Western political leader, but he still influenced the people, even though they would not vote for him or even rally actively to his cause. There is an obvious parallel between his death and Malcolm X's.

Albizu Campos' Party still lives on today, led by Julio Pinto Gandia, a lawyer and old comrade of Albizu's since the 1930s. Pinto Gandia and his few followers continue to boycott elections and to rail against America's presence on the island. Recently the Party has lurched to the left, influenced by the revival in radical left-wing activities. (Albizu's wife, for instance, is currently Fidel Castro's First Secretary at the Cuban Mission to the United Nations in New York.) Today it is often found cooperating with these newer groups. Indeed, it is too small to do otherwise.

The most radical of the new groups is the Movimiento Pro Independencia. Its history can be traced back to 1946 when a dissident group, led by one Gilberto Concepcion de Gracia, broke away from Muñoz's Popular Democrats to set up the Partido Independentista Puertorriqueño. Concepcion de Gracia's Party grew substantially in the next six years, receiving 125,734 votes for governor in the 1952 election, second only to the PDP. Since then PIP, as it is known, has declined, having been replaced by the Statehooders as the number one opposition party. PIP is fairly inactive today; it still is seeking independence through the electoral process and can barely corner 5 percent of the votes necessary to stay on the ballot. To its critics in the independence wing, PIP is a conservative organization, more vaguely socialist than militant Marxist, more pragmatic than dogmatic, more prone to democratic argument than to violence. As such it is suspect.

In 1958 the radical, Marxist-oriented wing of PIP broke away to form the Movimiento Pro Independencia. The leader of this faction was Juan Mari Bras, now the chief spokesman for the MPI and the heir to the mantle of Albizu Campos.

Mari Bras is a wealthy forty-year-old lawyer, the son of a founder of both the PDP and PIP. He was expelled from the University of Puerto Rico in 1947 for raising the Puerto Rican flag (at that time not allowed to be displayed) in the university's tower to celebrate the release of Albizu Campos from prison. He was later expelled from the George Washington University Law School soon after the Blair House shooting, although he was not involved. He eventually graduated from American University a few months after the shootings in the House of Representatives.

He is a heavy-set man with graying temples and a mustache that he continually fusses over. Although he is constantly quoting Marx, he told me: "I am not a Marxist; I am a Christian—very much so." He added, "I am a socialist and I aspire to be a revolutionary." Pictures of his two favorite revolutionaries—Simon Bolivar and Dr. Ramon Betances, the latter a wealthy nineteenth-century Puerto Rican who advocated violence as the road to freedom—hang on his office walls. His phone he claims is tapped by the FBI.

Mari Bras sees the U.S. wanting to take over Puerto Rico physically and to turn all islanders into waiters and dishwashers. He compares the situation to France and Algeria. "The Algerians took the war to Paris; we would take the war to New York too, and they know that," he said. "We are sure that if statehood comes there will be violence," he added, claiming that such a situation "would be an imposition over the Puerto Rican nationality."

He believes that the Commonwealth does not exist in reality. "What we have here is a typical colonial set-up which is rapidly coming to a crisis." He also sees the U.S. caught in a dilemma: if the Commonwealth is maintained in compliance with those U.N. resolutions that assert the right of people to self-determination, then it violates the U.S. Constitution;* if, on the other hand, it is set up in compliance with the Constitution, then it violates the spirit of the U.N. resolutions and is an embarrassment to the U.S. government because the relationship is a form of colonialism. His logic precludes any consideration of statehood as a way out of the dilemma. "Violence," he repeated for emphasis, "would be the result."

Mari Bras is an open admirer of the Cuban revolution. "Their National Liberation Movement," he said, "followed the Marxist-Leninist line; it might have gone in some other direction. How it goes in Puerto Rico is up to the Puerto Rican people."

The national secretary of the MPI, Pedro Baiges Chapel, puts it more bluntly: "If there is a conflict between the Unites States and Castro," he told me, "we would fight for Castro." As an afterthought he added, ". . . and the Vietcong too!"

Mari Bras' organization is the most activist of all the pro-independence groups. Its members number approximately five thousand, mostly students or young university graduates living on the island. His movement advocates non-cooperation with the authorities, and in this regard it carries on a number of protest demonstrations. The week I was in San Juan, the members were involved in an anti-registration drive; their newspaper was calling for immediate independence, the expropriation of all U.S. businesses, and agrarian reform; they were in the process of planning an anti-conscription march; and they had just finished a series of protests over university reform. They also hold, on a continuous basis, "micro-meetings"—short, ninety-minute street-corner harangues—of which they are very proud.

I attended one of these meetings, and they are not at all as effective as the members of the MPI would have one believe. It was held at night in a poor, crowded—but not a slum—neighborhood in a hilly San Juan suburb. The MPI had set up a microphone on the back of a pickup truck, parked on the sidewalk because there was no room on the curbs. Some fifty spectators—

---

* Article 1, Section 10, concerning the limitations of the powers of the several states. In this case, Mari Bras considers Puerto Rico a state with special rules governing it.

mostly men drinking beer and children—drifted by watching the proceedings impassively. "La Borinqueña," the Puerto Rican anthem, was played, and then three MPI speakers mounted the truck one after the other to give their speeches. Without exception, each one pitched his voice near the point of hysteria and kept it there until he had finished. An irate woman waving a broom kept interrupting one speaker, shouting that Puerto Rico had enough freedom already. Cars blew their horns as they passed; feedback from the microphone created a high-pitch screech; the MPI's truck overheated, covering the entire scene with steam and prompting a bucket brigade between a house and the radiator; a Tastee Freez truck passed the intersection a number of times, in each instance flashing its lights, ringing bells and playing an idiot jingle. One man drew laughs from the dwindling onlookers by mimicking the speakers. There was no clapping, no cheering, as each speaker finished his speech. Eventually, all three concluded their harangues over the screech of the feedback; the radiator was filled for the last time, and then everyone piled into the truck and went home.

The MPI also works closely with other pro-independence groups. The Progressive Labor Party and the Workers' World Party, both New York-based, are two of the more openly Marxist groups. Another is the Crusada Patriotica Cristiana, a small sect run until recently by a peasant-priest, Father Margarito Santiago. Fr. Margarito coats his desire for independence with a radical Catholicism. So too does another group with which the MPI works: the Partido Accion Cristiana, a recent dissident faction from PIP.

In early 1967, Mari Bras signed a "protocol of cooperation" with Stokely Carmichael, representing SNCC, in which both parties recognized each other as "being in the vanguard of a common struggle against United States imperialism."

MPI's largest associate is a student organization called the Federacion de Universitarias Pro Independencia, or FUPI for short. Although there is no official connection between the two, FUPI is the student training organization for the MPI. It can be more radical on occasion than its foster organization. For instance, it took an active part in the Castro rebellion, it is in the forefront of the agitation for a student revolt—what the revolt is to be about is seldom stated—and it was, until recently, raising money for the Dominican rebels.

Ramon Arbona, the MPI's current press secretary ($250 per month salary) and formerly President of FUPI said that the Federacion has been growing spectacularly since the Castro revolution. He claims the growth has been sparked by a renewed interest in independence and a dissatisfaction with the Commonwealth. "For the first time," he said, "students have not experienced the 'before and after' of Muñoz Marin's rule." He went on to explain that the "before and after" phenomenon stems from a parental attitude, often expressed as: "Before Muñoz it was bad, after he came to power it was better; I don't like the 'after' but we'll settle for it." Arbona, smoothing his mustache, continued: "We young students don't know the 'before.' Thus, today is *our* 'before' and we don't want it!" He added, "If this is true with me it will be more true with students six or seven years from now!"

Turning to his own MPI, Arbona noted that the organization does not advocate violence, although he qualified it by saying: "We believe in the people's right to self-defense, and when no avenues are open for grievances, then it is legitimate." The authorities, he believes, are frightened of the MPI and are trying to goad it into some rash act so that it can be closed down. One such provocation took place in November 1965, related Arbona. The MPI's headquarters were burned out, and Arbona, along with every other member of the organization, believes that the CIA did it.

The spacious offices have since been refurbished. (On one wall hangs a life-size oil painting of President Johnson in a Santa Claus suit, pointing to his abdominal scar.) They hum with activity: the MPI newspaper, *Claridad,* is being put together in one room, a FUPI zealot is running off leaflets in another ("MADRE—*No permitas tu hijo muera en Vietnam!*"), a lecture is taking place in yet another room, and a loudspeaker broadcasts music and speeches to the people in the square below.

"We consider ourselves a vanguard," said Arbona. "Our job is to educate and to organize and to agitate. Yes, we want to grow as an organization, but what we want to do first is to change the conditions so that eventually everyone is pushing with us." And, he added for emphasis, ". . . much like Castro in Cuba."

2

Another Spanish-speaking nationalist group in the United States is the Alianza Federal de Mercedes (Federal Alliance of Land Grants), one of the fastest growing minorities in the country. Its objective, simply stated, is to recover the more than 100 million acres of common lands originally granted to Spanish and Mexican settlers in the states of New Mexico, Texas, Arizona, California, Colorado, Utah and Nevada.

The founder, current president, and the man who provides the entire impetus for the organization is Reies Lopez Tijerina, forty, a one-time migrant cotton picker and Fundamentalist preacher and a self-taught lawyer. He is a short, powerfully built man with a square face, bushy eyebrows and a thatch of wavy hair. He is seemingly mild-mannered, was neatly dressed when I met him and gives an initial impression of being a bank clerk.

This, however, was misleading. He is considered a powerful speaker in his own language of Spanish and has a very loyal group of followers. Even when he spoke to me in English—which he speaks quite well—I could sense the depth of his feelings. He carries around at least a dozen legal books—all well worn, dog-eared and heavily marked—from which he documents the points he makes. He has the habit of pushing you on the shoulder or chest whenever he wants to emphasize a particular point.

Headquarters for this organization is located in a modest green-painted stucco building just outside the downtown section of Albuquerque. The rooms are bare to the point of appearing vacant. There is an American flag that has been tacked up backward on one wall. There is a small Mexican flag on a staff near an unused bar. The office and meeting room are almost devoid of furniture. Tijerina, as he prefers to be called, is assisted by his brother, Cristobal, who acts as the Alianza's secretary, and by a few other relatives and friends.

The organization was founded as a nonprofit group in 1963 and today claims 14,000 members, representing over 200 of the more than 1,700 Spanish land grants in the United States. It is financed by monthly contributions of one dollar from 3,000 families.

Tijerina says he is not paid for his work; when pressed about his own means of support he is rather vague.

The cornerstone of the Alianza's legal claim to these lands revolves around four documents. The first is Pope Alexander VI's papal bull *Noverunt Universi* (New Universe) of 1493—later incorporated into Spanish law—which specified that lands granted to settlers were to remain their perpetual property and that of their heirs. It added that taxes on and sale of the land were forbidden. Tijerina said that this document gave the Spanish authorities the Divine Right to distribute land.

The second document grew out of the first and is called Ordinance 99 of the Law of the Indias. It dates from 1573 and was the authority under which land was granted to the settlers by King Philip II of Spain and his successors.

The third document is the Treaty of Guadalupe Hidalgo, signed in 1848 at the end of the Mexican War, in which a large slice of Mexico was ceded to the United States. Article X of the treaty, concerned with land grants, was struck out by Congress, but a protocol was signed later, stating:

> The American Government, by suppressing the Xth article of the Treaty of Guadalupe, did not in any way intend to annul the grants of land made by Mexico in the ceded territories. These grants, notwithstanding the suppression of the Article of the Treaty, preserve the legal value which they may possess; and the grantees may cause their legitimate titles to be acknowledged before the American tribunals.[2]

The final document he uses is the New Mexico State Constitution, Article II, Section 5, which states that the rights, privileges and immunities guaranteed to the people of New Mexico by the Treaty of 1848 shall be preserved inviolate.

As Tijerina outlines it, his case seems clear-cut and just. He claims that there is no other cause better documented than this one, adding that none of the four documents above have ever been abrogated by another treaty or law. He says that less than one percent of the original land grant areas are still in the hands of the heirs of the original owners. He blames this situation on the "Anglos" (whom he admitted he calls "gringos" among his friends), in particular "Texans"—a derogatory term used by New Mexicans not only to mean Texans but all outsiders. These foreigners, he says, moved into New Mexico and by force or by chicanery took the land away from the ignorant settlers. He claims that the courts are biased in favor of the Anglos and that in many cases the validity of Spanish law is not even recognized.

"We haven't tasted justice, freedom and democracy for 120 years," says Tijerina. "We feel ridiculous when the President tells Castro to uphold the Treaty of Guantánamo. Why doesn't he uphold *our* treaty?"

Although Tijerina believes he has a clear-cut case in his favor, most other people who are familiar with the land grant situation in the Southwest refer to the problem as "a legal can of worms." There are many reasons why the situation is confusing. For instance, some lands were granted by the kings of Spain, some by the Mexican government between 1821 and 1846, and even some by the American government after 1848. Many of the grants overlap and conflict because there were no surveys at the time. Some of the titles to the grants were vague and legally confusing. For instance, the Anton Chico Land Grant was given to fourteen people by name "and six others." Squatters on that land today are claiming ownership of their portion by arguing that they are the direct heirs of the "six others."

Furthermore, some grants given by Spain were not recognized by the Mexican government because the owners did not support the revolution. There was further confusion when President Theodore Roosevelt created the national forests where boundaries again overlapped. The Homestead Act of 1862 encouraged a number of squatters to move into the territory. These people simply staked out some land and refused to move. Then, of course, there were the thieves and charlatans who took advantage of the ignorant and defenseless grantees. In many cases the land was simply abandoned by the grantees or their heirs.

The growth of the Alianza is due as much to a general dissatisfaction among Mexican-Americans as it is to any grievance over the ownership of land. To be sure, the land grant issue is what holds the members together—they see it as a road to a better life; but, essentially, Tijerina and his followers are complaining of their status as second-class citizens.

"What have we experienced in 120 years?" he asks. "Well, I'll tell you: State welfare powder milk instead of justice! It is an insult to mankind and justice!" He related his people's position on Vietnam: "When we are free and equal," he says, "then we could believe that the Vietnam war was being fought for some just reason, but to us now it looks as if they [the U.S. government] are going to treat them [the Vietnamese] as they have us to date."

Tijerina has faced and continues to face many potential stumbling blocks on his way to victory. He himself has, for instance, a flair for provocative statements. Recently he told an audience that the Watts riot was a preview to what could happen along the Rio Grande if his people didn't get a fair deal.[3] He is accused by some of being pro-Marxist; he is also denounced for his police record: in his youth he was jailed for petty thievery.[4] He has been bashed on the head with a hickory club by a fellow Mexican-American who disagreed with him. He also believes that some Anglo millionaires are out to kill him, because, he says, "they realize I can't be bribed."

Furthermore, there are groups of radical nationalists whose actions may discredit his movement. The most violent is a group of perhaps 200 individuals on or near the 594,000-acre Tierra Amarilla Land Grant in northern New Mexico that calls itself "Mano Negra" (Black Hand). It is no relation to the Sicilian variety but takes its name from the fact that it operates at night. These men are direct descendants of another terrorist organization called "Gorra Blanca" (White Cap). They believe in violence and "retaliation"—burning houses, cutting fences and killing cattle. Most of these men are armed. Tijerina emphatically disassociates himself and the Alianza from them.

The legal muddle is complicated enough, but one point is working to the Alianza's special disadvantage. Many grants were in areas that subsequently had cities built on them. This includes Los Angeles, San Francisco, San Diego, Tucson, Phoenix and El Paso. No one envisions the day when these areas will be given back to the heirs of the grantees. It does, however, raise the question of a cash settlement. Tijerina is blunt and to the point: "It is out of the question," he says.[5]

Tijerina, nevertheless, sees hope for the future. He has a small group of influential Anglos on his side—some in New Mexico, some in Washington. He speaks for five minutes each week over KOB-TV in New Mexico and plans to expand his talks to Texas and California. He writes a weekly news column, and he claims to have the moral backing of all Latin Americans.

He is considering initiating some civil disobedience demonstration—such as grazing cattle in land grant areas that are now national forests—because he claims it is easier to be accused than to accuse. Then, he added, "we don't carry the burden of proof and we can appeal all the way up to the Supreme Court."

Tijerina recognizes his debt to the Negro civil rights movement, first, because he believes that when the activist youths find themselves trapped in an "old" cause, they will turn their attention to "new" causes, such as the plight of the American Indian and the Mexican-American minority in the Southwest. He also recognizes that the Negroes have done a great service by "softening up the conscience of the U.S. government." He added: "When we go before the Supreme Court, they will be more willing to listen to us."

3

There are two other nationalist groups that deserve brief mention. One is the Guam nationalists and the other the American Indian nationalists.

Nationalism on Guam is primarily a sentiment and is not expressed in the form of a political group. Like Puerto Rico, this island was ceded to the United States in 1898; it, too, has its Spanish heritage; the mixture of its people is just as varied; the residents are American citizens and there is a local legislature. But there the similarities end. Guamanians, as they like to be called, have never had their own constitution, have never elected their own governor, have never benefited from an "Operation Bootstrap" and have, in reality, very little say in how the 209-square-mile island is to be run.

For the first time in over six decades the Guamanians are beginning to speak out. But what distinguishes them from the Puerto Ricans is that there is no three-way argument over status. In essence, what the Guamanians want is more home rule and less paternalism from America. They do not go so far, however, as to suggest any direct break from the mainland.

Carlos Taitano, a Georgetown University graduate, the owner of the local Coca Cola franchise, and the Speaker of the Gaum Legislature, is one of the leaders of the movement. "Guam wants three things," he says. "We want to elect our own governor, to be represented in Congress by a non-voting delegate, and to be able to vote for the President and Vice-President of the United States."

He goes on to suggest that the vast Trust Territories of the Pacific Islands, a U.N. area administered by the United States, be joined to Guam under the American flag. His proposal would bring together 2,000 islands with a total land area of 687 square miles. Already he has convinced the Saipan Legislature of the efficacy of a merger and is working on the other legislatures in the Marianas. "Whether the Trust islands and Guam should be united as a state like Hawaii, a territory like Guam today or a commonwealth like Puerto Rico, can be determined," said Taitano. "In any case, the United States should make a move before the 88,000 people of the islands start to lean in some other direction."[6]

Part of the agitation for home rule is economic. Guam, for instance, has 50,000 permanent residents and approximately 23,000 servicemen. Some 30 percent of the employed islanders work for the U.S. government and another 20 percent for the government of Guam. Most of the rest of the population is in school. Agriculture has declined and small businesses survive only on the trade with government officials. A 1966 survey showed that there would be a shortage of 2,000 jobs by 1970. In 1962 a typhoon called Karen flattened the island; Congress appropriated $45 million in disaster funds, of which less than half had been committed in 1966.[7]

Part of the agitation for home rule is also shrewd politics. There is no doubt that Guam and many other American territories or trusts in the Pacific have received relatively short shrift from Congress since World War II. Most of the islands have remained virtually unchanged since the time they first came under American jurisdiction. This is not the direct fault of Congress nor of the Navy and Interior Departments that between them administer the islands. Their remoteness, the limited resources, the general indifference of the natives to improvements and the prohibitive costs involved have all helped to block any economic boom in the area.

Nevertheless, many islanders, wanting to get ahead, have come to realize that the amount of attention paid to them and their problems by Congress is in direct proportion to the amount of noise they make.

4

The term "American Indian nationalists" is perhaps a misnomer for a one-man crusade of confusing proportions led by a retired brigadier general named Herbert Charles Holdridge. General Holdridge's political viewpoints are so diverse that to say he seeks only the restoration of Indian sovereignty in America would be misleading. He has, for instance, written for C. Leon de Aryan's *The Broom* and was once nominated as a candidate for the Presidency on the American Vegetarian Party ticket.

Holdridge was born in 1892 and was graduated from West Point in 1917. He spent most of his active military career in administrative jobs, claiming responsibility for devising an efficient system for handling military paperwork. In 1944 Holdridge was retired because, as he states, his "Plan for Economic Reconstruction" was so potent a document that its implementation would have toppled the existing power structure.

The Holdridge Plan called for the establishment of a fourth branch of government—"economic"—that would provide the proper balance to the judicial, legislative and executive branches. This branch would oversee all cooperatives (the "invisible empire of capitalism," he writes, is "DOOMED"), from the largest to the smallest. To complement his plan he would institute a "balanced, noncirculating system of exchange," which seems to translate out as a form of Social Credit; "People's Banks," similar to army commissaries, would be set up; taxes would be eliminated; states' rights would be guaranteed; businessmen would be ensured a minimum income "under the distribution of purchasing power," thus freeing them from "trying to survive on the crumbs which fall from the table of the International Cartelists"; and, to guarantee lasting prosperity, "Cooperation for Human Welfare" would replace "Competition for Profits."

The necessity for such a plan is obvious to Holdridge. He is convinced that the two major enemies of constitutional government are:

> 1. The International Moneylenders of Wall Street which have confiscated the total resources of the people of the United States through the instrument of the Federal Reserve Banking System, and
>
> 2. The Internationalists of the Vatican who have, since the Council of Nicaea, been engaged in their lawless ambition to create a theocratic dictatorship of the entire world; work in complete harmony with Wall Street "40 Thieves"; and have been responsible for most of the world slaughter throughout the centuries. These two forces are now in total control of the United States, our "dirty politicians" completely subservient to them, and are now in process of rigging an H-bomb war which will barbecue all life on this planet.

The Vatican is in league with Murder Incorporated and the Mafia, claims Holdridge, and is the force behind the scenes that enabled John F. Kennedy to come to power. In an issue of *Reveille,* his newssheet, he outlines the "cold, harsh, logical, legal facts":

> His accession to power is the culmination of a Vatican conspiracy, initiated over 100 years ago, when the Vatican decided to infiltrate Roman Catholic immigrants into key cities and states where they could control the election of president through control of the electoral college, and thereby overthrowing the will of the electorate of a non-Catholic country.
>
> . . . The numbers of Roman Catholics entering the United States have been illegally increased out of all proportion to the percentage of the Roman Catholic population, including the addition of Hungarian "freedom fighter" assassins, priests, nuns, and the most ignorant off-scourings of Roman Catholic European countries. . . .

President Johnson is considered a part of this conspiracy. Holdridge describes him as "an egocentric, homicidal maniac with overtones of acute alcoholism induced by his ambition to consume a fifth of Bourbon per day. . . ." He sees the President as engaged in a war of nerves, called a "Peace Offensive," that can only lead to an H-bomb war. But, "the providential assassination of LBJ predicted by many psychics would alter the situation. . . ." he assured me in a letter.

Holdridge believes that he, too, is doomed to be assassinated for his unorthodox views. The "Pentagon Brass" have already made one attempt, he asserts, as have the CIA, Vatican, FBI, Secret Service and Post Office. His wife has tried to have him put away as a "mental incompetent," and only recently he complained that he found ground glass in his oatmeal.

Holdridge believes that the world is divided into "two levels of beings," taking his cue from the Oahspe Bible.* One level is "the off-scourings of cosmic evolutionary processes; the sub-human, greedy, thoughtless, ignorant, brutish, lacking spirit, mind or soul; the 'Zombies'; the 'living dead' who respond to no 'human' im-

---

* The Oahspe Bible, 844 pages long, dates from 1881. At that time, John Ballou Newbrough, by profession a doctor and a dentist and by inclination a spiritualist, was, according to the Bible's preface, commanded by God to write a New Bible. For a full year Newbrough sat before his typewriter, his fingers pecking away at the keyboard without his conscious control. At the end of the year he was instructed to read what he had typed and to publish the manuscript as the Oahspe Bible.

The work purports to be "an analysis of today and a prophecy for tomorrow" and claims to offer a method of developing spiritual powers, prophetic abilities and extrasensory perceptions. To the casual reader the book appears to be a *mélange* of spiritualist, Christian, Hindu, Zoroastrian, Buddhist and vegetarian ideas that, together, are often incomprehensible. The preface to the thirteenth American edition (1955) recognizes the layman's difficulty and offers as aids a "glossary of strange words" and "hints to the reader." The latter lists the Oahspe order of the universe, beginning at the top with Jehovih (or Eolin, E-O-ih, Eloih, Egoquim and Ormazd), and descending into the lower heavens to Nirvanian Chief, Orion Chief, God, Lord God, Lord, Etherean Cycles, Chinvat, Atmospherean Heavens in Atmospherea, Atmospherean, A Vortex and, finally, to The Earth. Along the way we learn that God, as ordinary mortals know Him, "is not the Creator but is simply chief executive officer . . . for our planet earth." In addition, Christ, often referred to as either Kriste or Looeamong, is considered by advocates of the Oahspe Bible to be one of "The Four False Gods."

pulse. These are called 'DRUJAS.' " The other level he defines as "the kindly; cooperative; intelligent, HUMAN—the 'peace people' who understand the meaning of brotherhood; these who hold fast to inner consciousness of the universal presence of a Higher Power —a 'SOMETHINGNESS' which animates all forms of LIFE, and who are thus called 'FAITHISTS.' " The General considers himself of the latter category.

Holdridge qualifies as a nationalist only because he believes that the government in Washington is illegal, having been installed in power by the Wall Street-Vatican axis. He therefore set up a "Constitutional Provisional Government of the United States" in 1961, otherwise known as OOH-N-GWE-HOO-WEH ("True Americans"). The word "Provisional" was later dropped because Holdridge now considers himself actually to be in power. He has taken the title of "Chief Magistrate" and has installed one Abu Timbel as his "Assistant Administrator for Negro Affairs."

In an open letter to the United Nations' Secretary General, U Thant, he explains why such a government was necessary:

> This usurping "government" after almost 200 years of exploitation and massacre of the "OOH-N-GWE-HOO-WEH" ("True Americans"—Indians), has broken every solemn treaty negotiated with them. By thus voiding these treaties, their lands revert to the "status-quo-ante," thus cancelling all rights of occupancy of Indian lands and territories. Our "White" invading population reverts to the status of illegal "squatters," maintaining their control illegally and by violence. . . .

In fact, Holdridge no longer considers himself a white man but an Indian. He was initiated into the Wolf Clan, Mohawk Nation, of the Six Nations of the Iroquois Confederacy and was given the name BA-HA-RE-WHE-HA-WEH, which means "Bringing a Message." He claims one of his ancestors was Chief Joseph Logan of the Mohawk Nation.

Having set up the machinery for his government, Holdridge is confident that his views will prevail. "I have it from sound spiritual sources," he wrote me, "that . . . my legal status will soon be recognized and I will walk into the top office (which I already hold legally) standing up and without firing a shot."

THE
LEFT
REVOLUTIONISTS

PART FOUR

THE

LEFT

REVOLUTIONISTS

13

CPUSA: The Loneliness of the True Believers

The history of the Communist Party of the United States of America can be divided into four eras. The first was the Party's period of growth that ran from 1919 to 1932. In 1919 the left wing of the Socialist Party broke away from the more moderate Socialists who controlled the Party. It was not a clean break but an atomization of the left wing that resulted in a number of factions jockeying for position as the voice of Moscow. In 1921 the dispute was settled by Moscow in favor of the Workers' Party (the name was later changed to the present one), but it established a legacy of factionalism that has since been the hallmark of the Party's activities.

To an American accustomed to the normal excesses of his own electoral processes, the activities of the CPUSA during this period —and indeed in the present—seem Byzantine by comparison. There were the Fosterites, the Pepperites, the Lovestoneites, the Trotskyists, the Browderites, and a number of other passing groups, all pushing their own version of "the truth" as they interpreted it from Moscow, and all demanding absolute obedience to the particular dogma. There were not only *inter*factional fights but *intra*factional fights of the most bitter nature. They argued over tactics, such as whether to support elections and if so which and to what degree; they spent hours arguing over the definition of such terms as "right deviationist," "centrist" and "social fascism"; there were endless disputes over the way "monopoly capitalism" would be overthrown, how the "class struggle" was to be carried out, what the function of the American "proletariat" was. All this had little to do with what was going on in the real world.

The Party was hindered by a number of factors during this era. One was that the rank and file—estimated at 9,000 in 1929 (but with nearly a 100 percent turnover)—were almost entirely foreign-born. Because these people lacked a knowledge of the English language, because they knew little of American institutions and traditions, and because they thought it more important to fight among themselves, only the most submissive, the most disgruntled, the most naïve and the most idealistic gravitated to the Party.

At the height of the Depression, in 1932, the CPUSA candidate for President, William Z. Foster, could muster only 103,253 votes, or 0.3 percent of those cast. It was the highest total the Party was ever to receive.

The Party's second era lasted from 1932 until 1944. It was at this time that the CPUSA experienced some successes. Since its inception, the Party has concentrated its efforts on five major groups in America: the "working classes" (meaning the unions), the intellectuals, the Negroes, the Armed Forces and youth. The Communists have had virtually no success in converting the latter three groups to their cause: in spite of their past mistreatment, the Negroes are seeking more freedom, not less; the Armed Forces have always been hostile for obvious reasons; and youth only rallied to the Party in special circumstances such as the Spanish Civil War, and then only fleetingly. A considerable number of intellectuals, particularly university professors and clerics, joined the Party during the 1930s, but according to one source, "the honeymoon . . . seemed to have been nasty, brutish and short."[1]

The frequent ideological changes required of all Party members seemed too unscientific (ironically) except to the most cynical intellectuals. A few did stay on, Theodore Dreiser perhaps being the best-known American.

The CPUSA was able to gain a foothold within the trade union movement during the 1930s. Its favorite tactic was to have its zealots take control of the key positions in a union, thereby exerting an influence far out of proportion to their numbers. It never occurred to them to convert a majority of the rank and file to their point of view and then have themselves voted into power. One recent observer underscores the leverage the Communist minority had in the unions during the late 1930s:

. . . The largest number of members which the Communist Party has had in recent years is probably 70,000. Assuming that of this number one-half belong to the unions—and that would probably be an exaggeration—they would have had a maximum numerical strength of .0024 of the 15 million labor union members. Yet at the height of this power drive within the CIO, they dominated 12 to 15 of the 40 international CIO unions.[2]

Communists were partiularly strong in the Pacific Maritime Federation, led by Harry Bridges, the fur workers' union, the Transport Workers Union, led by "Red Mike" (as he was known before he turned anti-Communist) Quill, the United Electrical Workers, Mine, Mill & Smelter Workers, National Maritime Union and the American Communications Association.

It must be emphasized that the Communists were always in the minority, but they knew the tricks: they would caucus before a meeting and then vote as a bloc, they knew parliamentary procedure better than the rank and file, and they were prepared to stay late after their opponents had become exasperated and gone home. It was years before the anti-Communists—Phillip Murray, John L. Lewis, David Dubinsky, among them—were able to weed out the Communists. There is still some Communist influence left within the trade union movement today, but it has been isolated, fragmented and demoralized and is not nearly as influential as it was in the 1930s.

The Party was also perfecting other stratagems. For instance, it set up a number of front groups with innocent-sounding names: the Tom Paine School of Social Science, the Abraham Lincoln Brigade, the Jefferson School of Social Science, Commonwealth College and the American League against War and Fascism. Many naïve Americans, ordinarily not sympathetic to communism, were drawn into these organizations in the belief that they sincerely were promoting a better world.

In 1935 the Party dropped its revolutionary stance and began calling itself "progressive." Words such as "peace," "liberty," "freedom" and "equality" were used to describe its objectives. At one point Earl Browder described communism as "twentieth-century Americanism."[3]

One characteristic of the Party throughout its history has been its ability to reverse its "line" time and time again with a straight face. When former comrades Bukharin and Trotsky were denounced as traitors, the CPUSA (along with all the other satellite parties, to be sure) joined in the condemnation. When many old and trusted revolutionaries were suddenly condemned (and eventually executed) for their "deviationism" at the 1936 Moscow Trials, the CPUSA was the first to turn on its old mentors. Not a word was heard in protest.

In 1939 the CPUSA was to perform a classic change of the party line that left the hard-core Party members dazed. Before the Hitler-Stalin nonaggression pact of that year, the Party could not think of epithets brutal enough to characterize Hitler and his regime—"Nazi beasts," "fascist reactionaries" and so on. When the pact was signed, the Party (granted, after a few days' silence) obediently began to describe Germany as a "friendly neighbor" and former allies France and Great Britain as "imperialist warmongers." When Germany invaded Russia in June 1941, the Party reversed itself again calling on warmongers France, Great Britain and the United States to join Russia in her "war of liberation."

The CPUSA's third era ran from 1945 to 1956. It was its period of decline and persecution. From a wartime high of some 80,000 members (and perhaps one million sympathizers), the organization has declined to the point where it can claim today only 10,000 adherents (and less than 100,000 sympathizers), of whom a good number are either aged Party functionaries in semiretirement, informers or FBI men. Russia's conversion from a wartime ally to a cold war foe helped reduce the appeal of the Party. So did the rise of McCarthyism, the Berlin airlift, the fall of China and the Korean War. Numerous convictions of the Party's leaders under the Smith Act of 1940 and the McCarran Act of 1950 physically removed the more active Communists from the scene for a stretch.

Recently sections of the McCarran Act have come under fire as being unconstitutional, as indeed President Truman himself believed in 1950 when he tried to stop passage of the bill by vetoing it. "The idea of requiring Communist organizations to divulge information about themselves is a simple and attractive one," said the President. "But it is about as practical as requiring thieves to register with the sheriff."

What finally killed the American Party was Khrushchev's 1956 denunciation of Stalin and the suppression of the Hungarian Revolution later in the year. The enumeration of the many crimes by the late Soviet dictator once more required of the faithful a switch from adulation to condemnation. The revolt in Budapest further eroded the membership by showing up Russia to be what it truly was: a dictatorship that had no interest in granting freedom to its captives. Members resigned in droves from the CPUSA, embittered, disgusted, hurt, disillusioned, angry and broken in spirit. Only the most cynical, unprincipled and mindless of members hung on, most in the belief that outside the Party they would lose even more: their life's work, their "religion," their friends and their livelihood.

Today the Party is a blind and toothless tiger, despite the fears of the Fundamentalist right. Undoubtedly it is still capable of mischief on occasion, still willing to aggravate problems rather than solve them, still willing to ensnare innocent Americans into its front groups, still willing to repeat Moscow's line, still willing to attempt takeovers of non-Communist groups.

There are many external signs that indicate how weak the Party really is. At a time when the Negro struggle for equal rights is rising in tempo, the Communist influence is minor and inconsequential. To be sure there are a number of Communists lurking around the fringes of the movement, but more often than not they belong to the "Peking factions," those small and volatile groups that have spun away from the Moscow-bound CPUSA. Furthermore, the Vietnam protest movement grew out of other impulses —again the New Left—and the CPUSA only belatedly jumped on the bandwagon to embrace the cause as its very own. Likewise, the peace movement has seen no Communist leaders come to the fore. An inability to form independent judgments—one of the strengths of the peace movement—has accounted for this more than any other consideration. "There's a great tragedy about a movement that requires people to stop thinking as it did during the whole period of Stalin," says David McReynolds of the War Resisters League.

A rather perverse way to test the virility of fringe organizations is to note the nature of their slogans and denunciations. The CPUSA has not come up with a good anti-capitalist slogan in years. It should also be noted that when enemy flags are carried in protest parades, it is sections of the New Left that carry Vietcong flags, not American Communists carrying Soviet flags.

Other tests, less perverse, show that the Communist Party is made up mostly of over-forties with roughly one third of its membership in its sixties. Young radicals are joining New Left groups, not the CPUSA. Because the Party has a seemingly infinite capacity to believe what Moscow tells it to believe only the most dedicated cynics and escapists are lured into the ranks these days.

Nor has *The Worker,* formerly *The Daily Worker,* scored any newsbeats since it became a twice-weekly newspaper in 1957. Its pages are filled with announcements of seminars, bazaars, lectures, rummage sales, suppers, dances and picnics at which a call for funds is made to restock the Party's sagging finances. Many of these functions serve food to the impoverished faithful, who anticipate such gatherings with relief to fend off the monotony of their lives. "We try to eat our way into a state of solvency," said one Party leader.[4]

Only the West Coast Communist paper, *Peoples' World,* shows any spark at all, reflecting undoubtedly the iconoclastic nature of Communists in that part of the country.

The Party's theoretical organ, *Political Affairs,* is also dull and uninteresting. Its leading thinker is Herbert Aptheker, who has not come forward with many new ideas of late. I once heard him speak to a group of students at Duke University. He, more than anyone, reflected the ravages time has had on Marxist dialectic. He was sarcastic and bitter, comparing President Johnson with Hitler and Lincoln with Lenin. In every reference he made to the Vietnam war he would allude to Hitler's actions in Czechoslovakia.

The Party is currently in financial difficulties. Most of its income derives from speaking tours by its leading spokesmen such as Gus Hall, Arnold Johnson and Aptheker. Although it is believed that little money is sent from Moscow, there is some indication that the Party makes money on the stock exchange, being tipped off in advance by Moscow when the Soviets plan to dump some commodity on the world market. Not all Party members are poor, however, nor has this been historically true. Indeed, many of them have been quite wealthy.

Recently the Party has been embarrassed by the capitalistic activities of one of its members, Claude M. Lightfoot. Lightfoot, a Negro and Party boss in Chicago and the owner of property in that city, was charged in 1966 with a number of building violations concerning unsanitary conditions. He denied the charges.

The Party no longer contests elections. From the 1932 high of 103,253 votes, the electoral showings have dwindled to nothing. In 1936 the Party received 80,000 votes, in 1940 only 46,000 votes, less than the Socialist and Prohibition Parties. In 1944 it supported the Democratic Party as a show of wartime unity. In 1948 it dominated Henry Wallace's Progressive Party, and by 1952 it was in control of it, running Vincent Hallinan, an iconoclastic Marxist, for President. Since then it has abandoned the electoral way to power in favor of the propaganda approach.

In the 1930s it tried take-overs of the Black Muslims, the Socialist Party and the American Labor Party, only the last of which it succeeded in capturing. Since World War II, no take-over mounted by the CPUSA has been a serious threat except with the Progressive Party.

One of the dilemmas the Party faces today is whether it should remain a "Russian" Party or become an "American" Party. If it remains loyal to Moscow it will never have any significant following; if it becomes Americanized it then risks alienating Russia, with no guarantee that it could draw Americans into the fold.

In an effort to solve the dilemma the CPUSA issued a new draft program in 1966. It combines the old line with the new one. America, it declares, is in a state of crisis. Its government is "bent on an inevitable nuclear confrontation" due to the "rapacious and aggressive" nature of imperialism; poverty, repression and "jim-crow" are still rampant; the anti-Communists in America are akin to Hitler's variety in the 1930s; the federal government has become "an agency for taking from the poor to give to the rich"; and actual power is exercised by "a handful of financial-industrial monopolists" who have turned America into an "avaricious dairy-man's dream: a cow with three udders":

One to supply the manpower and resources to protect the neo-colonial empire abroad; one to yield profitable defense contracts; and the third to supply additional butterfat to lubricate the remainder of the monopoly-controlled economy, and, incidentally, to soothe sections of the people while they are being bilked.

So much for the hard line.

The soft line calls for a "socialist" America (not a "Communist" one), "a renewal and extension of American democracy" and the creation of "a new people's party." The document claims that the Party rejects the theory of "the worse, the better" (the worse shape America is in, the better for Communist growth) because "we Communists are part of those classes and groups that bear the brunt of misery in this society." Freedom of religion would be guaranteed in a Soviet America along with a number of other benefits. The new government would abolish private property and ensure "democratic control . . . of the entire productive economy." The document concludes: "We Communists are, therefore, defenders of the Constitution in principle and practice."

The Party has actually been calling itself "American" for years, particularly since the passage of the Voorhis Act of 1940 that required organizations affiliated with foreign governments to register with the Attorney General. Arnold Johnson, the Communist Party's current front man, affirmed the point to me, saying, "We don't dance to anyone's tune."

Johnson, a Communist for over thirty years, looks like a banker in his pinstripe suit and conservative tie. He is one of the few Communists that I met that made any effort to be amusing, although like most of his comrades he is not naturally so.

He and the other Party leaders work out of a three-story brick townhouse on West 26th Street in New York City. The building was once owned by William Astor. Today it is in poor repair; the front door bears the scars of many staples and thumbtacks as well as the faint outline of unfriendly chalkings. In 1966 the ground floor was demolished by a blast so powerful that it blew out windows in a church across the street. The meeting room in which Johnson and I talked had seats for twenty-one people. A bust of Lenin flanked one side of a coal fire, a bust of Elizabeth Gurley

Flynn the other. There was a portable blackboard standing unused to one side; books on Lenin, Lincoln and Negro history filled a bookcase. Back copies of *The Daily Review,* translations from the Soviet press ("published by Novosti Press Agency, Pushkin Square, Moscow. Telephone: 29–67–84"), lay scattered on the conference table.

Johnson is most uncommunicative, though pleasant. I suggested that, in light of his claim that the Party was "American," surely he could give me a few examples where he differed with Moscow on ideology and tactics. He demurred, saying he would have to think about it. Since I was returning in three days to see the Party's general secretary, Gus Hall, I suggested he tell me then, which he agreed to do. Upon returning, Hall was busy so Johnson again sat down with me to answer the questions I had for his boss. When I raised the subject of differences with Moscow there was a long silence, and then Johnson reluctantly admitted that he could not recall any.

Dorothy Healey has no qualms about talking to non-Communists. In fact she is quite voluble and is a charming individual. She is a bouncy woman in her mid-fifties who has been a Communist since she was fourteen years old. Her family were radicals, particularly her mother, who was a Wobbly, a Socialist, then a Communist. She has had three husbands, all of whom were Marxists, and she has one son—"the pride of my life"—who is a graduate student at a large and well-known university in the South. Currently, Dorothy Healey is the Chairman of the Communist Party of Southern California and a member of the National Board of the CPUSA. Of all the Communists, she is the most outspoken, a constant thorn in the side of her more reticent comrades back East.

"Unquestionably we have made mistakes in the past," she exclaimed, "such as the Hitler-Stalin pact. But taking the long view of history it will show that our views will be viewed more favorably than those who have done nothing but attack the Soviet Union, because," she went on, "the existence of that country at building a new socio-economic system is more important than the mistakes they made in the course of building that society."

She complained that Communists are often forced into the

position of muting their criticisms of the USSR because of the "distortions put forward by the anti-sovieteers." There are, she went on, "many who seek cheap respectability by denouncing the Soviet Union to show what loyal Americans they are. We don't want any part of them, even though many of them are 'liberals.' "

Healey has considerable scorn for the New Left, adding optimistically that the CPUSA has been recruiting at a far greater rate than any other left-wing group in the country. "The test is whether you adopt policies which will eventually change the system. Progressive Labor and the Socialist Workers Party have 'the itch for the revolutionary phrase' which is not synonymous with a revolutionary policy."

Revolutions, she avers, "can only take place when the majority come to realize they no longer can live under the old system. We adopt policies designed to encourage the millions to reach this conclusion."

She is critical of the American system as it exists today, which does not make her much different from other Communists. "Capitalism has been reforming itself for years," she said, "but through no virtue of the capitalists." She says that "exploitation" will still be exercised as long as the worker has no control over the means of production. She adds that the political superstructure in a Soviet America will have to reflect those aspects that are particularly American, based on the country's traditions.

"The content of democracy will be changed, not just the form," she told me. "For example, the legislature would be run by those who produce the wealth. That is to say, it is not a question of people being told to elect workers, but for the first time the worker will have access to the means of power. This implies that elections are not based on monetary considerations and implies a reform of the electoral system."

Having been persecuted as a Communist she strongly opposes laws which, she claims, are designed to limit the spread of ideas rather than to inhibit the actions of an individual. "It is ridiculous," she said, "to brand *ideas* as foreign. Marxism came from Western culture." She went on to lament that "You can be a dissenter only as long as you don't touch the tender subjects. The most tender, for instance, is the profit motive."

One of the few rebels in the CPUSA, she trains much of her fire on her own Party. She complains that there is a reluctance to discuss new issues and to acknowledge past mistakes. She denies the American Party is anti-Semitic but admits that such feelings exist in the Soviet Union. "The USSR carries on a very crude anti-religious movement. The result of any policy directed towards a minority such as the Jews makes it anti-Semitic." But, she went on, "I believe that once a system has been achieved in which men's desires can be satisfied, then religion will no longer be necessary."

The CPUSA, she said, "lacks a capacity for developing Marxism theoretically and intellectually," pointing to such potential areas as "regionalism as a new para-structure" and "structural reforms" as examples. "How do you solve problems without adding to the weight of a central bureaucracy?" is a question she thinks should be asked more often. "Nor have we thought through our relationship with other Socialist countries," she added, meaning Russia. "How was it possible to bring about a deformation of Soviet legality? How much omission and commission do we still have to grapple with?" she asks. "Discipline and dissent and nature and character of the Party are not debated enough to arrive at new answers."

Russia is a socialist state, declared Healey "and that's inequality. They are a long way fom communism." Socialism, she went on, "is a transitional period through which you travel towards communism," noting that the Party's new platform calls for such a route for America.

"No Communist thinks that what exists in the USSR is the ideal," she concluded. "We don't criticize as much as you think we should because we think they are generally going in the right direction."

14

Dissenters on the Left

1

The Industrial Workers of the World, otherwise known as the "Wobblies," have been close to the point of death and far from the headlines of the newspapers for so long that most Americans under the age of forty have never heard of them.

The Wobblies were the closest America came to having a revolutionary union movement. Their star was brief, running from 1905 to the 1919–1920 Palmer Raids, a euphemism for the "Red Scare," which witnessed the destruction of the group and the jailing of many of its leaders.

The organization of the Wobblies* in 1905 brought together a number of radical streams of thought. One of them was syndicalism (from the French *syndicat,* meaning trade union), which argues that the wage system is unjust and helps to sustain an "immoral" capitalist system. Syndicalists maintain that the communal ownership of the means of production—known as "Workers' Control" or, as the Wobblies prefer, "One Big Union"—is the only means through which a worker can obtain his freedom. They advocate the establishment of industrial (as opposed to craft) unions which would work in voluntary cooperation with one another. They seek to achieve their objectives by a "Social General Strike," boycotts, revolutions and sabotage.

---

* Tradition has it that the name Wobbly came from a Chinese cook in a lumber camp whose efforts to say "IWW" came out "I Wobbly Wobbly." The initials of the organization were often translated by detractors as "I Won't Work" or "I Trouble You Trouble You."

Another stream of thought was anarchism. Anarchism has two roots in America, one native the other foreign. Native anarchism draws its inspiration from the writings and activities of such men as William Godwin, Josiah Warren, Henry David Thoreau, Lysander Spooner, Benjamin R. Tucker and, to some extent, Ralph Waldo Emerson. Anarchism as a social doctrine is reflected in the many short-lived utopian communities that sprung up throughout the United States in the eighteenth and nineteenth centuries, such as New Harmony, Modern Times, Brook Farm, Utopia and the Oneida Community. Foreign anarchism came over with the immigrants of the late nineteenth century and draws its inspiration from the works of Pierre Joseph Proudhon, Mikhail Bakunin, Leo Tolstoi and Prince Peter Kropotkin.

Anarchists represent the extreme expression of individualism. They believe that all governments, laws and bureaucracies are unjust and unreasonable and exist only to maintain the power and privileges of the state. All authoritarian governments—both capitalist and communist—should be abolished along with the manifestations of that authority, such as voting, conscription, taxation, police forces and Congress. This authoritarianism, they say, should be replaced by a "libertarian" society of free people. The essential difference between a syndicalist and an anarchist is that the syndicalist talks in terms of freedom for the worker while the anarchist talks in terms of freedom for man.

Because anarchists have no leaders, no hierarchy, no formal organizations, no official membership and no clear-cut political structure, there exist practically as many different philosophical interpretations of the word anarchy as there are anarchists in the country. There are, for instance, the individualist anarchists who follow the teachings of Thoreau and Max Stirner. Stirnerites are such extreme individualists that they refuse to call themselves anarchists on the grounds that the name is authoritarian. There are also anarcho-syndicalists, who combine both points of view but usually emphasize one or the other. Many Wobblies fell into this category. There are also the anarcho-communists (communist in the old sense of the word), who believe that the community is the center of society, not the individual. There are pacifist anarchists (found in the Catholic Worker movement as well as in New Left groups) and the anarcho-Marxists, an apparent contradiction in terms, who fuse some of Marx's theories with their anarchist theories. In addition, there are the revolutionary anarchists who believe in the "propaganda of the deed," such as throwing bombs and shooting Presidents. Leon Czolgosz, who assassinated President McKinley in 1901, was a revolutionary anarchist, as was Alexander Berkman, who attempted to shoot financier Henry Clay Frick in 1892. And there are the "permanent protesters," those who believe that anarchy is impossible to achieve and that their job, therefore, is to protest permanently against the ills of society in hopes of somehow ameliorating them. And, finally, there are the anti-industrial anarchists, a group of contemporary Luddites, who believe that machines represent the basis of all evil and should therefore be destroyed.

Yet another stream of thought among the Wobblies was a radical socialism, some of it based on Marx and Engels, some of it on German State Socialist ideas, some on a vague egalitarianism defying description. It is no coincidence that the bulk of IWW members—estimated at 100,000 at the movement's peak—were Germans, Finns, Italians and Hungarians who had been schooled in such ideas either in their homeland or by their fellow workers in America who were leading the fight to establish unions. The IWW published *The Industrial Worker* for those who spoke English, *Bermunkas* for Hungarians, *Industrialisti* for Finns and *Il Prolatario* for Italians. The circulation of *The Industrial Worker* today is 3,000 per month, and that of *Industrialisti,* the only other paper to survive, is even less. The *Freie Arbeiter Stimme,* independent of the IWW, is a German-Jewish paper with a small Wobbly-anarchist readership.

All these and a number of other smaller streams of thought were brought together in 1905 with the formation of the IWW. For the next fifteen years the Wobblies were to be the terror of the industrial scene. Tough, idealistic, hardbitten, boisterous, contemptuous of politics and reform, with a streak of lawlessness and Western braggadocio in them, they were an extreme expression of the restlessness and discontent within the union movement at that time. They took the lead spontaneously in some of the most bitterly fought strikes in American history; the McKees Rock strike of 1909; the famous Lawrence textile strike in 1912; the eight-month silk mill strike the following year in Paterson, New Jersey, in which 1,400 people were arrested and five killed; and the Mesabi Iron Range strike of 1916. Wobblies also struck in lumber camps, in copper mines, on waterfronts, in agricultural areas and in industrial plants. They precipitated a number of "Free Speech Fights"—in San Diego, Spokane, Fresno, Portland, Oregon, for example—in which Wobblies were shot, killed, tarred and feathered, beaten and jailed.

They were led by a swashbuckling crew of radicals. For example, there was William D. "Big Bill" Haywood, the hulking, one-eyed boss of the Western Federation of Miners who was to die in exile in Russia; there was Daniel DeLeon, the founder and leader of the Socialist Labor Party; there was Elizabeth Gurley Flynn, later known as the Communist Party's "elderly wheel-horse," a sobriquet she was to protest up to her death in 1964; there was Eugene Debs of the Socialist Party and William Z. Foster, a proponent of "boring from within," the founder of the short-lived Syndicalist League of North America, and later a prominent figure in the CPUSA. There were Joseph Caruso, Arturo Giovannitti, Joe Ettor, Frank Little, William Trautman, Carlo Tresca (for a number of years Elizabeth Gurley Flynn's lover), Vincent St. John and, of course, Joe Hill, the movement's martyr and saint.*

After World War I the IWW fell apart. The reasons are many and complicated. The Bolshevik Revolution, for instance, had precipitated a "Red Scare" that concentrated on persecuting non-conformists such as the Wobblies. These chanting, marching militants who advocated "direct action" and "sabotage" were a threat to the orderly growth of unionism as preached by Samuel Gompers and therefore they had to be resisted. As if that were not enough, the CPUSA had penetrated the organization and had very nearly

---

* Joe Hill, born Jeol Haaglund in Sweden, was a Wobbly writer and balladeer ("Nearer My Job to Thee," "Workers of the World, Awaken!" etc.) who was convicted of murdering a Salt Lake City grocer. The case is a long and complicated one full of so much circumstantial evidence that his guilt is still a matter of dispute. He was executed by a firing squad in 1915 and immediately became a Wobbly martyr. He is still revered today by all aspiring anarchists. Ammon Hennacy, of an older generation of anarchists, dedicated his "House of Hospitality" to him in Salt Lake City, only one of numerous memorials throughout the country.

succeeded in capturing it. In addition, those unions affiliated with the IWW slowly isolated themselves from the mainstream of unionism because they refused to sign local contracts unless they were industry-wide agreements.

As is often the case when a group falls on bad times, there were a number of internal schisms that drove the members and recruits away: one during World War I over whether the IWW should support America's effort, and another in 1924—this one shattering the movement—over a host of differences. Later those Wobblies whose major concern was a good job and decent pay switched over to the growing and more stable AFL or CIO. Only the most dedicated revolutionaries stuck it out in the IWW, still calling for the establishment of One Big Union, for the downfall of the "ownership class" and for continued violence in the streets. By 1947 their inability to adapt to the times had earned them a place on the Attorney General's list of subversive groups, along with the CPUSA and others. As one old Wobbly put it to me: "The IWW was just too goddamn anti-capitalist to survive."

In their brief ascendancy on the scene the Wobblies left behind a legacy of Americana. There were the songs—"Halleluja I'm a Bum!," "Workers Shall the Master Rule Us?," "Dump the Bosses Off your Back," "The Internationale" and "The Rebel Girl"—all still sung today by ardent unionists everywhere, even in the AFL-CIO. There were the hobo jungles, the hobo "colleges," the lore of the open road, the bindle stiffs, the gandy dancers, Mulligan stew and Smilo joints. And the pungent language of a people fighting for their lives: blackleg, fink, *agent provocateur,* goon, scab, yellow legs and Pink (a Pinkerton detective).

Carl Keller, the editor of *The Industrial Worker,* is in his seventies and has been a Wobbly since 1919. He, for one, does not believe that the IWW cause is lost. "We feel confident that industrial unionism will eventually triumph," he said. "There is evidence that the old type of unionism is not growing," he added, noting that the growth of the AFL-CIO is proportionately smaller than the growth of the population. He believes that the high incident of wildcat strikes, the existence of some industrial unions already (United Mine Workers, Auto Workers, etc.), and the recent replacement of such moderate labor leaders as David

MacDonald (of the United Steelworkers) and James Carey (of the Electrical Workers) by apparently more militant men is indicative of the rank and file's willingness to try another type of unionism.

He went on to say that when it came to automation the current craft unions are outdated. "The IWW," he stated, "is a class organization and seeks to solve the industrial problems for the benefit of the entire working class. The concept of Revolutionary Industrial Unionism [Wobblies prefer this description of their activities over the term syndicalism] is that a man joins to take place in a struggle for the working man. In the present unions," he recalled, "a man pays dues for certain services, and if automation takes away his job he is fired and then the man has no more use for the union."

The Wobbly head office in Chicago, where Keller has been for thirty years, is extraordinarily neat. There is no sense of chaos that is so evident in other fringe group offices; everything is in order and clean, the floor swept and free of scrap paper. An oil painting of Joe Hill hangs on one wall, and a leaflet announcing a memorial program marking the fiftieth anniversary of his execution is tacked to the opposite wall.

Keller, white-haired, hard of hearing and a chain smoker, was wearing a Joe Hill memorial button in his lapel when I met him. He claims that the IWW still has some scattered strength throughout the country, notably in Cleveland among machinists and in the West among agricultural workers. He lamented that the poorly paid fruit and vegetable pickers were the hardest to hold in the organization because they are by nature a rootless group who are not joiners. Keller puts the blame for this situation on his own IWW, noting the lack of money and the absence of middle-aged organizers. He said that the IWW at the present time is composed of "grandfathers and grandsons." He failed to add that the lack of "fathers"—the middle-aged Wobblies—stemmed from their reluctance to join in the 1920s, 1930s and 1940s when the organization was on the downgrade.

The "grandsons" Keller refers to comprise about one-half the current Wobbly membership—which optimistically might total 2,000 people with another 10,000 inactive sympathizers.

The 1,000 or so youths who have suddenly in the last three or four years joined the Wobblies are mostly under twenty-five years old, a good portion under twenty-one. These youths reflect an increasing interest in anarchic and syndicalist sentiment throughout the country. The older Wobblies tend to be more syndicalist in their point of view; the youth emphasize the anarchism, although much of the syndicalism of their elders rubs off on them.

The bulk of the young anarchists are loosely associated with either the Wobblies, the Anarchist Federation, the Libertarian League or a group called Resurgence Youth. There are no clear organizational lines between these three; indeed there is considerable overlap. Most anarchists are found in New York City, Philadelphia, Chicago, San Francisco and the Pacific Northwest.

The Anarchist Federation grew out of a recent discussion group on New York's lower East Side. Its function, according to Walter Caughey, a computer programmer in a big department store, is to create an anarchist theory applicable to today's society. The nineteenth-century anarchist philosophies are inadequate to cope with current problems, he believes. Automation must be used, for example, to free man, not create unemployment and alienation. Anarchists, he says, must work out a way to accomplish this. Caughey also said that anarchism must become more of an ecological science, studying how people are being affected by their environment, particularly with regard to pollution, machines and government.

There is a strong antiwar tendency in the Anarchist Federation; most members are pacifists. Since they consider their function to be to change things, they direct their energies against the ills of society, putting, as Caughey says, "no emphasis on the few redeeming features of the U.S." Unlike some anarchists, this group is tolerant of most anarchist thought primarily because the members tend to be more anarcho-communist in spirit—thinking in terms of community living rather than in the extreme individualism of the Stirner school. There seems to be a division in the Federation between those who support the status quo because change is a part of the status quo and those who believe that the state will disappear only after a bitterly fought social upheaval. Currently the members are preoccupied with studying the Hungarian Revolution, a switch from their usual fascination with the Spanish Civil

War. Caughey explained that anarchists now believe that future revolutions will be against socialist governments; therefore more lessons can be learned from the Hungarian struggle rather than the Spanish one.

This group's leading theoretician is Murray Bookchin, an ex-Wobbly and ex-organizer for the CIO. He has written numerous works on ecological matters. The Federation's heroes would include the West Coast theoreticians, George and Louise Crowley, Prince Peter Kropotkin, Alexander Berkman, Emma Goldman, Nicola Sacco, Bartolomeo Vanzetti, and Sir Herbert Read, the last often referred to as "The Queen's anarchist."

One of the founders of the Federation is Paul Spencer, a student at City College of New York, who says he comes from a "conservative Staten Island family." He is starting his own anarchist magazine called *Good Soup*. "It will be just that," he told me, studiously rolling his own cigarette, "a little bit of this, a little bit of that."

Spencer runs the Torch Bookstore on the lower East Side. It caters to the tastes of anarchists, syndicalists and Wobblies. The first time I visited the place it was in chaos: chairs lined both walls, pillows were scattered all over the floor, the room reeked of foul-smelling smoke and two individuals lay in a stupor in one corner of the room. I was told that there had just been a "session." One hand-scrawled sign on the wall said, "I'm going to kill you!" A wildly colored Miro-like mural covered part of another wall. One poster proclaimed: "Malcolm X Lives!"; another read: "DON'T VOTE. Direct Action Not Politics!" When I returned a few months later the place had been put in order: the walls were washed down, the pillows removed, and more books put on display. Old wooden milk crates, turned on their sides and stacked one upon the other, served as bookcases, a standard lower East Side custom.

"When I was young, the life I saw around me just didn't make sense," said Spencer. "I was practically raised on the *Daily News*. I had no intellectual stimulation until I got to college. I was never in accord with the society around me." His readings in cybernetics and ecological studies helped him to form a modified view of anarchism. "I do not see it now in class terms; it does not depend on the political victory of one class," he added. C. Wright Mills' *The Power Elite* he believes is outdated because it talks in terms of influential families and not the anonymous power elite of the bureaucracies. For instance, he said, "it is clear in the Vietnam War that Congress does not make foreign policy," meaning Congress did not declare war. "Is bureaucracy becoming the functional equivalence of fascism?" Spencer asks. He and his followers are pondering the question.

Spencer would like to see America do away with all compulsory activities, particularly work. He believes that in order to get people to spend the time earning their livelihood, a set of repressive laws has been passed which has produced a repressed person. "Leisure is defined in terms of work, not in terms of creativeness," says Spencer. "Once compulsory work is abolished, all that is left is 'life activity,' which is naturally productive and creative."

Spencer looks forward to the day the state will be abolished along with all forms of centralized control. He would like to see the country, particularly the urban areas where most people live, return to the "isonomy of the Athenian system," which emphasized the family life, a rounded education, no specialization, public involvement and the amateur spirit.

Two of Spencer's associates in the Federation besides Caughey are Charles T. Smith and Mike Itkin. Smith is a full-bearded youth of unkempt appearance. He is a graduate of Harvard and a former Episcopalian turned Eastern Orthodox. Itkin, although raised a Jew, claims to be a priest in one of the "Old Roman Catholic Church" sects. He is young and of small stature. For a short period of time he was a Wobbly, later a marcher with the Committee for Nonviolent Action.

"I don't like anything to do with the scene," Smith told me. "I think cooperation with the state is anti-revolutionary." I asked Smith if he went so far as to boycott the ballot box. Before he could answer Itkin broke in and said, "Not at all. I've voted twice; once for Pogo and once for Donald Duck!" Caughey hastily added that while some anarchists feel it more effective to register a protest at the polls, most shun them, content simply to run anti-vote campaigns.

The Libertarian League is kept alive in America by the writings

and efforts of one Sam Weiner. He calls himself an anarcho-plural-
ist and proves it by writing under a variety of names, one of which
is his real one, known but to a few of his friends. Weiner is one of
the rare middle-aged Wobblies; he joined in the late 1920s. He is
still active, proudly showing me his red membership booklet with
the dues stamps inside.

The League is international in scope and has no membership as
such except those individuals who subscribe to the literature. A
great volume of dialogue flows between English-speaking anarchist
groups, particularly in Great Britain where they are much more
active. Weiner subscribes to *Freedom, Anarchy, Anarchy International* and *Anarchy Youth,* all British publications, as well as
Direct Action, the British Syndicalist Workers' Federation publication. Since Weiner can speak five languages he is in contact with
most libertarian groups on the Continent.

Weiner's own publication is a lively twenty-four-page quarterly
called *Views and Comments.* It is freckled with interesting wood-
cuts and drawings, and the articles themselves tend to be short,
provocative and of an intellectual cast. Like all magazines with a
small circulation, it is run in the red, being periodically rescued
from insolvency by successful pleas for money from its readers.

The last anarchist group associated with the Wobblies is also the
most violent. It is called the Resurgence Youth Movement and was
started in New York City by teen-agers in 1964. Its interests are
centered on teen-age subcultures: smoking marijuana, rock 'n' roll,
hallucinatory drugs such as LSD, and gang warfare. No more than
a hundred individuals are associated with this group; the turnover
is reported to be extremely high.

The Movement is obsessed with violence. One editorial in a
recent edition of their mimeographed magazine, *Resurgence,* began: "We notice with regret that the number of police casualties
has dropped to a pitiful low. . . ." Below the article was a
"curse" on all policemen "taken from the 'Necronomican.' " Below that were the statements: "Police = brutality. Let the State
Disintegrate."

Walter Caughey, who used to write for the magazine (one of his
editorials ended with: "Let the workshops of the underground
produce music as well as the weapons of death"), claims that the

person who wrote the article "is hip and not hung up on any hostilities in society." He says that these youths are interested in violence because violence is part of society. They take special note of all riots and other civil disorders to bolster their theory.

The magazine features considerable poetry of an inscrutable nature, much of it vulgar; there is a section called "Teenrevolt"; and most pages carry imprecations with a threat of disaster running through them. "Get Johnson's cops out of Vietnam and Wagner's troops out of Harlem" reads one. "LEVEL EVERY-THING! Then we'll talk about 'politics,' " reads another.

Sam Weiner is one of the Resurgence Youth Movement's biggest critics. He calls it "a group of middle-class neurotics who have never found anything to be committed to—the logical extreme of the revolt that has nothing to revolt about." Weiner's wife broke in to add that they were "tourists in the labor movement," romantics, exhibitionists, masochists and above all nihilists. She also characterized them as a *"Weltschmerz"* group, carrying around a pain for the world in their breasts. Sam Weiner claims that the Movement has been read out of the Wobblies; how successful this has been is moot, since the entire anarchist revival is fluid and unclear.

Carl Keller is also adamant in his rejection of the youths in these groups. He, of course, is seeking new members for the IWW but does not particularly wish to be saddled with youths whose interests fall outside the sphere of Revolutionary Industrial Unionism. In fact he is quite skeptical about the lasting value of recruiting the young. Said he: "Youth is a very brief period in a man's life, so I don't see it contributing much to long-term social change. All my ideas are colored by that thought. Any movement based solely on youth is not likely to be of much consequence. Once a man grows up he begins to face the same realities as older people so he forgets his youthful attitudes."

2

One of the groups to evolve out of the turmoil among socialists during the latter half of the nineteenth century was the Socialist Labor Party, the oldest Marxist party in continuous existence in the United States today. Its origins can be traced back to the First

International of 1864–1876, but the Party as it is constituted today dates from 1890.

Much of the socialist agitation in America in the four decades after the Civil War was conducted by German immigrants. Large numbers of German socialists fled their homeland after Bismarck's government passed the anti-socialist Exceptional Power Act in 1878. These newcomers exhibited an eclectic taste in socialist thought: they were not solely influenced by Marx and Engels but by Bebel, Kautsky, Lassalle, Eduard Bernstein and Wilhelm Lieb-knecht as well. Each one of these socialist prophets had his loyal band of followers who ardently promoted his interpretation of "the truth." Socialists have always argued among themselves over the road to utopia. Is the revolution to be violent or peaceful? Is the ultimate goal to be achieved by working within the unions and the existing political institutions, as a propaganda group or as an armed guerrilla band? Should the party work secretly or in the open? Is the revolution to be national or international? Can capitalism and communism coexist peacefully?

These questions and many more like them have always divided the socialist groups. It is little wonder, therefore, that there existed such a complexity of socialist intrigue in America during this period. It was reinforced by the struggles of the unions to achieve recognition and by the realization that the way to power for these then-impotent socialists lay in the organization of the workers. The difficulties were also aggravated by native prejudice toward the newcomers and the inevitable clash of personalities between one leader and another.

Within this morass existed "the old Socialistic Party," which was split in 1889 between the newspaper *Volkszeitung* (*People's Voice*) faction and the *"Richtung auf Reisen"* or "traveling" faction, so named because of its propensity to skip from site to site. Into the breach stepped Daniel DeLeon as editor of *The People* (later *The Weekly People*), who was to become the Socialist Labor Party's leader, philosopher and, in death, its saint.

DeLeon had cut his political teeth in the Henry George Move-ment and Edward Bellamy's "Nationalist" movement before he moved into the SLP. He quickly reoriented the Party along Marxist lines, cleansing it of other socialist dogma. He was an advocate of "Social Industrial Unionism," a plan not too far removed from the Wobbly goal of "One Big Union." He also believed in "boring from within," infiltrating unions for the purpose of seizing the positions of importance. The American Federation of Labor and the Knights of Labor were his two major targets.

But "boring from within" was never successful and was soon dropped. DeLeon later came around to the view that the trade union movement should be the industrial arm of a political movement. The precise political instrument to achieve his aim was, he felt, his own SLP.[1]

A humorless, intense man of Spanish descent, DeLeon wore a George V beard that was black at its roots and white at the tips. He was an intellectual Marxist who did not get on very well with his contemporaries. In fact, he fought with every socialist around him, both in and out of his Party. He survived a bitter internal fight over dogma in 1899 while at the same time carrying on a running battle with Eugene Debs and his Social Democratic Party, the predecessor of the Socialist Party. He fought Karl Kautsky, James Connolly and later the IWW. His opponents he would castigate as "kangaroos," "logical centrists," "ninnies," "slummists," the "overall brigade" and the "brotherhood of booze."

DeLeon helped found the IWW in 1905. He had always encouraged the unity of socialists, envisioning the Wobblies as the nucleus of his Social Industrial Unionism concept. Unfortunately, DeLeon demanded unity on his terms only—not a weakness by any means peculiar to himself, nevertheless one ensuring that the amalgamation of such individualists as Haywood, Debs, Foster and DeLeon would not be permanent. In the following year Debs resigned, complaining that the action-conscious Wobblies were not putting enough emphasis on political activities. He went back to the Socialist Party. In 1908 DeLeon broke away because he, too, was opposed to the "physical force only" tactics of the group. But he was not prepared to join Debs because he (DeLeon) was committed to working within his own SLP.

DeLeon then further muddied the waters a bit by setting up a rival organization, for a while also called the IWW. This he intended to be the "industrial arm of the political movement."

However, his "Wobbly" group collapsed in 1915, a year after his death.

The SLP has been contesting elections since 1892. It has put up candidates in every subsequent Presidential race and a host of others in gubernatorial, mayoralty and state assembly contests. It has never won any of them. An analysis of the Party's voting record shows that the mean number of votes received in all nineteen Presidential races from 1892 through 1964 is 28,500. In 1896 and 1960—two good years for the Party—the candidates received only 36,475 and 47,522 votes respectively. With the growth of the electorate this means that the Party's following has actually fallen in terms of percentage: from 0.26 percent in 1896 to 0.074 percent in 1960.

With the exception of the 1960 and 1964 elections, in which it placed third, the Party has never ranked better than fifth; on four occasions it was seventh and on three occasions it was last. Its advance to third in the 1960 and 1964 elections is more a reflection of the decline of the Prohibition and Socialist Parties than it is of its own prowess and vitality.

The Party admitted "lowering its standards" only once, in 1906 when it urged members to vote for "Big Bill" Haywood, who was running (unsuccessfully) for governor of Colorado. In 1908 the SLP nominated a convicted murderer for President, but the man turned down the honor on the advice of his attorneys. SLP candidates have not been so flamboyant since then.

It is interesting to note that although the Party has been running candidates for President, one of its major demands has been the

> Abolition of the Presidency, Vice-Presidency and Senate of the United States. An Executive Board to be established, whose members are to be elected, and may at any time be recalled by the House of Representatives as the only legislative body. The States and Municipalities to adopt corresponding amendment to their constitutions and statutes.[2]

In recent years this statement has been blurred over with a smoother blend of Marxist jargon.

Since his death in 1914 DeLeon has been canonized by the Party faithful. His socialist Holy Writ is considered nearly the equal of Marx's. In fact, surrounding the late leader is a personality cult reminiscent of others. DeLeon is described in gushing praise as a genius: "His was a master mind. His hand has drawn the strategic plans that will give the working class the power to destroy the forts of capitalism and rear the structure of the Socialist Republic." Another spoke of "the virile, clear cut, logical and inimitable style" of The Weekly People's editor adding, ". . . every article it [the newspaper] contained from DeLeon's pen was based upon facts, breathing that enthusiasm that only a sound, scientific posture can bring forth." Yet another was to write: "But the seas you charted we shall sail, O Pilot!"[3]

In the eyes of the current SLP faithful, DeLeon's genius lay in his "discovery and development" of the "Social Industrial Union." In other words, Marx provided the theology, DeLeon found the way to achieve it. If I understand the Party's literature correctly, under an SLP government there would be no private ownership, no "economic classes," no President, Vice-President and Senate, no craft unions, no "labor fakers," no capitalism, no wars, no political state, no political parties.

In their places will be a giant Social Industrial Union and an SIU Congress that will manage and direct all "social production." The country will be organized by industries, the rank and file voting progressively up the line for their worker-representatives. All people will be represented in the SIU Congress by their trade— construction, food supply, lumber, mining, etc. This, the literature tells us, will avoid the "chaos" that the "capitalist class" provokes. It also ensures the people against "the danger of bureaucratic usurpation." Organized in this manner, "the workers are invincible. No power on earth can stop them," states one pamphlet.

Two men have dominated the Party since DeLeon's death in 1914. One is Arnold Petersen, the national secretary since 1914, now semi-retired. The other is Eric Hass, the current editor of The Weekly People. Hass was raised in Nebraska and came from a family, he claims, who thought that socialism meant William Jennings Bryan. Disillusionment over the Kellogg-Briand Pact of 1927 was the straw that drove Hass into the political fringes. He settled on the SLP because he said it was the only group that did not give him three different answers to his questions. In 1938 he took over the reins of the newspaper and after World War II began running for office. He has run for President four times, which is only two less than Norman Thomas' record. Hass has written a number of books on socialism; he is a veteran lecturer at universities; and his favorite participating sport—even though he is in his sixties—is wrestling.

Hass is an enthusiastic promoter of DeLeon's policies. He reiterates the founder's thesis that capitalism is not capable of reforming itself—as the Socialist Party believes—but must be destroyed. Reform of such an unspeakable vice as capitalism, said Hass, is "like washing garbage before you throw it in the can." He believes that force may be necessary to overthrow the system but not necessarily violence; what distinction he makes between the two is not clear. Nor is he specific about the measures he would take against the "capitalist holdouts."

He claims that the actual number of votes credited to him in the four times he has tried for the Presidency was only one-tenth the vote actually cast for him. The rest, he said, were stolen. "But voters or dues-paying members at this time are not important," he added. "Every great revolutionary movement in history has not only started with small numbers, but has had them up to the very time the clock struck twelve for the old society."[4]

Hass' perspective of the causes of World War II are different from most people's. According to him, the American "ruling classes" provoked Japan, forcing her to retaliate. The American capitalists, he continued, actually wanted a war for three reasons: first, to defeat Germany because it was an impressive industrial rival; second, to defeat Japanese expansion in Asia because "American imperialism" in that sphere was being threatened; and third, to destroy British capitalism and to break up her colonial empire so that American capitalists could take it over.

Although "capitalists," "imperialists" and "labor fakers" receive a considerable share of the SLP's criticism, most of its invective is saved for the Roman Catholic Church. It is denounced as "a universal political machine, bent on world power, and less and less concerned about concealing its ends or disguising its means."[5] Its aims are considered ultramontane, its members "feudal-minded reactionaries." One recent headline in *The Weekly People* read: "THE POPE'S U.N. TALK OFFERED NO HOPE TO HUMANITY." Hass believes that there is a conspiracy brewing between the Vatican and American capitalists; such a situation is suspect to him. He said to me: "It is the only organization that wants to establish a world theocracy." He shook his head and shoulders at the thought of it.

Hass runs his newspaper from an old building near the Brooklyn exit of the Manhattan Bridge. The shop itself is spotlessly clean and is, according to him, neither an open nor a closed shop but a "socialist shop." All workers are members of or sympathetic to the SLP. "You can't have industrial unions in a shop like this," Hass, the leading proponent of Social Industrial Unionism, told me.

His newspaper has a circulation of 13,000 per week and loses money. Membership figures are secret, but 13,000 would be wildly optimistic. The "Arm and Hammer" emblem of the Party is prominently displayed on the masthead. "We are not related to the soda company," Hass said. "I wish it were true; we could use the money."

Ordinary citizens cannot join the SLP just by applying, says Hass. Recruits must go through a training program of from three to six months. This, he says, cuts down turnover and ensures doctrinal purity.

This exclusive posture of the SLP raises criticism that the organization is little more than a private fraternal order for socialists, grown quite conservative in its old age. Its critics point out that the SLP is virtually the only Marxist group that has never taken part in the activities of the moment: whether it be "organizing the unorganized," protesting nuclear tests or working in the current civil rights, anti-Vietnam and peace movements. (Historically the SLP has been so docile that it was never put on the Attorney General's list.) The critics add that, with a strict membership limitation, there is no threat to the leaders, who then have no need to come up with any new ideas—which is the way DeLeon would have preferred it. Ammon Hennacy, by no means an SLP friend, claims the Party is "humorless . . . and well-financed by the capitalist system"; Party members "never risk going to jail which might disrupt their organizing."[6] Hass replies that action is futile if undirected by theory. "Those youths are wasting all that good energy," he said, adding that the current spate of activity is in his opinion only a temporary phenomenon.

As for the future, Hass is not bubbling with enthusiasm, but, then, time has taught him to blend his confidence with caution. "We're not pessimistic about it," he said. "It may not work out in a storybook fashion, but sooner or later there will be a crisis and when that happens the people will turn to the SLP."

3

The phenomenon of the Trotskyists as an independent ideological sect of the Communist movement dates from 1927 when Leon Trotsky, the creator of the Red Army, was expelled from the Soviet Communist Party and its Central Committee. Trotsky was removed for two basic reasons: he was a threat to Stalin's precarious (at that time) supremacy as Lenin's heir, and he believed that the Marxist revolution had to be built around an international party as opposed to Stalin's contention that socialism was a Russian national movement—"socialism in one country," as it was called.

James P. Cannon is considered the father of American Trotskyism. He is now an old man living in retirement in California. Prior to 1927 he had been a member of the CPUSA. At one point he was a member of the underground section and was known as "Comrade Cook." When Trotsky was sent into exile, Cannon and a few associates—Max Shachtman, Martin Abern and others—defended the ideological position of their hero and were expelled in 1928. There were no more than eight to ten rebels in this group. The CPUSA was so outraged at this defection that it demanded that every one of its cells express its solidarity with the mother party with a denunciation of Trotskyism by name and by vote. Those who hesitated, out of either sympathy or ignorance of the argument, were immediately expelled. Most of those expelled, infuriated over their treatment, became Trotskyists. As a result the dissident faction grew. Within a year it had one hundred members, all ex-Communist Party members, and was putting out a newspaper called *The Militant,* still the major Trotskyist newspaper in America today.

Cannon called his group "The Communist League of America, Left Opposition of the Communist Party." He and his followers believed that Soviet Russia was a "degenerate workers' state" capable of being reformed. The League, therefore, technically considered itself to be a part of the CPUSA, in opposition to the Stalinists in control of it. The leaders of the CPUSA did not agree, having read the heretics out of the Party with totalitarian finality.

The Stalinists went to great pains to crush this revolt. Cannon's apartment was ransacked and all his correspondence stolen; his meetings were disrupted by hecklers; and his followers were beaten in the streets. He was forced to organize a Workers' Defense Guard to protect his men from physical harm. Members of the Guard were armed with oversized hatchet handles, which they used on a number of occasions to rearrange their opponents' sense of reality. Violence of this nature has become endemic to the organization and endures today.

The Trotskyists have always been plagued by two problems, still today not resolved. One concerns "theory" and asks: what is the Party's position toward such-and-such a development? There was always a "correct" theory that had to be adhered to strictly; and the Party suffered splits whenever the "incorrect" faction could not be reconciled. Members would argue over such "theory" as the terminology for Soviet Russia (Was it *really* a "degenerate workers' state" or a "bureaucratic collectivist state"?); whether to support certain Soviet actions; and whether it was possible to reform the Third International. As long as Trotsky was alive, the "correct" theory was picked by the man himself. But after the old revolutionary was assassinated at Stalin's order in Mexico in 1940, there was no oracle to settle disputes. His followers were thereafter forced to seek the "correct" theory in his past works. Because Trotsky was not always clear in his writings and because he sometimes took conflicting points of view, schisms among the faithful broke out frequently.

What was the maximum ceiling above which capitalism could not expand (it was periodically revised upward amidst assertions that such-and-such a limit was the *absolute* limit)? When was the

Trotskyist revolution to take place? Were the Soviet satellites different from Soviet Russia—were they "deformed capitalist states" or something else? Such questions kept the Party divided after their prophet had died. In fact, Trotskyists argued these questions among themselves with such little regard for the events going on around them that they acquired a reputation of being unrealistic to the point of creating a fantasy world all their own—a reputation they still have today.

The second problem concerned tactics. Trotskyists have never been able to resolve how they are to grow as a party. Are they to be an outcast appendage to the CPUSA? Are they to set up shop on their own? Do they grow by "boring from within" the unions? Are they to be an activist group or a propaganda group? Historically, the Party's leaders would decide on one tack, only to see dissident groups break away to follow some other course.

When the League was first organized in 1928, Cannon determined that his group would do best as an appendage to the Communist Party. He took a stand against the formation of "Red unions" and against outside agitation because he conceived his role as one of changing the CPUSA only. Within five years, however, he had abandoned this position when he came to believe that the "bureaucratic state capitalism" of Soviet Russia was incapable of reforming itself. Thereafter the League considered itself a new party and began calling for "mass work" and "boring from within." Recruits were sought outside the CPUSA, from the left wing of the Socialist Party and labor movement. Cannon threw his men into the thick of labor disputes—in Minneapolis, Akron, Paterson; he held rallies, picket lines, protest marches. Wherever there were difficulties, Cannon and his few men agitated with their customary zeal.

In 1934 a union was formed between the League and A. J. Muste's American Workers Party. The new organization was called the Workers Party. It was an unhappy affair. Within a year the Oehlerites, led by one Hugo Oehler, were expelled for "sectarian phrasemongering." Cannon wanted the Party to join the Socialist Party with the idea of taking it over. Muste was against this "French turn," as it was called. The two men split in 1935, Cannon taking his troops into the Socialist Party. The Trotskyists were received coolly and within eighteen months had been frozen out of all positions of power. Realizing the futility of belonging to the Socialist Party, Cannon set up yet another organization, the Socialist Workers Party, which is still in existence today.[7]

The Socialist Workers Party* was one of the few political parties during the war to support strikes. In 1941, one of the SWP's leaders, Farrell Dobbs (who, like Eric Hass, has also run for President four times), was convicted under the Smith Act for conspiring to create insubordination in the Armed Forces. The Party was such an uncooperative group that it was put on the Attorney General's list of subversive organizations in 1947.

After the war the SWP grew considerably—at least in Trotskyist terms—to seven hundred or so members, only to decline during the McCarthy period. It also suffered the usual quota of divisions, the "Cochranite" faction being the largest breakaway during this period. (One of the original Trotskyists, Max Shachtman, had previously led his faction out of the Party in 1940.) After Khrushchev's 1956 speech denouncing Stalin, the Trotskyists reaped a harvest of new members who were fleeing the CPUSA. As has historically been the case, these newcomers did not stick but fled in turn from their Trotskyist taskmasters. By 1960 the Party was back to its hard-core strength of seven hundred. There seems to be an unwritten rule that prevents any Trotskyist group from expand-

---

* The SWP should not be confused with the WSP, or World Socialist Party, located in Faneuil Hall Square in Boston. This group, forty or so strong today, was founded in Detroit in 1916 and has done nothing since except provide speakers on the Boston Commons. Its members claim to preach the purest form of Marxism; all other prophets are rejected as spurious. One spokesman, Harry Morrison, who describes himself as an "outdoor salesman," says that the Party does not advocate a violent revolution; rather, he and his comrades see the achievement of Marxist goals as a continuing educational process. He said that WSPers consider themselves as "philosophical materialists," not as the "physical" variety. Morrison, however, can still talk of the "twin horrors" of capitalism: "capitalist war and capitalist peace," both in his eyes part of a capitalist conspiracy. He sees the working classes today as a machine that needs more than "gas and oil" to sustain it.

The WSP's only publication is *Western Socialist,* a dull pamphlet with a claimed circulation of 3,200. The Party maintains close ties with the Socialist Party of Great Britain, also a tiny sect that has done little in its many years of existence on the British scene to warrant the changing of its nickname from "Small Party of Good Boys."

ing beyond the seven hundred mark without splintering into two or more factions.

Today there are four discernible Trotskyist groups in America and probably half a dozen more one- or two-man splinters that have not yet surfaced to tell the world that they and they alone know the true path to Trotsky's heaven. The largest is still the SWP, run by Farrell Dobbs, an ex-teamster and now the national secretary of the Party, Ed Shaw, the organizing secretary, and George Novack, the Party's leading theoretician.

Since it was founded in 1938 the SWP has chosen the electoral road to success, or at least on the surface it has. Its record at the polls is less encouraging than Eric Hass' SLP vote. In the five Presidential elections it has contested since 1948 it has averaged 21,000 votes per election. But this figure is misleading. In 1960 it received 40,165 votes. This probably is a reflection of the increasing interest in New Left ideas. In all the other elections, except the 1964 one (in which it got 32,720), its total was near or below the 10,000 mark.

In the past five years or so the SWP has strayed from the path of strict Trotskyism. For instance, it still contests elections, which to some militants is a form of coexistence. Also, the Party was reported to have sent a telegram of condolence to Mrs. Kennedy on the death of the President, prompting one breakaway militant to say that it just showed how scared it was. But then Lee Harvey Oswald was once in contact with the Party.

Furthermore the Party is embroiled among New Left groups which are made up almost exclusively of students. Critics point out that this is not the most fertile field to build a "revolutionary party of *workers.*"

These Trotskyists are also active participants in the peace groups. In fact, some of them seem to be genuine pacifists—a far cry from militant Trotskyism. They are also involved in the field of black nationalism. Malcolm X was desperately courted by them because he was a militant of their own stripe. But Malcolm X was by no means the ideal Trotskyist; nationalism and Trotskyism have very little in common except a mutual desire to upset the apple cart. Apparently some SWPers harbored the notion that if a nationalist state were ever set up it would be a Trotskyist one.

Malcolm X certainly never believed this. Malcolm later modified his antiwhite separatist stand, deemphasizing the Muslim aspect and calling for a militant all-black drive for equal rights. Again, it appears that the SWP—a predominantly white organization—believed it would lead this movement.

One of the ironies and enigmatic aspects of the SWP is that, if anything, it has moved closer to Stalinism in concept since 1956. It supports, for instance, the Red Chinese position against Moscow. Ideologically it is more akin to the Progressive Labor Party and its dogmatic pro-Stalin position than the CPUSA, the organization that dutifully denounced the enemy of Trotsky.

This is not to say, of course, that the Party has reversed directions ideologically. On the contrary. Party members—particularly their current star candidate, Clifton de Berry, an albino Negro housepainter from Brooklyn—still talk of overthrowing the capitalists. They would close down all foreign bases, give up the Panama Canal, level all salaries through taxation, allow enlisted military men to elect their own officers and nationalize everything in sight. "Committees of workers and technicians" would be in charge. The country would be run on Marxist-Leninist lines without Stalinist distortions.[8]

Trotskyists have expanded the concept of "boring from within" the unions to include the infiltration of all left-wing groups. Most left-wing activists jump from group to group as a matter of course and are welcomed wherever they go. But not the Trotskyists: they have a reputation of being the troublemakers of the left—destructive, cynical and uncooperative. As a result they are hated with uncommon passion by everyone.*

For example, Trotskyists believe that "the unorganized proletariat" will only come around to their point of view when they have become disillusioned with the American methods of reconciliation. To achieve this they will send one of their better organ-

---

* To say nothing of other citizens. In May, 1966, a man waving a pistol stormed into the SWP's Detroit headquarters and ordered three persons to throw their money on the floor and line up against the wall. Crying "You're all a bunch of Commies!" he methodically shot all three, killing one, and fled without taking the money. Within hours the police had arrested a suspect listening to Beethoven at the public library whose wife had reported him carrying a gun near the Party's offices.

izers into an area, have him organize the people and then, just as his labors are about to bear fruit, they will destroy the entire operation so that those who were anticipating better conditions become disgusted—not with the Trotskyist efforts, but with the entire American system. Trotskyists believe that some of the disgruntled will then drift into their own camp. They vehemently deny that they use this tactic, but many examples of it are on record.

One specific instance—the Peace March in Washington on 27 November 1965—will suffice. It was held under the auspices of SANE and the National Coordinating Committee to End the War in Vietnam, the latter founded by Frank Emspak, a recent graduate of the University of Wisconsin. Radicals of all stripes, approximately 1,500 individuals, converged on the capital the Wednesday before to attend the Thanksgiving Day convention which was to discuss strategy.

The Young Socialist Alliance, the youth section of the SWP, led off by suggesting the creation of an additional "workshop" discussion group that would examine the problems of all the other workshops. It was agreed that this maneuver by the Trotskyists was designed to create a cadre of hard-core radicals within the all-encompassing National Coordinating Committee. It was an attempt to take over the NCC, indeed the entire peace movement. Some saw it as a reflex action acquired from the struggles of the 1930s. "Every generation has got to learn," said Steve Weissman of the Vietnam Day Committee, that "the Trots have still got their sense of *imminence*. They're still listening to history and not to people."

It soon became apparent that the Trotskyists had packed the convention. On Friday, at a plenary session, they struck again, this time over a complicated issue of credentials. There was a long and bitter floor fight apparently designed to antagonize everyone. One man tore up his delegate's card in anger; another suggested a delegate card burning. "The Trots were making so many wild motions," Ringo Hallinan of the DuBois Clubs told me, "that we were forced to propose right-wing ones to counter them. They were using every dirty left-wing trick in the book," he added.

The Trotskyist youths struck again soon afterward, this time on the question of slogans for the march on Saturday morning. SANE had previously laid down guidelines, stating that no slogan except those suggesting a "negotiated withdrawal" would be acceptable to it. The Trotskyists therefore proposed that slogans demanding "withdrawal now" be used. This, everyone agreed, would have split the movement, obviously what the Trotskyists wanted.

After the march, the intrepid Trotskyists struck yet again. They held a meeting to set up a rival national committee to Emspak's. Guards were posted at the door to allow in only those pledged to the move. Some violence, reminiscent of old, took place, prompting one independent to shout: "Goons and Storm Troopers! This is supposed to be a *peace* movement."

"We've never advocated nonviolence," retorted one young Trotskyist.[9]

The net result of the conference has been that the peace marchers, for one, at best a fragile coalition of many conflicting points of view, returned to their local headquarters a little more confused, considerably more bitter and certainly more pessimistic about the probability of achieving peace on earth. And what did the Trotskyists achieve? From all indications, nothing except a certain pleasure in wreaking havoc and dissension wherever they go. Certainly they did not capture the NCC nor even a tiny segment of the peace movement; there was no notable rush to join the SWP or YSA afterward.

But the Trotskyists disagree with this point of view. One of them—Harvard-educated George Novack, a member of the SWP and its predecessors since 1933—claims that his Party has never refused to unite with any other organization "in defense of democratic rights." People who have definite convictions, he said, "are always considered disruptive and difficult to deal with." He was convinced, he added, that the SWP gained some converts that weekend.

The Young Socialist Alliance, "officially" independent of the SWP but, in fact, an SWP front, also disagrees. Its national chairman, Lew Jones, claimed with remarkable understatement that the infighting at the convention was due "essentially to differences of perspective." He disclaimed any attempt to grab the leadership.

Jones is a young and pleasant man, a recent graduate of Northwestern. He says he comes from an upper-middle-class family. "By instinct I was a rebel," he said, noting that he witnessed considerable brutality as a child in the South. "I am a socialist because I believe it to be the only system that can solve the problems in the world. I am a Trotskyist because I believe he, Trotsky, is the only one to correctly interpret Marx." Jones heads an organization of approximately five hundred individuals, most of them young college graduates. Some of them were formerly members of the Young People's Socialist League, or "Yipsels," as they are known, the Socialist Party youth group which is currently in a state of limbo.

Jones, like all other militant Marxists, does not believe in internal democracy within the YSA. Differences of opinion can exist only so long as a question is in the debate stage. Once a majority decides the "correct" theory, all the minority factions must fall into line or get out. "If a minority feels its differences are so great that they can't work with the majority," said Jones, "it is better that they leave and form their own groups." Strict adherence to "the line" and lack of a bothersome minority opinion, said the chairman, produces what he calls "political clarity."

One group to break away from the SWP is the Workers World Party, otherwise known as the "Marcyites," after Sam Marcy, the chairman, who is acclaimed among the left for his charisma. The Party was formed in 1959 by dissident SWPers, some ex-members of the Communist Party and a few independent radicals. All told it has perhaps a hundred followers today.

According to Vincent Copeland, the editor of *Workers World,* there was a demand for a new group because none of the "tired out phony parties," as he called them, were pro-China at the time. The split with the SWP was actually triggered over "the Hungary question," the rebel Trotskyists favoring the Russian intervention, the body of the SWP declining to do so. Copeland claims that the WWP is attempting to build a "genuinely revolutionary movement along true Marxist-Leninist lines"; but, he lamented, "we are often called an 'anti-intellectual movement' because our newspaper is brief and simplified." He was acknowledging that the lack of long, often inscrutable dialectical arguments in a sect's newspaper warrants instant scorn from other Marxists.

The Party, he went on, is not only pro-China but also pro-Cuba, pro-Deacons for Defense and pro-Robert Williams' Revolutionary Action Movement. The Marcyites support the activities of the Progressive Labor Party, the Vietnam Day Committee, Youth Against War and Fascism, and the Puerto Rican Movimiento Pro Independencia. There is considerable overlap here. For instance, Dixie Bayo, a young Puerto Rican who runs the MPI's New York City branch, is the wife of a Workers World activist. One of the *Workers World* staffers, Phyllis Fishberg, also writes for the YAWF publication, *The Partisan*. Some feel that the YAWF is so close to the Workers World Party that it constitutes its youth section.

The WWP is stridently anti-administration, claiming, for instance, that the CIA has hired Vietnamese to dress as Vietcong and commit atrocities. It is also a racist and anti-Catholic group. Furthermore, it suffers from a conspiracy complex worthy of some radical right groups. "But the real enemy, some are beginning to suspect," reads one editorial, "is not to be found in Vietnam but in Washington." It keeps telling the world that it is in favor of revolutions—"like the French Revolution and the American Civil War," Copeland told me—but when it comes to the moment of truth, the Party only takes part in "united fronts" and, at that, complained the editor, infrequently, since they are hard to come by.

The WWP resembles in many ways the SWP. It is, for instance, a nonexclusive group that sends its members into every other group to proselytize the locals. It has also supported Jesse Gray, the rabble-rousing Harlem rent-striker, when he ran for mayor of New York City in the 1965 Democratic primary. It too suffers from a lack of direction, raising the question among other radicals of why it exists.

The last major Trotskyist breakaway of recent vintage is a group of perhaps two hundred individuals who revolve around a magazine called *Spartacist*. The nucleus of this "tendency," as they prefer to call themselves, were thrown out of the SWP in 1963, in this instance over the "Cuban question." Apparently the Spartacists defended the Trotskyists that Castro had jailed while the SWP denounced them because it supported the Cuban Revolution.

This tendency is perhaps the most militant of all the Trotskyist sects. It is cynical enough to believe, for instance, that the USSR is almost a capitalist country. Spartacists hate the Socialist Workers Party (it is, they believe, going through "political menopause"), even though they are periodically begging to be readmitted into it; they also hate the Communist Party, the Socialist Party, the Workers World Party and particularly the Progressive Labor Party (whose "Stalinist" accusations they describe as "the syphilis of the working class"). Spartacists are stridently anti-American, anti-white and anti-Castro (but pro-Cuban Revolution); they are enthusiastically pro-Vietcong (its Cornell University branch raised money to send to the National Liberation Front), pro-Congo rebels and pro-Deacons for Defense (one ad in *Spartacist* soliciting money for the Deacons began: "Every dime buys a bullet . . .").

Although they are hard-line Trotskyist militants, the Spartacists still maintain characteristics similar to the groups they hate. For instance, they can castigate the WWP for supporting Jesse Gray for mayor, but they can then turn around and call for the support of some "Labor-Negro candidate." Eventually the Spartacists settled on backing the SWP candidates, not too original a revolutionary tactic.

"We're revolutionary politicians," says Jim Robertson, the sect's leader. "We want to rip this country up by the roots and substitute a rule by another class!" Robertson, a large middle-aged man wearing rimless glasses, has been a radical activist since he was eighteen years old. He has been a member of the CPUSA, the "Shachtmanite" tendency, and the SWP. In 1963 he was convicted of assaulting a police officer.

Like every other Trotskyist, Robertson claims he takes the "classical" Trotskyist line. "We plan to build a revolutionary working-class power in order to bring about an international working-class revolution," he said.

He considers his group to be an "Ostensible Revolutionary Organization," or an "ORO"; Robertson wants to build his revolutionary party around the many small, disorganized OROs that are now scattered throughout the country. He has already brought into his fold the "Wohlforthites," a small militant tendency that publishes the *Bulletin of International Socialism,* perhaps the most tedious of all Trotskyist papers. He has been able to split the "Yipsels," always a source of trouble to Socialist Party leaders. There are many other diverse groups, split-offs from Communist, socialist and Trotskyist groups, that have aligned themselves with the Spartacists.

One of Robertson's organizers, and his right-hand man, is Albert Nelson. Nelson—who wears an "anarchist" mustache—has been a member of the SWP and the YSA. In 1964 he lost his passport for going to Cuba as a participant of the Student Committee for Travel to Cuba, a May 2nd Movement front. "We're the only organization calling itself revolutionary that has a national spread," he said, claiming considerable strength in the South in particular.

The Spartacists, says Robertson, are a "factional democracy" where a wide range of views are tolerated. This, he states, will prevent the Party from splitting in the future. "PLP sees factionalism as divisive—the crime of the counterrevolutionary Trotskyist. The SWP, too, allows no divisions," he went on, "except through their safety valve: writing documents for two or three months every two years—*and that's it!* The rest of the time, their brains are turned off.

"We expect our members to present their different views and fight for them," Robertson said. Almost in the same breath, however, he added: "Of course, we are a 'democratic centralist' organization where, once a vote is taken, the public view is the majority view." He did not say what would happen to a member who publicly aired a minority opinion.

Spartacist, the news magazine, does not make money even though its backers claim 13,000 sales per issue, a highly exaggerated estimate. Its ratio of slogans and Trotskyist phrases is high in relation to other items. "VIETNAM, WATTS: IT'S THE SAME STRUGGLE" and "NO SECRET DIPLOMACY" are some of the slogans; "American bourgeoisie," "the struggle against revisionism," "the assemblying of a cadre of working-class militants" are typical phrases. The Party structure, according to Robertson, is the "standard old Bolshevik type" with a central committee, political bureaus (politburos) and local committees. Its members place great emphasis on winning over the Negroes (Spartacists prefer the more nationalist term "blacks") to the cause, believing that they would provide a short-cut to the proper working-class base they are seeking. At the moment the Party is in transition, says Robertson, "But we will win eventual recognition from all interested parties as *the only true* Trotskyist Party."

To be acknowledged as Trotsky's only heir is considered of vital importance to every sect within the entire Trotskyist movement. Undoubtedly much of the maneuvering for this dubious honor is related to the credibility of one particular Trotskyist sect's dogma; for if it can be "proved" that such-and-such a Trotskyist position descends directly from Trotsky himself, then it reinforces the group's conviction that its theory is the "correct" one.

At the moment Western Trotskyists are split into three major warring camps. (There are so many other minor tendencies at war with each other that, in delving into their affairs, one soon finds oneself talking solemnly to a one-man group whose political viability is perhaps sixty days.) Each one insists that it alone is Trotsky's only legitimate heir. One group is known as the Pabloites with headquarters in Paris. This group takes its name from one Michael Raptis, alias Michel Pablo, a Greek Trotskyist who was a minister in Ben Bella's Algerian government. In opposition to them are the Posadaites with headquarters in Montevideo, Uruguay. The Posada tendency takes its name from a hysterical Argentine Trotskyist, a man about whom little else is known. The Posadaites are the more radical of the two factions, being considered in some Trotskyist quarters as "ultra-left adventurist maniacs." The Posadaite, for instance, believes in the inevitability of a nuclear war and thinks therefore that Russia should start one with a preemptive strike against the United States before the West turns on the socialist states.

The third group is the Healyites, located in London. Gerry Healy, a Communist Party member at the age of thirteen, is, along with J. P. Cannon, one of the major figures in Trotskyist politics.

He runs one of the most militant groups in Britain, driving his few troops with such zeal that many are broken men before they become of age. A small man with a turnip-shaped head that turns bright red when he becomes angry, Healy is the dictatorial boss of the Socialist Labor League. He is a proponent of the "smash and grab," a short and intense campaign to expend the energy of his two hundred faithful. One week there will be a campaign to recruit "Mods" and "Rockers," the next week an effort to infiltrate the Labour Party, the following week agitation for strike action and the week after that a supreme effort to topple the British government.

Most American Trotskyists align themselves with one of these three groups. The SWP used to be close to Healy but broke over "the Cuban question" (Healy believes that Castro has not overthrown capitalism; the SWP disagrees). Today it aligns itself with no one in particular, although it leans toward the Pabloists. The Spartacists and Wohlforthites until recently sided with Healy; because of a disagreement in 1966, the two broke away, the Spartacists moving closer to the Posadaists. The Workers World Party does not express its preference clearly but seems to be sympathetic to the Pabloists on occasion.

The American Trotskyists—like all Trotskyists—are in a state of political decline today. The reasons are readily apparent. Because they continue to argue over ideological trivia they guarantee that they will never be unified into a potential force. They also argue over questions that are so unreal that they drive off all but the most escapist and disgruntled. In three decades few of them have come to realize that Trotsky was an imperfect prophet. The American "proletariat," upon whom Trotskyists base all their hopes, is not seeking a revolution, is not disillusioned and is not pessimistic about the future. In fact, most Americans today are optimists, not the pessimists they may have been in the 1930s. Far from despairing of American democracy, they seek more of it, not less. The Trotskyists, on the other hand, are still calling for solutions that mean nothing to Americans; they have the smell of the 1930s about them and, at that, someone else's 1930s, not America's.

Over the years the Trotskyists have proved their incapacity to grow, particularly after the golden opportunity of 1956 when Communists were fleeing in droves from the CPUSA. In the future we may see the Trotskyists moving closer to the Red Chinese position, reveling in the their outcast status and overlooking its Stalinist aspects with an ease comparable to the acquiescence Communist Party members showed toward Moscow's past revisions of the party line.

But the body blow that has felled the Trotskyists has been self-inflicted and is not solely the result of hostile forces ranged against them. Trotskyists, said one observer of the political fringes, "ever since they first appeared on the American scene in 1928, have been self-proclaimed experts on Russia and her revolution but, on the other hand, they have never understood the revolution that has been taking place in America."

15

The New Left

1

During the early 1960s there emerged on the American political scene a new phenomenon known now as the New Left. It is composed of many ill-defined groups whose policies, purposes and personnel overlap considerably with one another.

The roots of the New Left go back to the late 1940s and the 1950s. This was the era of the "silent generation"—those university students who thought in terms of a good white-collar job, a comfortable marriage, a patch of suburbia, a new automobile with fins and other dull middle-class values. Although this is an unfair description of all the students during those years (many of them went on to distinguish themselves in the civil rights movement, for instance), it is true enough as a generalization. There was virtually no visible ferment (panty raids were held in higher esteem, for instance, than anti-McCarthyism), no intellectual skepticism, no individuality, no social consciousness. With prophetic irony, University of California President Clark Kerr was to say of them: "The employers will love this generation; they aren't going to press many grievances. They are going to be easy to handle. There aren't going to be any riots."[1]

Only a subculture disturbed the calm and self-satisfaction, namely the Beats—those bearded bohemians who timidly withdrew from society into their own world of pot, poetry and melancholia. The writings of Kerouac, Corso, Ferlinghetti, Ginsberg and the rest of the dissenters of this period mark the beginning of the New Left upsurge.

Four incidents mark the point where the New Left began to grow. First came Fidel Castro's 1959 victory in Cuba. This was interpreted by the young as indicative of the power they themselves had to change the world. Soon afterward, in 1960, came Caryl Chessman's execution in San Quentin Prison. The case of this convicted murderer, exploited unmercifully by American Marxists, contained enough seeds of doubt concerning his guilt that it provoked the young to question the validity of all laws, the very foundations on which the country rests. Then in the spring of 1960 there was the first sit-in—in Greensboro, North Carolina—which marked the civil rights movement's shift into high gear. It also sparked the social consciousness of many American youths, who soon were streaming south as activists. Finally there was the House Committee on Un-American Activities' investigation of subversive activities in California of the same year. Anti-Committee demonstrations took place throughout the entire hearings; many of the protest parades turned into battles between the students and the police. Later the Committee was to issue for general release a film on these demonstrations, called "Operation Abolition." Ostensibly its purpose was to show how Marxists manipulated the innocent; in fact, it contributed significantly to the growth of the New Left. "We are indebted to the Committee for that film," said Clark Kissinger of the Students for a Democratic Society. "It showed those big cops clubbing students. . . ." Groups of every variety began to spring up in protest all over the country.

The New Left grew for other reasons. First of all, McCarthyism had died out, and all serious dissent was no longer considered un-American. Also the Cold War was thawing, which allowed a far greater breadth of internal dissent. In addition, the youth, dash and vigor of President Kennedy forced the world to listen to the views of the young. Finally, the financial prosperity that has attended these youths since their birth has had much to do with their heightened political and social consciousness. Never before in American history has there been such a large percentage of youths who, once past their primary schooling, have been relatively free from the worry of earning a living. As a result, and in no way implying they give less stress to practicalities, they could indulge in the luxury of being concerned with abstractions—principles, theories and ideals—much like the wealthy Founding Fathers could nearly two hundred years ago. The apparently hungry students of the 1950s were more the realists; these current well-fed ones have become philosophers.

One of the primary influences on the New Left has been the success of the civil rights movement. Many members of the New Left are veteran demonstrators in the struggle for Negro equality. There is, for instance, a considerable overlap in membership among SNCC, Northern Student Movement and CORE and Vietnam Day Committee, Students for Democratic Society and the W. E. B. DuBois Clubs. Tactics have been borrowed wholesale by the youths: the sit-in, the nonviolent demonstration, the strike, the boycott.

For the most part the young activists of the New Left are not doctrinaire: Marx, they will tell you, is outdated; Trotsky was irrelevant, Stalin was insane, Debs and Norman Thomas were losers. "We do not spend endless hours debating the nature of Soviet Russia or whether Yugoslavia is a degenerate workers' state," said SDS's Kissinger. A new set of heroes are now worshiped. All of them have "style," a very important quality to the young. There is Gandhi, Jesus Christ, Martin Luther King, Albert Camus, John Kennedy, Bertrand Russell, W. E. B. DuBois, Ernesto "Che" Guevara and Frantz Fanon, the last an advocate of global revolution. Lesser heroes include I. F. Stone because he is nobody's pet radical, Bishop James A. Pike because he is always in hot water, Bob Dylan because he talks like a poet and sings like a rebel, Stanley Kubrick because his anti-establishment films (*Dr. Strangelove*, for one) are funny and grotesque, James Bond because he is cynical and always wins, and Batman because he is absurd.

They tolerate a few others but rarely heed them. One is Norman Mailer. "That Mailer is so caught up on his balls that he is embarrassing," said one undergraduate after listening to him speak at a Vietnam teach-in. "He's an old man. He's like an old man playing with himself. But why does he have to do it publicly and say that it has political importance?"[2]

The New Left uses other words. Out are such phrases as "the class struggle" and "socialist realism"; in are "commitment," "involvement," "relevance," "integrity," "participatory democracy" and "one man, one vote." These terms reflect more of a concern for social and emotional problems than political and intellectual ones.

Essentially these young radicals are rebelling against their middle-class upbringing—suburbia (often referred to as "the white ghetto"), the American Dream and "don't rock the boat." They reject all the phoniness and corruption of American society— payola, deceitful sexual mores, fallout, brinkmanship, tokenism, police brutality, lack of privacy and the smug middle-class life. The promises of America, they will say, have not been kept: injustice has crowded out equality, democracy has been replaced by "establishment politics," dissent smothered in consensus, the clamor for "success" has replaced "significance," and "mass everything" has been substituted for individual importance.[3] Above all, they reject compromise. "Freedom," said one youth, "is not splitting the difference."

They are fed up by the contradictions in American society— widespread poverty in the midst of plenty, private wealth and public squalor, freedom for everyone save the Negro, and so on— and demand that the self-satisfied middle-class public look behind the rhetoric and press-agentry for the truth. They hate the impersonality of American life, where everyone has a number after his name, where excellence is averaged down to a common denominator, where they are told that cybernetics can solve human problems, where the government sometimes insults its citizens by acting as an all-wise father. During the University of California demonstrations at Berkeley in 1964, students hung around their necks IBM cards on which was written "Do not fold, spindle or mutilate." It was by no means a joke to them.

They see the world as corrupt, unloving, insane and doomed, but unlike the Beats of the previous generation they refuse to withdraw from it. They are not interested in finding a place in society; rather they are trying to change it. They have no particular utopias in mind. On occasion they appear to be more interested in tearing down society than building it up, but this they will explain is a temporary evil, necessary before any positive good can come of their efforts. There is a streak of anarchism running through the New Left that often equates powerlessness with purity. These youths, for instance, are anti-bureaucratic on the grounds that hierarchical structures are totalitarian and stifling to the human spirit. Therefore, the reasoning goes, the less power the better. Yet, ironically, they realize that they, too, must be bureaucratic if they wish to confront the existing powers with any organized strength.

From out of this ferment several goals have emerged. They are unclear, fragmentary in conception and still in a state of flux. One goal is equal civil rights for all citizens. The young radicals want to see everyone—Negroes, Puerto Ricans, poor whites, Indians, etc. —working within the American political mainstream. These people talk of "the dispossessed," "the forgotten" and "the unwanted" and are deeply committed to their struggles for equality. War on poverty is another goal, and it finds the young working in VISTA, the Peace Corps, community projects, slums and other depressed areas. Peace is yet another goal. It is reflected in the New Left's active participation in the anti-Vietnam movement. There is also a desire to alter some of the more traditional aspects of American society. This is usually expressed in garbled and vague phrases such as "seeking a sense of community" and wanting to "turn people on."

The best-known goal is university reform because it is closest to the student's scholastic life. This call for reform first received nationwide publicity during the 1964 student demonstrations in Berkeley, California.[4]

The ferment began on 16 September 1964 when the Dean of Students sent a letter to all student political organizations announcing that the "Bancroft Strip"—not a dance craze but a piece of real estate 26 by 40 feet long—could no longer be used to advocate political views. The letter went on to say that the tables set up on the "Strip" created a hazard to pedestrian traffic streaming in and out of the university. Advocacy of both political actions and views had been a traditional activity, and the students felt that this new rule was a restriction on their freedom of speech.

Within no time at all a picket line was thrown up in protest. Delegations from a "united front" of student organizations met with administration officials to seek the removal of the ban. Neither side would back down. Charges and countercharges soon were flying back and forth. Within a few days tables had been set up in defiance of the order.

On 30 September eight students were suspended for violating the ban. This provoked a sit-in of five hundred students in Sproul Hall, the administration building. It lasted into the early morning of the next day.

A "Free Speech" rally was scheduled to be held in front of Sproul Hall on 1 October, once again in defiance of the rule. One individual, a nonstudent named Jack Weinberg, was arrested for "trespassing" and for advocating political views at a nearby table. He was taken to a police car parked at the foot of Sproul Hall steps in the center of the plaza. Before it could be driven away a crowd of some three thousand students surrounded the car and refused to let it leave. Mario Savio, a straight-A philosophy student, jumped to the top of the car and held the rally as scheduled. The Free Speech Movement was born, and it had found its leader.

The crowd remained around the car until the evening of the next day. A marathon rally was held, the speakers and folk singers haranguing the crowds from the now-flattened police car roof. Eventually the demonstrators dispersed when the FSM leaders, the faculty and the administration agreed to a moratorium on further protests, a review of the cases of the eight suspended students, the creation of an ad hoc student-faculty-administration committee to discuss all aspects of political behavior on the campus and its control.

By this time Californians woke up to realize that they had a student revolt on their hands. What had started as a family quarrel now had become a national issue: who was to run the universities, the critics cried, the students or the administration? There were cries in the press of "riot," "communism," "mob rule" and "anarchy." The plaza in front of Sproul Hall was nicknamed "Red Square" by one newspaper. William Knowland's very conservative *Oakland Tribune* laid the blame for what seemed to be capitulation in the face of student unrest to the university's president at the time, Clark Kerr. "A once glorious name and tradition," read one article, "a hundred years in the building, have been damaged by the indecision and vacillation of one person."

Because concessions had been granted, the Free Speech Movement almost died out at this point. But it was rescued by the end of that November when the eight suspended students were given harsher punishments by the university's Board of Regents than the faculty committee had recommended. Some eight hundred students, led by Savio and folk-singer Joan Baez, staged a sit-in in Sproul Hall in protest on 2 December. The university authorities and Governor Brown sent the police in to clear the area. All the demonstrators, most of whom "went limp" at the sight of the police, were carted off to detention centers.

This action by the authorities created a surge of sympathy for the demonstrators. Many members of the faculty, wavering between loyalty to the students and the administration, threw their support to the students. Most of the bail money, for instance, was collected by the faculty; they circulated a resolution calling for the limitation of political actions only with regard to "time, place and matter," later accepted in part by the university.

A student strike was called that was to last nearly a week. It brought the university to a virtual standstill. Savio best reflected the mood of the demonstrators when he spoke to them in Sproul Hall before they were taken away into custody. He said:

> There is a time when the operation of the machine becomes so odious, makes you so sick at heart that you can't take part; you can't even tacitly take part, and you've got to put your bodies upon the levers, upon all the apparatus, and you've got to make it stop. And you've got to indicate to the people who run it, to the people who own it, that unless you're free, the machine will be prevented from working at all.

On 7 December, President Clark Kerr addressed sixteen thousand students and faculty in the Greek Theatre in an attempt to restore "peace and decency" to the campus. A compromise had been worked out, by no means satisfactory to all, calling for lawful procedures in the settlement of issues, the creation of new and liberal political rules, no academic punishment for the eight hundred demonstrators and an end to the student strike.

Savio, dissatisfied with the agreement, sat close to the stage shouting "hypocrite!" at Kerr. Later the FSM leader rushed to the platform to speak but was restrained.

From that day on, the Berkeley demonstrations lost any coherence they ever had. Other questions had by this time become intertwined with the one over advocacy. Students demanded that they have a wider range of subject choice, that they determine what is taught, that the university take a stand on Vietnam and sexual freedom, and that other rules on other subjects be changed, liberalized or abolished. A Dirty Speech Movement was created by a confused student who missed the point of the demonstrations. He arrived one day on campus carrying a large sign saying, "FUCK." He was arrested and within a matter of hours a Fuck Defense Committee had been formed. It was, however, soon to fade into obscurity along with many other groups of this nature. In fact the Free Speech Movement collapsed in 1965, giving way to another organization, the Free Student Union, created to provide a wider base for university protests. This organization never got off the ground.

A number of points need to be clarified. First of all, the demonstrations were not "riots" as they are so glibly referred to today. There were shows of force by the police, mass protests by the students, a little rough stuff here and there, but none of the activities got out of hand. Secondly, the "united front" of student organizations was composed of pro-Goldwater groups as well as radical leftists. It was only after the large Sproul Hall sit-in that the conservatives backed off, passing full leadership to Mario Savio and his group. Thirdly, the protest was not a call for revolution; indeed, it originally stood firmly for the status quo. Only later when other issues were brought forth did it seem like a revolution. Furthermore, the demonstrations were not dominated by any political group. There was a clutch of Marxists hovering around the leadership, some of whom were Communists. But the vast majority were only vaguely radical, honestly concerned with the problem of free speech at the university.

After all the commotion, then, who won? The only answer is

nobody. Clark Kerr, one of the ablest university administrators in the country, oversaw an educational system that spends nearly $500 million a year, employs 40,000 people, and teaches 10,000 courses to 100,000 students. He came out of the fracas with his composure ruffled and his university being subjected to a wave of criticism from the press, alumni, faculty and public. (The reasons for his abrupt dismissal in 1967 by the university Regents can be traced back directly to the 1964 demonstrations.) The student agitators did not win because they failed to achieve many of their objectives. Even today the local radicals still argue among themselves about exactly what they did achieve. It should also always be borne in mind that, at the very height of the demonstrations, never more than one third of the 26,000 Berkeley students were involved. Of those, a considerable number dropped out as the heat became more intense, leaving a hard core of 3,000 activists. But then there have *always* been 3,000 or so radicals on the Berkeley campus. These people are so quick to demonstrate that they are known as "the instant 3,000."

It is evident that the demonstrations were caused by more deep-seated complaints than advocacy on the "Bancroft Strip." Like the main body of New Left radicals, these protesters were expressing a frustration with an educational system that, because of its size, dehumanizes the individual. They were reacting to the impersonality of the institution whose instructors know them only by seat number, where classes are conducted by teaching assistants, where professors are nearly impossible to visit, where the professor himself often flees to the quiet of his home, hastening to publish lest he perish. "My mind is *not* the property of this university!" read one popular sign used during the demonstrations. "Shut this factory down!" read another. In the words of one commentator, these students had an "urge to be heard above the whirring of the machine." Such was the mood that prompted the Berkeley demonstrations of 1964.

The largest and most influential of all the New Left groups is the Students for a Democratic Society. It originally was the youth section of the League for Industrial Democracy, itself an amalgam of labor union and Socialist Party activists founded in 1905 by Jack London, Clarence Darrow, Upton Sinclair and others.

During the years 1960–1961 SDS fought with the League over whether students should take part in direct action protests. By 1962 SDS had won the battle in favor of activism; the League recanted and let the students operate on their own. Addressograph plates, files and the offices of SDS, confiscated by the parent organization during the argument, were returned at this time. SDS only formally severed relations with the League in 1965 in order to protect the League's tax-free status.

In 1962 SDS was composed primarily of young intellectuals, perhaps one thousand in all, scattered around the country. They produced research and political statements; they emphasized the economic side of the civil rights movement; they stressed the need for a domestic social movement as the most effective way to bring about a change in American political attitudes; and they talked vaguely of peace and university reform. By 1964 SDS had come to realize that, in order to help the dispossessed in America, rank-and-file organizations had to be developed. It created ten Economic Research and Action Projects in as many cities—the most prosperous being in Newark, New Jersey—in which the poor were organized for community action. These groups—in which the poor are encouraged to stand on their own feet—form an important cornerstone of SDS's activities today.

To the surprise of its own members SDS grew phenomenally in 1965 and 1966 and continues to grow at a rapid pace today. Much of this growth is due to the Vietnam War. SDS has turned its attention almost exclusively to this issue; the 17 April 1965 "March on Washington to End the War in Vietnam," for instance, in which some 25,000 people turned out, was sponsored by the organization. It has played a leading role in virtually every other war protest to date.

But the growth stems from other sources of discontent as well. One source is known as the "alienated youth culture" or the "campus underclass," a social phenomenon among young people who express little sympathy for the world in which they live. They have flocked to SDS and, according to Paul Booth, a former national secretary, the result has been that SDS "has become *the* instrument for a new radicalism—not necessarily *left,* but *radical* —which is what SDS wants to be." Currently there are over 100 SDS chapters through out the country with perhaps 8,000 activists. The organization operates on an annual budget of $250,000.

Carl Oglesby, a past president of SDS and highly regarded by everyone in the organization, gives his reasons why it has grown. SDS, he said, "is intentionally ambiguous. People do not want to oppress others with their views. We are realistic enough to know that there are not enough concrete problems that are clear." Oglesby, a bearded playwright who looks somewhat like D. H. Lawrence in his middle years, is one of the few SDSers who comes from a blue-collar background. He is a graduate of the University of Michigan, an occasional painter and a night owl who does not like to get up before noon.

This ambiguity has created a nonexclusive organization. Anyone can join, no questions are asked. (Previous references in SDS's Constitution barring "advocates and apologists" of totalitarianism and opposing "authoritarian movements both of communism and the domestic right" have been deleted because these sections were "negative and exclusionary" and "smacked of Red baiting"). A number of philosophical strains have appeared as a result, none of them dominant. The most obvious one is an anti-bureaucratic anarchism that rails against the injustices of a centralized government. SDS directs its fire, for instance, against the "welfare state," which its members hate. They feel that the government imposes its own rules of behavior on the poor which, rather than freeing a man from dependence on others, guarantees that he remains a public ward. "We feel people must get together," said Oglesby, "and form democratic institutions and become involved in their own destinies." The SDS slogan—"Let the people decide"—is one way this sentiment is expressed. Paul Booth puts it another way: "People should have control over the decisions that affect their lives," he told me.

SDS is the only left-wing group to emerge since World War II that is distinctly libertarian in attitude. Every other group has followed the bureaucratic tendencies of the CPUSA and the Trotskyists—with a rigid power structure and narrowly defined dogma. Not SDS: it is intentionally free and easy with its definitions, it deemphasizes titles and organizational structure. Because it is the only group on the left (outside of the anarchists, of course) which is not asking for more government controls, many young radicals have flocked to the cause, having always been uneasy over the rigidity and destructive tendencies of the other groups. Although it often talks of "the people," SDS in reality is concerned about the individual and his values.

This attitude, at first glance, sounds like something out of the pages of William Buckley's *National Review*. Clark Kissinger, for one, believes that there are some similarities between the libertarian left and right. "The Young Americans for Freedom and SDS in debates," he said, "can come to some agreement as to the structure of a particular problem—although they may disagree how it got there and how it should be solved; but SDS finds it has virtually no rapport with those in the government because they— government people—look at a problem through an entirely different rationale."

Another strain is a humanistic belief that one must organize to change individual values rather than the institutions of society. If the values are changed, so the reasoning goes, then the institutions will eventually change. SDS puts this idea to work in its slum projects, combining it with its efforts to organize the poor. Because SDS is anti-authoritarian it does not, like CORE, for instance, go into a community with a predetermined program; but through give-and-take debate, it hopes a plan of action that the people themselves want will emerge. How successful SDS has been with its community action projects is difficult to say. There have been no clear-cut victories nor any resounding defeats. Not enough time has elapsed for a clear picture to emerge.

Its hostility to existing institutions includes the political world as well. Here again SDS is vague. On the one hand, SDS is very political, being concerned with virtually every problem that faces America today. Yet one member, Richard Rothstein, a Harvard graduate and Fulbright scholar, can say: "We reject the idea that you can bring change through getting elected to the legislature and then handing down change from the top. Somehow, under that system, the poor still get treated poorly."[5] Paul Booth is one who realizes that SDS will eventually have to come to terms with the political system. "We must turn our attention to radical political education," he told me. "We would like to set up an independent political group; whether this evolves into a third party or not is not yet decided."

There are other strains besides anarchism, humanism, a dedication to community action and participatory democracy. Most members believe in nonviolence and are committed to equality for all Americans; others have an obsession against manipulating others or being manipulated themselves; a small group express nothing more than a frenzied rebellion, more noticeable on the West Coast than the East, that has neither direction nor purpose. Many seem to have an almost religious or mystical feeling about the poor, believing that because the poor are powerless they possess inherent goodness.

The closest thing SDS has to a policy is their Port Huron Statement, drawn up on 1962 by Tom Hayden, Al Haber and others during the organization's fight with the League for Industrial Democracy. ". . . We seek the establishment of a democracy of individual participation," it states, "governed by two central aims: that the individual share in those social decisions determining the quality and direction of his life; that society be organized to encourage independence in men and provide the media for their common participation. . . ."

The document goes on to recount the "paradoxes and myths" of the economy: a "remote-controlled" octopus where "the wealthiest 1 percent of Americans own more than 80 percent of the personal shares of stock"; the military-industrial complex that believes in "the permanent war economy"; automation that destroys "whole categories of work," forcing up unemployment to an "acceptable" five million; and labor, the "countervailing power" against the excesses of big business, itself becoming a part of the establishment. It notes the "inhumanity" of the welfare state, the "lunacy" of our deterrence policy, the "negative anti-Communist political stance" of our foreign policy, our "paranoia" about the Soviet Union, and "white American ethnocentrism" as a barrier to racial understanding.

According to the Statement what is needed is obvious: universally controlled disarmament and the creation of a world in which hunger, poverty, disease, ignorance, violence and exploitation are replaced by abundance, reason, love and international cooperation. Private enterprise, it goes on to say, is not up to the job of industrializing the world; it should be the preserve of the federal government. America should no longer aid "corrupt anti-Communist regimes." "To support dictators like Diem while trying to destroy ones like Castro," says the Statement, "will only enforce international cynicism about American 'principle.' . . ." Foreign aid should be given through international agencies, and we Americans should "anticipate more or less authoritarian variants of socialism and collectivism in many emergent societies." America should abolish its political party "stalemate" and create "mechanisms of voluntary association" which will encourage the people to participate in political activities. Finally "America should . . . abolish squalor, terminate neglect, and establish an environment for people to live in with dignity and creativeness."

SDS's strongest hold on the young stems from this nonrestrictive aspect of its vision. Unlike such groups as the Vietnam Day Committee, whose eyes are riveted on the war in Asia, SDS sees all problems as interrelated. None, they will tell you, can be separated out and solved independently of the whole. "The League for Industrial Democracy and SANE," said Albert Maher, "believe in putting forward clear, single programs of primary importance. SDS on the other hand will say 'No! Vietnam, for instance, cannot be separated out of context from other problems of the world.'" Maher is a lanky fellow, a Harvard graduate who is currently teaching at a well-known New England university. He is one of the wealthiest members of SDS, his father being a millionaire Houston industrialist. His brother-in-law is Levi Laub of the pro-Maoist Progressive Labor Party; Maher himself is a Cuba-trip veteran, a former member of the May 2nd Movement who considers himself to be an anarcho-communist.

He continued his point. SDS, he said, "takes the long-range outlook, the global approach. We realize that problems cannot be solved at once or unilaterally. It must be done slowly over a long period of time."

Oglesby agrees with Maher but puts it differently: "War is a product of America," he said. The Vietnam war "is not 'Mc-Namara's' or 'LBJ's' war but America's, an expression of imperialism." Oglesby, however, does not absolve the President of the United States. He sees a particular hardness in President Johnson's attitude toward the war. "LBJ's imagination," he said, "is not excited by what he might get out of the conference table. He takes considerable pleasure out of the map rooms, pointers, computers, 'war toys,' etc. LBJ is a violent individual," he concluded. Oglesby is particularly upset that the war-making decision is no longer in the hands of Congress and the President. "Primary research is necessary to find out who actually makes policy," he said, adding that the "cloak of anonymity" that surrounds the decision-making process is a potential danger.

Yet no matter how broad the scope of SDS's outlook may be, it always seems to come back to the complaint that America is deceitful, shallow and immoral. For instance, the uproar that followed the 1965 anti-Vietnam statements of Julian Bond, a young SNCC worker who was denied his seat in the Georgia legislature because of his views, is proof enough to Oglesby how two-faced Americans can be. "It is very revealing of liberals," he said. "They are saying, in effect: 'Nigger, you're talking out of turn; you can only speak on civil rights issues!' But when Martin Luther King spoke out on Vietnam there was no wild reaction."

"This generation," said Jeffrey Shero, an SDS vice-president, "has witnessed hypocrisy as has no other generation. The churches aren't doing what they should be doing. There is lie after lie on television. The whole society is run and compounded on lies. We are the first generation that grew up with the idea of annihilation. In a situation like this, you have to go out and form your own religion."

"What kind of a system is it that leaves millions upon millions throughout the country impoverished and excluded from the mainstream and the promise of American society," asked a former SDS President, Paul Potter, with considerable passion; "that creates faceless and terrible bureaucracies in which people spend their lives and do their work, that consistently puts material values before human values—and still persists in calling itself free and still persists in finding itself fit to police the world?

"What place is there for ordinary men in that system and how are they to control it, make it bend itself to their wills, rather than bending them to its? We must name it, describe it, analyze it, understand it and change it," he cried.[6]

Headquarters for the group was, until recently, a ragged suite of offices in a Negro section of Chicago. Elevated trains rumbled by at window level. Signs on the walls expressed the sentiments of the workers: "Chief Parker must *GO!*" read one; "President Ho Chi Minh sends New Year Message to the American people . . . ," "Burn, Baby, Burn!" and "Our neighbor was beaten bloody at Klein's. Don't buy from Klein's. It could happen to *you!*" When I was there a number of young students wandered in and out, a few were dressed flamboyantly, most of them not. The place hummed with activity; each of the four or five offices had someone inside stapling, folding, typing or talking.

From here all SDS activities were coordinated. (In 1967 new offices were acquired in Chicago's Skid Row section.) The organization has since given up running its own Vietnam protest demonstrations as too time-consuming. All antiwar activities are now run by Frank Emspak of the National Coordinating Committee. This leaves SDS free to do other things. Yet SDS's activities often seem uncoordinated and random efforts which have no particular goals in mind. "SDS stumbles upon a sensitive spot by chance," said Carl Oglesby, "and produces a reaction far out of proportion to its size. This is not planned as some say." But Oglesby sees some inherent benefit from these random attacks. "This stumbling," he said, "should be increased with the hope that more nerves will be hit."

This random approach takes SDS far afield: it supported the Berkeley Free Speech Movement, its members organized a sitdown in late 1965 in front of a troop train in Oakland (the protesters were routed by a blast of steam), it has led numerous student strikes and boycotts, it is in the forefront of the sexual freedom fight, it supports the Deacons for Defense and attacks Bayard Rustin as an "Uncle Tom," it has promoted a plan to clog the draft machinery with a booklet called "How to Cool the Military," it advocates "intelligence" work within defense plants to determine "when and where strategic materials were being produced and transported . . . ," and its members are some of the brains behind the activities of the Vietnam Day Committee and SNCC.

In keeping with the anarchic character of SDS, all activities are carried out at the whim of the individual or group. What this portends for the future is unclear. Some, such as Oglesby, believe that groping in this manner is vital, yet at the same time many SDSers seem to have a nostalgia for pure research. But this they realize would stifle action—to which they are dedicated—and would ensure the death of the movement. Albert Maher sees the possibility of SDS becoming "the anti-imperialist wing of the peace movement"; others see the necessity of linking their uncoordinated activities to their vague philosophies so that the movement will "become whole"; still others believe that it is vital that SDS avoid being absorbed by the liberal left during these formative years. As a natural consequence of time, many of the older leaders, particularly those pushing the dreaded age of thirty, realize that an adult group must be formed which can draw to it as wide a variety of people as, say, Mass Pax did during the H. Stuart Hughes senatorial campaign of 1962. In this regard, there has been some talk of changing the word "Students" in their title to "Movement." Undoubtedly this will be done before long.

Where that movement will go is moot at the moment; undoubtedly it will grow.

2

The Progressive Labor Party is known by other members of the New Left as the "glandular Marxists" or the "Mao now crowd." According to one campus radical they are "the real swinging cats. . . . They smoke pot, do what they please, say what they please. They've got the best-looking women on the left. . . ." One PLP leader lives on New York's lower East Side with a blond and beautiful heiress whom the admiring rank and file describe as "a real reefer-smoking chick."[7] These people read far-out poetry, take to beards and long hair, hang around the coffeehouses and scare the wits out of other Marxists with their revolutionary talk.

There are some twelve hundred members of PLP. Most are under the age of twenty-five. Approximately one quarter of the entire membership is Negro and Puerto Rican. New York, San Francisco and the Bay area are Party strongholds with lesser "clubs" in Portland, Seattle, Atlanta and Boston. The Party publishes a monthly organ, *Progressive Labor;* a theoretical journal, *Marxist-Leninist Quarterly;* an East Coast English-Spanish newspaper, *Challenge-Desafio;* and a West Coast paper, *Spark.*

Progressive Labor—then known as a Movement—was founded in 1961 by a group of Communists who had been thrown out of the CPUSA. The expulsions heralded the creation in American Marxist circles of a miniature Sino-Soviet split: the dissidents claimed that the CPUSA was a "revisionist" group bent on peaceful coexistence with the West; the Moscow-leaning CPUSA retorted that those expelled were "pro-Mao" and "agents of the Albanian party."

PLP literature is straight Mao. It calls for a "struggle on whatever level and with whatever forms are necessary . . . against the gas-chamber plans of this country's ruling class"; it calls for pulling the "nuclear teeth" of the U.S. "paper tiger"; it likens Watts to a "strategic hamlet" from which the "occupation troops" should be withdrawn; it demands that the government "be smashed and . . . replaced by a workers' government," noting ominously that, because of the possibility of a capitalist backlash, the workers "may be forced to defend themselves." The PLP stalwarts claim that they themselves are prepared to suffer "gestapo-style raids," frame-ups, physical assault and even assassination in order to bring down the hated capitalists. The fight, they add, will be long and hard, "the kings, queens and bishops of modern finance capital" will use, they are convinced, every form of violence to hold onto their "stolen" wealth. "Surrender is a word we will not know . . . for from the very flames of our fight . . . a new society shall be built . . . a world of revolutionary socialism. To this end, we here resolve to give our every energy, our resources, and our lives."[8]

The goal of the Party is nothing short of being a "vanguard . . . capable of leading millions directly." It also calls for a $2.00 minimum wage, eight hours pay for six hours of work, a police review board, unarmed policemen who must live where they work, the end of all sales taxes and free medical treatment for dope addicts. Internal discipline is strict: gossip is discouraged, factions and cliques are not tolerated. Jargon is mid-1930s in flavor: "democratic centralism," "the class character of the state," "the defeat of bourgeois ideology," etc. "The Party," said one leader, "must become first and foremost in our lives." Slogans run to the Chinese Communist variety, reflecting all their dissatisfaction with the division of world power: "GI'S IN VIETNAM SAY: GET THE HELL OUT!" is a typical one.

The Party leaders are surly, militant and uncooperative. They shun interviews and more often than not avoid the demonstrations they send their janissaries to join.

Milton Rosen, the Party's chairman, is a forty-one-year-old Brooklynite, the son of a garment worker. He fought in Italy during World War II and joined the CPUSA upon his discharge. He was influenced in his decision to join, he says, by the Italian Communist Party. He still affects the ex-GI's postwar uniform of sports coat, khaki trousers and white shirt. During the Harlem riots of 1964 he urged city-wide riots, "to spread the police thin."[9] Mort Sheer is the West Coast organizer. He was kicked out of the CPUSA along with Rosen; they had proposed, among other things, that the Party go underground, which the CPUSA leaders rejected.

Fred Jerome is the editor of *Challenge*. He is the son of V. J. Jerome, a long-time American Communist. His mother, Alice Jerome, is the chairman of the Integrated Workers Branch of PLP. Jerome himself graduated with a Phi Beta Kappa key from City College of New York in 1960 and soon thereafter joined the CPUSA. He spent eight months in Cuba during 1960–1961. "That, more than anything else," he said, "made me feel emotionally that it was necessary and possible to make a revolution."[10]

Two other leaders in the Party are Levi Laub and, as noted previously, Albert Maher. Laub is one of PLP's leading theoreticians. "When you first meet him it's deceptive," says a PLP stalwart. "He looks like an escapee from Zeta Beta Tau. He wears these vests and this big camel's-hair coat, incredibly clean cut, very Tab Hunterish, very all-American. Then you discover that he is a brilliant student of socialism and Jewish history, that he has this really big head."[11]

Albert Maher, the son of Houston petroleum toolmaker John F.

"Big John" Maher, had until recently been occupied with the affairs of the May 2nd Movement, a PLP front. Since that has been dissolved he has presumably moved back into the PLP. Maher is one of the Party's biggest contributors. It was he, for instance, who put up the $10,000 bond for Bill Epton when he was jailed in 1964 on charges of criminal anarchy. "I use my resources to help causes I think are correct," he said.

Epton, the Party's vice-chairman and its star political attraction, is a tall, handsome Negro, a Korean veteran and an electrician by trade. He, too, was thrown out of the CPUSA at the same time Rosen and Sheer were expelled. Until recently, Epton was PLP's Harlem organizer, operating out of a Lenox Avenue office above a barbershop, next door to a business specializing in "Mystic Readings."

He also ran the Harlem Defense Council, another PLP front. This organization published a "Wanted for Murder" poster, featuring a picture of policeman Thomas Gilligan, the one who shot and killed fifteen-year-old Negro schoolboy James Powell. This act allegedly triggered the 1964 Harlem riots (in which the Defense Council was subsequently involved). Gilligan was exonerated in both grand jury and departmental investigations, which held that he had shot the boy in self-defense after being attacked with a knife. The policeman later initiated a $5,250,000 libel suit, still pending, against the Defense Council, Martin Luther King and other civil rights leaders, alleging that he had been falsely accused of murder by them.

Epton was convicted in late 1965 of conspiring to riot, of advocating the overthrow of the New York State government and of conspiring to overthrow it. He was sentenced to one year in prison. The charges grew out of the Harlem riots of 1964 in which Epton, in a street-corner speech, is reported to have said:

> We will take our freedom. We will take it by any means necessary. . . . We will create a new government. . . . And in the process of smashing the state, we are going to have to kill a lot of these cops, a lot of these judges, and we'll have to go up against their army. We'll organize our own militia and our own army.[12]

One group of PLP critics believe that the organization was actually looking for a conviction of this sort in order to have a martyr, particularly a Negro martyr. PLP member Ed Lemanski, the only one I had a chance to talk with in the Party for more than a few seconds, dismissed such an idea with contempt. "The ruling class will give us enough martyrs," he said. "We don't have to go looking for them." On the other hand, Conrad Lynn, the radical Negro who had once been the Party's lawyer, sees a much more complicated factor. He believes that the CPUSA was behind Epton's conviction, pulling the strings in such a way that Epton's credibility as a true revolutionary was called into question. This, Lynn said, destroyed PLP's authority among left-wing radicals, thus eliminating the Party as competition to the CPUSA. "I charge that the Communist Party was *that* ruthless," Lynn told me; "that they knew *exactly* what they were doing by destroying the moral authority of PLP! I'm sorry for Bill," he went on, "because his credibility has been destroyed." Whether this is actually the case is impossible to prove, since everyone involved, Lynn included, has his own particular axe to grind.

Despite all this noise, PLP has not yet shot anyone. In a 1965 *Saturday Evening Post* issue, Phillip Abbott Luce, a young radical, wrote an article, "Why I quit the Extreme Left," in which he accused PLP, to which he had belonged, of several political indiscretions, namely sedition, the practicing of violent defense techniques such as karate and judo, the stockpiling of arms and supplies in New York City and the conducting of rifle practice on Long Island. PLP is suing Luce and the magazine. From all other reports PLP is revolutionary but not *that* revolutionary. It talks loudly of revolution and it will aggravate problems whenever it believes it advantageous to do so, but there is little public evidence today that PLP has crossed the boundary into the realm of outlaws. It is acknowledged by PLP that all its phones are probably tapped and that there are undercover FBI agents within the group. These infiltrators, claims Fred Jerome, are easily spotted because they are "supermilitants trying to urge us into something they could trap us for."

Nevertheless, PLP still talks tough. Ed Lemanski, for instance, a big, strapping fellow who seemed to pride himself on being "hip," told me: "We will come to power through violence and the ballot, but the emphasis is on violence." No one, he added, "is nonviolent anymore, not even the nonviolent civil rights movement. Violence is necessary and there is no point kidding people. We are not terrorists, we are not assassins, but we do believe in fighting." Lemanski admitted that he has on occasion carried a gun and that he is very pro-Deacons for Defense. He claims he has been in jail four times, the longest term for three months. He complained that over one hundred PLP members have been arrested and convicted of various offenses. "We weren't guilty of anything," he said. "This is not a persecution complex; that's just the way the game is played here."

On many issues Lemanski was quite vague, almost conspiratorial. However, his reluctance to talk extensively seemed to stem less from an unwillingness to impart PLP secrets to outsiders than from his attitude that I would not understand, so why bother to explain it; if it were explained, I would probably get it wrong.

As we parted, I said to him, "I'd like to ring you if there are any questions." He answered, ". . . If I'm out of jail!"

PLP can still cause considerable mischief on the political scene. Besides those examples previously mentioned, one other comes to mind. In 1961 Fred Jerome and Jacob Rosen, Milton's brother, went south. One was hired by the *Augusta* (Georgia) *Chronicle,* the other by the *Augusta Herald.* Jerome called himself Fred Reed; Rosen's alias was John Harnett. As reporters they began to operate beyond the beat set for them by the newspapers. They also bypassed their city editors and sent articles to newspapers outside of Augusta—a sin in journalism. These articles concerned incidents that they themselves helped to create. Jerome and Rosen readily admitted their disloyalty but excused it on the grounds that they disapproved of the newspapers' stance on racial matters. The two were fired but it was more than three years later before the *Chronicle* and *Herald* were to learn that Jerome and Rosen were more than journalists.[13]

What will happen to PLP in the future is anyone's guess. The government authorities have the organization under close scrutiny. Epton's conviction has sobered the group somewhat, and recently there has been a campaign among members to rid the organization of beards and marijuana. Their youth front, the May 2nd Movement, named after a 1964 demonstration of that date, was disbanded in 1966, its members moving directly into the PLP proper. (In the nature of moves such as this, it caused the creation of yet another splinter group, the American Liberation League, whose members did not want to be absorbed by PLP.) All this has produced a falling off of new members, particularly the "swinging chicks" who do much of the monotonous work. Said one young girl in 1965, then under indictment for kicking a policeman in the groin: "They want us to do the typing at the office and hold down the picket lines and—well, you know, do other things as well. They told us we couldn't drink at parties because we were supposed to stay sharp and corral some new boys into the movement. They haven't let one girl into the leadership group at PL. I finally got fed up and I told them, all right, go have your revolution in the little-boys' room."[14]

3

The W. E. B. DuBois Clubs of America is another New Left group, slightly smaller than PLP in membership. The organization was started in 1961 as a local discussion group in California. Three years later it went national and became an activist group. Its major strength today is still centered on the West Coast.

The group takes its name from William Edward Burghardt DuBois, a Negro educator and a lifelong leader in the struggle for Negro rights. He was one of the founders of the NAACP. In 1960 he received a Lenin Prize for "contributions to peace." The following year, at the age of ninety-three, he announced his conversion to communism. Soon thereafter he gave up his American citizenship and became a citizen of Ghana, then ruled by Kwame Nkrumah. DuBois died there in 1963.

The DuBois—pronounced Doo-*Boys*—Clubs* follow a close

* One group to suffer because of the similarity in pronunciations is The Boys' Club of America, a nationwide group that provides recreation, guidance and handicraft instructions to 750,000 boys, seven to seventeen. Former Vice-President Richard M. Nixon, the Club's national chairman, claims that the confusion in names is deliberate on the part of the Communists, "an almost classic example of [their] deception and duplicity."

CPUSA line. Peaceful coexistence, complete disarmament, a fight against the "racist and right-wing forces in coalition with the most reactionary sections of the economic power structure," the abolition of private property and the creation of a socialist state are all advocated. In fact, the lines are so close that J. Edgar Hoover and the Attorney General have labeled the organization as a Communist front and have demanded that it register as such.

Club members vehemently deny that they are CPUSA pawns. For example, Conn "Ringo" Hallinan, one of the leaders of the organization, said, referring to the government's charge, "It is a very nice compliment because it means we're doing something. We are not a CP front, but we have no objections to Communists joining."

In spite of this and other denials, the evidence is weighted fairly heavily in favor of the government's charge. The number of active Communist leaders is impressive. Bettina Aptheker, daughter of Marxist theoretician Herbert Aptheker, is a self-confessed Communist. At one point she was chairman of the DuBois Clubs; recently she has been active in the Vietnam Day Committee. Carl Bloise, editor of the DuBois magazine, *Insurgent,* was formerly a staff reporter for *People's World,* the West Coast CPUSA newspaper. There is Mike Myerson, who once told a reporter: "If it were up to me I would like to see passed a twenty-fifth Amendment to the Constitution abolishing private ownership of property, just as the Fourteenth [actually, the Thirteenth] Amendment abolished private ownership of people." Myerson has traveled without State Department permission to North Vietnam and is one of its most fervent apologists.

There are other indications that the DuBois Clubs are firmly under the thumb of the CPUSA. One of the organizers of the founding convention of the Clubs was Mortimer Daniel Rubin, then the National Youth Director of the CPUSA. Present at the convention was Archie Brown, who has run for office in California as a Communist, and at least four young offspring of old-line CPUSA members. Ringo Hallinan said that the organization's name was chosen because "DuBois himself seemed to sum up what we wanted to be." *The Worker,* never one to give much space to a competitor, felt in one issue that the founding convention was worth forty-three column inches of news. When the CPUSA youth magazine, *New Horizons for Youth,* folded, the DuBois Clubs took over its assets. Even Gus Hall, while not admitting that the Clubs were actual CPUSA fronts, did say "We've got them going for us."

One DuBois coordinator, Robert Heisler, a student in New York City, directly identifies DuBois goals with those of the Soviet Union. Said he: "The Soviet Union and the whole Socialist bloc are on the right track. They have broken loose from some of the basic problems that are at the heart of this country's social system. I don't mean that we're calling for a blueprint, a carbon copy of what they do. But I do believe that the Soviet Union and the Socialist bloc—including the new nations in Africa and Asia—are more on the way to getting this than is the United States at this point."

Because the organization is ideologically and physically close to the CPUSA, its members were considered "squares" by the other more hard-nose radicals. Some claim that the government's attack on them in 1966 has given them status that they ordinarily would not have. Others believe that this persecution has helped their cause, doubling membership figures, for instance (which is doubtful). The authorities know from experience, however, that once a group is officially branded as a CPUSA front, membership falls off and it tends to wither. This has not happened to the DuBois Clubs yet. There have only been two noted setbacks. The Bay area DuBois Clubs have shrunk in size but only because of the activities of the VDC, which many DuBois members have joined. Also, the Venice West Coffee House, a well-known haven for free-thinking, free-living and free-loving souls in southern California, and run by DuBois member John Haag, was closed down by local authorities in 1966. But, on the other hand, the bombing of the Clubs' national headquarters in San Francisco in March 1966 evinced some left-wing sympathy for the groups; likewise, the beatings suffered soon after the bombings by a group of DuBois members in New York City at the hands of some anti-Communists strengthened the resolve of the waverers.

The DuBois Clubs are dominated by the Hallinan brothers of

whom there are six. The father of this brood is Vincent Hallinan, the Progressive Party's Presidential candidate in 1952. Vincent Hallinan is a trial lawyer whose tempestuous legal career has brought him an eighteen-month sentence in McNeil Island Prison for income-tax evasion and a temporary decree striking his name from the list of lawyers licensed to practice in United States courts. He is a non-joiner, an individualist with a flamboyant courtroom style. One of his sons, Ringo, told me proudly that the only type of Marxist his father claims to be is a "Vincent Hallinan Marxist." He added that his father was planning to sue the Catholic Church to make it prove the existence of heaven, hell and purgatory.

Ringo Hallinan is active in DuBois affairs and took part in the Berkeley demonstrations. He lives with his wife and children near the Berkeley campus and is the only left-wing activist I ever visited who had a rifle hanging on the wall. He is a large fellow with reddish hair, an Irish face, a bushy mustache and a ready smile. His five brothers are all active politically and have nicknames such as he. There are Patrick ("Butch"), a lawyer, and Michael ("Tuffy"), once active in Berkeley campus politics. There is Matthew ("Dynamite"), Terence ("Kayo") and Danny ("Dangerous"), all of whom are active in the DuBois Clubs. Ringo told me proudly that Hallinans were chiefs in County Limerick and that his surname means "handsome" in Gaelic.

"We don't have answers in neat packages," Ringo said of the DuBois Clubs. "Part of our philosophy is that we can win things under this society but it will be a long, hard, dirty fight with no easy solutions." He noted that the DuBois Clubs are preoccupied at the moment with the Vietnam War and the recognition of the National Liberation Front. He added that the Clubs prefer the way Senator Fulbright approaches the problem rather than the "impeach LBJ" attitude that others prefer.

On occasion DuBois Clubs turn their attention to other problems: poverty, civil rights, jobs and housing. Most DuBois activities include only demonstrations, picketing and speechmaking. So far very little violence has been laid at their doorstep.

"We are disliked by everyone on the left," Ringo Hallinan said, "but they come to us when they need work to do." There is considerable truth to this remark. In the nearly six years of existence, the sole justification for the DuBois Clubs has been their ability to supply troops in quantity to other organizations when they need them.

One group it has backed and stocked with troops from the start has been the most unstable of New Left groups, the Vietnam Day Committee.

The VDC, as it is known by everyone, is concentrated in the San Francisco Bay area, particularly on the Berkeley campus. It was formed in 1965 and picked up where the Free Speech Movement left off. Virtually every campus left-wing radical is associated with it in one way or another: PLP members belong, so do DuBois members and Trotskyists, Communist Party members and pacifists. It is the home of the nonstudent, that particular breed of individual who hangs around the university long after he has left it (or never made it). It is the home of the LSD users, sexual freedom advocates and wearers of the "anarchist" mustache, a rage among radicals these days.*

The sole objective of the VDC is to protest the American involvement in Vietnam, although Jerry Rubin, one of the founders of the VDC, will tell you that the movement is also concerned with university reform. Its position on Vietnam is hard, uncompromising and anti-American. It calls for the immediate withdrawal of American troops, the recognition of the NLF and the impeachment of President Johnson. It has taken part in virtually every anti-Vietnam War parade; its members are usually the ones carrying the Vietcong flags. In 1966 it backed Robert Sheer as a peace candidate in the Democratic primary against liberal Democrat Jeffrey Cohelan, the incumbent California congressman for the 7th District. Sheer received over 35 percent of the votes. The VDC has sent antiwar literature to soldiers in Vietnam, causing a storm of protest from military commanders, congressmen and

---

* An anarchist mustache looks something like the Buffalo Bill variety: it is a full mustache that hangs over the upper lip and curls around the mouth. Fastidious wearers curl the tips up under the lower lip, others let the points hang down straight. Many radical leaders wear them: Jerry Rubin, Jack Weinberg and Stewart Albert of the VDC, Ringo Hallinan of the Dubois Clubs, Phillip Abbott Luce, formerly of PLP. The fad has spread to SNCC and the peace groups. Said Ringo Hallinan: "It's the kind of mustache Bakunin *should* have worn" (Bakunin was full-bearded).

senators. It has also been accused of making those anonymous telephone calls to widows of servicemen in which the caller gloats over the fact that the man has died.

Some of its followers are vocal supporters of "Granny Goose," the Vietnam War's version of "Axis Sally" or "Tokyo Rose." Granny Goose is the pseudonym for Ronald Ramsey, a twenty-eight-year-old Californian. He has made antiwar radio tapes for broadcast from Hanoi. (Recently Ramsey fled the United States and has been seeking asylum in either England or Czechoslovakia.)

Stewart Albert, a blond, nonstudent VDCer who has attached a beard to his anarchist mustache, sees no difference between the riots of Watts and the war in Vietnam. "Johnson is saying," he told me, " 'You be good niggers and we'll throw a few bucks into the slums and give you a few penny-ante jobs. If not we'll have some Wattses where we'll bust your ass if you don't behave.' We see no difference between that and Vietnam."

The VDC has "style," a very important commodity to the young radical. In fact, its activities, coupled with those of the defunct Free Speech Movement, have created on the Berkeley campus a particular style that is the envy of every other campus. It is expressed in intense, highly emotional, short-range, independent protests, one usually following on top of the other. The radicals there have no permanent commitment to any organization nor to any long-range activities; they float from group to group as the mood or circumstances warrant, adopting the style of the particular group of the moment. The VDC's style is a haranguing one, the DuBois' is more "coalitionist," the Trotskyists are rabble-rousers, and the independent and socialist clubs' and SDS's more intellectual. The combination of styles among all these groups—to say nothing of the right-of-center groups, on the whole less volatile—produces a wild, untamed melee of a bohemian, romantic and permissive character that no other campus can equal. All this is financed by a large number of "radicals in the hills," as they are called, older sympathizers living in the surrounding countryside. The VDC's budget, for instance, is a staggering $100,000 a year, an extraordinary figure for a group with such little overhead and one so tiny in absolute terms. The phenomenon of "the instant

3,000" also ensures that Berkeley campus politics continuously boils and froths.

Any day one can see this style in action. Around noon a rally or protest meeting of one kind or another is held on the steps of Sproul Hall. The Plaza below, flanked by the Commons, Sather Gate and the "Bancroft Strip," is jammed with students, some passing through, others eating lunch, still others manning the fifteen or so political tables. Over on one side is the table of the Sexual Freedom Forum, manned by a weak-eyed girl in blue jeans. A few children stand around snickering. "Legalize Abortion" reads one large sign in front of the table; "No more coat-hangers!" reads the smaller print. On the table there is literature advocating free love, public nudity, legalized prostitution, the repeal of anti-homosexual laws and the free distribution of contraceptives by the university health service. Buttons are sold for twenty-five cents each: "TAKE IT OFF," says one; "I'M WILLING IF YOU ARE," says another; "COPULATE FOR COEXISTENCE," reads a third. The best-known button of the SFF is one that says "MAKE LOVE, NOT WAR." It comes in a variety of colors, sizes and prices. One SFF zealot would, on occasion, hike her skirt over her head and lie bottomside up on the table.

Over in another corner of the plaza is the DuBois Club table, the Trotskyist table and the Cal Conservative table (with a sign advertising "White Backlash" and "Cream of Fluoride" soups). The men behind them sit within six feet of one another but exchange nothing more than frosty glances. Other tables are scattered in other areas of the plaza; knots of bearded youths argue in front of them; few of these people are carrying books. Some of the people are wearing black armbands indicating their displeasure with the Vietnam War. Outside on the "Strip," a white-shirted Fundamentalist preacher, his front teeth missing and seemingly in the last paroxysms of rage, is haranguing an amused crowd over by the student government table.

Up on the Sproul Hall steps Bettina Aptheker is shouting hoarsely into a microphone against some campus rule with which she and the VDC disagree. She is a poor speaker but she is well-known and the radicals show her deference. When she becomes angry her eyes flash, her ponytail flaps back and forth, and flecks of foam appear at the corner of her mouth. Then comes Jerry Rubin or Stewart Albert or Sue Stein or Ringo Hallinan or a striking grape-picker or someone else to harangue the passing crowd. Approximately three hundred people turn up to take part in this particular protest rally; another five hundred or so spectators mill around the fringes. Not all of these people are friendly. A knot of ROTC students in their uniforms look on impassively; some conservatives in the crowd let fly with a few unfriendly remarks. Many people pay no attention at all. "Hey, honey," says one perambulator-pushing student to his wife, "look at this nut," pointing to a demonstrator whose cranial and facial growth is so heavy that it is only his eyeglasses that keep his eyes and nose free of hair. This particular fellow also is wearing a button that says in Chinese: "Liberate the Middle Kingdom."

Eventually the crowd breaks up as a handclapping SNCC worker begins shouting some incoherent song into the microphone. The discussion among the radicals as they leave is over what is happening that night.

The VDC headquarters was, until recently, located within a few blocks of the "Bancroft Strip," in an old frame house with an elderly Wobbly living upstairs. A month after the DuBois headquarters was blown up, the back of this building was demolished by a similarly mysterious bomb burst that sent seven people to the hospital to be treated for cuts inflicted by flying glass. The back had since been repaired and housed the research section. By the front door was a small sign, ridiculing the John Birch campaign, saying, "Support your local anarchist." (When I returned for another visit in the spring of 1967, there was nothing left of the headquarters except a vacant lot. I was told that another bomb had completely destroyed the building.)

The day I was there two fully dressed individuals lay sprawled asleep on the couches in the meeting room, oblivious to the commotion in the back. One fellow's head hung mouth-open over a couch's edge, his lips barely an inch from the rim of a fruit-juice can spittoon.

Jerry Rubin explained that the seeming anarchy and lack of any definite policy are deliberate on the part of the VDC. Power seems to gravitate, he said, to those who assume it for specific purposes.

"The mood and the ferment are important," he added, "and the organization is not." But he does not like the crisis-oriented atmosphere of the VDC because, he says, it argues against strategy and philosophical analysis. He recognizes that the VDC itself will last only as long as the war does, the radicals then moving on to another coalition or back to their old groups. When it comes to university reform, Rubin takes a near-anarchist position. He does not believe, for instance, that the University of California, nor any other university, should have any rules at all governing students. Nor does he believe in diplomas or exams. There is no question that the bulk of the VDC agrees with this point of view.

4

Once one travels past such New Left groups as Students for a Democratic Society, Progressive Labor, the DuBois Clubs and the VDC (plus those New Left groups mentioned elsewhere, such as Spartacist, Workers' World, Revolutionary Action Movement), one enters the world of the *really* minute and unstable organizations. They should be noted if for no other reason than to mark their presence before they pass from the scene.

One of them is Youth Against War and Fascism founded in 1962 to protest the presence of George Lincoln Rockwell as a guest speaker at Hunter College in New York. It grew out of an organization called the Anti-Fascist Youth Committee, made up of young Jews and a few concentration camp survivors. Today the membership of Youth against War and Fascism—perhaps a hundred people—has been broadened to include many Gentiles as well.

It is run by Deirdre Griswold, a young and pretty widow with dimples who bites her nails and crops her hair close. She considers herself a Marxist, and a "hard-liner" at that. But she is quick to say that YAWF is not particularly Marxist. The general consensus among left-wing groups, that her organization is closely tied to the Trotskyist Workers World Party, is also denied by her. She is an editor of YAWF's magazine, *The Partisan,* which is very similar in appearance to the DuBois Clubs' *Insurgent.* Despite what she says, the magazine's political stance is close to that of Workers' World:

it is pro-Vietcong, anti-American, pro-Deacons for Defense, pro-Puerto Rican nationalists and violently anti-police ("only the color of their shirts has changed").

The whole point of the organization, she told me, is to bring the issues that face the nation's youth into the open and to oppose the "fascist tendencies which the Vietnam War has developed." She can, at times, sound a bit like a Birch Society member; for instance, she said, "We believe we know this society and that the dangers to this country come from within." Specifically, the dangers include "the military and industrial complex," the draft and "fascism."

The group's emphasis, she said, was on action—"getting out on the streets!" She went on, "We did not want to be another discussion group; we have no need for bleeding hearts." She prides herself on being able to organize a picket line anywhere in New York City within an hour or less. When I was in her office it had just been announced over the radio that the U.S. Air Force had bombed Haiphong harbor for the first time. When this was reported to her she picked up the phone, dialed a number, gave a few terse orders, and within an hour there were two dozen pickets in Times Square. I asked her if these people just sat around waiting for their marching orders, and she said no, they are mostly students with no classes to attend at that time. She and her followers have also picketed President Johnson and ex-Mayor Robert Wagner's wedding reception. They were also one of the organizers of the "stall-in" around the World's Fair in 1964.

This is not a nonviolent group. "We believe people have to fight and defend themselves," she told me. "We have our own self-defense groups at our meetings." Each issue of *The Partisan,* for instance, is filled with pictures of YAWF stalwarts in fights, in protest meetings, struggling with the police and in jail.

And as to why YAWF is necessary at all, Deirdre Griswold said this: "We want to be sure that when people want to intervene in history and so effect the state they wish to live in, they will have an organization to turn to."

There is another group whose only distinction seems to be that it has the longest name of any American fringe group. It is called the Provisional Organizing Committee to Reconstitute the Marxist-Leninist Communist Party in the United States of America. To the immense relief of those who care, it is otherwise referred to as "POC." This tiny, New York-based group broke away from the CPUSA in 1958. It is Maoist and neo-Stalinist in outlook but refuses for unclear reasons to join with groups pushing a similar line. It is predominantly run by Negro and Puerto Rican Communists. It publishes an eight-page newssheet called *The Marxist-Leninist Vanguard,* which is virtually unobtainable among New Left groups.

An even smaller group is that which revolves around *Red Flag* (formerly *People's Voice*). It is run by a Michael Laski and an Arnold Hoffman, two Communists from Los Angeles. This group is also pro-Mao, pro-Stalin and anti-CPUSA—to say nothing of its anti-American stance. Its crudely published literature features long, dull tomes on its heroes: Marx, Engels, Stalin, Lenin and Mao. The proper title of this organization is perhaps the second longest on the fringe: The Communist Party of the United States of America (Marxist-Leninist). In October 1966, this group's Harlem storefront headquarters was burned down by arsonists. Laski, surveying the wreckage, pointed to a large Red banner with a hammer and sickle hanging in the window. "The flag still flies," he said, "and it will continue to do so."

When I visited this group, the front of the Harlem office had been boarded up against further firebomb attacks. A large picture of Mao Tse-tung dominated one interior wall and pictures of Lenin and Marx were visible on the back wall. ("We're out of Stalins," said Laski apologetically.)

Laski is the type of person who speaks to an individual as if the latter were a crowd. His words pour out with machine-gun rapidity and his hands continually chop away at the air and table in emphasis. His eyes become glazed as his political passion rises, and his voice—when his thoughts excite him—takes on a shrill, metallic quality that is both unnerving and compelling.

He is unabashedly a revolutionary of the Bolshevik stripe. He cannot wait for the day when capitalist blood will run in the streets, and he is convinced that when the revolution comes that it will be "forceful and violent and terroristic." In preparation for that day,

Laski has created a People's Armed Defense Group, a small force of dedicated Marxists, mostly from Harlem and Watts, who have been organized in strict imitation of the Red Guards in China. He proudly showed me the uniform his janissaries wear: green fatigue cap with red star (a painted brigadier's star), green shirt with red collar tabs, black belt and green trousers. In one breast pocket of each shirt is a red plastic-covered copy of "Quotations from Chairman Mao Tse-tung." Laski hastened to add that his force (estimated at from two to forty individuals) are currently used only as a self-defense group. He refused to say with what his men were armed.

The smallest New Left group is the New England Party of Labor which publishes *Hammer and Steel,* a mimeographed sheet that some people believe expresses "pure Maoist views." The man behind the organization is Homer Chase from New Hampshire. He wants to have a hammer and sickle carved on his father's headstone and has been fighting the town fathers for years on this issue. "This headstone seems more important to Homer than anything else," says critic Communist Gus Hall. "But he gets written up by the press as a big factor in the Sino-Soviet split." For once perhaps Gus Hall is right.

Three other New Left impulses should be noted: one is the "free universities," another is "soul sessions" and the third is the unaffiliated newspapers which influence the thoughts of these radicals.

Free universities sprang up as the cry for reform in accredited universities took hold among young student radicals. The number of free universities—also known as "counter-universities" or "anti-universities"—varies from month to month, since their viability is precarious. There have seldom been more than eight in the entire country at any one time. The three most stable ones are the Free University of New York, the New School in San Francisco (run by SDS) and the New Left School of Los Angeles.

These universities are modest in size, often operating out of a loft. The Free University of New York, for instance, has three hundred students and thirty-nine professors. Three on the faculty are Milton Rosen of the Progressive Labor Party, Dave McReynolds of the War Resisters League and James Mellen, a political science instructor at Drew University. Tuition is nominal, seldom running past twenty-four dollars for a ten-week course. Students usually attend these classes outside the hours of their regular university classes.

The impetus for these free universities stems from some students' disenchantment with what they call the regimented, stifling, dehumanized and uncreative aspects of a large university. This, they say, results in their being "exploited." In order to free themselves, the creators of these universities have drawn up their own lists of courses, considered taboo at established universities. Typical courses at the Free University of New York include: "Life in Mainland China Today," "Hallucinogenic Drugs: Use and Social Implications," "Search for the Authentic Sexual Experience," "Marxism and American Decadence" and "How the *New York Times'* Straight Approach to the News is Funnier than *Mad Magazine*'s Self-conscious Approach to Boffo Laughs." These universities show no inclination to seek accreditation, nor do they seek the right to grant degrees or credits for these courses.

Paradoxically, these free universities are more confining than the accredited institutions which the radicals attack. The complaint, for instance, that only one-sided and slanted courses are offered by other universities is not ameliorated by their own curriculum. The range of free university courses is far more narrow and confining than anything offered elsewhere. It is a sign of the times, apparently, that these free universities—with all their anti-organization, anti-establishment attitudes—still feel compelled to operate under the corporate label of a university, complete with the old patterns of lectures, seminars, professors and students.

In many ways these universities resemble the radical bull-sessions of the 1930s whose members met in coffeehouses and private homes to discuss their unacceptable ideas. They seem more like an aberration on the politico-educational scene, and it is doubtful that they will have any effect at all on the accredited institutions.

A "soul session" is a private gathering of people—up to twenty or more—in which the participants believe that only through baring one's soul can people come to understand one another. It has grown out of the New Left and civil rights movements as a reaction to the very act of protesting. Says Ray Robinson, Jr., a tall Negro who started the movement in late 1965, "Picketing and demonstrations will not end the war in Vietnam. I'm sick of walking and being in jail. The people don't hear us cry out in jail. We've got to show the people the only way is love. . . . We've got to talk to each other about our pain and how it hurts us and let the tears come out. We've got to cry out to each other about our pain."

The sessions have all the earmarks of a Quaker Meeting combined with intensive group psychotherapy. People speak as they wish and are not interrupted until they are through. Very personal emotions are aired, usually about life, love, sex, hate, war, peace and President Johnson. All this is taken down on a tape recorder to be replayed at a later date. Sessions sometimes run for twenty-four hours with no break except for sandwiches, coffee and cigarettes.

The leaders of this amorphous, nameless, memberless movement travel about the country inviting people to "blow some soul" with them. SNCC, SDS, Quakers and some other groups often lend their premises for these sessions.

One advocate of soul sessions, a member of SNCC, was discussing on the Sproul Hall steps the advantages of such meetings with a Berkeley radical. I was listening in. His whole argument revolved around the thesis that there is always a wall of silence— or at least some lack of communication—between one man and another. In order to knock down this wall, he said, it is necessary for both men to bare their hearts to each other. Once this is done then all antagonisms, suspicions, misunderstandings and prejudices will vanish, and the two men can then start working for a common goal. Because this particular advocate was a Negro, he stressed how important it was that whites understand how a Negro feels and vice versa. The campus radical replied that his own white skin was something he was born with but that it did not preclude his trying to understand. The Negro replied that that was good but not good enough. "Only soul sessions can solve the problem," he said.

The final impulse worth noting on the New Left is the unaffiliated newspapers and magazines that influence the young radicals. No complete list can be given since so many of them come and go so quickly. However, there are some publications that seem more semipermanent and carry more weight than others.

One of the most influential is *National Guardian,* an "independent radical left" weekly newspaper with a circulation of 27,000. Its editor was, until recently, James Aronson, a Harvard graduate who has been in the newspaper business for twenty-eight years. He wrote for *The New York Times, Post, Herald Tribune* and several other papers before helping to found the *Guardian* in 1948. His newspaper has seldom taken a stance on any particular dogma other than to be fervently, but obscurely, socialist. The masthead lists as correspondents Wilfred Burchett, who covered the Korean War from the Sino-Korean side; Anna Louise Strong, a well-known pro-communist writer who now lives in Peking; and Cedric Belfrage who, in 1962, was listed as "editor-in-exile" in Havana. In late April 1967 Aronson and Belfrage resigned after a dispute over editorial policy. At this writing, no successors have been named.

Aronson says he tried to give coverage to all aspects of the radical movement in America. In the process, he usually antagonized nearly everyone on the left, because if a smaller group was given more coverage in any particular issue, then the larger groups were angered. Nevertheless, the paper is still read avidly by everyone on the left, if for nothing else but to see what the competition is doing.

Monthly Review is edited by Paul Sweezy, who once taught economics at Harvard, and by Leo Huberman, who taught economic history at Columbia. This magazine is definitely Marxist in outlook and sells 16,000 copies per month, over one quarter of which go overseas, mostly to the underdeveloped nations. It also publishes a Spanish edition in Argentina. *Review* recently came out in favor of the Chinese position in the Sino-Soviet dispute, arguing that although anyone would prefer to settle things peaceably, sometimes violence is necessary. The CPUSA is considered fairly right wing; the magazine believes that America is stagnant and that socialism is the trend of the future.

One of the fastest growing publications particularly favored by the New Left is *Ramparts,* a slick monthly whose hallmarks are controversy and iconoclasm. It was established in 1962 by real-estate investor Edward M. Keating. The San Francisco-based magazine claims a circulation of 150,000 and operates on a budget of $600,000, yet still loses money. One of the staff writers is Robert Sheer, the unsuccessful peace candidate for Congress.

The magazine has attacked the Catholic Church and the Warren Commission, it has supported ecumenicalism and Senator Fulbright, and it has exposed CIA cover projects at Michigan State University and within the National Student Association. It is definitely against America's position in Vietnam. American soldiers stationed there, according to one writer, are "Russian tanks blasting the hopes of an Asian Hungary." The June 1965 issue carried a series of articles on the Selma-to-Montgomery march. The "Battle of Selma," as the issue was called, featured elaborate battle maps showing "the charge of the bible brigade," "the battle of the bridge" and the "grouping of forces on Sylvan Street and Revolt of Jeunesse." Military symbols were used to indicate "platoons of Sheriff's men," the "Union position" and "Union line of retreat." At first glance the articles appear to be studies of some obscure battle during the Civil War. Clever presentation of stories such as this is widely appreciated among the New Left, and it augurs well for the magazine.

The Vietnam War has spawned two major magazines. One is *Viet-Report,* a monthly that has a press run of 40,000. Its editor is Carol Brightman, a young English instructor at New York University. According to her, one of the major reasons for starting this magazine was to supplement the meager, one-sided and "managed" news on the war provided by the daily press. *Viet-Report* stands four-square against America's policy in Vietnam. Stories are sympathetic only to the Vietcong; much of the material used comes from foreign correspondents who have visited North Vietnam.

Because it seems content only to denounce the U.S. and to praise the Vietcong, *Viet-Report* fails to provide any perspective on the problem; none of the gray areas are examined, only the black and white extremes. Its sole object, therefore, seems to be to feed the arguments of those who are already convinced that the U.S. is wrong.

The other magazine is *Vietnam Perspectives*, a bimonthly with a press run of 15,000. It is published by the American Friends of Vietnam, a ten-year-old organization composed of 150 citizens with varying views. Unlike *Viet-Report, Perspectives* admits that the U.S. has made mistakes but it refuses to condemn all American policies in Vietnam. It has attempted to show a balanced picture, scrutinizing American weaknesses at the same time it is analyzing the shortcomings of the Vietcong. It wants to show that extremes are not the alternative in Vietnam, which—because sales are mainly to individuals on the left—probably accounts for its circulation being far lower than *Viet-Report*'s.

There is *I. F. Stone's Weekly*, a muckraking four-page newssheet that finds its way into many liberals' homes. It is neutralist, insightful, intelligent and clear, and presents its arguments with a sense of integrity. Another favorite is the monthly magazine *The Realist*. Paul Krassner is the "Editor & Ringleader." His two assistants have the titles "Scapegoat" and "Featherbedder." It is a ribald, irreverent, satirical and slightly cynical humor magazine. Like *Mad Magazine, The Realist* walks a narrow line, stopping just short of advocacy. Finally there is *The Minority of One* edited by M. S. Arnoni. This magazine was first produced by the Leftists who were kicked out of SANE in 1960. *Minority* boasts Bertrand Russell, the Reverend Stephen H. Fritchman, Linus Pauling, Professor Albert Szent-Gyorgyi and Sir Robert Watson-Watt among its sponsors. The magazine reflects a pronounced antipathy for most things American and a joy in those things socialist—often the articles are so biased that they are even meaningless to the left. One writer, for instance, describing Puerto Rican politics, refused to believe that the six Nationalists who stormed the Fortaleza in 1950 were actually trying to assassinate Governor Muñoz Marin. Apparently, so the story goes on to relate, all they wanted to do was to raise the Puerto Rican flag over the fortress and were gunned down for their efforts by the "colonialists." *Minority* also entertains the notion that all four assassinated U.S. Presidents had something in common: ". . . in actuality," read the subtitle to one article, "each was the victim of an elaborate political conspiracy." Many on the New Left would agree.

THE MODERATE LEFT

16

Democratic Socialism

1

One of the most successful of all American minority parties has been the Socialist Party. It has never won an election but many of its views have nevertheless prevailed. Such proposals as a minimum wage, social security, fair employment practices, the right to strike, the forty-hour work week, public housing, civil rights and urban renewal were being advocated by the Socialist Party long before they were even considered seriously by the Republican and Democratic Parties.

The Party dates from 1901. Similar to the Socialist Labor Party and the Wobblies, the Socialist Party grew out of the ideological chaos that existed among American socialists around the turn of the century. The man who was to dominate the Party for the first twenty-five years of its existence was Eugene Victor Debs.

Debs was born in 1855, one of ten children. His parents, emigrating from Alsace in 1849, had settled in Terre Haute, Indiana, and ran a grocery store there. By the age of fourteen Debs was a locomotive fireman on the local railroad. Five years later he had joined the labor union movement. By his twenty-fifth birthday he was secretary-treasurer of the 8,000-member Brotherhood of Locomotive Firemen and editor of its newspaper.

Debs had been impressed by the growth of the Knights of Labor and the American Federation of Labor. He soon was calling for the amalgamation of all separate and disunited railroad brotherhoods. This was achieved in 1893 when the American Railway

Union was formed. Debs was elected president. Its membership stood at a healthy 150,000. The ARU took part in the Pullman Strike of 1895. The railway workers were routed and Debs was sent to prison for six months for contempt of court. But as a result of this bloody and bitter strike Debs became converted to socialism.

In 1897 the ARU voted itself out of existence. Debs and its members, along with groups associated with various radical magazines, formed the Social Democracy of America, which was designed to advance the cause of socialism. But within a short period of time this group split between a utopian-socialist faction and Debs' following, which sought to rally the workers into a third party. Debs then formed the Social Democratic Party of America which, after numerous amalgamations with dissident socialist groups, became the Socialist Party in 1901.

Debs was an extremely hard worker with an eloquent and inspiring way of speaking. He was tall, balding and somewhat of an alcoholic. As opposed to the craft union concepts of Samuel Gompers, Debs favored industrial unions, which he felt would give his followers far larger bargaining leverage than any other type of organization. Debs was not a revolutionary but a radical reformer, wholly committed to the electoral process. He saw the Socialist Party as the political arm of a large working-class movement, similar to that which was taking shape in England.

In 1905 he helped found the Wobblies with Haywood, DeLeon and the others. But Debs rebelled because of that organization's propensity for "direct action," and went back to the Socialist Party.

Debs ran for President in 1900, 1904, 1908, 1912 and 1920. His best showing was in 1920 when he received 915,000 votes. When America went to war in 1917, Debs came out strongly against our participation in it. "The master class has always declared the war," he told a Canton, Ohio audience in 1918. "The subject class has always fought the battles. The master class has had all to gain and nothing to lose, while the subject class has had nothing to gain and all to lose—especially their lives!" Debs was soon indicted for violating the Espionage and Sedition Act, tried, found guilty and sentenced to ten years in the Atlanta penitentiary.

His confinement, however, did not prevent him from receiving the highest vote for President in his career; perhaps it helped.

During his absence from active leadership a split developed within the Socialist Party. The pro-Bolshevik left wing of the Party broke away to form what was later to become the CPUSA. Debs was released from prison in 1921 and soon afterward entered a sanitarium in Illinois. He died there in 1926.

At this point the second and last well-known leader of the Party was emerging from political obscurity. His name was Norman Mattoon Thomas.

Thomas was born in 1884, the son of a fairly well-off Presbyterian minister. He entered Bucknell University in 1901 but switched to Princeton the following year. He was a member of the Triangle Club, Colonial Club, choir and glee club. When he graduated in 1905 he had a Phi Beta Kappa key and had been chosen the class valedictorian. For two years he worked in New York's Spring Street Settlement, then took a trip around the world. In 1908 he entered Union Theological Seminary and, after completing the courses, was ordained a minister in the Presbyterian Church. In 1910 he married Frances Violet Stewart, the daughter of a wealthy banker. At this point in his life, Thomas had renounced his parents' Republicanism in favor of the Theodore Roosevelt Progressive Party Philosophy. He still was not a socialist but found himself moving in that direction. He voted for Woodrow Wilson in 1916.

When World War I broke out, Thomas, then pastor of the East Harlem Presbyterian Church, came out against American involvement. He worked briefly for the American Union Against Militarism (which collapsed when the U.S. entered the war) and then helped to found the National Civil Liberties Union, later called the American Civil Liberties Union. He also became part-time secretary of the Fellowship of Reconciliation and was actively involved in 1917 in Sidney Hillquit's bid for the New York mayoralty on the Socialist Party ticket. The following year Thomas joined the Party. Because of his uncompromising stand against the war he was forced to resign from some of his Presbyterian posts. When hostilities had ended, Thomas began campaigning for the redress of conscientious objector grievances (one brother, Evan, refused to fight and was imprisoned for two years; two others fought in the war, one being badly wounded) and also for Debs' release from prison.

In 1921 Thomas became co-executive director of the League for Industrial Democracy; then he became editor of the New York *Leader,* on whose staff were Ed Sullivan and Edmund Duffy. The paper went broke and Thomas returned to the LID. He supported LaFollette for President in 1924 and the next year ran himself for mayor on the Socialist ticket against Jimmy Walker and Frank Waterman, the fountain pen king. He lost, and the next year he ran for a New York state senate seat and again lost. When Debs died in 1926, Thomas gave the eulogy at his funeral. He then campaigned for the reprieve of Sacco and Vanzetti, whom Harry Fleischman, Thomas' adoring biographer,[1] called "two warm-hearted anarchists."

In 1928 Thomas ran for President of the United States on the SP ticket, the first of six unsuccessful tries. He did not (and still does not) believe that the Party was ever likely to become a mass party but saw it then as a "spearhead" to a mass party. In his first try for the White House he called for low tariffs, free trade, unemployment benefits, federal public works, federal loans to states and cities, a reduction in the working day and week, federal old age pensions, inheritance taxes, world disarmament, United States entry into the League of Nations, the recognition of Soviet Russia, home rule for Puerto Rico, independence for the Philippines, abolition of "lame duck" Congresses and the collective ownership of national resources. The greatest opposition to his platform came from public indifference and he received only 268,000 votes. But the Democratic Party under Franklin D. Roosevelt soon appropriated his ideas, many of which were to become law. Because Thomas was the only one talking about public welfare before 1932, he is now known as "the father of the welfare state."

Thomas received over 880,000 votes in 1932, his highest ever. Within a year or so afterward he came to believe that Roosevelt's efforts would turn sour and that the people would turn to the Socialist Party. He was wrong: the SP had hit its peak in 1932, ever since drifting inexorably down the electoral ladder until it abandoned that road after the 1956 election (in which the candidate, Darlington Hoopes, received only 2,126 votes).

All through the 1930s Thomas was preoccupied with keeping his Party together. Factional fights broke out, and periodically he had to fend off the take-over bids of the CPUSA. In 1935 the SP became an "all-inclusive" Party: it welcomed every conceivable sort of radical, from Benjamin Gitlow to Jay Lovestone to the Trotskyists. Thomas has always emphasized that *democratic* socialism lay at the heart of the SP's philosophy. This implied that whatever socialist changes came about in America they would be enacted through the existing political institutions, not through revolution. This reformist attitude irritated the radicals in the Party and they eventually left or were purged. But the damage was done; the Party was never a cohesive body after the 1936 election: it has suffered split after split. (One of the splinter groups, for instance, breaking away over the Party's antiwar position, became the Union for Democratic Action, later the Americans for Democratic Action.)

Thomas was reluctant to run in 1936 but finally consented. His fears of a poor showing (a switch from his earlier optimism) were justified: The new American Labor Party, made up of right-wing SP dissidents, polled more votes for Roosevelt. When the Spanish Civil War broke out, Thomas favored the formation of a "Eugene Victor Debs Column" of volunteers, which infuriated the pacifist socialists. On the outbreak of World War II he again came out against American involvement. All through the war Thomas was a political gadfly, attacking the treatment of the Nisei, the conscientious objectors, and attacking those who were crying for appeasement or unconditional surrender.

In 1948, Thomas' last bid for the Presidency, he polled 139,000 votes—not his worst showing. But he considers it his proudest moment because many of his views had been vindicated.

Since that election Thomas, then sixty-four, has dropped out of active Socialist Party politics. He realized then that the Party had no chance to create even a new political alignment. But his political activities on the whole have not ceased. Considered an elder statesman by all socialists and many others, he has spent the last two decades stumping the country, calling for the control of the "commanding heights of industry" (similar to the British Labour Party), a massive war on poverty, urban renewal, complete disarmament, the outlawing of discrimination and segregation, the closing of income tax loopholes, socialized medicine, an increase in the minimum wage and, lately, American withdrawal from Vietnam.

Today he is almost blind, crippled by arthritis and physically infirm, but he continues to pursue a rigorous schedule of speaking engagements—from debating William Buckley to soothing the revolutionary passions of Berkeley radicals. Of all the over-thirties, Norman Thomas is the only one whom the radical young will listen to for any length of time. He looks like everyone's favorite uncle, he has an air of detachment and dignity about him, and he is an old war-horse that is of the establishment but not by or for it. When he speaks, his huge hands with their bent fingers flap up and down by his side, he shakes his wrists when he mentions something unpleasant, his mouth snaps open and shut and his voice, still strong, booms out his message. "If you cannot learn to *live* with the Communists," he tells a crowd of students, "then you might begin to think about *dying* with them!" To hard-headed radicals he has said: "You march off demanding the impeachment of Lyndon Johnson and what will you get? I'll tell you what. You'll get a lot of people who are fed up with him suddenly coming to his defense. Instead, go out and be missionaries. If you can convince enough American people that you have the right idea in wanting us out of the Vietnam War, then you'll convince Johnson."[2]

One of his biggest disappointments over the years, he told me, peering at my calling card through a huge magnifying glass by his desk, has been that the Socialist Party did not grow into a major force, or at least did not effect any meaningful realignment. He does see, however, a possible new alignment emerging out of the Goldwater phenomenon. "Perhaps my biggest disappointment, though," he said, "is that people seem somewhat less intelligent and less wise than before World War II and the Korean War—so inadequate to the complexities of our times." He cited our "absurd" China policy, saying, "We must begin *right away* to put Red China in the U.N.!" As for our adherence to the phrase "free enterprise," he burst out: "There is damn little of it. Small boys playing marbles for keeps is the only example of it!" America's handling of the Vietnam War is another example of how little we have progressed: "There is no possibility that the U.S. can maintain itself indefinitely in Southeast Asia, and President Johnson is *just beginning* to realize this." If America can avoid starting a world war there, he added, "in a generation or so there will not be many substantial differences between the U.S. and the USSR."

The Socialist Party considers itself a propaganda group today. It has approximately five thousand dues-paying members who fall into three categories: there is an older group, mostly immigrants, who preach a very rigid socialism; a middle group, recruited mainly in the 1930s, whose socialism has an American slant; and a younger group, whose views are confused and unconventional. "Ask any of the post-1962 SPers what they're against," said Michael Harrington, author of the best-selling book, *The Other America,* "and you will get a long list. But if you ask what they're for, they have only vague answers." Their socialism, he added, is closely interwoven with other interests such as folk rock, marijuana smoking and fashions, so that the message they impart to the world often seems incoherent to the untrained ear.

Harrington, nearing forty and one of the better known Socialist Party activists, says he comes from an "Irish machine-Democrat family from St. Louis which was anti-WASP and pro-Roosevelt." His transition to socialism, he recalled, was an intellectual one, picked up in college. "I got emotional and moral about it," he added, "only after I was a social worker in a white St. Louis slum." He considers himself of the middle group of socialists in the Party, even though he joined in 1948. "I am the last child of the 1930s, which was in 1948, because the election of that year was dominated by 1930s issues and attitudes." He says he is a nuclear pacifist but not a conscientious objector. "I would defend my family," he said, "and I believe in the just war." He also said that he has not been a practicing Catholic since 1953.

The biggest problem facing the Socialist Party today is similar to the Trotskyist problem: how is it to grow as a party? This has not been resolved since 1957 when the Party left the electoral arena.

"There is no ideological discipline; we are a multi-tendency Party today. I believe, for instance, that socialists should be a member of the left wing of the Democratic Party. As a result I am a registered Democrat," said Harrington.

Paul Feldman, who succeeded Harrington in 1964 as editor of the Socialist Party's newspaper, *New America,* agrees. "The conflict within the SP is over whether you can work with the liberal establishment when it seems like a cover for capitalism; others say, how can you work with Democrats when they belong to a bourgeois party; others are die-hard socialists. We wish we could have something like the British Labour Party in the U.S.," he said. "This is the hang-up; how do you form a party like this?"

Feldman went on to lament, "We have confronted more difficult problems than socialists in Europe and we have been unable to cope with them. We have no institutional power whatsoever. Therefore one attitude seems as good as another. If we had congressmen who won or lost we could at least find out how our policies are going."

He refuses to believe that the SP is a party without a cause. "There is no question that the U.S. is not a just society and that many things we have advocated have not been brought to fruition." He listed but a few of the inequities that the SP seeks to correct: no national ownership of natural resources, no "decent" minimum wage, no control over the "commanding heights of the economy," no end to poverty or discrimination, no planned economy, no socialized medicine, no disarmament and no peace on earth. "You can *re*form capitalism but it does not give you the necessary social justice that we advocate. You have to *trans*form it. It may not come about in one glorious day; it is part of a continuing struggle," he said.

The Young People's Socialist League, or "Yipsels," the SP's youth group, reflects all the unease in the Party. Periodically, groups spin off in anger and frustration over the questions of how the Party is to grow and how it is to relate to other social forces (unions, for instance). Recently YPSL has been suspended because a group of Trotskyist infiltrators nearly gained control of it. "This bitter infighting," said Feldman, "has made it impossible for anyone to assume leadership. The Party, therefore, has no image."

This situation, he believed, "is not really of our making but is due to the political situation in the U.S. which is so confusing."

"To grow," he added, "we must have a consistent program. Why should a person join a party that is vague?" he asked. Harrington put it another way: "If you can't reach out," he told me, "you fight within."

Feldman went on: "I think the Socialist Party has great possibilities. We have to be involved in a political realignment in this country. I spend my time trying to build a democratic left." Like Harrington, Feldman believes that there is a place in this country for "a serious and sane conservative opposition."

One aspect that haunts the future prospects of the Socialist Party is that it is only the magic of Norman Thomas' name that keeps the Party from disintegrating. Many groups among the Marxist left anticipate such a splintering and are waiting expectantly in the wings to siphon off the members. Feldman, for one, sees that possibility. "If the Party dies with Norman Thomas," he said, "then it is because the members have not developed a meaningful perspective."

2

New York's Liberal Party is one of those rare minor parties that can, on occasion, hold the balance of power in its grasp. In the 1965 New York City mayoralty race, for instance, it gave John Lindsay 282,000 votes. Coupled with the regular Republican vote of 867,000, the Liberal vote was sufficient to overcome the Democratic total of 1,047,000. Obviously Lindsay would never have become mayor without Liberal help. Thus this little party has power—to be reckoned with by all those who seek state office (or higher) in New York.

The Party's chronology goes back to 1936. At that time Sidney Hillman (of the Amalgamated Clothing Workers Union), Dave Dubinsky (of the International Ladies Garment Workers Union) and a number of disgruntled socialists and "progressives" formed the American Labor Party. Its purpose was straightforward: Franklin D. Roosevelt, running for re-election that year, realized that there were many votes to be had in the Empire State among those who were loyal to him but who hated the local Democratic machine. So another line was set up on the ballot for these voters.

By 1943, however, the Communist Party had worked its way into the ALP. Dubinsky realized the impossibility of working with the Communists and broke away in 1944. He and Alex Rose (of the United Hatters, Cap and Millinery Workers Union) and Ben Davidson (the Party's executive director since its founding) started the Liberal Party. Soon afterward the ALP came under complete CPUSA control; it played a part in the disastrous Wallace campaign of 1948 but died out soon thereafter in the early 1950s.

The purpose of the new Liberal Party was threefold: to provide that extra line on the ballot for dissident Democrats who were pro-FDR; to provide an anti-Communist alternative to the Marxist ALP; and to keep the Democratic Party in New York to the left of center.

The advantages of having another party on the ballot were quickly apparent to most politicians. The Democratic reformers, such people as Eleanor Roosevelt and Herbert Lehman, saw the Liberals as a lever to fight corruption and reaction in their own party. If the Liberals held a balance of power, they reasoned, then the Democrats would be forced to nominate high-quality candidates and present reasonable policies. The Republicans, whose control of the state legislature for many years could easily have abolished the multiple-listing ballot, were also quick to see that the Liberal Party was the only wedge they had in heavily Democratic areas such as New York City. Given good Republican candidates, they felt that there was a reasonable chance that they could get the Liberal endorsement, which in turn would lower the odds on an easy Democratic victory.

Even shrewder Republicans knew that from time to time the Liberals would *have* to declare their independence of the Democrats, if for no other reason than to keep the big city machine honest. To go off and nominate their own Liberal candidate, however, would ensure that the Liberals would run a poor third with no post-election bargaining power accruing to them. More likely, these Republicans reasoned, the Liberals would come to them whenever they had an attractive candidate. This was amply proved with Lindsay's victory in 1965. By backing Abraham Beame, the machine Democrat nominee for mayor, the Liberals would have helped entrench the very group they despise; to nominate a Liberal independently would have placed them in fourth position (behind Conservative William Buckley), and Beame still would have been the victor. They had no choice but to back Lindsay, and this time their leverage paid dividends.

In its first race, in 1944, the Liberals polled a startling 330,000 votes for Roosevelt. In 1949 they backed Republican Newbold Morris for mayor against Democrat William O'Dwyer. Morris lost, but his Liberal vote beat the ALP's for Vito Marcantonio. This put the Liberal Party in a key third position for the first time and ensured the eventual demise of the ALP. In 1951 the Liberals elected their own candidate to the City Council, Rudolph Halley, the Kefauver Investigation Committee counsel. Halley received 583,000 Liberal votes, the Party's highest total to date. Since then the average has fallen to 330,000 per major election.

Since the Halley high-water mark, the Party has seldom backed its own candidates independently. Most have been Democrats; for instance, Stevenson for President in 1952 and 1956, Wagner for mayor in 1957 and 1961, Morgenthau for governor in 1962 and Robert Kennedy for senator in 1964. It is worth noting, however, that only in four of the twenty-eight major contests in which the Liberals have participated since their founding have they provided the actual margin of victory: Herbert Lehman's in 1950 for senator, Averill Harriman's in 1954 for governor, John F. Kennedy's in 1960 for President and Lindsay's in 1965. All the others were won handily by one side or the other, the Liberal backing making no difference.

But the value of the Liberal endorsement cannot always be measured in votes won or lost. Many of the campaigns backed by the Liberals, for instance, were turned into runaway victories— Wagner's primary fight in 1961 comes to mind—due to the zealousness of the Liberal worker.

Who, then, are the people who make up this balance of power? The hard core comes from the 400,000-member ILGWU and the 200,000-member Hatters Union. Approximately 50,000 of the members can always be counted upon to vote Liberal.

According to John Burke, a young Liberal Party employee, the Liberal voter was originally a first-generation middle-European Jew who worked in the needle trade. Today, he says, this is no longer true. The needle trade still accounts for many votes, but there are now more middle-class voters whose strength is centered in Manhattan on the West Side, in Morningside Heights and in Greenwich Village. Many of them are former socialists, ex-Democrats or disgruntled ALPers. Burke says that intellectuals are drawn to the Party, noting that for many years the chairman was Timothy W. Costello, professor of psychology at New York University; that the honorary chairman is Adolf A. Berle, Jr., former Assistant Secretary of State; and that one of its vice-chairmen was Reinhold Niebuhr, the theologian.

Burke himself is not a typical member. He is a native of Connecticut and a graduate of Yale. His family was Democratic, and Burke himself was decidedly anti-WASP. But he claims that his liberalism evolved not from his background but from a belief that all the other parties were less sensible and humane.

The Party platform is far less bold than Socialist Party proposals because the Liberals tend to see themselves more as appendages to the two-party system rather than as radical innovators. Liberals favor such things as rent control, public power, urban renewal, more Medicare benefits, more unemployment insurance and economic planning. Most liberal Republicans and Democrats could feel at home with these proposals. The Party seldom tries to be more than just a few steps ahead, goading the two major parties into a leftward course.

This has its pitfalls because without a sense of urgency and without pushing for more than it reasonably can hope to achieve, the Party ceases to be a ginger group. The intellectuals are usually the first to become disenchanted when they see that practicality has triumphed over idealism. The rank and file sometimes follow suit, confused in their own minds over exactly what the differences are between the Liberal Party and the two major ones.

Liberals will say that their go-slow stems from their experience as trade unionists, that there is no point asking for the moon, that pushing things past the point of acceptance serves no useful purpose. But this is really no explanation at all. In fact, Liberals know that their Party's strength lies in its balance-of-power-at-the-polls position and not in its program. To be sure, their program cannot be reactionary; but it need not be, they say, so radical that it alienates the two parties they wish to influence.

The function of the Liberal Party, to many members, is to "purify" the Democratic Party alone. By and large, Liberals foster this image with the public: Liberals stand for honest government and reform, the Democrats are inert and corrupt, the less-numerous Republicans are the medium to change the dominating party, and so on. Yet the purifying agent, the Liberal Party, is, in order to survive, forced to be just as opportunistic and as devious as either of the two major parties. "There is this paradoxical situation, you see," said one loyal Liberal; "at times we have to make a coalition with crooked Democrats, at other times with reactionaries."[3] This statement, made without any trace of embarrassment, reflects the Party attitude that purists, idealists, sectarians, visionaries and the like are unfit for the rough and tumble of the real political world.

Recently the Liberals' very reason for being—as a balance of power in favor of decent left-wing government—has come under challenge. The rise of the Conservative Party of New York threatens to offset the Liberal leverage. Already several minor candidates have won because of Conservative backing, and many others, particularly for the state assembly, could not have won had they had that Party's backing. Because the bedrock Conservative vote appears to be larger than the Liberals', there may come a time when the Republicans and Democrats seek Conservative support. The probability of this ever happening, however, is remote, given the liberal flavor of New York politics. But if the country takes a swing to the right—as every conservative will tell you it will—then the situation may change. It may, for instance, create a realignment, the more conservative people gravitating toward the Republicans, the more liberal toward the Democrats. In such an eventuality the Liberal Party would most likely disappear into the Democratic Party.

John Burke, for one, views the Conservative Party in a different light. "It will collapse in a few years," he says, "no matter what pieties they put in their literature. They're fanatics. Buckley is a fanatic." He said that the Conservative Party was founded and exists only for racists. "Racism," he added, "is one manifestation of their fanaticism." He pointed out that the Democrats and Republicans are still only interested in Liberal endorsement, not the Conservative endorsement. "All the Conservative votes do," he said, "is reduce the number of real votes." The proper perspective, he concluded, was self-evident in the 1965 mayor's race: "Beame was the conservative, Buckley was the reactionary and Lindsay was the liberal."

Burke's bitterness toward the Conservative Party reflects the panic with which Liberals view the rise of this new party. The huge Conservative vote in the 1965 mayoralty race shook the Liberal leaders more than they will admit publicly; they realized that their hold on Line C was in jeopardy. Therefore, when it came time to choose a candidate for governor in the 1966 elections, they picked Franklin D. Roosevelt, Jr., a man with no Liberal Party background but nevertheless a man whose name the Party chieftains hoped would rekindle fresh enthusiasm for Liberal Party policies. Roosevelt received 507,000 votes but it was not enough and the Party, at least for the next four years, will be listed on Line D.

Why the Liberals place so much emphasis on regaining their Line C listing is unclear. Undoubtedly part of the answer is psychological. They believe that they may have lost a good deal of their bargaining leverage and without that they are dead politically. Alex Rose, the Party's chief tactician, has no doubt suffered a personal defeat with the loss; his political power is vulnerable and he is currently under attack by dissident Liberals within the Garment Workers Union. Few of the current crop of Liberals seem to remember that their Party did well on Line D from 1944 to 1950; and they also seem to have overlooked the fact that the Conservatives' success on Line D in 1966 proves that voters have no trouble finding it. The future of the Liberals will be decided on what they have to say and not where they are placed on the ballot.

Two other problems plague the Liberals at the moment. One is that they are always haunted by the specter that, were there no Liberal Party at all, most of the faithful would vote liberal Democratic anyway. This explains why the Party feels it very important to maintain the image as a pure, mildly crusading organization because, without it, no one could tell the difference between a Liberal and a Democrat. Secondly, the Reform Democrats, those hardy souls who always seem to be battling Carmine DeSapio, Tammany's man in Greenwich Village, are viewed as rivals to the Liberal Party. If these people can accomplish the necessary purification of the Democratic Party, the reasoning goes, then there is no need for the Liberals. This development has created the ludicrous situation in which two reform groups are battling each other for survival.

One critic of the Liberal Party, Jack Newfield of the *Village Voice,* believes that the Party is neither liberal nor democratic. He points out that it has not been pushing for a higher minimum wage for fear that the needle trade will move out of New York City (thus destroying the Party). Furthermore, over one hundred Liberals held patronage jobs in Mayor Wagner's last administration, which tied the Party very closely to the Democratic apron strings. (Backing Republican Lindsay, as noted, makes it no less close to the Democrats in sympathy.) The Party also takes no stand on Vietnam ("Because it would split the membership," Burke told me), nor is there much emphasis in its platform on civil liberties.

As for Party democracy, most believe that Dubinsky, Rose and the other leaders run the organization with an iron hand, showing almost total indifference to the opinions of other members. "We are about as democratic as Poland," said one disgruntled member. This is defended on the grounds that to be otherwise would push the Party into anarchy, a situation constantly retarding the work of Reform Democrats.

"Thus," wrote Newfield, perhaps a bit too harshly, "the Liberal Party slides gracelessly into old age, sucking up patronage, opposing the minimum wage law . . . and playing pinochle in deserted clubhouses."[4]

17

The Peace Movement

1

Any examination of peace-seeking activities in America must be predicated on one question: at what level is the subject to be discussed? There have always been, and still continue to be today, three identifiable spheres of peace activity in this country, only the last of which concerns us here.

The first sphere is nationwide in scope. All reasonable Americans—from the President of the United States, to the members of the Cabinet, the diplomatic corps, to the businessman, the professions, and to the ordinary citizen—are concerned with peace. The only argument among them is how it shall be achieved. Even the "hawks"—the reasonable variety—are for peace; they just happen to believe that the best way to ensure peace is by a show of military strength, at worst, by fighting a war.

The second sphere incorporates a large number of organizations in which peace is a major, but not a dominant, theme of their activities. These groups cover a wide spectrum of interests. One group, for instance, is oriented toward "world affairs" and includes such organizations as the Foreign Policy Association and the World Affairs Councils. Another group is oriented toward "world government" and includes the American Association for the United Nations, the United World Federalists, The United Nations Association, and the American for Democratic Action. Yet another faction is that which concentrates on "world law," such as the American Society of International Law and Arthur Larsen's

World Rule of Law Center at Duke University. There are groups that are socially oriented, others that are scientifically oriented, and finally those that are church oriented—undoubtedly the most important.

I hasten to add that I do not wish to imply that peace is the exclusive prerogative of one group or another. It is the difference of *approach* that concerns us here.

The final sphere of peace-seeking activities is dominated by those groups whose primary interest is peace, usually to the exclusion of other interests. These groups are by far the most active, the most volatile, the noisiest and the most publicized of all the peace organizations in America today. They are often referred to erroneously as the "pacifists," "the draft evaders," "the conscientious objectors" and "the peaceniks." The major organizations are the Quakers and Mennonites and their attendant bodies, the Fellowship of Reconciliation, the Catholic Worker Movement, the National Committee for a Sane Nuclear Policy, otherwise known as SANE, the War Resisters League, and the Committee for Nonviolent Action.

The most influential of all these groups are the Quakers, and, to a lesser extent, the Amish Mennonites. Both believe that war and violence are contrary to the spirit of the Gospel and are therefore obscene and immoral; war violates the divinity of man; it atrophies the human spirit; it is the organized killing of man by man, the domination of man by force, and the idolatry of power. They take the position that wars will cease only when there is a change in men's hearts. To this end, they practice "public witness," nonviolence and conscientious objection.

A pacifist is often described as one who subscribes to these three practices and, in many respects, this is so. But it should be noted that there is no strict definition of the term "pacifist." It implies a very personal interpretation of life based on an individual's social, moral and religious viewpoint. Perhaps the best general definition of a pacifist comes from Alfred Hassler, the executive secretary of the Fellowship of Reconciliation. "A pacifist," he says, "believes that in the settlement of conflict it is possible to introduce the element of love and concern and nonviolent reconciliation. It is not simply the rejection of war but the commitment of oneself to the process of building a peaceful world society."[1]

Not all Quakers are pacifists. There are those who believe in "the just war," or who join Ambulance Corps in the belief that such work is humanitarian. Still others reject such work on the grounds that it merely hastens a wounded man's return to the battlefield.

Pacifism is not the exclusive domain of the Quakers; it can be and is embraced by other Protestants as well as Catholics, Jews, agnostics, atheists and anarchists. Even though pacifism is one of the dominant influences within the peace movement, the actual number of people who consider themselves to be pacifists is quite small. The vast majority of others in the movement seek peace for a wide variety of other motives.

There are approximately 130,000 Quakers in America today.[2] Among peace groups, they have an influence that is extraordinary considering their numbers. Few aspects of the peace movement today are free from their influence; this has been true in the past as well.

The major Quaker agency fostering peace is the American Friends Service Committee, founded in 1917 in Philadelphia. It was set up primarily to help conscientious objectors find work of a constructive nature during wartime, particularly in Ambulance Corps and hospitals.

Over the years the AFSC has been in the forefront of peace work. It sent peace speakers and peace caravans around the world in the 1920s. It established the first Institute of International Relations at Haverford College in 1927. As war clouds gathered over Europe in 1939, it became perhaps the most vocal proponent of nonintervention and neutralism (often finding itself taking positions embarrassingly similar to those of the Bundists and America Firsters). After the war broke out, it took the lead in helping Jews and other refugees to escape from Germany. In America, the AFSC helped to form the National Service Board for Religious Objectors, which was established to help the thousands of Americans who had declared themselves to be conscientious objectors.

In 1947 the AFSC shared the Nobel Peace Prize with its British counterpart. Today, the emphasis of the AFSC lies in people-to-people communications in the belief that such exchanges destroy barriers to peace. In this regard, it promotes a seemingly endless series of seminars, programs and conferences.

Only a part of the Service Committee's activities concern peace. As its title implies, it is essentially a service organization, spending much of its efforts on international service, youth services, community relations and international affairs.

It is interesting to note that, with the general growth of peace activities in America and throughout the world, the AFSC's share of income devoted to peace has declined over the last several years. In 1958, for example, with an income of $4.8 million, $1.3 million—or 27 percent—was allocated for peace work. In 1964, the AFSC had an income of $5.2 million but spent only $561,316 —or 11 percent—on peace.[3] This undoubtedly has been due to the rise of other peace groups.

The Friends Peace Committee is another Quaker agency and is independent of the AFSC. It predates the Service Committee by a number of years, and its distinguishing mark is its *sole* concern for peace. It operates out of the same "Quaker Quadrangle" as the AFSC at 15th and Race Streets in Philadelphia. The chairman is Lyle Tatum, the brother of Arlo Tatum, who runs the Central Committee for Conscientious Objectors across town.*

According to Bob Eaton, a young youth worker at the FPC, Quakers "have great outreach." That is to say, they tend to encourage all groups in the right directions rather than proselytize. Quakers have the reputation of being the conscience of the peace movement as well as the mother-father image. The Friends Peace Committee, for instance, is considered by Eaton to be the "big daddy" of regional peace groups. Other regional groups look to the FPC for leadership. Whenever there is a peace march, the question is always raised: where do you stay en route? Inevitably, it is at the Quaker meetinghouses.

* The function of the CCCO is to give legal aid and council to conscientious objectors. It claims it is not a "draft-dodgers' school" but a legally oriented group. Its major publication, *Handbook for Conscientious Objectors,* seems to support this view and is a best-seller among youths who seek to avoid the draft.

Eaton is a pacifist and conscientious objector. I asked him if his conscientious objection had anything to do with cowardice. "There is a certain element of cowardice involved," he said, "but that is not the main reason why I'm a CO. I don't see how any government should be so strong as to make a slave out of a man. When you go into the Army you sign away your conscience for two years. Ultimately it comes down to: 'I don't want to kill people and I don't want to be in the position of killing people.' I wouldn't admit to the government that my religion is what makes me a CO because I think that is irrelevant."

Eaton became quite voluble, adding: "I would never restrain people from fighting a war; I would hope they thought pretty hard about it before they went. What I would really like to see is everyone a CO, and those who decide to fight a war, they can cease to be a CO and fight it. I also think that to let me off [because of religious convictions] and send an atheist CO to jail is wrong.

"War is a situation in which you demand a man to do something that he has no choice. The government has no right to make the decision of whether a man must kill. Every man must make that decision for himself."

2

One of the oldest pacifist groups in America is the Fellowship of Reconciliation, located in Nyack, New York. It was founded in Cambridge, England, at the outbreak of World War I; within a year an American branch had been established which has since grown into the largest section of their international organization, the World Fellowship.

The founders were a group of Christians who, although they could not bring themselves to participate in mass killing, nevertheless found no adequate direction to the abolition of war in their religion. The FOR was thus set up as a Christian vehicle to world peace.

The distinguishing characteristic of the FOR is that, although the Quakers had a hand in its formation, it was the first organized religious group that introduced the idea of Christian pacifism into the churches on a large scale. It did not and still does not confine itself—intentionally or otherwise—to the historical attitudes of the peace churches, principally the Friends and the Mennonites, even though these two denominations still play a leading role in the organization.

From a historical point of view, its formation was one of the major developments in the erosion of the long-held notion in America that the churches had nothing to say to the state.

The Fellowship has a membership today of roughly fourteen thousand, many of whom are clergymen, lay preachers or otherwise church oriented. This relatively small figure belies the organization's vigor. In 1916, for example, FOR members set up the National Civil Liberties Bureau, which later became the American Civil Liberties Union; in 1923 it established the National Conference of Christians and Jews; in 1942 it created a Committee for Racial Equality which soon became the Congress of Racial Equality, or CORE, as it is better known today; FOR was also a pioneer of the sit-in—for instance, the 1943 sit-in in Stoner's restaurant in Chicago, which lays claim to being the first ever in America. It provides a counseling service for COs; it has been involved in civil rights activities, particularly during the last five years, and it has recently promoted an ecumenical movement among peace groups by helping to establish the broad-front organization Turn Toward Peace.

Many well-known men have been associated with FOR: Norman Thomas, James Farmer, Bayard Rustin, Martin Luther King, Jr., George Houser and A. J. Muste are but a few of them.

A few words are necessary here about A. J. Muste. No man had a greater impact upon the American peace movement than he. At his death in 1967 at the age of eighty-two, he had long been known as "Mr. Pacifist" and was America's nearest equivalent to England's Bertrand Russell—at least as far as Russell's political activities are concerned. He was associated in one way or another with most other pacifist and peace groups. As he said to me six months before his death: "It would be risky to suggest a committee that I haven't been on."

Abraham Johannes Muste was born in the Netherlands in 1885,

the son of a coachman to a noble family. His parents immigrated to the United States in 1891 and settled in Michigan. Muste and his parents became citizens in 1896.

By 1909 Muste had been ordained a minister in the Dutch Reformed Church, and four years later he had graduated *magna cum laude* from Union Theological Seminary. There he first met Norman Thomas, who was two classes ahead of him.

Muste voted for Debs in 1912. He said he had never voted Republican or Democratic, believing that the old Socialist Party itself was insufficiently radical even at that time.

During World War I, Muste became the minister of the Central Congregational Church outside of Boston; by 1915 he had declared himself a pacifist; two years later he was forced to resign from this church because of his views. He then went to Providence and enrolled as a minister in the Society of Friends.

He was one of the leaders of the Lawrence Strike in 1919; for two years he was secretary of the Amalgamated Textile Workers of America; and in 1921 he became the director of the Brookwood Labor College at Katonah, New York, a job he was to hold for twelve years.

Brookwood was situated on the grounds previously occupied by a "progressive Christian Socialist school for children" run by a family called Fincke, who were members of the Fellowship of Reconciliation. The Labor College was independent of the American Federation of Labor and was supported by the Garland Fund, a left-wing foundation no longer in existence. The curriculum at Brookwood was based on "socialist," Marxist and radical points of view. The AFL, always at odds with Muste and the college, accused the institution of being anti-union, anti-religious and pro-Soviet.

Muste quit the college in 1933, as the result of an argument he had with the faculty, and formed the American Workers Party, which has been described as a "democratically organized revolutionary party."[4] Muste by this time has become less of a Christian and pacifist and more of a revolutionary.

It was not surprising, then, that his group merged with the Communist League of America, the Trotskyist group under the leadership of James P. Cannon. The new party's name was Work-

ers Party of the United States. Cannon wanted this new amalgamation to join the Socialist Party with the object of taking it over. "A
Trotskyist," said Cannon, "will do anything for his party, even if
he has to crawl on his belly in the mud."[5] Apparently this was too
much for Muste, and in 1935, after a European trip on which he
paid court to Leon Trotsky in Norway, he left the Party and
returned to the Fellowship of Reconciliation, with which he had
been associated off and on since 1916.

At this juncture Muste felt he had to reestablish a connection
between his Christian pacifist background and his political activities. He committed himself to a policy of Christian nonviolent
direct action in his quest for peace, a policy to which he held
to the day he died.

From 1948 on, Muste refused to pay his income taxes.
He was brought to court in 1960 and charged with owing $1,165
in taxes over a four-year period, 1948 to 1952, as well as facing
additional penalties for fraud, nonpayment and underestimating
his tax.[6]

Muste both won and lost the case. He was cleared of fraud and
the payment of penalties, but the tax court held that the tax itself
was still due. The money has yet to be collected. Muste had
virtually no assets; what little he made was insufficient to be taxed.
Many of his indirect expenses, however, were underwritten by a
few wealthy Quakers.

Muste was involved in virtually every phase of the peace
movement following World War II. He helped found the Central
Committee for Conscientious Objectors in 1948 and the Committee for Nonviolent Action in 1957. A "Walk for Peace Committee" was formed in the same year, which picketed the White
House; in 1959 Muste climbed the fence into a missile base in
Mead, Nebraska, in protest over the weapons stored there. (In
order to break the law, it was necessary for him to climb the fence
twice, which he did. He spent nine days in jail as a result.) He had
been involved in the San Francisco–Moscow Walk of 1961;
Polaris Action of the previous year at Electric Boat Company in
Groton, Connecticut; and the numerous Washington and New
York peace demonstrations of 1965–1966.

Muste was one of the first to take an "absolutist" position

toward conscription. He not only advised COs during the war not to register for the draft, but also suggested that it was morally right for them to refuse alternative service.

Physically, Muste was tall and thin to the point of seeming undernourished. His collars were too big for his neck; his hands were long and bony. He had a large nose, a small chin, swept-back gray-white hair and plastic-rimmed glasses, all of which gave him the appearance of a bemused parrot. He spoke very softly, seldom raising his voice and never appearing to become excited.

His long fight for peace, he told me, had not alienated him from American society. His grievances, he said, were those of a man who felt a part of it. But, he added, he long ago gave up vocal protests; he was, at the time of our interview, wholly committed to action. "Don't just stand around and say it's wrong," he said. "Get in there and *do* something!" Muste said he was still a Marxist, but one with reservations. He believed, for instance, that Marx's concepts of the impacts of economics on politics and culture were still valid and important.

Muste was particularly irritated by critics who harped on the facial growth of pacifist activists. "When they tell me that there are too many beards among the demonstrators and that the impression is of a beatnik picnic, I tell them that if they want the image changed, they can join the line."

Alfred Hassler, of the Fellowship of Reconciliation, put it another way: "If you can dismiss the criticism of American policy as coming from a beatnik, a bearded slob, then you don't have to deal with the argument he raises.

"We make a point," he continued, "when our demonstrations go on of putting on a necktie and jacket. We don't want this kind of thing to interfere with what we're trying to say to the public. We're trying to say we're fellow Americans."

Muste's attitude toward the Vietnam War was a combination of moral and political points of view. The U.S., he said, has no moral justification for being in Southeast Asia. Whatever morality we ourselves have assumed by our presence there is further weakened, he added, by our having supported the use of gas, napalm, torture and the killing of civilians—all used "in the name of peace and democracy." He saw Communist expansion being halted, not by

the presence of American troops in the area, but by local nationalistic feelings, such as those in Indonesia.

From a political point of view, he would have liked to see the
U.S. declare a unilateralist cease-fire which would, he believed,
open the way for negotiations between the Saigon government and
the National Liberation Front. Both North and South Vietnam
must be reunited, in Muste's view, even if it meant that the majority
of the government was made up of members of the NLF. The NLF,
he told me, is not entirely Marxist but mostly made up of nationalists who, he added, are closer to a Titoist position than blindly pro-
Mao.

In the back of his mind was the specter of China. "The U.S. has
established itself militarily in South Korea, Japan, Okinawa, Tai-
wan, the Philippines and Thailand," he said. "For us to intervene
in Vietnam in addition and to impose our military presence there,
we believe this situation poses a military threat to China. There is
no point telling people you have the best intentions when you
surround them."

"What the U.S. should do in Vietnam," he said, "is to relax
because we, the U.S., will never be able to run it or get any profit
from it.

"I think," he concluded, "this is the most realistic approach."

3

At the present moment, the American peace movement is transfixed by the Vietnam War—far more so than the ordinary American citizen. But there are widely differing attitudes toward the war
within the peace groups.

One point of view is essentially moral and is found primarily
among religious groups such as the American Friends Service
Committee, the Fellowship of Reconciliation and the Catholic
Worker Movement. There is also a secular morality running
through the Committee for Nonviolent Action that differs in
nuance. All these pacifist moralists are saying, in effect, "we
condemn evil and immorality of others—say, the Communists—
but we have become just as evil and immoral."

Another point of view is known as "survivalist." These people are essentially *nuclear* pacifists. They are adamantly against the use of the A- and H-bombs; they reject violence but under certain circumstances might accept a war or the use of force. The Committee for a Sane Nuclear Policy is the major group with this point of view. This strain is found among most other groups but does not seem to be emphasized as much as it is in SANE.

Those who are pro-Vietcong constitute another viewpoint. They want the U.S. to lose in Vietnam. In essence, these people are those who have taken such narrow ideological and moral positions that they have gone beyond the point of mere difference of opinion into the realm of revulsion and hatred. These are the people who carry NLF flags in peace parades. They are the ones who, at a "Read-In for Peace in Vietnam" in February 1966, shouted down a man who had the temerity to suggest that the audience join with him in singing "God Bless America."

Their viewpoint, however, is one of the smallest within the peace movement. In fact, the strongest strain of pro-Vietcong feeling is found among those New Left groups who find themselves in antiwar demonstrations: Progressive Labor Party, Youth against War and Fascism, Vietnam Day Committee, etc. Among peace groups there are shards of this attitude primarily within the Student Peace Union and the Committee for Nonviolent Action.

The most ubiquitous viewpoint of all is the political one. Every peace group argues the politics of the war in Vietnam. To entrap any particular political theme within any one organization is virtually impossible, for there are as many variations as there are individuals within an organization. There are those who believe that America made a mistake and should withdraw; there are others who compare our actions with Russia's in Hungary; there are those who want a cease-fire and negotiations with the NLF (Muste, for instance, favored this); there are others who see the conflict as one between the U.S. and China; and there are those who focus on U.N. actions, Geneva agreements, moratoriums on bombing the North, Congressional elections,* foreign aid, and so

---

* The only peace group that believes in running candidates for office is Massachusetts Political Action for Peace, or Mass Pax, as it is more commonly known. Mass Pax's most famous campaign was the one in 1962 in which Harvard professor H. Stuart Hughes, grandson of Chief Justice

on, until the minutiae of opinion create a fog of confusion and repetition.

Number 5 Beekman Street, New York City, just off the park in front of City Hall, houses the headquarters of many peace groups, much like the "Quaker Quadrangle" in Philadelphia. Clustered together on the top floor—the tenth—in a rabbit warren of rooms and cubicles, are the Fellowship of Reconciliation (the New York City office), the War Resisters League, the Committee for Non-violent Action, the Student Peace Union, the Catholic Peace Fellowship, and *Liberation,* a leading pacifist magazine. Where the offices of one organization stop and the next begin is impossible to determine, for there is no clear distinction. The confusion is visual proof of the overlapping of memberships, functions, techniques and attitudes so prevalent today among peace groups.

The walls are covered with posters and slogans of one sort or another, mostly strident in character, occasionally humorous. One 2½- × 4-foot poster proclaims: "Why are we burning, torturing, killing the people of Vietnam? . . . to prevent free elections. PROTEST this Anti-democratic war!" Another, pasted on a door, says: "This house has no fallout shelter. Peace is our only security." Still a third says: "NOW is the time for all good Americans to get the hell out of VIETNAM!" There are numerous bulletin boards which are covered with such items as news clippings, Jules Feiffer cartoons, personal letters from friends, activity rosters, peace advertisements from various newspapers, requests for rides to Boston, and a variety of small stickers which carry slogans of a pacific nature.

In one corner are the offices of the War Resisters League. This organization was founded in 1923 by Muste and a few others as a secular counterpart to FOR. Since the Fellowship was essentially limited to Christians, there was a need for an organization that drew non-Christians together.

Charles Evans Hughes, ran for the Senate against Republican George C. Lodge and Democrat Edward M. Kennedy. Hughes received 50,000 votes, or 2.3 percent of the total cast. "Hughes was an educational candidate," one Mass Pax stalwart told me. "We now want to back a candidate that can win!"

Originally, the WRL was a peace pledge group and a registry for COs. But during World War II there was a faction fight—one group wishing to keep the organization as a registry group, the other wanting to turn it into a general peace action group. The latter faction won.

Today the WRL is a prime initiator of activities in the peace movement. It has a small membership of five thousand or so, a few of whom are Marxists. Such a small group gains its effectiveness not through any extraordinary zeal on the part of its members but because it joins with other groups to present a temporary united front. It has had a hand in virtually every peace effort since the war, yet the general public is quite unaware of its existence. The actual work of running the League rests with three people: Jim Peck, Ralph Di Gia and Dave McReynolds.

If there ever was a veteran pacifist and civil rights worker, it is Jim Peck. He is an atheist, a veteran hunger striker and a graduate of Danbury Prison (in which he spent three years because he refused to register for the draft in World War II). He has so many scars on his head and neck from beatings by segregationists and police that it raises the question of what he looked like before he became a political activist. The worst beating he suffered was during the 1961 Freedom Ride in which fifty-three stitches were taken in his head alone. He is a quiet fellow who speaks with an ironic turn of phrase but has a blood-in-the-eye look that perhaps explains why he is the focal point for so much violence.

Ralph Di Gia has been the administrative secretary of the WRL since 1955. He too spent the war behind bars—in Danbury and Lewisburg Prisons where he first met many of his pacifist friends. He comes from a radical background; his father he describes as "an anti-fascist who once worked for Carlo Tresca," the anarchist Wobbly. The first time I met Di Gia he had just finished conducting a class on how to avoid the draft for about a dozen mothers and their sons.

One of the most articulate of all pacifists is David McReynolds, thirty-seven, the WRL's field secretary. He comes from a very stable middle-class background. His parents are Republicans; his father served as a colonel in the China-Burma-India theater during World War II; and his grandfather served as secretary to Admiral

Dewey during the Spanish-American War. McReynolds himself is a graduate of UCLA, a pacifist since 1949, tall, well-dressed, spectacled and tending toward baldness. He was once active in the Prohibition Party. "I was a Protestant, a puritan, and a prohibitionist," he said, "and also very lonely and very neurotic, which is true of most of us in the radical movement as leaders." If a label is necessary for what passes as his religion today, he says that it would be a combination of Buddhist, Christian and Hindu.

Whenever he speaks he shows evidence of extensive self-analysis. On the question of whether his pacifism was due to personal cowardice, he takes the same position as Bob Eaton of the FPC, but is far more explicit. "I know," he said, "without any question at all that physically I am a coward. The idea of being hit in the face terrifies me terribly. But I think I am a pacifist despite being a coward not because of it. . . .

"Sure I'm a coward, but that wasn't what put me in the pacifist movement; in fact, that is what kept me out of it for a while. I had long talks about going into a movement when the requirement is that you take risks which you cannot defend yourself against.

"We don't have defense guards for our rallies: we go out and if we're attacked, we're attacked and that's it. If being a coward were central to my activities, I would not have any activities; I would resign. I certainly wouldn't work at this kind of work. I would be terrified all the time."

McReynolds, on the subject of Vietnam, is opposed to anyone —Japanese, Chinese or American—"taking over Asia," as he thinks the U.S. is trying to do now. "I think American policy in Asia," he says, "is about as close to being irrational as it can be without being clinically insane."

He assumes a fairly common pacifist stance on the solution: "We have never before fought a war," he said, "where a large number of citizens thought we ought to lose the war. A lot of us feel that we ought not to win this war, including myself. I don't want anyone to win it but I most emphatically do not want *us* to win this war. I think it is unjust. . . ." He went on to say that Vietnam has not had free elections because Ho Chi Minh probably would have won them, which McReynolds feels would have been unfortunate. He does not believe that North Vietnam is either free or democratic, as some of the pro-Vietcong peace factions do; but he says that it is the right of both the North and South Vietnamese to choose what government they want.

It is often said that active pacifism is lonely, difficult and thankless work. Dave McReynolds agrees, but he sees some advantages. "I think the idea that a pacifist is a particularly lonely person—or one who walks a lonely road—is true, until you walk the road. When you first say no, you think you're saying no only to the draft. And then you realize that . . . you are also saying no to every law in the country. Because if you're going to put yourself in judgment over one law you have really to put yourself in judgment over every law. You have to think for yourself. At this point you're very lonely. The first year or two when you begin to make this shift is a very great agony, but the idea is not really that of being alone; it's the idea of accepting a personal set of values. It's the same agony if you change from a Protestant to a Catholic. But when you walk to the other side you find there is a whole crowd waiting to meet you that you never knew about before.

"The pacifist movement," continued McReynolds, "is in a very fundamental way an anti-Communist movement, or anti-totalitarian movement. And the appeal that it makes is not an anti-Americanism but rather to an anti-military position; obviously if you're going to make a break with American violence, you're going to fight it out with Soviet violence or Chinese violence."[7]

This does not discount the immense amount of verbiage emanating from pacifist and/or peace groups that sounds as if it were created by dedicated Communists. It appears this way, however, only because many of the youths speak the jargon but fail to understand its meaning. Tom Cornell, a member of the Catholic Worker Movement and, in this instance, speaking not only of those in the peace movement but of the New Left, said: "These kids really don't understand Marx or Lenin or Social Revolution. They're rather unschooled in most everything. Primarily their protests are against background. Many of them are middle-class; quite a few are middle-class Jewish kids who react against their upbringing, the regimentation of being Jewish, or wearing lovelocks when they were kids. They seem to be rejecting everything about society. They are not revolutionaries; they are only protesting and hollering and letting off their venom, but they are not a menace."

The Committee for Nonviolent Action was A. J. Muste's favorite protest group. Virtually every important person in the peace movement is connected with the Committee in one way or another. Muste was chairman until his death; Ralph De Gia is treasurer. On the Executive and National Committees are Dave Dellinger of *Liberation* magazine; Robert Gilmore and Robert Pickus, both of Turn Toward Peace; Bradford Lyttle, also of the WRL; Jim Peck, Bayard Rustin and David McReynolds. Some of the consultants are Henry Cadbury, the honorary chairman of the American Friends Service Committee; Dorothy Day of the Catholic Worker Movement; Ammon Hennacy, the well-known anarchist who is also associated with the Catholic Workers; and Mildred Scott Olmstead, the executive director emeritus of the Women's International League for peace and Freedom.

The Committee was founded in 1957 at a time when there was considerable concern over the rising intensification of the cold war. Largely through the efforts of Lawrence Scott, a staff member of the AFSC, the Committee for Nonviolent Action was formed for the purpose of seeking more imaginative and dramatic nonviolent actions in the cause of peace. The Committee has no membership. Its followers are essentially pacifist—but not necessarily Christian—in their outlook, and they tend to belong to many other left-wing and pacifist organizations.

Because it is only a committee and not a membership group, it allows people to demonstrate as individuals. The polling of a membership for a decision on a course of action is avoided, thus eliminating acrimonious debate and schisms. The CNVA, in effect, initiates an idea and then asks others to join in if they wish. Most people in the peace movement do, with enthusiasm.

Muste stated that the CNVA believes in civil disobedience and the Gandhian position of nonviolent political action. Most followers, he added, accept the unilateralist position that the U.S. must disarm—partly for moral reasons, partly for political reasons.

Perhaps the most important word in the Committee's title is "action," for there is no peace group more active than this one. It is the natural culmination of Muste's "Get in there and *do* something!" admonition which his admirers carry out with zest and passion.

The Committee's first action was against nuclear testing in Nevada in 1957. Some seventy-five persons held a vigil outside the testing grounds. On Hiroshima Day (6 August), eleven of the protesters tried to invade the test site, "to present their bodies," according to their literature, "as a living barrier to the continuation of tests." They were arrested for trespassing.

In 1958, the *Golden Rule,* a thirty-foot ketch captained by Albert Bigelow (now one of CNVA's consultants), tried to sail into the restricted Pacific test zone, but was stopped by the Coast Guard outside Honolulu. The five crewmen, including Bigelow, were given sixty days in prison. Later on, Earle Reynolds (also a CNVA consultant) and his family sailed their yacht, *Phoenix,* sixty-five miles into the test zone before he was stopped. He was sentenced to six months in prison, but the conviction was reversed on appeal.

The next year CNVA initiated Omaha Action, a civil disobedience effort to protest against the construction and possible use of intercontinental ballistics missiles located in the area. This was the time that Muste had to climb the fence twice before he broke the law. He and fifteen others were arrested, several of whom served six months in prison.

In 1960, Polaris Action was the Committee's biggest and most successful effort of the year. The Electric Boat Company in Groton, Connecticut, was picketed, and several acts of civil disobedience were committed, the most spectacular being the illegal boarding of the nuclear sub *Ethan Allen* by a swimmer.

The San Francisco to Moscow Walk for Peace was the big effort of 1961. It actually took place—ten months of walking by a number of different pacifists (as opposed to the 1963 Quebec to Guantánamo Bay Walk, which was stopped by the Feds at the water's edge in Florida).

The *Everyman I, II,* and *III* protest sailings during 1962 were unsuccessful. Two of the boats were stopped by the Coast Guard as they were heading for the Pacific test site. The third was refused entry into Leningrad. As that boat was being towed out to sea by the Russians, the crew tried to scuttle the ship. They were not even able to do that successfully. Members of all three of the crews were given sentences ranging up to six months.

Since that time the Committee has been in the thick of the peace movement upsurge. The members have intiated draft-card burnings; they have picketed the Oakland Army Terminal; they were instrumental in setting up the "Assembly of Unrepresented People" in the summer of 1965, in which 350 people were jailed for committing civil disobedience; they have tried to block troop-ships either by sailing outrigger canoes or, as a last resort, by swimming across their bows; they have organized literally hundreds of pickets and sit-ins in the last three years alone, at such places as the State Department, the Democratic Convention at Atlantic City (in 1964), the Sikorsky Aircraft factory, the Pentagon, Armed Forces Day celebrations, and virtually every chemical company that makes napalm. They were the prime movers behind the anti-Vietnam War parades down New York's Fifth Avenue as well as the antiwar demonstrations in Washington in April and November of 1965.

The Committee's volume of activity is so large in fact that it is difficult to determine where the major emphasis lies. For instance, the New York CNVA puts out *Action Bulletin* every two weeks or so. Taking one at random, dated 17 September 1965, the Committee, over an eight-day period, was involved in the following:

Friday, September 17:
> *Party,* for Flatbush Committee to End the War in Vietnam.
> *Debate,* "Politics and the anti-War Movement," at the Militant Labor Forum [an SWP organization].
> *Teach-in,* "Is Radical Dissent Possible in America Today?" Statler-Hilton.

Saturday, September 18:
> *Workshops,* Statler-Hilton.
> *Vigil,* "End the War in Vietnam,'" Times Square [also sponsored by 12 other groups].
> *Street Meeting & Vietnamese Literature Sale,* 6th Ave. & 8th St.
> *Forum,* "Vietnam and the Draft," Free University, 20 E. 14th St.

Sunday, September 19:
Street Meeting & Vietnamese Literature Sale.
Party, for the Medical Committee for Human Rights, "Village Gate."

Wednesday, September 22:
Demonstration, "Protest against American support of the totalitarian government of South Vietnam," walk from Washington Square to 39 Whitehall St.; sit in [at recruiting booth there].
Soap-boxing, Vietnam, 10th St. & Avenue B.

Thursday, September 23:
Demonstration, "Protest against torture and senseless killing in Vietnam," Vigil and leaflet distribution, 108th St. and Amsterdam Ave.

Friday, September 24:
Demonstration, "Protest against the violations of human rights and international agreements by the United States in Vietnam." Walk from recruiting stations at 24th St. & 7th Ave. to the United Nations.
Sing-in for Peace, Carnegie Hall, followed by walk to Washington Square led by "many of the performers."
Talk, "Leon Trotsky in the Age of Permanent Revolution," Militant Labor Forum.

Liberation is the voice of that section of the peace movement that stands for radical pacifism: nonviolence, direct action, civil disobedience. Because these ideas are concentrated within the CNVA, it is no coincidence that the leadership of both the Committee and the magazine are similar. Dave Dellinger is editor, and Staughton Lynd, Dave McReynolds, and Bayard Rustin are three of the associate editors. The forty-some contributors, however, cover a wider spectrum of protest: James Baldwin, Lawrence Ferlinghetti, Michael Harrington, Martin Luther King, Jr., and Linus Pauling are but a few examples.

Dave Dellinger is the spark behind *Liberation.* He has been its editor since it was started in 1956, and has built it into one of the most widely respected publications among radicals. Dellinger comes from a well-to-do family in Massachusetts. He graduated from Yale in 1936 and went on to study as a Henry Fellow at New College, Oxford. He has been a pacifist and a conscientious objector since before World War II.

Dellinger is the object of a certain personality cult. He is revered by a few and admired by most everyone in the peace movement. He spent three years in prison during the war because of his views; he has since been in jail a number of times, mostly for acts of civil disobedience, the latest being thirty days in August 1965 after his participation in acts of civil disobedience during the Assembly of Unrepresented People in Washington, D.C.

He also has the reputation of never—as the current slang has it—"losing his cool." He refuses to compromise his views in the slightest, he is a veteran hunger striker, he is totally committed to the cause of peace, and he is willing to suffer beatings, jailing, fines, insults and ostracism because of his views. Undoubtedly what sets him apart, however, is his masculinity. In a field where many men are not quite men and many of the women are suspect too, Dellinger stands out as—if you will—a masculine man.

Staughton Lynd is also the center of a personality cult. He was born in 1929, the son of the authors of *Middletown* and *Middletown in Transition,* the celebrated sociological studies of Muncie, Indiana. Lynd graduated from Harvard in 1951 and two years later, because he claimed to be a CO, was given noncombatant duty in the Army. In 1954, he and a number of others received undesirable discharges because of their views, but a later Supreme Court decision forced the Army to grant them honorable discharges. This made Lynd eligible for the GI Bill, which he used to get a Ph.D.

He worked for a few years at the Macedonia Cooperative Community in northeast Georgia, then briefly at the Glen Gardner Cooperative Community in New Jersey where he met Dellinger, who was in the process of setting up *Liberation.* He taught history at Spelman College in Atlanta for three years and, since 1964, has been an assistant professor of history at Yale.

Lynd differs from other leaders on the left because he belongs to no group within it. His only ties are as an editor of *Liberation* and *Studies on the Left.* His strength comes from two sources: his charisma and his radicalism.

He has a Kennedy quality about him: young, tousled hair, subdued passion, striking looks, the chopping motions with the hands when a point is made, a thin clear voice that deepens in seriousness. The appeal of these characteristics should not be underestimated, particularly among the young who have already canonized the assassinated President.

As for his views, they are quite radical. He is a proponent of the street demonstration, the confrontation, the dramatic act, the vigil, the sit-in, the picket, the act of civil disobedience—in the belief that action is the only method which will bring about a change. He believes that actions must be taken even if the consequences are not fully understood, in the hope that the actions will somehow lead to an improvement.

During the 17 April 1965 March on Washington, he had this comment to make about the demonstrators and their possible powers:

> Still more poignant was the perception . . . that as the crowd moved down the Mall toward the seat of government, its path delimited on each side by rows of chartered buses so that there was no where to go but forward, toward the waiting policemen, it seemed that the great mass of people would simply flow on through and over the marble buildings, that our forward movement was irresistibly strong, that even had some been shot or arrested nothing could have stopped that crowd from taking possession of its government.[8]

This view of the world has been described as romanticism and "putschism" by a number of Lynd's critics.

Lynd is also a Quaker, a tax-refuser, "a product of Marxist and pacifist thought"; he has a blind spot for communism, a well-developed sense of righteousness, a conviction that the best society may be akin either to "African socialism" or to that which is found in an Israeli kibbutz; and he has a desire, as Irving Howe recalls it, "to dance at all the weddings," to be all radical things to all radical men. Lynd's brand of radicalism is best expressed by his peace trip to Hanoi in December 1965 and January 1966, which he took with Tom Hayden of SDS and Herbert Aptheker, the Communist. Lynd first defied the U.S. government ban on travel to North Vietnam; he then went with no credentials except "good will" and a dozen potholders his children had made as presents for his hosts in Hanoi.[9] Once there, Lynd proceeded to make a speech over the radio in which he denounced his own country's policies in Vietnam as "immoral, illegal and anti-democratic."[10] Upon his return to America, Lynd's passport was cancelled, much to his surprise. He sued successfully for its return on the grounds that its cancellation abridges his freedom of speech.

Such diverse personalities on the board of *Liberation* naturally lead to many internal stresses and strains. In fact, there is a three-way split among the board members that is worth noting here only because it is symptomatic of the differences which divide many of the peace groups.

In one corner are the radical pacifists—Dellinger and Lynd—who are essentially "hard-liners" and revolutionaries. Opposing them are Rustin and McReynolds, who are more pragmatic reformers rather than revolutionaries. The followers of Muste sit in the middle—confused by the crescendo of polemics around them—sympathizing with both but agreeing with none. Muste told me, "The essential difference is over the position of non-violent revolution, which means you're for neither nonviolent pacifism nor acquiescence in the status quo. You are demanding basic change, but you reject violence; therefore; in the radical pacifist wing you will find certain tensions between support of revolution and support of violence."

Beverly Sterner, a veteran of Polaris Action and formerly Muste's personal secretary, says that the argument is really over to what extent the peace movement should cooperate with the New Left within the framework of the peace groups' nonexclusion policy. Do we, they ask, cooperate past the point of violence? Dellinger and Lynd, under certain circumstances, might agree; others would not. She also says that the split reflects the antagonisms between the "old left"—"coalitionists," "compromisers," "reformers," as they are called by their opponents—and the New Left, which considers itself pure and free and unblemished.

4

The National Committee for a Sane Nuclear Policy, or SANE, is hated with uncommon fervor by most of the above peace groups, primarily because it is not a revolutionary organization, and secondly because its members tend to be "liberals" rather than radicals. No one down at 5 Beekman Street has a nice word for the folks on the Committee up on East 47th Street.

SANE is considered the major "survivalist" group within the peace camp. That is to say, it is primarily concerned with solving individual problems, the main emphasis to date being the control of nuclear weapons. "It is not a question whether truth lies to the left or to the right," says Donald Keys, SANE's program director, "it is a question of defining step-by-step approaches to the solution of a problem." The organization has tried its hand at protesting the Vietnam War, but it is still interested primarily in creating a world—now that a nuclear test ban is in force—in which there is no possibility of accidental war or nuclear poisoning.

SANE was founded in 1957 by the pragmatists in the peace movement: the late Clarence Pickett, Norman Cousins and Norman Thomas, to name three. Ideologically, it has always been close to the Campaign for Nuclear Disarmament in Britain with its single-minded concern over "the bomb." (Similarly, the groups at 5 Beekman Place are close to Bertrand Russell's radical break-away from CND, the Committee of 100.) It is the only organization to have taken a stand on Communists. In 1960, it adopted a resolution condemning totalitarians of both the left and the right. This is one of the reasons why SANE is hated so much by the radical groups. It is also the reason why other groups sprang into prominence, particularly the Student Peace Union, a magazine called *Minority of One,* and a number of tiny Marxist groups, mostly of an ephemeral nature.

The Committee operates on three levels: first, by trying to influence the "thought leaders" at the centers of power. The organization has an impressive list of influential directors and sponsors: Dr. Benjamin Spock and H. Stuart Hughes are co-chairmen, Steve Allen is a vice-chairman. Sponsors include Pablo

Casals, Leonard Bernstein, ex-Ambassador James J. Wadsworth, and François Mauriac.

Second, it conducts peace education programs among the general public. Its well-known *New York Times* full-page ads are part of this effort. One ad, entitled "The Winner of World War III," showed a picture of only a tiny cockroach. Another one, entitled "Dr. Spock Is Worried"—perhaps SANE's most famous ad—shows the well-known pediatrician pondering the future health of a little child.

Last, SANE has been demonstrating in the streets. This is not of the Committee's choosing; it was forced upon it when it became apparent, sometime in the early 1960s, that the New Left and the more undisciplined peace groups were stealing all the peace headlines. So, in order to retain whatever influence it has had within the movement, it has turned activist.

SANE seeks to balance its advocacy of ideas against their acceptability in society. This is the classic dilemma of all "outside" groups: if your ideas are too radical, you scare off your support; if your ideas are too commonplace, you find that no one is interested. SANE is trying to find this middle ground. It seeks to create a broad-based, nonaligned (i.e., neither pro- nor anti-American foreign policy as dogma) group that is effective. This is why SANE insisted on excluding Communists. It knew that with Communists as members SANE would never be broad-based, nonaligned or effective.

"The muscle in the peace movement," says Keys, "is not in little units but in large groups like SANE."

SANE also seeks to be a bridge between the peace groups and the two major parties. This does not imply, however, that SANE shifts its position of a question in order to stay between the two. It just so happens that to date it has found itself in that position, and it is trying to put it to good advantage.

SANE claims to have approximately twenty-five thousand supporters. Most of those that I met seem to have gravitated to SANE because of some void in the major parties. They tend to be liberals of the ADA stripe and considerably more idealistic. Keys agrees with this. "Gutwise," he told me, "a large percentage of SANEers have adopted the philosophy that loyalty to Mankind comes before loyalty to country."

5

The most enigmatic of the peace groups is the Catholic Worker Movement. Deeply religious, moody, unpredictable, maddeningly vague and philosophically obscure, this group is the current terror of the peace front. Among other things, its members burn draft cards, applaud America's enemies and attack their own church. Their running battle with the authorities has sparked a renewed interest in anarchism among the young.

A French-peasant-scholar, Peter Maurin, founded the Movement in 1933 in New York. His closest disciple was Dorothy Day, then a recent convert to Catholicism, who came from a Wobbly-Socialist-Communist-Woman's Suffrage background. Together they put out an eight-page newspaper, *Catholic Worker,* which sold for one cent. It still sells for that today.

Maurin sought a new intellectual synthesis capable of creating a nonviolent revolutionary movement aimed at establishing a new social order. This synthesis was developed around Christian teachings: the Sermon on the Mount, works of Mercy, voluntary poverty, personal responsibility, the love of God, and peace.

Out of these views came the conception of "Christian communism"—an apparent contradiction in terms—which meant the communal ownership of the produce "as told of the just Christians in the Acts of the Apostles."[11] This Christian communism, he said, however, must be voluntary and must respect the right of private property—the ownership of tools, homes, land, etc. To practice these views, the Movement for many years ran an eighty-three-acre farm on Staten Island, since sold. There is, however, another farm in Tivoli, New York, overlooking the Hudson, to which members can repair to practice their Christian communism.

The Movement grew spectacularly during the 1930s. The *Catholic Worker* reached a peak circulation of 165,000 per week in 1938, an extraordinary figure for such a small group. But the Movement soon went into decline, primarily because it refused to condemn the Spanish Roman Catholic Church (which supported

Franco) even while it was attacking both the Nationalists and the Republicans as totalitarians. The group also suffered during World War II because many of its members were in jail as conscientious objectors.

Today, the Movement runs a number of "Houses of Hospitality"—a euphemism for flophouses—around the country. The two best-known are the one on Chrystie Street in New York's Bowery and the recently closed "Joe Hill House" in Salt Lake City, which was run by Ammon Hennacy.

The active membership is estimated at 500; but the *Catholic Worker*'s circulation is 80,000 or so, which indicates a wider, more passive support than would otherwise be supposed.

All those who take part in CW affairs are not of the same mind, but they do have certain traits in common. Most activists are radical Catholics, pacifists, young and fairly well educated. They accept a life of voluntary poverty and lay monasticism, in the old sense of the phrase. Rather than address problems with "sociological first-aid," they would prefer to break with what they believe to be an immoral and corrupt society and to return to a Christian way of life. They are anti-exploitation on any front—capitalist, socialist or nationalist; they sympathize with some of Marx's writings but are not necessarily Marxists; and most of them believe that Maurin, who died in 1949, is a saint.

Some members are doctrinaire anarchists; others are Catholic anarchists, who believe that their church should take over the function of the state.

The Chrystie Street headquarters, in the heart of the Bowery, is a three-story tenement in a distressing state of repair. On the first floor is the kitchen-dining room and the anteroom, where the derelicts can wait for their one meal a day without fear of being picked up for vagrancy. The second floor is a TV room with crude wooden furniture; and the third floor houses the editorial offices of the *Catholic Worker*. There are signs all over the walls. "Pax," says one. "This floor will safely sustain a load of 40 lbs. per square foot," says another. "Iesus caritas," says a hand-printed sign. Another reads: "With Resounding cymbals, cymbals that crash /Give praise/Let everything that has breath/All Living creatures PRAISE THE LORD.

The whole building smells musty and damp. Much of this is due to the anteroom, which is hosed down after most of the derelicts have returned to the streets. Every time I visited the building, there were a number of derelicts wandering in and out of the place. Some were asleep on benches, others argued incoherently among themselves. No one seemed to pay much attention to them. Whenever there was a need for organization, the Catholic Workers would give orders in a quiet voice—no pushing, no shoving, no shouting—and with great consideration for the feelings of the derelicts. One aged fellow, half of whose face had been frozen immobile apparently by a stroke, kept following me around asking through the working half of his mouth for a cigarette. Another kept telling me his life story over and over again.

The derelicts are fed only a lunch meal: soup, tea and bread. The soup has meat and noodles in it. The bread is either donated or bought as "seconds" from hospitals and other public institutions. The meat is bought fresh because the Chrystie Street building has no refrigeration equipment. Approximately 150 to 200 bums are fed there each day.

The evening meal is for "the community"—i.e., those who work for the CW—and is slightly more substantial: meat, vegetables, salad, dessert, coffee. Approximately fifty people are working in the New York area at any one time. They all live most frugally, being paid nothing save subsistence money.

I went to one of their Friday night meetings, which are convened "for the clarification of thought." It was held in the kitchen-dining room. There were about sixty people present, all of them well dressed, all types and all ages; no derelicts were visible. Before the meeting started, Chris Kearns—a pleasant, crew-cut anarchist dressed in a denim suit, and the roommate of David Miller—explained the Catholic Worker philosophy to me. He said: "We address ourselves to moral questions, not laws, because 'Caesar can always beat you at the law.' " It is for this reason that CWs commit civil disobedience and refuse to pay fines when arrested. They are taking a moral position rather than a legal one.

He added that they do not question their church on theology, but only on positions outside it. Their major attack is against what

Kearns called the "church corporate" attitude, or the "Wall Street mentality," which means the church's preoccupation with material ownership, fancy vestments and power. To illustrate the point, Kearns told an apocryphal story—apparently a favorite of most CWs—concerning Francis Cardinal Spellman, the man most disliked within the Movement. When Cardinal Spellman goes to Heaven, he knocks on the gate and says: "It's me, St. Peter—Cardinal Spellman." St. Peter looks at the paper in front of him and says: "I'm sorry, but I don't have you down on my list; but just a moment and I'll check my files." After a while, St. Peter returns and says: "It's okay, Cardinal Spellman, you can come in; we have you down under 'real estate.' "

"The church," says Kearns, "should be working for peace, to produce a Christian world. But what is it doing? It's more interested in its investment portfolio."

The main attraction of the evening was Murphy Dowouis (pronounced Dewey), who played his guitar and sang songs of protest—"Hallelujah, I'm a Bum," "Joe Hill," "We Shall Overcome" and so forth. Dowouis is a young Louisianan whose nickname is "Cajun." He has a shock of black hair that he constantly grooms and teases with a comb that he keeps in the back pocket of his levis. "Unless you face overwhelming odds," he told the audience between songs, "you don't sing." He went on to lament that "once you are respectable, you don't sing." (Dowouis was arrested by the FBI for draft dodging seven weeks after this meeting.)

The evening was obviously a moving experience to the audience. They often broke in and sang along with Dowouis. They all sang with passion and gusto. There were prayers at the beginning, prayers at the end, plenty of conversation before and afterward and, throughout, a general feeling of warmth, friendship and belonging.

The Movement has produced three well-known personalities of late: David Miller, the draft-card burner; Dorothy Day, the editor of *Catholic Worker;* and Ammon Hennacy, the anarchist.

David Miller is a graduate of Le Moyne College in Syracuse where he was greatly influenced by the radical priest Father Daniel

Berrigan. He comes from what he calls "a nonconformist" home. A pleasant person, quiet, well groomed, articulate, Miller is not the usual picture of a rebel.

Miller does not believe that there is any conceivable situation in which violence is justified. Even if he had to come to the rescue of someone else, he would "put himself in-between" the antagonists. "It's surprising, but it works," he says.

Fear of being hurt was not the primary reason why he took an anti-draft stand. "I think if I were really that scared of being hurt," he said in retrospect, "I wouldn't put myself in a position of facing a number of years of jail."

He says he could not fill out his draft classification questionnaire because "that would give sanction to the conscription system, and it's the very idea of conscription that I'm opposed to." Miller does not consider himself a draft dodger because a draft dodger falsifies "rather than confronts." Dave McReynolds feels the same way, for instance, when he says: "Don't evade the draft; resist it!"[12] They make the distinction between the evader, whom they dislike—who feints homosexuality, drug addiction and insanity—and the re-sister, whom they admire because he openly and honestly attacks a practice he does not like.

Miller believes that the anti-draft-card-burning law is unconstitutional because it has no function other than to curb protest. He says he has no regrets for having burned his.

Draft-card burning did not start with David Miller or with any other group in the 1960s. Muste and a group of his friends were burning draft cards as far back as 1948. Undoubtedly the practice goes back to World War I and conscription. Nor is David Miller the champion card burner. His friend Tom Cornell, also of the CW, seems to hold the record. He has publicly burned eight cards at one time or another.

Cornell is the son of a successful traveling salesman. As a youth he sang on local radio shows. By the time he had finished college he had accepted pacifism, although he was not opposed then to alternative service in place of military training. Eventually he came around to the view of noncooperation, the same position held by Miller and McReynolds.

When Miller burned his draft card in 1965, Cornell found that he was without any to burn, having put the torch to his previously. So he wrote to his draft board and said he had no draft registration or classification cards because he had burned them years ago and would the board please send him duplicates? Apparently the draft board did, because Cornell promptly went out and burned them in public.[13]

Dorothy Day, at seventy, is the link with the past. She is greatly respected by all those in the Movement and is undoubtedly the organization's most stabilizing influence. She is a tall, plainly dressed, grandmotherly type with bifocal glasses and a tiara of blond-faded-to-gray hair. She has high cheekbones and a look of infinite patience about her. Ammon Hennacy, in his *Book of Ammon,* wrote: "Everyone is enamored of her and calls her a saint. One woman wanted to know if she saw visions and she replied, 'Hell no.' "

She believes that the government's reaction to the draft-card burners and similar protests against the draft is indicative of the government's growing "fear" and "sense of guilt." This, she sees, may inhibit further attempts to deal with Communists by force.[14] Like many others in the Movement, she believes that professional anti-communism is obstructing the road to peace.

Although I never met any CWs who applauded immolations, Dorothy Day is definitely not one to encourage them. To her, immolation is suicide, which can never be condoned.

One CW has already burned himself to death. Roger LaPorte, a student at New York's Hunter College, set himself afire in front of the United Nations and died in agony thirty-three hours later.[15] The only witness to the entire episode, ironically, was a gasoline truck driver who asked that his name not be mentioned when he was interviewed by the press.

This immolation took place only one week after Norman Morrison, a Quaker from Baltimore, set himself alight at the Pentagon, scarcely a hundred yards from Secretary of Defense McNamara's office window. Morrison died almost immediately but the baby he was holding was saved before it was burned.

Although these two immolations were not the first in America (a woman burned herself to death in Detroit earlier in the year), they nevertheless sent waves of shock through the public. The peace movement was particularly hard hit. When I spoke to peace workers about these immolations I would receive, for the most part, inchoate explanations. Everyone seemed to be wrestling with some moral dilemma. I had the feeling that, on the one hand, they were horrified by the burnings, yet, on the other hand, were searching deep down in their consciences for some justification of what seemed to them to be the supreme expression of protest. They seemed to equate supreme expression with supreme nobility; yet they knew that the immolations, plainly put, were suicides— still not an acceptable practice in Western culture.

On Roger LaPorte, Ammon Hennacy had this to say: "Anyone who can do it is fine, but it takes an innocent to do it. I couldn't do it. . . ."

The Quakers have been particularly divided on the issue. Among conservative Quakers, there is general condemnation; they quote the Bible as proof that such an act is not in keeping with the Christian spirit. The more liberal Quakers, generally those who live along the East Coast, are not so horrified. Says Bob Eaton of the Friends Peace Committee: "It should not be encouraged, but it raises questions. That is to say, it is not for us to judge the act, but to learn from it."

Ammon Hennacy is the third personality to emerge from the Catholic Worker Movement. He is perhaps America's best-known anarchist. He actually calls himself a Christian anarchist—"one who turns the other cheek, overturns the tables of the money changers, and who does not need a cop to tell him how to behave." Bullets and ballots, he adds, will never achieve his ideal; only the "One Man Revolution"—which is a voluntary spiritual transformation within each person—will ever achieve it.

Hennacy is descended on his mother's side from an old rebel family, the Fitz-Randolphs. His paternal grandfather was an Irishman who fled the 1848 potato famine and who later fought for the North in the Civil War "when he wasn't fighting booze."

Hennacy himself was born in 1893 in a Baptist environment. He soon rebelled against that. He thought Billy Sunday was a blasphemous bigot. By 1910, Hennacy was a pacifist, a vegetarian, a socialist and a Wobbly. He studied Yoga, spiritualism and Theosophy on the side, has since been convinced that he is guided by a "Celestial Bulldozer," apparently a combination of God, luck and fate.

In 1917, he was sentenced to two years in the Atlanta penitentiary for refusing to register for the draft. He met Alexander Berkman, the anarchist, there and they became good friends. It was the first of his countless visits to prison.

Upon his release from Atlanta, Hennacy began his career as an itinerant rebel that has lasted up to the present. He is a rootless individual who always seems to be moving on to another job and another protest. At various times in his life he has been a Fuller Brush salesman; an itinerant cotton picker, fruit picker and vegetable picker; a sheep herder; a dairy farmer; a wood-chopping pioneer; a hobo; and a social worker among Hopi, Navajo and Zuni Indians as well as among derelict winos.

His life of protest has been extraordinary. He is probably the only American whose major form of protest is the fast. To fast properly, one must be conditioned psychologically. Hennacy writes that once he has fasting on his mind—that is, he is about to begin—no food tastes good to him. The first few days are the roughest: headaches, a growling stomach and obvious weakness. Eventually, a "second wind" is reached and water is sufficient to sustain oneself. Physical movements must be made slowly to guard against dizziness.

Ralph Di Gia, another who has fasted on occasion, says he would dream about food the first few days or so. At the end of one particular twenty-one-day fast, he wolfed down a huge meal to appease his appetite. He had agonizing chest pains for three days because his stomach had shrunk and had become very tender over the three-week period. Di Gia claims that what carries you through a fast is being involved in a cause, something with which Hennacy undoubtedly would agree.

Hennacy protests against many things, no one issue being paramount. He has never payed any taxes because they are used, he says, to wage war; he refuses to stand up for the "Star-Spangled Banner"; he has fought for the rights of the American Indians; he used to hold memorial services for Sacco and Vanzetti every August 23 (the day they were executed in 1927) but discontinued the practice in 1942 when only one person showed up; he has fasted as penance for our bombing of Hiroshima; he is anti-capitalist and anti-Communist because he is essentially anti-totalitarian; he calls American a "breakfast food box-top culture"; he has picketed the Atomic Energy Commission, missile sites, civil defense offices and a number of other organizations he does not like. He has been sent to prison for many of these activities. He was one of the ones, for instance, who received six months for going over the fence at the missile site near Omaha in 1959.

What then does he want? He writes:

> The Remedy is clear, but the trend today is deeper and deeper in the mire of government paternalism and war, and the distraction of the public by radio give-away programs, bingo, witch hunts, and escapist Youth for Christ, World Government, and such delusions. Decentralization of society with each family unit or cooperative group living simply on the land! Self-government and individual responsibility! Mutual credit and free exchange! Freedom instead of government! A realization that you cannot make people good by law and that the Sermon on the Mount surpasses all codes and dogmas![16]

Hennacy lives at present in Salt Lake City with his attractive second wife.* "Salt Lake City," he says, "needs an anarchist like me." He is an extraordinary-looking fellow. He has a great big hook nose, a shovel chin, and eyes that sparkle. From pictures, his white hair sat like a mop on top of his head and looked as if it had been electrified. Recently he has had it cropped back. None of the clothes that he wears has he bought; all have been made by friends. He says that wearing store-bought leather shoes does not offend his vegetarian instincts. "If somebody will make me a pair of vegetarian shoes, size 9½ B," he says, "I'll wear 'em." He used to wear a Gandhi-type hat; he does not believe in germs, but he does believe in reincarnation. He never wears a tie; he does not drink or smoke but he swears now and then. He often gives the impression in conversation that he is pulling your leg. There is also

---

* Hennacy's first wife went off and joined the I AM religion in the 1930s. According to Hennacy, she believes he is the reincarnation of Benedict Arnold.

virtually no subject on which he does not have an opinion, usually a pungent one.

He became converted to Catholicism and the Catholic Worker Movement in the 1930s because, he said, "I had a crush on Dorothy [Day] but I got over it in a few years. We come to the Catholic Worker for mixed reasons, not all of them noble," he added.

Recently Hennacy has had a slight falling out with Dorothy Day and has actually renounced his Catholicism. The argument was over Dorothy Day's apparent obedience to Cardinal Spellman over the church's view of the Vietnam War. Hennacy claims she would have rebelled previously.

"I don't believe in Hell," he said, "I don't believe in obedience. I would have joined the Mormon Church if Dorothy had been a Mormon. I joined the Catholic Church because of the Catholic Worker and Dorothy, and when she turns around and supports Spellman—then compromises—that was what made me say out loud that I was no longer Catholic. I haven't been to communion, I won't obey a priest, I won't confess, I won't obey the Pope; I'll obey my conscience first!"

"Spellman," he adds, "is such an ass."

He also thinks Dorothy Day is too serious about converting the world and has lost her humor. She does not think it very amusing, Hennacy claims, when he turns to her and says: "God tells you what to do but being Irish helps a little."

The one word that has most meaning to Hennacy is courage. "If you don't have it," he writes, "you cannot practice the other virtues." He has the utmost contempt for those who do not have the courage to stick to their convictions—the backsliders, those who lose faith, who give up, who have been bought off. He reserves a special dislike for the part-time anarchist, the one who says, as he puts it: "I'm for the revolution but—shhhh—not too loud or I'll lose my job." Hennacy has never wavered from his convictions—no matter how vague and utopian they might be— and is willing to go to extremes, even death, in support of them.

What is he trying to prove with his "One Man Revolution"? "I want to prove," he told me, "that some people in every generation must live up to what they know. I know better than not to seek anything but the best. I'm trying to be an example of the type of these heroes of mine."

Hennacy's heroes are Tolstoi, Debs, Jefferson, Abdul Baha, St. Francis, Vanzetti and Gandhi. By living up to what he knows, Hennacy hopes that someday his name will be enshrined along with the others so that perhaps the spirit of one more man will be awakened to carry on the revolution.

Until recently, Hennacy ran the "Joe Hill House," a Catholic Worker House of Hospitality, in Salt Lake City. The authorities closed it down because it was unsanitary. He also had problems with the neighbors because the derelicts, in their alcoholic confusion, would often knock on the wrong doors. "I'm the only one who won't call the police," says Hennacy, "so I get the full load of bums."

Once a man asked after his work at the mission, "Have you rehabilitated any of those poor unfortunates?[11]

"Hell no," said Hennacy, "I haven't rehabilitated myself yet."

PART SIX

THE
INDEPENDENTS

18

From Prohibition to Krajewski

1

In addition to those organizations mentioned previously, there are a number of political parties that can qualify only as "independent." One of them, and perhaps the best known, is the Prohibition Party, the third oldest political party in the United States.

Sentiment in favor of temperance can be traced back in America all the way to the Pilgrim fathers. Organized opposition to the sale and consumption of liquor, however, dates from 1826 with the founding of the American Temperance Society in Boston. For the next thirty years following its foundation, the temperance movement enjoyed some measure of success. By 1836 over 8,000 temperance societies had been formed with over 1.5 million members (out of a total population of 13 million). The movement rallied many famous men to its causes, such as the Reverend Lyman Beecher and General Lewis Cass. Its momentum helped to create the American Temperance Union, the Washington Movement—a forerunner of Alcoholics Anonymous—and the Sons of Temperance. It also succeeded in having five- and fifteen-gallon laws passed in a number of states; and it could claim scattered local-option-law victories across the nation.

But by 1856 the movement had gone into decline. Most Americans were preoccupied with the slavery question; the courts began to strike down some of the local-option laws; and there was a certain amount of backsliding on the part of both the ordinary citizen and the law enforcement agencies.

In 1869, the Prohibition Party* was founded. Its leaders felt

* The Party has changed its name from time to time. At its founding, it was called the National Prohibition Party; in 1876 it was called the Prohibi-

that prohibition would never be achieved until a political party and its members accepted it as part of their platform. They saw prohibition as a national question rather than as a local one. They abhorred the growing use of liquor during the Civil War; they opposed the taxing of liquor because it entrenched it in government and politics; and they complained of the poor enforcement of the existing liquor laws.

The cornerstone of the Party's platform then—and indeed, to this day—was the *total* abolition of liquor.*

From the 1870s to the outbreak of World War I, temperance sentiment grew considerably. It was not, however, an ordered growth, but a broad-front revival that saw the many prohibitionist groups fighting as bitterly among themselves as with the liquor interests.

The Party itself was split at various times into a number of factions. There were some members who saw the liquor problem as a political one, others who saw it as a personal one. There were some who in their hearts wanted to be Republicans despite their principles, there were others who saw the Party as a balance of power, and there was another group who set themselves up as "purists" because they detested the practice of the two major parties of appealing to both wets and drys at the same time. In 1896 there was a three-way split over the silver issue, one faction starting a short-lived National Party, another bolting to the Democratic-Populist candidate, William Jennings Bryan, and the third staying put in the Prohibition Party. Furthermore, the Party has always been split between the "narrow gaugers" (those advocating a single-plank party) and the "broad gaugers" (those seeking to create a multi-plank party).

The two largest of the rival prohibition groups, the Woman's

---

tion Reform Party; in 1881, the Prohibition Home Protection Party; and later on it reverted to its present name, which, for the sake of clarity, I use throughout.

The Party's symbol throughout its history has been a camel.

* The emphasis on *total* is deliberate and has an historical basis. The early temperance movements were opposed primarily to the consumption of "ardent spirits"—in particular, rum and grain alcohol. But the temperance leaders were soon calling for *total* abstinence when it was found that many of their own members were getting drunk on wine, beer and hard cider.

Christian Temperance Union and the Anti-Saloon League, never seriously cooperated with one another or with the Prohibition Party. The WCTU was then under the influence of two dominating females, Frances E. Willard and later Carrie A. Nation. The Anti-Saloon League was concerned solely with destroying saloons. Its members were essentially anti-political-party, and they believed they should support "people's views," not party views. This attitude they called "omnipartisanship."

In spite of the bickering, the Prohibition Party was able to show some growth at the polls. In 1872, it received only 5,588 votes; in 1884, it received 150,957 votes; and by 1892 it received 271,111 votes—the highest number it was ever to receive. Between 1900 and 1916 it consistently polled over 200,000 votes, which was roughly 2 percent of the entire vote in each election. Although small in absolute terms, this percentage does not reflect the fact that many more people voted for prohibition in local-option elections. By 1916, a considerable number of communities all over the United States and twenty-three states *in toto* had banned the sale of liquor on their own initiative.

A truce was called in 1913 among some ninety of the warring prohibitionist factions. These groups agreed to promote a common objective: the national prohibition of the liquor trade. It was apparent to them by then that prohibition was a national issue and that in the interests of success it was best if they tried to work together.

It is still questionable whether the growth of prohibition sentiment in America was due primarily to the efforts of these warring groups or whether it had come about in spite of them. In any event, their victory was crowned with the passage of the Eighteenth Amendment in the House and Senate in 1917 and its eventual ratification by the states in 1919.

Even after this victory, the Party felt it necessary to put up candidates in the Presidential elections. It was apparent to many in the Party by 1923 that prohibition was not working. Enforcement of the dry laws was in the hands of the wets. Consumption of liquor decreased, but criminal violations of the liquor laws increased considerably. The administration of prohibition, the Party believed, amounted to a national scandal, which in large measure it was. It was for these reasons that the Party went back to the polls.

Many other prohibitionists, however, left the Party and returned to the Republican or Democratic Party, believing that the victory was final. In 1924, the Prohibition candidate for President received 56,292 votes (a drop of 70 percent from the 1920 Prohibitionist vote) and in 1928 he received only 20,101, the worst the Party was ever to do.

When repeal was passed in 1932, the Party's heart was broken, and it has never recovered from it. It drifted aimlessly through the 1930s and 1940s with few plans and no confidence. It nominated Sergeant Alvin York for Vice-President in 1936, but he declined the honor. In 1948, its Presidential candidate received over 100,000 votes. This was undoubtedly a comeback of sorts, but it was not permanent.

In the 1950s the party suffered three more crippling blows: it had to fight off a take-over bid by a group of pacifists which further split the party; later there was another split which resulted in a group of radical youths leaving to start their own party, subsequently short-lived, called Democracy Unlimited; and finally the Party ran deeply into debt because of the deficit-spending policies of one of its chairmen.

In 1960, the Party was embarrassed to find itself the object of friendly overtures from the National States Rights Party. The offer of association was emphatically turned down.

Today the Party is so small that no one knows who the rank and file are or where they live. It *is* known, however, that its electoral strength comes from Indiana, Kansas, Michigan, California and Massachusetts. According to Earl Dodge, a young insurance executive from Kansas City, and an energetic and articulate ex-chairman of the Party, most members tend to be Protestants only because prohibition is in the Protestant tradition. There is no law against Catholics and Jews belonging; everyone is welcome, according to Dodge. Members take no pledge upon joining the Party.

Prohibitionists get moral support from the Salvation Army, from Free Methodist, Nazarene, Wesleyan Methodist, Pilgrim Holiness, Pentecostal and a scattering of Presbyterian, Lutheran and Baptist churches. Ex-alcoholics as a rule do not join the Party because, although they know that they themselves cannot drink, they usually have no desire to cure others.

The Prohibition Party is not associated with the WCTU because remnants of the old arguments still persist between the two organizations. There are those in the WCTU who despise the Prohibitionists because they are outside the Republican Party; there are those in the Prohibition Party who claim that the WCTU refuses to recognize the liquor question as both a political and a national question.

Since World War II, the Party has usually been governed out of the reigning chairman's hat. For many years the headquarters were in Chicago; then in the early 1950s they were moved to Winona Lake, Indiana (the hometown of Billy Sunday); later, they shifted to St. Louis; and now the headquarters are in Kalamazoo, where the Party's present executive chairman, Dr. D. D. Gibbons, lives.

Headquarters are actually two basement rooms of Gibbons' house. In one room there is a small printing machine and dusty back copies of the Party's newspaper, *The National Statesman*. In the other, there are a few cabinets with literature stacked on the shelves; on a wall there is a row of books that could be found in any number of conservative households; and there are a few tables with not too much visible work upon them.

Dr. Gibbons has been executive secretary of the Party since 1963 and is a chiropractor by profession. He is considered by many in the Party as a "plunger," that is to say, a promoter who takes chances. He seeks all the publicity he can for the Party, he feels the press is fair to him, he exudes optimism, and he is an indefatigable speaker. Gibbons is one of the few men at the head of the Party who had a drinking problem in the past, but he long ago cured himself and no longer drinks anything alcoholic.

The chairman of the Party and, in effect, the figurehead is Professor E. Harold Munn, sixty-two, the assistant to the dean of Hillsdale College in Michigan. He has run for office a number of times, three times for mayor of Hillsdale, once for Vice-President on the Prohibition ticket in 1960 and once for President on the same slate in 1964.

Contrary to most people's belief, the Prohibition Party has never been a one-issue party. Indeed, the abolition of the liquor trade has always been a cornerstone of its platform but never the entire platform. As pointed out previously, the Party has often been divided between the "narrow gaugers" and the "broad gaugers," but at no time in its history have the "narrow gaugers" prevailed. E. H. Munn told me, in his methodical but emphatic way, that "no political party is worthy of the support of its citizens unless that party offers a complete program of government."

What is most ironic about the Prohibition Party's platforms in the past is that they were often twenty to thirty years ahead of their time. For instance, in 1876 it advocated international arbitration over international disputes and the abolition of polygamy; in 1888 it advocated woman's suffrage, a civil service free of patronage, anti-monopoly laws, and statehood for the Dakota territories; in 1908, it advocated a graduated income tax, a guarantee on bank deposits, regulation of interstate commerce, uniform marriage and divorce laws and the abolition of child labor; in 1916, it was calling for independence for the Philippines, old age pensions, federal grain elevators to house surpluses, the single Presidential term and public ownership of utilities; and even today—while it is evident that the Party has lurched somewhat to the right—it can still demand electoral reform and the application of antitrust laws to trade unions.

The greatest hurdle the Party faces is its name, since according to its members it conjures up so many false images in the mind of the public. Munn, for example, would prefer that the Party be called the "Christian American" Party because, he says, "that is what the Prohibition Party is." Ex-Chairman Dodge is also in favor of changing the name but only if the Party had enough money and sufficient publicity to do it properly. Both men see hazards in a name change. Dodge says that it would seem as if the Party were backtracking on prohibition. He then asked: "If we change our name, how do we reach the people who voted for us as Prohibitionists when we don't know who many of them are now?" Munn points to similar difficulties. Much financial support comes to the Party, particularly from the Pennock estate in Pennsylvania, specifically because it is Prohibitionist. He adds that such a change would create considerable economic and psychological hardships among the members.

Dodge, for one, is proud that his Party stands for a set of principles. It opposes deficit spending, the spoils system and excessive governmental regulation. It is for the separation of Church and State and at the same time sees no conflict in asking that legislators acknowledge God in the conduct of government. It believes in the extension of individual liberties, civil rights and the strengthening of laws to curb public immorality.

Part of the problem today, says Dodge, "is the pragmatist who does not believe in right or wrong. We believe that there are those things that are right and those that are wrong.

"We do believe," he went on, "that unless a party is based on principle, we don't see how the nation can exist. We see the nation declining economically and morally."

As to the future, both Munn and Dodge are optimistic, although no immediate upswing is foreseen. Munn says it will take fifteen to twenty years before the Party's principles will be built into the fabric of the people. Dodge talks in terms of seeing a religious and moral reawakening sometime in the future.

The Party plans to campaign actively in the future, but complains, as do other groups, of the restrictive electoral laws, the waste of time it takes just to get on the ballot, and the failure of election judges to count their ballots.

"We're out to win," says Munn, "because we believe in these principles." He then added: "We may not win but at least we will be true to the cause."

2

The Greenback Party is the fourth oldest political party in America. It was first organized, unsurprisingly enough, during the Greenback era and, off and on ever since, has been running candidates for the Presidency.

The Greenback era ran from 1862 to 1879. Previous to 1862, the country's currency was gold. The failures of the Union Army and the successes of the Confederates, however, alarmed depositors, who began to withdraw so much gold that specie payments had to be suspended (except in California). Bank notes, therefore, became the only easily available cash. Because the government could no longer obtain gold from the banks, paper money advocates convinced Congress to pass a Legal Tender Act in February 1862. This act provided for the issue of $150 million in U.S. Notes promising payment in coin, no date being fixed for payment. Subsequent issues were authorized, and by the end of the Civil War $400 million of these notes were outstanding.

These notes were called greenbacks because of their color. They were legal tender for all payments but from the first were worth less than their face value in gold coin. In 1864, for example, $100 in greenbacks were worth only $40 in gold. Thus there was a considerable rise in the price of goods.

After the war, the greenback began to appreciate, but it did not reach parity with gold until late 1878 when it was redeemed in gold by the government in accordance with a law passed in 1875. But a large section of the country liked the greenback so much that it opposed the government's plan to retire it. Greenbackers wanted to make it the permanent money of the country. They had sufficient influence in 1868 to have Congress pass an act suspending further retirement and cancellation. The effect was so bad on the nation's credit standing a year later Congress passed the Public Credit Act in which a pledge was made that the obligations of the government (the greenbacks) would be redeemed in coin. The redemption period lasted from 1875 to 1879, and because of the guarantee by the government, the greenback enjoyed perfect acceptability as money; in other words it was "as good as gold."[1]

The Greenback Party was formed in 1875 by individuals who opposed the return to gold. It nominated for President eighty-five-year-old Peter Cooper, the philanthropist and glue manufacturer. In the 1876 elections he received nearly 83,000 votes out of 8.4 million cast.

From 1876 to the present, the Greenback Party's objectives have become increasingly murky. Cooper's candidacy was a protest against the redemption of the greenback; this much is clear. But in subsequent elections, as the greenback issue faded and others rose to take its place, the Party's goals became more confused and vague until today they are virtually unrecognizable and, in many instances, incomprehensible. From a demand for the return to paper money, the cry soon went up for a general reform of the monetary system; exactly what kind of reform has never been made clear. Then the Party developed anti-business and populist sentiments that churned the philosophical waters still more.

This is most evident in the names the Party adopted over the years. In the 1880 election the Party was called the Greenback Labor and National Party; in 1884 it was calling itself the Greenback and Anti-Monopoly Party; and in the next Presidential election the Union Labor Party. By 1892, the Greenbackers had merged with the Populist Party (which received over one million votes that year). In 1898 the Greenback faction burst asunder, over half the members following William Jennings Bryan into the Democratic fold. These rebels were convinced that the silver issue was the road to monetary reform. The rump faction stayed with the Populists.

From 1900 to 1918, the "true" Greenbackers staggered about with no party, no platform and no leader. They managed to run candidates in 1904 and 1908 (under the name People's Party) but could not hold 1 percent of the voters (as opposed to 9 percent in 1892 when they had joined up with the Populists).

The Party was reorganized in 1918, pledging itself to "rightful government" and monetary reform. It was under the leadership of one John Zahnd from Indiana, who headed the ticket in 1924, 1928, 1932, 1936 and 1940. Old-time Greenbackers that I met will complain that Zahnd was "a dictator." In any event, the write-in vote during these years was so small that in most instances it was not counted. The Party's history, published as a thin pamphlet around 1953, complained that LaFollette's 1924 campaign as a Progressive and William Lenke's 1936 campaign on the Union Party ticket confused the Greenback voters and contributed decisively to its poor showing.

In the post-World War II years, the Party has come under the control of Fred C. Proehl of Seattle. He ran for President in 1952 and 1956. Exactly what he has done for the Party is unclear, except perhaps to postpone its extinction.

The current Greenback message is difficult to comprehend and accounts in part, no doubt, for the Party's very poor showing at the polls. If I understand their viewpoint correctly, the present banking system should be abolished and the country should revert to a system whereby the money supply is under the direct control of the U.S. Treasury. Whenever money is needed by the people, they say, the Treasury should print the required amount of paper money for distribution, to be paid back at no interest. In this way, so their reasoning goes, there will be no inflation, no interest charges, no credit, no profits for "a private group of bankers," and on the positive side, the monetary system will be under the control of "we, the people."

The Federal Reserve System is a most sinister institution to Greenbackers. Everything about it is suspect. Its operations, they say, are carried out for the sole benefit of the member banks. Because it is relatively independent of government control, it only fortifies their belief that the country is run by bankers. Greenbackers claim that the Federal Reserve can determine the value of money at any time it chooses and that it can determine the amount of profit it wants to make. Party members speak despairingly of "checkbook money." Checkbook money, according to Edward Meador, the Party's 1956 Vice-Presidential candidate and a retired Boston publisher, means inflation on a grand scale that brings about boom-or-bust conditions—again manipulated by the Federal Reserve for its own benefit.

Meador is one Greenbacker who believes that Wall Street—particularly Kuhn, Loeb & Company—runs the country. In fact, in his mind it is an international conspiracy. "Jewish, English and American bankers," he told me, "are all in it together." The government, he added, has turned the country over to these bankers for exploitation.

Proehl believes that the sole purpose of the Federal Reserve is to create debt so that as the major creditor it can govern as it pleases. He insists that Federal Reserve Notes are not lawful money and that the American people are being swindled because the Federal Reserve can buy the notes from the Treasury for the cost of printing them and then can turn around and lend them out at interest. "The Greenback Party is opposed to such highhanded legalized robbery," Proehl wrote me, "and insists that no money should be issued (coined) except by the federal government itself.

And then, only for material and/or services rendered to the government."

For example, he said that when the government wants to build a public service project, it would issue money (greenbacks) as the project is being built, paying the builders or contractors with interest-free money. When the project is finished the government pays for it in full with more of the same money. It would get its money back when the profits from the project come in. Once the project is fully paid for, the money used is retired from circulation. "In this manner," Proehl writes, "we would save ourselves millions of dollars each year in interest which we are now compelled under the present system to pay to the bankers and/or other interest collectors for which we receive nothing."

In the beginning of his long letter to me, Proehl wrote: "If there is any criticism of the political philosophy of the Greenback Party it is most likely [to come from] the banking interests. . . ." Proehl understates the case somewhat. All the bankers with whom I talked said that the Greenback Party does not even begin to understand the monetary system as it exists today. Edward P. Stuhr, the chairman of the executive committee and director of research at the Fiduciary Trust Company and an acknowledged authority on monetary matters, said that it was "a darned good thing that the Federal Reserve isn't owned by the government." Its purpose, he said, is to act as a counterforce to the Treasury. "It is meant to be," he continued, "a stabilizing influence, an effort to remove the political influence from the monetary set-up." Otherwise, he pointed out, the monetary system would be at the mercy of the politicians, whose whims could cause chaos with the value of the country's money. He went on to say that although the Federal Reserve is independent of the political administration, it is still influenced by politicians through the appointment of members to the board.

Every other banker with whom I talked will refute the Greenback argument point by point. They will explain that the Federal Reserve does *not* determine the value of money but that the free market does; Federal Reserve Notes, they add, *are* lawful money because the Federal Reserve Act makes them lawful; the existence of the Federal Reserve itself is not, they say, in violation of the

Constitution; nor is the FRB a swindle; nor does it exist to enrich a few bankers; nor is it part of a conspiracy; nor does it arbitrarily decide how much profits it will make each year.

Many bankers will say that the Greenback Party viewpoint is difficult to refute—not because there are so many valid points in its favor but because so few of its views relate to what is actually going on in banking circles today.

It is apparent when reading Greenback literature that the complaints—although sometimes specifically stated—are in reality signs of a general malaise. For instance, one banker said to me, "If you want to talk about the wealth of the country, you must talk about credit. The entire economy is based on credit and to talk of the Federal Reserve is to talk of credit." Greenbackers are frightened of credit. They do not understand it and they attack the symbol of their hatred, the Federal Reserve Board, without connecting the two. Greenbackers would, so it appears, much prefer to return to a barter economy where credit is assessed by the number of greenbacks in one's pocket and where expansion would be financed 100 percent out of savings.

They believe that the expansion of the money supply through credit has no limits and that the Federal Reserve is an irresponsible body which is coining profits *ad infinitum*. Such thinking makes it easy for an individual with a weakness for the conspiratorial view of the world to succumb to this message. There are few limits to the possibilities: first the system seems corrupt; then the member banks are seen as schemers; the payment of interest is held to be unjust; banks make profits; when the dollar fluctuates so do Swiss francs and deutschmarks and pounds; there are a number of wealthy banking families with branch offices in major financial centers; and so on, until the point is reached where the Greenbacker is convinced that the whole financial structure is a plot to do him—"the little guy"—or the country in. Some variations to this put all the blame on Jews, others say the Communists are behind it, still others say it is English bankers, and nearly everyone refers to anyone even remotely connected with the banking world as "they."

America's financial situation is, in reality, only incidental to why people join the Greenback Party. Their vague and garbled goals are only manifestations of general frustration, anger, fright and inner turmoil that are similar to those sentiments found in such groups as the John Birch Society and the Constitution Party. Greenbackers just choose to voice them through their own particular organization.

3

Another small independent party is the National Woman's Party, located in Washington, D.C., within sight of the Capitol Building. Its members are known as "the last of the suffragettes." The Party was founded in 1913 as a temporary body to secure the passage of the "Susan B. Anthony Amendment" to the Constitution, which would enfranchise women. The adoption of the Nineteenth Amendment in 1920 accomplished this. In 1921 the Party was reorganized as a permanent body to secure the removal of all remaining discriminatory laws against women.

The story of the National Woman's Party is largely the story of one person: Alice Paul, the founder and, today, the honorary chairman of the Party. Alice Paul graduated from Swarthmore College in 1905 and went on to the University of Pennsylvania where she received her MA and PhD. She then served as a charity worker in the slums of New York City and Birmingham, England. While in England, she joined Mrs. Emily Pankhurst's suffragette movement. On a number of occasions Alice Paul was thrown into jail, mostly for breach of the peace, which usually meant heckling unmercifully such anti-feminists as Sir Edward Grey, Lord Crewe and Winston Churchill.

Alice Paul returned to America in 1912 and turned all her attention to women's suffrage. She moved to Washington and organized the NWP. For the next eight years she was to be the driving force behind the equal-rights-for-women movement. According to one source she built the Party up to fifty thousand members and raised three quarters of a million dollars, in those days a considerable sum.[2]

In the heyday of the suffragettes, two tactics were used by the Party to keep the issue of women's rights before the public eye. One was to put pressure directly on the legislators, either in

Washington or in their home districts, and the other was to picket the White House. Today, the Party seeks to gain its objectives only by trying to influence legislators. The tactics of activism have been abandoned; no longer are there any pickets, watchfires and squads of umbrella-wielding feminists. In its old age the Party has turned genteel.

The NWP operates today out of the Alva Belmont House, believed to be one of the oldest houses on Capitol Hill. At one time it was rented to Albert Gallatin, Secretary of the Treasury under Presidents Jefferson and Madison. The house takes its name from a generous donor to the Party, Alva Smith Belmont. She was the wife of William K. Vanderbilt, before her marriage to Oliver Hazard Perry Belmont, and the mother of Consuelo Vanderbilt, who became the Duchess of Marlborough.

The headquarters look more like a museum than a political center. The front hall boasts statues of Elizabeth Cady Stanton, Sybil Ludington, Susan B. Anthony and Joan of Arc. There are numerous portraits on the walls of leading feminists, including one of Alice Paul as a young suffragette. There is rosewood furniture from a Louisiana plantation, a "California Room" maintained by western Party members, china from Alva Belmont, a silver tea service from the friends of Clara Barton and a chair in the library, marked by a brass plate, that used to belong to President McKinley's wife.

The atmosphere within is more that of a club. There always seem to be a few suffragettes having tea in the garden, and there are usually a few elderly feminists reading or chatting softly in one of the rooms. Everything is very orderly, clean and relaxed. There is no hustle and bustle.

The current leaders of the Party fortify the impression that the organization is a genteel one. Mrs. Emma Guffey Miller from Slippery Rock, Pennsylvania, is president. She has been a Democratic Party national committeewoman since 1932 and a delegate to every Democratic Convention since 1924. She was the first woman to receive a vote for the nomination for President (1924), and she made seconding speeches for Governor Al Smith in 1924 and 1928 and for Roosevelt in 1932 and 1936. Her work for women's suffrage began in 1910 and continues to occupy much of her time today. Other well-known feminists working for the Party are Genevieve Blatt, an unsuccessful candidate for senator from Pennsylvania and currently a member of the NWP's national council. There is hostess Perle Mesta, who serves as the NWP's advisory council chairman. Pearl Buck, the Nobel Prize novelist, although she holds no official position in the Party, is one of its strongest supporters.

Officially, NWP membership is secret but it runs to sixty thousand, if account is taken of all the clubs that support the Party's stand: the General Federation of Women's Clubs, National Federation of Business and Professional Women's Clubs, etc. Some estimate that total support runs as high as ten million. Those very active in the Party, however, are limited to a few hundred. "We are not looking for supporters," Alice Paul told me, "we are looking for success!"

Since the passage of the Nineteenth Amendment, the National Woman's Party has sought to broaden the concept of equality for women to include all spheres of human activity. The Party takes no action on any other issue. The only way Party members believe that this equality can be achieved is by means of an Amendment to the Constitution. This Amendment is known either as the "Equal Rights Amendment" or the "Lucretia Mott Amendment" and has been introduced in Congress in virtually every session since 1923. It reads in full: "Equality of rights under the law shall not be denied or abridged by the United States or by any State on account of sex." It has never been put to a vote in either the House or the Senate, but this has not been due to any lack of friends among the legislators. The NWP's legislative friends include Senators McGee, Eastland, Dirksen, Smith, Hickenlooper, Fulbright and Eugene McCarthy, and Representatives Farbstein (D., N.Y.), Lipscomb (R., Calif.), Gonzales (D., Tex.), May (R., Wash.), Freling-huysen (R., N.J.), Patman (D., Tex.) and Conte (R., Mass.). Every Presidential candidate since Truman has publicly supported the Amendment, although one NWPer said that President Kennedy "thought it was a joke." Usually advocates of the Amendment can muster up nearly half of the legislators to declare in favor of it. The Republican Party has had an "equal-rights-for-women" plank in its platform since 1940 and the Democrats since 1944.

At first glance, to vote against equal rights for women would seem akin to voting against motherhood; but it is not as clear an issue as that. The NWP's friends never get a chance to vote for the Amendment because there are powerful opponents to it. They include Senators Ervin, Javits, Case, and Representative Adam Clayton Powell. The two most important opponents, however, are Representative Emmanuel Celler of New York and Senator Carl Hayden of Arizona. Cellar is chairman of the House Judiciary Committee and Hayden is the Senate's senior member and chairman of the powerful Senate Appropriations Committee. Celler refuses to report out the Amendment resolution for consideration by the House. The NWP's friend, Senator Eastland, chairman of the Senate Judiciary Committee, will report it out from his committee but, before a vote is taken, a rider is attached that reads: "The provisions of this article shall not be construed to impair any rights, benefits or exemptions now or hereafter conferred by law upon persons of the female sex." This is known as the "Hayden Rider" and has been attached to the Senate resolution ever since 1950. It serves to squelch the Amendment.

Celler opposed the Equal Rights Amendment because, he says, it is an attempt to legislate the whole sphere of human behavior. He believes that such an amendment would thrust the government into areas of jurisdiction in which it has no business being, such as divorce cases, custody cases and domestic relations cases. He states that he is in favor of the Nineteenth Amendment because it dealt with a specific ill, namely voting rights for women. He claims he is in favor of equal pay for equal work in industries where women work alongside men. But he believes that all inequities must be removed on a state-by-state basis and not by the force of a federal law. He also fears that the many protective laws established to safeguard the rights and safety of women would be swept away as well. "I remain convinced," he told the House Committee on Constitutional Amendments in 1963, "that no more mischief-breeding piece of legislation has ever been placed before Congress so disguised in simplicity and clothed with so righteous a slogan, that it survives on that strength alone."

The NWP claims that Hayden's rider not only annuls the Amendment but would, if accepted into law, actually write sex discrimination into the Constitution. By mentioning "female sex," women are immediately set apart. The original Amendment, NWPers note, applies equally as well to men. Emma Guffey Miller remarked in 1956 that the only prominent organization in favor of the Hayden Rider was the CPUSA.

The National Woman's Party also takes issue with Celler's point of view. Alice Paul, for instance, believes that it is futile to attempt a state-by-state repeal of discriminatory laws because, she said, "none of the repeals would have the force of permanency." Women, she complained, have no legal point on which they can fall back on. "The Fourteenth Amendment," she said, "does not really count when the chips are down." She pointed out that the Supreme Court has repeatedly held that this particular Amendment does not guarantee to women the rights which men possess as a matter of course.

She then said that the real reason Celler opposes the Equal Rights Amendment is because he is constantly being pressured to vote against it by the labor unions. Unions, Alice Paul said, are anti-women because women, if given equal status to men, would then constitute a threat to all men's jobs. She noted that most legislators who oppose the NWP's Amendment are dependent on union votes to maintain them in office.

Curiously enough, neither side questions the fact that inequalities do exist in regard to property rights, inheritance rights, divorce, education, the right to work for a living, the right to compete on equal terms, the control of one's own earnings, engaging in lawful occupations, jury service, government service and other aspects of life. Over the years a number of ludicrous situations have arisen, only a few of which need to be noted here. In a 1944 speech, Emma Guffey Miller noted that in Ohio no woman could drive a taxicab, that in six states the wife's earnings were under the control of the husband, that in some states women could not make a valid contract or act as a guardian, that in South Carolina a woman's clothes belong to her husband and that in Michigan her own hair was the property of her spouse.

"In most states," she said, "an unmarried woman is considered competent to handle her own affairs, but once she takes unto herself a husband, she somehow becomes incompetent. . . . Sud-

denly she becomes a widow, and then she again becomes competent." Is this a reflection on husbands, she asks? In twentieth-
century-enlightened New York a state law was passed forbidding
women to work after midnight. Telephone operators, printers,
proofreaders, secretaries and waitresses were those affected, but no
mention was made of women who cleaned offices, giving rise to
suspicions that the true reason for the bill was to eliminate female
competition from these jobs and leave to females only the jobs
men do not want.

Many of these laws have since been changed or modified, but
the fact that inequalities still exist has never been denied.

The NWP takes credit for many equal rights measures which
have been passed into law at the state level. Among those adopted
by the various states are those equalizing the rights of guardianship
of children, the responsibility for illegitimate children, property
rights, the right to sue and be sued, the right to act as administrator or executor, the qualifications for jury service, the right to
public service, the pay in public service, the conditions for making
a will, and the power to make contracts and to be officers in a
corporation.

The NWP advocates that all labor laws be based upon the
nature of the work and not the sex of the worker. It calls for all
laws to be free of discrimination based on sex. The Party opposes
just as strenuously laws that link women with minors, criminals
and the insane and that discharge women because of marriage who
are employed in work (such as teaching) maintained in whole or
in part by public funds.

Members of the Party reject the argument that certain laws are
needed to protect women from the difficulties of everyday life. To
NWPers, this attitude reflects a thinly disguised excuse to keep
women from competing with men in certain areas. "Men, as well
as women," wrote Pearl Buck, "suffer certain liabilities occasionally as to health and physical handicaps, and yet no one thinks of
laying upon all men the handicap of sex inequality because there is
need for special protective legislation."

This hard line has, over the years, created the impression among
outsiders that the National Woman's Party is militantly anti-male.
The charge is partially true because it is primarily male legislators

who shelve, bury, recommit, dismember or otherwise delay the Equal Rights Amendment. On occasion this can provoke wild outbursts of frustration and hostility.

I caught some of this frustration and hostility full force on one of the days I spent talking with NWP members at the Alva Belmont House. Mrs. Mary A. Birkhead, the current chairman of the Party, told me of her irritation with Senator Sam Ervin, who, when she entered his office, made light of the equal rights issue in front of his staff and then tried to brush off her presence by attempting to be amusing. But it was Mrs. Meredith Thoenen, the chairman of the NWP's Congressional Committee, who was boiling with anger. Her job is to line up the 535 legislators so that the Equal Rights Amendment, whenever it comes to a vote, will be passed. It is a frustrating job, and the day we talked must have been more frustrating than most. She complained that she was "fed up with the runaround" she has received from various legislators. Often, she said, she is forced to skulk about the office building corridors hoping to catch legislators as they enter or leave their offices. Their treatment of her in particular and the Equal Rights Amendment in general particularly irritates her. "It is an absolute disgrace," she said. "They should hang their heads in shame!"

Mrs. Thoenen is an attractive, middle-aged woman who is full of energy and who speaks rapidly and argumentatively. She chain smokes, and as I sat on the terrace listening to her speak she would point two fingers at me, a cigarette between them, and explain how "you men" were the cause of all the troubles. "We pay first-class taxes," she said; "we've helped men build this country. Why do they deny us equality? Well, I'll tell you why: it is psychological immaturity. You men are the ones who are the bad sports. We're not asking for privileges, just equal rights.

"Sometimes," she burst out, "I can't stand the sight of men!"

It is obvious that all NWP members are not totally anti-male. That hostility exists is certain, but even this ebbs and flows with events. Mrs. Thoenen certainly does not maintain a constant, high pitch of hostility. It is only the nature of the goal—equality for women—that casts men in the role of ogres because they will not legislate such a demand with the utmost haste. Furthermore, the anti-male bias has been mitigated somewhat by the fact that most of the ardent NWPers have taken husbands. (I must admit, however, that I never met any of the husbands, so I cannot vouch for their state of mind or status in the family.) This bias is also muted because some of the Party's most loyal supporters are men. The Party may be anti-male in the heat of controversy, but it is not true as a general rule of thumb.

Recently, the advocates of equal rights for women have received a big boost in their favor—namely, the passage of the 1964 Civil Rights Act. Title VII of the Act, Section 703(a), states that it shall be unlawful for an employer to fail or refuse to hire or otherwise discriminate against a person because of the individual's race, color, religion, sex or national origin.

A new federal agency, the Equal Employment Opportunities Commission, has been set up to enforce the anti-discrimination ban, and so far it seems likely to become one of the most embattled of Washington's agencies. Within eighteen months after the law went into effect, 306 complaints of sex bias were lodged with the Commission. Airline stewardesses have complained, for instance, that they, and not men, must quit flying when they marry or reach the age of thirty-two. A woman was barred from becoming a sausage stuffer in a meat-packing plant even though she presented credentials that showed she could stuff sausages as well or better than "the incumbent male sausage stuffer." Eventually, after conciliation, the company allowed her to move up to the sausage-stuffing machine.[3]

Two California prostitutes complained that they were discriminated against when the two men who were with them at the time of their arrest were released without charge. A woman assembler in an electronics plant complained that the management refused to promote her to technician, even though she held a degree in electronics, on the grounds that she might have to lift something more than twenty-five pounds, thus violating a state law.

These are just some of the problems the Commission faces.

Since a ban on sex bias is a relatively new trend in major legislation (except for the Nineteenth Amendment), the Commission is groping its way through uncharted seas. It hopes to avoid absurd situations—such as the man who loves children so much that he applies for a job as a nanny—so that the effectiveness of the law will not be destroyed and that there will be no revolution in job patterns.

Yet there is considerable pressure from lobbyists to have Title VII repealed. Both the House and Senate felt it necessary to submit bills in 1966 that would replace the controversial section with an "Equal Employment Opportunity Act." The NWP, however, is determined to see that no such change takes place. It is leading the fight against the repeal of Title VII. "We may be overapprehensive," said one member in the Party's *Bulletin,* "but 'a burnt child dreadeth the fire.' "

4

The Tax Cut Party is a one-man crusade of individualistic proportions run by Lawrence Joseph Sarsfield Daly, a furniture manufacturer from Chicago. Lar Daly, as he is known, has run unsuccessfully for public office seventeen times since he launched his political career in 1938: four times for President, five times for senator from Illinois, twice for governor, once for Congress, three times for mayor of Chicago (he is no relation to Mayor Richard J. Daley), and twice for school board positions. He has run under a variety of party labels: in primaries as a Republican and a Democrat; otherwise as an independent or as the Tax Cut Party candidate.

Daly campaigns in an Uncle Sam suit, complete with top hat, cutaway coat and striped trousers. When this is inconvenient, he writes, he campaigns in an Uncle Sam hat and a red, white and blue sash over his coat. His legal name on the Illinois ballot is "Lar (America First) Daly."

In the field of foreign affairs Daly is a hard-line hawk. He advocates the total destruction of Red China's and Cuba's military forces and the destruction of France's Sahara Desert atomic plant. "We should notify Mao Tse-tung that he and his barbarian gang have thirty days to surrender at Hong Kong," he told a college audience in 1966. "If they don't, then we should destroy her areas of military concentration with A-bombs." This could be done without unnecessary carnage, he said, because we have "clean bombs" with a limited range of destruction. Once the Reds have been wiped out, Daly suggested, then Chiang Kai-shek should be sent to the mainland with his troops—armed only with small arms—to police the area. Cuba, he said, should be subjected to the same treatment, except that only conventional bombs need be used. As for France, he said, "I have no use for French delusions of grandeur."

On the domestic front, Daly wants to legalize gambling—bingo, policy wheels, numbers games and slot machines—so as to reduce the sales and income tax in Illinois. He claims that such a policy would do away with "any alliance between crime and politics." He wants to abolish public schools in favor of private and parochial ones, and he wants to have religion taught in all schools for a minimum of forty-five minutes daily. Non-Christians in an America First society would only be tolerated; and to ensure that the proper Christian beliefs are being maintained, he favors the renewal of the Inquisition.[4]

Daly would kill all dope peddlers after giving them one week's warning to get out of town. The offenders would be declared "public bounty" and a $1,000 reward would be paid for every head brought in. In general terms, Daly opposes a mythical representation of evil that he calls "Dr. Cyclops," who represents "all the goofy crackpot elements who oppose Christian moral principles, and want to destroy our traditional American way of life." Dr. Cyclops is caricatured as a mad-scientist type with unkempt hair, a long nose, wearing glasses and dressed in a wing collar and bow tie. Tax Cut literature usually features the caricature next to a picture of Daly in his Uncle Sam suit and asks: "Which do you choose?"

Americans that Daly most admires are President Truman, Admiral Hyman Rickover, Dr. Edward Teller, Barry Goldwater, General Douglas MacArthur, Senator Joseph McCarthy (whom Daly calls "the Great Shield of the Republic") and John Foster Dulles.

Although Daly's long political career has been a fruitless one in terms of victories, it nevertheless has produced a number of legal precedents. In 1957, for instance, when Daly was running for Congress, it was established that a candidate for Congress did not have to reside in the district in which he is a candidate. One beneficiary of this ruling has been Robert F. Kennedy, a Massachusetts voter who was elected senator from the state of New York in 1964.

In 1959, Daly was responsible for the establishment of the legal principle in Illinois that permits a candidate to crossfile for any office in the state; that is to say, a person's name may appear on both major parties' ballots, plus any other, at the same time.

In the same year, Daly achieved considerable renown when the FCC ruled that Section 315 of the communications law—generally known as the "equal time rule"—required that broadcasting stations offer equal time not only to candidates of the two major parties but to every candidate of every party competing for the same office. This had the effect of blanking out all news where a candidate for office was involved. But in late June 1960, Section 315 was officially suspended in order that Presidential candidates Kennedy and Nixon might debate each other without the public being forced to listen to the views of the sixteen other candidates for the office.[5]

Daly lost this round and as a result Americans will be denied his views on radio and TV. In spite of this setback, Daly now calls himself "the undisputed 'Champion of Equal Time,'" who wants the communications media to be available to the "little guy as well as the big shot." Such a claim may conceivably bring him a few more votes.

5

Another party concerned with taxes is the United Taxpayers Party. It was started in 1957, claims a membership of five thousand and limits its activities to New York City. The founder and current chairman of the Party is Vito P. Battista, a fifty-five-year-old native of Brooklyn. Battista immigrated to America from Italy at the age of three, and by his fourteenth birthday he was a high-school dropout. For the next four years he was an ice peddler and claims to have made $20,000 profit in the business. With his new-found wealth he went back to school and soon thereafter could boast of degrees from Carnegie Institute of Technology, the École des Beaux Arts in Fontainebleau and Massachusetts Institute of

Technology. Today he is a practicing architect and the director of the Institute of Design and Construction, which he founded.

Battista, a short, dapper man with a pencil mustache, said that the Party originated as a protest against rent control. "It is making slums out of buildings," he said, "and it is only kept for political reasons." If rent control were abolished, he reasoned, "home-owners would fix up their properties; then there would be open competition." Rents, he insists, would not go up that much. "Rent control denies free enterprise to the real estate industry, particu-larly the small homeowner," he said. Battista claims that the majority of his supporters are small homeowners in the Brooklyn and Queens areas. He received 11,000 votes for mayor out of 2.2 million cast in the 1965 election.

Battista insists that his Party is a multi-issue party. He says that he "generally lines up on the right side—as an independent Republican." He opposes fluoridation, busing of school children, "give-away" programs and "free education for the rich." He would like to have enacted a law requiring a two-year residency for individuals before they are eligible for welfare payments.

But it is the tax structure of the city that preoccupies him the most. He campaigned in 1965 for a rise in the subway fare (since enacted); he believes that people with the ability to pay should pay their full share—exactly what he means by this is unclear, but he usually describes the present tax structure as one that "robs the poor to pay the rich." He wants rent controls to be abolished and an end to public housing. He opposes the city's income tax, and any increase in real estate, water and sewer taxes. "If you're a small homeowner, a small businessman, God help you!" he told me. "The man in the middle is being destroyed. The city could gain $600 million if the taxes were put straight."

Speaking from the top of a truck on Wall Street, he asked a lunchtime crowd, referring to the proposed 50 percent increase in the Stock Transfer Tax: "How many of you would vote for Lindsay now? Say yes or no [crowd: 'No!']! Well, the next time how about paying attention to Vito [laughter]!"

The sides of his truck were festooned with signs: "JOIN THE TAX REVOLT, MAYOR LINDSAY'S TAX PROGRAM WILL DESTROY OUR

CITY. SIGN UP WITH UNITED TAXPAYERS" was the most noticeable one.

Whenever tax proposals are being debated by the City Council, Battista and his small legion can usually be found protesting in front of City Hall. The debate in April 1966 was no exception. Battista had set up an exhibit which he called a "torture chamber of horrors." Pointing to a man with his head on a mock chopping block, he said, "This is a small taxpayer with his head on the tax block. And this," he said, pointing to a woman lying in a mock-up of a spiked coffin, "is a small property owner caught in Lindsay's iron maiden of taxes." The woman in the iron maiden smiled self-consciously. Another woman had a noose around her neck, which Battista explained represented "Lindsay's hangman's noose of taxes." Another individual, a United Taxpayer from the Bronx, had his head locked in a stock. He complained that his 15½ neck size was uncomfortable in the size 14 stock. And the star attraction was a man dressed in black leather with a hood over his face. He was brandishing a bullwhip and a cat-o'-nine tails and was muttering, "Down with Lindsay!"

Off to one side was another United Taxpayer. He was carrying a sign, apparently referring to the previous mayor, which read: "All is forgiven, Bob, please come back."[6]

6

The most elusive of all political parties is the American Vegetarian Party. Everyone has heard about it, but when it comes to specifics, very few people with whom I have spoken or corresponded know much about it. The chances are that it does not exist today; if it does, it is being carried around in the hearts of a few men who eschew publicity. In the best of times the Party was a vest-pocket affair.

In 1948, Dr. John Maxwell, a "naturopath" who operated a vegetarian restaurant in Chicago's Loop, ran for President on the AVP ticket. He expected to receive one million write-in votes. According to official government election statistics, he received exactly four, all in California. Maxwell was eighty-six years old at the time, and his campaign was enlivened somewhat by his announcement that he had just been married. Maxwell was ineligible for the Presidency because he was born in England.

Maxwell's platform avoided mentioning the benefits of vegetarianism; rather, it emphasized the economic aspects of his views. He wanted to give everyone over sixty years of age $100 per month with the stipulation that it be spent within thirty days. He believed that the government should own all major national resources and that the workers should own the factories.

The major force in the Party, however, was Symon Gould, who ran a secondhand bookstore on West 48th Street in New York City. He published a magazine called *The American Vegetarian,* which claimed to be the "exponent and representative of vegetarianism." Gould died of cancer in the early 1960s. Ammon Hennacy, America's best-known vegetarian today, had no sympathy for either the Party or its leader, Gould. "Vegetarians," he said to me, "don't die of cancer."

In 1952, the Party and the American Vegetarian Union had a fight over the use of the Party name. The causes of the differences are obscure. But Gould did say, however, that the Union, "to use non-vegetarian parlance, just had a beef." One of the Party's Presidential write-in candidates that year was General Herbert C. Holdridge. He claimed to the press that he intended "to use dark-horse stalking tactics to step into vegetarian triumph at the Democratic Convention in June if a stalemate should develop there."

Gould was the Party's Vice-Presidential candidate in 1956 and its Presidential candidate four years later. Both efforts seemed to be litttle more than rocking-chair campaigns.* In a letter to *The New York Times* in 1956, Gould explained the vegetarian view of things. Wrote he: "The American Vegetarian Party is not merely content with pursuing the material road to achieve its goals, but prefers to emphasize the ethical interpretation of issues, taking as its guiding force the teachings of Pythagoras, Plato, Aristotle, Thoreau, Shelley, Gandhi, Shaw and other celebrated vegetarian

* The only other postwar rocking-chair campaign worth noting was the one conducted in 1960 by one Connie N. Watts, who ran from the front porch of his house in Banks County, Georgia. One of Watts' planks was to "pass a law to keep them 'vine-ripened' stickers off them mushy green tomatoes."

philosophers which in the final analysis must be accepted by mankind if humanity is ever to rise to a higher level of international amity in all its phases of everyday living." In conclusion, Gould said that his program offered "some shred of hope in its ideas to a hydrogen-harassed humanity."[7]

7

The Theocratic Party does not believe in the separation of Church and State. It points out that the American Constitution does not order the separation but only forbids the government from passing any laws affecting the free exercise of any religion. Theocrats want America, and eventually all countries in the world, to be run by "men of God." It makes no difference to them whether the President of the United States is a layman or a cleric, just as long as he serves "in the name of Jesus, the Son of God." Of course, Theocrats would prefer that the leader of their own Party become President, and it is the goal toward which they work.

The Party was founded in 1960 in time to put up candidates for President and Vice-President. Homer A. Tomlinson, a bishop in The Church of God, was the Presidental candidate, and Raymond L. Teague, a bishop from Anchorage, Alaska, was his running mate. Tomlinson ran again for the office of President in 1964. His running mate was William R. Rogers, an ex-baseball umpire from the Mountain States League and the Kitty League, who later became an evangelist and minister in The Church of God. Rogers heads the ticket for the 1968 campaign.

Tomlinson is the guiding spirit behind the Theocratic Party. He is in his mid-seventies and is a pleasant, idealistic and warm-hearted man with a cauliflower nose. He is a natural storyteller who frequently wanders off the subject into whatever area of interest occupies his thoughts at the moment. His manner of speech is a combination of soft chuckles, Biblical quotes and his own unique form of phraseology.

The Church of God (not to be confused with the Church of Christ) was founded in Cleveland, Tennessee, in 1903 by Tomlinson's father, A. J. Tomlinson. The members of this church, considered part of the Holiness or Pentecostal movement, are sometimes known as "Holy Rollers." They believe in "speaking in tongues and faith healing" (the laying on of hands), taking as their inspiration the words from Acts 2:4, which reads: "And they were all filled with the Holy Spirit, and began to speak with other tongues, as the Spirit gave them utterance."

In explaining this to me, Homer Tomlinson said: "Well, I'll tell you how it comes. We speak as the Spirit gives utterance. There are those who have the special gift of tongues." An unknown tongue, he said, means unknown to the speaker. "It may be understood by the crowd, sometimes not, because he may be speaking to God." Tomlinson claims he has the gift of tongues and that he can speak twenty-one languages understood by others. He is reluctant to demonstrate this ability but does admit that he sometimes gets the languages confused. "In Jersey City, one night," he said, "I was preaching away to a group of Russians and not getting much response. I thought I was preaching in Russian until someone came up and told me it was Estonian, and then I knew what was wrong."

The Church of God was never a unified group. As has been the case among many Protestant sects, schisms have sundered the congregations until today there are, according to the 1965 *Yearbook of American Churches,* some ten Churches of God, all of which call themselves the one, true Church of God. They split over dogma: over Wesley's views on sanctification, over tithing, over the translation of tongues into English and over "sowing discord among the faithful." In 1923, A. J. Tomlinson was thrown out of his Cleveland, Tennessee, church and was forced to begin all over again, this time in Queens Village, New York. On his death in 1943, Homer succeeded as the church's overseer. The younger Tomlinson calls his church today *The* Church of God, to distinguish it from those who broke away in the past and set up their own churches. Homer Tomlinson's home in Queens Village also serves as the Theocratic Party's national headquarters.

In 1952, Homer Tomlinson ran for President on The Church of God ticket. He campaigned on a platform of "righteousness." He told me that members of his church were appalled at his move because they thought if he were elected he would compromise his principles. "My people figured me backslid when I announced for

President," he said, "but the only way you lead is by example." Tomlinson said that he chose to run because his followers were so religious that they would not vote nor take a government job. He was and is still convinced that the churches, particularly his own, should come into politics in force. "We were able to lead by the strength of our teaching," he continued. "Usually the other churches are three or four years behind my teaching, but eventually they will catch up." The success of his 1952 campaign, he pointed out to me, is reflected in the increased number of voters on the rolls. "In the nineteen and forty-eight election," he said, "the Presidential vote was forty-eight million. In nineteen and sixty it was nearly seventy million, and it was our folks that brought it up to that figure."

Tomlinson's 1960 campaign was highlighted by his pronouncement at Princeton University that he would be elected "by a miracle." As he toured the campus, he was followed by 1,500 wildly enthusiastic students chanting, "We want a miracle! We want a miracle!"

The Theocratic Party's platform and philosophy are based almost entirely on the teachings of the Bible. The core of the platform revolves around forty-eight "laws" divided into four groups of twelve each. When he was explaining them to me, he would thumb through his battered Crudens Concordance until he found the appropriate passage in the King James Bible. (The RSV Bible he does not like, he said, because it omitted Mark 16:9–20 concerning signs following believers, healing, taking up serpents and speaking in tongues.)

The first set of twelve is called "Laws for Individuals" and includes the Ten Commandments plus two more from the New Testament: Matthew 17:5, "This is my beloved Son . . . Hear ye him"; and John 15:12, "This is my commandment, that ye love one another."

The second set of twelve is called "Laws for World Government," which, Tomlinson explained, "are really doctrines of The Church of God which we are offering to the people of the world." The Theocratic Party, states the first law, believes in "one gathering of nations, one world ruler." The world ruler is God's representative on earth, and the gathering of nations implies a belief in the United Nations, also under God's guidance. Some of the other laws are a 10 percent tithe (Deuteronomy 14:22–24 and elsewhere); an October gathering of men (presumably the rulers) in Jerusalem where women are invited but who "will keep silent"; and nations that do not unite or resort to war to suffer drought and plague (Zechariah 14:16–19).

The third set calls for "Laws for Individual Nations" and includes the union of church and state; the maintenance of liberty, freedom of worship, a high standard of living, equality for all; the end to wars, crimes, delinquency, divorce, gambling and the use of tobacco, liquor and narcotics; the return of Bible reading and prayer in schools; and the abandonment of Roman law and English common law for the law of righteous judgment (Isaiah 11:3–4).

The final set of twelve concerns the establishment of new criminal and civil codes in place of the abandoned ones above. Criminals should be forgiven 490 times when repentant (Matthew 18:22, "seventy times seven"). The jury system should be discontinued and replaced by Godly judges—according to Tomlinson, "those who have the gift of wisdom, knowledge and discernment of spirits which are supernatural powers." Unrepentant sinners shall not be sent to prison but will be punished by the word of the judge—"like Paul made Elymas blind for a season" (Acts 13:10–11). Thieves may show repentance by restoring fourfold (Luke 19:8 and elsewhere; an old Mosaic law), and the covetous will be sentenced to lose all. (When I asked Tomlinson where this could be found in the Bible, he said, "Well, I guess you should say it just come from brother Homer.")

Were Tomlinson or any other member of The Church of God to become President, cabinet posts would be filled by well-known religious figures. The 1968 cabinet as of this writing has not yet been announced but the 1964 cabinet posts were to be filled as follows: the President and the Vice-President would have been members of The Church of God—specifically Tomlinson and Rogers—representing "thirty million members";* the Secretary of

* This figure is vastly inflated. According to the 1965 *Yearbook of American Churches,* there are 500,000 members in *all* Church of God sects. The *Yearbook* also states that the total membership in all churches in America

State would have been the president of the Protestant Council; Secretary of the Treasury would have been Maurice N. Eisendrath, the executive vice-president of the Union of American Hebrew Congregations; the Secretary of Defense would have been Richard Cardinal Cushing; Attorney General would have been the president of the American Baptist Convention; the Postmaster General would have been Methodist Bishop Fred P. Corson; Secretary of the Interior, a Lutheran, Reverend Franklin Clark Fry; Secretary of Agriculture, a Presbyterian, the Reverend Silas G. Keesler; Secretary of Commerce, Episcopalian Arthur Lichtenberger; of Labor, the Reverend Ben M. Herbster of the Church of Christ; and of HEW, the Reverend J. H. Jackson, president of the National Baptist Convention.

"So powerful is the word of righteousness on the lips of these, just twelve men," writes Tomlinson, "America will not be able to function except as they are beholden to the truths in righteousness the Lord has anointed us to bring forth."

Tomlinson sees the Theocratic Party eventually taking back the functions of healing, education, welfare, missionary work and scholarship—functions that were originally carried out by the church—that the secular governments have taken unto themselves. Since the government is now doing the work the churches used to do, Tomlinson believes that it is doubly important that the country be run by Godly people.

The man doing most of the promoting of Theocratic views is Bishop William Rogers. He began his bid for the 1968 Presidency in September 1965 with what he calls his "Courthouse Campaign" to "Make America a Holy Nation." He has resolved to campaign at every county courthouse in America before election day. He has

numbers 121 million people. If major denominations are subtracted from this figure—23 million Baptists, 3 million Orthodox churchgoers, 6 million Jews, 2 million Mormons, 8 million Lutherans, 13 million Methodists, 4 million Presbyterians, 3 million Episcopalians and 44 million Catholics—the remainder numbers some 15 million people, and that includes groups that Tomlinson does not consider part of his fold, such as Friends, Mennonites, Christian Scientists, etc. Tomlinson may include in his total, however, part of the 68 million Americans who do not acknowledge membership in any church, although it it doubtful that half of this group are followers of his.

adopted the tactics of Joshua at the fall of Jericho: he walks around the courthouse six times in silent prayer and on the seventh, recalling how Joshua and his company shouted, Rogers breaks into a sprint, leaping in exultation, calling on the people to "look to the Lord and live." He then enters the courthouse, passing out literature and shaking hands all around. "This is not a publicity stunt," said Rogers: "we're undertaking a far greater task than Joshua had at Jericho. But we expect the walls of opposition to righteousness to fall as miraculously today as in those Biblical days."

On one instance the walls almost did come tumbling down. The day after Rogers appeared at the Bowling Green, Kentucky, courthouse, a large crack appeared on one of the outside walls, but Rogers said that it may have been coincidental.

Rogers is financing this undertaking through "love offerings"— collections in churches at which he is invited to speak en route. One plank of his platform, not one of the forty-eight laws, is that public officials should serve for forty years, as did Moses.

One of Tomlinson's heroes is Sir Isaac Newton, whose works provide the "scientific" aspect of his philosophy. According to Tomlinson, Newton predicted long ago that peace on earth would come to be in the year 1966, and that a "long reign of righteousness" would ensue.

Thus fortified, Tomlinson has set out to create a kingdom on earth. Back in 1954, Tomlinson crowned himself "King of All the Nations of Men," as well as "King in Righteousness." The ceremony was held at the Andrew Johnson memorial in Greenville, Tennessee. He explained to me that while he, Tomlinson, was "King of Men," God was "King of Kings." In other words, he was God's leader on earth.

From there, Tomlinson set out on a worldwide trip to 101 nations to crown himself "King" of each country. The coronation in each country took the form of his inflating a plastic globe, setting up a portable aluminum folding chair, covering the latter with a richly embroidered cloth of silk, then dressing himself in a silk robe. He would place an iron crown, covered with gold leaf, on his head while he held the Bible, open at Isaiah 32:1 ("Behold, a king shall reign in Righteousness"), in one hand. He would then say, as he did, for instance, in London: "I crown myself King of England . . . for Good, in the Name of the Father and the Son and the Holy Ghost." He would then pray that there be no wars, plagues, famines or depressions in the country and that the nation enter a period of lasting prosperity. When he crowned himself King of Ethiopia he announced that Haile Selassie could keep his job.

When pressed by the curious onlookers with the question, "Who made you a king?" Tomlinson would reply: "I feel that Jesus, my King, has made me a king." A king, he told me, cannot be chosen by vote or by popularity anymore than a minister, a musician, an artist, a poet, an inventor or a writer can be. "Such," he said, "must have these gifts from God within them." Mrs. Tomlinson, the Bishop's wife, is reluctant to call herself Queen. "She says she isn't," insisted the Bishop, "but I say she is."

In October 1966, to fulfill Newton's prophecy, Tomlinson crowned himself King again in Jerusalem, next to the Tower of David, on the Jordan side by the Jaffa Gate. This, he notes, is also in keeping with the prophecy of Isaiah 2:3, where it states that "the Law shall go forth from Zion and the Word of the Lord from Jerusalem." His haste to crown himself again, he said, was also in anticipation of the return of the Lord. "The word of God," he said, referring to Jerusalem, "come pretty powerful from there, don't you think?"

Tomlinson went on to explain other facets of his mission. "Now I'm really a king and I have a country," he said. "I haven't set it up yet but it is called Ecclesia. I have this country, 330 square miles with eleven cities northeast of Jerusalem and east of the Sea of Galilee. It was given to me by the Druses and we have the deed." He would not show the deed to me but he did say that his title in the country was King Homer I of Ecclesia. Neither Jordan nor Israel acknowledges the existence of this "kingdom."[8]

Previous to his coronation in Jerusalem, Tomlinson and the Theocratic Party merged their political efforts with a new political entity on the scene called the National Hamiltonian Party. Exactly what form this merger took is unclear, for the Hamiltonians bear scant similarity to the Theocrats.

The National Hamiltonian Party was founded in December 1965 by what appears to be a group of bluebloods. Its candidate for President in 1968 is Eric Sebastian, a descendant of Alexander Hamilton and a graduate of Harvard and Oxford. At one time he worked in the Dewey, Eisenhower, Rockefeller and Nixon campaigns but gave up in disgust in 1960. He noted with sadness "the degradation of blintz-eating politics that was forced on a truly aristocratic man" such as Rockefeller.

Other leaders in the Party are Adrian Tilt, like Sebastian a stockbroker by trade; Lindsay Williams and Maxwell Byrnes, both bankers; J. Thomas Aldrich, who complained that he had to run against "an unbelievable assortment of ambitious politicians" in Maryland's Sixth Congressional District; and Mannings Claiborne Case, who claims relationship to a number of well-known Louisianans of the past and who is described as a writer, a political and philosophical commentator, a philanthropist and a plantation owner. Case unsuccessfully contested the Senate seat now held by Allen Ellender.

Eric Sebastian, in opening his campaign for the 1968 race, said on 4 July 1966: "We, of the National Hamiltonian Party stand proudly together, united and determined to return America to the hands of the aristocracy. We are now calling for a return to this form of government as set forth in the Constitution: Rule by the Aristocrats!" Hamiltonian literature notes that Sebastian has entered the 1968 race with several disadvantages: ". . . he is educated, he is intelligent, and he is disdainful of stupidity. As we all know, stupidity is the one quality that has been identified [with] the 'average American voter.' "

Hamiltonians have a five-plank platform: the return to the election of senators by state legislatures; the return to the election of the President by independent electors, not by popular vote; a reorganization of the tax system in order to "encourage success"; the abolition of Constitutional Amendments Thirteen through Twenty-two; and the restriction of voting rights "to educated landowning leaders." The Party's slogan is a quote from Alexander Hamilton: "Your People, Sir, Are a Great Beast."

Sebastian promises not to bow and scrape for votes. Nor will he accept support from any group that he considers to be beneath the dignity of the office. President Johnson and Vice-President Humphrey he refers to as "peasants" who have squandered the respect of the free world by such actions as riding on a merry-go-round and showing off an abdominal scar.

How the Hamiltonians and the Theocrats will work together may prove to be one of the most fascinating demonstrations of political skill of the twentieth century. Neither has very much in common except considerable idealism and patriotism. Tomlinson, for one, is unconcerned with the details, for he is serenely confident that government by men of God will prevail, perhaps in as short a time as five years. "All nations will be glad for this," he wrote, "and all nations will call us blessed."

8

One of the more colorful independents, until his death in 1966, was Henry Krajewski who ran for President in 1952, 1956 and 1960 on the Poor Man's Party and American Third Party tickets, political parties of his own creation. Although his political organizations died with him, he is mentioned here because he added considerable lore to the American political scene. When I met him, less than a year before his death, he was in ill health, suffering from diabetes and the effects of an amputated right leg. But his spirits were still high and he had lost none of his humor for which he was noted throughout his long and unsuccessful political career.

Krajewski was a Runyonesque character from an earlier age. He was all the things that most other politicians today are not. He was highly individualistic; he spoke with a classic Jersey City accent; he made ample use of his hands whenever he described something; he was soft-hearted and he had a rough-and-tumble wit. In recounting his career to me he would often break into helpless laughter until tears rolled down his cheeks.

The eldest of eleven children, Krajewski for many years owned a fairly large and successful pig farm near his home town of Secaucus, New Jersey. He gave up farming after the 1960 election to devote his full time to his tavern which he called "Tammany Hall." The Tammany Tigers Social and Athletic Club he founded met at the tavern. His name he pronounced Kray-ef-ski, although he did not mind if people pronounced it the way it is spelled.

Getting into politics, particularly Presidential politics, was not easy for Krajewski. He had already rejected the two major parties as "boids of a feather," and he had not in any way distinguished himself nationally. But he was fortunate in that he found in the early 1950s a public relations friend from New York, Max Rosey ("A swell fella"), who decided he would promote Krajewski free of charge.

First he was given an image: a bandanna around his neck and a six-week-old baby pig under his arm as a mascot. He was billed as "the poor man's candidate" for the 1952 election. He then advertised in the newspapers for a running mate.

Next came the stunts for publicity. To get his name known, a parade was held in his honor down Broadway. Krajewski was the center of attraction—with a fashion model on each side of him and a 200-pound pig on a leash.

This was the first time the press had ever heard of Henry Krajewski and, appreciating the value of local color, they liked what they saw. Because he had neither the necessary money nor the organization, Krajewski likewise knew that whatever political gains he could expect were to be obtained only through the publicity he received. Whenever an election rolled around, the press would appear at his door and ask him to pose with his bandanna and pig. "I didn't want to look silly," said Krajewski, "but that was the only way the press would pay attention to me."

When he filed for President in 1952 he took his baby pig with him to the courthouse. The room was packed with civil servants, candidates, interested bystanders and the press. The proceedings were disrupted somewhat when his mascot defecated on a few of the more vital documents. Krajewski told me that it definitely was an accident and that he had not planned it that way. He added that the looks of dismay on the faces of the state officials were most evident.

Later on in the campaign he was asked to visit Phillips Exeter Academy in New Hampshire. The students were holding a mock convention and a faction of them wanted to celebrate a "Krajewski Day." The students found him to be an appealing candidate and they gave him an enthusiastic welcome wherever he went. "Them kids," he told me, "were so good to me it wasn't funny. When I left I cried like a baby." In the school's mock election later on, Krajewski placed second behind Eisenhower. Of this, Krajewski was very proud; in fact, the entire episode was still most vivid to him, for he had tears in his eyes when he told it to me.

In 1956, Krajewski ran for the Senate from New Jersey. He drew 35,000 votes, enabling Clifford P. Case, the Republican candidate, to beat Democrat Charles Howell. This was the only instance when Krajewski received any appreciable number of votes. In all his other contests the votes cast for him were negligible.

During the election campaign of 1956, Krajewski held a pig-roast across the street from a $100-a-plate dinner for Eisenhower at Madison Square Garden. He had a big sign made that said: "Walk across the street and save $98.02. Pig roast $1.98 for Poor Man's Party candidate." Apparently the dinner in Madison Square Garden was nothing more than a fancy box lunch, for, according to Krajewski: "As soon as the $100 dinner was over, our place was *mobbed!* All them rich Republicans came over and pulled that pig apart, *bones and all!"*

In 1960, he made a cross-country speaking tour, stopping off at the convention cities of Chicago and Los Angeles on the way. He had a sign on the back of his trailer that said: "If you hate communism, blow your horn." Apparently this was a big success with other motorists during the trip. He picketed both conventions with a sign that read, "Please do not vote for any red-tinted candidates"; and in Los Angeles, he and his party were attacked by an anti-Johnson crowd. "They're pushin' us around, I'm telling you, 'cause we're wearing cowboy hats. They're throwin' bot'ls and stones! . . ." he reflected.

And no matter where he went he was greeted warmly by the press. He also met a few Communist reporters on the trip, whom he described to me only as "sonsabitches."

His political program can only be described as individualistic. He wanted, for instance, "no piggy deals in Washington." He sought the elimination of juvenile delinquency by forcing all youths to work on a farm for a year. "Let 'em rock 'n' roll with the pigs and chickens at five o'clock in the morning," he told me. "By the time the sun goes down they would be tired enough to go to sleep and not spend their time thievin' and driftin' around the streets at night lookin' for mischief. . . ."

He wanted to annex Canada, lower taxes to prewar levels, bring Red China into the U.N., and keep American soldiers on American soil because, as he explained it to me: "You see, if you and me is enemies, and I don't know how strong you are, and you don't know how strong I am, we won't fight each other."

Krajewski went into politics in the first place to prove to America and the world that a poor man could be President. He did not succeed but, he said, he had some satisfaction, particularly the day Pravda called him "a swineherder from the prairies of New Jersey." That newspaper then proceeded to chastise the United States for allowing such a man to be a candidate.

In the 1956 and 1960 elections the state of New Jersey disqualified him on technical grounds from appearing on the ballot. The only way to surmount this obstacle, as he saw it, was to take his case to court, which he was reluctant to do considering his deteriorating health. He told me that one state official confided in him, off the record, that his past disqualifications were due to his "lack of dignity."

It is apparent that, although most of what Krajewski did was intended to attract attention, it was often misinterpreted. It was assumed in many cases that he was just a glutton for publicity. This does not seem to be borne out in retrospect, for behind his genuine desire to do something for his country, Krajewski was, in reality, mocking the absurdities of politics in America. Everything he did was a gross exaggeration of the antics to which most of our legislators in Washington submit themselves. Krajewski had an uncanny eye for all that is ludicrous, ironic and idiotic about American politics. The press, by and large, often missed the point and wrote him off as just another pleasant screwball. As for the politicians in New Jersey who kept him off the ballot, it is clear that Krajewski was a burlesque of themselves, which they did not particularly appreciate.

If anything, Krajewski's tavern was the best reflection of his political career and attitudes. "Tammany Hall" was split up into a number of rooms; one was a bar with straw hats nailed to the ceiling. Polish beer and *kebasy* were the specialties. There was a dance hall in back with chairs stacked on tables and cheap decorations hanging from the ceiling. In a dark corner of the bar was a battered pool table around which a seemingly perpetual stream of men stalked. Framed on the walls were Krajewski's political memorabilia: newspaper clippings, photographs, bumper stickers and campaign literature. Among these mementos was a 45-rpm record of campaign music called "Hay! Krajewski! Hay! Hay!," music by Bernie Witkowski and his Silver Bells.

And for years there was a large sign outside the tavern that passengers traveling on the main Pennsylvania Railroad lines nearby could plainly see. It read: "Politicians are Jokers."

Indeed, American politics is poorer without the individualistic style of Henry Krajewski.

PART SEVEN

THE
FARTHER
SHORES
OF
POLITICS

19

The American Political
Fringe Today

After having spent over a year interviewing and corresponding
with many members of America's political minorities and having
studied their affairs and watched them in action, I have inevitably
come away with a few general thoughts on the subject.

Perhaps the first point that should be noted is that the political
minorities, so often referred to collectively and derogatorily as the
"lunatic fringe," are by no means inhabited by madmen. I was
threatened a few times, once considered part of some subversive
plot, and growled at on occasion, but on the whole I was treated
politely and with great consideration. To be sure, there are those
on the fringe who exude suppressed violence, who can barely
control their anger, hatred and feelings of hostility, but these
emotions are not the exclusive property of political minority
activists. Indeed, they are common to our society as a whole.

Dr. Robert Coles, a research psychiatrist at the Harvard University Health Services and an acknowledged authority on political
minorities, agrees with my views. He has spent a number of years
in the South trying to apply critical psychiatric knowledge to
everyday social situations, particularly in regard to racial problems. His research has brought him into close contact with whites
and Negroes alike—civil rights workers, Negro schoolchildren in
integrated schools, Klansmen, Nazis and anti-integrationists in
general. Speaking of those on the extreme ends of the spectrum—
those advocating black power as well as those advocating white
supremacy—he rejected the notion that these people are "lunatics," "kooks" or "psychotics." "I have never met any one of them

that I would ever commit to a mental hospital. None of them have been either homicidal or suicidal or significantly enough psychotic that I could not understand what they were thinking about, given their assumptions. Now I definitely feel that they have their problems," he added, "but I can say that about all kinds of people."

If a member of a political minority is not a madman, what then makes him different from everyone else? The difference is only a matter of degree and, at that, not one so great as to constitute a new breed of political animal. These people have a heightened sense of dedication, loyalty, stubbornness, passion, zeal, sincerity, rectitude and other qualities. They have an eye for hypocrisy, they are slow to change with the times, they tend to be literal-minded, and they have a world-view of things in which all phenomena must be correlated. They refuse to believe that their ideas are irrational, and they are convinced of the justness of their cause.

These people, said Coles, "lose that precious commodity that Americans have so much of: indifference, boredom and lack of interest." It means, he added, "that they're hung up on something, as we all are."

There is no one set pattern from which such people spring. In each life, said Coles, "There are a number of complicated factors; there is no set pattern of childhood, of development or ideology or experience. There is no one explanation—psychiatric, social or anything. These people come from all classes. You cannot say that there is a childhood of the fanatic with common themes in all of them. I've looked pretty hard; they come from different backgrounds and have different problems."

It is important to stress, he went on, "that these people are not always fanatics, that they haven't always been eccentric, that they haven't always been off-beat characters." But, he said, "A change in the social or historical situation is what enables them to emerge as fanatics." He noted that the process is a slow one, that it is built up over a long period of time and that often it culminates in an explosion in a given situation.

If the public chooses to call these people "lunatics," it is a social statement, not a medical one. It implies that the views and the activities of these political minority groups are unacceptable to those within the consensus. These groups can be criticized legitimately only from an ethical point of view; that is to say, one can fault them on the views they hold as being incompatible with the ones others hold. To call them lunatics in a medical sense is to say that we are all lunatics.

It would also be a distortion of the truth to conclude, as the term "lunatic fringe" implies, that the activists are, on the whole, less intelligent and less capable than the more "normal" political moderates. Undoubtedly there are those individuals within the fringe who are dull-witted, mean, slow, stupid and irrational but, again, they have no hammerlock on these qualities. These fringe groups cannot be written off when they can produce men with the organizational and intellectual capabilities of Norman Thomas, William Buckley, Dave Dellinger and John Rousselot, to name but a few of them. All of these individuals probably could have done better financially and certainly could have received the esteem of more of their peers had they decided to "go along." But they chose to rock the boat.

Some people contend that the talents of these few gifted individuals are being misused or even wasted. Every time I hear this argument I try to imagine myself back in the 1880s looking at the fringes as they existed then. First of all, you had a group of hot-eyed women screaming for equal suffrage, a goal that many of the "accepted" political pundits considered near-idiocy; then you had a group of smelly ruffians known as the "labor agitators," who were calling for better working conditions and more pay—demands that to many smacked of anarchy and socialism (today, the leaders of these groups are known as "labor statesmen"); and finally, you had a myriad of groups who were calling for such "un-American," "subversive," "seditious" and "foreign" changes as the exertion of more federal authority in the fields of health, agriculture, labor relations, banking, education, foreign trade, welfare and immigration, for reform of the electoral system, for equal rights, for the end to monopolies, and so on. Since many political changes are born in a seemingly "lunatic" environment, it can only be mooted whether, in fact, these assets are being wasted.

Many of the groups surveyed in the previous chapters do play a role in American society that cannot be overlooked or dismissed as inconsequential. In the first place, they articulate the thoughts of a far larger segment of the American people than might otherwise be supposed. No matter how crude, undiplomatic or raucous the message might be, these groups are the vocal apex of some significant segment of public sentiment. Thus, the black nationalists are a manifestation of Negro despair, the Ku Klux Klan reflects, in part, the belief by many Americans that integration is *not* part of the natural order of things, and the New Left is a revolt against the dishonest aspects of American life, where the facts do not always support the claims. Any worthwhile politician will listen to their words, evaluate them and store them away in his mind to be reissued in some other form at some other time. To ignore the words of all political minorities as the ravings of the mad, the disenchanted and the frustrated would be pure folly for anyone who had any pretensions to improving the welfare of the citizens.

Political minorities are possible sources for new ideas. Any group that might develop new ideas—no matter how remote the possibility—should be encouraged to put them forth for evaluation by the public. Perhaps none of the previously discussed groups have anything of a lasting nature to contribute to America or mankind; on the other hand, perhaps one of them does. Our political history shows that every once in a while these minorities can exert a considerable influence on those in power, even when the groups themselves are not in power; the Socialist Party is one, the Prohibitionists (albeit fleetingly) were another, and the Liberal Party is another. It therefore becomes vitally important that these minorities be encouraged to speak up.

Political minorities are also convenient outlets for the rebellious individuals in society. Certainly everyone would prefer to see these rebels express themselves within the political mainstream; but if this outlet is inadequate, then it is better that these people be members of a minority group than individuals venting their frustrations on the public at large with knives and pistols.

Perhaps the most important role the political minorities play is a convenient foil for the general public, who find many questions difficult to solve. In other words, the community needs vague and sometimes specific "enemies" on which it, too, can vent its frustrations. The enemy may be, of course, the government in general, President Johnson, bureaucrats, union leaders or bankers. In many cases, however, the enemy is a political minority because many of them on the farther shores stand for ideals that are completely alien to American ideals. The Communist Party and the American Nazi Party, for instance, are considered staple enemies; unlike the government, President Johnson, bureaucrats, union leaders and bankers, these groups are always out of favor.

There are two basic types of fringe groups in the United States: Those that grow up in bad times and those that spawn and flower in good times. The Wobblies, the Trotskyists, the Christian Nationalist Party and the Socialist Party are examples of the former. These groups are more concerned with the here and now. They perceive an ill or an injustice and demand that immediate corrective action be taken. The John Birch Society and many of the newer right-wing groups are examples of the latter. Although they concern themselves with economics, they are primarily concerned with status in a shifting, changing, amorphous society. Their hallmarks are frustration, vindictiveness, sourness and a search for scapegoats rather than the development of proposals for positive action. The New Left, also a product of good times, differs somewhat from the other groups that were spawned in the same era in that status is replaced by a search for new attitudes. The phenomenon of the New Left could only appear in times of prosperity because at no other time could the youths who populate the New Left afford the luxury of reflection.

On the whole, the minor political groups share a number of common characteristics. All of them, for instance, travel on paper, some obviously more than others. The Foundation for Economic Education is virtually all paper and very little action, as is the Socialist Labor Party; the John Birch Society and the Committee for Nonviolent Action are half-paper, half-action; and the Minutemen, the Vietnam Day Committee, the Black Panther Party are all action and very little paper. Usually, once the organization has been formed—a magazine published, followers rounded up, rules of behavior established, goals set, etc.—it creates its own momentum that sometimes carries it far past the point where it conceivably might have added something to American political knowledge and understanding. Thus such groups as the Socialist Party, the Wobblies, the Prohibitionists, even the Trotskyists are still with us, one of their primary functions being trying to decide what they ought to do and why.

Most leaders of fringe groups were not elected to the posts they hold but claimed the position in their own right. Subconsciously they have a vested interest in maintaining their opposition to the status quo lest they lose their *raison d'être*. This often leads to a situation where success is considered to be of secondary importance —in fact, in a few instances success is relegated to a position of trivial consideration. These leaders also revel in their role as outsiders, as pariahs, as political lepers. Their rank and file vicariously identify themselves with the outcast status of their leaders, as if it satisfied some inner need. Some leaders become political wailing walls where every rejection, every loss, every defeat becomes a tonic of sorts to the followers.

Many leaders reject respectability as being superfluous and, in some cases, an actual hindrance to their work. They will say, for instance, that respectability infers an acceptance of the status quo and that their organizations, if so labeled, would not draw the people they want. They also believe that what is disreputable today will be respectable tomorrow, and vice versa, basing their conviction not only on the tendency of the public to have a short memory but on the rather cynical belief that the ordinary American is sheeplike—that he will change his views if enough people tell him to.

Factionalism is particularly intense among these groups. Because the leaders have minor messianic talents and because they refuse to brook the slightest criticism, small splinter groups spin off with a new infallible leader at the helm, new followers, new rules and new dogma.

Lack of discipline is also a common trait. Although the ethics of group formation demand a certain code of behavior, the fact that these groups are outside the political pale often creates pressures enough for violence sometimes to break out. It is not a sustained violence but inchoate, indiscriminate, sporadic and purposeless.

Intellectually, the lack of discipline is too obvious to warrant much comment here. They use each other as source references, they ignore evidence they choose not to believe (but, then, we all suffer from this), and their logic is fallacious: "Communists are for peace, X is for peace, therefore X is a Communist" or, on the left wing: "Anti-Semitic fascist beasts are right-wingers, X is a right-winger, therefore X is an anti-Semitic fascist beast." (A number of critics of the political minorities, it must be noted, also use this tactic to discredit these groups; that is to say, by dragging a tarbrush over one man's record so, by inference, is it dragged over the entire group.)

One of the most ironic of general fringe characteristics is its ability to destroy or call into question the very thing it wishes to preserve. Thus, the advocates of states' rights have destroyed the concept by refusing to live up to its spirit; thus the Minutemen's insistence on the right to carry any arms has sparked an investigation into the more flagrant use of this right; thus the militancy of the black nationalists has built up a wall of white resistance, denying to the Negro—or, at best postponing—the equality he seeks.

The similarities between the left and the right are particularly close. Both sides see the major threat to the country as internal: the Marxists talk of "Wall Street" and "the Establishment"; the Birchers, for instance, of "Comsymps" and "traitors." Their vision is apocalyptical, where the world is on the verge of an explosion unless their particular brand of solutions be adopted. They have deep-seated prejudices bordering on bigotry: the Marxists are anti-clerical in general and anti-Catholic in particular; the right harbors anti-Semitic and anti-Negro sentiments. Both sides oppose the United Nations, NATO, UNESCO, the bipartisan approach to resisting the nation's enemies, the existing economic policies and the internal security measures. They would have the country revert to an older order: "pure" Marxism-Leninism on one side, un-fettered *laissez-faire* capitalism on the other. Few concrete proposals are offered by either side to alleviate the existing inequities other than the vaguest of platitudes. Usually both talk in terms of repealing existing laws, the dismantling of various institutions and the destruction of our basic rights. In both camps there exists the attitude of the avenger—destroy the old and build the right. Both sides are calling for a war of one kind or another.

The same type of people are drawn to the left and the right: dogmatic, totalitarian and radical. Many, in the words of G. K. Chesterton, glow with the memory of tomorrow afternoon. The character traits are so similar that there exists the phenomenon of individuals moving from one end of the spectrum directly to the other without pausing in the middle on their way (James Burnham, J. B. Matthews, Dave McReynolds and Louis Budenz are four examples). They express the "freedom" they seek by slavishly following orders from the top. They refuse to believe that America can not only exist but actually prosper by being flexible, pragmatic, reasonable and democratic. This, to both left and right, is sheer heresy.

Both sides are intolerant of the *idea* of a legal opposition. (I never met a right-winger who knew an active Communist nor a Marxist who knew anyone on Wall Street.) The members are incapable of articulating their criticism within the framework of rational discourse and civic responsibility. Both exploit the cult of martyrdom for all it is worth: the left has its Smith Act "victims," the Rosenbergs and Caryl Chessman; the right has General Edwin Walker, John Birch, Povl Bang-Jensen and Peter Fechter, and so on. Both camps advocate dirty tactics—infiltration, front groups, the smear, take-over bids and general harassment. They both have literary outlets for the propagation of the faith, and both have an in-group language all their own ("Jimcrow" on the left, "Comsymp" on the right, for example).

Most of all, they both suffer from a conspiracy complex. The Marxists see devious plots being hatched by the "Wall Street Internationalists," the "Establishment," the "White Power Structure" and the "Vatican Conspiracy"; the right talks darkly of the "Communist Conspiracy," the "ZIP (Zionists in Power) Code Conspiracy," the "Mental-Health Conspiracy," the "One World Conspiracy" and so on. Often the conspiratorial view is heightened when opposing political leaders act in accord. Thus there is "proof" of a conspiracy when liberal Republicans and Democrats *and* the Soviets together were "shocked" at Goldwater's statement in his 1964 acceptance speech when he suggested that a *détente* is not what is wanted in the world between the East and the West. Likewise, a convention of monetary experts from all over the world is seen by the left as a meeting to coordinate the bankers' selfish string-pulling activities. Both the left and the right fail to realize that moderates differ only on means and not on the ends. Furthermore, the mere fact of change in a society is often considered to be part of a conspiracy because any shift away from the status quo is seen as a retreat from the desired end.

But the left and right are not the sole repository for the conspiracy complex. We are all prey to it. Witness, for example, the upsurge of conspiratorial thinking on the part of ordinary Americans after the Kennedy assassination. Millions still believe that there was a conspiracy long after the Warren Report came out. Undoubtedly there have been, there are and there will continue to be conspiracies in this world, but what distinguishes the left and the right from political moderates is that the fringes see virtually every act of history as part of some conspiracy. "What separates these people," says Dr. Coles, "is their willingness to become more inclusively concerned about the world from the vantage point of their particular involvement so that conspiracy becomes for them almost the way the good Christian feels about life."

Those leaders of political minorities who are concerned with putting across a point of view live with a dilemma that none have ever been able to surmount; namely, if on the one hand they choose to be respectable, they realize that few people will pay any attention to their demands. On the other hand, if they choose to be disreputable, they may receive the attention they seek, but they know they will also alienate the very people they wish to influence. The secret of overcoming this dilemma seems to be to balance one against the other, never allowing the disreputable aspects to dominate the organization yet, at the same time, never earning the reputation as a toothless tiger. The task of balancing one with the other is often made more difficult because schisms among groups often produce a disreputable faction that clouds the reputation of *all* the other groups. Intramural bickering, therefore, often becomes bitter and fratricidal.

Many minority leaders will claim that as a group they do not need to grow, that all they require is a disciplined elite loyal to the cause. They view their organizations as fulcrums capable, at the proper moment, of toppling the present power structure and replacing it with their own order. Among right-wing groups this attitude is known as the "Hitler complex" and among left-wing groups as the "Lenin complex." They believe that if Hitler and Lenin could, with a handful of men, topple the old order, then they too can do the same thing. Since the Nazis and the Bolsheviks both rode to power on the backs of a crisis, these fringe groups similarly seek or predict such a crisis which will elevate them to the position they believe they deserve. Thus the apocalyptical vision looms large in their thoughts.

Do third parties have any hope of winning elections? History has shown that, although small parties can from time to time poll a significant number of votes, they have virtually no chance of gaining a plurality in a major election. As has been pointed out, their presence can be felt by the two major parties, and their ideas sometimes adopted, but beyond that there is little hope of winning. Many observers believe that the proper function of a minority group is to be a negative force—articulating problems that the Republicans and/or Democrats will eventually attempt to ameliorate.

More important, however, is the growing difficulty a minor political party has in raising its voice of protest at the polls. Any sophisticated society is rich in minorities and should encourage them to speak up. Unfortunately, American lawmakers are not sufficiently self-confident to encourage their existence. Part of this is due to the legislators' mistaken belief that the job of a minority party is to *win* elections. On the contrary, many of the parties only want to find support for a particular issue which, if demonstrated at the polls, might be adopted by the two large parties and, hopefully, eventually passed into law. In an era where the differences between the Republicans and Democrats are often undetectable, the minor parties can promote a consistent program that need not take into account the conciliation of incompatible interests.

Unfortunately, *access to the ballot*—these are the operative words—is becoming more and more difficult for the minor parties to achieve. There are fifty different sets of laws governing how a third party may qualify to have its name on the ballot. Most states do not permit a minor party primary unless that party received a certain percentage or number of votes in the preceding gubernatorial election. The minimum percentages range from 1 percent in Connecticut to 25 percent in Virginia; the minimum figures range from 500 in Delaware to 50,000 in New York. This forces the third party to resort to the independent nominating petition which, again, is inhibitive in its intent. It usually requires that a certain number of signatures be collected, that they be apportioned by county throughout the state and, in some cases, that each signature be authenticated.

The American Civil Liberties Union, in its Model Election Law, suggests that minor parties be required to collect only one tenth of one percent of the total vote cast in the previous gubernatorial election with a limit of 10,000 signatures. As it stands now, Missouri demands a petition with two percent of the voters listed (36,000), Massachusetts demands three percent (72,000) and Ohio 7 percent (259,000).[1] In addition, Missouri insists that all the names on the petition be certified by a notary who personally knows the signer or by two witnesses who can swear to his identity. Pennsylvania requires that all signatures be obtained within a twenty-day period, and New York requires that there be at least fifty signers from every county. Furthermore, early filing dates, sometimes six months before the election, prohibit last-minute protests.

These stumbling blocks create two hardships upon third parties. First, they must spend an extraordinary amount of time, money and effort just to get on the ballot—even before they begin to campaign—and, second, they must do it at a time when the public's political consciousness is still sluggish. If, however, the prospect of such a task seems insurmountable to the third parties, they can always resort to the write-in vote. But this privilege is illusory, since most election officials find the process unwieldy, time-consuming and a distraction. Undoubtedly many write-in votes have never been counted or recorded in the past because it was apparent that upon inspection they had no influence on the outcome of the election.

Opponents to more liberal election laws contend that to allow every minor political party on the ballot would produce a blanket-sized ballot. This has some validity but is, at the same time, misleading. Even without minor parties some ballots are already blanket-sized, listing all the state's Presidential electors down to the county coroner. The size of some of these ballots today indicates that reform is needed. To add a few minor parties to the ballot would cause no hardship to the major parties but would reflect a truer picture of public sentiment. If one of the major jobs of a politician is to heed the voice of his constituents, he is curtailing his opportunity of finding out what is on the minds of the people by limiting the expression of their views to only two alternatives. Most Americans will by tradition vote for either the Democratic or Republican Party, but now and again a third alternative should be available where the disaffected can say to the two giant parties, "Take note!" Furthermore, the maintenance of a democratic society depends on the widest competition of ideas. The suppression of comparatively insignificant views is the first step toward the suppression of perhaps more significant views, and such a course, no matter how unintentional it may be, is unworthy in a land that calls itself free.

The government's attitude toward minorities is not a particularly tolerant one, although within the past decade there has been an upsurge of interest in this area. Most governments have an instinct for self-preservation, not only from a political point of view but also in terms of the nation's welfare; and the politicians who make up these governments are most likely elected to office because they have this quality. No state, in its own interests, can tolerate the existence of any group which advocates the abolition of the state itself. But beyond this, there seems to be no reason for the harassment to which some groups are subjected. The amount of pressure applied by the government against a particular minority group depends on the group's distance from the consensus. There is obviously a gray area between blatant subversion and what might be called "legalized dissent," no matter how idiotic the latter may be. Sometimes the government harasses groups that are not even in this gray area, such as the pacifists, the bulk of the New Left and sections of the far right. Occasionally the government treats these people as if they were about to take over the reins of power.

The chief instruments of government intolerance are the House Committee on Un-American Activities and the Senate Internal Security Subcommittee. Although some of the investigations undertaken by these two committees have in the past uncovered information necessary for the proper formation of legislation, the two bodies also serve quite unwittingly to stifle dissent. Any particularly offensive remark is often grounds enough for the committees to issue a subpoena to the individual concerned demanding that his statements be explained. The late Representative Francis Walter once subpoenaed Professor Linus Pauling to appear before the HCUA for no other reason than an eccentric remark that Pauling had made in public.

The often-attacked McCarran Act was, until recently, another instrument of government persecution because, in part, it attacked the *idea* of communism, which in a healthy, robust self-confident society should be laughed to death in the marketplace of free ideas. To pass laws punishing those who plan revolts, sedition or the breakdown of law and order is one thing, but to outlaw ideas is a suppression of free speech.

The most obvious difference between the British attitude toward its minorities—which I examined for a year—and the American attitude is that the British authorities actually promote the expression of unpopular views. They go out of their way to encourage some eccentric to stand up on his soapbox and speak his piece because they know that he becomes less dangerous by doing so. The British public have come to expect and in fact demand that their government act in this manner. In America, on the other hand, although legally the right to free speech is extended to everyone and no politician would dare oppose it, one gets the impression—unintentional, I am sure—that government officials, at the moment of truth, would be happier if all those raucous, dissenting voices on the fringes were silent so that everyone could go on about their business without so much static in the air.

The Secret Service claimed in 1965 that it had files on 130,000 individuals or groups that may be dangerous to the President. If we say that in all categories there are one million people dangerous to the political stability in this country, that would still be only one half of one percent of the population. In the full knowledge that these people, individually or in groups, could and on occasion do wreak havoc on some sectors of our political system, surely the quality of the agencies assigned to protect us from these people is sufficient in most circumstances so that additional laws need not be passed that would erode the liberties of all other Americans. Perhaps some gun legislation is needed, but any law that curtails a man for his political views will certainly result in all of us being deprived of our liberties.

Any free government, in the last analysis, reflects the hopes, fears and aspirations of the citizens at large. America has never been a particularly tolerant place. Succeeding waves of immigrants were hated by their predecessors; ethnic animosities were transported intact to America from Europe; the lack of any social stratification has aggravated differences among people as they clawed their way up or felt themselves sliding down the economic and social ladder. The pressures on society as a whole, emanating from sources such as these, are inevitably reflected by the men in power.

One of the strongest and most sustained pressures found in American life has been the demand for conformity. A Louis Harris poll in 1965 found that two out of every three Americans felt that nonconformists were a peril to the nation. Nearly 90 percent of all Americans felt that Communists were harmful, 72 percent were suspicious of those who do not believe in God, 68 percent believed that anti-Vietnam pickets were harmful and 48 percent felt that Birchers were a threat. The survey also showed that 52 percent distrusted beatniks and that 36 percent objected to the wearing of bikini bathing suits. Harris found that the incidence of intolerance was highest among low-income people, those with grade-school education, rural residents and white-collar and laboring people. The most tolerant Americans tend to come from the East or West Coasts, live in the cities, are professional people or executives, are college graduates earning over $10,000 a year.

From my own experience, I have also found the general public's attitude toward political minorities to be intolerant. Much of this is due to ignorance and confusion. Most Americans fail to distinguish between the various minorities, usually bunching dissimilar groups together in their minds. It is not too uncommon, for instance, to hear someone say "left-wingers such as Gus Hall, Norman Thomas and Arthur Schlesinger," or "right-wingers such as Robert Shelton, Robert Welch and William Buckley." More surprising, however, has been the number of Americans unassociated with any fringe group that I have met who, in the course of discussing political minorities, have turned to me and said: "I not only will *not* defend their right to say what they want but I will go out of my way to prevent them from saying it!"

Part of this intolerance stems from the attitude of the press, the major source of information on political minorities. On the whole, the press is conscientious in its treatment of the nonconformist, but on occasion—more than I believe is justified—they are quite unfair to them. For instance, many reporters whom I met in the course of my research would privately refer to those on the fringe as "nuts" and "screwballs." These words never appeared in their articles, but their attitude reflected an unwillingness to try to understand them. The most common question asked me by pressmen during my research was, "Why are you interested in kooks?"

The press also uses a device known as "libel by juxtaposition," whereby a perfectly innocent story on a fringe group is placed next to a story calculated to bring laughs or sneers. It is impossible to prove this libel because in many cases the juxtaposition is accidental. But I have found the device too often to believe that it is always accidental. For instance, one large Eastern newspaper ran a fairly straight story on the Minutemen. In the adjoining column was a story entitled: "2 Men Attacked, Both Bitten on Ear." The article began: "A man with a penchant for left ear lobes . . ." Cissy Patterson, who edited the Washington *Herald* for William Randolph Hearst, once fired her make-up editors because they placed a story on General Douglas MacArthur next to a laxative ad. So the technique is not new.

Another thing that I noticed during my research was that photographs in major articles on political minority leaders were usually very uncomplimentary. Pictures are a powerful public opinion tool, for they set the mood for the reader. If, for example, a man is smiling, then the reader is prepared to like the person; if his mouth is twisted into a grimace, his hair askew and his tie knotted over by his left ear, then the reader is prepared to dislike him. I have never seen a picture of, for instance, either Billy James Hargis or Kent Courtney that had not been taken from a low trajectory, thus emphasizing their chins and darkening their eyes unnaturally. Part of the problem I had when interviewing these two—and many others as well—was simply recognizing them from the pictures I had seen in the major news media.

None of us, no matter who we may be in America—elected officials, members of the press, ordinary citizens—can afford to dismiss these groups as an aberration that is unworthy of our attention. Some groups are a potential threat to the stability of our society; others have ideas that at least deserve a fair hearing. Whatever is the case, we must learn to differentiate between the good and the bad. Too often we forget that many of these groups spring up to fill voids in our life that other forces in our society choose to ignore, just as groups spring up within the consensus to fill voids there. Sometimes we also forget that political minorities are filled with human beings with the same essential characteristics as everyone else. They are not mad, nor are they a different breed of animal; they are like many others—simply people who are concerned about, or who unconsciously reflect, various problems, the articulation of which is often unfamiliar and unwelcome by others. We also often forget that in many ways we all are members of one minority or another with distinguishing characteristics that set us apart from other men—whether it be in bed, in church, in our ethnic origins, on the playing fields, in business, in our tastes, in our habits, in our goals or, finally, in our politics.

Over and over again this thought keeps returning to me: in the last analysis, who's to say who's the fascist?

1

The Attorney General's List

The following organizations, designated under Executive Order No. 10450 (dated November 1, 1955), have been named as either subversive or fascist by the Attorney General of the United States **(some groups have been deleted and others may have been added):**

Abraham Lincoln Brigade

Abraham Lincoln School, Chicago, Illinois

Action Committee to Free Spain Now

Alabama People's Educational Association (see Communist Political Association)

American Association for Reconstruction in Yugoslavia, Inc.

American Branch of the Federation of Greek Maritime Unions

American Christian Nationalist Party

American Committee for European Workers' Relief (see Socialist Workers Party)

American Committee for Protection of Foreign Born

American Committee for Spanish Freedom

American Committee for the Settlement of Jews in Birobidjan, Inc.

American Committee for Yugoslav Relief, Inc.

American Committee to Survey Labor Conditions in Europe

American Council for a Democratic Greece, formerly known as the Greek American Council; Greek American Committee for National Unity

American Council on Soviet Relations

American Croatian Congress

American Jewish Labor Council

American League Against War and Fascism

American League for Peace and Democracy

American National Labor Party

American National Socialist League

American National Socialist Party

American Nationalist Party

American Patriots, Inc.

American Peace Crusade

American Peace Mobilization

American Poles for Peace

American Polish Labor Council

American Polish League

American Rescue Ship Mission (a project of the United American Spanish Aid Committee)

American-Russian Fraternal Society

American Russian Institute, New York, also known as the American Russian Institute for Cultural Relations with the Soviet Union

American Russian Institute, Philadelphia

American Russian Institute of San Francisco

American Russian Institute of Southern California, Los Angeles
American Slav Congress
American Women for Peace
American Youth Congress
American Youth for Democracy
Armenian Progressive League of America
Associated Klans of America
Association of Georgia Klans
Association of German Nationals (Reichsdeutsche Vereinigung)
Ausland-Organization der NSDAP, Overseas Branch of Nazi Party

Baltimore Forum
Benjamin Davis Freedom Committee
Black Dragon Society
Boston School for Marxist Studies, Boston, Massachusetts
Bridges-Robertson-Schmidt Defense Committee
Bulgarian American People's League of the United States of America

California Emergency Defense Committee
California Labor School, Inc., 321 Divisadero Street, San Francisco, California
Carpatho-Russian People's Society
Central Council of American Women of Croatian Descent, also known as Central Council of American Croatian Women, National Council of Croatian Women
Central Japanese Association (Beikoku Chuo Nipponjin Kai)
Central Japanese Association of Southern California
Central Organization of the German-American National Alliance (Deutsche-Amerikanische Einheitsfront)
Cervantes Fraternal Society
China Welfare Appeal, Inc.
Chopin Cultural Center

Citizens Committee for Harry Bridges
Citizens Committee of the Upper West Side (New York City)
Citizens Committee to Free Earl Browder
Citizens Emergency Defense Conference
Citizens Protective League
Civil Liberties Sponsoring Committee of Pittsburgh
Civil Rights Congress and its affiliated organizations, including:
    Civil Rights Congress for Texas Veterans Against Discrimination of Civil Rights Congress of New York
Civil Rights Congress for Texas (see Civil Rights Congress)
Columbians
Comite Coordinator Pro Republica Espanola
Comite Pro Derechos Civiles (See Puerto Rican Comite Pro Libertades Civiles)
Committee for a Democratic Far Eastern Policy
Committee for Constitutional and Political Freedom
Committee for Nationalist Action
Committee for Peace and Brotherhood Festival in Philadelphia
Committee for the Defense of the Pittsburgh Six
Committee for the Negro in the Arts
Committee for the Protection of the Bill of Rights
Committee for World Youth Friendship and Cultural Exchange
Committee to Abolish Discrimination in Maryland (See Congress Against Discrimination; Maryland Congress Against Discrimination; Provisional Committee to Abolish Discrimination in the State of Maryland)
Committee to Aid the Fighting South
Committee to Defend Marie Richardson

Committee to Defend the Rights and Freedom of Pittsburgh's Political Prisoners

Committee to Uphold the Bill of Rights

Commonwealth College, Mena, Arkansas

Communist Party, U. S. A., its subdivisions, subsidiaries and affiliates

Communist Political Association, its subdivisions, subsidiaries and affiliates, including:

Alabama People's Educational Association

Florida Press and Educational League

Oklahoma League for Political Education

People's Educational and Press Association of Texas

Virginia League for People's Education

Congress Against Discrimination (See Committee to Abolish Discrimination in Maryland)

Congress of American Revolutionary Writers

Congress of American Women

Congress of the Unemployed

Connecticut Committee to Aid Victims of the Smith Act

Connecticut State Youth Conference

Council for Jobs, Relief and Housing

Council for Pan-American Democracy

Council of Greek Americans

Council on African Affairs

Croatian Benevolent Fraternity

Dai Nippon Butoku Kai (Military Virtue Society of Japan or Military Art Society of Japan)

Daily Worker Press Club

Daniels Defense Committee

Dante Alighieri Society (between 1935 and 1940)

Dennis Defense Committee

Detroit Youth Assembly

East Bay Peace Committee

Elsinore Progressive League

Emergency Conference to Save Spanish Refugees (founding body of the North American Spanish Aid Committee)

Everybody's Committee to Outlaw War

Families of the Baltimore Smith Act Victims

Families of the Smith Act Victims

Federation of Italian War Veterans in the U. S. A., Inc. (Associazione Nazionale Combattenti Italiani, Federazione degli Stati Uniti d'America)

Finnish-American Mutual Aid Society

Florida Press and Educational League (see Communist Political Association)

Frederick Douglass Educational Center

Freedom Stage, Inc.

Friends of the New Germany (Freunde des Neuen Deutschlands)

Friends of the Soviet Union

Garibaldi American Fraternal Society

George Washington Carver School, New York City

German-American Bund (Amerikadeutscher Volksbund)

German-American Republican League

German-American Vocational League (Deutsche-Amerikanische Berufsgemeinschaft)

Guardian Club

Harlem Trade Union Council

Hawaii Civil Liberties Committee

Heimusha Kai, also known as Nokubei Heieki Gimusha Kai, Zaibel Nihonjin, Heiyaku Gimusha Kai, and Zaibei Heimusha Kai (Japanese Residing in America Military Conscripts Association)

Hellenic-American Brotherhood

Hinode Kai (Imperial Japanese Reservists)

Hinomaru Kai (Rising Sun Flag Society—a group of Japanese War Veterans)

Hokubei Zaigo Shoke Dan (North American Reserve Officers Association)

Hollywood Writers Mobilization for Defense

Hungarian-American Council for Democracy

Hungarian Brotherhood

Idaho Pension Union

Independent Party (Seattle, Washington) (See Independent People's Party)

Independent People's Party (See Independent Party)

Industrial Workers of the World

International Labor Defense

International Workers Order, its subdivisions, subsidiaries and affiliates

Japanese Association of America

Japanese Overseas Central Society (Kaigai Dobo Chuo Kai)

Japanese Overseas Convention, Tokyo, Japan, 1940

Japanese Protective Association (Recruiting Organization)

Jefferson School of Social Science, New York City

Jewish Culture Society

Jewish People's Committee

Jewish People's Fraternal Order

Jikyoku Iinkai (The Committee for the Crisis)

Johnson-Forest Group (See Johnsonites)

Johnsonites (See Johnson-Forest Group)

Joint Anti-Fascist Refugee Committee

Joint Council of Progressive Italian-Americans, Inc.

Joseph Weydemeyer School of Social Science, St. Louis, Missouri

Kibei Seinen Kai (Association of U. S. Citizens of Japanese Ancestry who have returned to America after studying in Japan)

Knights of the White Camellia

Ku Klux Klan

Kyffhaeuser, also known as Kyffhaeuser League (Kyffhaeuser Bund), Kyffhaeuser Fellowship (Kyffhaeuser Kameradschaft)

Kyffhaeuser War Relief (Kyffhaeuser Kriegshilfswerk)

Labor Council for Negro Rights

Labor Research Association, Inc.

Labor Youth League

League for Common Sense

League of American Writers

Lictor Society (Italian Black Shirts)

Macedonian-American People's League

Mario Morgantini Circle

Maritime Labor Committee to Defend Al Lannon

Maryland Congress Against Discrimination (See Committee to Abolish Discrimination in Maryland)

Massachusetts Committee for the Bill of Rights

Massachusetts Minute Women for Peace (not connected with the Minute Women of the U. S. A., Inc.)

Maurice Braverman Defense Committee

Michigan Civil Rights Federation

Michigan Council for Peace

Michigan School of Social Science

Nanka Teikoku Gunyudan (Imperial Military Friends Group or Southern California War Veterans)

National Association of Mexican Americans (also known as Asociacion Nacional Mexico-Americana)

National Blue Star Mothers of America (not to be confused with the Blue Star Mothers of America organized in February 1942)

National Committee for Freedom of the Press

National Committee for the Defense of Political Prisoners

National Committee to Win Amnesty for Smith Act Victims

National Committee to Win the Peace

National Conference on American Policy in China and the Far East (a Conference called by the Committee for a Democratic Far Eastern Policy)

National Council of Americans of Croatian Descent

National Council of American-Soviet Friendship

National Federation for Constitutional Liberties

National Labor Conference for Peace

National Negro Congress

National Negro Labor Council

Nationalist Action League

Nationalist Party of Puerto Rico

Nature Friends of America (since 1935)

Negro Labor Victory Committee

New Committee for Publications

Nichibei Kogyo Kaisha (The Great Fujii Theatre)

North American Committee to Aid Spanish Democracy

North American Spanish Aid Committee

North Philadelphia Forum

Northwest Japanese Association

Ohio School of Social Sciences

Oklahoma Committee to Defend Political Prisoners

Oklahoma League for Political Education (see Communist Political Association)

Original Southern Klans, Incorporated

Pacific Northwest Labor School, Seattle, Washington

Palo Alto Peace Club

Partido del Pueblo of Panama (operating in the Canal Zone)

Peace Information Center

Peace Movement of Ethiopia

People's Drama, Inc.

People's Educational and Press Association of Texas (see Communist Political Association)

People's Educational Association (incorporated under name Los Angeles Educational Association, Inc.), also known as People's Educational Center, People's University, People's School

People's Institute of Applied Religion

Peoples Programs (Seattle, Washington)

People's Radio Foundation, Inc.

People's Rights Party

Philadelphia Labor Committee for Negro Rights

Philadelphia School of Social Science and Art

Photo League (New York City)

Pittsburgh Arts Club

Political Prisoners' Welfare Committee

Polonia Society of the IWO

Progressive German-Americans, also known as Progressive German-Americans of Chicago

Proletarian Party of America

Protestant War Veterans of the United States, Inc.

Provisional Committee of Citizens for Peace, Southwest Area

Provisional Committee on Latin American Affairs

Provisional Committee to Abolish Discrimination in the State of

Maryland (See Committee to Abolish Discrimination in Maryland)

Puerto Rican Comite Pro Libertades Civiles (CLC) (See Comite Pro Derechos Civiles)

Puertorriquenos Unidos (Puerto Ricans United)

Quad City Committee for Peace

Queensbridge Tenants League

Revolutionary Workers League

Romanian-American Fraternal Society

Russian American Society, Inc.

Sakura Kai (Patriotic Society, or Cherry Association—composed of veterans of Russo-Japanese War)

Samuel Adams School, Boston, Massachusetts

Santa Barbara Peace Forum

Schappes Defense Committee

Schneiderman-Darcy Defense Committee

School of Jewish Studies, New York City

Seattle Labor School, Seattle, Washington

Serbian-American Fraternal Society

Serbian Vidovdan Council

Shinto Temples (limited to State Shinto abolished in 1945)

Silver Shirt Legion of America

Slavic Council of Southern California

Slovak Workers Society

Slovenian-American National Council

Socialist Workers Party, including American Committee for European Workers' Relief

Sokoku Kai (Fatherland Society)

Southern Negro Youth Congress

Suiko Sha (Reserve Officers Association, Los Angeles)

Syracuse Women for Peace

Tom Paine School of Social Science, Philadelphia, Pennsylvania

Tom Paine School of Westchester, New York

Trade Union Committee for Peace (See Trade Unionists for Peace)

Trade Unionists for Peace (See Trade Union Committee for Peace)

Tri-State Negro Trade Union Council

Ukrainian-American Fraternal Union

Union of American Croatians

Union of New York Veterans

United American Spanish Aid Committee

United Committee of Jewish Societies and Landsmanschaft Federations, also known as Coordination Committee of Jewish Landsmanschaften and Fraternal Organizations

United Committee of South Slavic Americans

United Defense Council of Southern California

United Harlem Tenants and Consumers Organization

United May Day Committee

United Negro and Allied Veterans of America

Veterans Against Discrimination of Civil Rights Congress of New York (see Civil Rights Congress)

Veterans of the Abraham Lincoln Brigade

Virginia League for People's Education (see Communist Political Association)

Voice of Freedom Committee

Walt Whitman School of Social Science, Newark, New Jersey

Washington Bookshop Association

Washington Committee for Democratic Action

Washington Committee to Defend the Bill of Rights

Washington Commonwealth Federation

Washington Pension Union

Wisconsin Conference on Social Legislation

Workers Alliance (since April 1936)

Yiddisher Kultur Farband

Young Communist League

Yugoslav-American Cooperative Home, Inc.

Yugoslav Seamen's Club, Inc.

2

Ku Klux Klan Organization

The following is a breakdown of Ku Klux Klan organization and terminology:

IMPERIAL (NATIONAL) OFFICES

Imperial Wizard: national president
 supreme chief executive officer
 supreme kleagle or organizer
Imperial Klaliff: national vice president
Imperial Klokard: national director of propaganda
Imperial Kludd: national chaplain
Imperial Kligrapp: national secretary
Imperial Klabee: national treasurer
Imperial Kladd: national secretary to the president
Imperial Klarogo: national inner guard of conventions or national executive board meetings
Imperial Klexter: national outer guard of conventions or national executive board meetings
Imperial Klonsel: national legal advisor
Imperial Night-Hawk: national auditor and chairman of 3–5 members of audit and advisory committee

} IMPERIAL WIZARD AND HIS GENI

REALM (STATE) OFFICES

ELECTED AT STATE KLORERO OR CONVENTION BY
DELEGATES FROM KLANS OR KLAVERNS (CLUBS)

Grand Dragon: president of klorero
Grand Klaliff: vice president
Grand Klokard: lecturer
Grand Kludd: chaplain
Grand Kligrapp: secretary
Grand Klabee: treasurer
Grand Kladd: conductor of ceremonies
Grand Klarogo: inner guard
Grand Klexter: outer guard
Grand Night-Hawk: auditor
Grand Kleagle: organizer of klan units (often
holds another post in the realm)

GRAND
DRAGON
AND
HIS
HYDRAS

PROVINCE (DISTRICT) OFFICES

Great Titan: highest officer of a province and
president of the klonverse
3 Great Klaliffs: advisory board
Great Kligrapp: secretary
Great Klabee: treasurer
Great Kludd: chaplain
Great Night-Hawk: auditor

GREAT
TITAN
AND
HIS
FURIES

KLAVERN (LOCAL) OFFICES

Cyclops: klavern leader
Klaliff: vice-president
Klokard: lecturer
Kludd: chaplain
Kligrapp: secretary
Klabee: treasurer
Kladd: conductor of ceremonies
Klarogo: inner guard
Klexter (originally Lictor):   outer guard
Night-Hawk: auditor

CYCLOPS
AND
HIS
TERRORS

KU KLUX KLAN TERMINOLOGY

Invisible Empire: The overall territorial jurisdiction of a Ku Klux Klan.
Kloran: The official ritual book of a Ku Klux Klan organization.
Klankraft: Ku Klux Klan spirit and knowledge of all matters pertaining
to the Ku Klux Klan.
Klectokon: The Klan initiation fee.
Kalendar: The special Klan terminology to designate days, months, and
years.

Imperial Klonvokation: A national convention of a Ku Klux Klan organization.

Imperial Kloncilium: The supreme advisory and governing board of a Ku Klux Klan organization.

Realm: A territorial subdivision of the Invisible Empire, embracing a state.

Province: A territorial subdivision of a realm, embracing a congressional district.

Klorero: A realm (State) convention; also the realm governing and advisory board.

Klonverse: A convention of a province.

Klan, Klavern: The smallest unit (local club) of a Ku Klux Klan organization.

Klanton: The territorial jurisdiction of a Klan or Klavern.

Klonklave: Secret convention or meeting of a Klan.

Aliens: All persons who are not members of a Ku Klux Klan organization.

KLORANIC ORDERS

K–UNO: Order of Probationary Citizenship in the Invisible Empire.
K–DUO: Knights of Kamellia—Primary Order of Knighthood.
K–TRIO: Knights of the Great Forest—Order of American Chivalry.
K–QUAD: Knights of the Mid-night Mystery—Superior Order of Knighthood and Spiritual Philosophies.

KLAN KALENDAR

Monday:	Dark
Tuesday:	Deadly
Wednesday:	Dismal
Thursday:	Doleful
Friday:	Desolate
Saturday:	Dreadful
Sunday:	Desperate

First week of the month:	Woeful
Second week of the month:	Weeping
Third week of the month:	Wailing
Fourth week of the month:	Wonderful
Fifth week of the month:	Weird

January:	Bloody	*July:*	Terrible
February:	Gloomy	*August:*	Horrible
March:	Hideous	*September:*	Mournful
April:	Fearful	*October:*	Sorrowful
May:	Furious	*November:*	Frightful
June:	Alarming	*December:*	Appalling

3
The Presidential Elections 1860–1964

The following is a list of parties and individuals who ran for President and Vice-President of the United States from 1860 to 1964.

Contrary to what is commonly believed, there has never been *one* official statistical record of popular votes cast for these two offices. The reason for this is quite apparent upon examination. The number of popular votes cast has no legal standing; the only *official* vote in American law is the electoral vote. How each state goes about deciding which slate of electors casts its vote for President and Vice-President is the state's business insofar as the popular votes cast for that slate are concerned.

Therefore, every statistician of American elections has his own set of popular vote totals. Joseph Nathan Kane (*Facts About the President,* H. W. Wilson Company, New York, 1960) uses one set of figures; the United States government uses another set (*Statistics of the Presidential and Congressional Elections,* compiled from figures supplied by "the various Secretaries of the individual States at the time of the general election"); Richard M. Scammon, the director of the Elections Research Center in Washington, D.C., has yet another set (*America at the Polls. The Vote for President 1920–1964,* University of Pittsburgh Press, 1965); and so on.

Scammon, in a letter to me, explained why the popular vote figures differ:

> These variations are due to errors in addition (which come to light when individual county and small area totals are combined into a total which sometimes isn't the same one the state

authorities have certified), partial reporting (or non-reporting) of write-in votes, differences in nomenclature, and the like.

While the variations have declined in recent years, they still occur. For example, in 1964 one state left out a county in adding up its Goldwater vote; in another a slip of the adding machine took 1,999 votes off the Johnson figure. . . .

When you go back further, the records are poorer, recollections of facts are dimmer, and the problem of individual balloting for electors is a great complexifying factor. In the 1890s, for example, the matter of getting the various fusion elector tickets straightened out is difficult, to say the least. . . .

I'm afraid I can do no more than welcome you to the small group of electoral statisticians who have wrestled with this reporting problem over the years, small comfort though that may be!

Scammon's reference to the individual balloting for electors as "complexifying" is perhaps understated. For instance, in the 1960 election Alabama had eleven electors on the Democratic ticket, five of whom were pledged to John F. Kennedy, six of whom were unpledged (eventually voting for Harry F. Byrd). The Alabama voter was supposed to cast his vote for eleven of the twenty-two electors on the ballot (there were eleven Republican electors as well). If he had cast his votes for all eleven Democrats he was, in effect, voting both for and against John F. Kennedy. As it happened, all eleven of these Democratic electors received different vote totals, so even today it is impossible to say exactly how many popular votes Kennedy received in the state.

If finding the correct popular vote for the two major party candidates is difficult, finding electoral information on minor parties verges on the impossible. For the most part, minor parties are ephemeral political entities. The candidate's name, the state he represents, the number of votes he received, and even the party name itself often slip into quick obscurity as the electoral support in his behalf is listed under "other" or "scattered." Sometimes these votes are not even counted at all, since they usually bear no weight on the outcome of the election.

The following popular vote figures I use come from two sources, both of which are considered to be the most accurate. For the elections from 1860 to 1916 I use figures from Svend Petersen's book, *A Statistical History of the American Presidential Elections* (Frederick Ungar Publishing Company, New York, 1963). From 1920 onward I use figures from Scammon's book, *America at the Polls. The Vote for President 1920–1964*. Rather than use electoral vote totals I use popular vote totals because the purpose of this appendix is to show the wide variety of minor parties running in each election and the support they received from the public at large. Electoral vote totals would not reflect this, since most minor parties receive no electoral votes.

Where I have decided it necessary, I have added minor parties and their popular votes from Kane's book, indicated by an asterisk (*), from U.S. government figures (compiled by the Clerk of the House of Representatives), indicated by a dagger (†), or from W. Dean Burnham's book, *Presidential Ballots 1836–1892* (Johns Hopkins Press, Baltimore, 1955), indicated by a double asterisk (**). There may be some overlapping of these figures with those of Petersen and Scammon.

DATE	PARTY	POPULAR VOTE
6 November 1860	REPUBLICAN PARTY Abraham Lincoln, Ill. Hannibal Hamlin, Me.	1,867,198
	DEMOCRATIC PARTY (Northern Democrats) Stephen A. Douglas, Ill. Herschel V. Johnson, Ga.	1,379,434
	DEMOCRATIC PARTY (Southern Democrats) John C. Breckinridge, Ky. Joseph Lane, Ore.	854,248
	CONSTITUTIONAL UNION PARTY John Bell, Tenn. Edward Everett, Mass.	591,658
	GERRIT SMITH	172
8 November 1864	REPUBLICAN PARTY Abraham Lincoln, Ill. Andrew Johnson, Tenn.	2,219,362
	DEMOCRATIC PARTY George B. McClellan, N.Y. George H. Pendelton, Ohio	1,805,063
	INDEPENDENT REPUBLICAN PARTY John C. Frémont, Calif. John Cochrane, N.Y. (both withdrew before election and supported Republicans)	

DATE	PARTY	POPULAR VOTE
3 November 1868	REPUBLICAN PARTY Ulysses S. Grant, Ill. Schuyler Colfax, Ind.	3,013,313
	DEMOCRATIC PARTY Horatio Seymour, Ind. Francis P. Blair, Jr., Mo.	2,703,933
5 November 1872	REPUBLICAN PARTY Ulysses S. Grant, Ill. Henry Wilson, Mass.	3,597,375
	DEMOCRATIC PARTY AND LIBERAL REPUBLICAN PARTY Horace Greeley, N.Y. Benjamin G. Brown, Mo.	2,833,711
	STRAIGHT-OUT DEMOCRATS Charles O'Conor, N.Y. Charles Francis Adams, Mass.	29,464
	PROHIBITION PARTY James Black, Pa. John Russell, Mich.	5,588
7 November 1876	REPUBLICAN PARTY Rutherford B. Hayes, Ohio W. A. Wheeler, N.Y.	4,035,924
	DEMOCRATIC PARTY Samuel J. Tilden, N.Y. T. A. Hendricks, Ind.	4,287,670
	GREENBACK PARTY Peter Cooper, N.Y. Samuel Fenton Cary, Ohio	82,797
	PROHIBITION PARTY Green Clay Smith, Ky. Gideon Tabor Stewart, Ohio	9,630
	AMERICAN PARTY James B. Walker, Ill. Donald Kirkpatrick, N.Y.	2,508
2 November 1880	REPUBLICAN PARTY James A. Garfield, Ohio Chester A. Arthur, N.Y.	4,454,433
	DEMOCRATIC PARTY Winfield Scott Hancock, Pa. William Hayden English, Ind.	4,444,976
	GREENBACK LABOR PARTY (National Party) James B. Weaver, Iowa Benjamin J. Chambers, Tex.	308,649
	PROHIBITION PARTY Neal Dow, Me. Henry Adams Thompson, Ohio	10,364

DATE	PARTY	POPULAR VOTE
	AMERICAN PARTY John Wolcott Phelps, Vt. Samuel Clarke Pomeroy, Kans.	1,045
4 November 1884	DEMOCRATIC PARTY Grover Cleveland, N.Y. Thomas A. Hendricks, Ind.	4,875,971
	REPUBLICAN PARTY James G. Blaine, Me. John A. Logan, Ill.	4,852,234
	GREENBACK PARTY AND ANTI-MONOPOLY PARTY Benjamin F. Butler, Mass. Absolom Madden West, Miss.	175,066
	PROHIBITION PARTY John Pierce St. John, Kans. William Daniel, Md.	150,957
6 November 1888	REPUBLICAN PARTY Benjamin Harrison, Ind. Levi Parsons Morton, N.Y.	5,445,269
	DEMOCRATIC PARTY Grover Cleveland, N.Y. Allen G. Thurman, Ohio	5,540,365
	PROHIBITION PARTY Clinton Bowen Fisk, N.J. John A. Brooks, Mo.	250,122
	UNION LABOR PARTY Alson Jenness Streeter, Ill. Charles E. Cunningham, Ark.	147,606
	UNITED LABOR PARTY Robert H. Cowdrey, Ill. W. H. T. Wakefield, Kans.	2,818
	SOCIALIST LABOR PARTY	2,068**
	AMERICAN PARTY James L. Curtis, N.Y. Peter Dinwiddie Wigginton, Calif.	1,591
	EQUAL RIGHTS PARTY Belva Ann Lockwood, D.C. Charles S. Wells	*
	INDUSTRIAL REFORM PARTY Albert E. Redstone, Calif. John Colvin, Kans.	*
8 November 1892	DEMOCRATIC PARTY Grover Cleveland, N.Y. Adlai Ewing Stevenson, Ill.	5,556,982
	REPUBLICAN PARTY Benjamin Harrison, Ind. Whitelaw Reid, N.Y.	5,191,466

DATE	PARTY	POPULAR VOTE
	PEOPLE'S PARTY (Populists) James B. Weaver, Iowa James G. Field, Va.	1,029,960
	PROHIBITION PARTY John Bidwell, Calif. James Britton Cranfill, Tex.	271,111
	SOCIALIST LABOR PARTY Simon Wing, Mass. Charles A. Matchett, N.Y.	21,561
3 November 1896	REPUBLICAN PARTY William McKinley, Ohio Garret A. Hobart, N.J.	7,113,734
	DEMOCRATIC PARTY (also NATIONAL SILVER PARTY and Bi-Metallic League) William Jennings Bryan, Neb. Arthur Sewall, Me.	6,516,722
	POPULIST PARTY (also MIDDLE-OF-THE-ROAD PARTY, PEOPLE'S PARTY) William Jennings Bryan, Neb. Thomas E. Watson, Ga.	222,583*
	NATIONAL DEMOCRATIC PARTY (also SOUND MONEY DEMOCRATIC PARTY) John McAuley Palmer, Ill. Simon Bolivar Buckner, Ky.	135,456
	PROHIBITION PARTY Joshua Levering, Md. Hale Johnson, Ill.	131,285
	SOCIALIST LABOR PARTY Charles H. Matchett, N.Y. Matthew Maguire, N.J.	36,475
	NATIONAL PARTY Charles E. Bentley, Neb. James H. Southgate, N.C.	14,003
6 November 1900	REPUBLICAN PARTY William McKinley, Ohio Theodore Roosevelt, N.Y.	7,219,828
	DEMOCRATIC PARTY (also SILVER REPUBLICAN PARTY) William Jennings Bryan, Neb. Adlai Ewing Stevenson, Ill.	6,358,160
	PROHIBITION PARTY John Granville Woolley, Ill. Henry Brewer Metcalf, Ohio	210,200
	SOCIAL-DEMOCRATIC PARTY Eugene Victor Debs, Ind. Job Harriman, Calif.	95,744

DATE	PARTY	POPULAR VOTE
	PEOPLE'S PARTY (POPULISTS, MIDDLE-OF-THE-ROAD ANTI-FUSIONIST FACTION)	50,605
	Wharton Barker, Pa.	
	Ignatius Donnelly, Minn.	
	SOCIALIST LABOR PARTY	33,435
	Joseph F. Malloney, Mass.	
	Valentine Remmel, Pa.	
	UNION REFORM PARTY	5,695
	Seth Hockett Ellis, Ohio	
	Samuel T. Nicholson, Pa.	
	UNITED CHRISTIAN PARTY	521
	Jonah Fitz Randolph Leonard, Iowa	
	David H. Martin, Pa.	
	NATIONAL PARTY	*
	Donelson Caffery, La.	
	Archibald Murray Howe, Mass.	
	(both candidates refused the nomination)	
8 November 1904	REPUBLICAN PARTY	7,628,831
	Theodore Roosevelt, N.Y.	
	Charles W. Fairbanks, Ind.	
	DEMOCRATIC PARTY	5,084,533
	Alton B. Parker, N.Y.	
	Henry G. Davis, W. Va.	
	SOCIALIST PARTY	402,714
	Eugene Victor Debs, Ind.	
	Benjamin Hanford, N.Y.	
	PROHIBITION PARTY	259,163
	Silas Comfort Swallow, Pa.	
	George W. Carroll, Tex.	
	PEOPLE'S PARTY	114,790
	Thomas E. Watson, Ga.	
	Thomas H. Tibbles, Neb.	
	SOCIALIST LABOR PARTY	33,737
	Charles H. Corregan, N.Y.	
	William Wesley Cox, Ill.	
	CONTINENTAL PARTY	830
	Austin Holcomb, Ga.	
	A. King, Mo.	
3 November 1908	REPUBLICAN PARTY	7,679,114
	William Howard Taft, Ohio	
	James S. Sherman, N.Y.	
	DEMOCRATIC PARTY	6,410,665
	William Jennings Bryan, Neb.	
	John W. Kern, Ind.	
	SOCIALIST PARTY	420,858
	Eugene Victor Debs, Ind.	
	Benjamin Hanford, N.Y.	

DATE	PARTY	POPULAR VOTE
	PROHIBITION PARTY Eugene Wilder Chafin, Ill. Aaron Sherman Watkins, Ohio	252,704
	INDEPENDENCE PARTY Thomas L. Hisgen, Mass. John Temple Graves, Ga.	83,739
	PEOPLE'S PARTY (also POPULIST PARTY) Thomas E. Watson, Ga. Samuel Williams, Ind.	29,147
	SOCIALIST LABOR PARTY August Gillhaus, N.Y. Donald L. Munro, Va.	14,030
	UNITED CHRISTIAN PARTY Daniel Braxton Turney, Ill. Lorenzo S. Coffin, Iowa	400
5 November 1912	DEMOCRATIC PARTY Woodrow Wilson, N. J. Thomas R. Marshall, Ind.	6,301,254
	PROGRESSIVE PARTY ("BULL MOOSE" PARTY) Theodore Roosevelt, N.Y. Hiram W. Johnson, Calif.	4,127,788
	REPUBLICAN PARTY William Howard Taft, Ohio James S. Sherman, N.Y. (votes transferred to Nicholas Murray Butler, N.Y., after death of Sherman one week before election)	3,485,831
	SOCIALIST PARTY Eugene Victor Debs, Ind. Emil Seidel, Wisc.	901,255
	PROHIBITION PARTY Eugene Wilder Chafin, Ill. Aaron Sherman Watkins, Ohio	209,644
	SOCIALIST LABOR PARTY Arthur E. Reimer, Mass. August Gillhaus, N.Y.	29,290
7 November 1916	DEMOCRATIC PARTY Woodrow Wilson, N.J. Thomas R. Marshall, Ind.	9,131,511
	REPUBLICAN PARTY Charles E. Hughes, N.Y. Charles W. Fairbanks, Ind.	8,548,935
	SOCIALIST PARTY Allan Louis Benson, N.Y. George R. Kirkpatrick, N.J.	585,974

DATE	PARTY	POPULAR VOTE
	PROHIBITION PARTY	220,505
	James F. Hanly, Ind.	
	Ira Landrith, Mass.	
	PROGRESSIVE PARTY	35,034
	Theodore Roosevelt, N.Y. (declined the nomination)	
	SOCIALIST LABOR PARTY	14,273
	Arthur E. Reimer, Mass.	
	Caleb Harrison, Ill.	
2 November 1920	REPUBLICAN PARTY	16,153,115
	Warren G. Harding, Ohio	
	Calvin Coolidge, Mass.	
	DEMOCRATIC PARTY	9,133,092
	James M. Cox, Ohio	
	Franklin D. Roosevelt, N.Y.	
	SOCIALIST PARTY	915,490
	Eugene Victor Debs, Ind.	
	Seymour Stedman, Ill.	
	FARMER LABOR PARTY	265,229
	Parley Parker Christensen, Utah	
	Maximilian Sebastian Hayes, Ohio	
	PROHIBITION PARTY	189,339
	Aaron Sherman Watkins, Ohio	
	David L. Colvin, N.Y.	
	AMERICAN PARTY	48,098
	James E. Ferguson, Tex.	
	William J. Hough	
	SOCIALIST LABOR PARTY	30,594
	William W. Cox, Mo.	
	August Gillhaus, N.Y.	
	BLACK-AND-TAN REPUBLICAN PARTY (in Texas)	27,309
	SINGLE TAX PARTY	5,833
	Robert C. Macauley	
	R. G. Barnum	
4 November 1924	REPUBLICAN PARTY	15,719,921
	Calvin Coolidge, Mass.	
	Charles G. Dawes, Ill.	
	DEMOCRATIC PARTY	8,386,704
	John W. Davis, W. Va.	
	Charles W. Bryan, Neb.	
	PROGRESSIVE PARTY	4,832,532
	Robert M. LaFollette, Wisc.	
	Burton K. Wheeler, Mont.	
	(the Socialist Party supported the Progressive Party in this election)	

DATE	PARTY	POPULAR VOTE
	PROHIBITION PARTY Herman Preston Faris, Mo. Marie Caroline Brehm, Calif.	56,292
	SOCIALIST LABOR PARTY Frank T. Johns, Ore. Verne L. Reynolds, N.Y.	34,174
	COMMUNIST PARTY (also WORKERS PARTY) William Zebulon Foster, Ill. Benjamin Gitlow, N.Y. (the Farmer Labor Party supported the Communist Party in this election)	33,360
	AMERICAN PARTY Gilbert Owen Nations, D.C. Charles H. Randall, Calif.	24,340
	COMMONWEALTH LAND PARTY William J. Wallace, N.J. John Cromwell Lincoln, Ohio	2,948
	GREENBACK PARTY John Zahnd, Ind. Roy M. Harrop, Neb.	
6 November 1928	REPUBLICAN PARTY Herbert C. Hoover, Calif. Charles Curtis, Kan.	21,437,277
	DEMOCRATIC PARTY Alfred E. Smith, N.Y. Joseph T. Robinson, Ark.	15,007,698
	SOCIALIST PARTY Norman Thomas, N.Y. James Hudson Maurer, Pa.	265,583
	COMMUNIST PARTY (also WORKERS PARTY) William Zebulon Foster, Ill. Benjamin Gitlow, N.Y.	46,896
	SOCIALIST LABOR PARTY Verne L. Reynolds, N.Y. Jeramiah D. Crowley, N.Y.	21,586
	PROHIBITION PARTY William F. Varney, N.Y. James A. Edgerton, Va.	20,101
	FARMER LABOR PARTY Frank E. Webb, Calif. Will Vereen, Ga.	6,390
	GREENBACK PARTY John Zahnd, Ind. Wesley Henry Bennington, Ohio	
8 November 1932	DEMOCRATIC PARTY Franklin D. Roosevelt, N.Y. John N. Garner, Tex.	22,829,501

DATE	PARTY	POPULAR VOTE
	REPUBLICAN PARTY	15,760,684
	Herbert C. Hoover, Calif.	
	Charles Curtis, Kan.	
	SOCIALIST PARTY	884,649
	Norman Thomas, N.Y.	
	James Hudson Maurer, Pa.	
	COMMUNIST PARTY	103,253
	William Zebulon Foster, Ill.	
	James W. Ford, N.Y.	
	PROHIBITION PARTY	81,872
	William D. Upshaw, Ga.	
	Frank S. Regan, Ill.	
	LIBERTY PARTY	53,247
	William Hope Harvey, Ark.	
	Frank B. Hemmenway, Wash.	
	SOCIALIST LABOR PARTY	34,043
	Verne L. Reynolds, N.Y.	
	John W. Aiken, Mass.	
	FARMER LABOR PARTY	7,431
	Jacob Sechler Coxey, Ohio	
	Julius J. Reiter, Minn.	
	NATIONAL PARTY (GREENBACK PARTY)	1,645
	John Zahnd, Ind.	
	Florence Garvin, R.I.	
	JOBLESS PARTY	740
	James Renshaw Cox, Pa.	
	V. C. Tisdal, Okla.	
	JACKSONIAN PARTY (in Texas)	157
	ARIZONA PROGRESSIVE DEMOCRATS	9
3 November 1936	DEMOCRATIC PARTY	27,757,333
	Franklin D. Roosevelt, N.Y.	
	John N. Garner, Tex.	
	REPUBLICAN PARTY	16,684,231
	Alfred M. Landon, Kans.	
	Frank Knox, Ill.	
	UNION PARTY	892,267
	William Lemke, N.D.	
	Thomas C. O'Brien, Mass.	
	SOCIALIST PARTY	187,833
	Norman Thomas, N.Y.	
	George A. Nelson, Wisc.	
	COMMUNIST PARTY	80,171
	Earl R. Browder, Kans.	
	James W. Ford, N.Y.	
	PROHIBITION PARTY	37,677
	David L. Colvin, N.Y.	
	Claude A. Watson, Calif.	

DATE	PARTY	POPULAR VOTE
	SOCIALIST LABOR PARTY John W. Aiken, Mass. Emil F. Teichert, N.Y.	12,829
	CHRISTIAN PARTY William Dudley Pelley Willard W. Kemp	1,598
	NATIONAL GREENBACK PARTY John Zahnd, Ind. Florence Garvin, R.I.	
5 November 1940	DEMOCRATIC PARTY Franklin D. Roosevelt, N.Y. Henry A. Wallace, Iowa	27,313,041
	REPUBLICAN PARTY Wendell L. Willkie, Ind. Charles L. McNary, Ore.	22,348,480
	SOCIALIST PARTY Norman Thomas, N.Y. Maynard C. Krueger, Ill.	116,410
	PROHIBITION PARTY Roger W. Babson, Mass. Edgar V. Moorman, Ill.	58,708
	COMMUNIST PARTY Earl R. Browder, Kans. James W. Ford, N.Y.	46,259
	INDEPENDENT DEMOCRATS (in Georgia)	22,428*
	PROGRESSIVES (in California)	16,506*
	SOCIALIST LABOR PARTY (in Minnesota, called the INDUSTRIAL GOVERNMENT PARTY; in Pennsylvania, the INDEPENDENT GOVERNMENT PARTY; and the LABOR PARTY of Maryland) John W. Aiken, Mass. Aaron M. Orange, N.Y.	14,892
	INDEPENDENT REPUBLICANS (in Mississippi)	4,550*
	ALFRED KNUTSON, N.D. (no party label; ran as an individual)	545
	GREENBACK PARTY John Zahnd, Ind. James E. Yates, Ariz.	
7 November 1944	DEMOCRATIC PARTY (including, up to the present, votes cast for the LIBERAL PARTY ticket in New York) Franklin D. Roosevelt, N.Y. Harry S Truman, Mo.	25,612,610
	REPUBLICAN PARTY Thomas E. Dewey, N.Y. John W. Bricker, Ohio	22,017,617
	TEXAS REGULARS	135,444

DATE	PARTY	POPULAR VOTE
	SOCIALIST PARTY Norman Thomas, N.Y. Darlington Hoopes, Pa.	79,003
	PROHIBITION PARTY Claude A. Watson, Calif. Andrew Johnson, Ky.	74,779
	SOCIALIST LABOR PARTY Edward A. Teichert, Pa. Arla A. Albaugh, Ohio	45,191
	REGULAR DEMOCRATS (in Mississippi)	9,964*
	INDEPENDENT REPUBLICANS (in Mississippi)	7,859*
	SOUTHERN DEMOCRATS (in South Carolina)	7,799*
	INDEPENDENT DEMOCRATS (in Georgia)	3,373*
	AMERICA FIRST PARTY Gerald L. K. Smith, Mich. Henry A. Romer, Ohio	1,780
2 November 1948	DEMOCRATIC PARTY Harry S Truman, Mo. Alben W. Barkley, Ky.	24,179,345
	REPUBLICAN PARTY Thomas E. Dewey, N.Y. Earl Warren, Calif.	21,991,291
	STATES RIGHTS DEMOCRATIC PARTY ("Dixiecrats") J. Strom Thurmond, S.C. Fielding L. Wright, Miss.	1,176,125
	PROGRESSIVE PARTY Henry A. Wallace, Iowa Glen H. Taylor, Idaho	1,157,326
	SOCIALIST PARTY Norman Thomas, N.Y. Tucker P. Smith, Mich.	139,572
	PROHIBITION PARTY Claude A. Watson, Calif. Dale Learn, Pa.	103,900
	SOCIALIST LABOR PARTY (called the INDUSTRIAL GOVERNMENT PARTY in Minnesota, New York, and Pennsylvania) Edward A. Teichert, Pa. Stephen Emery, N.Y.	29,241
	SOCIALIST WORKERS PARTY (called the MILITANT WORKERS PARTY in Pennsylvania) Farrell Dobbs, N.Y. Grace Carlson, Minn.	13,614
	CHRISTIAN NATIONALIST PARTY Gerald L. K. Smith, Mo. Henry A. Romer, Ohio	42†

DATE	PARTY	POPULAR VOTE
	GREENBACK PARTY John G. Scott, N.Y. Granville B. Leeke, Ind.	6†
	AMERICAN VEGETARIAN PARTY John Maxwell, Ill. Symon Gould, N.Y.	4†
4 November 1952	REPUBLICAN PARTY Dwight D. Eisenhower, N.Y. Richard M. Nixon, Calif.	33,936,234
	DEMOCRATIC PARTY Adlai E. Stevenson, Ill. John J. Sparkman, Ala.	27,314,992
	SOUTH CAROLINA REPUBLICANS	158,289*
	PROGRESSIVE PARTY Vincent W. Hallinan, Calif. Charlotta A. Bass, N.Y. (the Progressive Party was endorsed by the American Labor Party)	140,023
	PROHIBITION PARTY Stuart Hamblen, Calif. Enoch Arden Holtwick, Ill.	72,949
	SOCIALIST LABOR PARTY Eric Hass, N.Y. Stephen Emery, N.Y.	30,267
	SOCIALIST PARTY Darlington Hoopes, Pa. Samuel H. Friedman, N.Y.	20,203
	CHRISTIAN NATIONALIST PARTY Douglas MacArthur, Wisc. Jack B. Tenney, Calif.	13,883*
	SOCIALIST WORKERS PARTY Farrell Dobbs, N.Y. Myra Tanner Weiss, N.Y.	10,312
	POOR MAN'S PARTY Henry B. Krajewski, N.J. Frank Jenkins	4,203
	OREGON INDEPENDENTS	3,665*
	CONSTITUTION PARTY Douglas MacArthur, Wisc. Vivien Kellems, Conn.	3,089*
	PEOPLE'S PARTY OF CONNECTICUT	1,466*
	SOCIAL DEMOCRATS (in Virginia)	504*
	AMERICA FIRST PARTY Douglas MacArthur, Wisc. Harry F. Byrd, Va.	233*
	LIBERTY PARTY (in Georgia)	1†

DATE	PARTY	POPULAR VOTE
	AMERICAN VEGETARIAN PARTY	
	Daniel J. Murphy, Calif.	
	Symon Gould, N.Y.	
	CHURCH OF GOD PARTY	
	Homer Aubrey Tomlinson, N.Y.	
	Willie Isaac Bass, N.C.	
	GREENBACK PARTY	
	Frederick C. Proehl, Wash.	
	Edward J. Bedell, Ind.	
6 November 1956	REPUBLICAN PARTY	35,590,472
	Dwight D. Eisenhower, N.Y.	
	Richard M. Nixon, Calif.	
	DEMOCRATIC PARTY	26,022,752
	Adlai E. Stevenson, Ill.	
	Estes Kefauver, Tenn.	
	INDEPENDENT ELECTORS (in Alabama, Louisiana, Mississippi, and South Carolina)	196,318
	STATES RIGHTS PARTY	111,178
	T. Coleman Andrews, Va.	
	Thomas H. Werdel, Calif.	
	SOCIALIST LABOR PARTY	44,450
	Eric Hass, N.Y.	
	Georgia Cozzini, Wisc.	
	PROHIBITION PARTY	41,937
	Enoch Arden Holtwick, Ill.	
	Edward M. Cooper, Calif.	
	CONSTITUTION PARTY IN TEXAS	30,999*
	William E. Jenner, Ind.	
	J. Bracken Lee, Utah	
	INDEPENDENTS (in Wisconsin)	8,946†
	SOCIALIST WORKERS PARTY	7,797
	Farrell Dobbs, N.Y.	
	Myra Tanner Weiss, N.Y.	
	CONSERVATIVE PARTY OF NEW JERSEY	5,317*
	MISSISSIPPI BLACK AND TAN GRAND OLD PARTY	4,313*
	STATES RIGHTS PARTY OF KENTUCKY	2,657
	Harry F. Byrd, Va.	
	William E. Jenner, Ind.	
	SOCIALIST PARTY	2,126
	Darlington Hoopes, Pa.	
	Samuel H. Friedman, N.Y.	
	AMERICAN THIRD PARTY	1,829
	Henry B. Krajewski, N.J.	
	Anne Marie Yezo, N.J.	
	FOR AMERICA PARTY (in North Dakota)	483†
	VIRGINIA SOCIAL DEMOCRATS	444*
	NEW PARTY (in New Mexico)	364*

DATE	PARTY	POPULAR VOTE
	CHRISTIAN NATIONALIST PARTY Gerald L. K. Smith, Mo. Charles F. Robertson, Calif.	8†
	AMERICAN VEGETARIAN PARTY Herbert M. Shelton, Calif. Symon Gould, N.Y.	
	GREENBACK PARTY Frederick C. Proehl, Wash. Edward K. Meador, Mass.	
	PIONEER PARTY William Langer, N.D. Burr McCloskey, Ill.	
8 November 1960	DEMOCRATIC PARTY John F. Kennedy, Mass. Lyndon B. Johnson, Tex.	34,226,731
	REPUBLICAN PARTY Richard M. Nixon, Calif. Henry Cabot Lodge, Mass.	34,108,157
	UNPLEDGED DEMOCRATS (in Louisiana)	169,572
	UNPLEDGED DEMOCRATS (in Mississippi) Harry F. Byrd, Va.	116,248
	SOCIALIST LABOR PARTY Eric Hass, N.Y. Georgia Cozzini, Wisc.	47,522
	PROHIBITION PARTY Rutherford B. Decker, Mo. E. Harold Munn, Mich.	46,203
	NATIONAL STATES RIGHTS PARTY Orval E. Faubus, Ark. John G. Crommelin, Ala.	44,977
	SOCIALIST WORKERS PARTY Farrell Dobbs, N.Y. Myra Tanner Weiss, N.Y.	40,165
	CONSTITUTION PARTY IN TEXAS Charles L. Sullivan, Miss. Merritt B. Curtis, D.C.	18,162
	CONSERVATIVE PARTY OF NEW JERSEY J. Bracken Lee, Utah Kent H. Courtney, La.	8,708
	CONSERVATIVE PARTY OF VIRGINIA C. Benton Coiner, Va. Edward J. Silverman, Va.	4,204
	TAX CUT PARTY Lar Daly, Ill. B. M. Miller	1,767
	INDEPENDENT AFRO-AMERICAN UNITY PARTY Clennon King, Ga.	1,485

DATE	PARTY	VOTE POPULAR
	CONSTITUTION PARTY OF WASHINGTON	1,401
	Merritt B. Curtis, D.C.	
	B. M. Miller	
	INDEPENDENT AMERICAN PARTY (in Michigan)	539
	AMERICAN BEAT CONSENSUS	
	William Lloyd Smith	
	AMERICAN THIRD PARTY	
	Henry B. Krajewski, N.J.	
	AMERICAN VEGETARIAN PARTY	
	Symon Gould, N.Y.	
	Christopher Gian-Cursio, Fla.	
	GREENBACK PARTY	
	Whitney Hart Slocum	
	THEOCRATIC PARTY	
	Homer A. Tomlinson, N.Y.	
	Raymond L. Teague, Alaska	
3 November 1964	DEMOCRATIC PARTY	43,129,484
	Lyndon B. Johnson, Tex.	
	Hubert H. Humphrey, Minn.	
	REPUBLICAN PARTY	27,178,188
	Barry M. Goldwater, Ariz.	
	William Miller, N.Y.	
	UNPLEDGED DEMOCRATS (in Alabama)	210,732
	SOCIALIST LABOR PARTY	45,219
	Eric Hass, N.Y.	
	Henning A. Blomen	
	SOCIALIST WORKERS PARTY	32,720
	Clifton DeBerry, N.Y.	
	Edward Shaw, N.Y.	
	PROHIBITION PARTY	23,267
	E. Harold Munn, Mich.	
	Mark R. Shaw, Mass.	
	NATIONAL STATES RIGHTS PARTY	6,593
	John Kasper	
	Jesse B. Stoner, Ga.	
	CONSTITUTION PARTY	5,060
	Joseph B. Lightburn, W. Va.	
	Theodore C. Billings, Colo.	
	UNIVERSAL PARTY	19
	James Hensley	
	John O. Hopkins	

Notes

Part One: The Racists

CHAPTER 1

1. Rockwell, George Lincoln. *This Time the World* (privately published, 1963), pp. 245–246.
2. *The Rockwell Report,* February 1965, p. 18.
3. *Playboy,* April 1966, p. 156.
4. *Ibid.*
5. Rockwell, p. 383.
6. *Ibid.,* p. 146.
7. *Ibid.,* p. 154.
8. *Ibid.,* p. 194.
9. *Ibid.,* p. 193.
10. *Ibid.,* pp. 277–278.
11. *Ibid.,* p. 369.
12. *Playboy,* April 1966, p. 77.
13. *The Rockwell Report,* April 1965, p. 15.
14. *The Stormtrooper,* Summer 1965, p. 7.
15. *The Rockwell Report,* April and August 1965.
16. *Ibid.,* May 1965, p. 11.
17. London *Daily Telegraph,* 16 October 1962.
18. *Official Stormtrooper's Manual,* (no date), p. 6.
19. Lynch, Thomas C. "Para-Military Organizations in California," a report by the Attorney General of California, 12 April 1965, Section I, pp. 10–11.
20. *Kill* magazine, February 1963.
21. *New York Times,* 31 October 1965.
22. *Times Talk,* November 1965, pp. 7–10.

CHAPTER 2

1. Lynch, Section II, p. 2.
2. Thayer, George. *The British Political Fringe* (Anthony Blond, London, 1965), Chapter 1.
3. Cook, James Graham. *The Segregationists* (Appleton-Century-Crofts, New York, 1962), p. 178.
4. *Ibid.,* p. 179.
5. NSRP constitution and by-laws, p. 32.
6. *Ibid.*
7. *The Thunderbolt,* October 1965, p. 8.
8. *Ibid.,* November 1965, p. 4.
9. *Ibid.,* June 1961, p. 1.
10. Cook, p. 170.

11. *Ibid.,* p. 171.
12. *Ibid.,* p. 184.
13. *Ibid.,* p. 159.

14. *New York Times,* 1 December 1965.

CHAPTER 3

1. Roy, Ralph Lord. *Apostles of Discord* (Beacon, Boston, 1953), pp. 61–62.
2. *Ibid.,* p. 63.
3. *Ibid.,* p. 13.
4. *Ibid.,* pp. 15, 20.
5. Rockwell, p. 145.
6. *National Renaissance Bulletin,* February 1960, p. 4.
7. *SE Guard,* June 1963, p. 2.
8. *New York Herald Tribune,* 7 November 1965.
9. *National Renaissance Bulletin,* March-April 1958, p. 3.
10. Hoskins, Richard Kelly. "Two Controversial Ideas," *Western Destiny,* July 1964.
11. Varange, Ulick, pseud. (Francis Parker Yockey). *Imperium* (The Truth Seeker Company, New York, 1962), p. 404.
12. *Ibid.,* p. 418.
13. *Ibid.,* p. 608.
14. *Ibid.,* p. xxii.
15. *Ibid.,* p. xxxiii.
16. *Viking Age,* April-May 1965, pp. 5–6. Original punctuation retained.
17. Warner, James K. "The Law of Odin" (pamphlet), 1965, p. 3.
18. *Ibid.,* p. 4.
19. *Ibid.,* p. 7.
20. Roy, p. 97.
21. *Ibid.,* p. 107.
22. *The Beacon Light,* August 1939, pp. 4–7.
23. *Ibid.,* March 1940, pp. 11–12.

CHAPTER 4

1. Randel, William Peirce. *The Ku Klux Klan, A Century of Infamy* (Chilton, Philadelphia, 1965), p. 133.
2. Chalmers, David M. *Hooded Americanism* (Doubleday, Garden City, L.I., 1965), p. 131.
3. Alsop, Stewart. "The Loaded Pistol," *Saturday Evening Post,* 23 April 1966, p. 22.
4. Duke, Judge Daniel (then Assistant Attorney General of Georgia). "The Klan Unmasked," Unpublished ms., 1946, pp. 34 ff.
5. *Playboy,* August 1965, p. 143.
6. CBS Reports. "KKK: The Invisible Empire," 21 September 1965.

CHAPTER 5

1. Carter, Hodding, III. *The South Strikes Back* (Doubleday, Garden City, L.I., 1959), p. 71.
2. *Ibid.,* p. 72.
3. Cook, p. 60.
4. Figures from the June 1965 issue of *The Citizen.*
5. From the transcript of a speech given by W. J. Simmons to the Greater Los Angeles Citizens' Council, 30 June 1964.
6. Hearings before the Committee on the Judiciary, U.S. Senate, 89th Congress, first session on S. 1564, Part I (U.S. Government Printing Office, Washington, D.C.), pp. 307–582.
7. East, P. D. *The Magnolia Jungle* (Simon and Schuster, New York, 1960), pp. 176–177.
8. Cook, p. 86.

Part Two: The Far Right

CHAPTER 6

1. *Washington Post,* 6 March 1962.
2. Kansas City *Star,* 18 August 1964.
3. *Richmond* (Missouri) *News,* 22 April 1963.
4. *On Target,* 1 April 1964, p. 2.
5. Kansas City *Star,* 3 December 1961.
6. *Ibid.*
7. *New York Times,* 12 November 1961.
8. "The Armed Superpatriots," *The Nation,* 11 November 1961.
9. St. Louis *Post-Dispatch,* 18 June 1965.
10. Washington *Star,* 11 June 1965.
11. KLAC Radio, Los Angeles. "Hotbed of Hatred" transcript, pp. 22–23.
12. *New York Times,* 12 November 1961.
13. Lynch, Section III; and KLAC Radio, pp. 1 ff.

CHAPTER 7

1. Overstreet, Harry and Bonaro. *The Strange Tactics of Extremism* (W. W. Norton, New York, 1964) p. 141.

CHAPTER 8

1. Westin, Alan F. "The John Birch Society . . .," *The Radical Right* (Doubleday, Garden City, L.I., 1964), pp. 241–248.
2. *Blue Book of the John Birch Society,* fourth printing, 1961, pp. 19 ff.
3. *American Opinion,* February 1964, p. 18
4. Welch, Robert. *The Politician* (privately printed, 1958), p. 268.
5. *Ibid.* (Belmont Publishing Company, 1964; sixth printing), p. 279.
6. Overstreet, pp. 68–74.
7. Walker, Brooks R. *The Christian Fright Peddlers* (Doubleday, Garden City, L.I., 1964), p. 129.
8. Cain, Edward. *They'd Rather be Right* (Macmillan, New York, 1963), pp. 82–84.
9. *Ibid.,* p. 86.
10. Overstreet, p. 33.
11. Letter to members of CSA, dated 12 March 1965.
12. Constitution Party *Newsletter,* November 1965, p. 7.

CHAPTER 9

1. Walker, p. 178.
2. *Ibid.,* pp. 86–87.
3. Tulsa *Tribune,* 4 January 1966.
4. *Christian Beacon,* September 1945.
5. *Ibid.,* 18 November 1965.
6. Lowman, M. G. *A Compilation of Public Records of 658 Clergymen and Laymen Connected with the National Council of Churches* (Circuit Riders, 1962), pp. 125–127.
7. Walker, p. 39.
8. McIntire, Carl. "THE TRUTH . . . An Analysis and Refutation" (20th Century Reformation Hour, no date), p. 11.
9. Cain, pp. 199–200.

10. Schwarz, Dr. Frederick. *You Can Trust the Communists (to be Communists)* (Prentice-Hall, Englewood Cliffs, N.J., 1960), p. 147.
11. Testimony before the HCUA, 29 May 1957 (from a tract printed by the Allen-Bradley Company, no date). The Allen-Bradley Company is one of the biggest financial supporters of right-wing groups. It constantly extols the virtues of free enterprise in its advertisements. It was one of the companies convicted of collusive bidding and illegal price-rigging in the electrical equipment field.
12. Walker, p. 65.
13. *The Reporter*, 20 July 1961.
14. Walker, pp. 77–78.

CHAPTER 10

1. Braden, Charles S. *These Also Believe* (Macmillan, New York, 1949), pp. 257–307.
2. LeFevre, Robert. *The Nature of Man and His Government* (Caxton Printers, Caldwell, Idaho, 1963), p. 27.
3. Welch, Robert. "The Neutralizers" (John Birch Society pamphlet, 1963), pp. 42–45.
4. *New York Times*, 18 May 1961.
5. "Cliches of Socialism," No. 28 (FEE publication, no date).
6. Buckley, William F., Jr. *Rumbles Right and Left* (Macfadden, New York, 1963), p. 63.
7. *Ibid.*, p. 36.
8. Des Moines *Register*, 18 July 1961.

Part Three: The Nationalists

CHAPTER 11

1. Essien-Udom, E. U. *Black Nationalism, A Search for an Identity in America* (University of Chicago Press, Chicago, 1962), pp. 122–142.
2. *Ibid.*, p. 123.
3. Lincoln, C. Eric. *The Black Muslims in America* (Beacon, Boston, 1961), pp. 13, 204.
4. Muhammad, Elijah. *Message to the Blackman in America* (Muhammad Mosque of Islam No. 2, Chicago, 1965), pp. 170–171.
5. From a speech given by Malcolm X at the Boston University Human Relations Center, 15 February 1960.
6. *The Autobiography of Malcolm X* (with the assistance of Alex Haley), (Grove, New York, 1965), pp. 106–108.
7. *Ibid.*, p. 243.
8. Dennison, George. "The Demagogy of LeRoi Jones," *Commentary*, February 1965, p. 67.
9. *Ebony*, July 1965, p. 149.
10. *New York Times*, 17 May 1966.
11. Sackett, Russell. "Plotting a War on 'Whitey,'" *Life*, 10 June 1966.

CHAPTER 12

1. Aitken, Thomas, Jr. *Poet in the Fortress* (New American Library, New York, 1964), p. 29.
2. Morrow, Judge William W. *Spanish and Mexican Land Grants.* (Bancroft-Whitney, San Francisco, 1923).
3. *Newsweek*, 3 January 1966, p. 18.

4. *Ibid.*
5. *West Heights* (Albuquerque) *News,* 27 August 1964, p. 12.

6. *New York Times,* 20 March 1966.
7. *Ibid.,* 3 April 1966.

Part Four: The Left Revolutionists

CHAPTER 13

1. Howe, Irving, and Coser, Lewis. *The American Communist Party, A Critical History* (Praeger, New York, 1957), p. 400.
2. Kampelman, Max M. *The Communist Party vs. the CIO* (Praeger, New York, 1957), p. 4.
3. Overstreet, Harry and Bonaro.

What We Must Know About Communism. (W. W. Norton, New York, 1958), pp. 150–151.
4. Martin, Harold H. "The Communist Party, U.S.A.," *The Saturday Evening Post,* 19 May 1962.

CHAPTER 14

1. *Daniel DeLeon, the Man and His Works* (New York Labor News Company, 1934) Book II; and Joll, James. *The Anarchists* (Little, Brown, Boston, 1964) pp. 218–220.
2. Porter, Kirk H., and Johnson, Donald B. *National Party Platforms* (University of Illinois, Urbana, 1966), p. 96.
3. *Daniel DeLeon . . .*, Book I, p. 14; Book II, pp. 163, 171.
4. Shanor, Donald R. "The Politics of Dissent," *The Progressive,* September, 1965, pp. 36–37.

5. Key, V. O., Jr. *Politics, Parties, and Pressure Groups* (Crowell, New York, 1962), p. 297.
6. Hennacy, Ammon. *Book of Ammon* (privately printed, 1953), p. 314.
7. Cannon, James P. *The History of American Trotskyism* (Pioneer, New York, 1944).
8. Shanor, p. 36.
9. Adler, Renata. "The Price of Peace Is Confusion," *The New Yorker,* 11 December 1965, pp. 195 ff.

CHAPTER 15

1. Newfield, Jack. "Don't Want No Leaders Over Me," *Cavalier,* October 1965.
2. Burdick, Eugene. "The New Subterraneans," *ibid.*
3. "The New Radicals," *Johns Hopkins Magazine,* October 1965, pp. 9 ff.
4. See Lipest, Seymour M., and Wolin, Sheldon S. *The Berkeley Student Revolt* (Doubleday, Garden City, L.I., 1965) and Miller, Michael V., and Gil-

more, Susan. *Revolt at Berkeley* (Dell, New York, 1965) for the best accounts of the demonstrations on the Berkeley campus.
5. *New York Times,* 15 March 1965.
6. Hentoff, Nat. "We're Happening All Over, Baby!" *Playboy,* March 1966, p. 98.
7. Armstrong, Richard. "The Explosive Revival of the Far Left," *Saturday Evening Post,* 8 May 1965, p. 38.

8. Preamble to PLP Constitution, *Progressive Labor*, May-June 1965, pp. 4–5.
9. Armstrong, p. 37.
10. Brooks, Thomas R. "To the East of the Communist Party," *New York Times Magazine*, 25 April 1965.
11. Armstrong, p. 38.
12. *New York Times*, 30 November 1965.
13. *Augusta* (Georgia) *Chronicle-Herald*, 11 October 1964.
14. Armstrong, p. 38.

Part Five: The Moderate Left

CHAPTER 16

1. Fleischman, Harry. *Norman Thomas* (W. W. Norton, New York, 1964). Fleischman sketches Thomas as someone almost supra-human. The author also seems bent on convincing the reader that he, Fleischman, is as good and as pure a socialist as his long-time leader Thomas.
2. *Life*, 14 January 1966.
3. Rosenberg, Bernard. "New York Politics and the Liberal Party," *Commentary*, February, 1964, p. 72.
4. *Village Voice*, 10 December 1964.

CHAPTER 17

1. Interview from private source.
2. *Yearbook of American Churches* (National Council of Churches, 1965), pp. 52–53.
3. *Annual Report, 1965*. American Friends Service Committee.
4. Hentoff, Nat. *Peace Agitator, the Story of A. J. Muste* (Macmillan, New York, 1963), p. 88.
5. *Ibid.*, p. 91–92.
6. *Ibid.*, pp. 125–128.
7. Interview from private source.
8. *Liberation*, June-July 1965, p. 21.
9. Corry, John. "Spokesman for the Left," *New York Times Magazine*, 23 January 1966, pp. 30, 35.
10. *New York Times*, 12 January 1966.
11. Forest, James. "The Catholic Worker Movement," *Fellowship*. September 1965, p. 14.
12. Interview from private source.
13. *Ibid.*
14. *New York Times*, 21 November 1965.
15. *Time*, 19 November 1965.
16. Hennacy, page facing p. 1.

Part Six: The Independents

CHAPTER 18

1. Johnson, Joseph French. *Money and Currency* (Ginn & Company, Boston, 1905), pp. 263–284.
2. Irwin, Inez Haynes. *Up the Hill With Banners Flying* (Traversity Press, Penobscot, Maine, 1964), p. 4.
3. *New York Times*, 27 March 1966.

4. *The DePaulia,* DePaul University, 16 March 1966.
5. White, Theodore H. *The Making of the President 1960* (Pocket Books, New York, 1961), pp. 337–338.

6. *New York Times,* 21 April 1966.
7. *Ibid.,* 26 October 1956.
8. Whitworth, William. "On the Tide of the Times," *The New Yorker,* 24 September 1966.

Part Seven: The Farther Shores of Politics

CHAPTER 19

1. Nader, Ralph, and Jacobs, Theodore. "Do Third Parties Have a Chance?" *Harvard Law Record,* 9 October 1958.

Index

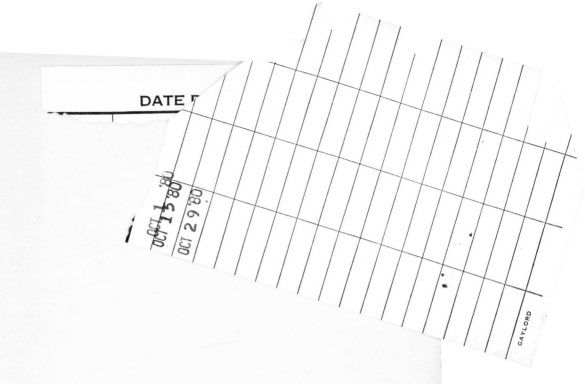